Parris, Guichard
Blacks in the city

DATE DUE

JUN 6 '73	MAR 7 79		
FEB 06 74	DEC 10 '80		
OCT 23 74	MAR 16 81		
JUL 30 75	JUN 17 80		
APR 28 '76	DEC 8 '82		
JUN 23 76	OCT 26 83		
MAR 3 77	FEB 15 84		
DEC 14 77	MAY 8 85		
FEB 8 78	MAY 14 '86		
MAR 22 79			

NOV 17 '80

Blacks in the City

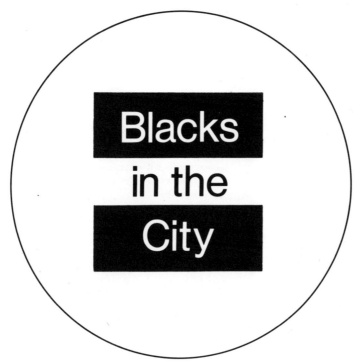

A History of the National Urban League

by

Guichard Parris and Lester Brooks

Little, Brown and Company—Boston—Toronto

Published simultaneously in Canada
by Little, Brown & Company (Canada) Limited

PRINTED IN THE UNITED STATES OF AMERICA

This book was made possible by the assistance of the National Urban League. The organization is not, however, the proprietor of this publication and is not to be understood as approving, by virtue of its assistance, any of the statements made, views expressed, or conclusions reached by the authors.

To the memory of
Whitney M. Young, Jr.,
executive director of the
National Urban League,
this book
is dedicated by
the authors

Preface

A generation ago, as the major nations of the world plunged into the maelstrom of World War II, an eminent foreign scholar was completing the most comprehensive study of black Americans ever attempted. Summing up his exhaustive findings, Gunnar Myrdal declared: "America is free to choose whether the Negro shall remain her liability or become her opportunity."

The passage of thirty years has not changed the pertinence of Dr. Myrdal's "either-or" conclusion. A major difference, however, is the fact that the "dilemma" now occupies a central, pivotal position in the affairs of the Republic. This was decidedly not the case earlier.

The concern of this book is the sustained and dedicated effort of an improbable group of citizens, white and black, unswervingly committed to the basic proposition that black Americans are and must be the nation's opportunity, not her liability. That is the heart of the National Urban League story, a noble enterprise for good and constructive ends, far too little known even to some who are associated with the agency.

A definitive history of the Urban League remains to be done. There is no such work and there will not be until the mountain of available material concerning both national and local Leagues is examined and evaluated.

The authors hope that this present work will serve as an interim exposition, help to throw light on the role of the League in "building for equal opportunity" and help to counter the tendency in some quarters to misconstrue the Urban League's efforts and denigrate or ignore its accomplishments. As Whitney Young often declared: "The League's shortcomings and . . . inadequacies are great. But they have not been for lack of spirit or tremendous effort by thousands of volunteers and Urban League staff members, both white and black."

American society appears to have arrived at a point of critical instability, seemingly ready to shatter at some crucial blow. We see ghettoes brimming with black resentment and hatred as nuclei of danger to the Republic. Once, half a century and more ago, the slums constituted an opportunity. We are so accustomed to the current condition of inner-city ghettoes as heavily, if not entirely, black enclaves that it comes as a surprise to realize that it was not always so. An 1894 Special Report of the United States commissioner of labor observed:

> The conclusions drawn from the comparisons of the slum with the total population are briefly, that in Baltimore the blacks, mulattoes, etc., in the slum districts canvassed is much less than found in the whole city being 4.12 per cent of the slums and 15.45 percent for the whole city; in New York .54 of 1 percent of the slum population are blacks, mulattoes, etc., while they compose 1.56 per cent of the total population; in Philadelphia they constitute 2.53 per cent of the slum and 3.76 per cent of the total population.*

How, then, did the slums turn black and many black Americans turn away from integration? Some little-known perspectives on those profoundly important transformations are in this volume. They may be glimpsed behind the chronicle of extraordinary efforts by blacks themselves to prevent such results. A pervasive element was the white myopia and worse that starved these efforts, foredoomed the blacks and made inevitable today's grotesque and gargantuan ghettoes, with their grave consequences to America.

The gloriously simple naïveté of those whites and blacks who organized the League and its predecessor agencies is apparent in their belief that life for blacks in the cities could and must be made safe and sound and that men of goodwill would share this view and support work toward such ends.

The agonizing truth is that there were always far too few such men and women and their support totaled but a token of the mountainous need. Today we can see the tragedy of the dissipation by whites of trust and belief and willingness on the part of blacks as they were excluded and their citizen rights callously denied or crushed. We can see the dismal results of the Establishment's undercutting of black leadership by design as well as obtuseness, resulting in increased instability in the black community and weakening of forces striving for an integrated society. There is tragic irony in the repeated pattern of ignoring the counsel of League professionals, then frantically appealing to them to restore "order" after a racial explosion the League had striven to prevent.

American racial policy, like its social and health policies until recently, has been one of emergency response, with clean-up, sweep-up action, Band-Aids and plastic surgery rather than sound, solid, preventive care.

---

* Carroll D. Wright, "The Slums of Baltimore, Chicago, New York and Philadelphia," United States Bureau of Labor, Seventh Special Report of the Commissioner of Labor (Washington, D.C., Government Printing Office, 1894; New York: Negro Universities Press, reprint 1969), p. 13.

The fact that black Americans are today in greater relative need, in unprecedented alienation, in more widespread despair, is not a condemnation of the League but of the society that too often limited its effectiveness when it could have been a more powerful factor in preventing today's conditions. One also can surmise from the record that black alienation might have reached critical mass a generation or more earlier but for the ministrations and efficacy of the League.

With uncommon perseverance and determination the Urban League has opposed the apostles of fear, division and social destruction, of whatever hue. It has, with the incredibly staunch faith and devotion of its board, staff and volunteers struggled incessantly for equal opportunity, equal life chances and equal life results for black Americans. Its work and achievements have been notable. Examining the record, one cannot help but conclude that the National Urban League's pioneering interracial work—a valiant endeavor—deserves high marks and a considerable measure of gratitude from its beneficiaries, the citizens of the Republic.

Acknowledgments

Whitney M. Young, Jr., observed that the achievements of the Urban League over the decades were all but unknown because they were buried in ephemeral or professional publications. He believed it was urgently necessary to make the League's history available in convenient form to remedy this serious oversight. For his initiative and leadership in this history project the authors are eternally grateful.

For his strong support and encouragement of this work Lindsley F. Kimball, honorary trustee of the National Urban League, has our deep appreciation.

We wish to thank the staffs of the many libraries and historical collections who helped in our research.

We are especially grateful to Mrs. George Edmund Haynes, Mrs. Eugene Kinckle Jones, and Mrs. L. Hollingsworth Wood, who made available the private papers and correspondence of their late husbands without which this work would have been incomplete.

Thanks are due to NUL Trustee Chester Burger for his careful reading and criticism of parts of the manuscript; to Mrs. Eileen Jennings, who gave us the benefit of her editorial and proofreading assistance; and to NUL staffer and long-time colleague Miss Ann Tanneyhill for her counsel and invaluable help at all levels of preparation.

Guichard Parris
Lester Brooks

Contents

Illustrations

Blacks in the City

1/ Ladies First

The first decade of the twentieth century saw an unprecedented burgeoning of social concern in American cities. It could be seen and felt, even documented and tabulated. One expert, in attempting to do just that, found in 1910 that "more social movements, national in scope, have been organized during the last ten years than the sum of all the movements organized before that date and still surviving." [1]

She found that most of these organizations were concerned with health, children, church, charity, industrial work and education, but two were concerned with city problems and one with immigrants. Changes caused by "shifting of races and nationalities within the city are," she said, "perhaps the most striking and the most rapid of those with which we have to do." [2]

To meet those problems, new agencies were begun and the activities of some existing agencies were extended. "While important new organizations were formed they were rather the natural outcome of preceding developments than fresh departures," observed another social work expert. [3] In no field was this more true or the need greater than in social services to black men in the cities.

The professionalization of social work had advanced remarkably in just a decade. Even in the late nineties "there were few 'surveys.' The people who really knew the neighborhood best were the priests, the politicians and the settlement residents." [4] But in the world of race relations, where every expression of need was met with flint-eyed skepticism, facts, surveys, dispassionate description of the realities seemed to be the most promising avenues to bring about improvements. These scientific approaches were taken almost as primary articles of faith by the Associations for the Protection of Colored Women, formed in 1905; the Committee for Improving the Industrial Condition of Negroes in New York (CIICNNY, 1906); the National League for the Protection of Colored Women (NLPCW, 1906); the Committee on Urban Conditions Among Negroes (CUCAN, 1910); and the agency that survived the merger of all of these, the National League on Urban Conditions Among Negroes (NLUCAN, 1911).

The year was 1905. The place, a small city in one of the southern United States:

> A procession comes into view. It is headed by a white man with a big drum. He is followed by a second man with a stick over his shoulder and tied to this is a bundle done up in a red and yellow bandanna handkerchief. Third—a woman—carries an old carpet sack, and is grotesquely dressed. These are followed by a straggling, wandering line of Negro women, some young, some old; some in sombre dress, others in gay-colored clothes of all hues. The second man is the cryer, and his voice rings out:
>
> "Any nigger woman wanting to go North and earn good wages, $16 to $30 a month, fall into line. Easy times and lots of money. Fall into line! Free passage! No fees!" [5]

The scene shifts to the outskirts of another southern city:

> A young, smartly dressed, sleek white fellow is driving about the southern country districts. He stops his rig here and there to chat at some plain little hut. In the evening he returns to town with two or three Negro girls.
>
> Whether we follow the procession headed by the drum, or this smartly dressed young man in the rig, we find ourselves in the same place—a southern employment agency. These agencies, located at the main ports of the south, with branches in the interior cities, are the distributing centers of domestic and other help for the northern cities.
>
> When they reach the agencies, these green colored girls are promised three things—good wages, easy work, "really nothing to do;" and good times. . . . To them, going to Philadelphia or to New York seems like going to heaven, where the streets will be paved with gold and all will be music and flowers! While these visions are still bright, they sign an innocent-looking contract. . . . This is all the southern agency does—gathers the women up, gets the contract signed, pays the fare . . . and puts them aboard the boat. . . .[6]

That was the beginning of the nearly air-tight system of depravity whereby the green Afro-American girls from the south were transformed into "white slaves" in the north. At the ports of Philadelphia or New York:

> Scores of eager Negro women come forth, and they find, what? Not the promised golden land, but ugly docks looking out to an unknown country, and instead of friendly faces, agency runners and sharks.[7]

The agency representative—the "runner"—tried to rob the girls of their small savings. He herded them to a lodging house—often the employment agency "office." This office, usually a tenement apartment with records, if any, kept in a cupboard or spare kitchen drawer, impounded the girls' luggage. Where would the girls stay while waiting for work? Why in the office/apartment of course, where:

> The mingling of the employees and family is very close and indiscriminate. Men and women are lodged under such crowded conditions (four in a bed in a room sleeping six, for instance) that the maintenance of morality does not seem possible.[8]

Each girl was charged for board and room and no effort was made by the agency to find her a job until her money had been exhausted. Streetwalkers and madams were welcomed by the agency and allowed (for a "finder's fee") to recruit girls fresh off the boat. The "runners" showed the newcomers the "sights of the town," ending up with "concert halls," after which work as a maid or laundress in a quiet home faded in attractiveness. As for that contract the girl signed before coming north:

> [The girl] owes not $7, but from $17 to $20, for she finds in New York that this sum is the price for her transportation and agent's commission—almost three times the regular fare.[9]

"When a girl without control over her person and baggage, $20 in debt, and a total stranger in the city, is sent to a disorderly place, upon threats or promises, can she be said to be anything but a slave?" [10] asked Frances A. Kellor, who was a leader in bringing this situation to public attention. Born at Coldwater, Michigan, in 1874, she was a distaff dynamo who had earned her law degree at Cornell, studied sociology and economics at Chicago and the School of Philanthropy in New York. While enrolled at Chicago she had written a sociology textbook and conducted a study of southern prison systems that resulted in basic changes in many states. During her studies she observed Afro-Americans and came to certain conclusions that were advanced for that time.

She advocated social settlements in the black sections of the cities and pointed out the need for trained social workers to minister to Afro-Amer-

icans. Frances Kellor urged unionization of black workers, called for public employment bureaus and said "some kind of protective agencies are
absolutely essential for women seeking employment, and legal aid societies are needed . . . to prevent fraud and injustice in the matter of wages,
hours, etc." Organized charity to help blacks rather than the "indiscriminate giving" that was "pauperizing" them was mandatory, she insisted.
Furthermore, coordination was needed. The situation as she saw it demanded systematic control of agencies.

Her observation of metropolitan labor conditions caused her to propose a study of job-seeking and job-getting in the big cities. The College
Settlements Association sponsored the project. Miss Kellor rounded up a
squad of eight young assistants and spent two years covering 732 employment agencies in the major cities. Sometimes the group members posed as
employers, sometimes as workers and interviewed hundreds of employers,
agency staff people and managers, jobless men and women. The results
were published in 1904 under the title *Out of Work,* which does not
begin to hint at the sensational contents of the book.[11]

Frances Kellor had written a bombshell that exposed the vicious system of exploitation of immigrants—foreign and black—by employment
agencies, the mainstay of prostitution in the big cities. She was one of
those formidable females who sparked reform movements at the turn of
the century.

In the spring of 1905 she wrote about the well-organized, comfortably
financed efforts on behalf of Jewish immigrant girls and contrasted this
with the desperate needs of black girls arriving in the cities. Jewish immigrant girls were met by a matron at Ellis Island, had the use of a model
East Side employment agency, could stay at the Clara de Hirsch Immigrant Home where they could learn a useful trade. There was a worker
to keep in touch with them, and a probation officer and other workers to
assist them.[12]

"A similar system is equally a need of the Negro women imported from
the south," wrote Frances Kellor.[13] She was not the first to note this nor
to act to bring it about. Mrs. Victoria Earle Matthews was the pathfinder
in this field. Born into slavery a month after the Civil War started, she
and her family moved to New York City from Georgia in the 1870's. She
became nationally prominent for her articles and stories in both black
and white publications and for books she edited, such as her *Black-Belt
Diamonds: Gems from the Speeches . . . of Booker T. Washington.*[14]

An activist, Victoria Matthews founded the Women's Loyal Union of
New York and Brooklyn to work for black women's rights. When the National Association of Colored Women was organized in 1895 she was one
of the leaders and was elected chairman of its executive committee.

Mrs. Matthews saw the viciousness of the employment agency racket early and in the mid-nineties acted against it. She opened the White Rose Mission and Industrial Association in 1895 at 217 East 86th Street in New York. Its primary function was to serve the migrant black girls, providing lodging for them, helping them find jobs, conducting free classes in cooking and sewing and black history. The mission also operated as a settlement house, with a recreation program and library of books on Negro life, Bible classes, facilities and social meetings open to the neighborhood.

It was Mrs. Matthews who first carried the message to the Hampton Negro Conference in 1898 about the exploitation and degradation facing colored girls in the northern cities.[15] She aroused the indignation of the conference attendees, who expressed their concern by organizing a volunteer effort at the Norfolk, Virginia, docks to counsel the black girls who were streaming northward. A major endeavor of Mrs. Matthews's White Rose Mission was travelers' aid work at Pier 26, North River in New York, and coordination with the volunteers in Norfolk. But despite dedicated efforts, Victoria Matthews and her Norfolk collaborators could not keep up with the growing numbers of black migrants.

Because of the need, Frances Kellor's Inter-Municipal Committee on Household Research took the initiative in organizing associations for the protection of black women in Philadelphia and New York in April 1905.[16]

The purposes of the "Associations for the Protection of Negro [*sic*] Women" as set down in the New York association's constitution were:

1. To prevent friendless, penniless, and inefficient Negro women from being sent north by irresponsible agencies which often misrepresented to them conditions in the northern city.

2. To promote action in the south for the placing of matrons in southern ports to advise with and direct women about to leave for the north.

3. To arrange better accommodations on the steamship lines for the use of such women.

4. To promote travelers' aid work, lodging-house work, training school work, and other helpful work for the protection of southern girls coming north.

With typical Kellorian thoroughness the activities of the associations were broken down into six categories and standing committees were set up to "provide for the various needs of southern women." These committees were: travelers' aid; lodging houses; education; employment agencies; finances; and membership.

Branches of the associations were needed in the south to complete the system. Moreover, because of the rampant abuses of the southern "employment" agencies in getting the unknown girls to sign exploitative contracts, state laws were needed to stop this abuse. "To accomplish this protection of the unemployed, and to secure better legislation," Frances Kellor reported, was the work of the new southern associations. And through Hampton Institute, she said, the northern associations already were in active cooperation with workers at the southern ports, as early as May 1905.[17]

The associations united a small army of workers in the honest employment agencies, the lodging houses, churches, working girls' homes, and training schools. The work needed to be expanded without delay, Miss Kellor urged.

These associations were made up of citizens of both races and sexes. "The Colored people are really doing this work of helping their unemployed women themselves, but there are many places where the white people can help them," said Frances Kellor. One important move was to distribute warnings in the south, telling the young women to think before rushing north. Next the preachers in the south were called upon to cooperate in spreading the word.[18]

By October 1905 the Associations for the Protection of Negro Women and their allies could point to substantial accomplishments. Investigations had been pursued from Richmond to Boston. A lodging house for forty girls was opened in Philadelphia at 714 South 17th Street. The YWCA in Brooklyn and in Germantown (Philadelphia) established classes to train the colored girls as domestics.[19]

From June through September the fledgling operation had assisted some five hundred women in Philadelphia and New York at a per capita cost of 88 cents. Mrs. S. Layten, who acted as the agent at Philadelphia, "took charge" of four hundred of these, which she estimated to be only a third of those needing help. Obviously the New York activity had barely begun.

The New York Association for the Protection of Colored Women rapidly developed into a "centralizing force for the various settlements, training schools, and agencies" that worked to help the strangers from the south. The association went to the people with its program, conducting special Sunday afternoon meetings in the Afro-American churches of New York City. The first was at Mt. Olivet Baptist Church on December 24, 1905. The meeting was planned and arranged by Fred R. Moore, a close associate of Booker T. Washington, Mary White Ovington, Elizabeth M. Rhodes (secretary of the Inter-Municipal Research Committee) and Mrs. Elizabeth W. Tyler. Future meetings were scheduled for January 1906 at several churches.[20]

After the Philadelphia and New York associations were well under way, other associations came into being in Washington, D.C., and Baltimore in 1906. And in that year the National League for the Protection of Colored Women was organized by the simple device of affiliation of the Philadelphia and New York associations and the assumption of the duties of secretary of both by Frances Kellor.

By 1909 the National League had local associations in New York (with its national headquarters at 43 East 22nd Street), Philadelphia, Memphis and Baltimore. The league had dockworkers in three of these cities plus Norfolk. A significant breakthrough was the establishment in 1909 of an association in Memphis to deal with conditions in the Mississippi Valley area. There a matron was employed to "meet the large numbers of colored women who come to the city on excursions, either to see the world a little and return home, or to seek permanent employment, and who are exposed to various temptations and deceptions." [21]

In New York, the association's work was diverse. In addition to travelers' aid a broad range of activities had been added: sick and friendless strangers were assisted; boarding places were secured for children of working mothers; fresh-air vacations for children were arranged; girls were placed in jobs; lodging houses were investigated (disclosing the fact that most private lodgings were unsafe for young girls); employment agencies were studied (seventeen of forty-four were "doubtful or unsafe for girls to patronize") and fifteen which were reported to the Commissioner of Licenses were severely reprimanded at a special hearing; a union of reliable black employment agencies was formed under the association's aegis; a study of amusement places open to black girls revealed many with "degrading influences," few with wholesome ones; and the association assisted girls convicted of petty offenses.

The statistics for the New York association's 1909 activities included meeting 238 boats and nine trains, aiding 843 "cases" and meeting 980 women and children. Fifty-one girls were placed in jobs, twenty-nine meetings "in behalf of the work" were conducted; and 391 "visits . . . in the interest of the work" were made. The league's report notes that 1,018 letters were sent out, but in addition, 3,639 letters were sent to the south warning against migrating to the city unprepared.

The statistics were equally impressive for Norfolk and Baltimore. The work in Memphis officially got under way in August and the worker met 685 trains and aided 1,715 travelers. A shelter at 936 McDowell Street was part of the operation, assisted by the National League.

By 1910 the leadership of the league had changed. Frances Kellor was no longer associated with it. Her close friend, Mrs. Ruth Standish Baldwin, was chairman of the national organization and a member of the

New York association, which had Fred R. Moore as its chairman. Mrs. S. Layten had succeeded Frances Kellor as general secretary of the National League as well as secretary of the Philadelphia association.

As the black migrants streamed north the need for the National League's ministrations was manifest. And as the number of Afro-Americans in major northern cities swelled, alert citizens were convinced that the black residents needed help urgently—even more urgently than the arriving blacks.

2 / The Industrial Concern

By 1904 there were local chapters of the Armstrong Association (named after Hampton Institute founder General Samuel C. Armstrong) with some five hundred members in major cities of the north. Annually they raised funds for both Tuskegee and Hampton Institutes (though originally they had been formed to support Hampton alone). The association intended to become national, to provide "a bond of sympathy between the north and the south." [1]

Over the years, the association had enlisted prominent men in its activities. These were the undisputed leaders of social and civic action, ranging from the President of the United States down through the mayors of cities, presidents of universities and industrial and business leaders. The 1904 Lincoln's Birthday public meeting of the New York Armstrong Association, for instance, featured Andrew Carnegie as chairman, Harvard President Charles W. Eliot, Grover Cleveland and Dr. Booker T. Washington. Theodore Roosevelt and William Howard Taft also participated in Armstrong Association activities.

With such high-powered support and endorsement from the Establishment, the association had the potential of becoming a forceful agency for Negro uplift beyond its simple fund-raising function. Some association members brought up the matter of devoting a portion of their missionary effort to aiding the blacks in their "own back yard," i.e., the cities, instead of concentrating on Tuskegee and Hampton alone. So it was that members of the New York association were preconditioned for a proposal advanced by Professor William Lewis Bulkley.

Bulkley was a giant in his time. He was one of those exceedingly rare birds, a black Ph.D. (Some authorities reckon there were fewer than twenty blacks with doctorates even as late as 1910.) He was born in Greenville, South Carolina, in 1861 to free black parents, who put him through Claflin University. He worked as cook, steward and janitor, sold baby supplies, steam cookers and pictures to finance his way through Wesleyan College in Connecticut. After a year at the Universities of Strasbourg and Paris and two years at Syracuse University, he had his Ph.D. in Latin and Greek. Bulkley returned to Claflin as vice president and professor.

He was active in Methodist church affairs and was elected a delegate to the World's Sunday School Convention in London in 1889. The professor and his family migrated to New York in the nineties. There he taught seventh grade in a Manhattan public school. In 1901 he became the first black principal of an integrated school, Public School 80 at 265 West 41st Street in Manhattan—a "problem" school.[2]

Dr. Bulkley was in the forefront of race uplift in the first decade of the twentieth century. His wide vision of the needs of blacks in the city caused him to initiate and lead in reform and social service efforts. Thus he was one of the original group called together by William H. Baldwin, Jr., president of the Long Island Railroad in January 1903 to consider conditions among blacks in the cities and to plan steps to improve them.

Bulkley was a charter member and treasurer of the New York Association for the Protection of Colored Women in 1905. That same year he was named to the pioneering subcommittee on tuberculosis among Negroes of the city's Charity Organization Society. The following year, when Mary White Ovington was looking for support for her drive to arrange summer outings for black children and their mothers, Bulkley was one of those she induced to become a member of her West Side subcommittee of the Association of Neighborhood Workers. It was in 1905 that the educator became a founding member of the Niagara Movement and, in 1909, of the National Negro Conference that evolved into the National Association for the Advancement of Colored People.

In Dr. Bulkley's view, the school's functions did not stop at its doors.[3] It should serve its community as an educational and social center. He saw that black families near P.S. 80 had to have some means of caring for younger children as much to relieve working mothers as to educate the youngsters. He therefore opened a kindergarten class that helped solve this problem.

Bulkley's teachers visited the homes, talked with parents and observed the home environment. He and his staff members spoke frequently in churches. He programmed parents' meetings and conferences and ten major in-school events a year to broaden the effectiveness of the school, improve the standard of living in the community and build trust, rapport and understanding between home and classroom.

It was to equip out-of-school youths and adults with marketable skills that Professor Bulkley in 1905 launched a night school offering industrial and commercial courses. (Included were the three R's plus such practical offerings as cooking, millinery, dressmaking, carpentry, cabinet work, mechanical drawing and stenography.) "We had expected to register possibly 200 people," he reported, "but we registered 1,500 people, of whom about 1,300 were colored." The enthusiasm, faithful attendance and excellence of achievement of the students, Bulkley noted, made the night school a showpiece of what could be done. It was visited by philanthropists, educators and reformers. The Board of Education even promised to enlarge the plant the following year.[4]

But having learned a skill, what about a job? "The colored boy," commented Bulkley, "runs sheer up against a stone wall here." It was the educator's concern with this basic matter that moved him to call a meeting of leading blacks and whites to consider this fundamental problem. It was at this April 19, 1906, meeting that Bulkley presented a paper about the economic needs of city blacks, especially for jobs and some mechanism to secure them. Mary White Ovington reported on her studies of the living conditions of Negroes on the West Side. It was proposed that a permanent organization of whites and blacks be formed "to consider the political, economic and social condition of the Afro-American."[5] To nominate permanent officers and define the scope of the organization a committee headed by Dr. William J. Schieffelin, president of the Armstrong Association, and the Honorable Charles W. Anderson, United States customs commissioner for New York, was appointed.

Following the formation of this committee, Schieffelin, true to his abolitionist heritage as a descendant of John Jay, wrote all the Armstrong Association supporters and other major public figures likely to be interested in black advancement. He pointed out that with some seventy thousand blacks in the city "we ought to feel a responsibility concerning them."[6]

During the next several weeks meetings were held "quietly." An important one was held Friday, May 11, 1906, at the home of Dr. Schieffelin in Manhattan's fashionable sixties—East 66th Street. There were forty whites and twenty blacks present.[7]

Schieffelin, Bulkley, and Anderson spoke and the entire group agreed to constitute itself a committee that "in due time would consider the matter of a large organization." As for priorities, the committee went for the jugular: "while mindful of other phases of the problem of the New York

Afro-American, [it] would consider, for the present, at least, the economic phase." "Economic opportunity" for blacks was the common bond uniting the two groups, and the committee's purpose would be to get the facts of industrial conditions affecting black city dwellers and take steps to improve those conditions.

Schieffelin was elected president, Bulkley secretary and George McAneny treasurer. The committee consisted of "an exceptional group of leaders among the colored people of Manhattan and Brooklyn, and a number of men and women, not of the race, whose interests hitherto have for the most part had to do with the work for the Negro in the south." "So far as is known," continued the editor of *Charities and The Commons,* the national journal of social work, "the committee is unique as a compact working body in which representatives of progressive elements among both white and colored populations meet on an equal footing." [8] Tracing the evolution of the committee's business the magazine noted that Dr. Bulkley's industrial classes at P.S. 80 were the beginning point, followed by a census of colored business, and then the April 19 meeting of professional people and leaders.

Meanwhile, the Committee on Social Research of the city's Charity Organization Society had decided to survey job opportunities for Negro craftsmen in New York and had prepared printed forms for that purpose. These, through the New York Armstrong Association's cooperation, would be used for a local study. Clearly, there would be overlapping of efforts unless there was some coordination. "A joining of forces resulted in the organization" of the Committee for Improving the Industrial Condition of Negroes in New York, with subcommittees on publication, craftsmen, tradesmen, social centers and trade schools, neighborhood work, employment, public meetings and publication.[9]

Actually, the New York *Age* headlines reporting the committee's birth are as timely as today's newspaper:

TO WIN INDUSTRIAL CHANGES

LEADERS OF BOTH RACES
FORM PERMANENT COMMITTEE

Will Try to Open Up Avenues of
Employment in Skilled Trades [10]

On May 16, the following Wednesday, the black members of the committee met at Dr. Bulkley's P.S. 80 to consider the organization's future. Bulkley outlined the problems and priorities:

The Afro-American population of the city was increasing yearly at an almost "alarming" rate, whose meaning thoughtful persons should consider. European immigrants were streaming in and seemed to have no serious problem in finding jobs. But blacks did. With perhaps 75,000 Negroes in New York, self-interest, if not humanitarian interest demanded attention to their needs. "It is possible to be ignorant of or even to ignore a malady in its incipiency; but let it threaten to become an epidemic, and every agency for its cure is aroused and active," said Bulkley.

"It is impossible for these increasing thousands of black humanity to settle in the city and find wholesome housing conditions or helpful vocations. The districts in which they are forced to live are . . . crowded with disreputable characters and every sort of vicious institutions. The work in which they are likewise forced to engage is either poorly remunerative and menial or more attractive but vicious." The Negro immigrants were handicapped, he stated, by "centuries of training" in dependence. "Initiative, self-reliance and the lessons of thrift and economy that the European immigrant knows" were denied black slaves.

Dr. Bulkley sketched the Afro-American panel's recommendations for organized efforts to grapple with the multiple problems:

1. A committee on publication . . . (for) printing . . . but particularly aiming to inform the public through the press of any encouraging steps of the colored men in trades or business. In other words, this committee shall feel it its duty to secure the friendship of the press to our cause.

2. A committee on public meetings . . . in the churches, especially among the colored people, to enlighten them as to their needs, their duties, their opportunities, and also in other places where the white man may be brought to think of his share in improving the industrial conditions of the black man, as well as what the latter is doing and of what he is capable.

3. A committee on securing employment whose duty shall be twofold: (a) an investigation of the number of colored craftsmen in our city, and their ability in their several lines; (b) an investigation of the attitude of employers and labor organizations and places where the colored craftsmen can find work. In other words, said committee shall act as an advisory body, and information bureau, and to a certain extent, an employment bureau.

4. A committee on the employment of women which shall have duties similar to the one just mentioned.

5. A legal committee whose duties shall be the investigation of all enactments which will be of interest to the colored craftsmen and shall further stand ready to protect him in his rights as a workman.

6. A finance committee which shall look after the raising of funds necessary for the work of the Association.

7. A committee on trade schools and social centers.

8. A committee on membership, to whom shall be referred all names of persons proposed for membership.[11]

This spell-out and the sequence in which the elements were set down are significant. (This was a full three years before the convening of the National Negro Conference.) In the ordering of priorities, first place went to public relations—winning the press and informing the public through the mass media and public meetings. The initial emphasis seemed to be on telling whites of positive gains by blacks to offset the prevalent negative news and to indicate that blacks were capable workers and business people.

Considering that the original impetus for organizing was to upgrade and place black workers, it is remarkable that on Dr. Bulkley's list the committee for this task was third rather than first. The over-all framework was squarely in the Hampton-Tuskegee tradition in its focus on jobs and training; it was consonant with Atlanta University's investigative approach. In its inter-racial make-up the committee was avant garde, providing that meeting ground for "the best of both races" that leading whites and blacks had advocated for years. It broke through in another area: knowledgeable black leaders—not some group of "enlightened" whites—drew up the "bill of particulars."

At the next meeting, Tuesday, June 19, 1906, the Committee for Improving the Industrial Condition of Negroes in New York (CIICNNY) was formally organized, with Dr. William Jay Schieffelin as chairman; Samuel R. Scottron, Brooklyn manufacturer of pottery lamp bases and (later) first Negro on Brooklyn's Board of Education and Seth T. Stewart, district superintendent of public schools as vice-chairmen; Dr. Bulkley as secretary; and Mary White Ovington as assistant secretary. The executive committee, subcommittee chairmen and members were, as the organization's "introductory" leaflet stated, "an exceptional group of leaders." [12]

The behind-the-scenes story of the committee's formation was given by Mary White Ovington in a "progress report" to W. E. B. DuBois:

[Dr. Bulkley] has been the prime mover in getting up [a committee]. He appealed to the Charity Organization Society . . . for help or advice in regard to the getting of work for Negro mechanics. They referred him to the research committee, and it decided that an investigation should be made as to the number of such mechanics in the city. Mr. Kellogg grew considerably interested in the matter and the next thing a meeting was called of prominent colored folk and a few white people to see if anything definite could be done to improve the economic condition of the Negro in New York. Just at this time the Armstrong Association had been talking about doing something in New York; it felt it ought to help the colored folk at home as well as abroad, and here was surely an opportunity to get them interested. Mr. Schieffelin came to the meeting and was interested at once, and the upshot is a committee has been formed with Mr. Schieffelin as

chairman and Dr. Bulkley as secretary to improve the industrial condition
of the Negro in New York. Two committees are to go at once to work, one
on crafts and one on small business enterprises.

I am especially delighted to have the committee definitely committed to
work on the industrial question. (We put it first "economic" question, but
Mr. Isaac Seligman, the banker, for some reason changed it to industrial
which we may have to stretch a little.) It would be easy for the Armstrong
folk to give money to a philanthropy and there have the matter end, but
this commits them to work on the most difficult of all the Negro problems
in New York, and they are just the men to be of help if they are ready to
meet the issue. . . . I am tremendously tickled myself to have the industrial
education men turned to this partical problem of how the Negro can use
an industrial education in New York, and also to the study of the occasions
in which he is successful, and where he can best be encouraged. But we
must wait a couple of years before we know what [they] will do" . . .[13]

DuBois's response was one of cautious optimism. He was especially glad
to see this "work committee" formed. It had men of varying competence
on it, but that was true in all things. He could not overcome his strong
distaste for Fred Moore even though he had not met him and Mary
Ovington's acceptance of him made DuBois reserve judgment—"but be
careful of him!" Dr. Bulkley was a fine person—Scottron meant well but
was soft-headed.[14]

In its first publication the committee credited Professor Bulkley with
"fathering" the organization, though William H. Baldwin, Jr., was also
mentioned: [15]

The development of the committee is in a sense the fulfillment of a plan
long cherished by the late William H. Baldwin, Jr.

The present movement had its inception in the social work carried on
by Dr. Bulkley among the members of his race as principal of Public
School No. 80, on West Forty-first Street. Here was brought out concretely
and in the large, what was already known to everyone who is in contact
with the influx of southern Negroes into the northern cities—that with the
ever-increasing Afro-American population, there is developing each year a
more serious industrial problem. Thousands of people are idle or, what is
infinitely worse, actively engaged in criminal practices. It is fair to ask to
what extent they are forced into these conditions by the attitude of some of
the labor unions; to what extent by their own unfitness or shiftlessness.
Whatever be the cause, there is beyond question too large a number in vocations more or less menial, and entirely apart from that skill of hand
which they acquired in the south or West Indies. City boys and girls can be
taught elementary subjects to a certain point, but after that there is little
to hold them in school—few openings in life other than as hall boys or in
other unskilled callings where education does not count. The difficulty of

finding desirable employment for colored men and women is increasing and not diminishing.

The committee plans to proceed slowly. The first work is to get at the facts—and then to enlist public opinion and the co-operation of colored people themselves in ways that will develop opportunities where they are now denied through opposition or indifference or lack of information. The response which leaders of the colored people have met in putting the plan before them, would seem to indicate that the organization of the committee may be the begining of a wide-spread cooperative movement among the Negroes of New York.[16]

It was not until September 20, 1906, that CIICNNY held its first public meeting. It played to a packed house at the Mt. Olivet Baptist Church in the heart of the black neighborhood on West 50th Street in Manhattan. Booker T. Washington was in the city and pinch-hit for the scheduled speaker, his longtime associate Charles W. Anderson, who had been called to Washington, D.C.[17]

The Tuskegeean gave the sweltering audience one of the thrift-diligence, upward-bound inspirationals for which he was famous. But something new was added by the committee. The blacks "were not told the usual political claptrap that they are progressing as no race has progressed. They were told that from an economic standpoint they are dropping behind in the great cities and that only by working together and standing for high standards of workmanship, is there a chance—and a large chance—for better conditions." [18]

Dr. Schieffelin presided. Mrs. Mary Schenck Woolman, of Columbia University and the director of the Manhattan Trade School for Girls, urged women to take advantage of opportunities at the trade school. Dr. Bulkley reviewed conditions in the city and impressed upon his audience how "the glamour of a great city, housing conditions, and restriction to menial employment are having a decidedly harmful effect upon the majority of Negroes who have come north." Just how bad and how many were affected would be revealed, he said, by the committee's planned investigations.[19]

T. Thomas Fortune's New York *Age* front-paged the report of this initial meeting of the CIICNNY, headlining it:

OPEN DOOR IN TRADES
DR. WASHINGTON ASKS
BETTER CHANCES FOR
MAKING LIVING;
CHIDES RACE PAPERS
Feature Bad at Expense of Good
News and Discourage the Young
—Bulkley Talks.[20]

But the news in that issue was dominated by the *Age*'s biggest type, screaming ATLANTA SLAYS BLACK CITIZENS—the headline over the report of the Atlanta riot September 20. "Scores Killed; *Infernal Result of Agitations by Whites;* Hoke Smith is Guilty; *Abominable Campaign of 'The News' also is Responsible;* Black Men Retaliate; But are Disarmed by Militia . . ."

The Atlanta riot sent a shudder of revulsion through the nation. It stirred Atlantans to action. Under the leadership of ex-governor William J. Northen of Georgia, leaders of the black and white communities did come together and established the Atlanta Civic League.[21]

Meanwhile, back in New York, the CIICNNY's subcommittees moved along their special avenues to help black New Yorkers. There was a determined effort to canvass all skilled Negro workers and build a file of their names and specialties. This information was fundamental to an employment bureau, which soon went into operation. There was also a move to organize the various tradespeople, dressmakers, waiters, carpenters, mechanics and printers. Over the months and years the committee cracked the prevailing wall of disinterest and/or prejudice, to place painters, bricklayers, decorators, masons, plumbers and construction workers. There was one signal success in prying a charter for a Negro local out of the Grand United Brotherhood of Carpenters and Joiners of America. It was, unfortunately, an isolated and limited victory.

The leadership of Seth Stewart, the public school official, brought into action a battalion of volunteer canvassers who collected hundreds of names on a petition for night schools for Negroes. The petition succeeded, and two such schools were soon opened. In February 1907 Stewart reported to the CIICNNY that one of these, Evening School 67, had "surpassed all expectations in the excellence of work and numbers in attendance." [22]

Throughout this period the CIICNNY used public platforms to report on the work to white and black audiences. More important still, many of the meetings were held in the black communities, in churches and meeting rooms where the people themselves could and were encouraged to bring up and discuss their problems. This was a logical outgrowth and corollary of the "investigations" which the various subcommittees made concerning conditions among blacks. Discontent and immediate needs were channel lights that guided the committee and set its course. The community meetings were sounding boards to direct the CIICNNY actions.

A close relationship soon developed between the CIICNNY and the League for the Protection of Colored Women. By 1907 the committee's letterhead announced that it was affiliated both with the Armstrong Association and the New York Association for the Protection of Colored Women. At the committee's February 1907 meeting in Dr. Schieffelin's home, Frances Kellor reported formation of the National League for the Protection of Colored Women.[23]

"One thing is quite apparent to our committees," CIICNNY secretary S. R. Scottron reported, "and that is that colored people are settling hereabout too fast, faster than they can be assimilated and adjusted to surrounding conditions." [24]

Scottron was concerned not only as a long-time Negro resident of the city, but worried, like his counterparts in Boston, Philadelphia and other major northern cities, about the impact of the new black immigrants on the relations between Negroes and whites and feared that they would worsen. "This matter of overcrowding here should have our earnest attention," he warned, "to the end that we may preserve what we already have attained . . . Already they [whites] are discussing a return to the separate school system of former days. Many very powerful and influential persons have their minds already in that direction." [25]

What to do? Disperse the blacks. Noting that the colored population was concentrated in four or five spots, Scottron advocated, "send the people over to the green fields and purer air of Long Island and New Jersey" which rapid transit, he claimed, made as accessible as the crowded tenements of San Juan Hill.

In the future, CIICNNY hoped to establish "a central office and headquarters that shall be readily accessible and a central point toward which all may turn and from which the most powerful aid proceed for the general uplift of the colored people of the city." [26]

During 1908 CIICNNY began paying the salary of the dock worker who reported to the New York Association for the Protection of Colored Women. During the year the Reverend Victor G. Flinn, a white Moravian minister with offices at 39 East 42d Street, was hired as secretary of the committees. CIICNNY through September of 1909 continued to focus on industrial training. It guided Negro youths to the two new evening industrial schools, one at 134th Street and Lenox Avenue, the other at 138th west of Fifth Avenue, where the latest instruction in machine shop practices, toolmaking, printing and woodworking was available.[27]

And in 1909 the CIICNNY employment subcommittee initiated a "Mechanics' Association," probably the first in New York City that brought together some fifty skilled black workers "to stimulate friendships that shall work for the solidifying of the race without creating . . . antagonisms" toward other races. The skills included bricklaying, hod carrying, painting, plastering, plumbing, lathing, goldsmithing, blacksmithing, and carpentry. Because of the committee's activity, reported Flinn, who was also association secretary, the City and Suburban Homes Company planned to hire more black mechanics. This company was about to build a large model tenement for Negroes on West 63rd Street, behind its successful Tuskegee Apartments, in the heart of a densely populated black neighborhood. CIICNNY backed the project, promoting sale of shares in Suburban Homes Company to committee members for this purpose.[28]

In Philadelphia, wealthy young Quaker John T. Emlen organized a social service agency in April 1908 to develop "life and opportunity" for blacks. Emlen called the organization the Armstrong Association of Philadelphia and it conducted one fund-raising event per year for the benefit of Hampton and Tuskegee. However, its primary program was ongoing effort to find work for black mechanics and even to act as a contracting agency when necessary.[29] Richard R. Wright, Jr. (who later became bishop of the African Methodist Episcopal Church and president of Wilberforce University), was the first field secretary. Three school visitors were employed to promote education and act as liaison between school and home. (They proved so effective that the city took over this function later.)

Wright organized more than two hundred workers into "The Colored Mechanics' Association of Philadelphia," which he described as a mutual aid organization rather than a labor union. Actually, it operated as a contracting agency through which bids were made on jobs ranging from 75¢ to $1,600 that first year. By 1910 there was more work than there were qualified black workers available. The Armstrong Association therefore campaigned for trade education for blacks and for industrial training and night school opportunities in the public schools.[30]

Like the CIICNNY in New York, the Philadelphia activity was interracial in its board and committee structure. Its fundamental difference was that its ongoing staff and program were manned by professionals rather than volunteers.

3/The Social Concern

Muckraker Ray Stannard Baker, who had become famous writing for *McClure's* magazine, examined Negro life in the south when he investigated lynchings in 1904 and 1905. In 1906 and 1907 Baker traveled widely in the south again and in northern cities gathering material for a series of articles on "Following the Color Line" for *American Magazine*.[1] His articles stirred up considerable controversy and discussion, though they were, by present standards, conservative. His observations became a valuable overview of race relations in the major cities of the south and north.

Baker was a natural choice to "headline" a meeting in New York City of people interested in aid to black citizens. Mrs. Ruth Standish Baldwin invited him to address a group at her home at 44 East 65th Street in Manhattan on January 20, 1910.

Mrs. Baldwin was the widow of William H. Baldwin, Jr., the extraordinary young railroad mogul whose death six years before at age forty-one had taken from the scene Booker T. Washington's closest white friend.

Baldwin had been president of the Long Island Railroad and was a Democrat in an era of Republicans. He had championed reform in New York City through selfless service on numerous civic commissions. Universally respected, he had been a director of thirty-seven corporations and dozens of civic and social agencies and was called "the Galahad of the Marketplace" by Dr. Felix Adler for his incorruptibility.

Ruth Baldwin was a blue-blooded Brahmin, daughter of Samuel Bowles, publisher of the venerable Springfield, Massachusetts, *Republican*. She traced her ancestors to Miles Standish, one of the first English colonists. She shared her husband's concern for blacks and for reform and enlisted her strength in respectable radicalism as a supporter of many pioneering labor progressive movements and as trustee of her alma mater, Smith College.

Mrs. Baldwin had become active in the work of the National League for the Protection of Colored Women, serving as the league's chairman. Frances Kellor, who had initiated the protective work in 1905, was then living in her apartment. In arranging the January 1910 meeting Mrs. Baldwin wrote Ray Stannard Baker that he would be the only speaker and the rest of the time was to be given to "practical discussion of difficult phases of the work to the end of greater effectiveness and more cooperation among those laboring in this special field." The only hint of what she meant by that was her statement "we feel that a lodging house, employment bureau and the subject of recreation need to be considered and discussed among other things." [2]

The meeting began in the afternoon and in addition to Baker there were fourteen speakers. The Brooklyn *Eagle* called the gathering a conference and both the *Eagle* and the New York *Age* noted that it was the

"National Association [*sic*] for the Protection of Colored Women" that had called the meeting to discuss conditions in the north. Mrs. Baldwin, as hostess, presided and was assisted by Dr. William Jay Schieffelin, who spoke about the late William H. Baldwin, Jr.'s, plans for cooperative work among black Americans.[3]

Ray Stannard Baker reviewed the attractions that pulled rural Negroes to the cities and the inhuman conditions they suffered in those cities. He complimented the league on its "first aid to the injured"—the women coming north by the hundreds—and the wisdom of the league's workers in shielding them from temptation.

Warning that it would be more difficult to protect them "in the midst of the fiercely competitive life of our northern cities" as the number of migrants increased, Baker pointed up a fine dilemma. There were already far too many blacks crowded into the cities, he said, and, "in one way, the easier and safer you make it for the girls to come, the more you will have coming." It was necessary to strike at fundamental causes to "stop the stream at its source." And basically, he stated, "the Negro problem is inextricably bound up with all the larger economic and political problems of today . . . essentially a problem of competition and of the distribution of wealth. We center wealth and opportunity in the city and it draws young men and women, white or black, as the flame draws the moth." [4]

Basic conditions had to be changed, said Baker, and this "great work is even now going on everywhere in the south." Sensible education was the beginning point, he thought, training both black and white children in the Hampton-Tuskegee manner. Cooperative efforts that would give blacks a greater share of the products of their labor were a paramount need, though he did not define these, and called for brotherhood, not charity.

The presentations that followed ranged from Dr. Schieffelin's calling for laws against cocaine and the Reverend William H. Brooks's solemn denunciation of dancing to Fred R. Moore's demand that the northern press quit temporizing and speak out against Jim Crow. The Reverend Henry L. Phillips, a member of the Philadelphia Armstrong Association, had seen the progress made by a coordinated approach in that city just since 1908 and reported on it. The main emphasis of the meeting, however, was on the need for recreational outlets for Negro girls.[5]

Curiously enough, none of the immediate reports on this meeting of thirty-eight prominent black and white citizens mentions any discussion of coordinating, merging or joining forces for black advancement. It was months before there was any such claim. And yet, the advantages of coordinated effort must have been self-evident to most of those present. Of the thirty-eight attending, eleven were CIICNNY officers or committee members in New York. Most of the leaders of the National League for the Protection of Colored Women were there.[6] The White Rose Mission had a contingent at the meeting.[7] Another person present who had worked with these organizations as a member of the Negro Fresh Air Committee was the Reverend William N. Hubbell of Judson Memorial Church. Among those attending were adherents of both the Booker T. Washington–Tuskegee and the militant Niagara Movement–National Negro Conference schools of thought. And also present were Professor Robert E. Park, Lillian D. Wald and Mrs. Schieffelin. Clearly, there was much overlapping of interest among the agencies represented at the meeting but all were concerned with the deepening need for aid to the city blacks.

During this period a young black Columbia graduate student named George Edmund Haynes had met with Mrs. Baldwin and Frances Kellor at offices of the National League for the Protection of Colored Women. Haynes discussed with the ladies the pressing need for social work among blacks in New York.

Solidly built, with the wide brow and firm jaw of the rugged, all-American cowboy, Haynes had covered considerable academic ground since his birth thirty years before in Pine Bluff, Arkansas. He had navigated through the institute in his home town, the A. & M. College at Normal, Alabama, and the prep school and college at Fisk University in Nashville, Tennessee, where he received the A.B. degree. He had piled up a fine academic record at Fisk. It was so good, in fact that he won a scholarship to Yale's graduate school. There he earned his M.A. degree, studying with men famed in their day, including Professor William Graham Sumner (a favorite of the Power Elite for such pearls of wisdom as "There is no reason, at the moment, why every American may not acquire capital by being industrious, prudent, and frugal, and thus become rich.") [8]

From 1905 on Haynes traveled the south as secretary of the International Committee of the YMCA. This was the Y's Jim Crow arm and Haynes's responsibility was to visit the 106 colored YMCA units, most of which were in the south, seventy-four of them on Negro college campuses. In the course of this work Haynes met the leaders of Negro education, church and fraternal work. His base of operations was Atlanta and he attended the Tuskegee and Atlanta Conferences. Haynes met W. E. B. DuBois during this time.

Haynes was convinced that he needed further grounding in economics and the social sciences. So, as he put it, "I found my way to Columbia University and the great laboratory of New York" in 1908.[9]

In the city Haynes met Dr. E. P. Roberts and William L. Bulkley. He was hired by CIICNNY to interview students at Bulkley's booming night school and help place them through the various employment agencies operating under the new New York Employment Office law. He quickly realized that the information he was gathering would be useful fodder for a Ph.D. thesis.

Dr. Edward T. Devine was then director of the Charity Organization Society's (COS) School of Philanthropy, which had a working liaison with Columbia University. A number of faculty members of each institution also held appointments at the other, and there was much crossover in coursework by students of the two schools. Devine also was a director of the COS Bureau of Social Research, established in 1906 "as a necessary adjunct to its teaching function." COS was intent on developing a coordinated employment agency locally, if not nationally, and as a first step wanted the Bureau to study work and migration patterns. This was a time in United States history when no federal, state or city employment agencies existed, only private agencies. Fellows of the Bureau of Social Research were assigned various parts of this study. Young Haynes landed a $50-a-month fellowship at the bureau and Dr. Devine assigned to him the study of the Negro migration to the cities.

Haynes talked with Columbia University Professor Samuel McCune Lindsay, his faculty counselor, and received approval to cultivate this field for his Ph.D. thesis. It was when he worked out the form of the inquiry and began sifting census data that another phase of the subject struck him. It was the question of the fate of those Negro migrants when they arrived in the northern cities. The only thoroughgoing work on the subject was *The Philadelphia Negro,* an 1898 study by W. E. B. DuBois. Haynes promptly decided to include this vital matter in his New York inquiry. (He finished his field work in January 1910 and acknowledged the help of Dr. Bulkley, Dr. Roswell C. McCrea and a fellow classmate, E. E. Pratt.)

Columbia was the ideal place for Haynes to develop his interests to the fullest. He concentrated on sociology and economics and social work administration, rounding out his studies with courses in education at Teachers College. Among his teachers were several who played significant roles in his later work. Professor Lindsay was one, Lillian D. Brandt another and, above all Professors E. R. A. Seligman and Edward T. Devine. Devine had an excellent opportunity to observe Haynes in his class, and what he saw he admired.

Devine also was in the midst of COS discussions about the black migrants in the city. In the years from 1903–1911 the number of blacks in just one six-block area of Manhattan's west side had soared from 300 to nearly 5,000 families.[10] Their problems were obvious to casual observers and the dimensions of their needs were being measured by trained observers. Mary White Ovington was one of these, and her study documented that in 1908 two of every seven black babies in the Bronx and Manhattan died before their first birthdays (white mortality was half that). The mortality rate was a staggering 290 per thousand live births. She found that the black babies succumbed mainly from improper nutrition because a disproportionate share of black income went into rent.[11]

There were agencies among the blacks attempting to deal with their problems, but a number of influential whites suspected there was waste, duplication, fraud, ineffectiveness and inefficiency in vital services to the city's blacks. As R. R. Wright, Jr., had observed, the one black agency most experienced in social service was the church, but the various denominations, unable or unwilling to cooperate, did not begin to meet the needs of the newly urban blacks. The COS kind of coordination, overview and long-range approach was mandatory.[12]

So Haynes, in those green years of professionalizing black self-help, was the man of the moment in 1910. He was about two years from the completion of his doctoral work, but his solid scholarship had impressed his Columbia mentors.[13] He was the number one candidate and obvious choice for any black-serving social agency.

Haynes's logic, academic background and force of character struck Ruth Standish Baldwin and Frances Kellor favorably and his conclusions about black migration and the need for social work for blacks mirrored their own. His emphasis on the need to train black social workers was eminently sensible. All three of them agreed that such efforts were overdue.

The time was opportune, for the CIICNNY was in the process of reexamining its program. It had appointed a subcommittee to propose plans for enlarging its activities. Mrs. Baldwin was a member of the committee and met with George Haynes once again as to his interest in the post of executive secretary of the new, expanded CIICNNY. In such an expansion, plans for social work and training of black social workers would receive primary emphasis. Such plans, wrote Mrs. Baldwin to Haynes, were "properly the work of the Committee and the reason the work has not been effective so far is because they have failed to see that such careful studies are necessary as the basis for any constructive work. . . . I want to see you put in as secretary of the Industrial Committee and given a free hand to work out plans and methods for getting at results decided upon by the Committee in consultation with you."[14]

Meanwhile, Fisk University president George A. Gates invited Haynes to join his faculty as a professor of economics. Haynes saw it as a golden opportunity to develop a center for training black social workers and continue his research in the social sciences. As he weighed the alternatives he conferred with Professor Edward T. Devine, who suggested, "Why not tie the two things together and focus your educational work with the students at Fisk University as a scientific foundation for their further education in social welfare and the organization of city agencies into which these trained workers might be introduced?" [15] Fisk seniors would do a specified number of hours of social work in the field each week under Haynes's direction. And Haynes would supervise the social welfare action for blacks in New York, ultimately using the trained workers from his Fisk "laboratory."

In the spring of 1910 a draft program proposing that CIICNNY expand its activities and institute social work coordination and training was formally presented by its subcommittee. In spite of strong endorsement of the plan from several CIICNNY members the organization voted down the expansion and the new emphasis proposed. Mrs. Baldwin, Frances Kellor and George Haynes were stunned.

Their consternation, however, was superseded by determination to go ahead nonetheless. They decided to organize an "urban committee" if they could assemble a nucleus of strong leaders pledged to cooperate. Haynes sought out Professor Devine, who promised that he and other friends of his would help with the organization work in New York. Members of the CIICNNY subcommittee who had pressed for expansion joined in. A memo outlining a prospective program was developed: [16]

> The whole scheme is meant to be initiated within a five year period, provided financial support and competent workers can be secured.
>
> A. For successful work of this character, it is evident that there is need of competent trained Negro men and women who shall also possess the spirit of social service.
>
> At the present time there is no adequate training for social workers given anywhere to Negro students. It is, therefore, desirable that some college for Negroes suitably located, well esteemed, properly equipped and possessing the necessary social spirit should be encouraged to offer opportunities for such training to its students. Fisk University meets these requirements, and it is moreover in an especially favorable condition for the work at present, as it is reorganizing its work in economics, sociology and history, and has appointed as associate professor of economics, Mr. George E. Haynes, who has seemed to the present members of the Committee the best available person to organize and supervise the work in New York City. . . .
>
> The practical program of work is in two parts: First, its application to New York and other cities. . . . Second, the training of workers at the University.

I. *The training of workers* (at Fisk University):

(a) Instruction will be given the students in economics, sociology, labor problems and social work.

(b) Special training will be given in methods of social work and in research and investigation. The students will study problems like housing, employment, delinquency, as they find them in Nashville. Courses of lectures, already arranged, will be given by experts on social problems from New York, Philadelphia, Chicago and Atlanta.

II. *Plan of procedure for New York City:*

Mr. G. E. Haynes to take position of associate professor of Economics at Fisk University, September, 1910, spending most of the school year 1910–11 in organizing the department; putting an assistant at work in New York City in September and returning himself in May or June 1911 to organize and establish the work here. Therefore he will divide his time and ability to train and install assistant and substitutes in either place.[17]

A meeting to consider the matter was called on May 19, 1910, in a room at the New York School of Philanthropy. Mrs. Baldwin was chairman and a number of prominent black and white leaders attended. It was decided that interracial cooperation was the basic principle on which the organization was to develop. Whites were to work *with* blacks for their mutual advantage and advancement rather than working *for* them as a problem, emphasized Haynes.[18] There was tentative agreement to go ahead.

George Haynes sent a copy of the proposed plan to President Gates of Fisk, underscoring the opportunity it presented to the university to train social workers. "Thus Fisk," wrote Haynes, "could lead the way for the Negro college to grapple with the city problem as Tuskegee and Hampton are working at the rural conditions." [19]

The cooperative arrangement was made with Fisk University without difficulty, for Paul D. Cravath, one of those deeply interested in organizing the urban social work, was the son of Fisk's first president, and Haynes had continued his close association with the school as a distinguished alumnus. Part of Haynes's time was to be spent in "development of the work in New York." [20] This, as it developed, was easier said than done.

The increasing concentration of Negroes in cities demands better methods of work and more efficient workers of their own race to help them meet the conditions they must face. In addition to the ordinary handicaps of life in cities, Negroes find it more difficult than do others of similar economic standing to secure good neighborhoods and houses in which to live; harder to get suitable employment outside of domestic and personal service, or recreation free from degrading temptations. They often lack experi-

ence and training such as are needed in industrial and business competition, and they meet a prejudice which restricts their activities in many
directions and single handed is often insurmountable.

The agencies for their economic and social improvement are often too
few in number and too weak in resources to give the service needed. In
New York and other cities, there is also a growing and justifiable demand
on the part of those doing and supporting such work, that the many agencies for betterment shall be standardized and united and that efficient
Negro workers be secured, trained and put in charge.[21]

In those words the "representatives from many institutions and organizations, and apostles of many points of view" described the needs they
sought to meet by coming together to form still another agency on September 29, 1910.[22] They met to form the Committee on Urban Conditions Among Negroes, which, as they put it, was "an outgrowth of a conference held last January of persons active in work among colored people
in New York City, at which there was strong expression of the need for
co-operation among existing betterment agencies, in order to avoid the
waste of effort and money due to duplication of work and to the starting
of new agencies without sufficient preliminary study of conditions and
needs." [23]

At this September meeting a plan for the committee's future work was
adopted, George E. Haynes was named director (1910–1918), E. E. Pratt
was elected secretary, a budget of $4,000 was approved and a committee
of three, consisting of Mrs. Baldwin, Dr. Bulkley and Professor McCrea,
was chosen to nominate officers and an executive board of seven members
in addition to the officers.[24]

The committee set forth a seven-point program of work that was
clearly in the COS tradition of professional, non-duplicative effort. Coming, as it did, after the 1909 meeting and before the 1910 meeting of the
National Negro Conference, its emphasis on human needs and exclusion
of political and civil rights action is significant:

The general purpose of the work outlined would be (1) to make a survey
of prevailing conditions; (2) to co-ordinate the work now being done; (3)
through the education of public opinion and the development of financial
support to create a standard of work; (4) to bring about the establishment
of agencies to meet needs not already provided for; (5) to see that the several Negro neighborhoods may be proportionately supplied.

Cooperation of agencies at work for the improvement of the community
at large. These general agencies have had very little success in reaching the
colored people; by conference, suggestions and information more effective
connection with the Negro population may be secured.

Improving of housing and neighborhood conditions; higher rents are usually charged to colored people than to white for similar accommodations. The causes and remedies, if any, need attention. Respectable Negro neighborhoods find themselves unable so far to keep out persons of doubtful or immoral character. There is a lodging house problem, especially with reference to domestic help.

The employment problem needs attention. It is the crux of the situation. Negroes are ill prepared to grapple with an intensive industrial competition, and, except in domestic and personal service, meet a race prejudice which is often insurmountable. In business lines, the development of many small dealers already in business could be furthered toward larger economic group self-dependence and cooperation.

Development of thrift agencies: (1) in connection with the general thrift agencies of the community which have little influence with the Negro population; (2) such agencies owned and operated by Negroes themselves.

Provision of such amusement and recreation centres as would lead to the profitable use of leisure.

The relation of the Negro church and other religious institutions to social conditions.

The whole scheme is meant to be initiated within a five-year period, provided financial support and competent workers can be secured.[25]

Meanwhile, down at the Charity Organization Society hall, the National Negro Conference had met for three days in May and transformed itself into what it hoped would be a permanent organization called the National Association for the Advancement of Colored People. As reported in the social work journal, the NAACP's object would be "to call the attention of the nation to the frequently unjust treatment of colored people in the United States and the danger to American democracy of continued and customary injustice. The methods of work will include careful investigation into present conditions and the publication of results, organized correspondence, a bureau of information, federating of Negro organizations and increasing cooperation among them and the holding of conferences and public meetings. Beside tracts and pamphlets the association expects to publish a small monthly journal." [26]

Though the emphasis on publicity and protest could be discerned in this outline, there were a number of points of possible overlap with CUCAN. Among these were the "investigation of conditions," the federating of Negro organizations and increasing their cooperation. Perhaps this challenge was responsible, in part, for the terminology in the CUCAN objectives when they were listed officially at the organizational meeting.

The committee's objects had been condensed to two: "First, the careful study of the conditions which result from the growing concentration of Negroes in cities with a view to encouraging helpful co-operation between betterment agencies already in existence and the establishment of such agencies where necessary; Second, the training of young Negro men and women for social work among their own people." [27]

Haynes had to scurry about to secure a field secretary. In the first place, there were only three trained black social workers in the nation. The ideal man for the job, Benjamin F. Lee, Jr., then field secretary of the Philadelphia Armstrong Association, vacillated when Haynes queried him about coming to New York. By the time Lee indicated that he could take the job full time after November 20, 1910, Haynes had already hired a man whose background looked promising. Savannah-born Emanuel W. Houstoun was twenty-seven, with an A.B. from Atlanta University and post-graduate credits there. He had Dr. DuBois's endorsement and had worked on investigations in Atlanta and Savannah, Georgia, Elizabeth City, North Carolina, and Jefferson City, Missouri. Houstoun was at the time mathematics instructor at Missouri State School. Haynes and the CUCAN held out to him the prospect of the big city, work he liked, and a part-time fellowship at the School of Philanthropy and Columbia University to continue his education. [28]

As Haynes saw it, Houstoun's first job was to research the city. He prepared an outline of work for the field secretary. [29] It called for three basic studies: (1) of agencies "for social betterment among Negroes"; (2) of agencies working for both blacks and whites; and if possible (3) of efforts to develop private employment agencies. Haynes spelled out questions to be covered and the schedules to be kept. In looking at the operating agencies he wanted facts as to personnel, plant and equipment; operations, boards and officers; paid and unpaid workers, their age, training, experience, salary, job descriptions and even a statement on their probable efficiency; also, he wanted information about the territory covered, the Negro population and its proportion of the total; socio-economic standing of the families reached and facts about the needs not reached or attempted.

Following the assembly of such data, Haynes planned to district the city, mapping locations of existing agencies and following the pattern of COS districts. A similar pattern was to be followed for the agencies serving both white and black citizens. Haynes believed that the facts collected would "probably give clues to the Negro leaders through whom connection with the neighborhoods was attempted and those leaders should be interviewed for record of successes and methods, as well as for information about and reasons for failure."

At some point during the winter of 1910 it became apparent that Houstoun was not working out as field secretary. The committee later called his hiring an "unsuccessful venture." Houstoun's replacement was a twenty-five-year-old Virginian who was "general assistant" at the Louis-ville, Kentucky, Central High School, teaching mechanical drawing classes. This young man was Eugene Kinckle Jones, with an A.B. from Virginia Union and an M.A. from Cornell University.[30] Jones came to the CUCAN job on April 10, 1911, but was prudent enough to do so on a year's leave of absence from the Louisville public schools. He need not have bothered with that precaution, for when the lanky, soft-spoken ath-lete joined CUCAN he had found his niche.[31] The Reverend A. Clayton Powell wrote George Haynes a few weeks later, "I have just had a long talk with Mr. Eugene K. [Jones] this morning and he is going to make good in this city." [32] Powell's forecast proved accurate.

By the following July, CUCAN could cite a respectable roster of achievements in its brief history. On the research front, it had collected "reliable facts" about eighteen institutions and filed them for reference. It also had cooperated with the National League for the Protection of Col-ored Women in a "preliminary survey" of the Harlem district that re-sulted in "a movement of the Colored residents to improve their neigh-borhood"; and formation of an amusement committee that began work to secure recreation and playground centers. The committee arranged for a model camp for boys, campaigned through letters, papers, and pulpits against children under sixteen attending picnics and dances at night, and organized a monthly conference of church and social agencies working with boys in Manhattan and Brooklyn (out of this grew boys' clubs for black youngsters). Two black graduate students had been selected for so-cial work scholarships at the School of Philanthropy. And a cooperative agreement had been worked out with the national and New York organi-zations for the protection of colored women.

CUCAN had under way a survey of rental rates and the beginnings of its housing and neighborhood organization efforts. The committee had agreed to take over the supervision of "fresh-air work" among the city's Negroes. A study was in process of conditions and facilities endured by black delinquent girls in both Brooklyn and Manhattan. And a confer-ence of social workers among blacks in Brooklyn and Manhattan was scheduled for fall.[33]

The new social work agency was up and on its way.

4/A New Era

As the second decade of the twentieth century began, it was clear that for economy of effort and money, the existing social agencies in the black betterment field in New York should coordinate and preferably amalgamate. There were three major ones. To bring them together would presumably strengthen all three and satisfy the tidying-up instincts of the Charity Organization Society leaders and other social work professionals.[1]

During the summer of 1911, Professor George Haynes was in New York City directing the work of the Committee on Urban Conditions Among Negroes and working up plans for a federation to include the two other agencies, i.e., the National League for the Protection of Colored Women and the Committee for Improving the Industrial Conditions of Negroes in New York. There was a good deal of momentum behind the Haynes project due not only to the push provided by the Charity Organization Society of New York but to the interlocking directorates of the three organizations.

So, a "plan for uniting the social betterment organizations among Negroes" was drawn up and circulated for consideration. It proposed to name the new organization the Social Service League Among Negroes. This new federation would consist of an executive board of three representatives each from CUCAN, NLPCW and CIICNNY. The new agency would "unite for mutual help and cooperation such social betterment organizations that have for their purpose the objects as are outlined in the statement of CUCAN."[2]

The new agency was to be a weak organization with limited powers:

> The general policy of the League shall be to act as a steering body for approval of plans, budgets, etc. of the organizations so united, but shall have only approving power. However, it shall be understood that neither of the organizations will undertake anything in the way of work or budget which is not first approved by the League or which has been disapproved by it. The officers and accredited agents of the League shall act as advisers and supervisors for the several organizations and as a central clearing house for information and methods of work and workers.[3]

Expansion of the organization was anticipated by the board's power to choose six additional members from the three agencies and to bring on the federation's "general committee" two representatives of organizations in other cities that might wish to "unite as branches."

Flawed though it was, this plan provided a basis for discussion. By mid-August it had been considerably reworked and the date for the organizational meeting had been selected: September 26, 1911. There must have been some heated discussion of the plan among CIICNNY leaders, for the Reverend Samuel H. Bishop, prominent in its activities and a CUCAN director, wrote Haynes about semantic questions raised in the proposed constitution. Article IV called for "supervision" by the new agency of its constituent organizations. This was too strong, advised Bishop; could the word "examination" be substituted? "Won't the use of that word help our cause with the Industrial Committee? I do want this thing to go, and therefore, I want to do everything to help make it go." [4]

Two weeks before the organizational meeting CIICNNY directors met and Bishop wrote Haynes about that event: "You will be glad to know, as you will be officially informed, that we carried our point (Sept. 12) with only one amendment, namely, that the three unified societies be named, the understanding in the committee being that the present Urban Committee (CUCAN) should continue its organization doing local work, and thus be not a rotten borough but one of the three integrating societies. I am very glad of this and am sorry personally that the Industrial Committee has delayed the consummation of so desirable an end." [5] So it was that the annual report listed as "united organizations" the CIICNNY, NLPCW and CUCAN. Each of these was allowed not more than nine representatives in NLUCAN. [6]

Any move to put together an agency affecting the lives of black citizens was bound to require the evaluation of the arbiter of Negro life in the nation. And, of course, Booker T. Washington knew of, if he did not actually stimulate, the consolidation of the three agencies. [7] Five of Washington's closest associates in the New York area were CIICNNY board members: Charles W. Anderson, P. A. Johnson, Fred R. Moore, Dr. E. P. Roberts and Mrs. Baldwin. Moore, Roberts and Mrs. Baldwin were associated with NLPCW and Roberts, Mrs. Baldwin, Schieffelin and William G. Willcox, President of the New York City Board of Education, with CUCAN. Furthermore, the last two were Tuskegee trustees. It is not surprising that Haynes, therefore, sent Washington information about the proposed merger and asked to discuss it with him when he visited New York that summer.

Washington was concerned because the rise of the NAACP was a visible, continuing index of the erosion of his influence. He had been concerned when the CIICNNY was formed, though his friend Charles Anderson had assured him that "our friends have control of the [CIICNNY] movement, so far as the colored men on the Committee are concerned." [8] Washington feared the CIICNNY, which he called "this important organization," might be taken over by the militants such as "Bulkley and his crowd." He therefore urged Anderson to attend the CIICNNY meetings and counsel its president, William J. Schieffelin, to keep the organization out of reach of Washington's adversaries.[9] Unquestionably Washington had similar anxieties about the consolidation of the three social welfare agencies. However, as the time of federation approached Bulkley and "the militants" were far outnumbered by the pro-Washington element, as was proven by the board membership, constitution, goals and program of the new agency.

So, after a working session on September 26, the delegates from CIICNNY, NLPCW and CUCAN met on October 16, 1911, and approved federation into the National League on Urban Conditions Among Negroes (NLUCAN). Officers and board members were elected, staff appointed, a budget and a plan of work approved.[10]

Mrs. Baldwin prevailed on a reluctant Professor Edwin R. A. Seligman to serve as chairman (1911–1913), at least during the beginning stages of the new work.[11] Jacob W. Mack, Mrs. Baldwin and William L. Bulkley were elected vice chairmen, E. E. Pratt was named secretary, A. S. Frissell, president of Fifth Avenue Bank, became treasurer and L. Hollingsworth Wood, assistant treasurer. Wood was also treasurer of CUCAN and of the New York Colored Mission, chairman of the Central Bureau of Negro Fresh Air Agencies, and prominent in Quaker charities in the city.

George E. Haynes was appointed director, and field secretaries were Victor G. Flinn, the part-time CIICNNY secretary; Mrs. S. W. Layten, the Philadelphia-based NLPCW general secretary; and Eugene Kinckle Jones, CUCAN field secretary.

NLUCAN's executive committee had "power of supervision and recommendation as to general plans, policies, budgets and financial appeals" of the constituent bodies—far broader powers than originally discussed. This meant "that instead of three distinct and separate organizations, acting independently of each other, duplicating each other's work, and burdening the public with financial appeals, there is now constituted one central body directing and supervising the work of all, issuing appeals to the public for all, and to which the public may look for responsibility." [12]

At that point in time NLUCAN assessed the three constituent agencies and described their purposes. CIICNNY provided for "mutual conference, consultation and the sharing of the experience and knowledge of both races, in order that the sympathy and helpfulness of the white people, and the deliberate will and sense of need of the Negroes may be expressed." With the flowery obfuscation removed, it meant that blacks and whites met and blacks set out their needs. Training, organizing and assisting Negro mechanics and finding them jobs were listed as the main activities of CIICNNY.

NLPCW's purposes were given as "first to check the emigration of Negro women from the south; and, second, to direct those who do emigrate to proper lodgings in the strange city and to assist them in finding suitable employment and wholesome recreation."

The purposes of CUCAN were stated as (1) a study of socio-economic conditions of Negroes in cities "with a view to securing cooperation among all agencies seeking to better urban conditions among Negroes"; (2) the development of other agencies, if necessary; and (3) training Negro social workers.

NLUCAN was to take over the national features of the CUCAN "at once" and do likewise for the NLPCW "as rapidly as possible." Significantly, no mention was made of the CIICNNY and its activities in the timetable. In the next breath, however, NLUCAN stated that it "supervises the work of the three organizations and presents their financial appeals to the public." The semantic niceties of taking over national features and supervising local work were open to interpretation, and it would be up to the director, George E. Haynes, and his clusters of directors to clarify such definitions.

As the new agency put it, CIICNNY would continue its work as a standing committee and integral part of NLUCAN. NLPCW would continue as a standing committee known as the Committee for the Protection of Women. CUCAN would carry on as a standing committee known as the Committee on General Welfare. These component committees would be able to move ahead with their programs, indeed, with added velocity due to reduced friction and overlap if the scheme worked out as expected.

Above all, the most significant aspect of the federation was that people concerned about social betterment for blacks in the cities had come together in New York under the aegis of the most enlightened social service institutions of the day—the Charity Organization Society of New York, the Association for the Improvement of Conditions of the Poor and the New York School of Philanthropy—and brought with them the people who could secure support—financial and influential—of the power elite, both black and white. A more auspicious send-off would be difficult to imagine. As the journal of professional social work saw it "with the con-

solidation of three bodies committed to constructive social work among
Negroes, a new epoch opens in the effective consideration of this phase of
the American City Problem." [13]

NLUCAN anticipated that there would be three types of organizations
in the federation. The first type was *United Organizations,* forming "a
very close union" such as the CIICNNY, NLPCW and CUCAN, and others that might qualify.[14]

The second type would be *Branches*—"bodies in cities other than New
York City; but doing a work similar to that done by the United Organizations in New York."

Affiliated Organizations would be the third type. These were various
social agencies in New York and elsewhere working among blacks and
wishing to ally themselves with NLUCAN.

This scheme anticipated the voluntary linking of all agencies in efforts
to improve city life for blacks. Already Nashville and St. Louis were
forming organizations that would qualify as branches. And in the social
agencies and colleges serving black Americans there would be many possible affiliates, perhaps even candidates for branches or united organizations.

NLUCAN set forth its plan of work in October 1911.

In carrying out . . . the purposes of the organization, the following definite
and constructive pieces of work are about to be undertaken:
     A definite, thorough and continuous campaign to bring about coopera-
tion among the various social agencies working with Negroes in this
country.
     The establishment of branch organizations in several cities.
     The holding of the first semi-annual conference of social workers
among Negroes in New York, on December 4, 1911.
     The further development of educational work along social lines at Fisk
University—work which has already been started under the direction of
CUCAN, and the extension of this work to other Negro colleges. The
specific additions to the work for the coming year are the following:
     Appointment of a teaching fellow at Fisk University.
     Establishment of additional scholarships at Fisk University.
     Appointment of additional graduate fellows for study in New York
City.
     Development of departments of social science along similar lines at
other Negro colleges.
     Appointment of scholars of this league at other Negro colleges.

From the first, the training of black social workers was a fundamental
commitment of CUCAN and its successor, NLUCAN. As the agency said
in its first annual report, it believed that it was laying the very foundation stones for work among blacks. "Such leaders the NLUCAN is train-

ing under the tutelage of its director, through its practical work, and in the best training schools that the country affords." [15]

The agency tackled this matter in two basic ways. First, George Haynes trained workers in his social work sequence at Fisk University and these students did their field work in Nashville at Bethlehem House under Haynes's guidance. Fellows at Fisk received a small stipend and their tuition was remitted. Also, they lived as residents at Bethlehem House near the campus.

Second, the New York School of Philanthropy made tuition grants to two League Fellows, accredited their field work and arranged enrollment and study privileges at Columbia University. The field work itself was supervised by George Haynes and/or E. K. Jones and approved by the fellowship committee of NLUCAN. The agency also provided a stipend of $50 per month per Fellow in the beginning. This was increased in later years.

The New York Fellows conducted girls' and boys' clubs and made investigations (such as those of black employees in apartment houses, of the Harlem housing for families of children sent on fresh-air outings, of social services to blacks in the city of "Dance Halls and Public Dances of the City" and the "Negro Woman Adult Offender"). They served also in district offices of the Charity Organization Society.

There was some concern about the qualifications of these black college graduates who were being appointed League Fellows. The level of instruction in the black colleges of the south was considered below the requirements for admission to graduate work at the New York School of Philanthropy and Columbia University. The stringent admission requirements of these institutions were waived, however, thanks to the intercession of Professors Seligman, Devine and Lindsay and the faith of these faculty people and the admissions officials in the selection processes of NLUCAN's fellowship committee and its director, George Haynes. This action on the part of the New York institutions was one of the first examples of "special effort" on behalf of blacks.

The shortcomings of black higher education were also of concern to NLUCAN executive Haynes. He found that the black colleges were not offering the necessary foundation courses in economics and sociology and with other black educators he reviewed the educational standards of these colleges. Through Haynes's initiative with these college leaders the Association of Colleges for Negro Youth was formed (later known as the Association of Negro Colleges and Secondary Schools). This organization moved to set standards of admission to and instruction in its member colleges.

Over the years more than two hundred Fellows were trained. A number of these were supported by special funds from the Ella Sachs Plotz and George W. Seligman legacies, the Benezet Association of Philadelphia and the Adam Hat Company. The program was expanded to many other colleges, including Carnegie Institute of Technology, the universities of Pittsburgh, Denver, Southern California, Chicago, and the schools of social work at Simmons College and Bryn Mawr, among others. The training program expanded through the action of the local Leagues as well. The Philadelphia Armstrong Association pioneered in this regard, and supported two or more scholars at the University of Pennsylvania for many years. Other local Leagues did likewise and also cooperated with schools of social work in their areas to provide field-work opportunities for graduate students.

Though the initial intention was to train social workers, League Fellows not only became League professional workers, but found their way into other private agencies and government where they distinguished themselves.

In 1911 the potentials for cooperation were apparent in the reports of projects carried out jointly by the protective and urban committees. In May, they had held a conference on conditions in Harlem and a survey was made. The result, announced CUCAN, was a movement by Harlem residents to improve their neighborhood and efforts to establish recreation and playground centers for the area. CUCAN took the lead and pressed the city administration and the Playground Association for a playground in Harlem. When rebuffed, CUCAN organized the community and raised funds to rent a vacant lot from a black Harlem tavern keeper, turned it into a playground and supervised its use. Thus CUCAN scored an early popular success with its grass-roots constituents.

CUCAN and the Protective Committee also cooperated to bring together persons concerned about care of delinquents. They jointly studied the city's treatment of and facilities for delinquent black girls. Though about half of the youngsters were committed to institutions, more than a third could not be accommodated. In Brooklyn, two of the eleven refuges had stopped admitting colored girls, five others accepted no more than five each; the others were lily-white. However, court officials, judges and probation officers (all white) were frankly unable to deal adequately with the problems of delinquent black girls.

To counteract this, the Protective Committee instituted a Conference of Workers Among Girls, meeting monthly, "for exchanging ideas and methods in dealing with girls." NLPCW appointed a probation secretary and worked with the New York Court of General Sessions to care for women offenders. The work, NLPCW reported, was successful in twenty-three out of thirty-six cases, failed in seven cases and was still under way or slightly improved in the remaining six. The committee also inaugurated an amusement club for girls where dancing was taught, "sociables" held, lectures on sex hygiene and etiquette given.

CUCAN picked up other responsibilities in this area, by conducting a campaign through the press, the pulpit and letters to keep youngsters under sixteen away from picnics and balls "at unseasonable hours." It instituted a monthly Conference of Workers Among Boys in the churches and social agencies, and this, by the fall of 1911, was evolving into a system of boys' clubs in Brooklyn and Manhattan. (The official Boys' Clubs were white and refused admission or cooperation to blacks and CUCAN.)

Carrying its interest in wholesome recreation a step further, CUCAN was asked to "take over, supervise and direct all the Fresh Air work among black Americans in New York City" from the Central Bureau of Negro Fresh Air Agencies. This bureau, whose chairman was L. Hollingsworth Wood of the New York Colored Mission, had inspected all facilities open to Afro-American children and had a registry of those who had applied and participated in the program (to prevent repeaters). This was the first assignment given CUCAN's new field secretary, E. K. Jones—the organization of the fresh-air summer work—under a two-year, $2,000 grant from the Russell Sage Foundation. In addition, a model camp for boys was operated under CUCAN direction for ten weeks for the first time in the summer of 1911.[16]

In many other areas of activity, the possibility of conflict among the three federating agencies was remote. The Protective Committee still concentrated on caring for the migrant girls as they landed in Philadelphia (270 cases during the year); Memphis (474 cases); Baltimore (386 cases); New York (225 cases); and left from Norfolk (693 cases). The agency was dissatisfied with its level of performance, however: "The work in Baltimore and Memphis has not reached the standard attained in Philadelphia, Norfolk and New York, because of the impossibility of finding trained women workers. The demand for such workers is acute." [17]

NLUCAN's finances in the year ending September 30, 1912 indicated where its backing came from and where its program emphases rested. More than half of its combined total income of $15,488.70 came from six contributions: John D. Rockefeller, $2,500; Julius Rosenwald, $2,000; Alfred T. White and his sisters, $1,500; Mrs. D. Willis James, $1,000; Godfrey Hyams, $1,000; and Mrs. Ruth Standish Baldwin, $785. Other influential contributors included Paul and Felix Warburg, Andrew Carnegie, Cleveland Dodge, the Seligman brothers (Edwin, George and Isaac), Dr. Felix Adler, Robert C. Ogden, Jacob Schiff, Oswald Garrison Villard, V. Everit Macy, George Foster Peabody, and William G. Willcox.[18]

That same year NLUCAN expenditures totaled $11,891.36, of which $2,198.71 was used by the women's committee (formerly NLPCW); $1,063.44 was spent by the welfare committee (CUCAN); and $632.10 by the industrial committee (CIICNNY). Executive and field services came to $5,992.66 and other requirements in New York took $1,246.25, while those in Nashville totaled an additional $711.20. Miscellaneous expenditures were $47.00.[19]

Though its panel of contributors was gilt-edged and the dollar was almighty, the contributions to NLUCAN, weighed against its optimistic goals and the inescapable needs, were little more than tokens. They were, unfortunately, accurate indications of the kind of support the agency was to receive in most of its years. Considering the obvious needs, the contributions were tantamount to opening a soup kitchen with much fanfare, charging it with feeding the needy and equipping it with a quart of milk and a medicine dropper.

5/Black City Pioneering

In its early years, the New York Local Committee worked on many fronts. Among its more fruitful efforts were the moves to secure union membership for black musicians and to organize a vocational exchange in which high school students advised other youths about employment opportunities and the preparation necessary for jobs. The committee assembled a directory of colored businesses out of which grew a businessmen's league for cooperative buying and publicity.

In the shrunken job market of 1914, NLUCAN worked with all the employment agencies but managed to find jobs for only 181 of the 800 who applied for work. The following year NLUCAN worked out a system whereby daily records from each employment agency funneled into the League and were exchanged with all other agencies. Thus, in the Harlem area a summary of all available jobs listed by the various agencies was on hand at NLUCAN's offices before 1 p.m. daily. That year—1915—NLUCAN processed 1,560 job applications and placed 308 workers itself.

It was under the Mayor's Unemployment Committee that the League made work for hundreds of men in the jobless spring of 1914. In the process it became a showplace of relief work and was visited by political and civic leaders, including Theodore Roosevelt.

NLUCAN's report for its New York work for 1914–1915 tells in the dry terms of the social worker something of that humanitarian effort.[1] In direct relief—the area of activity NLUCAN intended to enter only if a void existed—it doled out seventy gallons of soup to needy families and 12,739 lunches to 774 men (the food was bought from a colored grocer, it noted). Jobless were given emergency work—in a workshop, in preparing bandages and surgical dressings which were donated to hospitals and institutions serving blacks in New York and elsewhere. A breakthrough was scored when the League cracked the color line in subway construction, resulting in 400 jobs for Afro-Americans. Jobs were found for 148 other blacks (for wages totaling $19,000) after job opportunities were canvassed in suburban towns within a radius of twenty miles of New York; seventy-eight colored girls went through League-established six-week classes in household arts, receiving $3 a week each; and NLUCAN succeeded in placing blacks as special investigators with some local welfare agencies. The house-to-house study of "Housing Conditions in Harlem, New York City," completed in 1914, showed that an estimated 49,555 blacks by that year were living in 1,100 houses in a twenty-three-block section. Just four years earlier the census had counted a total of 60,534 blacks in all of Manhattan. Obviously, Harlem was where the action was, and NLUCAN cast its lot with the future, closed its downtown offices and moved to new headquarters at 2303 7th Avenue. NLUCAN staff was on the scene when a devastating fire turned five Harlem apartment houses into an inferno in 1914, making seventy-nine families homeless and destitute. Coordinating the relief effort, the League organized a committee and collected food, clothing and $700 for them.

Black people's needs were publicized by actions such as the appeal through the New York *Globe* for a building to use for convalescent treatment of Negroes in greater New York.[2] Since blacks were not admitted in the existing convalescent homes, the need was urgent, and E. K. Jones asked for "some liberal-minded person" who had or knew of such a suitable house to step forward. Actually, NLUCAN had carried out a survey with funds from the Burke Foundation to determine the need for such a facility. By July 9, 1915, a home serving twelve women had been opened at 85 North Kensico Avenue, White Plains, underwritten by the Burke Foundation.[3] This was a clear-cut case of carrying on functions undone by other agencies (even though it was in direct disregard of the provision in NLUCAN's articles of incorporation banning such operations).

Seeking to cut mortality rates (black male life expectancy in 1910 was thirty-four years; female, thirty-eight years), NLUCAN published a bulletin cooperatively with the city's Department of Health and distributed 5,000 copies each month. It initiated and cooperated with other agencies in a Health Week campaign that reached 18,000 Afro-American homes, held three public mass meetings, delivered talks in "practically all" the churches and Sunday schools and blanketed black New York with 111,-000 pieces of literature.

Boys' Work Secretary Charles C. Allison's description of the boys' work of the League gave chapter and verse of efforts to "save the boy." It also gave a penetrating insight into city crowding and black attitudes in 1913:

> The average boy between twelve and fifteen years is full of energy. Getting rid of this energy through play he is constantly brought into close contact with the law. The more energetic the boy, the greater the danger of his breaking the law. Many parents note these tendencies of waywardness and refer their boys to our Secretary of Boys' Work. He reaches them at once through the corrective control of a Big Brother, and saves many boys from falling into the clutches of the law. Often a boy reaches the Court and, placed on probation or suspended sentence, he is referred to our Secretary by the Court and a Big Brother is assigned.[4]

The attitude toward the law reflects distrust based on the southern experience, the deep and bitter antagonism between Irish and Afro-Americans and the fact that most New York cops were from the Ould Sod. The 1900 race riot in New York, when the police beat blacks unmercifully and without penalty, lived in the memory of the city's black Americans and in the dispositions of its law enforcers.[5]

A Big Brother, said Allison, "is any responsible and exemplary man who volunteers his service and is assigned to look after some boy who has gone or seems about to go wrong. By an interchange of visits a sympathetic interest develops which works wonders in improving the boy's character and ideals of life."[6] The Big Brothers reported constantly to Allison and occasional conferences of these volunteers brought them together to go over problems and improve their approaches. Allison reported that in 1913, 206 Little Brothers had been aided, 190 assigned by the courts, and only fourteen returned to the juvenile court. The following year 324 boys and 414 girls under sixteen were helped.

The heart and promise of NLUCAN's Big Brother, Big Sister and probationary activities are captured in a story that the late John Dancy used to tell. At the time, 1914, Dancy was working out of NLUCAN headquarters in Harlem, assisting the industrial secretary. In addition, he took on Big Brother assignments.[7]

One day, as he did regularly, Dancy visited juvenile court. The judge told Dancy about a fifteen-year-old boy who had gotten into some scrape and been picked up. The lad was well-spoken and the judge was impressed with his potential. He remanded the boy to Dancy's custody.

John Dancy took the youth home by subway, located just two blocks from NLUCAN's office. The boy's mother, a Mrs. Porter, was seated in a rocking chair. To Dancy, it looked as if she was there for life, because she was so fat. He told the woman what had happened and explained that he was interested in the boy, responsible for him and wanted to do what he could to help.

"He's a nice boy," Mrs. Porter said, "but he doesn't have anything. He has nobody to do anything for him."

Dancy could see the truth of this in a glance, because the boy's world was a single squalid room, dark and dingy, poorly ventilated, meanly furnished.

Since the woman's sole support was $10 per week from the Children's Aid Society, obviously the first thing needed was more income, and Dancy was determined to find a job for the boy. Dancy alerted the employment people at League headquarters and urged them to keep an eye open for a job the boy could handle.

They found one. John Drew, the famous actor, was appearing in *Dr. Jekyll and Mr. Hyde*. His part required lightning costume changes for which a coat-holder was needed and the boy could easily do the task. Dancy cleared it with the Board of Education. The youngster was enthusiastic and performed his exciting and crucially important job responsibly; whereupon he received $10 a week, which as Dancy put it, doubled the family income and practically made them plutocrats.

The boy "perked up" considerably and often called on his friend at home as well as at the office. Dancy found him to be intelligent and interested. Through Dancy's encouragement, the boy began to write, often showing his Big Brother poems he had composed. These he submitted to his high school paper, and before long he began to be noticed. While he was still in high school some of his poems were printed in magazines.

After midnight one wintry night, Dancy was awakened by a knock on his door. He found the boy, thoroughly frightened, imploring Dancy to come with him. His mother had been rushed to Bellevue Hospital and he wanted his friend to go there with him to see her.

Dancy did, of course, and they located the woman in a vast line of beds where privacy was unknown. The man and the boy stood at the bedside and talked with her. There, as her life ebbed away, she asked Dancy to care for the boy. Dancy promised he would do the best he could. After her death that night the Big Brother went to a neighborhood minister, the Reverend F. A. Cullen, to arrange the funeral. On what Dancy remembered as one of the coldest days of the coldest winters on record, the funeral was held in the presence of four people: the undertaker, Cullen, Dancy and the boy.

For a while Dancy looked after the lad. Then the boy went to stay with the Cullen family and after some time, Cullen formally adopted the youth. Thus his name then became Cullen also—Countee Cullen. Dancy kept in touch with him and was proud of his graduating Phi Beta Kappa from New York University, his increasing fame for his poetry, and his joining the staff of the National Urban League. The pride was justifiable. Both Dancy and the League had helped put on a constructive path one of the nation's great poets.

Another aspect of NLUCAN's youth program was organization of boys' clubs. They were recognized by NLUCAN staff as "another means to off-set the lack of playground facilities." Several of them were conducted in cooperation with neighborhood settlement houses. In addition NLUCAN held athletic carnivals in Harlem in summer and winter to burn up youthful energy and to raise funds for camp.[8]

Allison had a brilliant idea for constructive youth activity. He worked up a Juvenile Park Protective League in Harlem in 1914. In short order he enrolled 626 boys "who cooperate with city departments to make the city better and cleaner." The youngsters were on the lookout for ob-structed fire escapes, unlit hallways, the illegal sale of liquor and ciga-rettes to minors, and other infractions of city ordinances. Allison man-aged to have some badges made and these were awarded for meritorious service. The results were astonishingly good.[9]

"Mr. Allison's little boy citizens are enthusiastic," wrote E. K. Jones. ". . . They are beginning now daily to bring in reports concerning dead animals lying on the streets, the improper disposition of garbage and ashes, and general uncleanliness in the neighborhood."[10]

The activity rapidly built *esprit* in the youngsters. In fact, it was so successful that white boys clamored to join the squads. This had the highly desirable result of reducing interracial friction and, in Harlem, eliminating the "deadline" formerly crossed by boys of the opposite race only at their peril—or in gangs. The project was extended to other areas of the city. Allison reported one difficulty: he did not have badges for the white boys, and no money to purchase them.

The care of delinquent black girls had been largely ignored. It was NLUCAN's continual probing that stimulated formation of the Utopia Neighborhood Club to raise money and support for Sojourner Truth House for girls. The League, meanwhile, pressed to open state and pri-vate institutions to these girls. A study was made of reformatories in the area. Other related studies were made of "questionable houses" and street solicitation, dance halls, pool rooms in the San Juan Hill and Harlem sections, and of West Indian and southern blacks in New York City. There were also investigations of predelinquent cases and counseling of youngsters, their parents or guardians. Frequently the child was removed from a corrosive environment to a foster home in a suburb.

The "probation oversight of delinquents" was one of the cardinal functions of NLUCAN, listed from its earliest days under the heading "Why We Exist." NLUCAN had prevailed on the Phelps-Stokes Foundation to underwrite a probation officer for children in Savannah, Georgia, and by 1916 was working out similar arrangements in Little Rock and New Orleans.[11]

The overwhelming need for such care had been dramatically demonstrated in Atlanta, where League Fellow and Morehouse sociology teacher, Garrie W. Moore, had been appointed the first black probation officer in the city's history. In his initial year on the job, Moore had been swamped with more than 900 cases. His first-year salary had been paid by the Phelps-Stokes Foundation and had been taken over by the city of Atlanta after the worth of the service was amply demonstrated.[12]

In Louisville and Nashville volunteer probation work was carried on by League workers in the children's court. In Detroit, a study of juvenile court disposition of cases involving black youngsters was under way and the League there was pressing to secure a black probation officer in the city.

In New York, the League pulled its probation officer off the job after four years of supporting the activity. This was "in keeping with the plan of the volunteer organizations to induce the County to assume the financial burden of supplying probation officers . . . and place same under Civil Service," E. K. Jones stated. However, "our worker had continued . . . to interview those probationers assigned to him" before the cutoff. The city did pick up the work. There were too many other pressures on NLUCAN to continue what was clearly a community responsibility.[13]

Another pioneering program was begun modestly by John T. Clark in 1914. He had the vision to realize that the League could and should extend its employment services by counseling not only men looking for jobs, but youths thinking about their education. He took on the task of interesting young high school students in vocations and working with them to develop not only skills but character.

Clark got together with a small group of youngsters and started civic improvement projects. From this grew regular Friday evening meetings at which Clark and the youths held forums, debates, discussions of burning topics of the day and occasional social gatherings to which the boys as they grew older brought their girl friends. The youngsters adopted the name Douglass Student Club and Clark so inspired them that most of the original group of six boys carried through and had distinguished careers. One became a dentist, another an official in the New York school system, a third was appointed to the New York State Tax Commission, a fourth to the state insurance department, the fifth was a successful artist and the sixth unknown. So impressive was the record of this group that it became known as the "100% Club," referring to the high achievement of its original members. It was, said E. K. Jones, "an irrefutable argument for organizing young people during their school days and for placing before them living examples of successful achievement following early preparation and self-denial." [14]

In later years the club changed its name to Delta Sigma Kappa, the Greek letters standing for DSC. Under this fraternal banner, it expanded and became widely known in the New York City area.

In this 1914 clubwork the foundation was laid for NLUCAN's later programs in vocational guidance.

A major program innovation was NLUCAN's Housing Bureau in New York—literally a "Registration Bureau of Tenements." It opened in February 1913 at 127 West 135th Street in Harlem, thanks to a donation of $1,000 from the New York Foundation. Its mission was to improve the moral and physical conditions among tenement houses, principally of Harlem. It was run by John T. Clark. He called the Housing Bureau "the result of the just indignation of the residents at the indiscriminate mixing of reputable and disreputable persons in tenement houses." The Housing Bureau's job was to prevent this practice:

First, by furnishing lists of houses certified by investigation as being tenanted by respectable people and being physically clean and wholesome.

Second, by getting corrective action of agents and owners or of proper city authorities in case of infraction of Tenement House, Board of Health or Police regulations.

Third, by aiding in developing moral conscience on the part of Negro citizens of New York . . . that will cause tenants to refuse absolutely to tolerate carelessness and indifference in the management and control of houses advertised for rental to respectable tenants.

Fourth, by efforts to educate Negro tenants in practical knowledge of the sanitation and upkeep of properties they occupy.[15]

This was true pioneering. NLUCAN and John T. Clark were charting a new area in housing in the black community. In the first six months of its existence, the bureau handled 168 housing cases and was responsible for having a number of "undesirables" dispossessed. These were usually whores who set up shop in apartments or rooming houses (often with the encouragement of landlords, who received more rent from them) and disrupted the decent home life of other tenants. Clark continued the program originated by the Industrial Committee, holding public meetings at Public School 89 on tenement house regulations. These sessions featured representatives from the city's park and tenement house departments.

The Housing Bureau worked with tenants in 240 cases in 1914–1915 to correct violations of tenement, health and police regulations and to improve "the moral tone" of houses, the janitor service and disposal of garbage and refuse. The bureau's distribution of hundreds of leaflets explaining its functions and its aggressive action brought results—sometimes unexpected: the Reverend A. Clayton Powell reported that at least one landlord had raised his rents after the League inspected his tenement and put it on the "respectable, physically clean and wholesome" list.[16]

Housing then—as now—was a fundamental handicap to blacks in the city. John T. Clark and his clean-up activities in the Housing Bureau were, in sum, ameliorative. The major need was for basic changes in conditions and structure. But such changes could be successful only with sizable investment of money by influential citizens and this could be enlisted only when the needs and prospects were evident. Facts were needed. Therefore, the League carried through a study of 1,002 families in 726 apartments and 443 houses in Harlem between 131st and 142nd streets.[17] The research was ended in January 1915 and showed that blacks in the study area had an average income of $791 per year and paid $281, or 36 percent of it for rent. For comparison, NLUCAN checked 133 apartments "in the same character of houses, occupied by German Jews, in neighboring districts" and found their rents averaged only $207 annually and that 69 percent of these were for three and four-room apartments. The average income of these immigrants was much higher than that of the blacks; the slice of income devoted to housing, therefore, was proportionately much less. The black tenants, to make ends meet, resorted to renting out rooms in their apartments on a huge scale: 62 percent of the apartments had lodgers. There was a total of 16,000 lodgers in Harlem—42 percent of all the adults in the community.[18]

For 1915, NLUCAN's Housing Bureau goals were: cooperation with city departments, agents, owners and real estate dealers; lectures and talks with tenants on duties and rights; moves to raise janitor service standards. The major effort—meeting the lodger evil—was to be tackled on two fronts: first, by inducing responsible real estate companies to take over some apartment houses, modify them for small families, manage and rent them at reasonable fees with the goal of eliminating undesirable tenants. The use of black superintendents, rent collectors and agents was to be promoted. Second, NLUCAN would try to locate or establish decent accommodations for single men and women, perhaps in hotels, the Junior League Home or in additional space at the YM and YWCA.[19]

Eugene K. Jones followed through on this program when, at the sixth New York City Conference of Charities and Correction, on May 25, 1915, he cited the housing survey. The exorbitant rents had their impact in burdensome demands on the League, he pointed out:

> When the time of unemployment comes around such as we had last year . . . we have a much larger percentage coming to us for assistance than the other organizations have because the tenants have not prepared for this condition, for they must pay out of the remaining $500 of their family income [the balance after paying rent] for all of the necessities of life. . . . They are, therefore, unable to save anything through organizations or as individual families for this time of need.[20]

Jones had a suggestion for improving this situation. It was for the social workers to use their influence with potential investors to put some money in Harlem houses—build modern tenements with two, three or four rooms at rentals blacks could afford. "The vacancies in the Harlem district are from two to five per cent," he said, "much smaller than . . . other parts of the city; so the investment would be a wise one. The average rent, too, is much higher than in other parts of the city. I am not saying this is fair, but it does prove the fact that it would be a safe investment for someone to go in there for the sake of giving some relief to the situation and at the same time to invest in a profitable scheme for housing which would benefit a large number of people who are in need." [21]

It was this proposition that was put before the City and Suburban Homes Company, the organization that managed the tenement houses built by Henry Phipps and other philanthropic entrepreneurs such as Alfred T. White and the Phelps-Stokes family. The City and Suburban Homes Company was directed by a group of powerful New Yorkers. R. Fulton Cutting was chairman, Isaac N. Seligman was treasurer, and Joseph S. Auerbach, Sam A. Lewisohn, John H. Storer and Alfred T. White were on its board. Some of these men had been interested in the CIICNNY for years as members of its committees or had been associated with the New York Armstrong Association and supported education for blacks.[22]

With NLUCAN help, City and Suburban Homes looked into the Harlem situation. It found that poor accommodations and high rents explained "the bad social conditions." It was desirable for the city as well as for the blacks that a determined effort be made to house these people properly. "Good citizenship thrives poorly in bad housing conditions," the company concluded.

So the company developed plans for new, reasonably priced housing after conferences with Harlem property owners indicated it would be easier to build than "induce the present owners to improve their property. . . ." It stated that "the problem is not more difficult than that of housing white people. As a matter of fact our Negro tenements are as cleanly kept as those occupied by our white tenants; and the return upon the capital invested is just as satisfactory." [23]

City and Suburban Homes acknowledged that the plan for housing the black population of Harlem should be comprehensive, but believed that a start should be made as a demonstration project. It proposed to build tenements on a plot about 200 by 100 feet on which there would be a total of 190 apartments with rentals of $1.25 to $1.70 per room per week. Seventy of the apartments would have only two rooms; ninety-six would have three, and the remaining twenty-four would have four rooms each. Estimated cost of such a project was $288,000, including land.

The company said its experience had shown that such buildings would be filled at once with respectable blacks and the income from rentals would insure at least a net of 4 percent on investment. If $3,000,000 could be raised and the project expanded accordingly, there would be savings on operations, and the company expected it could pay 5 percent dividends. This was certainly a conservative estimate. The NLUCAN housing study found that earnings averaged 7 percent on Harlem properties. "The plan to properly house our Negro citizens," it concluded, "is one that ought to attract investment from all those who feel that their surplus funds might well be employed in serving the public as well as earning dividends." [24]

The scheme was launched on December 12, 1915, at a meeting in the New York Chamber of Commerce building, 65 Liberty Street, and the initial goal was announced as $350,000. Stock at $10 per share was to be offered with a 4 percent dividend and maturity of eighteen years. [25]

But perhaps more persuasive than the prospective profit or philanthropic advantages of the project was the rationale advanced by real estate experts at the meeting. They "showed how the operation of the new plan will keep the blacks within a certain section and restore real estate values to normal. For the last few years demoralization of values have followed the steady influx of the Negroes, to the wall. Mortgages have been foreclosed simply because they were unable to hold them with property value constantly decreasing, and many companies refused to grant mortgages there." [26]

The *Times,* in its coverage of the subject, noted that "one phase . . . presented by the Negroes themselves, has been the establishment of a Negro bank in Harlem, with a Board of Directors composed of Negroes and Whites. In this institution a large part of the money deposited by

Negroes, and in the aggregate that deposited would amount to considerable, could be placed and put at the disposal of mortgagors. This movement would necessarily invite competition, and banks and financial institutions would see the advantages in investing in property owned or rented by colored people." [27]

On another front, the new agency also blazed a trail. One of the most significant moves it made was its approach to labor. This was a matter of urgency and fundamental importance. By 1913 in New York strikes were a familiar aspect of city life. Likewise, the hurried recruitment of blacks as strikebreakers had become a reflex tactic. They had been thrown into the longshore strike in 1895, the laborers' strike in 1904, and the strikes of street cleaners in 1907, of baggage handlers in 1910, of hod carriers in 1911 and of waiters in 1912. Were the hordes of unemployed black workers always to constitute a pool of ever-ready recruits for breaking the back of organized labor's efforts to improve working conditions? [28]

In June of 1913, George Haynes took the initiative and called the American Federation of Labor in New York. He met with Hugh Frayne, a general organizer who worked out of the AFL New York headquarters. The question was, what would the AFL do in cooperation with the League in the matter of organizing Negro workmen, especially in unskilled and semiskilled occupations? Frayne, of course, was in no position to decide this portentous question. He arranged, however, for Haynes to appear before the AFL executive council at its Atlantic City meetings the following month.

Haynes hurriedly consulted with NLUCAN board members who were available and on July 21 presented a request for AFL cooperation along four avenues:

> 1. To correct the impression wide-spread among Negroes that labor unions and organized labor of white men in general are not friendly toward Negroes as members on full terms of membership.
> 2. To educate the Negro working men in correct ideas of the underlying principles of organized labor, and to show them that the interests of Negro labor are ultimately one with those of white labor.
> 3. To change the indifferent or prejudiced attitude of white union working men in their relation to Negro labor.
> 4. To assist in organizing associations in unskilled and semi-skilled occupations, bringing Negroes into local unions with the whites where they can, but organizing them into separate locals where they must, with full privileges and rights of representation in the central councils and in the National conventions.[29]

Reporting on the meeting later, Haynes said that President Samuel Gompers "called attention to the fact that the Federation is making every

L. HOLLINGSWORTH WOOD
Treasurer, CUCAN (1910); Assistant
Treasurer, NLUCAN (1911); Board
Chairman and President, NUL (1915–
1941)

WILLIAM H. BALDWIN
Secretary, NUL (1915); Board
Chairman and President, NUL
(1941–1945)

LLOYD K. GARRISON
Treasurer, NUL (1926);
President (1945–1952)

ROBERT W. DOWLING
President, NUL (1952–1956)

Theodore W. KHEEL
President, NUL (1956–1960).

Blackstone-Shelburne N.Y.

HENRY STEEGER
President, NUL (1960–1964).

Blackstone-Shelburne N.Y.

6/Beginnings

The healthy, vigorous agency portrayed in the first NLUCAN *Bulletin,* issued in the fall of 1911, was in reality the experimental amalgam of three disparate organizations, with fundamentally different approaches and structures. At the outset they had little more in common than some of their directors, their interest in aiding city blacks and a realization that it would be better to coordinate than conflict. True, each was directed by an interracial group of men and women; all three relied considerably on volunteers to carry the work; each organization employed at least one staff person; and none of these agencies had a 1911–1912 budget above $2,200 per year: CUCAN—$1,063; NLPCW—$2,199; CIICNNY —$632.[1]

It was not until May 1912 that NLUCAN leased joint offices for its three constituents. In the months that followed, committees on reorganization and incorporation worked up the plans which, when approved, were followed in consolidating into one corporate body. The keystone in this new edifice was Professor Edwin R. A. Seligman. Ruth Baldwin wrote him expressing "the deep appreciation that all the members of the new committee feel that you have consented to act as chairman." They would do their best to help. "Some of us can relieve you of most of the burden of the work, but just to have one thing more on your mind and that last inescapable sense of responsibility however slight—constitutes a burden for which there is no real relief. That you are willing to assume it at any rate for the present, is a real sacrifice that we fully appreciate." [2]

Seligman had served with Mrs. Baldwin's late husband, William H. Baldwin, Jr., on the reform Committee of Fifteen in New York City as secretary. Seligman had been a leader in progressive social service activities in New York. He was a member of Greenwich House, a settlement in Greenwich Village, and its Committee on Investigations that sponsored Mary White Ovington's study of the black workingman in New York, among others. He had served as chairman of the Columbia University Committee on Social Settlements and Allied Work (mostly Sunday schools) in 1903.

In 1907, Seligman became chairman of the Bureau of Municipal Research. It was he who urged establishment of a chair in social economy at Barnard (whose first occupant was Mary K. Simkhovitch, co-founder of Greenwich House). By 1908 he had taken on the chairmanship of a committee to manage the programs launched by Greenwich House. One of these programs was run by the Committee on Congestion of Population in New York, which included Ruth Baldwin (there was no black representation on this 1908 committee, which included the city's public and voluntary health and welfare agencies that served the poor).

On the face of it, NLUCAN was dominated by educators, religious, social and civic leaders. They might be expected to show preference for social work, education and training and to put less emphasis on industry or job placement—and that was precisely the way it developed.

The major program efforts of the combined agency did not come to grips with the job needs or opportunities in the New York area to the same extent that the Armstrong Association had in Philadelphia.[3] NLUCAN managed to place seventy-four persons in 1911–1912, its first combined year; this was an improvement on the job-finding record of CIICNNY alone.

NLUCAN's initial program was concentrated on survival services with only a passing nod to economic fundamentals. The same number of job placements and the limited number of workers reached in vocational training are indices of this; the meager approach to business aid is another. These shortcomings are particularly dramatic when one considers that the chairman of the organization in its first two years was Professor Seligman, the nation's outstanding economic theorist and a member of one of the most powerful financial families in the world.

The only evidence that the agency intended to devote attention to such economic basics was an item in the CUCAN report for 1910–1911, which called for "the development of thrift agencies and co-operative business enterprises." But instead of strong black banks, industrial and business institutions, CUCAN foresaw penny-savings plans for children and housewives and cooperative buying of supplies by neighborhood black barbers and retailers.

The operation of NLUCAN began to jell in 1912. At the same time, control of the agency began to shift. At the December 4, 1912, meeting of the executive board, there were seven members present, who elected the slate of officers and approved the committees appointed. At that meeting L. Hollingsworth Wood replaced E. E. Pratt as secretary and a special committee was named to oversee the Welfare Committee's scheduled housing bureau and the vocational exchange planned by the Industrial Committee.

The vital Membership Committee was appointed; it included Roger N. Baldwin (nephew of Ruth Baldwin) of St. Louis, the Reverend William H. Brooks, Elizabeth Walton and L. Hollingsworth Wood. This was the group largely responsible for the make-up of the organization's board of directors and, therefore, its future. The members were a young man who lived hundreds of miles away; a venerable black pastor of a mixed congregation; a highly moralistic Quaker spinster and an aggressive Quaker lawyer. None of these had sufficient influence to bring to the board leaders of industry and finance required to strengthen NLUCAN.

The major national events of 1913 were the inauguration of Woodrow Wilson, the institution of the federal income tax, creation of a department of labor and drastic reorganization of the banking system. For NLUCAN, the major events of the year were its incorporation, the remarkable development of social work training under George Haynes's direction in Nashville, and respectable achievements in carrying out the agency's objectives.

Its incorporation was one of those necessary acts that gave additional stability and permanence to NLUCAN. In its statement of objectives for the record, it also gave a picture of the agency as of March 26, 1913, according to its thirty directors. The "particular objects" of the corporation were to be:

(1) To establish and maintain for Negroes exclusively employment bureaus; playgrounds; travelers' bureaus for meeting, directing and advising strangers in the cities; fresh air outings for women and children; and, bureaus for better housing conditions. (2) To employ probation officers for Negroes exclusively and to encourage the development of the probation system among Negroes and to assist in the reformation of Negro offenders and the prevention of crime among Negroes; (3) to encourage, assist, employ and train Negro social workers; (4) to make studies of and distribute informa-

tion concerning the industrial, economic, social and spiritual conditions among Negroes; (5) to encourage, promote and assist in establishing institutions and agencies, whose objects are the improvement of industrial, economic, social and spiritual conditions among Negroes. Provided, however, that nothing herein contained shall be regarded as giving to this corporation any power to actually establish or maintain institutions for the care of inmates.[4]

The League's constitution, filed with the articles of incorporation, was a perfunctory document. It contained definitions, prerogatives and duties of the executive board, officers, and committees. It clearly stated that the executive board of thirty members (with a quorum of ten) was to meet in February, June, October and December each year—a directive honored largely in the breach. Also, the board was to elect all new members. Yet, simultaneously, League literature was being distributed that solicited memberships : "active members pay $1 to $5, contributing members $5 or more annually; all members have the same powers and privileges." [5]

Article IV called for an auditing committee of three executive board members—another provision overlooked in practice. But in drawing up the constitution, its author had made the organization an easy one to manage. The League was to have a membership committee of seven, elected by the executive board; four members of this committee would constitute a quorum. Under Article VII, other committees could be appointed by the executive board "to do work in any city in the U. S. or Canada." And under Article X, the constitution could be amended by a two-thirds vote of the executive board present at a regular or special meeting—providing at least seven members voted for such an amendment.[6]

In practice the chairman, Professor Seligman, seldom had time to attend to his NLUCAN duties. In Seligman's absence, Mrs. Baldwin or Hollingsworth Wood generally chaired the board meetings. Attendance was usually from seven to twelve board members, a number which seldom met the quorum requirement except for the annual meeting in December, or for a special meeting.

This relaxed approach was extended still further by the establishment of powerful committees. A Finance Committee was the first, a Membership Committee second, and a Committee on Conference (to work out intramural problems) was third. On each of these committees representatives of the original three organizations were included. By 1913, a "Committee of Chairmen" had evolved, consisting of the chairmen of the standing committees—Improvement, Dr. William L. Bulkley; Protective Committee, Elizabeth Walton; General Welfare Committee, Edward E. Pratt; Finance, Paul Sachs; and Membership, L. Hollingsworth Wood.

As time went on the Committee of Chairmen took on the functions of an ad hoc directing group or steering committee.

One of the developments that indicated a new stability in NLUCAN in 1913 was the integration of the Industrial Committee. It became one of the standing committees of NLUCAN. Also, with the affiliation of Richmond as a branch in June 1913, and the establishment of offices at 185 Duffield Street in Brooklyn and 127 West 135th Street in Harlem, the agency claimed six additional affiliates.[7] It was beginning to look like the national organization its title claimed to be.

For the first time in its literature the League began to use the phrase "Not Alms But Opportunity," from William L. Bulkley's 1909 speech to the National Negro Conference. And on the letterheads and reports the agency's official seal began to appear.

Financial malnutrition forced hard choices between support of training—contributions to black colleges and professional social work education—and programs aiding blacks in the cities. There was growing awareness that the agency could not possibly do all the things it had projected for itself. Difficult, fundamental decisions had to be made and priorities had to be set. Those choices, once made, would take the League down one or another road to an increasing degree, and the direction taken would make fundamental differences in such disparate areas as black education, social work, the cities of the north and relations with labor and government. More and more, the alternatives evolved as: 1) concentrating the agency's major energies and resources on the immediate and urgent—the tactical or "emergency room" approach; or 2) increasing the emphasis on the basic elements in the William H. Baldwin–Booker T. Washington approach—that is, bring together the best whites and blacks in the cities, train Afro-American youths for leadership in dealing with the city problem and improve rural conditions.

George Haynes had been true to the Baldwin vision of raising the rural areas to relieve the pressure on the cities. Haynes had carried this gospel to the black preachers and teachers in summer institutes. And he had seen social work training as a key to coping with the city problems of migrants. Through his leadership at Fisk, training was combined with practical work, linking the university and the community. His goal was to spread the success of Fisk to other black colleges, setting up social work training centers that would educate dedicated black youngsters in perhaps a score of vital southern cities and in the process set them to work on the abysmal conditions in those communities.

Set off from the main currents of Afro-American life in his ebony tower at Fisk, Haynes became more convinced of the fundamental, overriding correctness of the educative approach. His elaborate plan for a training center in Nashville would multiply the number of youths to be trained for service in the urban centers of the south.

The necessity of the training center grew in Haynes's perspective until it loomed as the major element absorbing his NLUCAN attention. Most of his correspondence from 1913 to 1917 was devoted to this project. It brought him increasingly into contention with his junior, Eugene Kinckle Jones, with a NLUCAN executive board that had, by late 1915, changed markedly and with conditions in the major cities of the north that had altered radically.

Though Haynes later considered Jones the antagonist in the conflict, he was, perhaps, more the focus of the opposing viewpoint. It was Haynes, after all, who had brought Jones from Louisville and directed him to follow a program drawn up by Haynes with the counsel of COS and the School of Philanthropy experts on the one hand, and the black community leaders on the other. Jones had relatively little supervision from the professor. He had displayed initiative and professionalism in carrying out the surveys of Harlem housing, organizing and expanding fresh-air programs and recreational opportunities for blacks, and establishing the housing bureau and youth guidance services and probation work. The lanky Virginian was a quick learner, made efficiency his watchword, and impressed board members with his honesty, diligence and administrative ability. When the black migrant flow quickened in 1913 and 1914, Jones had the city's resources as well as NLUCAN's firmly in mind and marshaled these effectively.

The situation at the end of 1914 was clear-cut: In New York, trained and experienced in pragmatic responses to pressing emergencies, oriented to the industrial climate and pace of the northern metropolis, was young Jones, ambitious, eager and ready to extend the New York-type NLUCAN operation to other northern cities. In Nashville, oriented to the south and concerned about grounding the vital social workers of the future in a southern training center so they would be acceptable to southern cities, was Haynes, diligently perfecting the training work and indoctrinating southern teachers and preachers about the city's pitfalls so they could warn the black peasants and keep them south.

In New York and the east were the major contributors to NLUCAN, nearly all of them white industrialists and businessmen who lived in the cities. These wealthy city people saw black faces with increasing frequency and read about black crime and indigence in the north with growing disquiet.

The city fathers in the south saw what appeared to be a relatively static situation—the poor blacks were still living in squalor, as they always had. There was no drastic change, and no emergency or sense of urgency pressed southern white leaders to seek the services of George Haynes, NLUCAN or their trainees.

In New York and other major northern cities by the end of 1914 what had been a drift of Afro-Americans to the city had taken on a new timbre. It was different in purpose and texture. It had been mostly women before; now there were more men and families. They were fleeing hunger as well as seeking fortune—and with the drying up of European immigration because of World War I this movement quickened and had the feeling of the groundswell that precedes something greater.

Jones and the New York NLUCAN staff had demonstrated considerable agility in coping with the dynamics of black immigration. Furthermore, control of the agency had shifted from the hands of George Haynes's mentor, E. R. A. Seligman (who had been NLUCAN chairman); Haynes's Columbia schoolmate, E. E. Pratt (NLUCAN secretary); and Frances Kellor (executive committee member), all of whom had been his original backers. By the end of 1913, Mrs. Baldwin had superseded Seligman as chairman, but was often incapacitated by illness. Frances Kellor had left the agency and was devoting her time to foreign immigrant problems; Seligman and Pratt were still board members, but not officers, and were largely inactive.

In 1914, with NLUCAN's newly elected vice chairmen remote from the scene (Kelly Miller at Howard and R. R. Moton at Hampton) the agency direction devolved on its secretary, L. Hollingsworth Wood, and a small nucleus of board regulars. Elizabeth Walton and L. Hollingsworth Wood had unbroken attendance records; the Reverend William Brooks, Abraham Lefkowitz, Fred Moore, Dr. E. P. Roberts and lawyer George W. Seligman (brother of E. R. A.) seldom missed meetings. Wood shouldered more and more responsibility. By mid-1914 Ruth Baldwin had decided that Wood should succeed her as chairman. And at the September 1914 board meeting, L. Hollingsworth Wood was authorized to sign the agency's checks in the unavailability of either its treasurer or assistant treasurer. With his keen fund-raiser's eye, Wood saw where the philanthropic support and potential contributors were—in the northern cities. As the confrontation of the two basic philosophies and programs approached, Professor Haynes was hopelessly outweighed. He did not have the votes where it counted.

In the fall of 1914 a drastic reorganization of NLUCAN was voted. The Committee of Chairmen had met and developed a plan of work and a division of the directors. The scheme was approved by the executive board for the coming year at its December 16, 1914, meeting.

A "Local Committee" was named. It was to have charge of the combined work of the Industrial, Protective and Welfare Committees.

The other committee was to have charge of "the national and educational features of the work of the League."

Certain aspects of this reorganization stand out: The Educational Committee contained a number of nationally known persons, foremost of whom was Booker T. Washington. It had broad geographic representation, from Miss Sophonisba Breckinridge of Chicago to John Hope in Atlanta, Talcott Williams in Philadelphia to James Dillard in New Orleans, from Kelly Miller in Washington to R. R. Moton at Hampton. All of these were leaders in their professions and their presence on the committee lent great prestige to the League. There were nine executive board members on the committee. The Local Committee had only five board members; the majority of its members were young, just coming into their own in their professions. The result was an excellent paper Committee on Education, dispersed around the nation to such an extent as to be impractical. The New York Local Committee, by contrast, was largely concentrated where it was needed—in the city. Thus Jones had support and counsel for his program activities readily at hand on short notice. Haynes was operating largely by himself with a restricted budget (retrenchment was in full swing).

There were two persons who were members of both these committees: Elizabeth Walton and the Reverend John Haynes Holmes; Miss Walton was the only board member on both. She was unique in being a member of more league committees than any other person. Her committee memberships included: Membership, Education, Women's, the New York Local Committee and the Committee of Chairmen; she was, therefore, in a key position to see more of the working aspects of the organization than any other board member.

Elizabeth Walton had a strong sense of rectitude and group solidarity. Her Quakerism was deeply felt, and she characteristically used "thee" and "thou" in addressing fellow Quakers such as L. Hollingsworth Wood. Her sense of group identity confused some of her League associates when she would question a black worker about some person proposed for committee membership, saying, "is he one of us?" (To James H. Hubert, head of the Brooklyn and later the New York League, it was not clear whether she was asking if the person was a black, a Quaker or one simply dedicated to black advancement.) She was a close friend of Ruth Baldwin and Frances Kellor and like Miss Kellor shared an apartment with Mrs. Baldwin for a time.

Miss Walton thought it scandalous that the general welfare agencies ignored their responsibilities to black citizens. And she was highly opinionated about NLUCAN staff members and their understanding and execution of their missions. She wrote Hollingsworth Wood in exasperation

after reviewing the agency's program efforts in the fall of 1915, "Every
one of the workers but [Charles] Allison are drifting back to individual
case work whereas our work should be organization, cooperation and
putting [the burden] over on white societies. I wish thee would read
them the riot act on this question." [8]

As a member of the committee on reorganizing NLUCAN work, Miss
Walton had considerable influence on the new structure. When this restructuring of NLUCAN's work was discussed at the December 16, 1914, executive board meeting,[9] E. K. Jones was present; George Haynes, for reasons unknown, was absent. When the secretary, L. Hollingsworth Wood,
sent out invitations to the first meeting of the Education Committee, he
redefined its functions. It would, he said, "be extended to take in work of
a more national kind, having in view the educational features throughout the country, i.e., the lecture courses and conferences, the choice of the
'fellows' from the Negro colleges, the developing of the Training Center
at Nashville, and in general the work which brings us in touch with the
educational opportunities for the Negro." [10] Mrs. Baldwin saw another
dimension to this committee's work, however, and at her suggestion the
committee's area of activity was expanded to include the cultivation and
development of affiliates.[11]

In a memo prepared for the next executive board meeting Jones, who
now styled himself the "resident Director," gave his view of the priorities
and approaches to these plans. Calling his observations "Second Step in
Plans of the League," Jones started by recommending the phase-out of
work with delinquents by May of 1915. "Notice should be served on the
workers supervising this department and white organizations doing similar work in the community that the change will be made on May 1st. Efforts should be made to have the white organizations commit themselves
to taking up the work with colored children and employing colored
workers." [12] (This move was only partially successful. Instead of taking
over the work, the white agencies underwrote part of the salaries of
NLUCAN's chief men and women workers.)

NLUCAN staff should be used in five "distinct directions," said Jones:

First, the staff should be used in educational work—lectures, national
conferences and worker training.

Second, the staff should set up and supervise branches.

Third, especially in New York, frequent conferences should be held
with city officials, representatives of private organizations and corporations, including department stores, factories, construction companies, etc.,
to encourage a more favorable attitude on their part towards the Negro
population and to execute the appropriate plans in the program outline.

Fourth, Negroes should be organized into neighborhood groups and shown "the opportunities for improvement afforded by the various city departments and private organizations existing for the good of all New York citizens."

Fifth, the public relations and publicity functions should be centralized in one person's hands. (This Protean individual was to publicize public meetings, prepare for meetings of local and national League committees, write all releases, reports, appeals, carry out occasional fund-raising among colored people, oversee the office work and also act as secretary to the resident director.) Jones had hired the man for this job in April 1914; he was T. Arnold Hill (acting executive, 1934–1936).

E. K. Jones suggested that special committees be appointed by the chairman on a task-force basis. Each would aim at eradicating a specific evil. Examples were: 1) A committee on better playground facilities for Harlem. It would tackle the Parks Department.[13] 2) A committee on "cleaner tenements from a moral point of view." This group would work with the Harlem police inspector and Committee of Fourteen in "getting evidence against buffet flats." 3) A committee on possibilities of a Negro bank to consider the question from all sides and also to cover development of Negro business. 4) A committee on vocational guidance for colored children. 5) A committee on ample provision for the Negro lodger to secure a hotel or institution for single men and women with small incomes. 6) A committee on fresh-air work to supervise the league's boys' camp and arrange for more fresh-air outings through white organizations.

"Other special committees, whose life will be of very short duration (for example, a committee on unemployment among Negroes) could be appointed from time to time."

Jones then made a pitch for "trained, intelligent, sympathetic workers whose disciplined minds and enthusiasm will keep them constantly and untiringly working for more favorable conditions among their people." This, of course, would take salaries that were competitive, so that the agency would not be constantly having to seek replacements. With that in mind, Jones set his salary at $1,900, those of his three key assistants at $1,200 each, and the clerical and other workers ranging downward to $360 for Mrs. H. A. V. Proctor of Virginia, Travelers' Aid Secretary, then in her eighth year as a human revolving-door serving hundreds of black migrants at Norfolk's docks.

After reading the scheme, one has no doubt as to which was the body of the canine and which the tail. The accompanying budget bore this out: New York was budgeted at $12,820; Nashville at $1,030 (plus the expected stipend from Fisk for Haynes's salary).

7/Inside Story

The year 1915 was one in which dwindling immigration and the sinking of the *Lusitania* struck home to Americans the nearness of the European war. In the cities the impact of economic dislocation hit those who could not tide themselves over the Depression. The New York Charity Organization Society labeled 1915 a "year of unusual distress and unemployment." [1] It was a year in which NLUCAN, according to Hollingsworth Wood, "gathered the strings of tragedy and comedy, of failure and success, of want and degradation, relieved here and there with gleams of golden self-sacrifice and unselfish service." [2]

This was the year of Booker T. Washington's membership on the agency's board, and his death. He had declined earlier invitations to board membership, one as recent as February 1914, with the statement that the time was not psychologically right, but that he would help any and every way possible and come on later. [3] The death of P. A. Johnson in late 1914 opened up a board slot and Fred R. Moore nominated Washington for it. His acceptance was a valuable endorsement of the organization and a great psychological boost. It also was an indication that Washington considered the agency strong enough then to bear whatever slings and arrows might be directed at it because of his open association.

Washington attended his first NLUCAN board meeting in February 1915. The minutes report that he suggested that the local New York committee get the facts on Negro enrollment in the city's high schools. Washington's announcement of National Negro Health Week sponsored by the National Negro Businessmen's League was read. NLUCAN voted to participate in this and develop a plan for a model campaign which was widely copied later in cities with large black populations. It was kicked off Sunday, March 16, with mass meetings in four different spots in New York and Brooklyn. Beginning at 11 a.m., Booker T. Washington participated in these meetings, addressing the crowds until 10 p.m.

During Washington's February visit to New York, Ruth Baldwin, at George Haynes's insistence, discussed with him the proposed training center at Nashville, with its implications for serving cities in the south.

Haynes at this time was calling the center scheme an "interchurch college." Ruth Baldwin reported to Haynes that the Tuskegeean thought "the idea which was proposed for the Interchurch College would be an excellent one and could probably be secured." She footnoted this, "All this is speaking of big things when we haven't yet accomplished little ones, however!" [4]

In April 1914 Washington spoke in Memphis before the Southern Sociological Congress and strongly endorsed NLUCAN's work. This endorsement was all-important to the agency at a time when its support came largely from the major philanthropists and business and industrial leaders who respected Washington above all other blacks. The great man's death in November 1915 was unfortunate for the agency on several levels, but was not a mortal blow.

A second blow to NLUCAN was the resignation in mid-1915 of Mrs. Ruth Standish Baldwin as chairman. Ruth Baldwin's resignation took from NLUCAN an individual who was highly respected, whose name was favorably known among the social and civic elite, who could call with poise and the expectation of a hospitable reception upon leaders of finance, industry, philanthropy, education and society because of her own family background as well as her husband's widely admired public service. Her no-nonsense, nonpatronizing approach to race relations was rare. Feminine, fashionable, highly intelligent but frail of health, Ruth Baldwin had taken the leadership of the agency when E. R. A. Seligman stepped down in the fall of 1913. But by May 1914 she found her health suffering and wrote confidentially to George Haynes, telling of her intention to resign in June that year. A strong and energetic man was needed for the leadership, she said, and hoped L. Hollingsworth Wood, then secretary, would be elected chairman and her son, William H. Baldwin, would move into the secretaryship. [5]

Ruth Baldwin did not resign according to her timetable. She stayed on as chairman for an additional year. During that period she was concerned about the seeming ceiling of $15,000 on contributions to NLUCAN; about the withering away of interest in the League in Chicago; even about the unwieldy name of the agency (L. H. Wood, she said, had suggested National Urban League be the official name; this name had appeared in the minutes of the agency as early as October 1913). [6]

In her correspondence with Haynes, Mrs. Baldwin confided her dissatisfaction with the national program, though she did not specify her complaints, and lamented that the major energies of the executive (George Haynes) were tied up to such a degree in the college work. She commented also about the disadvantage of having Haynes in Nashville when problems were so pressing in New York. [7]

But the organization was moving. It was a going concern. Ruth Baldwin, who was so ill that frequently she could not write and had to dictate to her daughter, could take pride in its accomplishments. Had she been of stronger constitution and sterner stuff it might have been different. She was not the sort to lead a suffrage parade or a temperance raid. The small gathering, not the public occasion, was her forte. However, the work, more and more, appeared to require going to the public.

On June 1, 1915, Ruth Baldwin sent her resignation from her summer home in Washington, Connecticut. It was addressed to Hollingsworth Wood. She resigned from the chairmanship, the education and extension committees and the League, to take effect immediately. The reasons, she said "are so familiar to you as to need no repetition." She expressed keen regret at withdrawing from the work and the associations which had been so congenial and inspiring.[8]

Saying that she had only accepted the chairmanship because no more suitable person had then been available, Mrs. Baldwin confided that she had "chafed during all this time under the knowledge that the League sorely needed a far different leadership from that which I could give." She then defined the kind of leadership she meant: "Leadership, at once aggressive and tactful, from one also who can and will represent it on all suitable public occasions and also is in a position to seize and develop opportunities for its growth, both in New York and elsewhere, and whose wide knowledge of other efforts which are being made from various angles to better the conditions of colored people in all parts of the country, will enable him to guide the work of the League wisely and, so far as possible, in cooperation with such other efforts, whether their emphasis be on the economic, educational, religious or other needs of the Negro population." [9]

She looked back over the record and thought the progress greater in some directions and less in others than expected in the time spanned. "No one not closely associated with the work can realize how serious have been the difficulties and discouragements which we have faced, nor appreciate how far short of our ideals our accomplishment frequently has fallen." The past year, she believed, had brought a realization that the labor had not been in vain and that a future of increasing usefulness lay ahead. Barring United States involvement in the war, she foresaw better financial support and, consequently, more freedom to develop work in other cities "where earnest groups are already struggling with their local problems and looking to us for encouragement and guidance." More money would make it possible, she said, "to increase the value of the work which Dr. Haynes is doing among teachers, ministers at their summer institutes and conferences and to strengthen the Training Center at Nashville." [10]

Mrs. Baldwin's view was that "as far as may be, the two parts of our work should be developed in unison: on the one hand the arousing of Negroes in urban centers to an appreciation of their own living problems and the creation of a desire for the intelligent study and improvement of conditions, and, on the other, the training of young Negro men and women to be leaders of the practical work in communities where the sense of the need has been previously aroused." She expanded on this theme:

> The civic usefulness of groups of colored men and women, stirred to a realization of their own living problems and ready to cooperate with the best and most forward-looking white people in the community towards a bettering of the total community life, should naturally be very great, and just here is the point at which I hope we may continue to emphasize: that, altho' the problem which we have set ourselves is one of definite limits, namely the improvement of all the living conditions of *Negroes* in cities, the best spirit in which to approach it is by considering it as a part of the larger problem of developing a more wholesome community life in general and a sounder national democracy.
>
> That is to say, when we, colored and white people, banded together in our League, seek to better conditions among the *Negroes* of Harlem or San Juan Hill or Brooklyn, we seek also to make a better New York City for *everybody* to live in, and to help in some measure towards a truer realization of the ideals of sound community living in our great Republic.
>
> Similarly, the affiliated organization in Richmond or Savannah, or Augusta works not only for the Negroes of each of those cities but for the city itself, because, as loyal citizens of Richmond or Savannah or Augusta, the members of the League are bound to do all possible to enhance her fair name in state and in nation. Let us work, not as colored people nor as white people for the narrow benefit of any group alone, but *together,* as American citizens, for the common good of our common city, our common country.[11]

Ruth Baldwin was not asking for the moon; it was all common-sensible, even practical. The fact that it seemed to be a major liberal statement tells a great deal about the America of that time. Her words, proclaimed L. Hollingsworth Wood in the next annual report, were a "ringing resignation message" that "cheered on every man and woman who has a spark of metal in his or her nature." [12] A committee consisting of Fred Moore, L. Hollingsworth Wood and the Reverend William H. Brooks drafted a sentimental response on behalf of the NLUCAN board and sent it to Mrs. Baldwin.[13] Then they proceeded, without a quorum, to elect L. Hollingsworth Wood to replace Mrs. Baldwin and her son William III to replace Wood as secretary.[14] So began the long period (1915–1941) of L. Hollingsworth Wood's leadership of the League.

Wood, then forty-two, was by this time one of the most prominent Quakers of his generation and a leader of the peace movement in the nation. Educated at Haverford College, he had studied law at Columbia and built up a thriving estate practice after his admission to the New York bar in 1899.

"Due to a strange set of impulses which affect one's thinking, and starting with a small mission class which developed into a debating society for young colored boys," wrote Wood later, his attention and interest were "more and more focused on the problems which beset the Negro in our country and in our day and generation." [15] He and his sister Carolena became active in the New York Colored Mission and Wood was elected an officer of it. Hollis B. Frissell of Hampton interested Wood in the Penn School, a community school for blacks off the coast of South Carolina, and he soon became a trustee and fund-raiser for it. Later he was elected to the board of Fisk University and was the vice chairman of its trustees and its fund-raising chairman for decades.

The association of both Wood and his sister with the New York Colored Mission brought them into the orbit of the New York Association for the Protection of Colored Women and the League that evolved from it as well. By the time CUCAN was formed, large, jovial Hollingsworth Wood was prominent enough in activities on behalf of blacks to be a natural choice as a trustee and officer of the new organization. His interest and faithful service to the agency (along with his sister and fellow Quaker Elizabeth Walton) put him in line for a top position. By 1915 he was nationally known as an organizer and leader of antimilitary activities (the American Union against Militarism) and civil rights concern (the National Civil Liberties Bureau—the predecessor of the American Civil Liberties Union), along with social workers such as Jane Addams, Socialists such as Norman Thomas, J. Q. Phelps-Stokes and Crystal Eastman, and Progressives such as John Haynes Holmes, John N. Sayre and Judah L. Magnes.

With a ready smile and outgoing warmth, Wood was in the forefront of humanitarian efforts during this period. After World War I he was a member of the American Committee for Irish Freedom, the Committee on Feeding of German Children and voluntary agencies formed to relieve suffering in Russia and the Far East. He continued his Quaker activities as a member of the board of managers of Haverford and assistant clerk of the New York Yearly Meeting of the Society of Friends. The burden of his fund-raising efforts and his organizational interests caused him to give up the active practice of law in the early twenties.[16]

8/Migration and Expansion

Though neither George Haynes nor NLUCAN realized it at the time, the shot that shattered the Austro-Hungarian empire on June 28, 1914, also pierced the dike that had kept blacks from coming to the cities in even greater numbers. On July 31, 1914, the Sarajevo shot struck the Cotton Kingdom. Thousands of tons of cotton had been sold to Russia and Central European nations. With the start of World War I, these contracts were canceled, and even cotton that wasn't canceled couldn't be shipped. Cotton prices hit bottom—a dive from twenty-five or thirty cents per pound to five cents. The cotton exchanges slammed their doors and panic-stricken investors threw their stocks, bonds and commodities on the market for whatever they could get. Southern Negro workers threw their assets—their labor—on the market and got few takers. Thousands left the land and headed for city streets.

In 1915, too many bugs ("the eevil boll weebil"), too much water (floods) and too many workers resulted in too little work and starvation wages (seventy-five cents per day or less). This was the year after Henry Ford had rocked American industry by instituting an eight-hour day and a five-dollar minimum wage. No wonder tens of thousands of those who could (primarily the young, single and rootless but also families or parts of families broken by agricultural disaster in the south) hurried to the cities.

In New York the depression of 1914 and the surplus labor of 1915 had pushed NLUCAN into emergency action to scare up jobs—any kind of work.

Northern industry had fed and increased on cheap labor, mainly immigrant. But the outbreak of war in Europe drastically cut the flow of workers and started a reverse trend. As one example, the Slovaks and Lithuanians who had been arriving at the rate of 50,000 a year in 1914, were trickling in at the rate of about 700 per year in 1917. At the same time, armament contracts to American companies changed the labor picture overnight. In Connecticut and Massachusetts the munitions makers were paying sixty-five cents an hour and siphoning workers from industry and agriculture. The shade-grown tobacco industry was one of those hit earliest and hardest. When fieldworkers deserted for the factories, the Connecticut tobacco men simply went to New York in 1915 and advertised for women to replace them. They signed up two hundred young white women in short order. For the girls it was a paid vacation in the country, and they cultivated the tobacco fields by day and the streets and saloons by night, scandalizing the staid New England communities. After the harvest the tobacco men shipped the whores back to New York and, on an inspiration, one company called NLUCAN.[1]

In the middle of December, 1915, after a howling snowstorm NLU-CAN's John T. Clark arrived in Hartford to investigate the situation. There was an unreal quality to the whole mission and there is a note of incredulity in Clark's reports on it. Only a few months before, he had been struggling to find emergency work to keep hundreds of black New Yorkers alive. Suddenly, he was in a remote, frigid town in Connecticut to discuss not a handful of temporary jobs but scores of permanent jobs— maybe more.

He learned that the company had three plantations, tenements to house workers, and paid wages averaging from $11.50 to $13 per week. Clark cautiously verified this by inspecting the payroll, noting that one woman even earned $20 a week on piecework.

The company wanted fifty black families as an experiment, and expected an average of two workers from each family.

What about schooling for the children? The owner told Clark that he had a large family himself and his children went to the same school with the children of the employees, that the law was compulsory: each child must get an education. He said, furthermore, that the transportation and moving expense of the families would be paid and they would be guaranteed immediate employment at the going wages—under no conditions did he intend to lower wages.

Clark made another trip to Hartford on January 9, 1916. In the twenty-five days since Clark's last visit, the situation had changed. Representatives of *all* the tobacco companies had met and "quite a number . . . were intensely interested in this proposition."[2]

This was not a philanthropic, but a strictly business matter. "Their purpose," he reported, "is not to import Negroes in order to cheapen the labor, but rather to provide steady sources of labor." The work ranged from clearing land to weeding, harvesting, leaf processing and packing. For harvesting, it developed, college students—1,000 of them accustomed to farm life—could make from $1.50 to $3 per day and the companies would pay transportation from Norfolk to Hartford. In subsequent discussions, the Connecticut Leaf Tobacco Association became the agent for the growers.[3]

In 1914, NLUCAN found jobs for 181 blacks; in 1915 it placed 358. Suddenly, the agency was faced with an embarrassment of riches: 500 permanent and 2,000 harvesting jobs at top wages, transportation and expenses paid, facilities for workers, schools for dependents, enlightened employers, red carpet treatment . . . the abrupt turnabout from the soup kitchen and emergency relief "made-work" conditions of spring, 1915, was enough to set the head spinning. The workers would make two dollars per day with prospects for an increase and the positions would be permanent if work was satisfactory.

The twelve tobacco companies would accede to terms the League might suggest, even to paying travel expenses all the way from the workers' homes to Hartford and return (for the harvesters). Further, NLUCAN's expenses, estimated at $2,250 for securing the workers (and Clark's trips to Hartford), would be paid.

This was the point of no return for NLUCAN—and the decision was to help bring southern blacks to the tobacco fields of the Connecticut valley. The project sped along. On June 2, 1916, E. K. Jones reported that twenty-five Morehouse College students from Atlanta, Georgia, had arrived that morning en route to Hartford. Nearly 100 permanent workers had already been sent up and almost 1,000 student contracts for harvesting were signed and in hand.[4]

"Thus was born, right in the heart of Yankee land," exulted the New York *News,* a black weekly, "the first significant move to supplant foreign labor with native labor, a step which has resulted in one of the biggest upheavals in the North incident to the European war, which has already been a boon to the colored American, improving his economic status and putting thousands of dollars into his pockets." [5]

It was a black Klondike! It was irresistible. Before midsummer, 1917, there were 3,000 Afro-Americans in Hartford—above and beyond the students hired for summer work. The railroads, especially the Erie and Pennsylvania, were quickest to seize on the "new" source of labor.

One NLUCAN report describes this:

> From Jacksonville, St. Augustine, Pensacola and other cities in northeastern Florida, the first train loads of Negroes were picked up promiscuously. They were at first organized into camps. The promise of a long free ride to the North met with instant favor and wild excitement ensued as the news circulated. Carloads of Negroes began to pour into Pennsylvania. When they had once touched northern soil and discovered that still higher wages were being offered by other concerns, many deserted the companies respon-

sible for their presence in the North. Some drifted to the steel works of the same state: others left for nearby states. Letters back home brought news of still more enticing fields, and succeeded in stimulating the movement. Of the 12,000 Negroes brought into Pennsylvania by the Pennsylvania Railroad, less than 2,000 remained with the company.

Thus began in the year of 1916 a flood of Negroes from the south which neither the dread of northern winds, nor the persuasion of their leaders, nor the intimidation of authorities, nor the withdrawal of facilities for travel, could abate until it had spent itself.[6]

It was ironic that the very agency that said one of its cardinal principles was to discourage the flood of black Americans to the cities was the instrument that triggered the greatest exodus in the nation's history. Once the movement started, the League could no more have turned it off than it could have prevented iron filings from flying to the poles of a magnet.

In November 1915 L. Hollingsworth Wood stated in the NLUCAN annual report, "Because of the shortage of funds, early in the year the Executive Board of the League decided not to attempt to form new organizations in other cities, but to concentrate on the organizations already formed." [7]

Yet, that very month Eugene Kinckle Jones was away from the New York office in a major effort to develop new branches. It was a twenty-four-day trip that took Jones to Detroit, Chicago, Indianapolis, Louisville, Cincinnati, Columbus and Pittsburgh. The results were depressing. Jones came back with no new branches, only promises.[8]

The most recent affiliates had been the Armstrong Association of Philadelphia in 1914, the Atlanta Neighborhood Union in 1914 and an Augusta, Georgia, branch on December 4, 1914. The great pressures, problems and opportunities for branch organization lay in the huge manufacturing cities of the north. Yet, in them the progress had been small. This was the reason for Jones's trip.

His first trip to Detroit had been in the spring of 1915. It had been a humiliating disaster. Detroit's leading Negro pastor, Robert L. Bradby, of the Second Baptist Church, had heard about the League's work and invited Jones to tell the city's leading ministers about it, with the possibility of organizing a League branch as the ultimate goal. He was to make a one-hour presentation before the clergymen. Jones wrote Dr. Bradby that he was coming and hopped a train. Meanwhile, Bradby had written Jones not to come, but the League executive was on his way when the letter was delivered in New York.[9]

Jones was allowed five minutes for his presentation. When he finished, the ministers decided that since organizing a League would be extremely involved and difficult in Detroit, it would be best to consult the laity. They proposed a public meeting that same day where Jones could present his case to a larger group for a public response. They immediately telephoned their parishioners and that evening a group of seventy-five or more met in the basement assembly room of one of the churches.

At the close of Jones's NLUCAN presentation, the pastor of the church relieved his soul of his thoughts on the subject, saying that "we have excellent race relations in Detroit." Following that, Jones recalled, "I was attacked from all sides by leading citizens of that city. I was told that there was no Negro problem in Detroit and that the night before at one o'clock one of the colored pastors was called from his bed to tell the white Travelers' Aid worker at the station what disposition she should make of a colored girl who had come to the city without knowing where she was to stay or where she was to work. This was as evidence of the fact that there was no discrimination practiced by social workers in Detroit. The audience at once saw the point when I asked the question whether the white pastors were called from their beds at one o'clock at night. . . . There was a girls' home in Detroit for such cases." [10]

Though he made his point, he lost his opportunity. The meeting said no. But as Jones was leaving the hall a young man in the audience called him aside. The youth told Jones that there were several young men who had decided Detroit really needed a League because there was no social service work for blacks and that the older residents simply had not observed the problems that were thrust upon the city with the increase in black population.

Jones stayed overnight and got together with seven young men the next day. They said they would work to establish a League in the city and they wrote NLUCAN's secretary in New York for memberships. Jones then went to the Associated Charities offices and spoke to the secretary. The League was known to the Associated Charities and its credentials were unimpeachable. Jones was given the name of Henry G. Stevens and was told that this was the one person in the city who would see that the League was established in Detroit if he was convinced of its importance. Jones could not reach Stevens. He kept trying, however, and out of the blue, months later, he received a telegram one day in New York to be in Detroit the following morning for an eleven o'clock meeting with a group of interested persons to consider the possibility of a League in the city.

E. K. Jones boarded the "Detroiter" at Grand Central, due in Detroit the following morning. To Jones's increasing agitation, the train was delayed by a snowstorm and arrived at noon, five hours late. Frantic because he believed the group must have dispersed, Jones rushed to the meeting place. He found that Stevens had held the men when they learned of the train delay and Jones had until 1 p.m. to make his pitch. The men listened, lunchless, as Jones told about the League program. They asked to meet with the seven youths whom Jones had spoken to earlier, and a meeting was arranged at the Associated Charities offices the next morning. Again, Jones presented his case, the youths verified the need and reaffirmed their willingness to help, and the Associated Charities vouched for the League and its national directors. The white leaders were impressed, Mr. Stevens and others promised their support. They began with a city-wide meeting of organization representatives two weeks after Jones left Detroit for Chicago. The Detroit Urban League was actually established in 1916.

In the Windy City a luncheon had been arranged by the secretary of the NAACP, to which the city fathers had been invited. It was a capital occasion, Jones was in good form and his audience was receptive. Only a blind and deaf citizen would have been unaware of the burgeoning black population and the friction that was the daily fare of the newspapers. Jones convinced the group that the NLUCAN program was reasonable. He received a vote of approval and the ball, in effect, was handed back to him. The decision of the meeting was to invite E. K. Jones to return with a proposed plan of work to deal with the needs of Chicago's blacks. January 6 was the date set. The National League had many friends in Chicago, of course, in Jane Addams of Hull House, a former board member; Sophonisba Breckinridge, of the Chicago School of Civics and Philanthropy, a current board member; the social workers at Wendell Phillips settlement house, which the League had been subsidizing; and friends in the black community.

Out of this visit grew, at a later time, a committee to consider launching a League in Chicago. However, nothing crystallized. Jones thought he knew why when he learned that the executive secretary of the Jewish charities organization had developed something similar to the League and had told the committee leaders that it would take at least five years for the NLUCAN movement to develop in Chicago. This, Jones believed, froze out the members of the temporary committee, people who did not expect to devote that much of their life to forming a social service agency in the black community. The committee effort dragged along but was mostly dormant. (The Chicago Urban League was established in 1917.)

Indianapolis was a complex problem. E. K. Jones talked with business and professional leaders at one conference and with social service agency representatives at another. He also called on the Associated Charities and the superintendent of the Flanner Guild settlement house. There was much talk, and there was to be a meeting after he left to decide whether to organize within the existing central council of social service agencies and experiment with this approach, or to set up a League-type operation —perhaps even a League. (The Indianapolis Urban League was established in 1966.)

In Cincinnati, E. K. Jones found the most difficult situation. "There are," he said, "five distinct factions working largely in the field of education, but whose prejudices reach out into other fields of labor whenever one of the opposing interests is interested in their development." In this highly charged atmosphere, Jones prudently avoided any public meeting and concentrated on locating a leader with the least explosive potential. He thought he found one and she was willing to call a meeting in January to which representatives of the jealous agencies and others would be invited. Jones would make his presentation at that time.

It was not his original plan to spend time or effort on Columbus, but Jones visited the city and conferred with a group of leaders. He tartly concluded, "I found a disinclination on the part of those present at the conference to organize for social betterment." [11]

E. K. Jones's missionary effort in Pittsburgh bore fruit—but not for the League. He called on many leaders, spoke about the League's program at three public meetings, conferred with black and white social workers and the leaders of the Associated Charities. The upshot was a decision to organize a "general committee" of white and Negro social service workers linked by a liaison man who would be a black added to the Associated Charities staff, trained by that agency and guaranteed a salary for six months. If it developed as expected the general committee would add workers and open a district social service office as funds became available. Over the months it might ripen into a League-type operation, even an affiliate. Watchful waiting and friendly assistance were called for. (The Pittsburgh Urban League was established in 1918.)

So, after the facts were sifted, there was not too much to celebrate in Jones's branch development trip. Yet, by the end of 1916 the spadework of this series of meetings had produced favorable results in a number of those cities. The Detroit situation was nailed down when Jones bundled NLUCAN Fellow Forrester B. Washington onto a train and delivered him in Detroit to serve as first executive secretary of the new Detroit Urban League. Washington was the tenth League Fellow to go through the New York School of Philanthropy–Columbia University academic training and NLUCAN field work to qualify for professional social work. By the fall of 1916, many more students had completed similar work in Nashville with George Haynes at Fisk University and Bethlehem Center, and two others had been supported at Chicago.[12]

George Haynes had created an impressive educational institute at Fisk University in Nashville to train graduate students for social and religious service. In 1916 eight courses were taught by Haynes, Paul F. Mowbray, Joseph N. Haskell, Helen A. Walker of Fisk and Estelle Haskin, supervisor of Bethlehem House. Among the courses were Negro history and problems of Negro life, using "all available data to acquaint the student with the part the Negro has played in the developing life of America and with the economic, political, intellectual, social and religious forces that enter into the condition and relations of the Negro and white people in America. Particular attention is given to urban conditions . . ." [13]

The special aim of the training, said Haynes, "is to link the growing enthusiasm and knowledge of educated Negro youth with the pressing needs of the toiling thousands of the Negro people . . ." [14]

Haynes was working to build in Nashville a model training center as a pattern to stimulate other institutions "to emulate and draw experience from." Such a center, Haynes was sure, would act like the NLUCAN work in New York, as a demonstration. The New York "center" had been "a powerful lever with which to lift the lethargy from other localities." [15]

Meanwhile, Haynes was teaching undergraduates in sociology and economics and had eighteen upperclassmen enrolled in the 1915 school year. NLUCAN offered fellowships to promising students; they were modest, but tuition and fees came to only $12, and monthly room, board and laundry totaled $14 in 1916. Partial fellowships were available to teachers and others wishing a month or more of "trial training." [16]

No question but that George Haynes was doing a basic job. By training two NLUCAN Fellows per year at the New York School of Philanthropy, one or more at Fisk, plus his graduate students at the Nashville Training Center and undergraduates in sociology at Fisk, the professor was inevitably influencing social work among blacks by preparing professionals. Furthermore, his theory of providing a pattern for other institutions was sound. By 1914, Morehouse was incorporating sociology courses and Talladega was looking at the possibility of developing social work sequences. However, the most outstanding outgrowth of this activity came about when the Atlanta School of Social Work was organized in 1920.

The League had built up a group of trained professionals by 1916, in the form of its Fellows and through its "broken" fellowships (partial tuition and on-the-job training at NLUCAN). Thus, the agency was prepared to some extent when the migration surge inundated the cities in 1916. In addition to the scholars it had trained, the League had stimulated interest among blacks in social work. The public meetings, in-service courses taught by George Haynes reaching preachers and teachers, the publications and news reports of NLUCAN activities helped carry the word of a new horizon to Afro-American youths. Word of the League and its program was spread by the black opinion leaders, and because it had unassailable credentials in its purposes, programs, personnel and its leading board members, it won almost automatic and universal acceptance. But it had even more going for it.

It beckoned to young, well-educated blacks and was able to recruit them with relative ease at this time, because of its various and powerful appeals. The League and social work among blacks were synonymous. And, because career avenues open to middle-class black college men were circumscribed, NLUCAN quickly became one of the desirable professional career possibilities.

Teaching and preaching were crowded and old hat; law, medicine and dentistry were solid but delimited to the race; social work was something new and had many attractions. It was respectable and prestigious, sanctioned by church, civic and social leaders and poor citizens alike. It was not a "hustle" or fly-by-night operation; social work looked to be a long-term career—both the poor and prejudice were likely to be around for some time. The work offered opportunities where the action was, in the cities, and the pay was competitive with teaching and preaching, certainly. Mobility was a factor—there was the possibility of changing from one city to another. And the intangibles were appealing: entry into the highest reaches of white/black civic, political and social circles; insight into the power structure, being privy to its plans concerning blacks; the prospect of operating as a local Booker T. Washington in the community —even the state.

In a word, the new field of social work had much in its favor; and the major factor in black social work was NLUCAN. Thus alert, ambitious young men from the best families and finest universities came to this rapidly developing new organization in its first decade. Among them were William T. Ashby, a Lincoln University and Yale graduate who became executive of the Newark League; John T. Dancy, Jr., out of Exeter, Livingstone College and the University of Pennsylvania, executive of the Detroit League; Forrester B. Washington, Tufts graduate and Detroit executive; John T. Clark, Ohio State graduate and Pittsburgh executive; T. Arnold Hill, from Virginia Union University, Chicago executive; and, Charles S. Johnson, University of Chicago, the research director of the Chicago League. There were many others, and as the Nashville training center and the NLUCAN Fellows program got under way there were even more.

There had to be. The migration pressure had sufficient impact on city fathers in many industrial areas to cause a veritable blossoming of local Leagues.

9/Anatomy of a Conflict

Though Eugene Kinckle Jones was invariably quiet, reserved and as soft-spoken as a silken scarf, the tensile strength of the ambitious administrator could be glimpsed occasionally. It was unconcealed in Jones's letter to Hollingsworth Wood following the February 1916 Steering Committee meeting:

> I write to inform you concerning those things which you are supposed to do in keeping with the resolutions passed. . . .
>
> You are to write to Miss Breckinridge requesting her to remain on the Executive Board. You are to write to Dr. Haynes informing him that his and my titles have been changed to "Executive Secretary." You are also to inform Dr. Haynes that the Steering Committee will recommend to the Finance Committee and the Executive Board of the League that the League attempt to raise the $3,800 for Nashville expenses, only after the regular budget of the League is assured.
>
> Please send me the resolution which was drafted in regard to the death of Dr. Booker T. Washington. I think you took it at the Executive Board meeting.[1]

The actual control of the agency on an operating basis was concentrated at this time in the hands of Wood as chairman and in the seven-man Steering Committee of the executive board (although only three or four members attended meetings). Of those few, however, L. Hollingsworth Wood and Elizabeth Walton were invariably present. Nevertheless, the tone of E. K. Jones's letter accurately reflected the true locus of power. Kinckle Jones was in the driver's seat. If any part of the League program was to suffer in a budget cutback, it would be the educational work under Haynes's direction.

Perhaps Dr. Haynes's reaction to this challenge was predictable. Perhaps it was what Jones and Wood had in mind when the changes were proposed. At any rate, George Haynes wrote Hollingsworth Wood with his analysis of the situation:

> It works itself out in concrete terms thus: Whether now that the New York work is well on its feet, the necessary financial increases and other ef-

forts shall now be made to put the Nashville work on its feet in a similar way before financial increases are made for supervision or other things. Travelling supervision is only incidentally needed—particularly in the South where social work must be demonstrated before people really will know what we are talking about. These people need an example to copy and trained workers to lead more than they need the visits of a secretary. Mr. Victor McCutcheon [NLUCAN assistant treasurer] the other day in talking with Jones and me seemed to think that the New York work could spare Jones and he suggested the idea for him to move to Chicago for two or three years to develop work there.

During the past five years when questions have been raised as to where Nashville and Fisk stand in the League's plans, I believed there was warrant for assuring people that Nashville's turn would come when we had put New York on its feet. My discussion with you and Mr. Jones, your letters, and the steering Committee's vote on Nashville's next year's financial increases lead me to fear that the case is different. Since the matter has been brought up I shall be glad if it may be determined what we have meant by Nashville as Southern Headquarters and training center.[2]

The basic question was whether to shift a major portion of the budget into building a training center or into moving to develop new branches. The fact was that Haynes had not sold the executive board or the Steering Committee on any urgent need for the training center; and the showdown choice between a full-dress Nashville training facility and new branches had already been voted by the steering and finance committees in their budget allocations.

Considering the unsettled relationship of Haynes and the Nashville work to Jones and the New York and northern work, it was injudicious, to put it mildly, for Haynes to have leaped at the opportunity to take on an outside contract in mid-1916.

From his summer session teaching at Wilberforce University, Haynes wrote Hollingsworth Wood that he had been asked to take part in a Harvard study of Hampton Institute and its work. Haynes's part would be investigation of the graduates, visiting them in their home localities. His expenses would be covered, of course; the work was to be spread over the next year or so and thus would not interfere with his other duties. He would, said Haynes, "be willing to make adjustments for any time actually taken from League work should that occur. . . . It looks like a big lead for our work. . . . I think it will give us touch with the field and in many directions." [3] However, from the vantage point of national overview with the pressures of black arrivals in the cities building up daily, Haynes's personal project must have appeared diversionary at best.

One resolution of the basic dilemma was attempted in a joint meeting of the NLUCAN's steering and finance committees on April 11, 1917. Actually, only Fred Moore, Elizabeth Walton, Abraham Lefkowitz and Hollingsworth Wood were present plus E. K. Jones, who was a staff, not a committee, member. This committee voted to authorize Wood to present the following plan of work to both Jones and Haynes:

> Mr. E. K. Jones is to continue as Executive Secretary of the League, whose national headquarters should be New York City, to which office all matters pertaining to the League's general development should be referred.
>
> Dr. George E. Haynes to be given the title of "Consultant," with the understanding that the Board should have the right to refer any matters pertaining to the League to Dr. Haynes for advice—Dr. Haynes to continue in charge of the Nashville field; to give lectures in schools and colleges when called upon and in other ways to further the work of the organization.[4]

There was no mention of budget; and there was considerable disparity in spelling out Haynes's specific duties and leaving all else to Jones (apparently Haynes never received official notice of this plan).

Meanwhile Haynes developed a scheme "for further executive organization of League work." [5] He suggested two basic plans—the first to divide the educational and practical field work, each with a responsible head. The second would be a division of labors "growing out of the existing conditions" into what Haynes saw as a model northern center and a model southern center. From these, the League "could send efficient and experienced workers, trained at the centers, into such localities as are ready to support them and, as the League's finances increase, workers could be supported and loaned, so to speak, to new fields (meaning cities) for varying pioneer periods."

Either plan, he said, would be headed by the executive board acting through special standing committees (a new proposal) and the staff head at each center. Thus there would be a standing committee of southern black and white people "to advise on matters relating to the Southern field." [6]

The first five years of League functioning were evidence that the second plan was best, he said, quoting literature and letterheads which listed Nashville as NLUCAN's southern headquarters. He described the southern state universities' extension work with public school supervisors; Peabody College was working out a similar extension system to have its graduate teachers visit alumni in the field. And he noted the failure of the YMCA efforts in the cities (which he had experienced at first hand) as an object lesson. The Y, he said, "started on a theory of organizing the city fields and supervising them at first, giving much less attention to the problem of the workers. They have been driven around to the necessity of placing the emphasis upon trained workers and the movement has its great weakness in the lack of trained workers. Workers hold the keys to success in such a movement. In recent years they have started attempts the other way round. . . ." [7]

There were "rising forces of religion and democracy," said George Haynes, not understandable to or to be dealt with successfully by persons living outside the south. If furnished with a demonstration in a southern city, "they themselves will be eager to copy [it] . . . and our task of stimulation and guidance will then be easy. By hurrying into these localities and trying to organize committees and work before the demonstration has created a belief of its possibility and has shown correctly what can be done is to court failure and mushroom success." [8]

The second plan, Haynes said, was favored by "those of large vision who are best acquainted with the Negro situation." He named Dr. Wallace Buttrick of the General Education Board as one who had spoken favorably of such approaches; and Dr. Bruce Payne, president of Peabody College and Major R. R. Moton favored this specific plan.[9]

Anyway, the first plan was impractical, argued Haynes. "It is contrary to one of our underlying ideas, 'the articulation of the Negro college with the life of the Negro people.' It weakens the connections between the workers in training, the workers who go forth into the cities and those who are to train and to supervise. The best thought of modern education is to prevent as far as possible the break between the practical life of the world and the preparation for that life." [10]

Undoubtedly George Haynes's design would have advantages—the League effort in the south would be indigenous and more acceptable; all the key League workers would be professionally trained; "mushroom success" would be avoided. But Haynes had failed utterly to come to grips with the urgency of the developing situation. NLUCAN's work, its methods, its staff and resources—all of these had been hopelessly overwhelmed by the human and institutional demands that were pouring in on the League. These demands, growing out of the migration surge, were conditions that Haynes, as the nation's foremost authority on black urban migration, should have recognized first of all. There was truth and poignance in his observation about the separation of colleges and their communities; but the larger need was for League organizations where the masses of black people were flocking—in the cities of the north.

At the end of June 1917 a special meeting was held to consider the division of work between the two executive secretaries. Hollingsworth Wood chaired the meeting and Miss Walton, Fred Moore, Roger N. Baldwin and William H. Baldwin III were present—plus E. K. Jones. Roger N. Baldwin (who had just moved from St. Louis to New York at Wood's invitation to assist in the work of the American Union Against Militarism and to head what became the National Civil Liberties Union) spoke as a southerner and emphasized Haynes's point about developing work in the south more easily from a southern headquarters. E. K. Jones agreed that the country should be divided into districts with centrally located headquarters in each. But when the question of overall supervision of NLUCAN's work came up, the committee asked Haynes and Jones to outline their recommendations and tossed the matter into the laps of Roger Baldwin, Wood, Jones and Haynes to work out in consultation.

Ruth Baldwin wrote Hollingsworth Wood the following week: "I do not envy you and Roger your job, and of course I hope that the result may not mean the loss of either Haynes or Jones, but even if it should mean the loss of both, somehow or other the organization has got to be worked out." [11]

Roger Baldwin believed that one executive should be responsible to the Steering Committee, which would be situated in New York. He doubted that the plan of dividing responsibility would work out; and he thoroughly agreed that a southern headquarters with a secretary in charge was desirable.[12]

Meanwhile, E. K. Jones submitted to Wood an organization chart and letter setting out his idea of the agency's "ideal arrangement." He recommended that one person be the executive or general secretary, "through whom all reports of the workers should be made to the officers and Executive Committee . . . and through whom all instructions and decisions made by the Executive Board should be officially transmitted to the various employees and affiliated organizations." [13]

Jones brought up a new thought for developing affiliates: that T. Arnold Hill, his secretary from New York, and Paul F. Mowbray, Haynes's assistant at Fisk, share responsibility for new affiliates, reporting to and receiving instructions from the general secretary at the national headquarters (that is, Jones). They would divide their activities geographically along a line following the Potomac and Ohio Rivers. This was a suggestion not likely to appeal to Haynes, who was complaining that he needed additional assistance even with Mowbray's full service.

"The work of educating the teachers and students in public schools and colleges of the South, to an appreciation of the possibilities of organized social work, the raising of the standards of social science training in Southern Colleges, and in cooperation with the national headquarters, the work of finding and training women for the field, [should] be entrusted to one person—logically Dr. George E. Haynes," wrote Jones. "He should so correlate these activities with those of the organizers on the field as to have workers prepared for assignment to new fields when the new organizations are ready to employ them." [14]

Jones's organization chart was headed by the NLUCAN executive board, "to whom all reports of outline accomplishments, problems as to policy and methods of organizing locals, etc., are to be made." The Finance Committee was shown beside the executive board. The Steering Committee was below it and was to be chaired by the League president. It would consist of "certain members of the Executive Board" and would act between board meetings.

The next level on the chart was the executive staff, with the executive or general secretary heading it. Below this was a new administrative layer: four regional directors, known as the secretaries of the northeastern, southeastern, northwestern and southwestern fields. Also on this level was a fifth secretary, the educational secretary. George Haynes, in other words, would be in the same administrative stratum and co-equal to four other secretaries. Jones's plan also foresaw that local Leagues in the various cities would each have a board of directors and local secretary, reporting to the appropriate regional secretary.

George Haynes sent his suggestion to Roger Baldwin. His covering letter displayed unusual defensiveness. "Lately," he complained, "questions were raised about my ability to get hold of and train capable young people. In reply I point to the following: Robinson in Cincinnati; Anderson in Nashville; Uxenia Scott in Houston, Texas; Sophia Boaz, Juvenile Court, Chicago; Birdye Haynes in New York; Myrtle Alexander, Augusta, Ga.; Rosalie Singleton, New Orleans; A. F. Williams, Newport News, Va. I pass over my part in finding and training E. K. Jones, James Hubert, Garrie Moore and others. I pass over the fact that some of the most active board members, including the Chairman [Wood], came into the League at my solicitation." [15]

Haynes foresaw development of state organizations, with local committees and local executives responsible to them. He had two states under way toward such development, he said, urging local autonomy.

The professor suggested that there should be one central city for each of the regions—New York, Nashville, and Chicago. In each region, there should be an executive secretary, responsible to the executive board and Steering Committee, Haynes suggested. He wanted to be independent of a New York administrator because "executive control from New York will not get hearty cooperation of [southern] whites in dealing with Negroes. Even colored people who may be disgruntled will use this with white people against us as was so disastrously done in Richmond." [16]

Furthermore, said Haynes, the success of the city work depended on efficient workers. "A general program of short secretarial visits to cities before these workers are available has not proven of great value." Though Haynes was highly critical of "mushroom efforts," referring to attempts to form branches overnight, only to find them as insubstantial as fungi, a number of the affiliates he had developed had been rent by internal strife and had subsided into nonactive status.[17]

To justify the co-equality of the three executive secretaries Haynes suggested that general executive matters be parceled out to them. For example, one would handle all monies; another the convention and summer school supervision, and so on. In the professor's view, division of responsibility was practical if the intentions of the individuals were pure.

Worker training and field work should be developed at each regional center, Haynes recommended. Thus local workers would be available and could be offered to any locality that was willing to undertake systematic work. "If the locality cannot take over the salary . . . the national organization should put the locality on probation for a number of months, with the understanding that support for the worker will then be provided by the locality. The crucial time in a city is the first six months or year of its effort." [18] Though George Haynes touched on the vital matter of finances, neither he nor Jones came to grips with underwriting the movement via fund-raising nor with the impact of the migration or the war.

As an outgrowth of Haynes's suggestions, Roger Baldwin drew up a proposal for reorganization and forwarded it to Wood. Meanwhile, Wood sent to board members a suggested outline for their reactions.[19] James Dillard wrote that the outline was too skeletal for him to understand it well, but recommended an early meeting to settle the matter. "The increasing importance of the League," he wrote, "demands that we should have such a meeting so that no time be wasted in any further discussion of methods." [20]

In Wood's papers a draft outline containing seven points appears to be the agenda for discussing the scheme. The framework outlined called for southern and western advisory committees consisting of board members and others appointed by the board. The southern field would be centered at Nashville, with Haynes as secretary of the committee and Paul Mowbray as field secretary; the western field headquarters would be at Chicago and T. Arnold Hill would be field secretary but the advisory committee secretary (parallel to Haynes's position in the southern field) was to be filled after consultation with Hill. These two committees would advise on both educational and field work. NLUCAN's executive secretary under the orders of the "Board of Directors and Steering Committee" would have direction of field work and general organization as well as direction of local work in and about New York and on-the-job field work.[21]

The educational director ("with committee on education of Board") would have as his functions the training of workers, securing and placing them; supervising the southern field as advisor, with the committee; cooperating with educational agencies; and directing local Nashville work.

The last category on this agenda was that of field secretary—for the south and west; and under this was the item "Local secretaries—New York (?)."

The controversy simmered along without resolution until the end of August 1917 and then a special meeting was held on "neutral ground" in the office of Dr. Thomas Jesse Jones in the Federal Education Building, Washington, D.C. Present at the session were board members Robert R. Moton, John T. Emlen, John Hope, William H. Baldwin III and Hollingsworth Wood. Also very much present were Dr. T. J. Jones, Haynes and E. K. Jones. After discussion, a formal conference memorandum was drawn up:

> It was agreed that the activities of Dr. Haynes and Mr. Jones should proceed on the following general lines:
>
> Mr. Jones to be called the Executive Secretary.
>
> Dr. Haynes to be called the Educational Secretary.
>
> Dr. Haynes to cover as his field the southeast of the Mississippi with the exception of the Atlantic Coast states. Mr. Jones to have general oversight of the other territory in the United States, developing local or district leaders as the exigencies of the situation require.
>
> The report to be made to the Board through the New York office.
>
> In the above general outlines, it is intended that the work shall be carried on with complete frankness, and with the fullest confidence—information being exchanged and the question of individual influence in each particular part of the territory considered, rather than making a hard and fast geographic line.[22]

This agreement was approved by NLUCAN's Steering Committee on October 10, 1917. And so it seemed the major questions had been resolved to the satisfaction of all concerned. Second thoughts, however, assailed George Haynes. In November he complained to Wood that two of the points were not as he had understood them. "Both at Washington and in my discussion of details with Mr. Jones; it was definitely the understanding that he is to have general executive matters and that general educational matters are to come under my supervision. This is also stated in the outline of your committee. Does the memorandum mean this?" [23]

Haynes pointed out that the discussion had said no hard and fast geographical line was to be drawn. Yet, in the memo the south was defined as "east of the Mississippi" and the Atlantic Coast states were under Jones's supervision. This, he said, obviously called for readjustment.

Wood's reply ten days later hints at exasperation. "I am interested that you thought those questions important enough to write a letter about," he wrote the professor. "Certainly everything in anybody's territory is subject to adjustment between you, as was, I thought, indicated by the memorandum." As to the general educational matters, Wood said he thought it would be all right to consider them as coming generally under Haynes's oversight, but they should be reported to Jones so that he could keep in touch with all activities of the agency.[24]

By this time (mid-November 1917) World War I was absorbing America. Blacks were rushing from southern lands to city factories. Manpower crises were developing and the government was hastily shaping plans to regulate labor and expedite war production. It was this national crisis that ultimately resolved the controversy over NLUCAN's direction.

10/Farm to Factory

There were some who realized that the pressures set in motion by the exodus would have profound effects. It was partly for long-range, but even more for immediate reasons that NLUCAN called a Conference on Migration in 1917. It was held in the Russell Sage Foundation building in New York on January 26 and brought together an extraordinary collection of interested persons.

Movement of Negro Labor from South to
North Is Seriously Considered by
Thinkers of Both Races

UNDER AUSPICES OF NATIONAL URBAN LEAGUE

All Phases of the Question are Discussed by Both Radicals and
Conservatives, and Practical Experts Gave the Actual Result So
Far Resulting from the Migration of Southern Labor Into Northern
Industrial Communities

headlined the New York *Age*.[1] Dean Kelly Miller of Howard University chaired the afternoon session; L. Hollingsworth Wood presided in the evening. Among the program participants were the U.S. Commissioner of Immigration; the New York City Tenement House Commissioner; New

York *Evening Post* publisher Oswald Garrison Villard; Principal Hollis B. Frissell of Hampton Institute; C. T. Erwin, president of the Negro Organization Society of Virginia; R. R. Wright, Jr., editor of the *Christian Recorder* and NLUCAN representatives from the national office and local branches plus industrial agents.[2]

There were three subjects discussed at the Conference: the causes and consequences of the migration; the condition of the migrants; and how to aid their adjustment. The audience, representatives of national organizations and local agencies that one way or another were concerned with Negro life, heard Dr. Frissell speak on "The Negro's Industrial Opportunity"; Dr. Wright, Jr., on "The Economic Power of Negroes"; and J. H. Butler of Savannah's League on Urban Conditions on "The Futility of the 'Strong Arm' Methods to Stop Migration from the South."

Erie Railroad representatives praised the majority of black workers brought from the South. "A few have been, like any other race or any other men, shiftless and ready to 'jump their jobs,'" one commented, "but the majority are otherwise."[3] A Mr. Jackson of Lukens Steel and Iron Works, Coatesville, Pa., stated that black workers were making more money than ever before and were making good.

John T. Emlen, secretary of the Armstrong Association of Philadelphia, reported on the status of black migrants in and around that city. The association's employment secretary had visited Coatesville and been appalled at the miserable housing and social conditions. The town "had large bodies of men who have no families and no home environment; they were living in company provided barracks . . . the social conditions are extremely bad, and one of the leading colored citizens reports the increasingly noisy condition of the town at nights on account of the newcomers."[4]

But it was Forrester B. Washington, the young Detroit League executive, who stole the show at the Migration Conference. In eight short months he had made the Detroit League an indispensable institution. The kind of thinking he had to contend with was well represented in a reply he received to one of his first inquiries. He wrote the Bay Court Home run by the Associated Charities of Detroit about admission of black mothers. "We have never had colored mothers and children," replied a Home official, "because we were afraid they would not be contented."[5]

There were a lot of discontented blacks in Detroit in 1916. The black population had zoomed to 20,000 and the trains were bringing 100 more every day. Where the other Leagues—even in New York—were dealing with several hundred job placements each, Washington actually placed in his hectic first year 6,993 men and 1,279 women. Furthermore,

2,100 of these were skilled and semiskilled jobs. He was lucky—he had an "employment secretary" whose salary was paid by the Employers' Association of Detroit. Most of the Leagues had neither assistants nor the financial backing which Detroit enjoyed.

Forrester Washington gave the Migration Conference a how-to-do-it-in-the-northern-city description of his Detroit activities. His talk stressed constructive action in employment, housing, recreation, crime-prevention cooperation and industrial services. The first week, he contended, was the most critical one for the new arrivals. They were easy prey of exploiters and were welcomed only by the "vicious element." It was important to bring the new migrant into contact with the "good elements" and find him a job at once. Therefore, the Detroit League circulated cards in black districts with this message:

NEWCOMERS TO DETROIT—You can find employment and be directed to decent lodgings FREE of charge at the Detroit League on Urban conditions Among Negroes.[6]

A similar announcement was flashed on the screen at a local movie house, and Washington expected to place agents at the railroad stations as soon as he had funds for this purpose.

Hundreds of migrants arrived with little or no money. Their immediate problem was bed and board. Washington had worked out a scheme with some employers by which the factories issued checks to guarantee restaurant and boarding house bills of migrants who came to work for them.

Calling for wholesome recreation facilities for the immigrants, the Detroit League executive said it was sad but true that the newcomer did not receive a warm welcome from the great majority of colored citizens of the better class, but while these solid citizens "are trying to decide whether his coming is a benefit or an injury to them," he receives red carpet treatment from the saloonkeepers, pool-room proprietors, "blind pig" (gambling club) managers and madams.

Washington advised his audience that to be useful, a housing bureau should "scour the city for every available house, tenement or room inside or outside the recognized Negro district. It should make a thorough investigation of comparative rents charged Negroes and whites, and give the findings the fullest publicity. The Bureau should constantly remind employers of Negro labor that it is to their advantage to see that the Negro is well housed and that, if nobody else will build, it is good business for them to do so." [7]

This was not empty talk. The Detroit League had induced two of the large foundries to build low-priced homes for black employees near its plant. And in another ingenious move, the League had bought up leases from the madams in charge of whorehouses closed by the police. Most of these were in the black district. The League then persuaded local manufacturers to take over the leases, thereby providing housing for a large number of colored families. Also, the League's housing bureau kept a list of vacant houses and was surprised at the number of them not listed with commercial real estate agents. A list of respectable furnished rooms was supplied to Detroit employers for the use of new employees. In this way, said Washington, the immigrants were steered away from the open arms of the disorderly houses.

The Detroit League also scored another notable victory in the housing field. In a spasm of blind hatred a mob of two hundred whites had descended on a house into which twenty-five Negro newcomers had recently moved. It had been an all-white neighborhood until then. The whites evicted the blacks, tore up the house, threw the furniture out in the yard and destroyed it. The League stepped in, arranged a conference between the migrants and the whites, and brought them to mutual understanding. The whites agreed to pay for the damage, the blacks moved back in and harmony was established in the newly "integrated" neighborhood.

The young Negroes' Protective Association was an instrument developed by Washington to spread the word in the black community about health, housing, employment and other matters of common interest. It consisted of young college men. The association also carried out a program of noon-hour talks at factories where black workers were employed, talks on fundamentals such as hygiene, health, tardiness, how and where to save and purchase Liberty Loan bonds, and especially, about the Detroit League—what it was and how it could help the men.

The League executive even enlisted the police in his work with migrants. The police commissioner appointed a special officer to mingle with the newcomers on street corners and public places "to dissuade them from blockading sidewalks by boisterous behavior, using loud and obscene language, etc., and directing the unemployed to the League office for jobs."

The League covered its community. Washington had put together an "executive council" composed of chief executives of the black churches, fraternal, literary and welfare organizations. He had formed an employment committee with representatives of three churches. He was cooperating with the mothers' clubs, had established his agency as the channel through which the city Recreation Commission furnished coaches, umpires, auditoriums and baseball fields, and was the black "mayor" of the city so far as the Detroit Board of Commerce, Employers' Association, police and other city departments were concerned.

But what really clinched the high evaluation of the Detroit League operation was not only the superb job Washington and his staff had done, but the chilling occurrences at East St. Louis, Illinois, in mid-1917. In that grimy outpost of manufacturing and meat packing exploded a bloody pogrom whose ferocity shocked the public from coast to coast and especially jolted industrial leaders in northern urban centers.

East St. Louis was a classical confrontation of forces. Sociologist Graham R. Taylor described the place as a satellite city where absentee capital had only one interest—getting the largest possible dividends—where community spirit was zero and where politics of the worst sort was the result.[8]

When the workers of a major aluminum plant in the city struck for higher wages the company promptly hired black workers to replace them. Anonymous racist ads appeared in the local newspapers. The union leaders issued inflammatory bulletins denouncing blacks and in a mass delegation met with the mayor. They demanded that no more blacks be allowed to enter the city. As the men were leaving City Hall

> they heard that a Negro had accidentally shot a white man during a holdup. In a few minutes rumor had replaced fact: the shooting was intentional—a white woman had been insulted—two white girls were shot. By this time, 3,000 people had congregated and were crying for vengeance. [White] Mobs roamed the streets, beating Negroes. Policemen did little more than take the injured to hospitals and disarm Negroes.
>
> The National Guard restored order. When the governor withdrew the troops, tensions were still high, and scattered episodes broke the peace. The press continued to emphasize the incidence of Negro crimes, white pickets and Negro workers at the aluminum company skirmished and, on July 1, some whites drove through the main Negro neighborhood, firing into homes. Negro residents armed themselves. When a police car (filled with white officers) drove down the street, Negroes riddled it with gunshot.
>
> The next day a Negro was shot on the main street and a new riot was under way. . . . The area became a "bloody half mile" for three or four hours; streetcars were stopped, and Negroes, without regard to age or sex, were pulled off and stoned, clubbed and kicked, and mob leaders calmly shot and killed Negroes who were lying in blood in the street. As victims were placed in an ambulance, the crowds cheered and applauded.
>
> Other rioters set fire to Negro homes, and by midnight the Negro section was in flames and Negroes were fleeing the city. There were 48 dead (only 9 whites), hundreds injured, and more than 300 buildings destroyed.[9]

Suddenly, to a degree unequalled in American history, the enormity of the black potential forcefully impressed itself on the men in power. In a time of national peril, the blacks were in the centers of the nation where the necessities of battle were being forged. They were there in force, a mass that could be a threat or a huge advantage. But what—or who—was to control them?

The New York *Evening Post* editorialized that the Detroit League's work was a lesson for other cities. "Neglect the Negro emigrating northward, make him feel an outcast, allow him to be exploited by influences which demoralize him, and you have helped prepare the powder for such an explosion as took place in East St. Louis. The human material coming from the South is plastic. It can be made industrious, law-respecting, and progressive, or can be abandoned to the saloonkeeper, gambler and drug-vender to be made into the criminal character which furnishes the excuse for white violence. The Detroit League does what a similar body of whites and Negroes working together could do anywhere in guiding colored newcomers. . . . It should be imitated." [10]

NLUCAN for the first time moved to center stage nationally. L. Hollingsworth Wood announced that the League planned to contact mayors and responsible citizens of all industrial centers where serious problems had been created by the arrival of untrained blacks from the South. The purpose, he said, would be "to affect organizations which will forestall repetitions in other cities of the recent mob outrages in East St. Louis, Illinois." [11]

"What precautions are the other cities taking with their thousands of migrants that some day similar outbreaks may not occur with mobs, black or white, running through their streets, murdering and pillaging as they go? The National Urban League, which is organized in eighteen cities North and South, is doing its utmost to turn this raw, ignorant labor from a possible threat into a civic and industrial asset. It is eager to aid other cities to meet their problems in a constructive way, but the scope of its work is dependent entirely upon the cooperation of the best white and colored elements in the communities, as well as upon the financial support of its contributors." [12]

Wood's words fell on receptive ears. Interest in the League spurted.

With its network of affiliates, the League was the intermediary for scores of thousands of black workers in their new, unfamiliar role. In 1916 and earlier a telephone call for black workers was a request for porters, domestics, elevator operators or janitors. By early 1918 the calls included many for skilled and semiskilled workers. Requests for engineers, draftsmen, carpenters, shoemakers and brass molders were among them. And black women were being placed not only as domestics, but in the garment and silk industries, also as designers, machine operators, milliners, toymakers, "even stenographers in private firms, federal and municipal positions." [13]

"Formerly, Negroes were seldom hired," said E. K. Jones in February

1918, "except in the traditional occupations, to do even unskilled industrial labor. Foreigners were preferred in the cruder tasks in the factory, on the railroad, etc. Today the Negro has a chance to do the kind of work that is the foundation for skill. Our main objection to menial labor is that it leads nowhere." [14]

There were some exceptions to the generally favorable labor scene. The Interborough Rapid Transit in New York was "almost unapproachable when it comes to giving the colored man a chance." However, "in cities like Detroit . . . one sees a colored motorman almost every few minutes on the most important streets. The best he could hope to get [in New York] is a porter's job." [15]

The "commercial field" had its strictures too. Jones found the department stores generally had not hired Negro girls as clerks though one of New York's largest shops had several black saleswomen. "I don't believe in this period of change it would have shocked this store's trade to see twice the number at the counters," Jones said. "The patrons would attribute the increase to the general war situation." (This rationale had the obvious weakness of being easily invalidated by peace; expediency dictated.)

Though there were gains in the professions as well, there was still a long way to go. Prejudice in the professions, Jones noted, had scarcely been jogged. He pointed out that not a single hospital in New York would accept a black intern. The situation for black teachers was somewhat better, he judged. There were between 125 and 150 of them in the city schools. The opportunities in the professions were great, Jones said; the trouble was that the black man could not find the initial opening. Color barred him.

"The only remedy for this prejudice lies in the conduct of the individual Negro plus a constant campaign of education and drilling of the people who are withholding these opportunities," said the League executive. In his view there was no "open sesame." "Every Negro must persist in demanding consideration in a respectful and intelligent way and in doing his utmost to make good," said Jones.[16]

The disastrous East St. Louis massacre had broad repercussions in industry. At the Congressional hearings on the riot, the testimony etched a shocking picture of callous indifference to the human needs of workers and citizens. Since the riot disrupted production of war goods vitally needed by the United States Army, the War Department became alarmed and responded with a crash program to rehabilitate East St. Louis civically, socially and industrially through the War Community Services Committee of its Community Organization branch. The WCSC had been allotted an emergency $100,000 for the purpose, and this was matched by citizens and corporations of the city for underwriting a three-year program. It was out of this fund that the budget of the fledgling Urban League in East St. Louis was underwritten.

Not all of the industrial jobs for black workers were confined to the northern cities. In the pressure of war, industrial manpower needs expanded overnight. NLUCAN found itself expanding also, and not only in terms of the cities it served, but the services it was called upon to give. An excellent example was its emergency aid to Newport News Shipbuilding and Dry Dock Company, then America's largest shipbuilders. There was only one labor pool with the needed manpower for America's shipyards: black workers. The company, with the aid and counsel of George Haynes, acting officially for NLUCAN, went all out.

By the fall of 1917, Newport News Shipbuilding had a qualified black social worker on its payroll and had just hired a second (a former Haynes trainee). It pulled together the story of its personnel policies and published it in a leaflet with the notice on the cover "Under general supervision of the National League on Urban Conditions Among Negroes, of New York. Southern Headquarters, Nashville, Tenn." [17]

"A BETTER CHANCE IN THE SOUTH," blared the headline on the leaflet. Under it were listed eight points—for steady work, high wages, fair treatment, a safe home, friendly neighbors, schooling for the children, good churches, and pleasure in spare hours. "Can you hold down a man's job?" it asked. "Do you want a man's chance?"

But along with these promising, provocative phrases were the clinchers. The company president, H. L. Ferguson, was quoted as saying, "This Company probably employs, under satisfactory conditions, a larger number of skilled Negro men in iron-working trades, than any other company." Following this were the nigh-unbelievable figures that bore this out: The company had 7,000 men on the payroll, about 3,500 of whom were *colored men* (company italics) and they planned to increase the total to over 10,000. Hundreds of colored men had worked there up to twenty-five years. "The work is heavy," said the company, *"but the pay is high.* Men at rough labor begin at 24 cents an hour." And the scale rose depending on ability, to 48 cents an hour, plus overtime after eight hours at the rate of time-and-a-half. Skilled workers were on piecework rates and were earning from $27 to $30 weekly.

Beyond the wages, the company promised fair treatment. The entire shipyard was divided into departments and from each there was one Afro-American to serve on a "grievance committee" to "bring to the attention of the management anything that the men at work feel should be spoken of. Besides, *any man,* no matter where he works or what his job, can see any of the head officials up to the President about any matter where there is trouble."

The company answered basic questions in its leaflet. It described a suburban residential district just being opened up for occupancy. Only a 2½ cent streetcar ride from the yards, the houses all had gas, running water, electric lights, baths and inside toilets if desired and sold for from $1,050 to $1,700 on easy terms: $50 cash and the balance on monthly payments. A photo showed huge two-story houses with ample porches, many windows, large, open yards set off from the sidewalk by hedges and saplings. Houses in other sections were said to be available at corresponding prices. "There are no saloons as Virginia has prohibition; no places of vice in Garden City. Vicious persons cannot have houses there."

As for schools, churches and recreation, no need to look further. In Newport News there were grammar schools and a public night school; Garden City children went to a county school but ground for a school had been donated and it was up to the citizens to secure one through their own efforts. With fifteen Baptist, three Methodist and six other churches in the town, religious needs were amply covered. A ball park, bathing beach, movie hall (showing only "Censored" films) and YMCA game room were the recreation complement. Hampton Institute and Virginia State Normal Institute were close by.

Such an open invitation to black workers had seldom, if ever, been given by a southern company. It was revolutionary, and many a black who read the leaflet headed for this mecca; others shook their heads in wonder. Vouching for the authenticity of the offer was NLUCAN, already known and respected as reliable and nonprofit.

The League's participation in the project was unprecedented. George Haynes reported to Hollingsworth Wood that the company's model camp "is highly praised." Finding good men seemed to be the major problem for Haynes's protegé (Paul G. Prayer) at that point. "Because of so many 'floaters' and 'deadbeats' the company had stopped advancing transportation expenses of new workers," Haynes said. They modified this to refunding such expenses over several pay periods to prevent the men from taking off after the first payday. Also, "they have had their fingers burned by labor agents," observed Haynes, "and are, therefore, cautious." [18]

In 1918 when E. K. Jones addressed 800 members of the Employment Managers' Association at Rochester, N.Y., on "Psychology in the Employment of Negro Working Men," he struck a lode of response. He described League programs serving workers and management, such as in Detroit; the training and recruitment of industrial welfare workers, such as Paul G. Prayer with the Newport News Shipbuilding Company; and the League's stand on collective bargaining and strike-breaking, as spelled out in the resolutions at its Negro Labor Conference the previous January. He also cited the final resolution in which delegates called on employers to realize that the efficiency of their employees depended largely on proper housing, decent amusement, fair wages and proper treatment.[19]

As a result of this presentation Jones and the League were swamped with requests for counsel, aid, assistance and for black labor advisers and welfare workers. The list of corporations asking for such aid reads like a roster of American industrial giants of that day: National Lead, Swift and Company, Armour, Morris, Missouri Malleable Iron, Mississippi Glass, Buckeye Steel Castings, Etna Chemical, Carnegie Steel, Westinghouse, Dodge Brothers, Packard, American Car and Foundry, Detroit Motor, Old Hickory Powder, Rockford Malleable Iron, J. I. Case, National Carbon, American Rolling Mills, American Brass, Consolidation Coal, DuPont, Ohio Glass, American Zinc, Bush Terminal and scores of others. To each, the League gave counsel and service.

Seven of the affiliates (New York and Brooklyn included) placed 28,000 men in the League's fiscal year 1918. And the agency placed twenty-two black welfare workers in major corporations such as DuPont and Carnegie Steel during that period. In addition, both national and local staff workers of NLUCAN made innumerable trips to the hundreds of plants requesting League services.

The American Brass Company experience was a typical case in point. The company had seven branches where it produced brass shell casings, critically important for army artillery. In May 1918 production was far below quotas. Alarmed, the company called NLUCAN. E. K. Jones went to the plants and consulted with them concerning the irregularity and inefficiency of workers.

Jones inspected the conditions in the plant and in the community. Then he gave the workers the "jawbone treatment" at noon assemblies, exhorting them to be more prompt, regular, conscious of their health and "guarded in their moral life," more efficient in their labor and more friendly toward their fellow-workers, stressing the importance of increasing production. To the company he counseled specific action to improve housing, recreation, clinics and health facilities.

When Jones returned from this mission, an emergency at the Jenkins, Kentucky, works of the Consolidation Coal Company was described and his help requested in a telegram. The problem, management said, was one of "stabilizing" the black miners. They had become disturbed about

rumors that as Kentucky went dry, Alabama would again become "wet."
Though unfounded, the rumor had caused some miners to pack up and
leave for Alabama, even though they were receiving high wages.

The availability of liquor was beyond the powers of E. K. Jones and
NLUCAN to command. However, with essential war production at stake,
Jones went and in a series of mass meetings stirred up the patriotic impulses of the miners to produce for the war effort. He also inspected
housing, recreation, health and other facilities and made recommendations for improvement of living conditions.

The crises, of course, came in all shapes, sizes and varieties. One
of them, illustrating a familiar pattern, occurred in New Jersey in
1918.[20]

The women were crying. They stood in the Newark Urban League office, looking beaten and baffled. They had gone to the Standard Oil
Company plant for their interviews. They were on time. They told the
personnel man that the League executive had asked them to report. The
Standard Oil plant had a United States government contract for war
products. It had fallen far behind and the government complained that
it wasn't delivering according to its contract. The company, like so
many others during World War I, was desperately searching for workers.
When men became scarce, it had employed women. Now even the women
were scarce and there were vacant machines on the production line and
quotas were not being met. Pushed to the extreme, the company considered hiring black women. An executive at the plant had called Newark
League executive William Ashby about this, invited him to lunch and explained their needs. Could Ashby help?

"Sure," he had said. He knew that he could round up some qualified
women with a little effort. And whatever the effort, it would be worth it
to "crack" Standard Oil. Whatever Jersey Standard did set the pace; if it
hired black workers, other employers in the Newark area would follow
suit.

Ashby went out and carefully selected the women he was going to refer
to Jersey Standard. He was determined to have them make good, for on
their performance would depend future hiring of perhaps hundreds of
other black workers. So he coached the women in what to expect and
how to act, how to dress and about the importance of punctuality and efficiency on the job. They were bright girls and well able to do the work;
he was certain they would be excellent on the job. They had gone for
their interviews with his blessing and he was confident they would measure up.

Now here they were in his office, weeping and carrying on. What had
gone wrong? The man had said he couldn't hire them. Ashby's blood

pressure went up twenty points. "This guy is making a fool out of me," he thought.

"What reason did he give you for not hiring you?"

"He wouldn't tell us anything," the girls said. "He wanted to see you."

Burning with rage at the girls' humiliation, Ashby jammed on his hat and dashed out of his office. He drove immediately to the Standard Oil plant and went in to see the executive in his office.

"I'm terribly sorry we couldn't do this," the official began, in a placating manner. "The company attitude on this kind of thing, you know, simply made it impossible and I'm sorry that we just can't do it."

"Well what specific reason do you have for turning them down?" Ashby snapped.

"To tell you the truth, our white women workers said they wouldn't work with the Negro women."

"My God!" cried Ashby. "All right, tell me specifically the reason they wouldn't work with them."

"Well," he replied slowly, "they said if you bring in colored women we'll leave our machines."

"Why?" demanded Ashby.

"Well," he said, reluctantly, "they say colored women smell under their arms, that their feet smell bad, that they're not clean personally, that all colored women have venereal disease . . ."

"Good God!" blurted Ashby. "All crap stinks, no matter where or what color people it comes from!"

The corporation executive was rocked back in his chair. "You can't say a thing like that to me," he stammered.

Sizzling, Ashby shot at him, "Now, I'm not shocked by what the women did. What shocks me is that a company like Standard Oil would let some women who just got off the boat from Italy or Ireland yesterday dictate whom it should hire and whom it shouldn't hire."

His audience of one was staring at him, mouth agape. He sat, stunned, for what seemed to Ashby to be five minutes. Then he rose quickly. "Mr. Ashby, I've never heard anything like this before. Come with me."

Ashby had his hat; he was ready to leave. He felt better for getting the burden off his chest. He followed the company official into one of the plant buildings. The official motioned him inside, went in with him. They entered the production area and the executive went up to the fore-woman and ordered, "Stop these machines."

A flicker of anxiety swept her face and she shut down the production line. The official called the workers together and said, "Girls, this is Mr. Ashby. He is from the Urban League. He is going to send us some women who will help us in our production. They will be colored women.

Today is Friday. It's payday. Some of you have said that if we bring in colored women to work beside you, you'll walk away from your machines." He paused. "Now, you all receive your pay tonight. If you don't want to work with colored women, don't show up Monday morning."

That ended the teacup rebellion, the company's employment problem, Ashby's rage, and the plant's lily-white personnel status. Ashby followed up and found that only one woman had walked off the job. Her place was taken by one of the black girls. Additional black workers were placed with the company and it was indeed a significant triumph. As a result, many other companies followed Standard Oil's example in the New Jersey area.

Bill Ashby's experience was not unique, nor was it typical; League staff members ran into such situations daily. In most instances during World War I, industry was eager to hire men and women for the unskilled jobs that constituted 90 percent of those in which blacks labored. In such jobs, need outweighed niceties such as considerations of personal prejudice by production workers.

NLUCAN had the knowledge and experience to help black workers keep pace with the revolution of which they were a part. From this time forward the destiny of the black worker was not bound to the land but to the machine—and the machines were in the cities.

11/ The Federal Government Enters

The move from farms to cities and the drafting of men for the armed services indicated that a farm crisis was coming and that food production might be drastically curtailed in early 1917. Both butter and guns were subjects of overriding concern to the Wilson administration. So, when a black lawyer named Giles B. Jackson proposed in July of 1917 that the government create a "Bureau of Negro Economics" to mobilize "Negro labor for the farms and industries of the country as a means of helping the nation in the production of food," both Samuel Gompers and Labor Secretary William B. Wilson were receptive.[1]

Jackson proposed that the bureau be set up under the supervision of the Department of Labor, as a private operation with a budget of $700,-000 and himself as head. It would, he said, "operate to give the Negro an opportunity to cooperate with the government . . . in solving the food and labor problem . . . and serve as a basis from which to solve the many problems that may confront the government with respect to the Negro." [2] Jackson was president of an organization called the National Civic Improvement Association, Inc., in Richmond. It had, he wrote Secretary Wilson, "been doing considerable work among the race within the last eight months and is prepared to launch a successful campaign at once as soon as authorized by the government to do so." Secretary Wilson's response was polite; Samuel Gompers thought it preferable that any such operation be run by the government.[3]

Jackson continued his self-promotion, but nothing materialized—for him.

NLUCAN executives and board members at their January 1918 conference in New York had urged "the appointment of one or two competent Negroes in the Department of Labor to serve as assistants in each of the Bureaus in adjusting and distributing Negro labor to meet war and peace needs." [4] The following day NLUCAN's executive board met and decided to send a committee to Washington to talk with appropriate officials of the Department of Labor.[5]

The department had been backed into a corner by the conflicting demands upon it regarding black workers. Back in 1916 the department had as part of its "Immigration Bureau" an employment service. This service was intended to help place all Americans in jobs wherever these might be, if the individual was qualified. As the black migration stepped up in 1916, the federal employment service helped hundreds of black workers find jobs in the north. Inevitably, cries went up from southern congressmen that the Labor Department was using federal machinery to take black workers from the south.

The department immediately stepped on the brakes. It issued orders to all its local offices in the south not to cooperate in making large shipments of workers to the north.[6] This, of course, upset northern industrialists who needed workers. Other northerners charged that the blacks were being shipped north by railroad companies to be used as strikebreakers.

With America's entry into the war and the emphasis on boosting output, southern industry yelped that it was being handicapped by the black exodus and that production in the south would suffer as a consequence. To get the facts, Labor Secretary Wilson appointed Dr. James H. Dillard to survey conditions and advise him as to what path to follow. Dillard recommended that the Labor Department set up machinery to keep in touch with the race question on a continuing, if not permanent basis.

Meanwhile, Secretary Wilson was under attack for not moving to meet the accelerating problems growing out of the black migration. Many individuals and groups urged him to act. A committee to consider the situation and come up with recommendations was established under former governor of Minnesota John Lind, with representatives of industry, labor and government. It had no black members.

This was the situation when, on February 12, 1918, NLUCAN presented a memorandum to Secretary Wilson, urging that a black be appointed to the Lind Committee and that the Department of Labor hire black staff members to advise and work on these matters. The memo was signed by E. K. Jones, R. R. Moton, L. H. Wood and James H. Dillard of NLUCAN, John Shillady, secretary of the NAACP, and Thomas Jesse Jones of the Phelps-Stokes Fund.[7] Assistant Labor Secretary Louis F. Post sent a recommendation to Secretary Wilson, advising against adding an Afro-American to the advisory committee because it was too late. He recommended instead that a black adviser be appointed. Secretary Wilson approved this plan.[8]

Eight candidates were actively considered by the department, and NLUCAN backed George Haynes for the post. Haynes himself heard little about this, he said, until President F. A. McKenzie of Fisk called him in and asked if he would be interested in the position.[9] He was. McKenzie, the Nashville Chamber of Commerce and others strongly recommended Haynes, and on April 15 he received a telegram from the Secretary of Labor formally asking if he would be available. He was appointed Director, Division of Negro Economics, and took up his work on May 1. He was given leave of absence from NLUCAN for one year, without pay. Secretary Wilson's office announced Haynes's appointment as follows:

> Dr. Haynes will act as advisor to the Secretary on all questions affecting the Negro race. His appointment places him in what is probably the most important position ever held by a Negro in the United States.[10]

Haynes was asked to prepare a statement outlining his conception of the work, the basic policy that should govern, and his relationship to the secretary and other divisions of the department. Haynes studied the units operating in the department and proposed that "the advice of the Director of Negro Economics should be secured before any work dealing with Negro wage earners is taken and that he be kept advised of progress of such work so that the department might at all times have the benefit of his judgment in all matters affecting Negroes." [11]

Haynes immediately visited major centers where problems of Negro workers were pressing, talked and corresponded with black and white leaders. On June 19, under the auspices of the governor of North Carolina, a formal state conference of representative white and black citizens was held. Haynes spoke, suggesting ways and means of increasing morale and efficiency of black workers and improving their relations with white workers and employers. The conferees discussed conditions and the governor appointed a committee to draft a constitution setting up the first state Negro Workers' Advisory Committee. Haynes's plan was to organize such committees in the counties and cities as well.

In the five months that followed, similar state organizations were set up in four southern and four northern states. The Secretary of Labor appointed a black supervisor of Negro Economics in each of the states where these committees were formed. His job was to conduct work to improve "racial labor relations and assist the several divisions and services of the department in mobilizing and stabilizing Negro labor for winning the war." [12] Two of these men were League executives. Bill Ashby was appointed for New Jersey; Forrester B. Washington for Michigan (later transferred to Illinois).

As Haynes saw it, there were two main problems to be faced:

1. The difficulty of forestalling a strong feeling of suspicion on the part of the colored people, growing out of their past experiences in racial and labor matters.
2. The difficulty of forestalling a wrong impression among white people, especially those in the south, about the efforts of the department, and of having them understand that the department wishes to help them in local labor problems by means of its plans.[13]

An example of the retrograde white attitudes was the following statement by John H. Kirby, president of the National Lumber Manufacturers' Association, speaking on labor problems in the south: "The Department of Labor in Washington, when it sends these emissaries into this country, more especially white emissaries, for the purpose of organizing your labor and taking charge of the industrial forces of this people, is sending 'carpet-baggers' just as certainly today as they sent them then. And there can be no peace—there can be no prosperity—there can be no tranquillity in any community in this country where this kind of thing is recognized or tolerated." [14]

In the face of this virulent hostility, the advisory committees were circumspect and carefully restricted themselves to their stated purposes: "To study, plan and advise in a cooperative spirit and manner with employers of Negro labor, with Negro workers and with the U. S. Department of Labor in securing from Negro laborers greater production in industry

and agriculture for winning the war, through increasing regularity, application and efficiency, through increasing the morale of Negro workers,
and through improving their general conditions." [15] After the Armistice,
the reference to the war was dropped, of course.

On August 1, 1918, the United States Employment Service was made
responsible for recruiting and allocating labor for war industries employing 100 or more workers. Through his network of state supervisors of
Negro Economics, Haynes helped name black examiners for the USES
and find locations for USES offices in the black communities. A number
of these were located in Urban League offices, as adjuncts of their industrial relations operations, particularly in Chicago and Detroit, two of
the busiest centers.

Through the Negro Economics network Haynes and his associates distributed information on the dangers of venereal disease, in cooperation
with the Public Health Service, and with the Labor Department's Housing Bureau. They worked to secure war housing in Washington and
other cities, developing room registries for housing war workers and veterans. Haynes's network also carried out surveys of labor supply in various cities and counties to assist in allocating labor. The Mississippi supervisor requested help in recruiting surplus black labor for farm operations
and his counterparts in Illinois and Ohio quickly canvassed through the
state and local Workers' Advisory Committees, advertising the Mississippi
openings.

The Negro Economics supervisors helped the USES in a variety of
ways. One of these was to organize volunteers, as in the District of Co-
olumbia, where seventy-five persons helped recruit workers, referring them
to the local USES offices. In Chicago, a branch office of the USES was organized, which Haynes and Forrester Washington claimed credit for
helping to arrange and for working up a panel of Negroes to manage the
office. Its special work was assisting returning black veterans and this it
did by soliciting some 1,000 firms for jobs.[16]

Haynes brought together in Washington a conference of leaders interested in the labor scene. In February 1919 for two days 150 delegates met
and learned about the programs, plans and coordination going on within
and in cooperation with the Labor Department. The conference determined that there were two basic areas requiring immediate attention—
working conditions and living conditions. Furthermore, analysis showed
that to affect them required local work, that national coordination had
little chance of success. So, Haynes and his associates worked with local
conferences of welfare organizations, boards, and agencies (as did the
local Leagues), employer representatives, and spokesmen for white and
Negro workers. The conferees expected to work on neighborhood condi-

tions where special needs were evident in housing, sanitation, recreation, thrift, vocational and literacy education programs. Health, housing and work efficiency programs were planned. The League was represented at this meeting by E. K. Jones, R. R. Moton and John T. Emlen.

Much of Haynes's program was identical to the NLUCAN program in terms of helping black workers in industry. It was inevitable, perhaps, that some confusion, friction and misunderstanding should develop among Haynes's associates and advisory committee members, League staff and board, USES state and local staff members. There simply were too many cooks, too much duplication, too much mutual distrust and too much overlap to make for tidy results. So heated did some of the Urban League executives become about operation of some of the state supervisors and Haynes's apparent insensitivity to the conflicts, that E. K. Jones was urged to take "drastic action."

Jones resisted, however, for by mid-1919 the future of Haynes's operation was self-evident: none. Congress cut off the appropriation and so, after about half a million dollars was spent on the Division of Negro Economics, it died at the end of June 1919.

Haynes's operation had been a center of controversy. The manufacturers in Illinois had pictured the USES and Division of Negro Economics as a "union machine." The unions, on the other hand, saw it as a vehicle for supplying strike-breakers to industry. The south saw it as a "movement" that was "being used by agitators and unscrupulous propagandists . . . to propagate a feeling of unrest and dissatisfaction among the Negroes and to arouse in them a desire to dominate." [17]

Furthermore, the Negro Economics operation had been a blow at the sanctified mores of the sovereign south in that white industrial leaders and employers had been requested by the Department of Labor to confer with Negro officials. "When it comes to sitting in council with Dr. Haynes, a Negro, you will have to excuse me," shrilled one southern businessman. "In the south we tell them what to do, and we do not sit in conference with them and accept their suggestions to us, as to what we should do. The best thing you can do . . . [is] cease to interfere with industrial conditions down there—not because industry resents it, but because the races resent it, and you will only promote race conflict, and confer no good upon anybody, and, for God Almighty's sake, let it not be said that a Democratic administration is promoting carpet-bag rule in the south." [18]

The Department of Labor and Secretary William Wilson considered Haynes's division so valuable that the secretary made an unusual effort to help extend it during the postwar period. Wilson released a letter to Haynes on July 1, 1919, saying that "so important do I consider the in-

formation, advice, and departmental aid furnished through your work
. . . to harmonize the labor relations of white workers, Negro workers
and white employers, and thereby to promote the welfare of all wage-ear-
ners in the United States, that I hereby request you to continue the
service." [19] Wilson acknowledged that the lack of an appropriation meant
Haynes's staff would have to go, but he had arranged to carry the professor and two assistants on reduced salaries for a while. Haynes would have
to accomplish his work by mail thereafter and Wilson hoped he would
enable the Department of Labor to continue to deal with delicate and
difficult problems touching Negro labor, thus serving employers and
workers of both races and all sections of the land.

Meanwhile, NLUCAN Executive Secretary Kinckle Jones had been offered a tempting opportunity. A young Harvard graduate named Alexander L. Jackson, who was working at the Chicago YMCA, was interested in
transferring to educational work with the League. NLUCAN had been
without an education secretary since George Haynes entered government
service and Haynes's leave of absence had expired May 1, 1919. Best of
all, Jackson's salary as education secretary would be covered by a special
grant for that purpose by a new contributor.

That was the situation when George Haynes met with Hollingsworth
Wood at the end of June 1919. Haynes described his status with the Department of Labor. He was to be continued for three months with the
hope that funds could be raised outside the government to finance lectures by Haynes at Howard University and Hampton which would make
it possible for him to continue the Negro Economics skeleton activity.
Hopefully, Congress would bring in a new appropriation for the work.
The League, said Haynes, "can be of great use to the cause of cooperating with the Department now that we have no field service." [20]

Wood followed this meeting with a letter July 1 that shocked Haynes.
"In view of our conversation on last Saturday, I am writing to ask for
your resignation as Educational Secretary so that I may be free to go
ahead with our plans for the development of this work." [21] The League
chairman offered to assist Haynes "in any way that you feel that I can" to
scrape up additional financial assistance to keep Haynes going, preferably
by writing letters of explanation and appeal. "Of course," he continued,
"I have written the above letter in view of your statement that you had
made your choice to be retained in the skeleton organization in the Department of Labor, and with no view to cutting you off from the Urban
League and its work. Only to-day Mr. Jones and I have been discussing
the possibility of the Urban League being of further use to the Department, now that you will be faced with a shortage of men in your service;

and as always, we will be most happy to render every service that we can." [22]

Haynes responded predictably to Wood's letter. The Labor Department post was precarious at best; the League "should be willing to go half way." Wood had the wrong impression, Haynes contended. He discussed it with James Dillard, who happened to be in Washington, and at his urging wrote R. R. Moton for counsel, enclosing a proposed reply to Wood and a white paper on a Labor Department–local League controversy that had developed in Chicago, which Haynes blamed on Jones and vice versa. Moton received a letter a few days later from E. K. Jones that all but ended the matter. "Our Steering Committee," Jones reported, "on Thursday formally accepted Mr. Jackson" as educational secretary of NLUCAN. [23]

At the same time, the Steering Committee decided to invite George Haynes to become a member of the NLUCAN executive board for a term expiring in 1920. Haynes wrote Jones that he hardly saw how he could become a member of the board in view of the fact that he had not resigned as educational secretary. The committee's action, said Haynes, "was taken probably upon mistaken information, as the question of how long I shall be here [Washington, D.C.] is yet uncertain." [24]

Haynes sent his delayed response to Hollingsworth Wood and scrapped the contentious letter he had planned to send E. K. Jones. Wood must have written "with an incorrect understanding" of the facts stated, said Haynes. "I could not . . . have stated that I made a choice to stay permanently [in the Labor Department]," because no permanent position existed.[25] He did not, however, state clearly just what he intended to do. In other words, Dr. Haynes once again was astraddle: he desired to continue on leave of absence as NLUCAN educational secretary and as director of Negro Economics, so long as possible.

He had good reason to hedge, for the stakes were high. After the Chicago and Washington riots in 1919 (which he investigated) George Haynes told his supervisor that racial tension was so widespread as to be a national concern, calling for federal attention. He recommended to the secretary of labor that a coordinator of government activities concerning blacks be established. This person would carry on exchange of information and cooperation with other departments of government, state and federal, "through which a large, National constructive program for bettering the living and working conditions of Negro workers and improving their relations with white workers and white employers may be outlined and put into operation."

George Haynes cited cooperative efforts he had taken with the State

Councils of National Defense, the United States Public Health Service, the Treasury Department and the special assistants to the secretary of war and the Agriculture Department. He urged Secretary Wilson to take steps to secure and publish statistical data on Negro workers and their relations to whites and to work out plans for practical cooperation with other executive branches that dealt with workers. The Negro Workers' Advisory Committees should be used to minimize racial friction. In cooperation with other federal agencies, investigations of race relations "in as many localities as possible [should] be undertaken as a means of having information and advice to improve conditions and race relations." The kingpin in this plan would, of course, be Dr. Haynes. The recommendations were approved by the secretary of labor on September 29, 1919, and George Haynes's hopes soared.[26]

Hollingsworth Wood, confronted with the nightmare of a new educational secretary due to start August 1 while another was on leave of absence, perhaps to return within three months, wrote to Haynes: " [I] am at a loss to understand why you should desire to stand upon the technicality as to the wording of my letter. What was evident in the letter was that in my judgment the work of the Urban League at the present time requires that, as President, I should have in my hands your resignation as Educational Secretary." [27]

Haynes did send his resignation some two weeks later but he requested that it be passed on by the executive board. This Wood wished to avoid because, he said, "it will make a partisanship question out of one that is now quite simply explained on grounds of efficiency and divergent interests." [28] The Steering Committee had considered the inability of Jones and Haynes to get along and all of them—Dr. Roberts, Dr. Powell, Emlen, Miss Walton and Wood—concluded that the League was being injured by the continuing controversy. If Haynes insisted on a long wrangle before the board, thought Wood, even though he explained himself satisfactorily he "never could convince the Chicago group that he did not intentionally attack the Urban League there. The result will be that . . . after such a meeting many members will not feel like doing anything with him . . . even those whom Dr. Haynes regards as his friends on the Board will not feel that they know enough about the inside problems of the running of the League to try to oppose the unanimous recommendation of the Committee." [29]

To Dr. Haynes, Wood wrote that his resignation had been received and would be submitted to the executive board. He hoped it would not be made a subject of controversy for that would only lead to "the taking of issues" which would hardly prove beneficial for either Haynes or the League. "As it is now," he said, "we are all ready and willing to aid you in any way and the general public and membership need never know that anything has occurred beyond a selection of different fields of effort." [30]

There is in the papers of Robert Russa Moton an unsigned draft of a letter to Wood which says: "My request that my resignation be submitted to the Executive Board was not made in order to raise a controversy but to have a chance for my connection with the League to be informally considered when I can have a hearing. I have done everything I could to avoid controversy and have the facts to show what has been done. My connection with the League since its origin, its plans and work have been such a part of me that fair play demands a full consideration of the question of my future relations to it. The facts and interests of all concerned should be weighed and the matter settled upon that basis." [31]

Whatever the intervening correspondence, now lost, the matter was settled, even though Haynes may not have understood it so. At the executive board meeting in October there was a laconic entry in the minutes: "It was recommended that the League accept the resignation of Dr. George E. Haynes as Educational Secretary to take effect August 1, and give him a note of appreciation." So ended Haynes's formal tie to the League, in an acrimonious exit. It was not his last association with the agency, however.

He was invited to participate in the League's October 1919 conference in Detroit on industrial problems of the Negro, and Jones urged him to attend the National Conference of Social Work, and to help secure proper representation of black speakers on the program. Beyond that, in December 1919, when Secretary Wilson had managed to put an item in his budget for $15,000 to cover "Negro Economics," Jones wrote Haynes that "practically all our local secretaries report that they have received very favorable responses from the Congressmen representing their local districts relative to the Bill which the Secretary of Labor is presenting to Congress in the interest of continuation of the Department of Negro Economics." [32]

Though Secretary Wilson carried Haynes on a part-time consultant basis, Congress in May 1920 scratched the Negro Economics appropriation from the Labor Department's appropriations.

12/World War I Readjustment

"The extraordinary year which has passed with its problems of war," announced Hollingsworth Wood at the end of 1918, "has been succeeded by this year in which we find ourselves with the terrific responsibility of the problems of peace for which we are so unprepared." [1]

The fiscal period from October 1917 to the end of 1918 had been a pinnacle of NLUCAN usefulness and effectiveness. [2] On the national scene the agency had succeeded in placing its education secretary in the Wilson administration; the AFL had been persuaded to promise to organize blacks; scores of welfare workers in industry had been placed through League efforts; and scores of thousands of workers had jobs as a result of League action. In some cities the Leagues were concentrating on "breakthrough" jobs—employment in occupations never before opened to Negroes—and training and upgrading ambitious black workers for skilled work and more responsible positions. "Missionary work" about black workers had been carried out through appearances and addresses, talks and counsel at national conferences of business organizations, at state and local conventions of officials and civic leaders, at industrial plants, mines, shipyards, steel works, and so on. For the first time, black clerks were placed in sizable numbers (especially with Pittsburgh department stores, and Montgomery Ward and Sears, Roebuck in Chicago) and at least one lily-white hospital (Bellevue in New York) was opened to black interns.

Locally, the Leagues had cooperated in war support activities such as bond sales drives, aided draft boards, served as black community centers for the United States Employment Service offices, the United States Food Conservation Campaign, Red Cross work, the Council of National Defense, and War Camp Community Services.

NLUCAN's work during this year of World War I is described in a publication entitled "A Contribution to Democracy." In prosecuting that work, said Hollingsworth Wood, "we have tried to look far ahead to the future—gauging our stand on the questions of policy and human affairs in the light of possibilities and justice. 'Results' has been our slogan throughout wherever effort has been expended—whether it was the publication of a news article, attendance at a conference, organization of a new city, or the presentation of a need to some person or agency that might help in the common Cause!" He reported on the work of the year, giving "account of our stewardship to those who have so generously and so unselfishly aided us by their financial and moral support as well as by their counsel and personal service." [3]

A quick glance at the balance sheet would have revealed the fact that NLUCAN was long on moral and short on financial support. In this, its most successful year to date, it operated a national activity, serving scores of the nation's industrial giants, the bluest of the blue-chip companies, helping them use the essential but volatile ingredient of imperative wartime production—black workers.

Through a network of thirty cities in the nation, and eighty-one paid staff workers the League had drawn glowing tributes for its work: [4]

> It is developing 10,000,000 Negro Americans in loyalty and citizenship and is instructing many communities in the valuable service Negroes can render.
>
> Judged by tangible, practical results the most successful organization working for the welfare of our people is the National League on Urban Conditions Among Negroes, which is now extending its activities to many cities throughout the country.
>
> The grand total of the value of [the Philadelphia affiliate] placements mounts to more than $250,000, and indicates a degree of efficiency which if widened by more work of this sort, eventually would do more to lift the Negro out of his rut than all the efforts of less practical "reformers" could accomplish in decades.

The fact was that eighty-one paid staff workers of the League movement around the nation were supported and program expenses were met out of consolidated total expenditures for the year of $102,000—slightly more than $1,200 per worker for salary, expenses and overhead.

In its annual report for the year, NLUCAN listed sixty-seven corporations that the agency had served in specific, substantial ways. The list stretched from American Brass Company to Westinghouse Electric & Manufacturing Company. In many places and in many ways, NLUCAN had given these corporations thousands of dollars worth of service—in referral of laborers, counseling on production, efficiency, morale and advising on personnel policies. Some local secretaries even acted as what the New York *Times* called "general supervisors in factories . . . often successful in obtaining greater industrial efficiency." [5] In all cases, NLUCAN acted to minimize friction between races and stabilize living and working conditions in the larger community. These were services for which the

League was uniquely qualified, services upon which price tags could have been established, but were not. There were even a few board members capable of such cost accounting: A. S. Frissell, of the Fifth Avenue Bank; George W. Seligman, lawyer; and investment banker Paul J. Sachs. In practice, of course, neither the League board members nor the corporations did anything of the sort. Therefore, no League representative asked for *quid pro quo*. While the profits of DuPont, Carnegie, Swift, Armour, Dodge Brothers, National Carbon, Consolidation Coal Company, National Lead and scores of other beneficiaries of NLUCAN activities soared into the millions, the League's tin cup turned out to have a hole in its bottom.

After this yeoman service, the National League on Urban Conditions Among Negroes wound up the year with an income of $35,000 outweighed by expenditures of $37,000.

That sobering fact should have been sufficient to red-flag the agency's leadership that the League had problems and chief among them was its fund-raising.

NLUCAN had unquestionably saved the Connecticut tobacco industry from disaster in 1915 and from costly labor difficulties in 1917 and 1918. In the light of this, the League's executive secretary wrote to the head of the Griffen Tobacco Company in Hartford on October 2, 1918:

> By the way, Mr. Griffen, do you not think that the Connecticut Leaf Tobacco Association [might] make a contribution on its own behalf for the support of our Organization? You know that we made absolutely no charges for the services which we have rendered because we felt that we were helping our boys as much as we were aiding the Tobacco Corporation, but we are passing through a crisis, a financial crisis in our work at present and need about $2,225 to keep out of bankruptcy. Five hundred dollars will save us from a deficit on October 15th, which could be extremely embarrassing if this sum is not realized.[6]

In other words, after the tobacco crop for the year was safely harvested, E. K. Jones was asking for a pittance, a tip. He requested the tobacco growers to contribute $500—about $167 per year, amortized over the three years of the rescue operation for recruiting, screening and overseeing the supply of nearly 3,000 high-quality workers per year.

On Armistice Day, E. K. Jones shook another apple tree. He wrote the Carnegie Corporation of New York asking for a grant.[7]

Before he came to the actual purpose of his letter, he spent two pages, single-spaced, telling the philanthropic foundation of (1) NLUCAN's service as headquarters of the War Savings Stamp Campaign among colored people; (2) its responsibility for opening soldiers' clubs under the War

Camp Community Service; (3) the League's part in arranging a 4th of July parade in Augusta, Georgia; (4) its efforts to speed production of war needs by exhorting workers and counseling employment managers; (5) some of the corporations with which the league placed welfare workers and labor advisers; (6) NLUCAN's primary role in inducing the United States Labor Department to hire George Haynes; (7) the Red Cross's seeking for advice about black soldiers and their families; (8) the League's role in "adjusting the differences" in East St. Louis after the riots.

The League was now about to face the problems of reconstruction in more than thirty cities and would apply itself to "showing the Nation the great service that Negroes in our midst can render and are anxious to give in their Country's Cause. We shall work among the Negroes themselves to try to make them more efficient, more reliable and therefore, effective in their country's service." [8]

Then he came to the specific request. The League wanted between $2,500 and $3,000 to put on payroll an industrial field worker for a year. This industrial secretary's duties would be to "intercede with the largest employers of Negro labor in the country . . . [to get] Negro welfare advisors appointed on the staff of these industrial plants to aim at larger industrial efficiency of the Negro working-man and to bring the employers to the realization of the large possibilities that lie in the use of Negro labor, especially at a time when there will probably be a shortage of labor due to the return of a large number of foreigners to European points for obvious reasons—this statement being made on authority of a very high official in immigration circles who has estimated that at least two million men will be leaving this country within a short period following the signing of the armistice." [9]

The Carnegie Corporation of New York made no contributions to the League in 1918. Not that one could blame them. The request E. K. Jones sent them might better have been directed to the National Association of Manufacturers or the United States Chamber of Commerce.

The proposal had dollars and cents value to manufacturers; it was of limited interest to a foundation specializing in uneconomic projects of an educational nature. And the strongest case for supporting the League, the East St. Louis service, was presented as but one of eight reasons for contributing.

This weakness, the inability to talk the language of the prospective donor, to convince him of the necessity of his support and ask for the money, was to plague the organization for another forty years, with consequent blighting of its policies, programs and personnel.

The blame, if any, for this unrealistic approach cannot be laid to E. K.

Jones any more than to NLUCAN chairman Hollingsworth Wood or the executive board. By 1918 the only businessmen on the board were Fred Moore, George W. Seligman, A. S. Frissell and Paul J. Sachs (who had betaken himself to the Fogg Collection at Harvard). The rest were clerics, educators, physicians and reformers. The strong panel of industrial and financial leaders brought to NLUCAN through the Committee for Improving the Industrial Conditions of Negroes in New York had fallen away over the years; even William J. Schieffelin and Paul Cravath had dropped by the wayside.

It is instructive to note that NLUCAN's support from industry in 1917 came from six companies: Fiberloid Corporation ($8.90); Buerney Ball Bearing ($25); Isaac G. Johnson & Company ($25); National Sugar and Refining Company of New Jersey ($10); du Pont ($8.33); and Worthington Pump ($25). By 1920 only National Sugar and Refining Company ($20) and National Malleable Castings Company ($50) were among the industrial supporters. (The only union contributions—$153—in this period were from two locals of the Brotherhood of Dining Car Employees, to which the League gave office space.) [10]

There were, therefore, few businessmen to advise the League about the approaches to industry and to make clear the revolution that had taken place. The agency's leaders were captives of their former experience, acting still as though they were soliciting for a leper colony instead of for the delivery of valuable, vital services.

As for approaches to philanthropic foundations, Dr. James H. Dillard, the executive of the Jeanes-Slater Funds, was on the board and there were also representatives of Howard, Tuskegee, and Morehouse. They had had experience with foundation grants—but did not extend it to the League's financial needs. In fact, when Hollingsworth Wood wrote to League vice chairman R. R. Moton of Tuskegee for assistance in securing support, the turndown was a sharp one:

> I need not reassure you of my interest in the work of the League, but because of the peculiar position I have it will not be possible for me to solicit funds for the Urban League or for any other organization with which I am identified outside of the Tuskegee Institute. As you know, it is necessary for me to raise something like two hundred thousand dollars a year for our work here, and I could not go to the same people who give aid for Tuskegee and ask them to give to some other cause, that would not be fair to them or to us.[11]

The fact that it did not have such backing was too bad, but Moton saw the League as a competitor for philanthropic dollars.

Fundamentally, the very base underlying the NUL operations was unsound because of its financial weakness. And this weakness was not likely to be improved by the attitude of three of its most active white board members, Hollingsworth Wood, its chairman; Elizabeth Walton, head of the New York League and long-time member of the powerful steering, nominating and membership committees; and John T. Emlen, secretary of the Philadelphia affiliate, League vice president and Steering Committee member. Wood's attitude seemed to be that "God would provide"; that the agency's good works would be rewarded. Unfortunately, the agency's workers could not live on approbation alone.

If NLUCAN could not cover expenses in the peak year of 1918, the prospects for the uncertain postwar times ahead were not as reassuring as Hollingsworth Wood seemed to think.

What was to be the agency's stance for the imponderables of "reconstruction"? According to NLUCAN chairman Wood, "As we think into the future and plan for what we have to do, I am sure of only one thing; and that is, along the line of the spirit of cooperation; our faith in our fellowman is the road and there are no other sign posts as I can see, as to which way we must go. The problems are problems of human relations, and only as we recognize humbly our fundamental belief in our fellowman as longing to do right, if he can be shown it is only along that line that we can hope for success. So in greeting the problem of the returned soldier, we must pin to that the opportunity of brotherhood, which can and will bind people together." [12]

A somewhat different view was offered by one of the most eminent white men in the field of race relations, Jeanes-Slater Funds executive and NLUCAN board member James H. Dillard:

> I wish I had a voice that could reach our good colored people everywhere to beg them to act wisely and not do anything rash. They must have patience, while I am a revolutionist myself, a little bit, I cannot keep from feeling that there is a great deal of good being done in the south which might be upset if there were any ill-advised, unwise outbreaks. We know that the colored people are not going to have things as they were before, but let us go wisely, if possible.[13]

On the very day the Armistice was signed, the War Department telegraphed defense industries around the nation canceling war contracts. With what appears to have been prescience, NLUCAN three days before that had sent out a call to its affiliates and interested agencies for a conference on "The Reconstruction Period." This two-day meeting, November 25 and 26, 1918, at the public library in Columbus, Ohio, was the earliest recorded annual conference of the Urban League movement. Seventeen League executives (of the twenty-eight affiliates, only seventeen had paid secretaries at this time) plus board members and representatives of other agencies (such as the NAACP's John Shillady) dug into community needs (as presented by T. Arnold Hill and John C. Dancy), ways in which local Leagues could help the nation (John T. Emlen's presentation) and the national organization could help the locals (by John T. Clark). The welfare worker, the unions and migration in "reconstruction," were discussed by Paul G. Prayer, A. L. Manly and James H. Hubert, respectively.

The conferees looked at the successful techniques used by school visitors in improving education of grade school youths and examined the hard fundamentals of financing locals and the national League, training workers, publicizing the work and the development of the East St. Louis emergency operation.

With a magnanimity not reciprocated, the conferees voted against the proposed federal restriction of immigration for ten years. The Urban Leaguers were opposed, said Hollingsworth Wood, to "depriving European immigrants of the same rights which the colored people are gradually being able to enjoy." [14]

An extraordinary "Reconstruction Program" was proposed by the Chicago League.[15] Two problems were pre-eminent in postwar readjustment, said the Chicagoans. First was "reabsorption" of excess labor from war industries, second was "the welcoming and returning" of black troopers. "For the Negro the problems are accentuated in proportion as each separate community regards him as a 'problem,'" and NLUCAN, it pointed out, was the only national organization prepared to handle the interests of colored men and women in these two matters. The plan called for the League to offer its services to federal government agencies, organize in more cities, and set up a listening post in the national capital.

To "reabsorb" Negro labor, an NLUCAN "reconstruction committee" was recommended to organize and oversee efforts in which at the local level all possible sources of jobs would be investigated. Local Leagues were to establish connections with local manufacturers and commerce associations, federal, state and city employment bureaus, major construction companies and the municipal building departments to gain and use information helping to secure work for blacks.

A number of these recommendations were taken up by the Steering Committee of the League. E. K. Jones was instructed to write all government departments, boards, bureaus, and committees that would have any part in reconstruction offering League services and cooperation, and also to write to private agencies. The Steering Committee asked Hollingsworth Wood to inquire "as to how legislation could be watched and influenced in Washington insofar as the welfare of Negroes might be concerned." [16]

A study of Negro labor and the effects of postwar change was recommended by the conference. The purpose would be to circulate the information to all League cities "to prevent any unnecessary migration of labor." The Steering Committee tabled this one, to discuss ways and means of securing the necessary personnel, but also with grave reservations about preventing "Negro labor from migrating for advantages other than those offered by labor itself." [17]

To help the League assist in a "satisfactory adjustment of the Negro population—civilian and soldier—in their respective cities," the agency was urged to contact national organizations. These agencies, in turn, would be asked to alert their locals, urging them to cooperate with the NUL locals in this effort.[18]

There was a new sense of self-confidence reflected in the Chicago proposals. The postwar black was as different from the prewar black man as the 1919 vehicle—the auto—was from the horse and buggy.

13/Moving West

NLUCAN's experience in establishing locals varied widely. In the case of post-riot East St. Louis it had been an emergency action, like that of a fire department damping down a blaze and acting to prevent another. In most cities formation of League affiliates was an urgent necessity to cope with the migrant deluge; in still others, Leagues were seen by the enlightened whites as vehicles for keeping the "natives" from becoming restless. From the perspective of the black community the League offered varying advantages, but perhaps its primary recommendation for being was its regularizing of communication between whites and blacks. The original concept had been Booker T. Washington's, wherein the best whites and blacks would come together to meet and discuss their common problems. There were many cities where this was exactly what happened; there were others, where this concept was almost nullified. In the south, for instance.

The south was a tough row to hoe, no question about it. True, a number of southern Leagues had been launched during George Haynes's time. Some had been launched and launched again; and again. Nashville was one; St. Louis another; Louisville a third, Richmond a fourth. The trouble was not in Haynes as an organizer alone, nor in massive prejudice alone, but in basic misconceptions as well.

Social service for blacks in southern cities was largely left up to them. The cities generally had meager provisions for social services, and these were directed toward white citizens who paid the major portion of taxes and held all but the menial jobs in city government. The fact that the needs of blacks were greater was subordinated to these two overriding determinants. The private agencies were also largely directed toward whites because white money supported them and white boards and staffers ran them. For the most part, social service among blacks was carried out by the churches, the most progressive of which had "social service departments." These departments were supported by contributions of the parishioners in what were called "after collections"—following the passing of the plate for the weekly offering after the Sunday service. The money collected in this way was then distributed by the pastor in his wisdom to the members of his flock who needed it most—the shut-ins, the sick, lame, halt and aged.

Dependent as it was on the vagaries of weekly collections from persons hard-pressed to make ends meet, distributed by empathetic but untrained and overburdened preachers, this kind of social service was inadequate before 1912 and absolutely overwhelmed by the migration to the cities that came afterward. Inevitably, pressures built up in the black belts of the southern cities and it was to civic leaders, black and white, who recognized this fact that George Haynes talked when he moved to organize local Leagues in such cities. In those early days of the work Haynes generally helped bring together a committee of whites and one of blacks— all volunteers—along the lines of the original Committee for Improving the Industrial Conditions of Negroes in New York. With no ongoing secretariat and no executive, no budget, few if any interracial meetings and only volunteer action to accomplish program objectives, it was not surprising that these early southern Leagues were unstable. Such Leagues were easily organized, quickly set up—relatively—and were, despite Dr. Haynes's belief to the contrary, the very "mushroom" growths he intended to avoid.

The reasons for the decline and demise of these early Leagues were many. In St. Louis, the first affiliate, the organization got off to an excellent start, but petered out when its leading light, Roger N. Baldwin, turned his attention to probation work. In Nashville, the League was initially the Bethelem Center settlement house operation; it was succeeded by the Public Welfare League, a more rounded organization which grew out of joint white-black relief activities after the Nashville fire of 1916 and the center's highly lauded work in that emergency.

In some cities blacks and whites never really did function as a team. In fact, in Augusta and Savannah, to name two, they never once came together in the same room. The complications of prejudice were a formidable handicap. They constituted at once a checkrein in the form of a veto that could not be appealed and a throttlehold (because of the dependence on whites for financing) that could not be shaken—except in rare instances. One such instance was that of the Richmond League. At a conference in the Virginia governor's mansion to discuss the League's program and its "revolutionary" interracial aspects (meaning its black and white board), the black delegation was led by Mrs. Maggie L. Walker, first woman president of a bank in the United States. E. K. Jones tells about the meeting:

> The governor's secretary kept addressing Mrs. Walker as "Maggie." The blacks took offense at it, but they thought it was up to Mrs. Walker to handle the situation. She did, in a magnificent fashion. Whenever any question would be addressed to her she would with deliberation, unusual poise and an excellent choice of words, answer them directly in a manner which showed the questioner to be inferior in choice of words and in intelligent selection of points at issue. Before the meeting was half finished, there was a complete change of attitude on the part of all the whites present. They were addressing her as "Mrs." It ended up in their requesting her to restate for the group assembled the conclusions reached and the program proposed. Thus the first Richmond Urban League was born.[1]

E. K. Jones revealed only in the late 1940's that Mrs. Walker carried the local League during the first years of its existence, paying the rent, operating expenses and salaries. The least she could do, she told E. K. Jones, was to stand back of William Colson, the local League executive, who was so splendid and courageous a person.

Colson had been an early Urban League Fellow and proved to be what Jones called "a man of somewhat radical ideas—frank, intelligent, decisive, unbending when it came to demands for opportunity on an equal basis for Negroes." [2] Colson had "frequent clashes" with the children's court judge, the white newsmen and city fathers, according to Jones. But he got results: he won better jobs for blacks and recruited workers for the Connecticut tobacco fields. Colson organized a committee on neighborhood improvement that kept the courts, health department, board of education and sanitation department constantly on the defensive because of demands made on them for better services to blacks.[3]

Finding a black community with enough financial resources to carry the cost of a local Urban League operation, even a minimal one, was not easy. Richmond was almost unique in finding a single "angel" to underwrite its work, and absolutely unique in having a black angel. Savannah was a city with a thriving and prosperous black community, much like those in Winston-Salem, Greensboro and Richmond. In Savannah the local League, in E. K. Jones's estimate, began with the greatest promise in the south. It never had white members on its board, though it had the sympathy and approval of the secretary of the Associated Charities, Miss Helen B. Pendleton, who later helped organize the Urban League of New Jersey and the Atlanta School of Social Work.

The fact that it was an all-black operation caused some soul-searching on the part of NLUCAN's board before Savannah's affiliation was approved. The winning point, of course, was that the city needed social work for its black citizens, and if the whites could not be engaged to cooperate in it, the blacks would have to carry through themselves—which they did.

The president of the Savannah League was the editor of the local black weekly newspaper; the treasurer and part-time executive were both on the staff of a black bank in the city; the secretary was a public school teacher. The agency was a going concern, with relief, probation, Big Sister, health, athletic, recreation and other valuable programs. But when economic disaster struck the south in the early years of World War I, one of the casualties was the Savannah bank owned and run by blacks. As it suffered, the League suffered, inasmuch as two of its key persons were associated with the bank. Both bank and League went under.

Some Leagues were starved to death. The southern Leagues were highly vulnerable for they had so little margin on which to operate. As E. K. Jones put it:

> The question of financial support was paramount. In order that we secure secretaries of needed training, understanding and skill, it was necessary to pay salaries in excess of the normal pay available to Negro professional workers in the southern communities. With white welfare agencies supported begrudgingly by these communities, it was all the more difficult to get support for Negro social work agencies. The Negroes themselves were always as liberal as their circumstances permitted, but their position in the lower economic bracket of the economic scale foreordained them to meager support of their own charitable and benevolent movements.[4]

Though NLUCAN's board might waive the requirement about an integrated board of directors (as it did in three instances in the south), it could not sidestep the fundamental requirement that the local Leagues had to be self-supporting; in fact, after 1920 they were supposed to pay 5 percent of their budget to the national League. NLUCAN could not possibly do anything but throw the financial burden on the locals because it was chronically in financial difficulty itself.

In securing support, NLUCAN had problems with both whites and blacks, however. White philanthropists, E. K. Jones found, would squeeze out a bit of guilt money for a single black agency. That single contribution would then be evidence of the Great White Father's "interest in the Negro" while simultaneously he would support scores of different white agencies engaged in social work in dozens of fields from athletics to workingmen's education.

Whites characteristically would consider the logic of support for social work among blacks and, especially in the south or backward cities elsewhere, would turn down the request with a surprised "We're not doing that for white people. Surely you wouldn't expect us to discuss such programs for Negroes!" [5] Corollary to this, whites in authority often would decline to go along with a program because of what was conceived to be (by the official) the public's attitude against such a measure.

There were problems with the black community also. Especially in northern cities, E. K. Jones observed that he often was rebuffed when trying to form Leagues where black leadership had coalesced around the fight against segregation. In such circumstances, he found, "any social welfare effort in the interest of Negroes was immediately branded as an attempt to segregate them." [6]

Another sticky situation was that in which existing black organizations (such as churches, clubs, and fraternities) and black leaders in a city perceived the entry of the League as a competitor for power, prestige and patronage. In such cases, formation of a League was frequently stymied for considerable periods. A case in point was Boston.

Though the Cradle of Liberty was a city where blacks historically had enjoyed considerable freedom, there was a color line that was rigid and unyielding. Blacks could go to the theaters, stay at the hotels, eat in the restaurants and enjoy the concert halls, museums and public places of the city, but they were locked into "Negro jobs." As waiters, liverymen and domestics they were welcome; though even these traditionally segregated jobs were being taken over by immigrants in the first decades of the century.

By the time of America's entry into World War I, the NAACP had its largest local branch in Boston, and it was working energetically for black civil rights. Neither the blacks nor the whites, either as individual leaders or in voluntary or public agencies, were meeting the social and economic needs of Boston's Negroes, however. Housing, health, jobs and improved living conditions were not the concern of any organized or systematic program, such as the League could bring to bear.

NLUCAN was interested in organizing in Boston, and there were friendly whites and blacks there who encouraged the effort. E. K. Jones made several visits to try to establish a local there. He called on both

black and white leaders, among them the fiery Monroe Trotter, arch-foe
of Booker T. Washington and anything smacking even faintly of accommodation or compromise. Yet, when Jones presented the arguments in
favor of a League for Boston, carefully delineated the differences and
complementary activities of the NAACP and NLUCAN (as he had to a
dozen other influential Bostonians in private conferences), Trotter
seemed won over. Suddenly Trotter's wife, sitting at a desk in the room,

> dropped her pencil, turned and faced us both [said Jones] and with accus-
> ing finger pointed at Mr. Trotter said: "Don't let that New York youngster
> fool you! I have listened to everything he said and I do not believe in him.
> I am against all of these segregation Negroes coming into Boston to lull us
> into false security. Don't you fall into his trap, Monroe!"
>
> She evidently felt sincerely that Mr. Trotter's and her mission was [to]
> keep all of Booker T. Washington's ideas out of Boston. Anything that was
> not calculated to lend strength to the forces for equality for which the Bos-
> ton *Guardian* at that time was the champion, was to be discouraged. She
> felt that any new movement, even though desirable *per se,* would dissipate
> the strength of the chief effort being fostered by blacks in Boston at that
> time; so the Urban League, instead of adding to the solution of the prob-
> lems, would really tend to weaken the forces for good by putting additional
> burdens on the limited number of persons already occupying positions of
> leadership.[7]

Actually the serious opposition was not from Trotter. Butler Wilson,
head of the Boston NAACP, suggested that E. K. Jones ask Joseph P.
Loud, civic leader, to send out a call for a meeting to hear the proposal
for a Boston Urban League, which he did. However, it wasn't until Jones
arrived in Boston for the meeting that he learned what Loud had said in
his letter. The invitation had stated that he (Loud) was not in favor of
organizing the League, in fact was opposed to it, but since Jones insisted
on being heard he thought it was only courteous that this privilege be
extended.

With this inauspicious prelude, the meeting was held June 5, 1918, just
off Boston Common at the Twentieth Century Club. The audience of
seventy-five was about 60 percent black. Loud introduced Kinckle Jones,
who gave a history of the League movement and a projection of what a
Boston League could accomplish. A letter from Moorfield Storey, national president of the NAACP and one of the nation's legal giants, was
then read. Storey said he thought an Urban League would be a duplication of effort.

There was a short discussion from the floor and Loud called on Butler
Wilson, the NAACP official. Wilson, with a carefully prepared speech,
torpedoed the whole idea of a League. There was, he said, a plan that

black leaders had discussed, under which all of the social work agencies in Boston would be asked to include black workers on their staffs for work not only among blacks but whites as well, across the board. "It all sounded very good," admitted Jones. "There were a few people who were apparently impressed, but the overwhelming majority of Negroes present and many of the more practical minded whites knew that this was a chimerical dream which had been discussed and fostered in the minds of idealists for many years. In fact, I had mentioned it as the League's ultimate objective. Up to that date it had not been realized anywhere." [8]

The question of an Urban League for Boston was put to a vote. To the amazement of all concerned, the vote was overwhelmingly in favor of establishing a League.

Butler Wilson adroitly sprang forward with a motion to appoint a committee to study the matter and devise means for meeting the needs of the situation. The following day the committee met in the office of Mr. John F. Moors. Wilson presented his proposal and Mr. Moors demanded something more than a paper program. Wilson asked that the group of which he was a part be given one year to work on their program before the League be allowed to proceed. Jones, sensing "that Mr. Moors' inclination seemed to be that the strategic thing to do would be to give Mr. Wilson every possible opportunity to carry out his idea," reluctantly agreed to this. He knew that there would be less opposition to the League if it could be truthfully stated that it had not "forced itself upon the community too precipitously." The meeting adjourned; Wilson left "with great glee" and Jones "with some disappointment and regret," Wilson to celebrate his "victory," and Jones to find a date pad on which he promptly circled June 6, 1919.

On that day in 1919, Kinckle Jones again was in the office of John F. Moors in Boston, with the other members of the committee. Butler Wilson was asked for his report and to the surprise of all concerned—even Jones—he had to admit that not one black social worker had been placed with any Boston agency. Still unwilling to concede defeat, Wilson called for extension of the deadline. But Moors, an overseer of Harvard College and experienced in public affairs, snapped his watch shut and called for action. The group voted on the spot to constitute itself the organizing committee of the Boston League. Mrs. Moors became treasurer of the local League and for several years, before it was admitted to the Boston Community Chest, the agency was largely underwritten by Mr. and Mrs. Moors, when half or more of the fund goal was unmet. [9]

Such decisiveness and financial support of the League were rare in most cities during the second decade of the century. The needs were enormous and the cities beckoned, however. The western field, with its many industrial centers, cried out for organization. Chicago, that huge magnet at "the top of the world," as southern blacks called it, pulled Negroes from Dixie by the thousands as the exodus accelerated. It was too important, too vital, too dynamic and too big a black community—more than 100,000 Negroes—to overlook or set aside. To the NLUCAN board and officers by 1916 Chicago was the number one goal for affiliation, and as a base of operations for the prospective western field office. For these reasons, not to mention the obvious need of providing and coordinating professional social work in the brawling, burgeoning black community, Chicago demanded NLUCAN attention.

E. K. Jones's first visit to the meat-packing capital of the world had ended in "no verdict." He returned in January 1916 with the auspicious welcome of Robert S. Abbott, whose Chicago *Defender* wrote about Jones and the prospect of a League branch with a news article and a glowing editorial endorsement of NLUCAN, urging blacks and their organizations in the city to help establish a Chicago League.[10] But it was an uphill struggle. Chicago was seething with ambitious, eager, black citizens and organizations, each with his own goals, petty jealousies, suspicions and vested interests.

The churches, of which there were dozens, operated employment agencies as part of their concept of "family service" to their black parishioners. A pastor's success in finding jobs for his flock seriously influenced the prestige, power—and income—of his church. Likewise, the social clubs and settlements were deeply involved in civic and welfare projects. Their support from the community depended on the attractiveness of their programs and their ability to serve their constituents. They were not keen on sharing with some new organization.

It was into this unusually active scene that Jones and the League wished to come. They had certain strengths: Miss Sophonisba P. Breckinridge had been a League board member since 1911, and was a highly respected member of the faculty at both the University of Chicago and the Chicago School of Civics and Philanthropy (of which she was dean). Active in social work and progressive circles, she was a good friend of such eminent citizens as Jane Addams, Celia Parker Woolley, Robert E. Park, Amelia Sears and Horace Bridges. It was her Wendell Phillips settlement house that NLUCAN had subsidized since 1913, in the form of a portion of the headworker's salary. In addition, some NLUCAN Fellows had trained in Chicago at the School of Civics and Philanthropy. Further, in the black community there were many prominent admirers and friends of Booker T. Washington. Washington's membership on the NLUCAN board until his death in 1915 and the membership of his wife and his successor, Robert R. Moton, afterward helped swing both black and white support behind the League in Chicago.

Yet, in spite of many trips by both Kinckle Jones and Hollingsworth Wood it seemed impossible to jell the situation by remote control from New York. At last, the decision was made that by devoting one month of intensive effort to organizing the Chicago community a branch could be launched there. The man for this nettlesome assignment, it was decided, would be E. K. Jones's secretary, protégé and assistant, T. Arnold Hill. Hill's background was similar to Jones's—both were born and reared in Richmond, Virginia, had attended Wayland Academy and Virginia Union University. Hill, an intense, vigorous young man whose steel-rimmed glasses gave him a scholarly look, was warm, affable and very approachable in contrast to the "correct" and formal Kinckle Jones.

So, taking the initiative, Jones and Hill entrained for Chicago and met on December 11, 1916, a group of eighteen citizens of the city at the Wabash Avenue YMCA. Of these, twelve were women, representing various social service and civic organizations; two were representatives of the Boy Scouts of America, and Dr. George Cleveland Hall, chief surgeon at Provident Hospital, presided.

Kinckle Jones described the nature of a local League program and proposed that a permanent organization for Chicago be set up then and there. He laid it on the line about finances: $3,000 would be necessary to keep the organization afloat through its first months. Of course NLUCAN would help—that was why Hill was there, to get things under way and start bringing in the sheaves.

A month later Dr. Hall chaired another meeting. T. Arnold Hill acted as secretary and the election of board members and officers was held. The constitution was read and a program of work was discussed. The budget was announced and inside thirty minutes the Chicago Urban League was formally launched and the meeting adjourned.

Robert E. Park, distinguished professor of sociology at the University of Chicago, was the League's first president. For his work among blacks in the Congo and the United States before coming to the university he was considered an authority. And his studies of the sociology of cities gave him further background for heading the local League. It was he, with Hill, who set the path of the League. He saw the black man in the Windy City as an immigrant, with the immigrant's immediate problems of work, wages, health, housing, and adjustment to city surroundings. The League must, therefore, do for black migrants what various organizations did for white immigrants.

The Chicago League, Park believed, had three major objectives: First, through research, it would give a solid base on which to improve the effectiveness of the welfare work carried out by black organizations. Second, it would deal with the city and county welfare agencies on behalf of blacks, interpreting black needs to the boards and administrators of social service and citizen-serving agencies. Third, the League would educate the black population as to the sources of public and private services open to them. Research, Park believed, was fundamental because efficiency rested upon knowledge.[11]

After one month of rallying support and collecting money, Hill was making progress. But even though he threw himself into the effort, calling on as many as sixty club presidents in one week, he and the local League had considerable construction ahead before the ship was ready to sail. Therefore, the NLUCAN board extended his stay an additional two months. With an introduction from Dr. Felix Adler of the NLUCAN board, Hill called on Horace J. Bridges, leader of the Chicago Ethical Culture Society. Doors were opened for Hill to call on many important persons in the city—Charles G. Dawes, president of Central Trust Company; Arthur Francis, head of the Chicago Community Trust; James G. K. McClure, president of McCormick Theological Seminary; Mrs. Louise deKoven Bowen, president of the Juvenile Protective Association; well-known feminists Jane Addams, Amelia Sears and Celia Parker Woolley; Judge Edward Osgood Brown, president of the Chicago NAACP; and federal Judge Julian Mack, leader of Jewish welfare movements.[12]

These were influential people. One of key importance was William C. Graves, "almoner" to Julius Rosenwald. Graves was impressed with the need for and potential of the local League and decided to become a director. This endorsement-by-proxy from Rosenwald was almost as valuable as the magnate's support in cash. Rosenwald gave $1,000 the first year and agreed to give up to $3,000 the following year, on a matching basis. Many prospective donors were influenced by Rosenwald's support.

The League, judged Graves after its first year, "is bringing cooperation from scores of Negro civic and philanthropic organizations which have been working at cross purposes and with much jealousy. It has received the migrants from the South, has advised them, has helped them secure homes and has found work for them. It has been their constant friend and advisor. On the other hand, it has been of assistance to many employers whose forces have been reduced by employees volunteering and being drafted for military service. It has opened kinds of employment hitherto closed to colored people." [13]

In February 1917 the deferred decision was faced: T. Arnold Hill would stay in Chicago. He would remain as executive of the Chicago Urban League and devote part time to work as western field secretary for NLUCAN. Hill's one-month trip to Chicago became an eight-year stay.

As might have been expected, the plan for the western field worker to split his time between administering Chicago and organizing work in other cities was practical only on paper. By mid-1919 it was evident that Chicago alone was more than enough to keep Hill occupied even though he had built a staff of thirteen. He had visited Milwaukee to help the local League, and gone to Kansas City and Lansing, Michigan, to stimulate formation of Leagues there. But the burden was too great for him to handle, and the demands too immediate in Chicago, as the eruption of a race riot in 1919 dramatically proved.

So a conference was held between members of the Chicago and NLUCAN boards to work out a formula for Hill's efforts. "It is thought," reported E. K. Jones, "that an agreement may be reached by which Mr. Hill will be able to leave Chicago periodically with the approval of the President of the local organization [for] supervision of local fields in the north." [14]

14/A Reorganization

During World War I, NLUCAN climbed to a new peak in services and demands on its staff. Its executive board eyed the growth of League affiliates in cities widely disparate geographically, temperamentally, sociologically and economically. The board also saw a national organization acting too much as a fire department, responding to conflagrations rather than working according to plan and preset pace.

The board designated two study groups to bring in recommendations to guide the national and local agencies. These committees reported on February 1, 1918. The first, a special committee of six chaired by Roger N. Baldwin, was charged with suggesting "a more effective organization of the League's work." [1]

They came up with a tightly reasoned, seven-page document that began by describing the current situation as one of "revolutionary change" brought about by the black migration in both northern and southern cities. This, they said, placed on NLUCAN an obligation to extend its work immediately. "Instead of confining ourselves as we have in the past to the training of a comparatively few Negro social workers and to organizing social work in a comparatively few centers, our efforts should reach practically every city of any size north and south, and should be brought forcibly home to white social workers throughout the nation, to public officials in cities, and to the business and labor interests who are so closely concerned with the new industrial problems involved."

There were two means to these ends, the committee affirmed: organization and publicity.

The organization, it was urged, "should be extended as rapidly as possible to all cities of 25,000 and over in which there is a considerable Negro population." For closer supervision, the work should be districted, rather than run from New York alone.

To carry out this plan, there would be three districts, with Arkansas, Louisiana, Oklahoma and Texas thrown into the southern district. Each district would be supervised by a committee of twenty-five persons from the area, appointed by NLUCAN's executive committee. These district or regional committees would have officers, and the executive secretary would be a paid League field worker. Regional headquarters would be established in New York, Chicago and Nashville. The League in local cities would report monthly to the districts and the district secretary and his committee would "supervise, aid and advise on conduct of local work."

Roger Baldwin's committee recommended establishing three special subcommittees of the NLUCAN board, one on publicity, one on cooperation with national agencies, and a third on education. The *educational* work would be supervised by a subcommittee of three. "The proper conduct of our work demands George Haynes should have that help from NLUCAN's executive committee." Baldwin had checked with George Haynes for suggestions on recruiting and training black workers and Haynes proposed that "definite arrangements" be made with black colleges which taught sociology or economics. Baldwin called for continuation of the scholarship program at social work schools, notifying black students in colleges about the League's work and opportunities. NLUCAN should confer with professors of sociology in northern colleges to advise black students about their studies as a preparation for social work. Haynes suggested "drafting" the scholarship students and the northern sociology students into "regular routine League work at New York, Chicago, Detroit, Nashville and Atlanta."

The *publicity* function should be designed "to get more action on the Negro problem in our cities," by directing itself to white social workers, public officials, Chambers of Commerce as well as "leaders in the labor, socialist and radical papers" and the black communities. "A news service to weekly and professional papers, pamphlets, circular letters, and speakers should be the means used."

(By the end of the year Roger Baldwin had worked up an additional plan "for securing more definite expression of public opinion in the matter of racial troubles." He wanted NLUCAN to adopt the methods used with such success in the selling of war bonds in the Liberty Loan drives. "Monster mass meetings," widely advertised, using parades, pageants and race relations experts as speakers, would put before the public the Negro's cause. The board pushed this one over to the Steering Committee, where it apparently died.) [2]

"In order to get public officials to pay more attention to the Negro, a circular letter campaign should be planned at intervals through the year addressed to city officials, county officials dealing with city problems and to such state officials as supervise work in cities, such as, for instance, superintendents of schools and state boards of charities." [3]

The committee called for two pamphlets, one to help white social workers and public officials solve black problems in the cities, and another to present essential facts about Negro city life.

Concerted and continued action was needed, the report said, to put the work of the League before national audiences on all aspects of city problems. The League should appear on programs of national organizations such as the National Municipal League, American Federation of Labor, American Public Health Association, National Housing Association, and so on.

Other specific recommendations were that the local work in New York City be split from the national; that the "lengthy and awkward name should be shortened to the National Urban League for Negroes"; and that the Steering Committee should be renamed the Directing Committee and given authority in the by-laws to act for the executive committee between meetings (thus the NLUCAN board was formally notified that for seven years the major decisions which guided the agency, namely, those of the Steering Committee, had been without legal sanction).

All of these plans could be implemented, the committee reckoned, for about $3,100. They put in an item of $2,000 for New York local work, salaries and additional expenses, and the remainder was allocated to publicity, including services, postage, and printing. They expected that the district work would be organized without additional funds "at present" by assigning George Haynes to the southern, E. K. Jones to the eastern, and the secretary of the Chicago branch (T. Arnold Hill) to the western district.

In keeping with the special committee's recommendations on publicity,

E. K. Jones devoted greater attention to this activity. By the year's end he could report dozens of addresses by NLUCAN staffers before city, state, federal government organizations, national agencies and associations, fraternities and professional groups ranging from the Baptist Convention to the committee investigating the steel strike. Also there were published articles and editorials in many journals, including the *Crisis, Southern Workman, Independent,* the *Survey* and both daily and black newspapers.

The second major proposal to NLUCAN's board was that of the "Committee on Standardizing Work of the National Urban League." Chaired by Horace J. Bridges of Chicago, this committee included T. Arnold Hill, George Haynes, the Reverend T. H. Dwelle, president of the Chicago League, and E. K. Jones ex officio. None of these was a NLUCAN board member.[4]

The heart of the committee's proposal was a model program for a local League. The committee stressed that it did not expect every branch to undertake all the elements immediately, and each branch was free to take on tasks not specified, tasks required by local conditions. The categories in the standard program were: inquiry into the actual condition under which the colored people lived, taking account of existing agencies, their aims and accomplishments, in delinquency—adult and juvenile; employment opportunities; recreation and amusement; housing; health and sanitation; education; and travelers' aid (for large cities and railroad centers).

Calling for tact and "greatest care," the committee recommended that the next step be to decide which problems could be met by coordinating existing agencies and which needed new machinery. A joint committee to coordinate had proven a wise technique. Overlapping efforts were to be avoided and/or brought to a close by definite allocation of responsibilities. The committee suggested goals.

"It is of the first importance that the attention of organizations devoted to the amelioration of specific evils . . . should be directed to the phase of their work that especially affects the colored population." In employment, the emphasis should be on opening work for black citizens in industries formerly closed; job-finding agencies should be developed, under League auspices or public authorities, or otherwise. Where there were large forces of black laborers, welfare workers should be urged on management; the local League should have such a person on the staff where needed; and the local League should prevent exploitation of black migrants. There was no specific comment about organized labor or strike-breaking.

In recreation, the ideal was to be equal opportunities for white and black citizens, including playgrounds, pools, bath-houses, youth clubs, settlements and schools, and supervised outings and social gatherings.

The housing proposal said "the ideal to be aimed at is the provision, either by civic authorities or by private investors, of model houses and apartments to be rented at a fair commercial rate. It is unwise, dangerous and self-defeating to provide accommodation at rentals that are not commercially remunerative as those it is intended to benefit are pauperized and spiritually injured. But experience has shown that responsible capitalists can be induced to invest their money in such enterprises on a five or six per cent basis."

Such housing "rescues a considerable proportion of the community from exploitation by the unscrupulous landlord or real estate speculator, but also sets a standard to which other owners of house property are obliged to conform. This, in fact, is its chief social value.

"Independently of such schemes, the Urban League should everywhere agitate for the enactment of legislation governing housing conditions; not simply for colored people. Although our task is primarily the amelioration of conditions among Negroes, yet we are a general *community organization,* and our chief desire is, by cooperation with other bodies, to render service to the whole community."

(Note the phrases "agitate for . . . legislation" and "our task is . . . primarily amelioration." Considerable controversy whirled around those two concepts in the years that followed.)

The committee called for action to secure cooperation of existing health agencies, especially city health departments. Hiring of black nurses and physicians were urged. After a six-year siege by the League, Bellevue Hospital in New York finally admitted black interns. The New Jersey League succeeded in having three black nurses appointed in Newark. As a direct result, black infant mortality dropped from 170 or more —where it had been for years—to 106.[5] Also, black migrants needed health and hygiene campaigns.

> With regard to education . . . the idea of the League is to secure equality of opportunity as between white and colored children. This refers particularly to trade and vocational education, and higher education generally. Experience has shown that, where the cooperation of the Superintendent of Schools can be secured, the public schools (whether colored or mixed) can be made a valuable channel for the propagation of the Urban League's message and ideals. The schools can be used as community centres. Home and school visitors (men and women) can reach the parents through the children; and even to the children many of the leading principles underlying this programme can be successfully imparted. It should be a constant

element in the policy of all centres of the League to utilize the machinery of public education to the utmost extent practicable.[6]

Such was the thinking of NLUCAN advisers concerning local League programs as of 1918. One of the earliest efforts to settle on a standardized program, for many years it served as a functional framework for local League activity. There were many attempts to regularize local programs and to define what constituted a local League in terms of services over the years. It was a matter that remained unsettled throughout the League's history. Because of the widely disparate conditions faced by the local Leagues, their autonomy and varying degrees of financial health, it was inevitable that local programs deviated from the "ideal."

As a study in contrasts, the problems occupying the Atlanta League and the Cleveland League in mid-1920 are instructive. Here is Jesse O. Thomas's catalog of Atlanta League activities:

Following a brief housing survey made in the Fourth ward, where a great many people are living in (uninhabitable) houses . . . through the housing committee for the League . . . a recommendation [was made] to the City Planning Commission for the Passing of a Housing Law . . . that will make it felonious for an agent to rent or collect rent for a house that leaks and that is generally out of repair.

The Legislature's attention was called to a man . . . who was beat up by a policeman named Pope in Pittsburgh and to a conductor on the West Fair line placing a revolver in the face of a Morehouse student a few days ago. The League made a careful investigation . . . that resulted in both these men being indicted before the Grand Jury.

On the night of the 4th a Colored boy, employee of the Western Union Telegraph Company while delivering messages near Tenth and Peachtree Streets was assaulted by four White boys. . . . In self-defense, he stabbed one of them in the fray, who died. One of the boys shot at him seven times. These boys and a lawyer organized a frame-up to send this Colored boy either to the gallows or the chain-gang for life. The Urban League got busy on the job and secured a preliminary hearing, where stenographic record was made of the testimony. . . . The League had a lawyer in court. If the League does nothing else this whole year than to save this boy from the gallows or the penitentiary for life, we feel that it has been a success.

Through the Big Brother and Big Sister Movement, we have enrolled thirty-five Big and Little Sisters, seventy-one Big and Little Brothers. . . . If out of these one hundred six Little Brothers and Little Sisters, we can save six, the Urban League will have justified its appeal.

These are perhaps the most important things we are doing after all, investing in human life and character. Through our Probation Officer, we have discovered that in the waiting room at the Police Court, where men, women and children are detained for hours waiting to be called for trial, that there is only one convenience, that is a pail or bucket, that is used by all in the presence of each other. We are now organizing our forces to remedy this situation. This condition is unbelievable in any civilized community.

In an effort to secure a Colored City Physician, the Urban League has had a meeting with the Finance Committee of the City Council. . . . The mortality rate of our group will be materially reduced if we can get a colored physician for our city to look after the health of the poor.

We are fighting now to have one-third of the play-ground facilities given to our Colored Children. The original plan was to give us one out of eleven.[7]

Hundreds of other things, less spectacular but of equal importance, were done.

In the city of Cleveland the local League had been in operation for one year. At mid-1920:

Classes in foremanship are being conducted by the Cleveland Organization, William Connors, executive secretary, through cooperation with the Board of Vocational Training which prepares men for opportunities as foremen. Through the training department of the Associated Charities it also conducts classes in social work both for paid and for volunteer workers. . . . "How to handle labor," "How to increase output," "How to hire men" and "How to maintain friendly relations between employer and employee," are some of the subjects. . . . Volunteers from churches and social organizations with interest and some experience anxious to increase in efficiency form the main body of attendants at the classes in social work in which case work, hygiene, how to teach home economics to ignorant mothers and civic responsibilities are taught.[8]

The needs of the black citizens in these two communities seemed light-years apart and typified the disparities found from one city to the next.

A number of Leagues operated settlement houses or community centers during this period, although the official agency position was against it. "While the League's specific objects do not include the opening and operation of community houses, it bends its efforts towards creating such institutions if the community feels the need of them" but usually preferred to turn them over to others for operation. In 1919 local Leagues in Youngstown, Detroit, Cleveland, St. Louis, East St. Louis, Atlanta, Savannah, Philadelphia, Springfield, Massachusetts, and Louisville were supplying recreation, health and education needs to their black constituents through settlement centers. Through their home economics departments they taught housewives not only how to cook, but nutrition, economy, home care, family budgeting, how to save in shopping and the importance of depositing savings regularly in a bank. These home economics departments were important forces in acculturation of the raw city immigrants.[9]

NUL leaders were not unsympathetic to the settlement house activities. Rather, they saw such operations as diversionary. "It is one of the most dangerous experiments which we try with the Urban League," warned Hollingsworth Wood, "for the problems of the settlement are so much closer-up than the community problems which the Urban League is designed to tackle that they almost inevitably swamp and cramp the activities of the League." [10] Advising the Boston League against settlement work, Wood revealed his own attitudes toward black control of such a community facility: "The problem also of joint responsibility on the part of the Negro group has to be solved and I should think this would be extremely difficult in the case of a property-owning enterprise like the Robert Gould Shaw House, and that the white group would be very loath to let Negroes into anything like an equal share of responsibility and control. And yet I think this is essential for the successful working-out of the Urban League program of mutual confidence and cooperation." [11]

Nevertheless, even as close to home as Brooklyn, the League took on settlement work. In that borough, it was to prevent what Hollingsworth Wood characterized as "the catastrophe" of giving up a settlement for blacks "which had been run by the NAACP that the Brooklyn League took it on and has been struggling along under it ever since." [12]

It was difficult for NUL to disentangle itself from settlement work to press forward its community work. Wood likened settlement work for an Urban League to the process of whipping up public interest in some reform activity, then "having a big public mass meeting and letting all the energy and steam off by means of adopting resolutions of protest or denunciation or acclaim, as the case may be." [13]

In a local League operation, Wood believed, a settlement house as a center from which to radiate into the community would be "very useful" but "the greatest watchfulness is required to prevent the immediate problem of the settlement . . . [from becoming] so pressing upon the notice and attention of the responsible parties that the larger aspects of the community service are relegated to tomorrow." [14]

As for national program, the most important question, as we shall see, was, "What does E. K. Jones think?"

15/Wooing Organized Labor

In January 1918 NLUCAN held a three-day conference in New York. Originally it had been planned as an opportunity for urgently needed co-ordination of programs among Leagues. Its purpose became more specific, however, as its opening day approached, and it evolved into a conference on "Negro Labor in America," perhaps one of the most significant subjects at that moment in history. The American Federation of Labor at its convention in Buffalo just a few weeks before had held out a welcome to black workers. The League considered what attitude blacks should take toward this new AFL posture. It recalled the limited practical results stemming from the organization's first meeting with the AFL leadership in 1913.

Dr. R. R. Moton presided. Horace J. Bridges, head of the Chicago Ethical Culture Society and board member of the Chicago League, gave a strong keynote address characterizing the League as neither a union nor a strike-breaking organization. He explained the even-handed way in which the agency worked with organized labor, or, where shut out by the unions, with management. "If the labor unions refuse [entrance] to the colored laborer, then the labor unions are themselves putting into the hands of the masters a weapon to use against them. Because the men must live," he exclaimed.[1]

George Foster Peabody said he firmly believed things would be different after the war and also that by being righteous, patient and living "close to God" the Negro would finally win entrance to trade unions as well as other forms of equality.

Dr. A. A. Graham, chairman of the Negro Organization Society of Virginia, advised adhering to the old sentiment, "If it pays to educate the Negro, educate him; if it pays to keep him well, keep him well. . . . If the American Federation of Labor opens its doors to the Negro . . . he should walk in. The question with the Negro is not what is the Negro going to do, but what are the white people going to let him do. Going to let him be an officer in the army—yes, but just so far; . . . going to let him go into the unions—yes but just so far."

The NAACP's new secretary, John R. Shillady, was convinced that the war would bring about in one year what might have taken fifty or a hundred otherwise. The AFL, he asserted, had shown more willingness than before to admit black men only because economic conditions had changed so drastically that they had to.

Emmett J. Scott, still new at his job as assistant to the Secretary of War, told of the education black recruits were receiving in army camps and cantonments he visited. They were learning the fundamentals of civilization, he said, citing health rules and obedience to authority as primary elements.

Hollingsworth Wood summed up on a spiritual note, asking blacks who had suffered so much prejudice, to "be awfully careful about prejudice against us. . . . Believe in the impossible. . . . It is to that wonderful glory of youth; that stupendous postulate of belief that the Urban League's spirit, I think, calls all our community."

The meeting passed a resolution directed to organized labor, specifically to the AFL:

I. . . . We would ask the American Federation of Labor, in organizing Negroes in the various trades to include: Skilled as well as unskilled workmen; Northern as well as Southern workmen; Government as well as civilian employees; Women as well as men workers.

We would have Negro labor handled by the AFL in the same manner as white labor: When workmen are returning to work after a successful strike; when shops are declared "open" or "closed"; when union workers apply for jobs.

We would have these assurances pledged not with words only but by deeds—pledged by an increasing number of examples of groups of Negro workmen given a "square deal."

With these accomplished, we pledge ourselves to urge Negro workingmen to seek advantages of sympathetic cooperation and understanding between men who work.

II. We would also address ourselves to the Labor Bureau of the United States Government:

In our national effort to speed up production of articles essential to the conduct of the war as well as the production of other goods, let us not lose sight of the loss to our country in quantity production by an unreasonable prejudice in many quarters against the use of Negro labor. Negro workmen are loyal and patriotic, cheerful and versatile. In some sections there is an oversupply of such labor; in other sections a shortage.

We would urge the appointment of one or two competent Negroes in the Department of Labor to serve as assistants in each of the Bureaus in adjusting and distributing Negro labor to meet war and peace needs.

III. We would urge Negro workmen to remain cheerful and hopeful in work; to be persevering in their efforts to improve in regularity; punctuality and efficiency; and to be quick to grasp all opportunities for training both themselves and for their children. Success lies in these directions.

IV. We would impress upon employers the fact that the efficiency of their employees during work hours depends very largely on the use made of the non-working hours. Most of the complaints against Negro labor can be removed if proper housing, decent amusement, fair wages, and proper treatment are provided.[2]

The Negro press carried word of this new overture to organized labor into the black community. The New York *Age* gave it a banner three-column headline on page one:

NATIONAL URBAN LEAGUE ADVISES
NEGRO WORKMEN TO AFFILIATE
WITH THE FEDERATION OF LABOR [3]

Following up on this almost immediately, the League dispatched a committee to Washington in February 1918, to call on the AFL. Augmented by the NAACP's John R. Shillady and Archibald Grimke, plus Dr. Thomas Jesse Jones and Emmett J. Scott, it asked the AFL executive committee to respond to the NLUCAN resolution by naming representatives to a joint committee to work out problems of recruiting and organizing Negro labor.

Six weeks later, Samuel Gompers named five AFL representatives to meet with the NLUCAN committee "to consider and prepare a plan of organization." He appointed the presidents of the Plumbers and Steam Fitters, AFL Metal Trades Department, Building Trades Department; the AFL secretary, Frank Morrison; Newton A. James, president of Central Labor Union 606; and himself as ex officio member. An April date was set for meeting.[4]

The other half of the joint committee was to consist of R. R. Moton, Fred Moore, E. K. Jones, James Dillard and Dr. George C. Hall, a member of the Chicago League's executive board, Shillady and Grimke from the NAACP, plus Emmett Scott and Thomas Jesse Jones from the Phelps-Stokes Fund.

In preparation for the AFL meeting, E. K. Jones canvassed the local League executives. The conference, he told them, was to plan ways of reducing friction between white union labor and Negro labor. Therefore, he needed to know in what lines of work Negro workers were employed in each city; were they in the AFL or another organization? Jones asked for the names of "potential labor leaders" among black workers. What was the relationship between white and colored labor in that city—cordial? Strained? Was the outlook for Negroes to enter skilled lines hopeful? What was the attitude of black workers toward the unions and vice versa? [5]

One of those who replied was William J. Ashby, of the Newark League. Black workers in his area believed the unions would take them, but would not interest themselves in getting work for them; and in fact, some unions were openly against them.

Many NLUCAN members were skeptical of the high-flown resolutions of the AFL conventions and its national leaders. Several League executives looked into their local labor situations.

John T. Clark in Pittsburgh rounded up a group of twenty-three "mechanics" and talked with them at some length. They unanimously approved the resolutions adopted at the League's labor conference, and opened up about their experiences with organized labor. Eight of the men were union members and fifteen were not; they worked in twelve different trades. Clark reported that the electrician in the group had never attempted to join the union because "he knew of the experience of too many men to make such a foolish effort." [6] Although there were more than 200 Negro plasterers in Pittsburgh, only two were members of the union. Black plasterers were bitter toward the union and said it was well known that no black application would be considered for membership.

Three of the men Clark talked to were railroaders—two firemen and an engine inspector. None of them had had a chance to join the union because the railroad organizations were lily-white. Consequently, these three men were working at other trades.

The two structural ironworkers in the group had specifics to relate. They had been brought to Pittsburgh by the Turner Construction Company to work on the construction of the Pennsylvania Chocolate Factory.

> After the job was well underway and quite a few white Union iron workers were on the job, the government took over the supervision of this construction and limited the time for its completion. The business agent of the iron workers, Mr. Wilson, called on the men and ordered a strike if the superintendent, Mr. W. Ryan, did not at once remove the two Negroes. He considered his Negro iron workers expert men and plead [sic] with the Union to let him continue to use them—that he would stand any expense in having these men taken into the Union. They positively refused to consider these men. The heads of the local would not be prevailed upon to let these Negroes join the Union under any circumstance. Mr. Ryan, the Superintendent, is temporarily using one of the Negroes as a general laborer around the plant and the other one as a foreman at the Structural Iron Works (as a foreman he is not considered a structural iron worker).[7]

"There are many other trades in Pittsburgh," stated Clark, "in which the Negro absolutely will not be tolerated." As proof, he cited a study by

Henry Epstein of the Negro migrant to Pittsburgh, in which the researcher found that there was an understanding among most trade unions that no member would bring in a membership petition for a Negro. And the mechanics he interviewed, he said, "seem to doubt the sincerity of the American Federation of Labor about their fair attitude toward the Negro and ask that the executive heads of the labor movement should exert a greater influence on the business agents of the various locals to see that they practice less discrimination toward the Negro. They claim that there are many instances almost daily in which preference is given even the foreigner who does not speak our language." [8]

Meanwhile, George Haynes had learned of the NLUCAN–AFL conference and wrote Moton, "In view of this question coming up at several points now in our Southern territory do you not think it advisable for me to attend this conference [?]" [9] But the committee was set and Haynes was not to be part of it, even though he had initiated the NLUCAN–AFL dialogue in 1913. Back in Washington, D.C., in preparation for the AFL meeting the NLUCAN committee met the night before the conference to hammer out strategy. [10]

When the committee was received at AFL headquarters on April 22, 1918, Gompers announced that the union welcomed Negro workingmen to the ranks of organized labor. Both black and white workers had common interests and must fight unfair wages, hours and bad conditions. He admitted that it was "difficult" for the national AFL organization to "control the actions of local unions in difficulties arising within the trades in any particular community" but that "we can and will use our influence to break down prejudice on account of race, color or previous condition of servitude." He hoped that the NLUCAN group would use its influence to show black workers the advantages of collective bargaining and AFL membership. The AFL had many black members, though, he averred, few outside the movement knew how sizable their numbers were. [11]

It was true, said Gompers, that there had been "unpleasant incidents in connection with efforts of colored men to get recognition in trades controlled by the AFL." But the AFL had been the victim of a bad press, for though these incidents had been publicized, he complained, "the good effects of wholesome and healthy relationship have not been given publicity." This was the reason that "a general attitude of suspicion has been developed towards union labor on the part of colored working people." Gompers hoped that "a more cordial feeling of confidence by working men in each other" would spring from this conference. He agreed to give the special committee the right to name an additional AFL Negro organizer whose duty would be missionary work among black workers, explaining labor organization to them. [12]

The NLUCAN group followed up with a letter, June 6, 1918, to Gompers. It affirmed willingness to cooperate:

> First, we suggest that you prepare a statement, along the lines of [your words at the Conference], and send it to us for joint approval and then to be given to the Negro press throughout the country as expressing your position on matters connected with the relationship between Negro and white working-men.
>
> This statement, in our judgment, should contain a clear exposition of the reasons why certain internationals may exclude colored men as they do by constitutional provision and still be affiliated with the AFL whose declared principles are opposed to such discrimination. This we think necessary because the stated facts above alluded to will be familiar to the leaders among the colored people, particularly to editors and ministers whose cooperation it is essential to secure if the best results are to be obtained.
>
> We would suggest further that you consider the expediency of recommending to such internationals as still exclude colored men that their constitutions be revised in this respect.
>
> Second, that a qualified colored man to handle men and organize them be selected by us and recommended to you for employment as an organizer of the American Federation of Labor, his salary and expenses, of course, to be paid by the American Federation of Labor.
>
> Third, that for the present we meet at least once a quarter to check up on the results of our cooperative activities and to plan for further extension of the work, if satisfactorily conducted.
>
> Fourth, that you carry out your agreement to have your Executive Council voice an advanced position in its attitude toward the organization of Negro working-men and have these sentiments endorsed by your St. Paul convention in June, and this action be given the widest possible publicity throughout the country.[13]

The signers of this memorandum were Eugene Kinckle Jones and Fred R. Moore, for the committee which consisted of R. R. Moton, John H. Shillady, Fred R. Moore, Archibald Grimke, Emmett J. Scott, Eugene K. Jones, Thomas Jesse Jones, James H. Dillard and Dr. George C. Hall.

Gompers referred the document to the AFL Committee on Organization which reported:

> It is with pleasure we learn that leaders of the colored race realize the necessity of organizing the workers of that race into unions affiliated with the American Federation of Labor, and your committee recommends that the President of the American Federation of Labor and its Executive Council give special attention to organizing the colored wage workers in the future. We wish it understood, however, that in doing so no fault is or can be found with the work done in the past, but we believe that with the co-

operation of the leaders of that race much better results can be accomplished.[14]

This report, with its unctuous self-exoneration, was appended to the League memorandum, presented to the 1918 convention of the AFL and adopted unanimously. The concrete results were all but invisible, though it gave a benchmark from which to judge future hypocrisy.

By mid-November 1918 the evidence indicated that the sweet music orchestrated by the AFL chiefs in Washington was being played sourly by its internationals and their locals. E. K. Jones wrote R. R. Moton that word had come of "numerous instances" of "gross discrimination" against black workers by the AFL locals. In fact, there had been so many instances, he said, that some members of the labor committee wanted another meeting with the AFL "to check up on the results of our previous conference and to devise ways and means of making the decision which we reached more effective." [15]

By 1919 the tide of black workers in industry had crested. As early as mid-May serious labor surpluses were cropping up in the manufacturing centers. John Dancy in Detroit had been asked by T. Arnold Hill to help in finding work for black laborers from Chicago. Dancy demurred: "Inasmuch as we are having lots of strikes on here and Negroes breaking them . . . we might on the return of the white strikers find ourselves flooded as you people are now [with unemployed] . . . if [Hill] sent on twenty or thirty clean fellows . . . we could use them, but I am averse to having them send great groups only to find ourselves in Chicago's present predicament. It is far better to have a condition of that sort in one city than to have it in two." [16] Dancy went on to say that Detroit's housing facilities were impossible. There was not a single room available, and Negroes were actually sleeping in the streets.

It was in this uncertain situation that the AFL held its convention in 1919. Whereas the year before only six Negro members reached the lectern, in June 1919, twenty-three black delegates spoke. Among them were representatives of the Freight Handlers and Helpers, the Shipbuilders' Helpers, Janitors, Stationary Firemen and Oilers, and Longshoremen. They protested discrimination and exclusion by many AFL affiliates, especially the Railway Brotherhoods. The AFL Committee on Resolutions introduced a proposal that

the Executive Council give a particular attention to the organization of colored workers everywhere and assign colored organizers wherever possible; [three specific places mentioned were Jacksonville, Raleigh, North Carolina, and the state of Virginia] and that in cases where International

Unions affiliated with the AFL refuse admittance to colored workers, the AFL organize the workers under charters from the Federation.[17]

There were additional resolutions against the Metal Trades International; for a study of organized labor conditions among Negro workers; and for a Negro union to be granted an international charter.

A demonstration broke out, following the authorized resolution. Heads of international unions rose and spoke, claiming they had black workers in their ranks. Among those present and accounted for were the International Ladies' Garment Workers (claiming 6,000 black members); the Meat Cutters and Butchers (with its thousands of Negroes in the packing plants and its five black organizers); the building trades, laundry workers, teamsters, barbers, printers, letter carriers and nearly forty more.[18]

The resolution was passed and Samuel Gompers gave it authority it otherwise would have lacked when he said, "The action of the convention in removing every class and race distinction from trade unionism should mark an era in the struggle of the Negro for equal rights, as well as an advance in the history of political and economic liberty in America." [19]

According to Fred Moore, Negro leaders agreed that if the resolution was sincerely carried out by the AFL, there had not been any step so important since the abolition of chattel slavery. They still had their doubts, however. Said Moore, other black leaders wondered "after treating the colored laboring man with rank indifference all these years, what has prompted the Federation to make overtures to him at this time?" [20]

Moore listed some answers. Most of them were rooted in expediency: the decrease in immigration; the interracial disturbances growing out of strike-breaking; the constant threat of a large pool of unorganized labor available for strike-breaking. Another reason Moore cited was because of the record made by colored soldiers in the war.

If carried to its logical conclusion, the AFL decision would necessarily mean better chances for Negroes to become skilled or semiskilled workers. "The real extent of this forward movement," said Moore, ". . . can only be gauged by the spirit in which it is carried out. The AFL must deal fairly with the Negro, and at the same time the colored man must be required to measure up to the standards demanded of all." One black worker told the AFL convention, "We don't ask any favors, we ask for a chance to live like men, with equal rights and democratic rule. The Negro can read now, and the man who can read can think." [21]

Carrying the battle to those who could both think and read, E. K. Jones, in an unusually pugnacious stance, called on national labor leaders to implement their policy decision. In an article in *The Crisis* entitled "Fight the A F of L," he beckoned to black workers in communities around the nation. The AFL convention decision, he said, "will mean a great deal provided that in every locality throughout this country the colored men and women come together and demand of the various labor locals recognition of Negroes as working men." [22]

The annual conference of the League in 1919 took this statement one step further. There the delegates passed a resolution that enunciated the League policy position on labor unmistakably:

> We believe in the principle of collective bargaining and in the theory of cooperation between capital and labor in the settlement of industrial disputes and in the management of industry. . . . We advise [Negroes] to take jobs as strike breakers, only where the union affected, has excluded colored men from membership. We believe they should keep out of jobs offered in a struggle to deny labor a voice in the regulation of conditions under which it works.[23]

Kinckle Jones expanded on this in an address before a "Reconstruction and Readjustment Congress" at Howard University and mused about the problems of unionizing blacks. "As a rule," he said, "Negroes are suspicious of unions, with but little sympathy towards other Negroes who advocate affiliation on the part of Negro working-men with white unions. However, the union will never be able to muster their full strength in their fight with capital without the recruiting of Negro workmen now constituting one-seventh of the labor supply of America. And Negroes will be unable to attain their positions in the labor world without in a large measure affiliating with organized labor groups.

"It is inevitable that an adjustment of some kind must be made. Whether it will be through the affiliation of Negroes directly with white labor organizations or through the formation of Negro labor organizations that will eventually affiliate with labor but in the meanwhile will bargain with labor and capital alike, is the question which the local situation in any industry must determine. The fact remains, that Negroes must organize in industry for self-protection and self-preservation." [24]

Haunted by the gory spectre of the Chicago and other riots and aware of unsettled labor conditions, the League decided to press forward in its attempt to move the AFL off dead center. At the 1920 convention in Montreal, one delegate was Dr. Abraham Lefkowitz, a long-time NUL board member, New York City school teacher and president of the local teachers' union. The NUL executive board approved a set of resolutions which were introduced by Dr. Lefkowitz at the AFL meeting:

> WHEREAS, the American Federation of Labor has taken a firm position on the claims of Negro labor to fair and impartial sharing of the benefits of organized labor, and

WHEREAS, despite this attitude of the American Federation of Labor encouraging results have not followed and millions of Negro working-men continue ignorant of the benefits of collective bargaining, thus militating against the successful operation of the Federation in its fight for a square deal, be it

RESOLVED, that the American Federation of Labor engage upon a campaign of education among both white and colored working-men to convince them of the necessity of bringing into the ranks of labor all men who work regardless of race, creed or color.

RESOLVED, that with this end in view there be called into periodical conference with the Executive Council of the American Federation of Labor, white and colored leaders who can suitably represent and express the point of view of Negro working-men and can convey to Negro working-men the good will and sympathy felt by the American Federation of Labor towards them.

RESOLVED, that there be employed in headquarters at Washington a competent Negro agent who will express the hopes and yearnings of Negro working men to the American Federation of Labor and in turn be the mouthpiece of the Federation for such messages and information as the Federation may from time to time wish to convey to the Negro workers throughout the country, said agent to be the Executive Secretary and official representative in the interim of meetings of this special committee on Negro workers described above.

RESOLVED, that this Conference endorse the appointment of Negro organizers in all states in which Negroes are or may be employed whose duty will be to build up Negro membership.[25]

It was a spirited convention. One observer reported that the local and federal unions that had been organized by the federation attacked the AFL indifference to black workers.[26]

Though there were the usual expressions of universal brotherhood, the AFL resolutions committee saw to it that most of the NUL resolution was not reported to the floor. The suggested educational campaign and the proposals for a special standing committee and permanent secretary at AFL national headquarters were stricken out in committee.

The gutted final form of the resolution as passed was:

WHEREAS, the American Federation of Labor has taken a firm position on the claims of Negro labor to fair and impartial sharing of the benefits of organized labor; and

WHEREAS, despite this attitude of the American Federation of Labor encouraging results have not followed and millions of Negro working-men, continue ignorant of the benefits of collective bargaining, thus militating against the successful operation of the Federation in its fight for a square deal for labor, be it

RESOLVED, that Negro organizers be appointed where necessary to organize Negro workers under the banner of the American Federation of Labor.[27]

And so the matter rested unrequited so far as League efforts at the top were concerned, until A. Philip Randolph began to organize the sleeping-car porters and maids with the active support of NUL and until T. Arnold Hill went after the AFL with bulldog determination.

16/The "New Negro"

At the turn of the century Booker T. Washington had written about the "New Negro," the black man of the twentieth century. Though his vision was clear, his timing was off. It was not until the cataclysmic changes and unprecedented inputs of World War I transformed hundreds of thousands of blacks from peons to cosmopolites that the New Negro emerged. He made his greatest impact on the consciousness of white Americans in the postwar period, in new voices, new leaders, new attitudes and new strength. It became apparent that the blacks had developed 'a spine.

The New Negro did not burst upon the American scene fully formed like some genie from Aladdin's lamp. Rather, his outlines, his strengths, his potential were revealed as much by his reaction to virulent white racism as by his own positive acts. In the year 1919, the perverse persecutions of white Americans served to form and reveal a New Negro in much the way a lapidary brings out the inner reality of a rough gemstone by chipping and honing its surfaces.

Nineteen nineteen was the year that the nation dedicated to making the world safe for democracy demonstrated what it meant in practice by flaying, burning alive, lynching, massacring, driving from their homes and farms, jobs and schools, burning the houses and possessions of hundreds of American citizens because they were black.

Returning regiments of Negro veterans were cheered as heroes as they paraded up Main Street—and berated, insulted, beaten and lynched for being "uppity" and not "knowing their place"—as individuals on the side streets.

Black workmen, who during the pressure of war production had been hailed as vital workers for victory, became, as war contracts were canceled and jobs were eliminated, a menace to "labor peace."

The tensions and inconveniences of overcrowding and overloaded facilities in the major industrial cities had been endured as patriotic during the war; with peace, and continued black migration to the cities, patience—by both blacks and whites—wore thin. Extemporaneous interracial violence and crimes of passion were augmented by the fruits of organized white racism, such as the bombing of Negro homes on Chicago's South Side by "patriotic" young men.

Far-sighted citizens realized that it would take organization to prevent widespread race conflict. The blacks with such vision enlisted in the efforts of the NAACP to eradicate lynching and disfranchisement, in the development of Urban League efforts to provide a vehicle for black progress and communication across the barricade of skin color, and in efforts of organizations such as the Association of Colored Women's Clubs, black Masons, Elks and fraternal societies and business groups.

Far-seeing whites went two different routes: The primary example of the ameliorative route was the formation and operation of the Commission on Interracial Cooperation. The antithesis was the re-emergence of the Ku Klux Klan, with its gory Christian hypocrisy of "uniting native born white Christians for concerted action in the preservation of American institutions and the supremacy of the white race."

Examining the record of 1919, one might conclude that mob action against blacks had become the new national sport, replacing baseball and boxing. In addition to the lynchings, there were twenty-five riots logged in the last half of 1919.

Much of the bloodiness of that year was caused by Negro adaptability and gullibility. The blacks had proven highly adaptable. They quickly learned to run the unfamiliar machines of American industry and the lethal devices of the American military. New literacy and new exposure to freedom and new ways of life in the industrial centers had taught by word and influence that black men were meant to share in the benefits of American democracy. They read the basic documents of America and heard the Wilsonian pronouncements and were gullible enough to believe that they applied to black Americans as well as white. They had shown similar gullibility after the Emancipation Proclamation nearly sixty years before.

Or were they gullible? Were they not rather the products of America's highest aspirations and expectations? With no allegiance to imported "isms" or nations, their beliefs and views had been taught by Americans and experienced in America alone. Their God-fearing faith in a higher destiny had sustained them, and the experience of being wanted and needed as free men in large numbers by industry and the armed services tended to justify their belief in the system. Up until this time the major thrust of black thinking and leadership had been centripetal—moving toward the center of American life, working for, believing in, demanding inclusion, even integration, in the system, in the society if not in social life. In spite of the contrary efforts and examples, the mass of black Americans held the ideal of eventual integration as an article of deepest faith. Thus the wartime evidence of a new degree of acceptance of blacks gave a new sense of self, of realization that they were on the threshold of a new and truly democratic era.

Therefore, when the lash of white hatred struck in an epidemic of unprecedented lynchings, intimidation and riots, blacks were stunned. However, they quickly demonstrated their recent learning and their adaptability. They showed, by retaliating, that they were not supinely going to allow their rights to be abridged and their advances to be annulled by white repression. This was the message of the Washington riot in July 1919, when mobs of white sailors, soldiers and marines went on the rampage against blacks. For three days they indulged in an orgy of shooting and brutality, injuring scores of innocent blacks and killing several who happened into their paths. But the turning point came on the third day when a band of thugs started into the black community to set it afire. This rallied black resistance and in defense of their homes and their rights black men set upon the invaders. A number of whites were killed and wounded before authorities managed to bring the riot under control.

Even in the backwater areas a fresh spirit was apparent. In Elaine, Arkansas, blacks met to work up a plan for forcing their landlords to deal fairly with them. When a posse led by a deputy sheriff arrived to break up the meeting, there was a general uproar. In this confusion the deputy was killed, and this set off a vicious pogrom by whites in which several Negroes were killed and scores shot. Here the significant action was that of blacks coming together to force action from landlords—unheard of in Booker T. Washington times.

But the "civil disorder" that cast a pall over the country and a shadow into the future was the Chicago riot that flared on July 27, 1919. Its real causes were complex and deeply rooted in racism and "gut" issues.

In growing from 59,000 to more than 100,000 during the war years, Chicago's black population had, in its quest for housing, pushed and frightened out many whites from once all-white neighborhoods. In the three years preceding the 1919 riot twenty-seven bombs had been thrown at Negro homes in formerly white neighborhoods and at homes and offices of real estate men who sold to blacks.

Blacks and whites clashed in the job market, also (and had since 1894 when blacks had first been used as strike-breakers at the stockyards), with consequent violence and bloodshed. In 1904 a mammoth stockyard strike set the scene for use of 10,000 black strike-breakers, and in 1905, less than eight months later, a teamsters' strike saw black strike-breakers brought in again. In both these latter strikes violence occurred, but in the teamsters' strike there was a decided shift. In that one, the concept of strike-breaker was generalized by whites to apply to all Negroes, and blacks became targets for calumny, epithets, stones and attacks not only from white strikers and union sympathizers, but generally from blue-collar whites and their families, including children.

By 1916 between 10,000 and 12,000 blacks were at work in the stockyards, Chicago's largest industry. This was nearly half of the total meatpacking industry work force. By 1919, 90 percent of the whites were union members, but only 25 percent of the blacks, and this fact created much friction, for both union and nonunion workers were paid the same.

War contract cancellations hit Chicago after the Armistice, and Negro women were the first to be laid off, followed by black men and then white workers. Unemployment among blacks hit at least 10,000 early in May 1919. The pinch was on and made more acute by demobilization of veterans and continuing migration of southern blacks to Chicago.

The 1919 riot was triggered when whites and blacks, escaping the torrid July heat, clashed at a Lake Michigan beach. A young black boy drifted into an area claimed by the whites, and they threw stones to drive him away. He drowned. Blacks charged he had been murdered and demanded of a policeman that one white, presumed responsible, be arrested. The policeman refused and arrested a Negro instead. From this event rumors and hatred fueled action in both the white and black communities. Clashes between mobs broke out during the night, and the war was on. (The drowned boy's body was recovered later and examination disclosed no evidence of injuries from stoning, but by that time whites and blacks were beating and killing one another with a vengeance.) The governor of the state sent in the militia on the fourth day, but for nearly two weeks Chicago suffered mob rule before reason prevailed.

The toll, insofar as it could be assessed, was thirty-eight dead—fifteen white, twenty-three black; 537 injured—178 white, 342 black, seventeen unspecified; more than 1,000 families homeless—mostly black—from fire and mindless, furious destruction of property.

The riots in Chicago and Washington shook the nation. Two of its major cities, one of them its capital, had been in the control not of elected authorities but the madness of race war. These riots, warned the NUL, "are solemn warnings to our country of the dangers that we are facing in our own body politic. They emphasize anew the fact that after all, human relations can only be satisfactory when founded on conditions which are based on justice and equality." [1] What these lofty sentiments meant in terms of preventing future riots, the League took pains to point out:

> In the past Negroes have suffered from mob attacks on individuals for crime or alleged crime committed by the individual while the bulk of the Negro population was left unmolested; but at East St. Louis, Washington and Chicago, Negroes were attacked as a race and at Washington and Chicago, they retaliated as a race. . . .
>
> The conditions obtaining after a riot has started require the most effective and impartially strict administration of the law. Unfortunately both in Washington and Chicago, the colored people and the whites who know the facts are convinced that the police have not administered their office with fairness. . . .
>
> It is the condition which makes for these racial outbreaks that demands the immediate attention of all public-minded men and women. . . .
>
> Only by improving the housing, health and recreation opportunities of the Negro at the same time that we demand of him the contribution of his hands and brain in industry can we look for fundamental improvement in race relations. Organized labor as well as organized capital must understand him and his human longings and both must give him justice and a chance to make his contribution to the common life of our communities. . . .
>
> It is the duty of every agency of public expression, public officials, especially those of the police departments, doctors, lawyers, clergymen, teachers and all who have the opportunity to express themselves in public to bring to bear the forces of public opinion to rectify the abuses which produce conditions of distrust and almost of despair.[2]

The League held up as an example of outspoken responsible comment the statement of Illinois Attorney General Edward J. Brundage:

> . . It is a reflection upon Chicago that black men could be mobbed in broad daylight in the heart of the business district without a single member of that mob being arrested. A mob is the most horrible of all brutal aggregations, and a few determined police officers could have made it possible for the State's Attorney and a Jury in the Criminal Court to have given a wholesome lesson to mob leaders.[3]

In point of fact, of what use was an Urban League in a cataclysm such as the Chicago holocaust? The local agency, under T. Arnold Hill's leadership, abandoned its ongoing programs and became an emergency outpost, relief station, rumor-quencher, paymaster and island of sanity providing vital lines of information and action into both white and black communities.

Black workers were afraid to go to the stockyards, understandably, either to work or to collect pay checks. In the black section of the city, meanwhile, Jewish merchants became alarmed that thousands of Negroes without income might, in desperation, loot the stores. To help out, the League served as a pay station for the Morris packing plant during the riot.[4]

Here is E. K. Jones's eye-witness Chicago report (written August 12, 1919):

The League . . . is a God-send to the community . . . [it] is headquarters for Red Cross Relief Work and one of the four relief stations for the homeless and foodless Negro victims of the riot. Lines of men and women all day for more than a week have been coming to the station to get their regular allotment of meal checks and food.

The industrial situation for the Negroes in Chicago is serious. Many Negroes who could not safely reach their work during the time of the riot returned to their places of employment last week to find their positions filled by white workers, who in many instances, are being retained. The League with its employment force of some five or six workers, is attempting to get work for the unemployed either in their old jobs or in new places as speedily as possible.

The most ominous situation is that at the stockyards where before the riot about 15,000 colored men were employed, of whom 3,000 are union members. The white union members have struck against military and police guards remaining at the yards to protect the colored workers, who in large numbers are returning. Simultaneously the union officials are publicly claiming that the packers are responsible for the riots.

The Urban League has demanded that the Unions as proof of the good faith of their claim that there is no race feeling against Negro workers at the yards issue a statement urging all union members to refrain from all hostile acts against Negro workers—union or non-union and is urging all Negroes to return to their respective places of employment. Any efforts to unionize Negro workers whom they claim they would welcome to their ranks can follow the return of tranquility. Prominent union leaders promised us they would use their influence to have such a statement issued.

In consultation with certain influential men representing the packers, we learn that it is their intention to have all colored workers return to work. This will have a salutary effect on the question of the Negro's right to work in Chicago wherever he is wanted by employers and as a test case will be of value in similar disputes in other locations. These representatives of the packing interests in Chicago who shape the policies of the large plants in other cities will give financial help to our efforts to organize branches of the League in Kansas City and Omaha, Nebraska.[5]

Shaken by the riot, civic, social, business and religious leaders met during the conflict to try to end it. Illinois's governor Frank O. Lowden was asked to appoint an emergency committee to search the event for its causes and recommend action to prevent any repetition. Two Chicago Urban Leaguers—executive T. Arnold Hill and board member William C. Graves—were named to a group of six citizens who were to secure the governor's action on this request.[6]

This was the genesis of the Chicago Commission on Race Relations which for a year dissected the riot and its causes. Its report has influenced every serious study of violence in the nation since. Though its conclusion was that there was no ready remedy or "quick means of assuring harmony between the races," the commission laid bare the conditions which brought Chicago to the brink. There was a catalog of fifty-nine problems, grievances and misunderstandings. Those fifty-nine were, unfortunately, almost as valid half a century later in most American cities.

The commission's report, entitled *The Negro in Chicago: A Study of Race Relations and a Race Riot,* suggested remedies. These effectively served as a guide for the action of community agencies for the two decades that followed. Much of the basic material for the report was based on information and studies from the Chicago Urban League files. The associate executive secretary of the commission was Charles S. Johnson, a young black protegé of the University of Chicago professor Robert Park. Johnson was research director of the Chicago League, and was boosted to national prominence by his work on the *Study.*

There were some, of course, who embraced the "devil theory," believing that the sudden upsurge of racial strife around the nation was inspired by some malevolent outside force.

FOR ACTION ON RACE RIOT PERIL
Radical Propaganda Among Negroes
Growing, and Increase of Mob Violence
Set Out in Senate Brief for Federal Inquiry

headlined the New York *Times,*[7] noting that in ten months there had been thirty-eight riots and clashes. It was a time when the New York State Lusk Committee was riding high, and the Bolshevik menace was thought to lurk around every corner if not under every bed.

Gleefully, southern labor agents circulated in the troubled cities of the north. In Chicago, the Mississippi Welfare League agent recruited a select "commission" of blacks to observe and report on the shiny new welcoming attitude of the south toward Afro-Americans. T. Arnold Hill and the Chicago League secured statements from blacks in the southern states, giving the lie to the propaganda. Hill also wrote newspaper and magazine articles ridiculing such spurious southern concoctions.[8]

The National Urban League, sifting the ashes of 1919, had its own analysis of riot causes. The world war, it said in its annual report for the year, had enhanced the value of the Negro as a productive force in the nation. But he was, "through no fault of his own—ill equipped to meet the responsibilities which they entail. At the same time the employers are as ill-prepared to make intelligent use of his great potential services, and the white labor of all ranks including the most unskilled and ignorant foreigners, greet his arrival with widespread and unreasoning hostility— all this at a time when profound economic and political unrest are racking the country!" [9]

The League formula for solution of these difficulties was easily stated: ". . . salvation from destructive bitterness and riots rests upon getting these conflicting elements to understand each other and pull together fairly and harmoniously. That means education all around and the development of confidence between white and colored leaders upon which to build the larger confidence of the rank and file of both races." [10]

That was League philosophy and it pursued it in its thirty-two locals and at the national level by pushing to organize more interracial Leagues in cities north and south to train more professionals to serve, in Charles S. Johnson's phrase, as midwives in the urban rebirth of the rural Negro. It did this and updated the NUL board and staff members through its combination institute and seminar known as the annual conference.

In this work it was not without criticism. In fact, some of the severest criticism came from one of its own, a young radical named Chandler Owen who had been one of the first NLUCAN Fellows. He studied at the School of Philanthropy and Columbia and worked with NLUCAN on investigations. Almost overnight, he became a national figure and a leading spokesman in the black community—much to the chagrin of his NLUCAN sponsors.

A half-generation after DuBois challenged Booker T. Washington, Owen and A. Philip Randolph challenged the new black establishment —including DuBois. Through the pages of a monthly magazine called *The Messenger* they advocated socialism and pacifism, attacked institutions and excoriated leaders for their inconsistency, timidity, stupidity and worse.

They blasted DuBois and *The Crisis* for urging in 1917 that blacks "close ranks" and fight the American battle during the war, putting aside the struggle for Negro rights for the interim. *The Messenger* denounced war profiteers such as the Morris brothers who overnight boosted their salaries from $25,000 to $75,000 per year, while their packing-house workers were eking out an existence on a few hundred annually. War and capitalism victimized the poor and helpless, said Owen and Randolph. They told Negroes they had good reasons to be pro-German (though anti-Kaiser), because they were treated as men in that country. For this editorial in the wartime hysteria of "100% Americanism," the editors were sentenced to jail for two and a half years.

Meanwhile, they shook up their elders. They called for new leadership for Negroes. They said that DuBois, Kelly Miller, William Pickens and James Weldon Johnson had simply held jobs, produced schoolboy rhetoric and lulled blacks into a false sense of security. George E. Haynes, Emmett J. Scott, Robert R. Moton, Fred R. Moore and T. Thomas Fortune, they charged, had preached the gospel of satisfaction and contentment. These leaders had demanded nothing during the war and therefore after it was won they had no claim on anyone, accused *The Messenger*.

"The Negro soldier is not asking for rhetoric and praise," Owen and Randolph editorialized. "He wants just and fair play—a chance to work with a decent wage, freedom from discrimination . . . protection of his life from lynching and his property from mob violence . . . the right to vote and education for his children. Leaders who have not the courage to demand these things are worthless." [11]

Attacking George Haynes's speech on the "Negro and National Reconstruction," *The Messenger* said, "The amazing lack of the slightest conception of the problems of reconstruction confirms the repeated charge . . . as to the ignorance of Negro leaders. If all which Mr. Haynes demands were granted, the Negro would be in no better condition than that in which he now is." [12]

Robert Russa Moton was, in *The Messenger's* view, a white man's Negro, put in charge of Tuskegee by the white industrialists who controlled Tuskegee. "Moton," they taunted, "has neither the courage, education or opportunity to do anything fundamental in the interest of the Negro. . . . There is a mortgage upon his mind and his brain is in pawn" to the Tuskegee trustee board of white capitalists.

As for the 1919 breakthrough in securing from the AFL both an endorsement of and announcement of organizing Negroes into its unions, *The Messenger* waved off as laughable the thought that the "old Fossils" —Moton, Moore, Archibald Grimke, Emmett Scott—had been responsible. No, said Owen and Randolph, it was the threatened withdrawal of tens of thousands of Negro workers from the AFL, the formation of the National Brotherhood Association (by Owen and Randolph) as a competitor to the AFL and *The Messenger's* editorial campaign that had forced the AFL to "come clean." [13]

The young editors roasted the Urban League movement in an article on "The Invisible Government of Social Work" in their December, 1920 issue. The work of the League secretaries in thirty-two cities, they said,

is largely the collection of scabs for the industrial magnates and capitalists . . . who finance the League. . . . [It] is more completely dominated by capital than any other organization among Negroes. It is the Booker

Washington's northern and western propaganda tool. It is the northern
clearinghouse of the Major Moton idea. It is the instrument of Wall Street.
. . . The Urban League is an organization of, for and by capital. . . . The
capitalist Urban League cannot represent the working class Negro race.

Suddenly, in *The Messenger* articles, there was an utterly irreverent
candor and radical advocacy speaking to a constituency of educated, dissatisfied blacks. The message was that the institutions were corrupt because they were controlled by whites, hopeless because they were run by
ignorant, aged or ill-trained blacks, and that accommodation and gradualism were doomed to fail. Radicalism and socialism and immediate,
uncompromising assault on the system were the only answers.

To the League, all this was very painful. After all, NLUCAN had
footed Chandler Owen's graduate-school expenses and made him a
League Fellow. NLUCAN had, it appeared, nourished a viper. Embar-
rassed, George Haynes wrote his friends at Columbia University that the
agency was tightening its screening of fellowship applicants even more.[14]

It was true that times had changed, the nation had changed and blacks
had changed. But the perspective of Owen and Randolph was not the
only one from which to observe these changes. Nor was it the only valid
perspective on the future of black citizens and the options open to them.

When one looks at race relations over the carnage of 1919, several promontories loom above the turbulence: First of all, blacks could not out-
fight the whites because they were hopelessly outgunned, outnumbered
and overwhelmingly handicapped because they had no industrial, financial, police or military power, and relatively little economic or political
weight. Therefore, all-out confrontation—race war—would be suicidal
and had to be avoided.

Race conflict might be avoided by making the black a doormat for
whites—returning him to slavery *de jure* or *de facto*—but this was obviously unacceptable to ten million blacks and patently impossible.

There appeared to be two remaining alternatives to conflict.

The first was interracial cooperation. In this, black Americans would
have to acquaint white leaders with actual conditions among blacks and
both would then press for genuine progress—that is, reduction of white
racism and centripetal movement along the continuum toward integration. Relatively few Americans were so outspoken as to suggest at that
time that no-holds-barred integration was the ultimate goal. Those who
did so were considered wild-eyed radicals or insane. Almost all black
leaders and organizations and interracial agencies advocated more côm-
plete integration of blacks into American life rather than revolution—the
destruction of the American system.

The second alternative was so ridiculous on the face of it that it could scarcely be mentioned seriously. It was separation of the races—a centrifugal movement of blacks away from the integration goal. In this alternative, the vain dream of inclusion in "white America" would be abandoned. Such a notion had usually been expressed in terms of colonization of blacks somewhere—anywhere but here—and had been rejected and derided by blacks. Then along came Marcus Garvey and he made plausible what had previously seemed absurd.

The first alternative, integration via gradualism and cooperation within the system, was pursued with varying degrees of vigor and pressure by almost all the black and interracial organizations and advocated by nearly all black spokesmen. The annual convention in 1919 of the "radical" NAACP called not for revolution in the face of shattering evidence of widespread and murderous white hostility but for eliminating bigotry, lynching and injustice to move black Americans further along that continuum toward the center, toward integration into the system and society.

Other black organizations echoed this stand. The 1919 meetings of the National Equal Rights League, the National Race Congress and others protested lynching and disfranchisement and the National Baptist Convention went on record favoring centripetal action—more integration of blacks in American life.

The NAACP's vigorous attack on denial of civil rights focused on lynching. It used propaganda, publications, politicking, prosecution and public meetings. The agency brought men such as Charles Evans Hughes to this cause, giving it the endorsement of enlightened white leadership of national prominence. The NAACP's documentation in *Thirty Years of Lynching in the United States, 1889–1918,* proved to be a revelation and gave a sound base for attack on the unspeakable horror. And the association scored notable successes in its civil rights drive when it won the Supreme Court's decision against the "grandfather" clauses, residential segregation, peonage in Arkansas and all-white primaries in the south.[15]

Supposedly at the opposite extreme from the NAACP, the "conservative" Urban League almost without exception aimed its programs and efforts at making middle-class Americans out of black peasants. To blacks only hours removed from the hard scrabble, the location of a bed, a meal, even clothing, housing and medical care and a job with no peonage strings, these were radical changes. The Urban League, which was the key to these changes, was therefore, a radical force in the lives of scores of thousands of city blacks.

The League was radical also to many whites, especially those in the south. The basic NUL concept was still that fundamental faith that the best blacks and whites counseling together could improve race relations.

The radical aspect of this to southern whites was the word *together*. In such circumstances it was a triumph every time whites and blacks were brought together in the same room (other than a courtroom) and this the League managed to do in thirty-two cities, north and south.[16]

17/A Change in Pilots

The exit from NUL of George Haynes left lean, handsome Eugene Kinckle Jones as undisputed master of the agency. Young Jones (age thirty-four at the time) was to remain on the League's quarterdeck for more than two decades and his character and leadership shaped NUL during those crucial years.

Jones was born into the black bourgeoisie. His parents were both educators, respected members of the black establishment in Richmond. Joseph Endom Jones, his father, was born in 1850 to a slave girl owned by Maurice Langhorne, member of one of Virginia's aristocratic families. (On a trip to Europe E. K. Jones called on Lady Astor, *née* Langhorne, who gleefully introduced him to Lord Astor as one of her "Virginia cousins.") Jones *père* was taught to read and write by an invalided Confederate soldier. He was educated at Hamilton Academy and graduated from Colgate in 1876, thus becoming one of the first college-educated blacks in the state of Virginia. (His northern education was underwritten as an experiment by Henry Bill, a bookbinder from Norwich, Connecticut, who, after visiting Civil War battlefields, met the youth and another youngster named R. R. Wright. Bill decided to send one to school in the north, the other in the south. Wright, consequently, was educated at Atlanta University and became an educator. He was for years president of Georgia State College at Savannah.) For forty-seven years the elder Jones taught at Richmond Theological Seminary (which later became Virginia Union University).[1]

Rosa Daniel Kinckle Jones, Eugene's mother, was born to free black parents, educated at private schools, Howard University and the New England Conservatory of Music. She taught music for forty years at Hartshorn Memorial College. Eugene was born in Richmond in 1885 and during his youth became aware of not only the race antagonism that blacks faced but an additional aspect that was particularly evident in that city. This was the resistance of black leaders to segregation, Jim Crow and disfranchisement. Richmond had many prominent blacks who actively promoted race pride, business ventures and political action. Jones's father, in fact, had led the successful fight for black teachers in the city's black public schools. Both Jones's parents served on mixed faculties and the white and black faculty members regularly dined together and visited in one anothers' homes. Such a milieu contributed to E. K. Jones's firm belief in the equality of men and the capacity of blacks to measure up to any racial type, given opportunity.

Jones completed his undergraduate work at Virginia Union, where he played on and managed the baseball and football teams. He followed this with two years at Cornell where he shifted from civil engineering to the social sciences, in which he earned the M.A. degree. In 1906, the year that Jones arrived at Cornell, Alpha Phi Alpha, the first black college fraternity, was organized there and he was its first initiate. The following year he became president and under his leadership the fraternity decided to go national. Jones personally organized the first two chapters in other colleges and the first graduate chapter. (By 1920 there were some twenty chapters and 1,500 members.)

It was from Cornell that the young man went to Louisville where from 1909 to 1911 he was instructor at that city's Central High School. He was classified as "general assistant" and was assigned to teach mechanical drawing. Jones voluntarily served as assistant to the football and baseball coach, trained the track team and refereed many college and school games in the area. He also organized a social study club among young business and professional men in the city. From this position at Central High Jones took a year's leave of absence and on a spring day in 1911 went to New York to serve as field secretary of CUCAN.

According to Jones (writing in his "Abridged Autobiography" about 1940) self-confidence was the factor in his life primarily responsible for his success. "No man," he asserted, "can succeed in any undertaking unless he has confidence in his own capacity and believes sincerely in the principles underlying the policies formulated for the work he is doing." Jones's personal social philosophy was based on the belief that man is an economic animal:

> Early in my career I was influenced by the argument made by Negrophobes that prejudice was based on people's belief that some races were inferior to others and therefore the inferior groups should be segregated for the protection of the so-called superior groups. As I began more carefully to study and to observe, I came to the conclusion that these racial and group prejudices were moulded to accommodate themselves to the desire of one group

to have economic advantage over another and that fundamentally people do not hate other people because they are of different color or possess different physical characteristics. . . . the only superiority that [a white] possesses is that which he shares physically with his group in its control of the powers of government and the forces of man.[2]

These were judgments shaped over the years. But in 1919 the NUL's new leader was brimming with optimism and foresaw a rosy future. "Now is the time for Negroes to come into their own in American life," he told a Baltimore audience in April, because:

1. Democracy is in the air;
2. Men are feeling an obligation towards their fellows and a responsibility in their needs;
3. America is offering a larger opportunity for all of its citizens;
4. Negroes have gained a foot-hold in industrial life and a larger knowledge of methods and plans by which their lives may be made sweeter and more attractive.[3]

Jones had reason to be optimistic. The League, by the spring of 1919, was a network of thirty affiliates in major cities.[4] It had played a tremendous role in acculturation of black migrants to the cities. NUL income had reached a peak of $35,000 (only four years before, Mrs. Baldwin had lamented that $15,000 seemed to be the ceiling), indicating considerable support for the agency's programs and accomplishments. Expansion seemed to be foredestined. One manpower expert (Colonel Arthur Wood, of the United States Army and former New York City police commissioner) estimated that American industry would require 7,000,000 men by the fall of 1919. This inevitably would mean vast new job opportunities for blacks.

It was in these apparently favorable circumstances that Jones enunciated a "Reconstruction Program for the Negro." [5] As a preamble to his "Program," Jones listed the *needs* as (1) education of blacks—in formal schooling, in acceptable behavior, dress and language, in cooperation and in taking a longer view of things; (2) education of whites in fairer attitude toward blacks and to the contributions blacks have made and will make if given half a chance; (3) opportunities for blacks to work wherever they can "fill the bill"; to live in decent homes; to think as free men and speak openly without fear; to prepare for more difficult and intricate tasks.

Jones went on to stress that it was imperative that blacks hold the ground gained during the war, such as their broader distribution and widened industrial horizon—through more and better jobs, and training received in the military.

"Any reconstruction program for the Negro," stated Jones, "in addition to the work of consolidation of positions gained as suggested above must include forward steps." Those he recommended were, first and foremost, continuation of the Bureau of Negro Economics with its state and local advisory committees·and its cooperation with local organizations such as the League, YW and YMCA's, and the job placement duty by the United States Employment Service. Jones wanted George Haynes's operation in the United States Labor Department to expand its activities to include investigation of industrial conditions and to take in the distribution of labor within the various states.

Next Jones called for formation of a "national council" composed of two representatives from each of the agencies active in welfare work among blacks—the YMCA, YWCA, NAACP, churches and, of course, NUL. This council would meet annually (later he suggested more frequent meetings) "to compare programs and agree on terms of cooperation and coordination." Several times during the year Jones repeated this proposal, but apparently it received a chilly reception and he abandoned it.

At the local level Jones insisted that existing agencies include blacks in their programs both as "clients" and as staff members, that special services be established to get jobs for black veterans, that intensive health campaigns be conducted using New York's experiment as a model and that a national health organization be set up for this purpose. Further, he insisted that black accomplishments be publicized, that the "good of the race rather than the evils" receive emphasis.

In addition to the machinery in hand to carry forward such programs Jones listed several elements as necessary. Among these were: (1) National industrial workers (to coordinate the activities of the black industrial welfare workers and encourage appointment of more of them). (2) A national group to organize workingmen by vocations—that is, to bring them together for their protection and to secure higher wages and better working conditions. (Among the groups he cited as prime prospects for such organization were the dining car waiters, Pullman porters, hotel waiters, unskilled and domestic workers. They should, he counseled, "dicker with employers and union labor alike" and not .affiliate directly with the AFL unless assured proper treatment.) (3) A department of investigations to examine conditions of city life.[6]

Though he did not state it in so many words, apparently Jones had in mind that NUL would play significant roles in these matters. His own priorities for the agency were outlined in a presentation he made to the League's Steering Committee at the end of March 1919. It proved to be the pattern for major expansion of the agency:

We are now at the point in the development of the work . . . where we must make definite steps forward in order to accomplish the great results for the colored people and for America that an organization such as ours can bring about. We must not forget that this is the first time in our history that an organization interested purely in welfare matters has been able, in a national way, concentrating its efforts purely on the questions affecting Negro life, to gain the attention of a large number of trained social workers and of persons interested in forward movements. . . . The following is my suggestion for an immediate forward step, and we plan to engage at the earliest possible date, the following workers in their order:

1. Southern Field Organizer—duties obvious—to organize cities in the south and to keep them up to the League standard;

2. A Western Field Organizer—which means releasing Mr. Hill for full time on the field.

3. An Industrial Field Worker, preferably John T. Clark of Pittsburgh, this requiring us to find another man for Pittsburgh; Mr. Clark to give his full time primarily to mapping out a standardized program for local organizations, and working with large industrial plants not located in cities where affiliated organizations of the League exist. Also to conduct a campaign among Negroes to secure an interest in trade-training and other preparation for life work.

4. Educational Secretary to carry out the plans of the Educational committee for without trained social workers, as it were on "tap" to be assigned to fields as vacancies occur and as positions are created, it would not be possible for us to accomplish very much no matter how many fields we organize.[7]

Jones wanted a fifth member for this new team. This was to be a "financial agent," actually a fund-raiser, who would be a speaker of "national reputation, capable of presenting our cause well before both white and colored audience [s]." The man would have the burden of raising some $15,000 to $18,000 beyond the current League budget, in order to finance the additional work proposed. Kinckle Jones already had his candidate for this job—Dean William Pickens of Morgan State College. "We could arrange to employ each person as the money to guarantee his salary and expenses is assured, starting off on a long chance, of course, by employing the financial agent with an appropriate title." [8]

As it turned out, the League did not hire Pickens. (He went to the NAACP soon after.) And less than three months later, in mid-1919 Jones had refigured the costs involved in this expansion. He told the executive board:

We are failing during this period of wonderful opportunity, to prepare the Negro mind from a national viewpoint, for the big industrial chance that is before him in the "NEW ERA." This work should be done by a national industrial secretary "a northern organizer and a southern field organizer." Twenty thousand dollars (20,000) in addition to the funds that we can reasonably raise would do the trick. Considering the job, this is a small amount of money and it is certainly in America, and at our disposal if we can bring our plans forcefully to the attention of the philanthropically inclined.[9]

In his conclusions Jones was correct: He had placed a bargain price tag on the jobs to be done and there certainly was $20,000 of philanthropic money available in America. However, as he noted, the problem was to bring NUL plans forcefully to the attention of the philanthropists. This was not done and the money was not forthcoming. Consquently Jones had to be satisfied' with continuing the western field operation as a part-time activity of T. Arnold Hill; hiring a southern field organizer and reestablishing the southern field office in the hope that it would somehow be self-sufficient (Jones purposely selected a man known for his fund-raising ability for this post); hiring an educational secretary, Alexander L. Jackson, to replace George Haynes, thanks to an extraordinary grant for the purpose from a wealthy white sponsor of the young black who was hired.

As the American economy turned sour in the waning days of the year the projected industrial shortage of black workers rapidly became a surplus. Workers were laid off their jobs, country-wide, blacks above all. With this employment shrinkage and the uncertainties it forecast went the hopes of E. K. Jones for an industrial field worker. The major achievements in Jones's 1919 program were, then, the addition of the educational secretary (which we shall examine later) and the re-establishment of operations in the south after a lapse of more than a year.

The League board and staff knew well that the bulk of the black population still lived in the south and believed that part of its responsibility as a national agency was improving the existence of blacks in the cities of the region. Though it remained the most difficult of fields for League expansion it could not be abandoned. E. K. Jones was anxious to put someone on the job in the south. He found his man in 1919 in New York.

The candidate had a strong record: He was a Mississippi country boy, from Pike County where the subsistence level of white and black sharecroppers alike caused common interests to supersede racial antagonisms. He had slipped away from home at fourteen and worked in a sawmill. He had learned about Tuskegee and had saved his money to enter it. Clad in a flashy Rampart Street suit, sporting a genuine Panama hat bought for the occasion and smoking a Cremo cigar, he had driven up to the commandant's office one Sunday afternoon to apply for admission. He learned almost immediately that this was a prize gaff—Tuskegee was a highly religious community; smoking was *verboten;* students wore simple uniforms and the splendiferous attire of young Jesse O. Thomas marked him as a "city slicker," not the humble, diligent Tuskegee product. Flamboyance and aplomb were characteristic of Thomas, and his innate jauntiness and gift of gab carried him through this emergency and later ones.[10]

Thomas was accepted at Tuskegee, excelled in organizing and public speaking and impressed Booker T. Washington. Upon graduation from the institute, Thomas, then twenty-six, was appointed a field secretary for Tuskegee with headquarters in Rochester, New York. From this outpost he covered New York and western Pennsylvania, calling on white philanthropists and soliciting contributions in church meetings—both white and colored. He managed in his first year on the job to raise more money for Tuskegee than any other field man for the institute. It was a job he enjoyed, for he relished meeting people and the interplay of discussion. The entrée to the "upper crust"—both black and white—were his through the magic of Booker T. Washington's name and the Tuskegee cause.

In 1918, Thomas became one of George Haynes's associates as supervisor of Negro Economics for the state of New York, with his headquarters in New York City. In this job he worked closely with NLUCAN staff and even had his office in the League's Harlem building. The major function of the work was finding and placing men and women in essential jobs and to advance this Thomas established advisory interracial committees in nearly every industrial community of the state.

When the Division of Negro Economics folded in 1919, E. K. Jones hired Thomas as NLUCAN's southern field secretary.

The decision was made at this time to re-establish the southern field office not at Nashville, but Atlanta. When Thomas went to Atlanta in the fall of 1919 to set up shop, the divorce from George Haynes's operation at Nashville was completed. It had begun the summer of 1918, when Hollingsworth Wood had visited the president of Fisk and first pared to the bone NLUCAN's contribution to Fisk and the support of Haynes's assistant. (This was cut altogether in 1919.) With the move of southern operations to Atlanta, George Haynes's duties had been taken over and his patient nurturing of an educational center to serve as a pattern had been superseded by the E. K. Jones "New York model." Through this model, an efficient League program would provide the pattern for other cities with similar problems.

Jesse O. Thomas was a "new breed of Urban League cat." He was ebullient, was as self-confident as a tank and radiated enthusiasm, in contrast to the scholarly Haynes and reserved, quite correct E. K. Jones. Yet,

Thomas's different approach produced no miracles in the organizing of southern cities. In fact, E. K. Jones was impatient with him in 1921, although the southern field secretary could claim new or reconstituted local Leagues in Sumter, Birmingham, Richmond, Atlanta, Savannah and Albany, Georgia, and a hand in establishment of the Atlanta School of Social Work by that time. Thomas was traveling extensively to the colleges, churches, clubs and institutions of the south making speeches and racking up considerable transportation expenses. To Jones the results seemed meager:

> . . . I remember that you made a trip of this kind to Denmark [South Carolina] last year and we have seen no results so far as the Urban League work is concerned. You also went to Tuskegee at our expense to deliver a Class-Day address. I think that it is about time for us to be observing some actual Urban Leagues in some of the cities which you are visiting from time to time. It would be much better to concentrate on a few visits to one place than individual visits to a number of places with no apparent results so far as this organization is concerned.[11]

For his part, Thomas, with all his drive and energy, had an understanding of his Herculean task that gave him inner strength. In 1922 he reported to Jones about the demise of the New Orleans Civic League. The labor situation, Thomas wrote, had materially changed the attitude of whites in that city.

> Two or three years ago when Negroes were still going north the anxiety of the white man made it possible to get the cooperation of white groups in seeking to improve the conditions of the Negroes in a very much larger measure than is true today. Organization work in the south is going to be very slow as long as there is as much unemployment, that is general throughout the south at the present time. While this is the time we need social welfare work more than ever, it is nevertheless more difficult to get it established. The Negro is feeling especially poor because of unemployment and its kindred effects. The white man . . . feels that the Negro is compelled by circumstances to remain in the south at the present time. . . .
> A good deal of our work in the south has got to be that of the creating atmosphere for social work . . . program or propaganda must be directed toward both groups, white and colored. The white man has little or no conception of the social needs of Negroes and Negroes in this section of the country are getting, in many cases, their first conception of organized social welfare work. When you realize that this side of the Potomac River there is just one modern YMCA building and not a single YWCA building for colored people you appreciate how much of a problem it is to get an atmosphere created for social welfare work.[12]

E. K. Jones understood. Though temperamentally poles distant from his southern field secretary and exasperated frequently by Thomas's dramatic approaches, Jones developed a great fondness for the man he called the most colorful Urban Leaguer. Jones admired Thomas's agility and courage in working within and frequently beating "the system" in the south.[13]

Jesse Thomas's whole approach was different from the general tenor of NLUCAN staff members in the early days. He delighted in tackling the tough erstwhile contributors—persons who easily could and should have supported the League because of their profit from Negro customers. He saw his responsibility as including the burden of raising the budget for new Leagues for their first couple of years, until they could demonstrate their worth and be accepted into the local Community Chest. And in this fund-raising he was generally successful. E. K. Jones gave Thomas credit for bringing in some $3,000 to $4,000 annually to NLUCAN coffers from wealthy donors.

Thomas's first task in Atlanta was to set up a southern advisory board. By March 1920 he had thirty-nine members on this board, many of them widely known in the south, some of them nationally. Chairman of the board was James H. Dillard; there were seven vice chairmen, including R. R. Moton and F. A. McKenzie, president of Fisk. Mary McLeod Bethune was assistant secretary. The ten-member executive committee included Moton as chairman, Governor Thomas W. Bickett of North Carolina and Will W. Alexander, director of the Commission on Interracial Cooperation. Some other board members were John Hope, Mrs. B. B. Mumford, Bruce R. Payne, and Mrs. Booker T. Washington, all NLUCAN Board members as well.

Though the League had established its regional headquarters in Atlanta for the south, headed by a southern black (Thomas) and with an advisory committee of distinguished white and black citizens of the region, there were eruptions from the yahoos. After Thomas had (he thought) brought about the formation of a local League in Jacksonville through the painful, time-consuming process of collecting a board of directors, outlining an agreed-upon program and settling on a budget so that the organization could be launched, he received a frantic wire from that Florida city. Arriving, he learned that a crisis threatened the formation of the local League. Some white board members had discovered that NUL headquarters were in New York and they were frightened that whites in Jacksonville would charge them with being tools of northerners. They wanted to know if the local League could be called the Negro Welfare League. Disgusted, Thomas told them they could change the name to "the Jacksonville Sunday School Union" if they wanted to, so long as they carried out the program.[14] It was some fifteen years before the Jacksonville League adopted the standard Urban League name.

Community Chest acceptance of the local Leagues was extremely important. Without inclusion in the annual fund drive for Community Chest agencies, the Leagues had an uphill battle for dollars, recognition and effective operation with other social agencies and governmental units. Even when the local League proved its worth by conducting a vital program and demonstrated the degree of support from the black community and concerned whites, it still was subject to pressures that made its existence precarious. League policy of hiring professionals to head local Leagues generally kept them from criticism on the score of competence. But there were other pressure points.

In Tampa, for example, Benjamin E. Mays was the executive. He wrote an article for the local black newspaper criticizing the Jim Crow seating used for a special program presented by black high school students. The balcony, reserved for blacks, was jammed, and people could not even get in to stand, while the orchestra, reserved for whites, was sparsely occupied. Mays's article was headlined "It Costs Too Much in Terms of Manhood and Womanhood." Before sending it in for publication he had the foresight to read it to the ministers' alliance, of which he was a member, and it was approved unanimously.

When the newspaper came out the article created a sensation. The black supervisor of schools took it as a personal attack; the white school officials saw it as dangerous outspokenness. To this negative view of Mays was added the fact that his wife, a caseworker, addressed her black clients as Miss, Mr. or Mrs. and Mays, when reporting on his wife's work at League board meetings, referred to her as Mrs. Mays. One day Mays drove into a gasoline station and the attendant greeted him with, "What can I do for you, boy?" Mays immediately backed up and drove away, boiling mad. He wrote a hot letter to the filling station manager protesting the treatment, which he described. The manager sent Mays's letter with a message of his own to the Community Chest, complaining about the Urban Leaguer's behavior.

The executive secretary of the Community Chest wired Jesse Thomas to come to Tampa at once. He did, and attended a special meeting that included the Community Chest executive, its president (who also was president of the local Bell Telephone Company) and the superintendent of schools. The indictment against Mays was detailed, and he was damned for his "unorthodox" behavior which, the Community Chest people contended, unfitted him for the position of executive of a Chest agency. They had decided that Mays must go.

Thomas countered by citing the support of the ministers' alliance and a majority vote of the Urban League board backing Mays's criticism of Jim Crow. He took up the matter of the gas station incident, noting that even if Mays had not had degrees from three colleges, he was entitled to civil treatment simply because he was an adult citizen. Therefore, Thomas said, he would take no official cognizance of the conduct of the League executive. On that note the meeting adjourned and Mays continued in charge of the local League.[15] Years later Mays became president of Morehouse College in Atlanta and a member of the board of the National Urban League.

18/The Spread of Information

The major direction taken by NUL in the twenties was to institutionalize its fact-gathering, its interpretation and information and its industrial relations. The agency continued to organize new Leagues and it coordinated and advised the local League operations in major cities through staff visits, conferences and get-togethers at National Conference of Social Work annual forums.

The purpose and programs of the agency were not evident to persons who casually came upon the name Urban League in those days. When revision of the NLUCAN constitution was discussed in 1919 the changes sailed through the board without incident. But the matter of a name change for the organization produced lengthy debate. Someone proposed that it might better be called "the Baldwin League," in honor of Mr. and Mrs. William H. Baldwin, Jr. Mrs. Baldwin, who was present, "promptly squelched the idea. She wanted immediately to make it clear that her interest in the movement was entirely impersonal," reported E. K. Jones. Others agreed that to name it after an individual could leave the impression that the agency was getting its main support from that family.[1]

The objections to the name Urban League centered on its nondescriptiveness. Yet, there was consensus that no name should be adopted that could lead people to believe that the membership was of one race. Names such as National Negro League or National League for Negroes were, therefore, out. Finally, the board agreed on "National Urban League" as the easiest and most memorable of the titles proposed and this was adopted as the legal and official title on February 4, 1920. It was also decided that the phrase "for social service among Negroes" should be linked with the official title wherever possible.[2]

With that monumental matter decided, the agency could then proceed unhindered about somewhat more pressing tasks. One of these was to keep ahead of the local Leagues and the other agencies, public and private, schools and fact-consuming institutes or associations, that were in need of solid information about American blacks. The League was not a census bureau or a bureau of labor statistics, but it did have unique access to the centers of the nation where the change in status of blacks was happening fastest. The League naturally looked at the business of assembling facts about black urban life as its chosen province. After all, the organization had been conceived, so to speak, through research efforts that documented a need for it. And this pattern of study and response had guided the League from the first.

From the early days of the Committee for Improving the Industrial Conditions of Negroes in New York many industrialists and financiers had given small contributions to that agency and the NLUCAN which succeeded it. E. K. Jones, as part of his fund-raising efforts, annually called on Andrew Carnegie at his mansion at 91st Street and Fifth Avenue and was regularly turned aside by Carnegie's "man." Every year Jones would make a scatter-shot appeal to the Carnegie Corporation of New York (a philanthropic foundation set up by Andrew Carnegie) for support, only to be turned down.

There was a change at the top of the Carnegie Corporation of New York in 1920. Dr. James Rowland Angell of the University of Chicago became its president. E. K. Jones looked into Angell's background and found that he was interested in human progress and its measurement through recorded social data. He thereupon drew up a proposal that the Carnegie Corporation underwrite the establishment of a department of research and investigation for the League. This department, Jones said, would supply expert services to local Leagues and agencies and cities working on problems among blacks. It would also conduct the research basic to establishing new Leagues and supply facts about blacks for the use of writers and lecturers on "the Negro question, thus guaranteeing that the American public will receive authentic and reliable data on the Negro. We in time would accumulate sufficient facts to serve as gauges of Negro progress in America."[3]

Jones noted the interest of Dr. Angell's brother, federal Judge Alexis Caswell Angell, in the formation of the Detroit League, the fact that Dr. Angell's colleague at Chicago, Professor Robert E. Park, was head of the Chicago League, and that Charles S. Johnson, a Park protegé who was the Chicago League's director of research, was to head NUL's Research and Investigations Department. The price tag for this function was put at $8,800 per year, and Jones requested financing for three years "as an experiment." [4] This appeal to the foundation struck paydirt. The Carnegie Corporation gave $8,000 per year for a three-year period. NUL's Research and Investigations Department was established and Charles S. Johnson moved to New York to head it.

Johnson's approach to his job was far broader than that of a technician alone (though he was highly skilled in methodology). Research, as indicated in the outline for the Chicago research department, covered far more than simply statistics. Research had a job to do, believed Johnson, that was fundamental to "solving" the race problem. As he saw it, observers, regardless of their intentions, were often blinded by preconceived theories or notions which caused them to overlook factual contradictions and stimulated hallucinations to support their theories.

> This body of beliefs compounded of this mixture of truth and fiction, self-interest and passion, forms the structure of public opinion on the question of the Negro. These beliefs unchallenged not only magnify themselves and breed others, but react upon the Negro group, distorting its conduct. This distortion provokes in turn a sterner application of these beliefs and so on indefinitely, and with each step the isolation increases, each group building up its own myths and stiffening its own group morale. If the myths can be dissolved, if indeed the beliefs can be honestly questioned, many of our inhibitions to normal, rational and ethical conduct will be removed.[5]

With this view of interracial conditions, Johnson inevitably looked to research to provide ammunition to destroy the myths and, furthermore, he wanted to develop ways of getting the findings out of the files and into the hands and minds of people who could act upon them.

Charles Johnson, from 1922 on, made the League's Department of Research and Investigation a fundamental source for statistics and information about black Americans. He had the scholar's eye for the significant and knowledge of where to seek information that, in one way or another, was important to the living conditions of Afro-Americans. Under his direction the NUL Research Department was a repository for studies made by local Leagues, Urban League Fellows, other social workers and social scientists.

Meanwhile, Johnson undertook studies on behalf of the NUL. At the invitation of local Community Chests or interracial committees, Johnson studied communities in Hartford, New London, and Waterbury, Connecticut; Baltimore, Maryland; Morristown, Plainfield and Trenton, New Jersey; Akron, Ohio; and Westchester County, New York. In Hartford, 65 percent of the black population was covered in the research. In Baltimore, the focus was on industrial conditions and jobs for Afro-Americans. These studies were trailblazing events for the communities because they revealed, often for the first time, the actual conditions within the black community and the specific points that were most sensitive between the races—from the standpoint of Afro-Americans themselves. Equipped with a bill of particulars developed by the survey a local community could set its course. Many cities moved to organize local Leagues as a result.

There were urgent reasons for these surveys. One reason, strangely enough, was the success of the Community Chest movement, with its emphasis on responsible, planned social services financed by a federated campaign once a year. As Jesse O. Thomas observed, "With the coming of the Community Chest movement into operation in most southern cities the effort in organizing a welfare program among colored people has been made more difficult." [6] He explained:

> In the first place, no southern city consistently raises the amount of money necessary for the agencies already participating . . . the effort to establish a local Urban League encounters opposition frequently and very often a development akin to discouragement on the part of Chest officials. The second consideration that one faces is the amount that Negroes contribute from year to year on the basis of their obvious financial ability. . . . Negroes in Atlanta subscribe around $5,000 and pay between $2,600 and $2,900. On this account you cannot use the potential financial response of the Negroes to have Chest officials include a new agency for their special benefit in the schedule. . . . Therefore the effort to have surveys made as a means of graphically contrasting the service rendered the general population with that rendered to Negroes is most desirable and most fruitful. As a matter of fact it is fast becoming the only weapon that can be used effectively in getting Negroes in.[7]

The major research effort of the NUL Research Department under Johnson was the most comprehensive study of *Negro Membership in American Labor Unions* (published under that title in 1930) since the *Atlanta University Studies* in 1902 and 1912 and Charles Wesley's 1927 *History of Negro Labor in the United States*.[8] The project was made possible by a special grant from the American Fund for Public Service. The scope of the job was impressive. It covered the national, international, federated and local unions, independent black unions, the experience of black workers in selected cities with unions, strikes and organized labor. Category by category the study looked at the experience of black workers in the various trades and major divisions of the labor movement.

By 1926 Johnson had in hand some of the returns, and was able to give a preliminary report of progress on the study. However, it was not until 1928 that enough data were in hand to do an exhaustive treatment of the subject. At this point, Dr. Johnson moved on to Fisk, and was succeeded by a former League Fellow, sociologist Ira deA. Reid. It was Reid who put the report in final form and saw it through the throes of publication.

The 175-page volume, in Reid's words, enabled one "to obtain a fair estimate of the status of the Negro worker in the American Labor movement . . . [and] to present a picture of the method by which Negro workers have entered labor unions, the exclusion policies of national bodies, the types of union membership, the extent to which Negro workers are organized, and their experiences within and without the union." [9]

The result was devastating. It showed that "the Negro is yet on the fringe of America's industrial life. He continues to be the marginal worker. . . . He remains, however, the ominous threat to American labor." [10] By this Reid meant that unless they were welcomed into the unions, blacks would, by strike-breaking or organizing their own competitive unions, exert collective pressure on unions that excluded them. The report gave chapter and verse on the experiences of black men with organized labor. The study would, it was hoped, provide the League with ammunition to blast a way into the ranks of organized labor for black workers.

But research alone was not enough. It was because of the larger needs that Charles S. Johnson not only conducted research but found himself, in December 1921, editing the first regular publication designed to reach the League "family" and the "outside world" as well: *The Urban League Bulletin*. The League executives at the 1921 NUL conference had practically demanded that some regular information bulletin be circulated by the national office to keep them informed of conditions and programs.

The first *Bulletin* showed evidence of Johnson's skill as an editor as well as an "information processor." Johnson brought together data from government and Urban League sources to review the current status of the Depression. He quoted government estimates that there were about half a million blacks unemployed in the nation, then gave figures for Chicago, New York, St. Louis and Louisville that showed 46,000 unemployed in those four cities alone. "The Chicago office is now so swamped with clerical routine as a result of the crush of applicants for jobs that registration has been suspended on all but special workers," he noted. In New York, the local League was emphasizing its industrial program for boys and girls and reported that there had been a drop in wages of up to 40 percent and "a marked decrease in the number of calls for skilled and factory workers, leaving domestic service as practically the only opportunity for workers." [11]

Johnson devoted a section to "Special Studies and Statistics of the Negro" covering survey results from various Leagues, and a section on industrial relations in which significant speeches from the NUL annual conference were reprinted. Pertinent articles on migration and reports on conditions, such as the packing-house strike in Chicago, were reprinted also; in a general clearing-house section news of local Leagues was featured; and a grouping of news notes of interest to social workers was included. The first issue totaled twelve pages.

The *Bulletin* was published bimonthly throughout 1922, and it became the vehicle for carrying NUL's annual report, strong editorial statements by Johnson on current situations, and information on current books and articles and events of importance to the race.

The *Bulletin* was clean-cut, full of useful information and stimulated much favorable response. But in the view of some Urban Leaguers, it was only a step toward an even larger goal. The leading spokesman for this stand was John T. Clark, then executive of the Pittsburgh League. "At every annual conference held by the National Urban League," recalled Kinckle Jones, "John T. Clark made his appeal for an official organ. . . . Members of the organization listened patiently and finally . . . the *Urban League Bulletin* . . . made its appearance. But this did not satisfy John. He still demanded a more formal publication—with advertisements and second class mailing privileges. By the time of the National Urban League Conference in Pittsburgh, October, 1922, sufficient interest in a magazine had crystallized to forecast the early publication of an official organ under Urban League aegis. So on January 19, 1923, *Opportunity: Journal of Negro Life,* made its first appearance."

The magazine's name came from the NUL slogan, "Not Alms, but Opportunity," and Charles S. Johnson was its editor. Its purpose, he stated, was "to present, objectively, facts of Negro life. It hopes thru an analysis of . . . social questions to provide a basis of understanding; encourage interracial cooperation in the working out of these problems, especially those surrounding the emergence of the Negro into a new industrial field and the consequent reorganization of habit and skill." [12]

But, most significantly, Johnson added a new dimension to the magazine beyond its attention to factual reporting. He took it into the realm of the arts. "There are aspects of the cultural side of Negro life that have been long neglected. There are facts of Negro progress as well as handicaps that should be known not only for the stimulation which comes from recognition but as an antidote to a disposition not infrequently encountered to disparage unjustly the capacities and aspirations of this group." [13]

With Abram L. Harris as *Opportunity*'s business manager, Johnson put together a thirty-two-page first issue that featured articles, book reviews, abstracts, pictures and reports on local Leagues. In that first issue the articles covered a range of topics: child placement (by Edith Sampson of the Illinois Children's Home and Aid Society); zoning plans and their relation to Negro housing by a member of the Chicago Zoning Commission; social work in the south (by Jesse O. Thomas); social work in the church (by A. Clayton Powell); the American Negro and the world-wide color conflict (by the Reverend S. Parkes Cadman of Brooklyn's Central Congregational Church); the doctrine of human equality (by Horace J. Bridges); and two articles on Negro labor in the industries by the personnel managers of Westinghouse Electric and the National Malleable and Iron Castings Company.

Before the year was out, *Opportunity* had attracted the work of some of the leading black writers of the day, providing them with a welcome outlet. Among those featured during that first year were Gwendolyn Bennett, Countee Cullen, Abram L. Harris, Alain Locke, Kelly Miller, Robert R. Moton, C. C. Spaulding, Eric Waldron, Monroe Work and William Leo Hansberry. As its monthly issues came out, *Opportunity* stirred up increasingly enthusiastic responses among those interested in literature and quickly became a focal point for creative writing. Langston Hughes's seven-line poem, "The White Ones," was published in the March 1924 issue. In May 1924, in *Opportunity*'s African Art issue, Carl Van Doren lauded the literary talents of the new crop of black writers who were coming to light through the magazine's pages. In that same issue Claude McKay and Lewis G. Alexander had several works.

Down this bright, unanticipated avenue of cultural flowering *Opportunity* raced, pacing the development of black artists in what came to be known as "The Negro Renaissance." It offered its pages and its help, it brought the works of these talented people to a nationwide black audience and also to a widening audience of interested whites. In 1924 the first *Opportunity* Literary Prize Contest awards were offered in the fields of short story, poetry, plays, essays and personal experience sketches, thanks to a gift from board member Mrs. Henry Goddard Leach.

In contrast to the seven entries in the NLUCAN's short-lived essay contest in 1913, there were 732 entries in this literary event. The judges were some of the best-known whites and then little-known but highly qualified blacks. Among them were Carl Van Doren, Zona Gale, Fannie Hurst, Dorothy Canfield Fisher, Alain Locke, Witter Bynner, James Weldon Johnson, Van Wyck Brooks, Alexander Woolcott, and Robert Benchley.

The entries were richly varied, and from the prizewinners rose new stars in the literary firmament, such as John Matheus, Zora Neale Hurston, Eric Waldron, John Davis, Langston Hughes, E. Franklin Frazier.

After the *Opportunity* Awards dinner presentations, the New York *Herald-Tribune* editorialized:

> The significant thing in all this . . . is not that people with more or less Negro blood can write . . . but that these American Negroes are expressing for the most part essentially Negro feelings and standing on their racial inheritance.
>
> These young people—and youth was another striking thing about this gathering—were not trying to imitate the white man nor repeating the professional white story-teller's dreary stencils of the "darkey." They were expressing their own feelings, frankly and uanbashed, even if it took them back to the jungle. . . . A novel sight that dinner—white critics, whom "everybody" knows, Negro writers whom "nobody" knew—meeting on common ground. The movement behind it doubtless means something to the race problem in general; certainly it means something to American literature. . . And it would be one of fate's quaint but by no means impossible revenges if the Negro's real contribution to American life should be in the field of art.[14]

Underwritten by $1,000 in prize money from a black New York businessman named Casper Holstein, *Opportunity* expanded its contest in 1925, adding the categories of musical compositions, constructive journalism and a special Alexander Pushkin poetry prize. Among the judges in the second contest, which drew almost 1,300 entries, were William Rose Benét, William Stanley Braithwaite, Robert Frost, Vachel Lindsay, David Belasco, Paul Robeson, Benjamin Brawley, Frank Damrosch, David Mannes, John Hope and Emmett Scott. Among the winners (in addition to those who had scored in the previous contest) were Arthur Huff Fauset, Dorothy West, Lee Wallace, Eugene Gordon, Claude McKay, Waring Cuney, L. Ariel Williams, Joseph S. Cotter, Frank Horne, F. H. Wilson, May Miller, Warren A. McDonald, Miles Mark Fisher, Anita Scott Coleman, Edmund T. Jenkins, Hall Johnson, Arna Bontemps and, for editorials, the New York *Age* and the *Amsterdam News.*

In 1927 the contests were repeated, thanks to another $1,000 from Casper Holstein. Five more awards were added through a gift from George W. Buckner, former executive of the East St. Louis League and by this time a highly successful black businessman in St. Louis. Art was a new category in this year, and it brought to the fore artists Aaron Douglas, Allan Freelon, Antonio Jarvis and Richard Bruce.

In addition to the concentration of literary work that fell into the *Opportunity* contest category and was published in the contest issues, the magazine was an ever-hospitable showcase for the work of the black writers and artists it helped develop. Some who were in the midst of the extraordinary flowering of black culture in Harlem at this time applaud *Opportunity* for its part in that development, even attributing the "Negro Renaissance" to the magazine.[15]

At this point in time there was an expanding interest in the black past. E. K. Jones fed it and drew upon it in his speeches and editor Johnson promoted it with articles in *Opportunity*. The League interest converged with the remarkable achievement of scholar Arthur Alfonso Schomburg. Schomburg, employee of a large New York bank, had been born and educated in Puerto Rico. His parents were black Puerto Ricans. One of his early teachers had commented that blacks had no history. Fired by this assertion, Schomburg became obsessed with disproving it and spent the rest of his life searching the bookstores of major cities of the world for evidence. In this he was a pioneer and amassed an unrivaled collection of priceless books, documents, art and artifacts from, by and about blacks throughout the ages, to establish beyond question that there was a glorious black history.

In 1926 this superb collection was offered by Schomburg to the NUL. However the agency had neither the facilities nor staff to do justice to it. Therefore Charles S. Johnson and Kinckle Jones with Hollingsworth Wood worked out a plan for purchase of the collection by the Carnegie Corporation of New York. Schomburg's collection was presented to the New York Public Library's Division of Negro Literature, History and Prints which had been opened in 1925 in Harlem. The Carnegie Corporation paid $10,000—only a tiny fraction of its market value—and a few years later made an additional gift that enabled the library to hire Schomburg as curator. He held this position until his death in 1938.

Thus the magnificent Schomburg Collection was secured for the enjoyment and use of the world's largest black community—Harlem—and for serious scholars of black history. The collection has served as a fundamental resource over the years. It has fulfilled its original purpose which was, to paraphrase Schomburg, to bring together materials to help blacks develop a group tradition to compensate for persecution and to give pride of race as an antidote for prejudice. "History must restore what slavery took away," he said, "for it is the social damage of slavery that the present generations must repair and offset." [16]

Though history had its place, and a featured one, in *Opportunity*, editor Johnson did not neglect the other areas of concern for which the magazine had been fashioned. In its pages appeared the latest findings of experts in health, housing, sociology, anthropology, economics and many other disciplines as they looked at black men. Through *Opportunity* readers became acquainted with African culture and the views of black men of other nationalities, as well as the condition, history and projected future of American blacks. And, of course, nowhere else was there any coverage to compare with *Opportunity*'s reportage of the social needs and social services to Afro-Americans.

Editor Johnson's point of departure was decidedly different from that of editor DuBois of *The Crisis* and purposely so. Johnson's editorial philosophy delineated the differences:

> It [*Opportunity*] has tried to assemble in its columns the best minds this country will yield in its dispassionate assault upon the traditional errors of our tangled relations, in its equally dispassionate quest for truth, and in its revelation of the negative aspects of Negro life. Its policy has been intelligent discussion rather than fireworks; of calm analysis rather than tears. The race has been spared the morbid spectacle of eternal crucifixion on a billboard; it has capitulated to no wrong, or vanity, or arrogance. Its shibboleth has been facts—facts useful, incisive, stimulating. These carry their own light.[17]

There was a change in 1928 when Charles Johnson stepped down as editor and left the League to become professor of sociology at Fisk University. His successor was Elmer A. Carter, who had experience as a former League executive in three cities, Columbus, Louisville and St. Paul, and had worked for Robert S. Abbott's Chicago *Defender*. Editor Carter, when he took over in October 1928, wrote:

> Slowly but surely the idea of interracial cooperation . . . becomes the accepted approach to the so-called race problem. *Opportunity* must make that idea articulate by presenting to the intelligent minority a new picture of the Negro. . . . But before the new picture can be completed, an old picture must be destroyed—a picture which is framed in facts—a picture which was framed in conjecture and myth and designed in antagonism and bitterness. It is the purpose of the Urban League to obliterate the outlines of that picture by the delineation of the new picture through the pages of *Opportunity*.[18]

Carter made changes in the magazine. Where Johnson had marshaled the forces of research and brought them to bear on the injustices visited on blacks—his scientific attack on the validity of the intelligence quotient as a measuring device was a classic case—and used the pages of *Opportunity* to propel black talent into the American cultural scene, Carter's editorship produced a different product. *Opportunity* continued to be the organ of the Urban League and of social work among blacks; it continued to showcase Afro-American talent; and it continued to print the significant articles on sociology, economics, health and so on. But the thrust of the Negro Renaissance dispersed under the impact of the Great

Depression and the opening of other journals, the previously closed "white" magazines, to black authors and artists. Though *Opportunity* continued to open its arms to black writers, it was no longer one of two outlets for such works. And, inevitably, the lively personality of Elmer Carter, with his militant rejection of caste, was reflected in his editorial philosophy and his editorials. Editor Johnson's editorials, in the view of E. K. Jones, were "somewhat heavy in their expression," but deep and searching. They were, in Johnson's own word, "dispassionate." Elmer Carter, in contrast, specialized in strong and impassioned expression which appealed especially to younger blacks.[19]

Nevertheless, factual articles remained the lifeblood of *Opportunity*. But unfortunately, calm analysis and facts did not have the box-office appeal of "morbid spectacle" and tears and fireworks. Though its circulation was respectable and the League took pride in the number of institutions and states and nations to which it was distributed, neither its advertising nor its sales were sufficient to cover its costs. Yet as a setting for talent, a marketplace for ideas, a vehicle for informing the League family and others about social service to black Americans and their unmet needs, *Opportunity* was invaluable throughout the twenties and thirties. It served as the memory bank of a complex system of interrelationships, stabilizing and helping give direction to positive efforts on behalf of blacks. Even a casual sampling of the thousands of pages of *Opportunity* stagger the observer with the quality of the work included and the range of subject matter.

The *Opportunity* deficit cast a pall over meetings of its editorial board. According to Carter, Hollingsworth Wood, Roger and William Baldwin seemed to think that the fault was the lack of circulation, to which Carter retorted, "How much money do you think the *Economic Review* makes? How much money from circulation and advertising does the *Harvard Monthly* make?" The rhetorical questions were never answered and the dilemma between making *Opportunity* an Urban League house organ or a popular-appeal magazine was never successfully resolved.

Carter brought to *Opportunity* the work of E. Simms Campbell, Otto Klineberg, Ralph J. Bunche, Clarence Darrow, Sterling Brown, George Schuyler, H. L. Mencken, Roy Wilkins, Carl Carmer and Pearl Buck, among hundreds of others during the fourteen years of his editorship.

In the post-Carter years, editorial management of *Opportunity* was in the hands of Edward Lawson, Jr., Madeline L. Alridge and Dutton Ferguson. The magazine continued to draw outstanding contributors and was an essential outlet for news of developments in civil rights and race advance as well as literature and the arts of Afro-Americans.

Through the years *Opportunity* served as a primary vehicle for introducing black talent to the American scene. The list of awards and prizes and recognition bestowed on the authors of works presented first in *Opportunity*'s pages would be too lengthy for inclusion here. It should be mentioned, however, that selections from *Opportunity* appeared year after year in *Best Short Stories,* an annual anthology edited by Edward J. O'Brien; the O. Henry Memorial Awards similarly cited outstanding selections in *Opportunity*.

The fate of *Opportunity* was determined in part by its own success in opening broader fields for black writers, in part by the stringencies of 1949 that forced NUL to terminate the magazine in a desperate cost-trimming operation. This dry-eyed epitaph for the magazine was penned by its first editor, Charles S. Johnson:

> *Opportunity* magazine once performed an invaluable service in serving as a medium of expression for Negro writers who found other channels closed to them, and as a place where studies of problems and conditions could be reported and publicized. Partly as a result of this service, Negro writers now command a far wider audience and have access to larger and more general periodicals; the same is true of factual articles relating to Negroes and race relations. The discontinuance of *Opportunity* magazine, therefore, while a wrench to all of us who have worked for it and with it, can be regarded as marking a milestone of progress.[20]

19/Focus on Industry

The optimism with which E. K. Jones observed the future in 1919 received a merciless buffeting in the next two years. The postwar depression struck and instead of millions of jobs there were millions of jobless and among them in disproportionate numbers were black workers. From this grim experience came the all-too-true phrase "last hired, first fired." The promise of a halcyon age which had filled Jones's vision in 1919 had disappeared in resurgent antiblack violence, segregation and prejudice.

For blacks, Jones told the 1921 annual conference of the League, the American ideals of "harmonious and profitable existence" had been suspended or nullified. However, farsighted persons knew this to be a false doctrine, he said, and were seeking to "set matters aright" by educating the public, thereby reducing or removing prejudice, and by "increasing the intelligence of the maligned and mistreated groups." [1]

In 1919, at the time he had recommended to the NUL board that an industrial secretary be hired, Jones had addressed the AFL convention in Atlantic City and stated that America's greatest problem was the Negro but that the greatest problem before the American Negro was industrial. The greatest problem that America has attempted to solve, said Jones, is the adjustment of labor in its relation to capital. He did not need to point out to his audience how imperfectly that "adjustment" had been made.[2]

Eight months, numerous speeches and considerable disillusionment later, Jones narrowed his subject to "The Negro's Future in Northern Industry," in a talk in Pittsburgh.[3] The question was, Jones said, whether black workers would be demanded by northern industry and if so in what capacities and under what conditions. And that question, he declared, brought up others: Will blacks be able to change their southern psychology? Will they have real hope for the future in their present occupations? Do they take advantage of the opportunities that are theirs?

There were forces holding them back—widespread prejudice which was possibly stronger among white workers in the north than in the south. There was the action of the law of supply and demand for labor, in which immigration was the most potent factor affecting black workers. Unions, he said, "have been genuinely stupid in their handling of the question involving white and colored workers." In spite of "beautiful platitudes" from the labor leaders and international unions, blacks had been excluded from locals. "This attitude on the part of the alien, has been the cause of the length of many strikes by organized labor and caused to keep Negroes out of the skilled and semi-skilled trades to the extent of making the Negro worker a potential enemy of organized labor." [4]

Jones stated that "employers of labor, have with remarkable uniformity failed to appreciate the worth of the Negro workman"; those who had really encouraged him and been interested in him gave him high marks and preferred him to Europeans.

Jones urged organized labor to take in blacks and encourage their loyalty. Black workers, he advised, should accept membership in organized labor as often as bona fide chances came. But black workers needed careful guidance in the matter of unions. Under current 1920 economic conditions, advised Jones, "the Negro should let the white workers take the leadership in organizing" because:

> *First,* organized labor has in the main during the past ignored Negro workers or deliberately excluded them from affiliation.

Second, when considered as an obstruction to the attainment of the end sought by organized labor feeble efforts have been made to bring the Negroes in. Of course failure had attended these efforts making the feeling of union white workers much more intense against the unorganized Negro.

Third, frequently feeling is gradually aroused against Negroes and results in violence being shown them.

Fourth, the employers and the ruling classes have drawn up resolutions representing their protest against such violence, but usually during the progress of the race conflict nothing of great consequence is done and never is an effort made to get the actual participants in the struggle between the various race elements together. [Jones noted that the old familiar phrase, "Get an understanding between the better and thinking elements of the two races," was still current. "What we need most," he said, "is to get a better understanding and a feeling of sympathy between the thoughtless and worst elements of the races—since the leaders have made such little progress in recent years."]

Fifth, the Negro should knock for admission to organized industry in lines where he has not had access, but should be expected to act as a strikebreaker or scab if his plea is met by deaf ears.

Sixth, Blacks should not take the initiative in organizing because employers will fire them and white fellow workers will keep them out.

Seventh, wherever an industry is being organized with the [tacit] consent of the employing group, as in the stock-yards of Chicago, the Negro should enter without hesitation the ranks of organized labor. Encouragement should be given to the employment of colored welfare workers in industrial plants. Thru them the Negro would be assured of a fair return from his labor and a more congenial atmosphere in which to work and would receive inspiration to develop those characteristics essential to attaining his place [and] retaining it in the future.[5]

Such were the basic currents of Jones's thinking at the time he called for addition of an industrial secretary in 1919. He did not get his man in 1919. The money was not there. Every year following this Jones called on the NUL board for the addition of the industrial secretary, and every year, the money was lacking.

In January of 1923 Jones asked John D. Rockefeller, Jr., to underwrite the salary of this staff person with $4,000, but was turned down. Three weeks later Jones went back with an expanded, more grandiose conception for which he solicited Mr. Rockefeller's support at just double the previous figure. The League executive requested $8,000 toward the budget of a new Department of Industrial Relations, which would:

(1) Standardize and coordinate the local employment agencies of the League so that exchange of information and more regular correspondence between them can assure applicants for work more efficient and helpful service and employers of labor a more efficient group of employees;

(2) Work directly with large industrial plants both in cities where the League is established and the communities removed from such centers to prepare larger opportunities for work and for advancement on the job for Negro workers and to stimulate Negro workers to a fresh determination to "make good on the job" so that their future place in industry may be assured.

(3) Work with organized labor to the end that Negroes employed in the trades represented by the unions may be given an opportunity to affiliate with organized labor on equal terms.[6]

This proposal sparked some interest in the Rockefeller establishment, and by the end of October Mr. Rockefeller had in his hands a report from one of his philanthropic advisers detailing the working conditions among American blacks and the position of the national and local leagues in that picture. A November 2 memorandum to John D. Rockefeller, Jr. endorsed the establishment of an industrial department in the NUL, approving its objectives as well as the basic principle. There was but one reservation: "They should forget and eliminate entirely the question of the labor unions. . . . They should devote their efforts to assimilating the Negro in northern industry, which will automatically place him in the position where he can demand recognition by the union." [7] The case of women in the printing trades was cited as an illustration of this point, with the notation that attacking the problem directly was like starting from the top down. This astute observation may have been passed along to NUL but failed to influence its activities, as we shall see.

In February 1924, John D. Rockefeller, Jr., pledged $4,500 per year for three years to support an industrial relations operation in NUL, on a matching basis—that is, a dollar for every dollar raised by the League, up to a maximum of $4,500. On the strength of this Hollingsworth Wood asked Julius Rosenwald for a contribution to underwrite the industrial activity. His reasons were somewhat different from those outlined by Jones:

> The problem of the Negro ought not to be complicated by the irrational attitude of capital and labor, the frequent use of the Negro as a strike-breaker and then heartlessly turning him off when the strike is broken. It is an economic stimulus to any racial prejudice that may already exist and every one of the riots that has taken place so far has some very firm basis on the economic side. Again, we want to set up some intelligent machinery to help distribute the migrant hordes of labor to centers where there are jobs rather than flood a place like Detroit during the periods of depression in the automobile industry which actually did happen. Again, it is necessary to have a man with a national viewpoint to talk to the big national officers of the corporations located here in New York, like the steel company, etc.[8]

In 1925 the money was available, at last, and an industrial secretary was hired. The man for this position was E. K. Jones's former staff secretary, one-time field secretary, later (and most recently) combined western field secretary and executive of the Chicago Urban League, T. Arnold Hill.

The timing was favorable for Hill. He had suffered a crushing defeat in the 1923 Chicago elections as a candidate for alderman from the South Side. He ran on a nonpartisan reform ticket with the endorsement of influential supporters of the Chicago League, the Municipal Voters' League and the Chicago *Daily News*. As one observer sagely noted, in the Chicago of 1923, "the Negro community, however, was not a strong territory for reformers." [9] The Chicago *Defender* opposed him and Hill was hit with a mudslinging campaign from his opponent. Inevitably, his usefulness was damaged by the defeat and the inspired rumors; likewise, the local League suffered.

The new NUL position offered Hill an opportunity to move to the national scene. To the job he brought ten years of League experience and a record of distinguished leadership in Chicago during the time of the League's most effective expansion and service. He had built the Chicago organization to a staff of sixteen with a budget of $30,000. Hill made the transfer as of March 15, 1925, but he actually arrived in New York April 8, having stopped en route at five League cities.

T. Arnold Hill had a clear view of his responsibility as director of the new Department of Industrial Relations:

> Economic advancement for the Negro will, for a long time to come, be one of the most important functions of organized social service. In it are involved the solutions of practically all problems that retard his social progress. In the working out of a program of a Department of Industry, it is necessary to bring to it full realization of not only the Negro's economic need and contributive ability, but the extent to which industry is, or can be interested in the Negro as a dependable industrial quantity.[10]

Sounding more like Madison Avenue than South State Street, Hill wrote:

> Before attempting to sell a product a knowledge of that product should be had; not only the quantity but the quality. To do this requires that the Industrial Secretary should visit the sections from which the labor is to be obtained. He should acquaint himself with the industrial processes and the extent to which Negroes are employed. He should visit the various schools to acquaint himself with the extent of training for productive employment the students are given. He should make contacts with key men in the centers of supply in order to meet quantitative and qualitative demands.
>
> Secondly, he should make a study of industrial needs and seek to acceler-

ate the introduction of Negroes in plants where none are being employed and to advance those who are being employed. Having a knowledge of the Negro's equipment at the source of supply, he can assist employment managers in selecting the types best adapted to a particular industry or job.

Having the essentials indicated above, he will be in a position to advise principals of schools as to the curricula for industrial training. He should make a close contact with bureaus of education, especially the *Land Grant Division of the U.S. Bureau of Education* so that the training of Negro youth should conform to the general demands of industry instead of the usual training for local or community need.[11]

Hill's priorities are of great interest, as is the extraordinary fact that nowhere in his outline of duties does he mention the subject that was to absorb his primary attention: the relationship of organized labor and black workers. Perhaps this is understandable, considering the official announcement made by NUL in which the program of the new industrial department was spelled out. Headlined "The National Urban League Launches Industrial Program—T. Arnold Hill Heads up Work," the release trumpeted a "strenuous nation-wide campaign for larger opportunity for Negro workers" and gave Hill's background, including his age (thirty-nine), alma mater (Virginia Union University plus social science specialization at New York University) and his service in Chicago.[12]

The program announced for the new department had three parts. They were identical to those spelled out by E. K. Jones in his letter to John D. Rockefeller, Jr., in January of 1923 with one significant exception: The third point concerning "work with organized labor" had been dropped and in its place was this:

To help through available channels of information to ascertain points at which there is an oversupply of Negro labor, and to use existing agencies of publicity and placement to direct Negro Labor, including migrants, to those points where they are most needed and where their families will most easily become adjusted.[13]

Nowhere in the announcement was there any mention of organized labor.

The New York *Age* applauded the new department and editorially advised that "particular emphasis should be placed on the training and preparation on the part of those applying for places requiring any degree of skill." [14]

By the end of June 1925 Hill had shifted his priorities. His "Prospective Immediate Program" called for (1) intensive industrial campaigns in three cities; (2) work with trade union organizations; (3) opening new opportunities for Negroes; (4) inducing the National Industrial Conference Board to survey the current and future picture of Negro employment;

and (5) continued mutual action with the Workers' Education Bureau.[15]

By the end of October, Hill reported to the NUL board, "We conceive our main objective to be . . . creating public sentiment favorable to [Negro] employment. The successes and availability of Negroes should be emphasized . . . to the labor union officials, to individual employers and associations . . . and among the general public—in order to create a larger and better field for the use of Negro labor. . . . With this as our main objective, we have given special attention to the relationship of the Negro to the trade union movement." [16]

Hill had moved the industrial campaign to the second priority and made trade union organization of black workers his first item of business. He decided to develop a special issue of *Opportunity* on industrial questions and began a regular column of his own in the magazine reviewing matters of interest concerning black workers. He reported also, "We have made very little headway with industrial corporations to whom we wish to present the problem of Negroes in industry. We want to reach the presidents of larger corporations, particularly the public utilities, in order that a policy favorable to Negroes might be adopted for their branches and subsidiaries in various parts of the country. . . . We need . . . direct lines of connection . . . to executive officers in order that our story might be told direct to them." Hill called on board members to help provide such contacts.

As for the NICB project, the industrial secretary noted that such a survey of present and future use of Negro workers would help in planning the preparation they should make for industrial jobs. "We have received from a number of technical and trade schools of the south," Hill said, "endorsement of this plan through the assurance that they would be aided thereby in shaping their curricula." [17]

Nevertheless, the unionization of blacks was the primary effort. T. Arnold Hill's initiative with the AFL was well timed. The year 1925 saw the demise of the IWW—the Industrial Workers of the World—notable as one of the few labor organizations that had welcomed blacks as members. Some 100,000 Afro-Americans had carried IWW cards at one time or another, most of them in the Texas and Louisiana lumber and turpentine industry or as longshoremen in the ports of Norfolk, Philadelphia and Baltimore.[18]

The AFL bestirred itself and appointed Hugh Frayne as its consultant and liaison person with the NUL. A dozen years before, Frayne had accompanied George Haynes when the NUL executive called on the AFL executive council and in 1920 he had addressed the NUL annual conference. It was Hill's belief that the League "should seek an audience with the officials of the various international unions that do not admit colored people . . . in order to break down the discrimination that exists. A general conference of the Urban League, the American Federation of Labor and the unions involved should be held. At least three internationals should be approached in this connection." [19] The same procedure, Hill recommended, should be used with unions that were not AFL affiliates, such as the Amalgamated Clothing Workers.

Hill had sold the NUL Steering Committee on his plans to interest black workers in trade unions and this, it should be remembered, was a courageous, against-the current position in 1925. The plan, Hill reiterated, would not require that the League "actually participate in securing members for [unions] but that in certain cities, through committees or organizations to be formed for the purpose, an attempt is to be made, with the National Urban League taking the initiative, to educate the colored workers on the advantages of collective bargaining." This would be done through study classes. The cities under consideration were Philadelphia, St. Louis, Newark, Chicago, Richmond, Cleveland, Milwaukee, Akron, Atlantic City, Toledo and Harrisburg. It was ten years before Hill was able to put this plan into operation.[20]

This was the year in which a wide campaign of unsigned antilabor advertisements ran in the largest black newspapers and the effort of A. Philip Randolph to organize the Pullman porters had been condemned by a conference of more than fifty black leaders assembled in Washington, who also turned down organized labor in general.[21]

The League for many years had a close relationship with the Dining Car Employees Union, which in fact received office space from the League. And, through T. Arnold Hill, NUL supported the struggle of the Brotherhood of Sleeping Car Porters for recognition. NUL was faithful and strong in its backing of A. Philip Randolph and the porters in their ten-year battle, in decided contrast to substantial sectors of black leadership (except the NAACP) which opposed the campaign or were indifferent to it. Randolph acknowledged that only NAACP and NUL had seriously turned "to the question of improving the lot of Negro workers" in the mid-twenties.[22]

Black newspaper editors and preachers had sided with the company in large numbers in the Pullman strike. Influential leaders such as Kelly Miller wrote that "logic aligns the Negro with labor, but good sense arrays him with capital," and the black Improved, Benevolent and Protective Order of Elks (IBPOE) went on record at their August 1925 convention in Richmond, Virginia, as follows:

> Whereas, it is clear to those of us who have studied the bad results of other like movements where those of our race-group lose positions through union agitators and strike leaders, that unionism is calculated to do our

people all sorts of harm and injure them with the employing class in America; therefore be it

Resolved . . . that it be the continued policy of our people everywhere to line up with the best class of American citizenship, which in the last analysis all over our great country constitutes the large employers of labor.[23]

On this issue NUL took a diametrically opposite stand, firmly backing the porters. Kinckle Jones spoke in support of their organizational effort in January 1926.[24] It was their right, he maintained, to bargain for better conditions, hours and wages, for mutual protection and for being considered as worthy of respect as other railroad employees and indeed, as necessary for proper operation of the roads. They should be able to approach company authorities directly with their grievances and to consider causes of complaint as a group without outside interference. In November 1926 Jones was guest speaker at the porters' labor dinner. The speech was a strong one endorsing their organizing drive. When he mentioned the right to organize for mutual protection the NUL executive declared that workers were justified in being suspicious of big business.

Another indication of the League attitude toward organization was the fact that it was not put off by the formation in 1925 of the Negro Labor Congress. The congress, with its sponsorship by Communists, served to confirm and inflame the antagonism of black workers and the middle class to unionization of Afro-American labor.

With these facts in mind, it is even more remarkable that the NUL consistently and unflaggingly promoted collective bargaining. One of the avenues pursued was to aid formation of the New York Trade Union Committee for Organizing Negroes. The committee actually took shape in the office of the New York Urban League. Its purpose was to spread the word about unionism and encourage blacks to take advantage of it. It also hoped to discourage the use of black labor for strike-breaking.[25]

Early in 1925 T. Arnold Hill addressed an open letter to Chambers of Commerce, employers and employees, union and nonunion members, employment agencies and the public at large, offering the services of the NUL Industrial Relations Department. Its objectives, he said, were:

1. The further use of the Negro in industry.
2. The dissemination of information on successful experiments with Negro workers.
3. The abolition of restrictions of Negroes to certain stereotyped lines of work.
4. The dissipation of antagonism between black and white workers.
5. The removal of barriers against Negroes by labor unions.
6. Better training of Negro workers in trade schools.
7. Better apprenticeship opportunities for Negroes entering new occupations.[26]

It was a manifesto for NUL industrial relations work that was to guide it for the next four decades.

In his first two and a half years as industrial secretary T. Arnold Hill made repeated efforts to "effect reconciliation between prejudiced nationals and internationals of the AFL and Negro workers." He appeared twice before the AFL executive council, had several interviews with President William Green, AFL Secretary Frank Morrison and Hugh Frayne in Washington, plus labor officials in Washington, Philadelphia, New York, Chicago, Boston and other cities.[27]

A candid article by Hill had been printed in the *American Federationist* and an article by Green had been printed in *Opportunity*'s industrial issue.[28]

Through Hill's monthly information releases to the press, local Leagues and "industrial associates," reliable information about labor market changes fed into the black community. Not only did NUL report the losses and gains of Negro workers, but opportunities and remedies were mentioned. Through it all ran the thread of "efficiency," advising "the proper attitude toward work" and encouraging training and vocational study.[29]

By the end of 1927 the New York Urban League was a sponsor of the first Negro conferences convened at League headquarters by A. Philip Randolph at the time when a decision had been made concerning the emphasis of NUL's industrial program.[30] John T. Clark (then St. Louis League executive) and T. Arnold Hill had concluded that the next step was to organize a nationwide "Negro in Industry Week." Local Leagues would take the lead in their communities, enlisting cooperation of other interested agencies. The NUL would attempt to cover cities where no affiliates existed, through cooperation of national organizations such as the National Negro Business League, YMCA, YWCA, Rotary, Kiwanis and Lions clubs, Greek-letter fraternities, lodges, churches, women's civic and social groups.[31]

When he proposed the idea it had not been decided whether the thrust should be to "propagandize" the white public and leave individual conferences with employers for later follow-up. Clark recommended that the "celebration" be the last week in March, covering two Sundays and tying in with Negro History Week and Interracial Sunday. Making it clear that the national office could supply coordination, literature, and some speakers but no cash (though it would attempt to get a special appropriation for the project), the industrial secretary warned that travel expenses of NUL speakers would have to be picked up by the local Leagues.

Hill queried the local executives on the content and emphasis of the campaign. Should it, he asked, concentrate on prevalent restrictions, prejudices, traditions, habits and customs that exclude Negroes? "Or should it stress what the Negro himself can do to improve his own status?" Responses suggested improving his proficiency, learning trades and "building up public sentiment that will be assertive when efforts are initiated to find opportunities in business places his patronage helps to make possible." [32]

Though Hill did not know it, the timing was too late. "Through the fall and early winter months of 1927 the Urban League has experienced an increasing number of persons looking for work and a decrease in the number of calls for workers. This unusual lack of employment furnished the occasion for some well organized and extensive effort to bring to the attention of the public at large this very hazardous situation." Clark, Hill and other Urban Leaguers could not have foreseen it, but this was the beginning of the toboggan slide that accelerated throughout 1928 and widened and deepened into the disaster of the Great Depression. [33]

20/Black Social Workers

During the twenties professionalization of social work among black Americans was a primary and continuing NUL goal. Through college and on-the-job training of workers NUL increased the supply of qualified black social workers. And through attendance and participation in its own annual conferences and special meetings, in conventions of such organizations as the National Conference of Charities and Correction (this later became the National Conference of Social Work), the American Association of Social Workers and their local and state counterparts, NLUCAN staff, board and other volunteers sharpened their techniques and grew in the social work profession.

This drive for professionalism began early. The first public meeting of the newly consolidated League organization (NLUCAN) was an open all-day conference of social workers held on December 4, 1911. Featured speakers for the occasion were Dr. W. E. B. DuBois, the Reverend William H. Brooks, Mary White Ovington, William L. Bulkley, Edward E. Pratt, Fred R. Moore, George E. Haynes and Eugene K. Jones.

George Haynes's pioneer work in training blacks for social work began at Fisk in 1910. Three years later (1913) he announced the negotiations which NLUCAN had started with leading black colleges (Howard, Fisk, Talladega, Knoxville, Virginia Union and Wilberforce) to raise the standards of these colleges and add to their curricula courses in sociology and economics.[1] In his summer extension work from 1913 onward, Haynes lectured to teachers and preachers in at least five institutions, stressing not only the facts and problems of black migration but also the urgent need and opportunities for social workers.

NLUCAN's centripetal thrust was clear in this professional area. The major event for American social workers was the annual forum of the National Conference of Charities and Correction. George Haynes was the first NLUCAN official to appear in person before this conference when in 1911, he addressed the section on "Cooperation with Colleges in Securing and Training Negro Social Workers for Urban Centers." In the spring of 1912, Eugene K. Jones addressed the New York City Conference of Charities and Correction, pleading for facilities and provision for black girls who were running afoul of the law. NLUCAN approved George Haynes's proposal to accept the invitation from the National Conference of Charities and Correction for the League to host one or two sessions during the 1913 Memphis meeting. Haynes was authorized to spend up to $100 for printing, speakers and meeting place.

At the 1915 conference, NLUCAN sought to have "the Negro health problem" presented and was told that there would be no opportunity for such a discussion. However, Mrs. Ruth Standish Baldwin pressed for a program slot to present a twenty-minute paper in the health section of the conference to describe the National Negro Health Week campaign. The rejoinder stated that the health section was limiting its subject to the relation of hospitals to the community and to social workers and therefore NLUCAN's health campaign would not be appropriate. Mrs. Baldwin pointed out in reply that the health campaign in Alabama stemmed from the Tuskegee hospital nursing staff and that the entire campaign was simply an extension of courses in health and sanitation that the Tuskegee staff was teaching in the local community. She cited also the case of Dixie Hospital in Virginia and offered to have the paper presented by a physician, if necessary.

Disavowing overpersistence, Ruth Baldwin pursued the reluctant head of the conference health section nevertheless: "It does seem to us that as the Negroes are constantly blamed and looked upon as a menace to the health of the communities in which they live because of their carelessness in health and sanitary matters, that it would be exceedingly useful to white people to know what efforts they are themselves making to better these conditions." [2]

In 1916 there was a breakthrough at the Indianapolis meeting of the National Conference of Charities and Correction. The conference steering committee had asked George Haynes to arrange for a discussion of "Negro betterment work." NLUCAN was offered a slot on the program on the subject of child welfare—the effect of the relation of home and school on the black child. In addition, NLUCAN had a table of its literature in the conference headquarters lobby. NLUCAN scheduled two sessions of its own outlining betterment work among blacks in various cities: Chicago (by Sophonisba P. Breckinridge); St. Louis (by Roger N. Baldwin); Nashville (by George Haynes); Washington (by Howard professor George W. Cook); and Indianapolis, Cincinnati, Columbia, South Carolina, and Savannah. The black delegates to the conference, white social workers and a number of interested persons from Indianapolis attended the sessions which were widely reported by the daily newspapers. "So successful was this meeting," judged George Haynes, referring to NLUCAN's entire conference participation, "that I am fully convinced that we should hold a similar gathering next year at the Pittsburgh meeting of the National Conference . . . [it] is making a special effort to encourage more colored people to attend, welcomes us to meet with them and the opportunities for publicity are greater than we could get in any convention by ourselves." [3]

By the time the 1917 Conference on Charities and Correction rolled around the nation was at war. With a heightened sense of mission Urban Leaguers from many cities flocked to Pittsburgh and NLUCAN held a series of meetings in conjunction with the conference. NLUCAN activities included a public reception at the (colored) YMCA in Pittsburgh, thanks to the local League affiliate then led by John T. Clark. The newspapers, particularly the black weeklies, gave the NLUCAN meeting broad coverage. The Atlanta *Independent* pulled out the stops to declare that "The National League on Urban Conditions Among Negroes has been holding the second annual meeting of social workers in [Pittsburgh] in cooperation with the National Conference of Charities and Correction, the greatest gathering of social workers of its kind in the world." [4]

Speakers at the NLUCAN sessions included Dean Kelly Miller, and Professor George W. Cook of Howard University, Roger N. Baldwin of St. Louis, Professor Josiah C. Morse of the University of South Carolina (talking about prospects for improvement of race relations in his state), Helen B. Pendleton, district supervisor of Associated Charities Auxiliary of Atlanta, and E. K. Jones, who described NLUCAN's work during the recent months. "An attractive feature of the meeting," reported the *Bulletin* of the National Conference of Charities and Correction later, "was the singing of familiar hymns and folk songs."

The following year, after holding a January conference on labor and being caught up in the frenzy of emergency war work, NLUCAN executives changed their approach. During the war period the agency was represented, as before, at the annual social work forum (which changed its name to the National Conference of Social Work). But in addition, NLUCAN participated in other meetings such as those of the National Housing Association, the National Municipal League, the Illinois and New Jersey State and New York City Conferences of Charities and Correction, the National Medical Association, the National Negro Business League, National Association of Colored Women's Clubs, the National Conference of Housing Bureaus and Room Registries, and the special Conference on Demobilization and the Responsibilities of Organized Social Agencies, which was held in New York.

This last was an extraordinary meeting held less than three weeks after the Armistice. A hundred executives of the largest and best-known social service agencies in the nation met to consider postwar conditions. At the end of the parley a lengthy bill of resolutions was adopted, calling for enlightened social welfare in the nation, and incorporating in its opening remarks this statement, urged on the meeting by NLUCAN and the NAACP jointly: "That every program for demobilization and for national and community reconstruction shall adequately and consciously include provision for our Negro fellow-citizens and for their cooperation therein." [5] Just words? Not entirely. These resolutions were endorsed by the nation's leaders in social work. The inclusion of black delegates at the meeting was significant progress and the resolution was evidence of great forward motion, especially when all this contrasted with the resistance in 1915 to the request merely for NLUCAN's participation in the National Conference health panel.

It was in November of 1918 that NLUCAN broke away from the National Conference of Social Work and held its own annual conference, for the first time, in Columbus, Ohio. Seventeen *paid* League executives attended plus volunteers, board members and persons from interested agencies. The program was, quite simply, to discuss the problems confronting the local Leagues.[6]

In 1919, through a joint committee of representatives from the NAACP, YMCA, YWCA, National Federation of Women's Clubs and NUL, letters were sent to the heads of the various departments of the National Conference of Social Work. As a result, at the Atlantic City conference that year the 5,000 delegates had constantly before them problems of black Americans, for these were incorporated in nearly every session. Forty black delegates were present, including League executives, and white and black board members. One session was devoted entirely to living conditions and problems of blacks. E. K. Jones addressed the industry session on "The Negro and Labor." A committee was appointed to call on the head of every NCSW department to see that adequate attention be given to problems of blacks at the next conference.

The other major meeting for Urban Leaguers in 1919 was the second annual conference of the NUL. It was a five-day affair, held in Detroit, with seventy-seven delegates attending. The focus was on "The Negro in Industry." The conference's major achievement was direction of attention to "reconstruction" and postwar readjustment.

E. K. Jones's keynote address, "Why We Are Here," focused on blacks in industry "because it is one of the most important questions now before the race and its friends." [7] Industrial problems, he noted, were the basis of many race disturbances. The basic question was, "Shall the Negro work?" He reported on southern efforts to induce blacks to return, on minimum standards and investigations in the south. Jones cited Pittsburgh's welfare work to assure workers good health, decent housing, wholesome recreation and a chance to advance as an ideal to be sought elsewhere. "How much further shall we go in the union movement?" he asked. The resolutions of the NLUCAN labor conference in 1917 had been fruitful, he claimed, pointing to AFL pronouncements that followed it. He also reviewed the activities of the federal Bureau of Negro Economics, stated that employers had become "more liberal" and pointed to League placement of twenty-two social workers in industry in 1918 alone as evidence of this fact.

For its educational work, the League at this time hired the young man who had helped bring about the formation of the Chicago League, Alexander L. Jackson, secretary of the Wabash Avenue YMCA. Jackson had been an honors graduate of Harvard and class orator. He began in mid-1919 as NUL educational secretary, succeeding George Haynes. The demand for trained, professional black social workers had far outstripped the supply—industry was crying for them, the League needed them and dozens of cities and even some states had become aware of the need for knowledgeable persons to work among migrant blacks. With George Haynes's training center program discarded, the alternatives were to screen the colleges and universities, north and south, for promising young blacks who were interested in careers in social work, and to stimulate white students to work in the field also.

Jackson became the first recruiter of black college youth. He traveled the Ivy League circuit and major colleges and universities in the northeast and midwest, making an estimate of blacks in college, and meeting and talking to many of them in an effort to interest them in social work. He also conferred with faculty members of the institutions, acquainting them with the opportunities in the field and the operations of the League, as well as impressing upon them the fact that the League was truly the clearing-house for jobs—and professional training—in the field.

By December the educational secretary had visited twenty-two campuses and discovered more than 300 black students enrolled in the north. His survey was fragmentary, he admitted, but he had found and interested "several splendid young men and women in social work as a vocation." [8]

Through Jackson's efforts the number of graduate schools offering openings to League Fellows was expanded. Ultimately it included the schools of social work of Simmons College, Boston; the University of Pennsylvania; the University of Pittsburgh; Carnegie Institute of Technology; Bryn Mawr; Mount Holyoke; Ohio State University; New York University; and the University of Chicago in addition to the New York School of Social Work. Jackson and the pressure of the times successfully stimulated the interest of blacks (and white students as well) in social work. The number applying annually for the League Fellowship grants climbed to nearly 200 in the thirties. The actual number of full-time Fellows expanded to as many as six in one year, plus an unrecorded number of "broken" Fellows—i.e., college students doing their field work under local League direction.

Furthermore, sponsorship of League Fellows expanded also. Julius Rosenwald, for example, underwrote grants in 1928 to train three Fellows as future League executives. The black Improved, Benevolent and Protective Order of Elks sponsored two grants that, with the aid of the Columbus League, helped two Fellows at Ohio State University. At one point the Pittsburgh League had six scholarship students at Pennsylvania colleges. The first League affiliate to sponsor black scholars was, however, the Armstrong Association of Philadelphia.

The training center for black social workers that George Haynes had striven to establish in Nashville continued to function. Its program consisted of sociology courses at Fisk and field work at Bethlehem Center as before, but without the strong direction and guidance of a George Haynes.

The most vital element in the training of black social workers was the Atlanta School of Social Service at Morehouse College, begun in 1920 on the impetus of NLUCAN Fellow Garrie Moore. Moore was a Haynes protegé who had observed the Fisk training center and sociology curricula closely. He was joined in efforts to form a similar training institution in Atlanta by Miss Helen B. Pendleton, supervisor of casework for the American Red Cross in Atlanta, and R. C. Dexter, secretary of the Atlanta Charity Organization Society. Dexter had found that black social workers were more effective than whites in working with Afro-Americans and he urged John Hope, president of Morehouse, to consider such a training facility at that institution. Moore also enlisted Jesse O. Thomas, NUL's southern field secretary, in the project and Thomas was named chairman of the committee for the school. Professor Moore was the school's director and among its executive committee members were John Hope, Plato T. Durham, Lemuel L. Foster of the Atlanta League and William J. Trent, secretary of the Committee on Church Cooperation in Atlanta.

It may seem strange at this distance to hear that missionary work was necessary to educate local leaders of the black communities in major cities to the necessity and urgency of social services among Afro-Americans. Such was the case, however, and NUL's extension secretary traveled in 1922 to eighteen cities or more (and three times as many in 1923) explaining and educating. This man was J. R. Lee, Jr., a Kansas City school principal formerly on Tuskegee's staff. He had the unenviable task of trying to raise funds in black communities for support of the NUL and local Leagues.

During the twenties the need for professional social workers to deal with the needs of black citizens was also impressed on white community leaders by Urban Leaguers. "Almost invariably now [1929]," wrote Jesse O. Thomas to Kinckle Jones, "when a request is made for a social worker anywhere in the south, they require that the worker be trained. In many cases they ask that in addition to having social service training the worker should have a college education as a background." [9] Whites in many cities learned that trained black social workers were a distinct advantage if not a necessity. Atrocious events such as those in Memphis could be prevented by professionals. Jesse O. Thomas outlined the deplorable Memphis circumstances:

The morning I reached [Memphis] Miss Bessie Simon was sentenced to three months in the workhouse and a fine of $400. . . . Mrs. Bolton Smith who was the person responsible for the organization of the settlement house 10 years ago when Miss Simon began her activities as a social worker, after being let out of the public school system, was the most active person in an effort to get Miss Simon convicted. . . .

Several children in the Home were found to be suffering from rickets and from other forms of malnutrition. Some were victims of other forms of punishment where Miss Simon had them put their hands down on something solid and would strike their joints with a shoe heel, thus disabling the child so that all through life, he would never be able to completely close or open the hand.

The outcome of the Simon controversy turned a critical eye of the community toward Negro social work. There was an interracial organization there, headed up by Dr. Fuller, which received $2500 a year from the Community Fund and which investigation revealed had not had a meeting in 18 months. There was another "sister movement" headed up by Miss Jenny Moore, whose activities have also been discovered as being far below the standard and it is agreed she does not have the ability to develop the type of social service program that the community ought to support.[10]

An indication of the professional standing of Urban Leaguers was their acceptance in the social work calling indicated by the appearances on the NUL annual conference program as early as 1923 of both the current and past presidents of the National Conference of Social Work.

The year 1924 was a landmark for black social workers. In that year there were nineteen NCSW program presentations by or about blacks— many made by Urban Leaguers. Moreover, E. K. Jones was elected to the executive board of the conference, a signal honor conferring recognition to the whole NUL movement. In addition, both Jesse O. Thomas and John T. Clark were elected to NCSW committees.

From that date on, Urban Leaguers appeared often on programs and participated in the activities of the NCSW. In 1927, E. K. Jones was re-elected to the conference's executive committee and furthermore was appointed one of ten delegates to the International Conference of Social Work which met in Paris. That year Charles S. Johnson, Jesse O. Thomas and R. Maurice Moss, Urban League executive in Baltimore, were named to special committees of divisions of NCSW.

The participation of Urban Leaguers in the National Conference of Social Work programs as officers, committee members, speakers and panelists plus the adjunct meetings in local churches, special luncheons and dinners in the conference city at the same time gave the NUL two major rallies during the year. The other, of course, was the League's annual conference (with the exception of 1925, which was skipped). Through these two yearly conclaves the agency took its message to the social work profession and those interested in it, and also to the black community and whites interested in it.

Typically, NUL annual conferences were part workshop and part information exchange and, perhaps even more important, were updating sessions on urgent topics. Generally they centered on a central theme and then examined specific aspects of that subject.

For example, "Present Day Problems of Social Life" was the general theme of the 1926 conference. This was viewed by E. Franklin Frazier (then director of the Atlanta School of Social Work), who spoke on "How They Affect the Negro," and by Forrester B. Washington (then executive of the Armstrong Association of Philadelphia) speaking on "A Program to Meet These Needs" in the north and J. Marshall Ragland, executive of the Louisville League, giving the view from the south.

"Experience of Negroes with Labor Unions" was reported by Charles S. Johnson and discussed by Hugh Frayne, AFL general organizer, Ira Reid (then industrial secretary of the New York League) and James Brady, director of industrial relations of the New York State Department of Labor.

"Training for Industrial Opportunities" brought out T. Arnold Hill, the presidents of A. & T. College at Greensboro, North Carolina, and of Antioch College, plus a New York City public school official and the superintendent of a New Jersey brick plant. Later, Hill reviewed the industrial work of the NUL and was joined on the rostrum by James Weldon Johnson, then secretary of the NAACP.

A fresh concept was explored by Jesse O. Thomas, George W. Thompson, executive of the Akron affiliate, and Roger N. Baldwin, then director of the American Civil Liberties Union. They discussed "Community Competition for Negro Labor," reviewing the appeals of southern and northern cities and the differences in living conditions that influenced migration of blacks.

Health was the topic that drew the health commissioner of New York City, the president of the Liberty Life Insurance Company of Chicago, the medical director of the North Carolina Mutual Life Insurance Company, Dr. E. P. Roberts, long-time NUL board member, and the consulting statistician of the Prudential Life Insurance Company, Frederick L. Hoffman. This session was especially notable for presenting the extraordinary spectacle of a nationally known expert eating his words in public. Hoffman, who had been called "the insulting statistician" and worse by blacks, was the man whose book *Race Traits and Tendencies of the American Negro,* at the turn of the century, had branded blacks as constitutionally inferior. American Negroes, he had concluded from his intensive combing of the data, were doomed to extinction. At the conference, he took almost all of it back, reversing himself on the basis of later and more reliable data, stating that disease afflicted blacks not because of racial tendencies but because of environment.[11] Naturally, this statement had wide significance and was reported in white and black newspapers across the land.

Annual NUL conferences were of growing interest because of the caliber of experts and the topicality of their subjects. Sometimes the heat of the discussions was news in itself. In 1928, with the Negro Renaissance in full swing, the subject matter that year of the NUL annual conference in Philadelphia included color preferences of employers; race and crime; health and social work.

In a session on emergency relief, decorum was stretched thin when a representative of the American Red Cross spoke about its policies as exemplified in the 1927 Mississippi flood disaster. The Red Cross, he stated, gave relief in the form of food and clothing, and so on, directly to sufferers. He estimated that three fourths of the 600,000 beneficiaries in the flood were Negroes and told how his agency sought group and race cooperation in stricken communities. However, there were two ways, he said, in which to halt cooperation: by baiting or snooping around to get information and by injecting issues not related to the immediate necessities of relief.[12]

Jesse O. Thomas and E. K. Jones had been appointed by United States Commerce Secretary Herbert Hoover to a special Negro advisory committee on Mississippi flood relief to investigate sensational charges of rampant brutality, exploitation and peonage in relief distribution. Thomas, who covered hundreds of miles of the flooded area, had witnessed some of these lapses by local distribution committees and had found that "without exception in every camp where the local colored leaders had been called in for consultation, cooperation and advice, that the conditions there were more like those provided for the white and were more satisfactory." But it had taken investigation and strong representation to get the Red Cross to cooperate and act.[13]

Consequently, "a rather animated discussion" with the Red Cross representative ensued when Kinckle Jones pointed out that "the Red Cross learned the value of cooperating with Negro social agencies especially after the race problem had complicated the issue of relief." [14]

It was the function of both the annual conference of the League and the annual forum of the National Conference of Social Work to bring together the professional black social workers to concentrate on the overriding problems and apply in their localities the techniques learned at these information exchanges. The conferences served as a giant step for the League professionals and the communities they served.

21/Other Forces at Work

By the mid-twenties the pool of American leaders interested in race relations had expanded greatly. Instead of a cluster of progressives in New York and a scattered handful outside it, as at the turn of the century, most major cities had developed nuclei of concerned citizens. In the post-World War I years the southern Commission on Interracial Cooperation and the Federal Council of Churches' Commission on the Church and Race Relations, headed by George E. Haynes, had brought still more citizens into the arena.

While the number of persons with at least some knowledge of needs of black citizens increased, the conditions that called for single-minded, hard-driving effort on the part of the NUL had diffused. From 1916 through 1921 the central concern of black adjustment in the cities had been jobs. All other aspects of migrants' problems radiated outward from that core. And throughout this period the League used its experience and expertise in the employment field with great effectiveness. It was *the* source of counsel, aid and leadership at the national as well as local levels.

From 1921 on, however, there was a decided change. The urgency of war and reconstruction were over and the emphasis on work (particularly for blacks) was not a matter of popular national concern. The NAACP turned increasingly to issues that were of grass-roots interest, particularly housing segregation, lynching and discrimination. The "goodwill" agencies, those headed by George Haynes and Will Alexander, turned to positive, educational programs, bringing together the "best" whites and blacks. The League, as the "magic" faded from employment as a central focus for its efforts, turned to fundamental research and propaganda (in the form of *Opportunity* magazine) and launched its industrial relations department.

In the early twenties two interracial organizations had been formed which NUL leaders, rightly or wrongly, saw as competitors. These were the southern Commission on Interracial Cooperation (CIC) headed by a young minister, Dr. Will Alexander, and the Department of Race Relations of the Federal Council of Churches of Christ in America, with George Haynes as its executive.

The CIC began in Atlanta after World War I. (Community officials who were collecting money to benefit returning veterans were persuaded to give the allotment scheduled for black soldiers to the CIC as an interracial effort to minimize tensions.) It started and continued with solid foundation support (from the General Education Board, Carnegie Corporation of New York) and perennial gifts from philanthropists (Rockefeller and Rosenwald), assuring it of a six-figure budget.[1]

With a white and a black paid worker in each southern state plus many volunteers, the CIC grew into a sizable regional network. There was a central committee in Atlanta, plus state committees (many of them appointed by the governors) and local voluntary committees that met once a month or more.

The CIC moved in highly genteel ways to counteract friction. Alexan-

der hired a newspaperman who visited editors and stressed the importance of printing positive news about blacks, pointing out the results of
sensationalizing crimes by blacks. CIC also hired a research director who
discovered that there was a huge void concerning race relations in the
south. The commission stimulated research at southern universities and
conducted studies of its own.

In many communities, believing that "by and large, [they were] very
much in advance of what the official church [position] was in relation to
the application of their doctrines to social and human problems," the
CIC mobilized church women. Alexander believed this helped educate
communities and reduce suspicion between the races. Frequently the organization called special meetings of educators—college presidents, deans
and faculty members. These conferences attempted to impress the educators with the need for research, curricula and course offerings and teacher
training in race relations.[2]

Another ambitious program in the field was initiated in 1922 by the
Federal Council of Churches with a grant from the Carnegie Corporation. Dr. George Haynes was appointed secretary of the council's Department of Race Relations and continued in that post for twenty-five years.
Haynes was a strong churchman and became vice moderator and first
vice president of the Congregational Christian Churches' Home Board. It
was he who originated Race Relations Sunday, which was widely observed throughout the nation's churches.

Haynes's major effort on the national scene was the development in
thirty-five states and 135 cities of councils of churches under the leadership of his organization. Each council was reported to have a paid executive. These councils were intended to "improve" race relations and had
no programs for delivery of services.

Both Haynes and Alexander were energetic, southern-oriented and
church-centered. They operated in the region where the NUL was weak-
est and most blacks lived. They had reservations about NUL's likelihood of achieving substantial gains for southern blacks and sincerely
believed that the CIC and Department of Race Relations educative-
dialectical efforts would be more productive.

No doubt on the part of George Haynes there was an added element
involved. He was convinced that he had been squeezed out of NUL by
Kinckle Jones and his subsequent relations with the League executive
were frosty. (Jones had invited Haynes to participate in NUL's 1919
"Negro in Industry" conference. Haynes, the nation's leading expert on
the subject, accepted. Jones then assigned him to speak on housing.
Haynes was furious at being asked to talk on a secondary subject and at
being shunted to a minor place on the program.)

By the mid-twenties, the initiative in race relations had shifted from the League's leaders. The shift was manifest in a 1925 special conference held in Cincinnati. Its theme was "Toward Interracial Cooperation," and it was sponsored by Will Alexander's Commission on Interracial Cooperation and George Haynes's Commission on the Church and Race Relations of the Federal Council of Churches. To this well-financed, broad-based three-day meeting were invited the nation's leading authorities in the fields of welfare, sociology, education and race relations.

Some two hundred black and white delegates were brought together to "exchange their experiences in dealing with conditions and race relations in their communities." [3] The goals of the conference were to define and set before the nation the purposes of the "interracial movement" and its methods, in which conference, understanding and goodwill achieved more than force, violence and hostile contention. The fourth purpose listed by the conference sponsors was to represent the agencies "that are making efforts day by day" to work out the ideals of brotherhood in a democracy.

This last point was especially interesting because mention of the League was conspicuously absent from the conference discussions and presentations, even though Urban Leaguers attending included Dr. Gilbert S. Cox and Nimrod B. Allen of Columbus, Samuel A. Allen of Boston, Forrester B. Washington of Philadelphia and Jesse O. Thomas, who also was a member of the executive committee. One presentation, a description of forming and operating a local League, was an exception to the general oversight of NUL activities. This talk was given by former League Fellow James H. Robinson, executive of the Cincinnati League.

The subjects discussed by the conference were all areas of League concern and operation: health, housing, social agencies, church, industry, courts, schools, "publicity" and interracial cooperation. The conference was, in fact, the kind of effort that would have been organized and led a decade before by the League itself. That others had brought it into being and executed it was an indication that the NUL had lost its monopoly on initiatives in the field of interracial social action. That the NUL view of the proceedings of this 1925 conference was less than enthusiastic can be deduced from the fact that no mention of the meeting is to be found in *Opportunity* magazine, in E. K. Jones's reports to the NUL board or in the League's annual report.

The results of this Cincinnati conference were not visible in specific accomplishments. They were not apparent in abrupt changes of attitude or policy toward the League, either. But clearly there had been erosion of the leadership role of the League, and some of the League's long-time friends and supporters began to be uneasy about its grasp of conditions in its chosen field and its ability to accomplish the necessary work. The major contributors had some flutters of doubt as a result of the exposure of Marcus Garvey's success in attracting hundreds of thousands of dollars from black citizens to his efforts while the NUL was unable to raise even $68,000 (for both national and New York operations) from wealthy contributors, foundations and black community combined. A crisis of confidence was building.

The year 1928 brought further evidence of this crisis in a special conference entitled the "National Interracial Conference for the Study and Discussion of Race Problems in the United States in the Light of Social Research." Held in Washington for four days in December, it was organized by Miss Mary Van Kleeck, of the Russell Sage Foundation, who had played an important role in the 1925 Cincinnati conference. She had, as a fellow of the College Settlements Association in New York, led the investigation of women factory workers in 1905. When the Russell Sage Foundation established a division of industrial studies in 1916 Mary Van Kleeck became its director. From this post she went to the Department of Labor as director of its newly created Woman in Industry Service in 1918 and it was there that she met and worked closely with George Haynes, then the director of Negro Economics of the department. Following that service she returned to her position at the Russell Sage Foundation. Dissatisfied with the limitations of the 1925 conference, she moved in 1926 to bring together national leaders to construct "a reasonably faithful contemporary picture of Negro life and relationships with the white race in the United States." It was this effort that culminated in the conference of 1928 and a book, *The Negro in American Civilization*.[4]

This 1928 Washington conference was more inclusive than the 1925 meeting and it avoided the petty mistakes of that previous conclave by including the NUL as one of the sixteen sponsoring organizations, putting E. K. Jones in charge of the membership committee, and Elizabeth Walton, John Hope, Hollingsworth Wood and Jones on the executive committee. (Will Alexander's Commission on Interracial Cooperation and Haynes's Department of Race Relations played key roles.) Moreover, the wheelhorse of the conference was Charles S. Johnson, who was lent to it by the NUL for six months to serve as organizer and officially listed as Conference Research Secretary.

This gathering was attended by representatives of the major foundations, leading university departments of sociology and economics, and agencies active in work among blacks. The purpose, wrote Elmer Carter, was "to pool all the available information which has been collected by public and private agencies and to interpret this information for the future guidance of interracial endeavor."[5]

Observing the conference as an obvious endorsement of the NUL's interracial approach, *Opportunity*'s editor both approved the conference's findings and chided it:

> Experience has shown that the problems of the Negro cannot be adequately met by discussion, no matter how erudite and dispassionate. . . . It is only when the question of the Negro is lifted out of the realm of the academicians and placed into the stream of actual life and living that all of the contending forces—the conflicting ideas, the inhibiting traditions—are exposed to the influences of racial good-will and understanding. . . . We must know the causes and the rate of Negro mortality. We must also be able to bring to bear upon the community a sense of its responsibility for the ignorance—the pitifully inadequate housing—the low incomes which contribute to the Negroes' high mortality rates and menace the health of the entire community.
>
> In other words, social research must be made to live through organized social efforts designed to meet the problems which research reveals. The Interracial Conference at Washington is a recognition of this principle, a principle which the founders of the Urban League established as the dominating element in their program for better race relations.[6]

For the evident success of this conference, E. K. Jones claimed a portion of credit for the NUL. In his annual report for the year, the League executive recorded the facts: not only did Charles S. Johnson give more than half of his time for the first nine months of the year but the NUL also gave office space and incidental services, such as those of Johnson's secretarial assistant, and the New York Urban League lent its industrial secretary, Ira deA. Reid, to assist Johnson. "The success of this conference," said Jones, "is now well known to persons interested in improving the technique of service in the field of race relations and the League is pleased with the contribution it made towards effecting this result." [7] It was also a fact that NUL lost its director of research, Charles S. Johnson, who took a post as professor of sociology at Fisk in the fall of 1928.

In this period of general malaise, when there was no single focus to interracial efforts, there were those who were dissatisfied and said so. One such was Alfred K. Stern, son-in-law of Julius Rosenwald and a member of the board of the Chicago Urban League. Stern had succeeded William C. Graves as Rosenwald's representative on the Chicago board in 1925 and had considerable influence with the newly formed Rosenwald Fund. Stern was, according to those who worked with him on League matters, opinionated, dictatorial and uncompromising.[8]

He was not easily pleased, and the Chicago League's problems displeased him greatly. At one point he urged E. K. Jones to remove the Chicago executive, but was rebuffed. The industrial relations program needed more attention and manpower, he believed, but the man hired for these purposes was, in his view, unqualified. The action of the local League board in censuring the University of Chicago's Billings Hospital for discriminatory practices upset him (the university received substantial Rosenwald support). He opposed hiring E. Franklin Frazier as the Chicago League's director of research but was overridden by the board. As Arvarh E. Strickland, chronicler of the Chicago Urban League, concludes, "many of Stern's criticisms of the League's work were justified, but his attitude was more likely to destroy the organization than to make it a more effective agency." [9]

Stern had grandiose ideas about the national race relations scene as well. He had conceived the notion that consolidation was needed for the good of all concerned. The fund-raising difficulties of the separate agencies and the weaknesses in administration, he believed, could be overcome if the NAACP and NUL were merged under the leadership of Will W. Alexander. In this scheme, Kinckle Jones would be Alexander's assistant, supervising programs for economic improvement of blacks.

Needless to say, the plan did not arouse enthusiasm in either NAACP or NUL leaders. Lloyd K. Garrison, NUL treasurer, had at one point toyed with the thought of merger (without any such third force as Will Alexander) simply as an expedient way of getting money to support the work. He had explored it with the NAACP and abandoned it, realizing that it would only result in limiting the effectiveness of each agency.[10]

Rumors of a merger under the Rosenwald aegis persisted as late as 1933, nevertheless, and were vehemently denied by NUL officials.[11] The following year James Weldon Johnson, general secretary of the NAACP, published his proposal for a "correlation of all forces" in which blacks would "channel our forces so that they will function through a central machine." This, he declared, would create a "super-power." He called for coordinating the strength of black religious, fraternal, political, economic and press power in such a way as to make the NAACP "the spearhead of our forces, in a way that will enable it to shift the emphasis more and more from protest to action." [12] Johnson's seeds fell on barren ground. NUL was not the only agency that expressed no interest in the plan.

Stern had discovered some others who were dissatisfied in one way or another with the NUL. One of these was Beardsley Ruml, of the Laura Spelman Rockefeller Memorial Fund, which was supporting the NUL generously at the time and had, in 1929, made a three-year commitment of up to $15,000 on the basis of the NUL's raising four dollars for every one from this fund. Ruml told Stern that he had spoken to both Hollingsworth Wood and E. K. Jones "expressing dissatisfaction as to their properly covering the field of work in which they are operating." [13] Ruml, according to Stern, told the NUL men that the Laura Spelman Rockefeller Memorial Fund would not contribute to the agency after the pledge was fulfilled, as far as he was concerned.

Stern, advising his father-in-law, Julius Rosenwald, stated that E. K. Jones was "the dominating influence in the entire organization" and that it was "our opinion" (his and Edwin Embree's, the head of the Rosenwald Fund) that Jones was "incompetent to fill that position." Stern said that Jones controlled, "for the most part, both the policies of the organization and the appointment of local secretaries." The secretaries of the Chicago, Springfield, Illinois, Richmond and Atlanta local Leagues were incompetent, charged Stern, and the "capable" New York secretary "has had considerable difficulty with the national." [14]

Locally, Stern resigned from the Chicago League board and Rosenwald notified it that he would not contribute in 1929–1930. Stern also carried his antipathy further, and with the head of the Wabash Avenue YMCA, tried to persuade other contributors to turn against the Chicago League. In this, he had little success.[15]

Nationally, Stern influenced the Rosenwald Fund to cut back its program support to the NUL, limiting it to $1,000 plus underwriting one or two NUL Fellows for future service as League executives. For the League it was a sorry decline from the days in 1911 when Rosenwald underwrote, on a matching basis, up to 20 percent of the NUL budget.

There were others who were critical of the League at this time. Will Alexander was one. He called the full-time League leadership in the south inadequate in training and temperament to deal with the complicated, "little understood" fundamental question of race relations in the region. However, the southern staff was, he noted, doing "some excellent social work for Negroes in communities." [16]

Even Charles S. Johnson had serious doubts. NUL programs, he said, had been somewhat "diffused and uncertain" and the current work was "ineffective." Its southern headquarters, Johnson suggested, should turn to expanding both policy and program by enlisting the practical working interest and confidence of influential southerners.[17]

Though Alfred Stern was highly critical of E. K. Jones, there were those who were disenchanted with League president L. Hollingsworth Wood also. One of the Carnegie Corporation specialists jotted down a brief evaluation calling "the League's work . . . fairly effective, though tending to be assertive through its Executive Secretary Jones." The reporter stated that he was not "sold" on Hollingsworth Wood, calling him vocal, aggressive and a "carpet bagger who does not go well in the south." [18]

Mary Van Kleeck advised the Rockefeller interests of her reservations about the League. "There is some question whether with the opportunity at hand the Urban League could do more effective work among the Negroes." [19] With its forty local Leagues, should the work of the national office be primarily service or should it develop its own policies and activities? she asked. Coordination of the work of the locals might be more effective in obtaining the acceptance of League policies through concentrated effort rather than through individual spasmodic efforts. She criticized the fact that the NUL had no field secretary, so visits to branches occurred only when some pressing situation developed.[20]

She might also have reported that without the money to hire a field secretary and carry out the program she suggested it would be impossible to judge accurately the League's ability to make its work more effective. Would the economy of withholding a few thousand dollars (perhaps eight or ten) justify restricting the agency? Was lack of money crippling it like a Chinese bound foot, preventing it from exercising wider services in its natural field? What could the League have accomplished if it had received even one quarter of the support of the CIC? How else could it add a field secretary except with a larger budget?

No one will ever know, for economy rather than expansion was the decision. It was, indeed, the order of the day.

22/Anchor and Hope

For blacks, the Great Depression began in the winter of 1928—a full year before the crash. At that time, layoffs of black workers and rise of black unemployment were what today's economists would call "leading indicators." They pointed to worsening business conditions—and they were deadly accurate.

T. Arnold Hill attributed the unemployment to two factors: continuing migration of both blacks and whites to the cities (census figures would later show that the black migration continued throughout the twenties at the average rate of some 75,000 per year); and technological displacement, or the replacement of men by machines.

"For almost two years," stated Hill, "attempts have been made to trace the cause to vicious design on the part of prejudiced whites. Investigation has failed to reveal concerted effort in this direction, but it has shown the uncontrollable impulse to preserve one's self at the expense of social prestige and tradition." [1]

As a consequence white men are driving trucks and express wagons in the south, repairing streets, doing the scavenger work, delivering ice on their backs where formerly Negroes delivered and white men collected for deliveries, serving as waiters and bellmen in hotels and doing other tasks which were once regarded only fit for Negroes. This same practice passes beyond menial occupations to the building trades where impressive losses are felt keenly. . . . The transformation goes on in the north as well where elevator operators, doormen, house servants, and hotel men are more often white than colored. [2]

Further on in his review, Hill noted that black workers were trickling into various vocations, many of them for the first time and some of them as skilled workers. However, job conditions among black workers in general were precarious. At the end of the twenties Hill found that:

Of the 1,000,000 Negroes engaged in industry the majority are unskilled workers in steel and iron plants, lumber and turpentine mills, slaughter houses, railroad construction, and the like. Of the 1,500,000 women in gainful occupations, all but 80,000 of them were in agriculture, domestic and personal service, dressmaking, tobacco factories and teaching. No other classification had as many as 10,000. [3]

President Hoover's tenacious dedication to the principle of "rugged individualism" meant that government employment policies would not be used to compensate for the failure of the private sector to sustain American workers, black or white. The fact was that at the beginning of the 1929 fiscal year the United States government had on its payroll only 51,882 black citizens, who received aggregate wages from the federal treasury of $64,483,133; an average of less than $104 per month. Half of these (25,390) were in the Post Office Department; the War, Navy and Treasury departments had more than five thousand each. Only five other executive departments or sections had as many as 500 black workers. Clearly, federal employment was not a major factor as an underpinning for black workers, and with a President dedicated to individual initiative for workers and *laissez-faire* for employers, the prospects were dim for opening federal careers for Afro-Americans. [4]

The focus in the Hoover era, therefore, would have to be the private sector, as it always had been.

As Hill surveyed the gloomy prospects for black workers in the widening unemployment of May 1929, he concluded that "the pressing need of the hour is a plan for the Negro's occupational future." This, said Hill, blacks had never had. The Afro-American had come north "to meet industrial exigencies created by the war crisis," and otherwise had made his entry into industry when there was a strike to be broken or a labor shortage or onerous or low-paid work to be done—conditions that made his labor expedient, following which, as the emergencies subsided, "he was discharged and left to find his way as best he could." [5]

Considering the uncertain industrial conditions of 1929, Hill alerted black workers that they must prepare themselves for the future. "Lacking opportunities for apprenticeship [the Negro] can make effective demand upon Land Grant college and trade schools for thorough courses in mechanical arts. Our losses in building operations have been due in part to our failure to apprentice or to follow courses of instruction in schools." [6]

Hill's comments reflected the thinking of NUL's executive secretary, E. K. Jones, who, in an unusually acerbic speech scrutinized the American economy and educational system in the fall of 1929. Jones attacked the inadequate schooling of most American children in regard to term, quality and applicability. Though the phrase "drop-outs" had not come into use, Jones spoke of Massachusetts boys, 75 percent of whom did not finish school, as "occupational nomads." Schools should take over the function formerly assumed by apprenticeship, that is, develop work-study plans that would prepare youngsters for jobs and for "a complete life." [7]

In a remarkable spell-out of goals, Jones called for education adapted to individual needs; consideration of social conditions in which the child lived; vocational counseling geared to the child's capacity and available occupations; adult education for those denied educational advantages; more money to train teachers and provide equipment—therefore "adequate occupational or vocational training"; and a higher compulsory education age limit. And yet, said Jones, education must not simply prepare men and women only for work that returns the largest financial profits to others. "Higher forms of socialized happiness must be secured" by cultivating (among other things) respect for justice, personal honor, independence and self-support. He noted that "breaking down of spirit increases dependency (the Negro needs a renaissance in this particular . . . .)." [8]

Jones reviewed the "difficulties inherent in our present day society," which included subordination of workers by masters in slavery and by "the factory system and the laissez-faire political economy." These conditions required development of plans of cooperation between employers and workers to reduce unemployment and low wages; and special attention to securing educational advantages for blacks in the south, thereby "emancipating" all workers. Solution to such education problems would require much larger expenditures of public funds, said Jones, and then quickly sketched the disproportionate distribution of income in the United States, stating that "the corporate form of concentrated control makes for irresponsible control and accentuates operation for profits only."

"Palliative work can be done through case work . . . [and by] helping the family to take advantage of existing facilities through better training and vocational guidance for the children in the home, but the big job is that of influencing our political systems to the end that more adequate provision may be made for the development of our school systems taking into consideration the total educational needs of the people, approached through the children. . . . The dependency due to lack of industrial training can only be removed by making provision for more adequate training through the channels of the public school, supported by the taxes of the people." In this conclusion Jones was right back where Booker T. Washington had been thirty years before.[9]

NUL effort in the industrial education field came after T. Arnold Hill had traveled through the south, midwest and west coast searching for some solution to the disastrous unemployment among blacks. He found only despair and more despair, even among youths.

Having put together an industrial relations advisory committee with League treasurer Lloyd K. Garrison as its chairman, Hill proposed to this group that NUL's Industrial Relations Department be enlarged for a greater effort. To buttress his case, he supplied his committee with a ten-page paper backgrounding the needs, present activities, proposals for enlarging the program (under eight headings) and five points for consideration and decision before he came to the price tag: for two staff assistants, one clerk, funds for additional travel, publicity, and so on—$12,000 additional.

Hill's "Proposals for Enlarged Program" were the heart of his memo and consisted of a distillation of his fifteen years experience in League work. The "Proposals" constituted a perceptive projection into the future as well. The nine areas he discussed were the local Leagues, black workers, white workers, employers, public opinion, training facilities, public agencies and research and publicity.[10]

Pointing out that black workers needed incentive, Hill also urged that they be told of opportunities to train and advised to take advantage of them. White workers, he noted, had been all but overlooked in League efforts and to meet objections of whites to employment of blacks, Hill recommended "taking our propaganda directly to groups of employees in meetings called for the purpose using appealing speakers such as attractive and knowledgeable black and/or white girls and specially-designed literature." [11]

Hill called for approaches to large national multiplant companies. Furthermore, he struck a note of new militancy: "Companies that are known to have a number of Negro patrons should certainly be asked to give employment to Negroes . . . chain stores, certain insurance companies, the telephone company and five and ten cent stores." And he called for moving in on manufacturers in new industries where traditions against blacks had not solidified.

Local Leagues soon seized this technique. The Chicago *Whip* had started it with a campaign to put black workers in the stores selling goods in the black community. With persistence, irrefutable logic and an unforgettable slogan, "Don't Buy Where You Can't Work," the upstart *Whip* had united the black masses behind its campaign. As the Pittsburgh *Courier* observed, "Because of the campaign of the *Whip* there are more colored folk employed in the business establishments on the South Side than ever before and the white people concerned in the change have a greater respect for the group. . . . There ought to be such a campaign in every city in the United States." [12] And the word had spread. In Philadelphia, the local League affiliate had launched a similar campaign with the black weekly Philadelphia *Tribune* and placed a clerk in a chain grocery. In St. Louis, the League had put pressure on the St. Louis Dairy Company and it had hired blacks.

In New York, Samuel A. Allen, industrial secretary of the local League, had formed the Co-operative Committee on Employment made up of representatives of social agencies in Harlem. This committee took on the task of placing black clerks in Harlem stores. As a direct result, seven elevator operators were placed in the largest department store near the district and the Western Union Telegraph Company put in an all-black staff in its 135th Street branch.

Public opinion, said T. Arnold Hill, should be approached on a broader basis, through use of radio and more literature. Training facilities should be looked into by a subcommittee of the NUL industrial committee and "the whole question of manual training for Negroes in the light of present day potentialities" should be studied, with particular reference to trade schools in the south. Vocational guidance and instruction of black youths should be changed. "Many counselors do not know of the lines of work open to colored people and are still advising menial and domestic occupations as the only certain fields of employment." Time and effort should be devoted to opening union and corporation apprenticeship training.

Public agencies, Hill stated, should be approached via procedures worked out by the NUL industrial committee. "Our duty here is to point out to the Department of Labor in Washington, the New York State

Labor Commission . . . and similar state commissions tasks they might assume with reference to colored workers. The Department of Commerce now has a colored employee who visits colored communities in order to assist them with their commercial problems. He is encouraging business among Negroes. Does this offer a suggestion of a possible service by the Department of Labor?" [13]

Hill, in this outline for the future, had the program. He did not get the staff nor the money to carry it out. In fact, having begun 1929 with a deficit of $4,300, NUL's prospects for expansion were slight. As the year progressed, and after the October crash, the financial situation turned from serious to grave. With staff paychecks weeks late, both E. K. Jones and Hollingsworth Wood frantically beat the bushes for contributions.

T. Arnold Hill called two conferences of League executives in the fall of 1929. At the first one, in Columbus, Ohio, eleven Leagues were represented. The second, at the New York Urban League, drew together eastern League representatives. John Dancy of Detroit and William L. Evans of Buffalo agreed that industrial problems were largely an indication of other interracial problems and the group consensus was that "an approach to the problem of the Negro in industry can probably be better made through interracial understanding." [14]

Hill suggested a campaign using two approaches: (1) getting blacks to think industrially; and (2) moving employers to think in terms of black workers. William Conners of the Cleveland League said emphasis should be placed on preparing blacks for industrial opportunities and participation in industries. Evans questioned the encouraging of students to enter trade and technical schools if there were no opportunities for using such training. Conners said that was the policy of the Cleveland schools, but he believed that students should be shown there was opportunity to use such training and then the question should be raised with the school superintendent.

The discussion moved again to what the League could do and it soon was apparent that John Dancy, for one, was apprehensive that in Detroit a campaign aimed at industry and black workers might be dangerous. He had discussed this matter with both whites and blacks and with 40,000 Afro-Americans in Detroit plants; "any little rupture might make things hard." What Dancy and others feared was a boycott campaign of the sort launched in Chicago by the Chicago *Whip*. The stridency and uncompromisingly militant stand were too far out for Dancy and some other League secretaries. Such approaches might "upset their apple carts."

Hill suggested emphasizing conduct; someone else recommended that opportuntities be stressed. The local League executives agreed that the program should vary with the local conditions and the committee appointed to suggest a name for the observance (A. C. Thayer of Pittsburgh, William Evans of Buffalo and J. A. Thomas of Louisville) recommended "Opportunity Campaign." After much discussion, this was modified to "Vocational Opportunity Campaign."

John T. Clark proposed that NUL attempt to secure President Hoover to make a one-minute radio talk in connection with VOC, and that NUL should use most of its energy through radio to publicize vital facts. Others proposed that NUL produce appropriate literature and that the churches be enlisted in the VOC.

As a parting shot, T. Arnold Hill raised the question as to "how far are we going to back any effort to get Negroes in stores; to what extent are the Urban Leagues trying to get . . . solidarity." John Clark responded that "we have got to develop such a desire in us" and there was a suggestion that the League focus on occupations in which blacks did not then have jobs.[15]

Soon after his return to New York, Hill received a letter from W. Robert Smalls, the Minneapolis executive, about the campaign. "I feei that we ought to lay stress nationally on just what the Negro himself can do in improving his own status," emphasized Smalls. He told Hill how hard it was to get black boys to attend Dunwoody Institute, one of the finest vocational training schools in the country. And he related his bitter experience in losing the opportunity to place twelve black girls as stenographers because he could not locate a qualified bookkeeper with experience to head up this operation for a mail-order house. Even before that, the Minneapolis League had missed out in placing several black workers in a large machine shop because they were not to be found "and you know the spirit of this locality toward importing workers." [16]

The loss of customary occupations, said Hill, "has left Negroes without anchor and without hope. As a consequence they are depressed and need the stimulus which a national campaign in their behalf will generate." [17]

So, in the period of April 20 to 27, 1930, the first Vocational Opportunity Campaign was held. The NUL issued two modest leaflets, one of them telling the VOC purposes, specifically:

First: To emphasize the importance of work and wages in the scheme of life for all peoples, particularly the American Negro. We should stress not only that it is necessary for Negroes to think more of their economic life, but also to pursue accepted practices and theories in their search for a larger place in occupations.

Second: To expose the fallacies respecting the ability of Negroes to do only the laborious and menial types of work they are most often permitted to do. While this is a bad time to appeal for jobs, it is not a bad time to put forth the achievements we have made in industry, professions, transportation and trades in general to propagandize for a larger place in the productive and professional pursuits of the country.[18]

The other leaflet was entitled "Unemployment and Vocations" and was a reprint of T. Arnold Hill's March 1930 article in *Opportunity*. In this the campaign purpose was given more succinctly: [19]

To improve the Negro's conception of his own part in his struggle for place in industry and to expose the fallacies respecting the ability of Negroes to do only the laborious and menial types of work.

Our reaction to this economic philosophy of the Negro must of necessity be a more serious emphasis upon vocational training and guidance. Our private colleges have come in for much criticism of late because the quality and quantity of preparation have not met the need. Counselors in public school systems must encourage Negro boys and girls to train for whatever occupation they lean toward rather than for the courses they are always advised to take—domestic science and commercial subjects. The standard by which Negro capacity has been gauged has not been the ability of the student but the limited classification of occupations open to members of their race. Thus this practice has limited our boys and girls to what they were allowed to do rather than to what they could do. Mothers and fathers have discouraged the pursuit of trade training, content to have their sons and daughters follow the usual occupations open to Negroes. The Industrial Relations Department of the National Urban League senses *vocational variation* as an essential step in our occupational advancement. It will loom up in the League's program with increased emphasis as a main feature toward which the national organization and its various locals will address its best efforts [emphasis added].[20]

In those words, T. Arnold Hill sketched the misapplication of education, counseling and training that had given black Americans far too little ammunition in their battle for economic survival. Now, at the pit of the Depression, this visionary sounded the trumpet for action and the NUL launched a campaign not geared to immediate relief, but to the ultimate hiring on their merits of skilled Afro-Americans. Though some believed the timing was all wrong, Hill and the League began the VOC in 1930 and expanded it in succeeding years, reaching millions with annual themes such as "Plan and Prepare, the Future is Yours."

It was none too early to move. In many cities, vocational education and trade training for blacks were under attack. In 1926, the white bricklayers in Nashville had petitioned the city council to halt trade training for black youngsters in the school. Charles S. Johnson noted that seventy-five years before it was the white carpenters of Atlanta who similarly petitioned the city council.

In some cases blacks themselves joined in the assault. A survey of in-

dustrial conditions in Richmond, Virginia, in 1930 showed that blacks
had lost skilled jobs in alarming numbers in recent years. One of the important factors in this loss was found to be a shortage of vocational training opportunities. Yet, when the Julius Rosenwald Fund offered to establish an industrial school similar to those in other southern cities, the
board of education declined on the ground that trade training had been
"tabooed" by Richmond blacks. An impartial investigator reported that
the Richmond Board of Education's statement was, by and large, correct.
This was the kind of self-defeating view of the future among blacks that
the League, through VOC, was determined to turn around.[21]

As *Opportunity* put it, "for this campaign to achieve complete success,
it must accomplish even more than a change of attitude on the part of
white employers and employees. It must break the spell which the van-
ishing 'Negro job' has cast over Negro youth and infuse him with courage 'to strive, to seek, to find, and not to yield.' For after all, the power to
win a place in industry rests with him." [22]

In that first VOC, fifty cities cooperated, 177 employers were interviewed, talks were made before luncheon, fraternal, women's and other
clubs, literature was distributed and some 58,000 people attended 164
meetings on the subject during the period. The message was broadcast
thirteen times and newspapers such as the Richmond *Times-Dispatch*
and Cincinnati *Post* endorsed the effort.[23]

In its second year it was evident that the VOC had struck a vital note.
Eight black universities included VOC Week in their curricula, featuring
assemblies, faculty conferences and job forums. League literature went to
450 secondary schools for blacks. (This literature included a question-
naire asking youngsters' thoughts about their futures. The responses
helped plan future VOC's.) More than fifty cities, seventeen radio stations, many daily and weekly newspapers and twenty-nine other social
agencies promoted the VOC in 1931.[24]

The VOC in 1932 had as its theme "After the Depression—What?," a
question whose answer was attempted by the League in emphasizing career preparation. In this bleak Depression year the VOC offered some so-
lace to blacks by underscoring the broadening of opportunities from the
formerly narrow service and agriculture ruts. The 1930 census had found
that blacks were engaged in 530 of the 534 major occupational groupings.
The inference was that no field was now proscribed to blacks—if they
were prepared. Unfortunately, the color bar and the drastic, absolute
shrinkage of the job market relegated this conclusion to the realm of
theory—unemployment rates among blacks in Chicago, Cleveland and
St. Louis were running 40 to 50 percent and as high as 75 percent in
Birmingham.

Kinckle Jones commented, in an inspirational talk on "Why a VOC?," that certain occupations normally showed increases in blacks employed (stationary engineers, plant foremen, mail carriers, musicians, insurance agents, store clerks, plumbers, retailers, machinists, garment workers, and so on). Whites "conveniently" questioned the capacity of blacks, Jones stated, and should be told about the race's progress in vocations and potential as well as the availability of workers. VOC was designed to carry such messages to the white community. Further, it was necessary to educate the schools about the need for vocational advice and important to encourage and bring to the attention of black youngsters the career possibilities stemming from well-directed initiative.[25]

Economic conditions became so desperate and the League staff stretched so thin that VOC was suspended for the next three years. In 1937 NUL planned a campaign to reach 3,000,000 youths.

The week-long VOC drive began with a nationwide broadcast on NBC featuring United States Commissioner of Education John W. Studebaker. Some 170 black schools participated and Greek-letter fraternal organizations, the YM and YWCA, state employment services, the United States Office of Education and Department of the Interior cooperated. A breakthrough was the extraordinary aid extended by the National Youth Administration, whose state offices distributed VOC literature and promoted the campaign where there was no local League. In Ohio, Pennyslvania, and Illinois the NYA sponsored the VOC program throughout the states.

Associated closely with the VOC was the NUL Industrial Relations Department's effort to get a stream of press releases to the black newspapers. These releases alerted readers to federal, state and municipal civil service jobs coming up. Local Leagues conducted classes, gathered libraries of pertinent materials and bibliographies and even furnished typewriters which black civil service candidates could use to prepare for examinations. As a result, blacks in many states, even in the deep south, qualified for civil service jobs.

The VOC had proved its worth and was repeated annually thereafter. Each year new literature was prepared and distributed; radio was used with increasing effect locally and more pamphlets came from the NUL.

In 1935 T. Arnold Hill penned the foreword to a booklet called *They Crashed the Color Line* in which he capsulized the goals of VOC during the thirties:

> That driving spirit which impels success must be the possession of a large number of Negro young people. It must be accompanied by training to the point that they will develop definite skill for definite vocations. The chances of killing this spirit are greater than are those of keeping it alive. Toward this end the public schools and all agencies interested in Negro youth must plan definitely to render service.[26]

23/The Great Leveler

The forced impoverishment of millions taught Americans a lesson—the hard way—that black citizens had been trying to get across for sixty-five years. The lesson was that forces beyond their control could and did make beggars of people. Always before there had been enough Americans who were either prosperous or able to "get by" until the wheels started turning again and their fortunes brightened. Suddenly, the whole machine ground to a halt, and there was no family untouched by the icy freeze that struck the economy. It was clear to millions that what had hit them was not some righteous moral judgment of a wrathful God, nor had they brought on their personal calamity by their individual actions in most cases. The forces at work were far greater than any individuals could change. In fact, even groups of individuals—corporations, trusts, cartels—all the most sophisticated and sensitive constructions of modern man—were inadequate in the massive debacle of the Great Depression.

So, among the lessons that became manifest, the basic ones had huge significance for American blacks. For the first time in history whites understood to a degree never before so widespread that there was no moral judgment on the poor. If the good, the bad and the run-of-the-mill all were suffering, something had to be done for that suffering and, as rapidly became apparent, private welfare and social work agencies could scarcely skim the surface. Even the emergency efforts of the towns and cities were good for a few weeks at most. But as the conditions worsened and, like an open wound, became inflamed by the many inadequate patent medicines applied, the clamor for relief on a meaningful and sustained scale became insistent, even frightening.

There was only one possible resource big enough to respond to the gargantuan needs, and that was the federal government. Even under the celluloid-collar administration of Herbert Hoover the federal government began to move, began to be pushed and forced into accepting responsibility—temporary and piecemeal only—for aid to the newly indigent. For by 1930 the poor were everywhere and might be anybody—

one's neighbor, one's brother-in-law, the shopkeeper and grocer, the boss
—if you still had one—even oneself.

The year 1930 was a turning point for millions of Americans and for
NUL. It was the year that the League's monumental study of Negro
membership in American labor unions was completed and once and for
all the NUL stopped pursuing the chimera of an unbiased AFL.

It was the year that NUL moved to a militant stance in dealing with
employers, unions and government.

It was the year that the agency pushed as never before to get black representation on public agencies, commissions and committees that dispensed relief or jobs.

During 1930 the Urban Leaguers at their annual conference redirected
the agency toward economic basics—getting education and training for
youths to qualify for jobs; counseling with employers for jobs; pressing
local sales outlets of national firms to employ blacks and pressuring black
community retailers to hire blacks or face boycotts; retraining and giving
supplemental training to blacks who had the background but did not
qualify when they applied for skilled jobs.

The year 1930 was one in which some local Leagues were forced back
to fundamentals: operating survival centers, dispensing food, clothing,
"made" work, finding shelter and providing services to refugees from the
economic ice age.

In March of 1930 the NUL research department estimated that at least
330,000 black wage earners were no longer wage earners. Six months
later, the agency found that instead of decreasing, the unemployed had
increased. In November Ira Reid and T. Arnold Hill collaborated on a
special report, *Unemployment Among Negroes, Activities of the National
Urban League, Data on 25 Industrial Cities.* They found that in those
twenty-five cities there was a decrease of 34.5 percent of available jobs for
blacks and an increase of 40 percent in job applicants over the same period the year before. The drop in available jobs in leading cities registered as:

Cleveland	62.1 percent
Philadelphia	51.3
Chicago	50.1
Cincinnati	47.3
Brooklyn	21.4
New York	21.3
[Manhattan]	
Pittsburgh	13.5

In Cincinnati, though blacks constituted 7.5 percent of the population,
they made up 25 percent of the unemployed. In Gary, though they were

10 percent of the population, they were 50 percent of the out-of-work. Detroit had 27 percent of its black families on "the dole" from the city. In Buffalo, "streets are lined with unemployed men and evidence of privation and suffering is beginning to manifest itself in every section." [1]

League officials were serving on various relief and emergency employment committees in ten major cities. Understandably, the relief measures and organizations varied considerably from city to city. In Pittsburgh a $100,000 city appropriation for relief was administered by black case workers. Cleveland planned to provide three days a week of "public employment" every other week, at $4.80 per day. A League staff man was helping to register the unemployed for such jobs.

In some places the radicals of both right and left had surfaced. Communists were promising relief to blacks who joined the party. The Black Shirts of Atlanta boasted a membership spanning the south and demanded blacks be fired from any and all jobs wanted by whites.

Concluding that "the problem of unemployment among Negroes is serious enough to demand special attention," Reid and Hill called on official agencies "to offset the inequalities usually found in work relationships involving Negroes and certain to appear during a crisis such as this." They frankly admitted that "what the League forces are doing and causing to be done locally is not sufficient." And they ended on the ominous note: "Violent competition between white and black workers comes to the front in times like these to prove the weakness of an industrial system that pushes one group forward at the expense of another. The removal of this artificial barrier is the challenge to American industry." The NUL executives had not yet brought themselves to the Rubicon of calling for government action instead of private. [2]

Actually, T. Arnold Hill was appointed liaison officer between Hoover's Emergency Employment Committee and the Negro population. Hill used the post to put before the committee the facts about black unemployment throughout the nation and in turn drew from the committee facts about projected public works. This information Hill fed to black citizens in the areas concerned via the local Leagues, *Opportunity* magazine and the black press. The purpose was to help Afro-Americans get in on the ground floor as the plans were unrolled in the local communities.

Hill also wrote the governors of all states plus the Agriculture and Interior Department secretaries, calling on them to give fair recognition to the dire needs of black workers as public projects were inaugurated and jobs assigned. [3]

Hill's wider exposure to the national pressures of the period included his generalship of NUL's nationwide industrial relations campaign, the planning of the annual conference in Buffalo on the theme "Vocational Opportunities for Negro Workers"; his scorching attack on the AFL and his service on the White House Conference on Child Health and Protection. Hill was one of ten who signed the authoritative report on *The Economic Status of the Negro* requested by President Hoover and financed by Julius Rosenwald in 1930.

It was at the White House Conference that E. K. Jones stated the principle that the League recommended to secure care for black adults as well as children:

> In the matter of operation and control of agencies for Negroes, we believe it is beneficial to have mixed boards of control. We believe it would be desirable to have Negro dependents handled by agencies responsible for the whole community rather than to organize special agencies just for the care of the Negro group and that whenever it is possible, we believe there should be Negro representation in administration and support of these agencies.[4]

This was just one step short of demanding that community agencies should serve blacks and place them on their boards. Blacks had learned the hard way over the years that segregated social services were inferior social services, doled out from a disproportionately small slice of the total community welfare budget. The only way to get a fair share was to be in on the slicing. Atlanta's handling of relief was a liberal and enlightened (for the south) example. Even there the relief efforts that were attempted were not only inadequate but doled out with an uneven hand. Jesse O. Thomas took up this matter with the mayor of Atlanta:

> We have received reports from various sources relative to discrimination practiced in the city warden's office in giving assistance to the needy who apply at the office for aid in getting food, coal, etc. A social worker whom we had investigate the rumors reported that the method . . . is this: A representative of the warden's office comes out into the hall and takes the names of those who are to be given consideration as they are permitted to pass inside the office. No Negro names are taken by this individual so that when a Negro goes in, the person whose duty it is to dispense material relief, finds that his name does not appear on the list, and therefore he cannot be considered. We will appreciate it very much if you will investigate this situation and will lend the influence of your office in clearing it up.[5]

The reply was short and quick. The mayor's executive secretary wrote Thomas:

> An investigation of this matter has been made by me and Miss Ivey, who works in that department, states that this is a falsehood and that no discrimination is made between white and colored. That they serve the most

needy ones first as they find them, and if there is anything left, they serve the others.[6]

The roll call of local Leagues in 1930 found many of them deep in relief work with at least one staff member serving on some community-wide emergency organization:

Akron—Arrangements made for Negroes to secure odd jobs . . . care also arranged for homeless men; *Atlanta*—Urban League Emergency Relief Committee organized, serving destitute Negro families with Research Department of Atlanta School of Social Work investigating; *Brooklyn*—Emergency Work Bureau placing persons 3 days a week, reconditioning churches, Y's, club houses; *Boston*—Latter part of year devoted largely to relief of unemployed; *Chicago*—concentrated on skilled and semi-skilled placements, and made 1666; fostered schools for salesmen, office workers, household employees and for waiters, in cooperation with board of education; *Cleveland*—Intensive campaign to register and place unemployed, even if part-time jobs (300 placed in casual jobs, down from 1200 previous year); *Detroit*—Swamped; 1500 placements (mostly temporary) out of 8500 applications (smallest number placed in years); *Kansas City*—4750 applied for work, 765 were placed; League was headquarters for unemployment relief for Greater Kansas City Employment Committee; *New York*—Conducted workshop with temporary jobs three days a week for men and women; placed 2,000 in temporary jobs; added 14 emergency workers for family rehabilitation—finding temporary quarters for dispossessed, placing children in homes, sending needy to relatives and friends; organized Harlem Housewives League to work for the employment of Negroes in stores catering to Negro business; *Omaha*—Swimming pool incident nearly sparked race riot; UL secretary one of three appointed by mayor to "adjust the situation;" *Philadelphia*—In cooperation with the Philadelphia *Tribune* campaigned to get jobs for blacks in stores patronized by them; 18 men placed as clerks in stores such as A & P, American Stores, etc.; *St. Louis*—Labor conferences resulted in forming "mechanics associations" of electricians, plumbers, plasterers, draftsmen, engineers, bricklayers, etc., excluded from local unions; these quasi-unions located jobs for black workers; Hotel Employees Conference resulted in representative using League office space as center for placement of workers in hotels, country clubs, restaurants, etc. and training course for hotel service organized at local vocational school; League, as part of Vocational Opportunity Campaign, "convinced" chain stores, laundries and dairy firms of importance of "extending opportunity to Negro workers; . . . one dairy turned over eight routes to black drivers; three laundries hired from one to three blacks for laundry routes and a chain grocery hired black clerks in three of its stores. (The dairy and laundry drivers were immediately taken into their respective unions). With five full-time workers in the industrial department, the League received 40,500 job applications and placed 3,550; the League led the fight to se-

cure state licenses for a black plumber and an engineer—firsts. *Toledo*—
with other agencies, got stores to hire black clerks; distributed 15 tons of
coal to needy families.[7]

As NUL President Wood put it, the League offices across the country
constituted "a very delicate and responsive barometer to industrial
changes," and in 1930, local League activities showed clearly "the usefulness of the organization and the increasing dependence of other agencies
upon us in meeting their problems." [8] But if Wood's view of the League's
services in this critical year harked back to the depression of 1921 or even
that of 1914, he had miscalculated the trend of the times and the temper
of the nation's blacks. The new stance of the agency was typified in
T. Arnold Hill's year-end memo to E. K. Jones urging that NUL go right
to the top—to the President of the United States:

> Unemployment has been especially severe among Negro workers. . . .
> They are getting relief in all cities from which we have records, but they
> are not getting work. . . .
> Nothing will strengthen the heart of Negroes more than a meeting in
> the White House with the President . . . of a group of outstanding Ne-
> groes to discuss this question. . . . If the President hears the case . . . what-
> ever disposition is made—the fact that it gets before him will have favora-
> ble psychological reactions among Negroes, whether the practical results
> will be all that we can hope for or not. Of course we should hope to have
> definite benefits result, because we should want the President to say that
> the system is regrettable, and is working hardships upon Negroes. We
> should wish him to say that he would consider the matter and refer it to
> Governmental agencies that can effect relief. . . .[9]

Although Hill's recommendation did not result in the hoped-for White
House meeting, it was a portent of the future. It indicated where Hill believed the locus of power was shifting, in terms of psychology if not actual delivery. In earlier times, the NUL would have called a meeting of
top social workers, or educators, perhaps even industrialists. But not in
1930, when the impotence of the old idols had been exposed.

A year later, careful investigation by the NUL Research Department
showed unmistakably that conditions were worse. Ira Reid estimated that
as 1931 ended there were some 750,000 black workers unemployed. (A
year later Reid found one and one-half million blacks out of work.)
During the year he had examined information from sixty-two cities for
a report entitled *How Unemployment Affects Negroes,* and in the fall
106 cities were studied in detail and reported in *Unemployment Status of
the Negro.* Both of these studies were distributed widely to press, legislators and welfare and relief administrators in the nation. The second
report carried a section on "the unemployment contacts of the affiliated

branches of the National Urban League," spelling out the agency's activities and aid, in the form of staff workers lent, office quarters opened, volunteers recruited and committee services supplied to community-level unemployment relief efforts.[10]

T. Arnold Hill summed up the conclusions of the studies with a memo to the assistant director of the President's Organization of Unemployment Relief:

> First—Negroes are suffering to a greater extent than others.
>
> Second—As the first persons fired and the last hired, they have been longer exposed to unemployment than others and as a consequence have used up all surpluses or resources they may have accumulated.
>
> Third—There are employers who are discharging them in order to make room for white workers.
>
> Fourth—The Negro unemployment situation is too often incidental in our emergency set-ups when because of the very nature of the factors involved, their problems should have larger place and more sympathetic treatment.
>
> Fifth—Negroes with leadership qualities, social service training, and general knowledge of problems affecting their people are not being used to the extent that they should by the various relief agencies throughout the country.[11]

Consequently NUL, joined by other organizations, urged President Hoover to appoint a black member to his organization on unemployment relief. As a result, John W. Davis, head of West Virginia State College and NUL board member, was named to the Committee on Administration of Relief. Ira Reid and T. Arnold Hill kept Dr. Davis well supplied with factual data to feed into the committee.

But, as events so overwhelmingly proved, tossing data into the maw of the federal government during the Hoover administration was not enough. "We thought that in 1931 we had reached the bottom of the downward grade of business failures," lamented E. K. Jones, "and that 1932 might bring some evidence of the turn toward recovery; but there were no signs recorded of the return to normal business in our land— and our citizens again had to resort to most sacrificial and heroic efforts to save themselves from the fate of utter despair." [12]

> If the country as a whole was drifting along in its utter helplessness, the Negro—the economic pariah of the American family of peoples—found his lot a sad one indeed. He still represented the largest group proportionately of the army of the unemployed; he was pushed further down in his choice of occupations; he received a smaller proportion of the emergency jobs and of the national relief—and, to clinch the situation and to establish this condition practically as the universal policy in America, he had no repre-

sentation nationally or through state agencies, and but scant representation through local relief-giving agencies to assure himself equitable treatment.[13]

The League had acted both locally and nationally, said the executive secretary. The locals had tied into the central relief committees and had established at the neighborhood level "every conceivable relief agency— employment bureau, lodgings, food and clothing distribution station, temporary material relief facilities, even the antiquated soup kitchen in one community." [14]

Even the "bright spots" were only relative in the numb grayness of 1932. One of these was the organization of a new League in Macon, Georgia, which Jesse O. Thomas called "one of the most backward cities in the whole south." [15] As one indication of its backwardness, he said, "the board of education does not employ a janitor for Negro schools, the teachers rotate in doing the work of the janitor. The teachers also carry kindling from home to make the fire in the stoves in the morning. In the section of the city where the most colored people live, the majority of whom are property owners, there is no sewerage. . . . They have two college graduates in the school system and this is their first year. One teacher, who has been teaching in the high school for 20 years, is studying in the summer to get her high school diploma."

In this backwater the local League was, by the fall of 1932, providing essential relief. It "distributed 16,000 sacks of government flour to the poor and has been responsible for the organization of the Boy Scouts among Negro boys in Macon and the setting up of a two troop unit. They have kept an office open with three women employed for the distribution of the flour, paying them out of after-collections taken at the churches from time to time." [16]

In St. Louis John T. Clark applied the techniques that he had pioneered in Harlem as early as 1913. At that time, as head of the NLUCAN Housing Bureau and the agency's chief representative in Harlem, Clark had instituted the Negro Civic and Improvement League. This was composed of leaders from the various neighborhoods "whose integrity and whose general acquaintance with neighborhood conditions render them especially fit to lead such movements." The plan was to organize "neighborhood unions" in each black community in New York, with "volunteers residing in the districts under consideration" coming together to secure their rights and take action to fulfill their needs. Clark, by the end of 1914, had fifty men enlisted in the Civic and Improvement League in Harlem.[17]

This neighborhood union dovetailed with NLUCAN's Housing Bureau. Clark had developed the bureau into what he described as "a center for consultation on practically all matters concerning the home life of

Harlem Negroes who cannot solve their many problems." Clark and his assistants investigated reported violations of tenement house, Board of Health and police regulations and reached appropriate city authorities for action. They also conducted public meetings featuring experts to "educate the people of the community in the rights and duties of landlords and tenants." Real estate agents worked closely with the bureau, providing lists of vacancies and, conversely, checking the credentials of tenants who applied.[18]

Through the intensive investigation of living conditions of 1,002 black families in Harlem, Clark's Housing Bureau knew more about the needs and resources of citizens in that community than any other agency, public or private. And, through taking the initiative to form an emergency citizens' committee for the relief of seventy-nine families burned out in a devastating fire in 1914, the Housing Bureau had solidly demonstrated its dedication and worth to the community. It was thus that NLUCAN had become a major resource in the black community in the early teens.

In St. Louis during the Depression, the local League under Clark's leadership played a similar pivotal role. A major problem with which black citizens had to contend was the Depression-accelerated disintegration of their neighborhoods. Zoning laws were flouted as the properties of white absentee landlords were remodeled for maximum earning power. Barracks-like flats had been built on vacant lots—against the zoning laws; city service had dwindled to near-zero as street cleaning and alley cleanup were cut back and garbage collection became irregular at best. In addition, the black communities were awash in door-to-door salesmen peddling every kind of notion and appliance. These hawkers, in their feverish zeal to cover as many households as possible in the shortest time, leaped or pushed through fences, traipsed over lawns and through flower gardens making a sorry mess. These forces of deterioration were exacerbated by the sheer numbers of blacks living in the area.[19]

When the disgust of the residents of one block rose to the point that they came to the St. Louis Urban League for help, John T. Clark aided them in forming a block unit. Eleven families met in that first effort and invited every resident of the block to membership. They formed committees specifically aimed at tackling the nuisances that afflicted them from outside and from thoughtless residents in the block itself. Committees called on the theaters, department stores and merchants whose ads and leaflets littered their lawns and streets and asked them to cease and desist. The residents took a firm and unanimous stand against postmen, ice and other delivery men, salesmen and others trampling lawns, fences and gardens underfoot. A lawn improvement campaign was started that developed into a contest with prizes for the best and most beautiful yards.

Within weeks, Block Units 2, 3, 4 and 5 had been organized. One block committee made a point of demanding services from the superintendent of streets and succeeded in having the streets in its section cleaned and flushed every day. In another block, the Health Committee was particularly active, caring for each sick person and bringing group condolences when deaths occurred.

Clark assigned Mrs. Patty Cox Hall, his staff woman in charge of household demonstration, to work with the block unit program and soon it was bubbling with activity and improved *esprit.* The constitutions developed with the League's help called for improvement and cleanliness of lawns, streets and alleys; group action to check unwholesome influences; and group action to build, give support or arouse opposition to city ordinances that would affect their neighborhoods. Partisan politics and religious matters were taboo, there were no dues (unless the block unit itself voted them) and all residents, including lodgers, were eligible to belong.

By April 1933 there were twelve block units and a federation of these was organized to coordinate action on neighborhood projects. Among the projects were the cooperative buying of coal through the League's direct contact with a coal mine operator (nearly a thousand tons of coal were purchased by residents through this program) and an enlarged "lawn beautiful" contest. This became a big event, with the state horticulture society supplying the judges and the mayor donating a loving cup as first prize, plus garden tools and merchandise contributed by merchants. A gala lawn party signaled the end of the contest, and in this atmosphere of accomplishment and group solidarity the Federation of Block Units presented to the city a six-point list of policies recommended as necessary for black citizens to share in St. Louis's New Deal. These points included (1) removal of Jim Crow and the opening of all recreation facilities to black citizens; (2) replacement of trees destroyed by a tornado in residential areas and plantings on important streets; (3) correction of violations of zoning laws (that had been protested vociferously by black residents); (4) opening of Tandy Park as an "adults only" playground, enlarging the wading pool into a swimming pool; (5) installation of a separate children's playground near the city, with tennis courts and community center also; (6) more job opportunities for blacks.

From each block unit committees were appointed on each of these points. As a result of their follow-up pressure, John Clark reported a year later that 17,000 trees were planted throughout the city, but the first were installed in the black areas; a $500,000 bond issue for two community houses for blacks was pushed through and voted; recreation facilities were investigated by the city administration and inequities were ordered corrected. By mid-1934 there were seventeen block units functioning.

The potential of these units was just being explored at that stage. Some of them had boycotted unsanitary markets in their blocks; others called city sanitation officers about "odorous" butcher shops; four units joined in a boycott against a chain grocery that had fired a black clerk and shifted a white from another store. Two units boycotted a market that extended its curb market beyond the building line and forced the market into bankruptcy.

On another occasion the city levied assessments for a street-widening project on properties fully a quarter mile away. A petition by 223 black property owners denied any benefits from the widening and opposed the assessments. They presented their case so forcefully that the assessments were canceled and the board of aldermen dropped seven other street-widening projects until "more modern and fair methods were developed to pay for widenings." [20]

The block units refined their techniques early for putting the heat on city departments, and the police felt the fire on many occasions. The block units compelled the closing of lottery headquarters, "hooch joints" and other nuisances in their areas. Other city departments that received delegations and protests from these citizen organizations included the city's legal, sanitary, streets, zoning, health and forestry departments. The units were active in civic welfare projects, especially health education campaigns, and were supplied with literature and information about political issues.

John Clark reported that the total value of the properties occupied by blacks in the blocks covered amounted to more than $6,000,000, of which more than $5,000,000 was owned or controlled by blacks. At this time, he noted, there were no black aldermen, nor commissioners of education or welfare, nor commercial or trade organizations.[21]

(By 1939, block units in St. Louis had 4,152 members and had come to exert their power in boycotting and buying campaigns to strengthen black business and land jobs for blacks in theaters, stores and service outlets.)

Nationally, in 1932 E. K. Jones counseled action to keep up the morale of Negro workers in industrial centers, for "extending the whole interracial frontier by bringing into action such forces as would influence attitudes and policies." The formula he gave included (1) investigating the facts; (2) informing the public; (3) seeking the remedies for social maladjustments; (4) training and stimulating blacks "to approach the solution of their problems in a calm, determined, intelligent manner"; and (5) promoting sympathetic cooperation of thoughtful whites and blacks in "discussing and programming solutions of the social problems that become intense because of friction in interracial contacts." [22]

Jones cited the studies of the Research Department, the issues of *Opportunity* and other publicity that came via radio and public appearances, articles in newspapers and magazines; the VOC campaign in sixty cities on "After the Depression, What?"; T. Arnold Hill's intercession in the Share-the-Work Campaign; the President's Organization on Unemployment Relief, the New York State Home Relief Bureau, Emergency Work Bureau and Temporary Emergency Relief Administration, the Federal Children's Bureau, the United States Chamber of Commerce and American Legion "War Against Depression" activities, and the National Committee on Care of Transient and Homeless (Hill was a member of the committee).[23]

An example of NUL service to the local Leagues was the two-page work-up of information by Ira Reid in response to the telegraphed appeal of Floyd Covington, industrial secretary of the Los Angeles League. Covington wired:

NEED ADVICE AND AVAILABLE FIGURES IN ASSISTING DINING CAR COOKS AND WAITERS LOCAL RECEIVING A FIFTEEN PERCENT CUT IN WAGES STOP SEND COMPARATIVE DATA AVAILABLE ON WAGES COSTS AND STANDARDS OF LIVING ON ALL GROUPS FOR PERIOD OF NINETEEN TWENTY FIVE TO NINETEEN THIRTY ONE JANUARY TWENTY SEVENTH IS DATE OF ARBITRATION CONFERENCE ADVISE ME AT ONCE STOP [24]

The data were assembled and rushed to Covington. But such efforts, valiant as they were, counted for little against profit and loss statements that dictated drastic cuts. At a time when many believed they caught the distant rumblings of the tumbrels and predicted blood in the streets the League at the national level had to become more relevant or go under. Hill's glimpse of the future was an open-ended query:

Must Negroes threaten or fight their way into employment? If this were a temporary cycle of unrest, we might shrug our shoulders and forget about it. Unemployment has not ended, and when the acute form of it does pass, we are destined to have more than we have been accustomed to experience. Restlessness throughout the world is on the increase, and the Negro is in league with certain forms of it in this country.[25]

Of course there were private attempts to do something about the "restlessness" caused by the Depression. In Birmingham, the manufacturers' association met the challenge in its own inimitable way. It offered Dr. Henry W. Edmonds, president of the city's Interracial Commission and pastor of the Presbyterian Church (white), $1,800 "to inaugurate some work for colored people that would offset Communistic propaganda." [26]

At this news, E. K. Jones urged Jesse O. Thomas to hasten to Birmingham and discuss with Edmonds the possibility of developing a local

Urban League. Thomas visited Birmingham and reported back to Jones. The $2,000 raised for Dr. Edmond's campaign against the Reds was being used, said Thomas acidly, "In a recreational program which terminates in June. Hungry, unemployed Negroes are taken out in parks and open spaces and taught to dance, sing and play games in order to prevent them from becoming Communists." [27]

The measure of black restlessness was not alone the growing appeal of the Communist party (which was significant though numerically small) but disaffection with the party of Lincoln. *Opportunity* magazine's 1932 presidential poll showed the Democratic party to be more popular, and the top candidate was New York's governor, Franklin D. Roosevelt, who outdrew the leading Republican—President Hoover—about five to four. Even former governor Alfred E. Smith outran Hoover in the poll by nine to eight. The Democrats and Roosevelt promised changes and black Americans were ready for change—almost any changes would be for the better, they believed.[28]

Opportunity magazine opened its pages for messages from the presidential candidates. The Republican reponse was a directive from Treasury Secretary Ogden Mills to district engineers. It was a starchy policy statement directing that in public building and public works, labor preferences were to go to local workers without discrimination.[29]

Democratic party chairman James Farley spoke for Governor Roosevelt, promising that as President the candidate would "do nothing inimical to the welfare of any group. . . . He is not unmindful of the American Negro's plight. . . . Grover Cleveland said that the Negro was entitled to the helpful hand of the President. In that Governor Roosevelt concurs." Those who could remember Cleveland's uncertain "helping hand" must have had second thoughts about Roosevelt after reading that.

Socialist Norman Thomas struck at capitalism and upheld the banner of the classless society in which social justice and material abundance would be the lot of all in the society of workers. "The Negro in America," he said, "is a proletarian; he should be proud of it." Strong anti-lynching legislation and enforcement of Constitutional guarantees would be the Socialists' achievements for blacks. "More, the thoughtful Negro should not and will not ask," Thomas stated, and attacked the Communists for promoting apartheid.

Communist candidate William Z. Foster came down hard on the economic discrimination issue. He cited discrimination at Hoover Dam, Harlem Hospital and a government project in Jackson, Mississippi, where few if any blacks worked. He contrasted these with El Capitan dam in San Diego where "white and Negro workers, under the leadership of the Communist Party, stormed the City Council, demanding a proportion of the jobs for Negro workers, with equal conditions of work and equal pay." The Communists, Foster insisted, led the fight for (1) hiring of blacks on public works in proportion to their unemployment, not their percentage of population; (2) equal pay for equal work; (3) identical conditions for white and black workers; (4) hiring of black workers in all crafts and trades.[30]

If people voted according to logic, Communist Foster should have walked away with the black vote. He was the only candidate who truly came to grips with the severe tribulations of Afro-Americans and his running mate was a black, James W. Ford.

However, the overwhelming majority of Afro-Americans still had their eyes on the goal of inclusion—their inner urgings were centripetal. The Communists' doctrinaire solutions to problems repelled most black voters and Foster fared poorly. In the 1932 Presidential election, as *Opportunity*'s poll predicted, Roosevelt captured the votes of the black middle-class and the Republican tradition accounted for the rest.

To the percussion of closing banks, failing businesses, foreclosures and tax auctions of farms and homes, to the swelling of breadlines and floodtide of impoverishment of millions punctuated by occasional suicides of formerly rich persons, the New Deal moved into the nation's capital. Blacks, remembering the traditional southern bias of the Democratic party and the antiblack actions of the last Democratic administration— Wilson's—were apprehensive.

24/Focus on Washington

The new crowd in Washington in 1933 had some high-ranking members who were old familiars to the NUL. Roosevelt's cabinet included as secretary of labor Frances Perkins, who had been active in settlement work in New York City with Frances Kellor, Mary Simkhovitch and Mary White Ovington and knew many of the Urban Leaguers from social work activities in the city and from serving on committees and conferences with them.

Another familiar friend of the League was Harold L. Ickes, the new secretary of the Department of the Interior. Ickes had been president of the Chicago NAACP and close to the Chicago Urban League. He had been a foe of discrimination during his days as a prominent lawyer and member of the Progressive party.

The newly appointed head of the Federal Emergency Relief Administration, Harry L. Hopkins, was another old friend. He had pioneered broadening of health services as chief of the New York Tuberculosis Association and had shown a fine contempt for prejudice by installing a clinic and dental equipment and underwriting a nursing program and health services in the New York Urban League quarters in the teens and twenties.

So it was that the New Deal came on the national scene to high expectations. The major concern haunting black leaders was that Afro-Americans would be dealt out, as before. Thus the League acted quickly to press the new administration to deliver on its mandate. A quick trip to Washington early in 1933 convinced T. Arnold Hill that the entire federal system was in a state of flux and that if NUL moved to present its views to the new administrators who were arriving by the trainload it might favorably influence new programs.

Hill wrote:

> Not yet have important officials decided what they can do to lift discrimination against Negroes [which is] evident to a more or less degree in every national activity. . . . I have seen bewilderment, hesitancy, and doubt in the countenances of almost every one with whom I have talked. No one is certain about anything. It is all an experiment. Just to see the whirl and buzz in the Federal department buildings is sufficient to convince one of the magnitude and confusion. And so the controversial race question, though it bobs up always and everywhere, has thus far had to wait until other things have been settled.[1]

To capitalize on this amorphous situation, "the first move made by the League to galvanize sentiment on behalf of Negroes was to launch letter and telegram campaigns on the President, Cabinet members, and all persons in administrative positions in Washington. For a period of at least a year there was no let-up on this by either the national organization or its locals or other bodies and numerous individuals they were able to influence," reported T. Arnold Hill in 1935. Without question, he said, Washington was moved to "let down some of its restrictions" because of the insistence and persistence of the League's campaign.[2]

In many states a program of reforestation had been launched to put young men to work in constructive efforts to conserve natural resources. It was labeled the Civilian Conservation Corps. But in the south particularly, blacks were not allowed to enroll. NUL filed a written complaint to this effect about the camps in Georgia and Florida.[3] The director of reforestation enrollment telephoned NUL for definite data and reported back later by phone that enrollment centers for blacks had been designated in those states. Furthermore, he reported that a directive to the state enrollment directors instructed them to sign up black applicants.

This was not a satisfactory answer. T. Arnold Hill wired Secretary Frances Perkins:

HIGHLY RESPECTED SOUTHERN INFORMANTS ADVISE THAT STATES OF GEORGIA AND FLORIDA HAVE MADE NO PROVISION FOR NEGRO QUOTA IN REFORESTATION CAMPS EXECUTIVE ORDER FROM THE GOVERNORS OF BOTH STATES NECESSARY IN ORDER TO PREVENT DISCRIMINATION STOP THE MATTER IMPERATIVE AND IS CAUSING CONSIDERABLE CONSTERNATION IN THE SOUTH.[4]

He received a reply the same day from W. Frank Persons, for Mrs. Perkins. The labor official telegraphed that he was "taking the matter up energetically at once." [5]

The lesson that NUL learned from this episode was that it was necessary to know how the government programs were structured in order to come to grips with them. And if they were being set up in such a way as to permit local administrators to introduce discrimination, the NUL and the black community should know about this before the programs were solidified into regulations and codes.

Such thinking, plus T. Arnold Hill's abiding belief that it was necessary to go to the top, stimulated NUL to draft its first memorandum to an American president. Entitled *The Social Adjustment of Negroes in the United States,* the forty-three-page document was the work of NUL research director Ira Reid. Addressed to Franklin D. Roosevelt, it was delivered in April 1933, and copies were sent also to influential individuals around the nation.

The document reviewed black employment during the century and recommended that the federal government aid in "a more satisfactory readjustment of Negro life" through action by the Department of Labor. An expert should be appointed to help in the special problems of unemployment that demanded federal relief. NUL had some pertinent comments about both of those matters. It estimated that there were one and one-half million unemployed black workers at that time.

Squarely raising inequities such as discrimination on government jobs and projects, the memo received a quick reply from Labor Secretary Frances Perkins on behalf of the President. "I can assure you," she wrote E. K. Jones, "that as this Administration undertakes the problems of relief administration, of providing work opportunities, of raising basic wage levels, etc., etc., we shall not forget the special problems of . . . your race." [6]

The League specifically questioned abuses in the Mississippi flood control projects and Boulder Dam construction under the Hoover administration. Secretary Perkins promised that "as far as it is legally possible under the contracts already made the President will leave nothing undone which will prevent or stop the exploitation of workmen, whether white or colored, by Federal contractors. I am personally at work on the problem of making sure that labor standards will be more fully provided for in future government undertakings." [7]

The United States Employment Service came under the Labor Department directly and was, Madame Perkins told Jones, being completely reorganized. It would take some time, she said, to put the system on a basis that would "insure real service for working men and women." And she invited suggestions on improvement of the USES at any time.

All signs pointed to the need for increased action on behalf of black workers and citizens to include them in the relief activities of the new administration. This was the single most urgent conclusion of the high-powered Rosenwald-financed Conference on the Economic Status of the Negro, May 11–13, 1933. There, the nation's most prominent blacks, representing every shade of economic philosophy from "Communism to prayer," assessed the past and present.

T. Arnold Hill had worked on the conference with Ira Reid. One of the conclusions was that the federal government's new regulatory interest in business, coupled with unprecedented participation of organized labor, pointed the direction that planning for black workers must take. "Various bureaus entrusted with working out policies and procedures in connection with the control or regulation of private business, work and building projects, agriculture loans, etc., can be expected, if history is not changed, to neglect Negroes, or leave them only that which is the most disagreeable and burdensome." [8] This was at the time that the National Industrial Recovery Act was proposed and the National Recovery Administration was being put together.

Kinckle Jones spoke on "Next Steps Towards Improving the Lot of the Negro Economically." He called for great educational efforts along lines that would help decentralize the black population by informing of employment needs; diversifying employment of blacks by better vocational guidance, industrial and occupational education, professional training (and lifting the standards of black colleges). Leadership training was essential, he said, to bring blacks into the general life of the community and nation. Black leaders to serve on central boards and committees governing community-wide activities were needed. Both in government and private agencies black experts should be employed, Jones said, not just to work on problems of blacks but mainly to relate blacks to the program at large. To produce black leaders Jones recommended establishing a fund "for financing especially gifted or talented youths [in a] program to include selection of individuals on a nation-wide scale." The funds would finance special training. He also called for raising funds to test legality of the notoriously unfair division of school funds between the races in the south. He attacked the practice of denying blacks the right to study vocations in state institutions without making some provision to cover the cost of black students' securing professional training outside the southern states. These were but factors in the larger picture, he indicated, concluding "if health is purchaseable, better economic conditions for the Negro are purchaseable." [9]

NUL monitored the Washington scene closely as the Democrats moved in. Before the new administration was twelve days old E. K. Jones wrote an extraordinary letter to all League executives "on a matter of grave importance in the lives of the Negroes in America." The Industrial Relations Department, he reported, had studied unemployment and relief exhaustively and concluded that gross discrimination existed. In New Deal legislation organized labor obviously was going to play an important part and "it has never done things which will encourage us to feel that it will adequately represent Negro labor." [10]

Jones underscored as of "special interest" three specific actions in Washington during the last week of March, 1933: (1) passage of a bill to employ 250,000 men in reforestation and other public works programs; (2) a conference the day before (March 31, 1933) between government officials and leaders of organized labor who will be recognized in the administration of government funds and the employment of workers on government projects; (3) passage by the Senate of a bill providing $500,000,000 for relief of the unemployed.

Jones urged his co-workers to write immediately and get at least ten others to write or wire to the secretary of labor to conserve the welfare of black workers and their families.

The League pushed aside its normal activities and shifted to emergency operations. Hill interviewed the secretary of labor several times, submitted plans for incorporating blacks into government programs and data to support the proposals. He conferred with Interior Secretary Ickes, requesting public works jobs for blacks. Calls were made on officials of the CCC, the United States Employment Service and Federal Emergency Relief Administration, the NRA and other agencies, requesting appointment of blacks to boards, bureaus and committees and the elimination of discrimination.[11]

As highest priority Hill and Ira Reid pulled together all available information on the new administration's programs and projects, its policies and plans. When they added them up, the sum was a picture of callous discrimination throughout the nation:

Racial differentials in wages were written into the National Recovery Act (NRA), which meant that blacks had the alternatives of lower wages or no work to choose from if they were fortunate enough to find a job. "Negro jobs" were practically exempt from the codes, meaning that most blacks had no wage protection. And when blacks suffered discrimination that fell under code regulations, redress was nearly impossible because compliance machinery was under local control where bigotry could be—and was—most effectively applied.

The Agricultural Adjustment Administration (AAA) put into effect a crop-reduction policy in an emergency effort to save hundreds of thousands of farmers. In the process black tenant farmers and sharecroppers were pushed off the farms they had worked for years.

The bright promise of the Tennessee Valley Authority was tarnished by southern social customs that meant blacks were hired for unskilled labor and excluded from training programs and better jobs. Blacks were even banned from living in Norris, Tennessee, the model town created by the federal government.

Subsistence homestead programs in the south consistently excluded blacks.

The Civilian Conservation Corps used army officers for its administrative staffs and these members of a segregated institution continued the army's discriminatory practices in excluding blacks from administration and training.

"We differ from others," stated T. Arnold Hill, "in that we are not merely protesting, but we are providing service. We are submitting facts, programs, and recommendations. Some results have come from our labors. . . ." He cited appointment of a black to the USES Advisory Council; the recruitment of black workers in the reforestation camps; the settlement of a labor dispute in St. Louis. He told of proposals made to government bureaus about labor, NRA and relief, calling and participating in two conferences with government officials, one on housing, another on the double standard for wages—a lower pay scale for black workers. The League had called on the Commerce Department and influenced it to establish an advisory council. But Hill voiced serious doubts about the future for blacks under the NRA.[12]

There was, he said, a persistent effort to put blacks on a lower wage schedule in the regulatory codes for the laundry, textile, lumber, steel and other occupations NRA was establishing. Furthermore, agriculture and domestic service, where two thirds of blacks worked, were not under the NRA codes. As Hill put it, "adjustment of all NRA matters is made difficult because of the absence of Negroes [from] . . . the Industrial Advisory Board, the Labor Advisory Board, and the Consumers' Advisory Board, as well as in the employed personnel of the entire NRA."

This was one of the basic points in the League's formal memorandum to the administration.[13]

T. Arnold Hill, who had just completed his investigation of conditions in Alabama, Arkansas, Florida, Georgia, Louisiana and Texas, reported his observations of the outer reaches of hell, American-style:

Houston—When Negro persons apply [for relief] they are given an appointment for three or four weeks hence when they may come in for registration. Thereafter, an investigation is made and the quantity of relief determined. In this way, approximately one-third of the Negro relief applicants are eliminated.

Charleston—[Blacks] are given 30 per cent of the work relief, or three days' work a week at one dollar a day. White workers are given 70 per cent of the work—at $1.50 a day.

Atlanta—Lunches have been provided for white children attending the public schools . . . as late as February, 1933, not one cent had been allowed colored schools for this purpose.

Kansas City, Mo.—Black relief applicants waited in line from as early as five o'clock in the morning until late in the afternoon in order to plead for a chance to work. They were told there was 'no work for colored today,' or 'Democrats only need apply,' or 'see your precinct captain.' In some instance they were sent on a wild goose chase all over the city in order to find politicians who would certify them for work designed as 'unemployment relief.' [14]

The moral from all this (which haunts the nation today) was underscored by the League in its memo to President Roosevelt:

Wise administration of relief funds during this period of national emergency demands that relief be apportioned on the basis of need. In many instances the practices followed in local communities tend to make chronic paupers out of the Negro population and to create a permanent dependent class.[15]

The special memorandum to the President also cataloged an agenda of outstanding abuses, shortcomings and neglects dealt black citizens in the fields of education, health, housing, recreation, delinquency and civil rights. In sum, said the League, "these problems are more social than racial. In approaching them no special provisions are asked except as the necessity of discrimination and exclusion has demanded them. The mere fact that rights which inhere in the very nature of citizenship must frequently be re-established by law indicates the responsibility faced by the Government in this connection." NUL recommended that a "liaison person" be appointed to see "that justice is done to all groups without discrimination." [16]

At the Commerce Department, Secretary Dan Roper appointed NUL's E. K. Jones as adviser on Negro affairs. The NUL staff and board were convinced that the fast-breaking developments in the Roosevelt administration could best be monitored and influenced from inside that administration. Jones's appointment was seen as having great potential for those purposes. It had other significance as well. Said *Opportunity* editorially:

> Nothing has served to sustain the Negro's faith in the sincerity of the Administration's attitude toward his status as much as the recently announced appointment of Eugene Kinckle Jones as Adviser on Negro Affairs in the Department of Commerce. . . . [This act] has done more than any other thing to dissipate the doubt which had unquestionably begun to pervade the Negro group as to the ultimate results of the New Deal. The valiant efforts of the Administration to launch the Recovery Program have been enormously complicated by the perplexing and vexatious problems of race adjustment.[17]

The time when one black man could advise the federal government had gone with Booker T. Washington. Government and the black community had changed too drastically to give Jones the kind of pre-eminent prestige and power enjoyed by Emmett Scott and George Haynes in World War I.

With Clark Foreman, in the Interior Department, E. K. Jones became part of something unique, foreshadowing the future. These two, with Foreman's newly hired assistant, Dr. Robert C. Weaver, set up an "Interdepartmental Group concerned with the Special Problems of Negroes" within the administration. Together they worked to stimulate appointment of blacks in other departments and attempted to keep blacks from being left out or crushed under federal emergency programs. This "Inter-departmental Group" laid the groundwork for the informal but powerful "black cabinet" that came later in the New Deal.

Jones was able to influence substantially certain staff moves that the New Deal made. According to his own summary of NUL activities for 1934, Jones got what he called "Negro set-ups" in the Department of Labor, Department of Commerce, and Federal Emergency Relief Administration and obtained approval for setting them up in the Federal Housing Administration and Federal Credit Unions. He also persuaded the director of the Press Intelligence Service to subscribe to black newspapers in order to keep abreast of current editorial opinion in the black community.[18]

Jones was successful in having blacks appointed to the national advisory committee of the United States Employment Service, to National

Industrial Recovery Act (NIRA) compliance committees, relief commissions and regional labor boards, as well as to various bureaus in the Commerce Department.

Jones saw to it that black workers were hired to assist with the Commerce Department's real property inventory, its Negro Homes Rent Survey, its two censuses of American business, its studies of air pilots, insurance failures, trade associations, chambers of commerce and black periodicals, and its compilation of a bibliography of black business and convention dates. A special office was created in the Bureau of the Census, headed by a black who was entitled specialist in Negro statistics and had his own staff. Black card punchers, enumerators and supervisors, copyists and clerks were hired within the Commerce Department for these functions and for public addresses and articles on black business, and the planning and execution of the black participation in the Texas Centennial Exposition.

In May of 1936, Kinckle Jones listed nearly four dozen top-rank blacks who had been appointed to high federal positions in the New Deal. The number in the Department of Interior led the rest, with twenty-two blacks in supervisory, technical and administrative positions. Kinckle Jones's major contribution during this time was in representing black interests at the inner core of the federal establishment. He participated in conferences on crime, child welfare, relief programs, black education, subsistence homesteads, NRA violations, and in the regular and continuing meetings of the Negro Advisory Group in the Commerce Department as well as the interdepartmental group with Clark Foreman, Robert Weaver and others.[19]

Though the New Deal and the Roosevelt administration had serious faults, the problems they were attempting to cope with were nearly overwhelming. They did not release blacks from discrimination and segregation, but, in contrast with previous administrations, there were sincere efforts and some respectable accomplishments in the right direction. NRA did not, as FDR and others jested, stand for Negro Relief Association, but when blacks in Georgia received the prescribed $12 a week wage under a federal work program—twice as much as common labor in the area had ever been paid—it was evident to blacks and whites alike that a new spirit and interpretation of the rules were being applied. When Harold Ickes hired black lawyers, architects and engineers and threw out segregation in the Department of Interior, Afro-Americans knew they had something going for them in Washington.

Another of the things they had going for them was T. Arnold Hill. The NUL industrial relations secretary became acting executive secretary during E. K. Jones's detached duty at the Commerce Department. Jones spent one day a week in the NUL office and the balance in Washington. These two, plus Ira Reid, with their incessant shuttling between Washington and New York, became known as "the brief-case boys." Hill spent alternate weeks in the national capital "interceding with all of the emergency administrations on behalf of the Negro." [20] He called on legislators, bureaucrats, talked to new administrators and acted as liaison man. It was he who brought together housing specialists when subsistence homesteads were up for discussion, and it was he who spread the word about new federal programs to Urban Leaguers and the black elite through special memoranda, the pages of *Opportunity* and the Emergency Advisory Councils, set up in 1933.

During 1935 Urban Leaguers participated in "scores of important conferences" at all levels, including such unusual assemblies as the 1935 Mobilization for Human Needs and the President's Conference on Economic Security. The NUL did not hesitate to go straight to the President with telegrams, letters and memoranda. It had access to Mrs. Roosevelt through some of her black friends, notably NUL vice chairman Mary McLeod Bethune, and drew the First Lady into activities concerning the problems of youth and domestic workers.[21]

It was in 1935 that the NUL's government liaison was first institutionalized when it opened a Washington office and Reginald Johnson served as a two-way facilitator, transmitting information about government activities to the NUL family and taking up with government officials the most urgent complaints that came in. Johnson also arranged appearances before congressional committees where NUL expert testimony was put into the record and given due weight. During this period the charges of discrimination against the Public Works Administration (PWA) and Works Progress Administration (WPA), CCC and NRA were carried by NUL before the appropriate authorities and action secured to open up opportunities in the first three agencies.

In 1936 T. Arnold Hill had been brought in by Aubrey Williams, National Youth Administration's chief executive, as a consultant in basic planning of the National Youth Administration. Another NUL stalwart was made a member of the NYA advisory committee—Mrs. Mary McLeod Bethune. When NYA decided to hold a conference on Negro activities early in 1937, Hill was one of those who helped plan it and chaired one of its four sessions.

There were other types of government cooperation. When Dr. Ira Reid left the NUL in 1934 to become professor of sociology at Atlanta University he was hired by the Federal Emergency Relief Administration (FERA) to supervise a nationwide study of the black population. In this work Reid parceled out contracts for data collection to many local

Leagues around the nation. To a great extent, such federal contracts and the workers supplied for League activities under federal programs were the cement that bound together the sorely pinched local Leagues. As E. K. Jones put it,

> The salaries of several of our workers were placed in whole or in part on public agencies which agreed to prosecute types of work in line with the League's program and ideals, but we did not release for full time a single employee nor was a single local organization discontinued throughout this period [through the end of 1936].[22]

Though the League had not "released" any employees, the part-time government work that many of them found during this period made it possible to cope with payless NUL paydays that stretched over periods of months. The Depression dollar drought had shriveled local Leagues. Chicago, for instance, had been reduced to the executive secretary and one clerical worker.

Urban League services to government were a two-way street. For in more than one local League office many of the tasks were carried out by blacks on the payroll of the Federal Emergency Relief Administration or NYA. There were nine FERA workers in John Dancy's Detroit League and ten NYA workers on assignment in the research department of the NUL, for example. Many League staff members were named to state and city commissions.

By 1939, NUL's headquarters staff was active in multiple activities within many government agencies. T. Arnold Hill was serving as consultant to the Federal Work Projects Administration; E. K. Jones was on the New York State Unemployment Insurance Advisory Council; Elmer Carter was a member of the New York State Unemployment Insurance Appeal Board; Lester Granger was secretary of the Committee on Negro Welfare of New York City's Welfare Council; and the managing editor of *Opportunity* was on loan to the Census Bureau to help publicize the census among blacks.

What the service of League staff members on various government boards meant in actual practice is illustrated at the local level by the New Jersey experience. There, the executive of the League was a member of the Newark Housing Authority and was able to secure the adoption of a nondiscrimination policy by that agency. This meant that selection of tenants, administrative personnel and construction workers was all to be without bias. The New Jersey League also was responsible for appointment of a black as a state employment interviewer for the first time, the appointment of black nurses on the staff of the Newark Board of Health for the first time, and the securing of two state scholarships for black students for the first time.

Furthermore, local League facilities were widely used in WPA and NYA programs in the black communities. In Springfield, Illinois, the League headquarters in 1939 was host to seventy-two WPA and NYA groups who used the facilities regularly, for an annual attendance of 15,-000. Leagues in Canton, Ohio, Waterbury, Connecticut, Milwaukee, Brooklyn, Memphis and Lincoln, Nebraska were similarly active in federal programs.

The cooperation from government often was generous.[23] When the fifth Vocational Opportunity Campaign was launched in 1937, the United States Commissioner of Education, John Studebaker, appeared on the nationwide NBC network program that opened it. Furthermore, the NYA in Illinois and Pennsylvania were especially cooperative in distributing literature and opening facilities. And the WPA Washington offices arranged a tour of midwest centers with speakers and movies.[24]

After Ira Reid left, NUL was without a research director until 1936 when an Urban League Fellow from the University of Pittsburgh was hired. He was Warren M. Banner, then working for his doctoral degree. Banner drafted a 1937 memo to the WPA about juvenile delinquency among blacks, which was used to support a proposal that WPA establish church projects to combat delinquency. The research department prepared for the Senate Committee on Unemployment and Relief a report on those two crucial subjects. In 1939 the NUL research unit issued a revised edition of its pioneering *Selected Bibliography on the Negro and Source Materials on the Urban Negro in the United States.*

Warren Banner also put together a 1937 memorandum to President Roosevelt, which E. K. Jones called a "sequel to the one four years before." It was entitled *The Negro Working Population and National Recovery.*[25] Since, as Jones noted, most of the social problems outlined previously remained substantially the same this memorandum was confined to problems of blacks as workers.

Using the government's own statistics and reports, the League memorandum etched a picture of black misery and suffering. The number of blacks on relief had actually risen from 2,118,000, or 18 percent of the total Afro-American population, to 3,030,000. In the cities it was even worse—the proportion had climbed to 39.5 percent of all blacks in the cities. The figure for whites was 14.6 percent. In Norfolk 81 percent of the working-age blacks were on relief; in Charlotte, 75 percent; in Atlanta, 66 percent; in Birmingham, 63 percent and so on. At one point, 70 percent of the blacks in the entire state of New Jersey subsisted on public relief.

The deadening hand of the Depression had seized not only unskilled and blue collar workers, but also white collar and professional people, too. In Harlem, 60 percent of the black physicians were dependent on relief. And 63 percent of Harlem's schoolchildren were reported to be suffering from malnutrition. Also in New York, in the summer of 1936, with 60,000 blacks on relief, only eighty-two Afro-American men were placed in jobs in private industry by the local League.

E. K. Jones wound up this memo to the President with recommendations for federal action. Government departments, he said, should appoint more black assistants and increase their fields of authority. Disciplinary action should be taken against contractors who were proven bigots in their hiring policies. The Labor Relations Act should be amended to prevent union bias from excluding black workers from jobs while unions simultaneously excluded them from membership. The social security law should be extended, the NUL declared, to cover domestics and agricultural workers (the categories in which there were 65 percent of working blacks). The memo urged that the study of farm tenancy, then about to begin, be broadened to examine civil liberties and that legislation protecting sharecroppers and agricultural workers be enacted.[26]

These were the things the League requested of the national administration on behalf of black citizens. And if the government did not act? As Jones put it:

> The Negro has the balance of power in the pivotal states. He should exercise that power wisely and judiciously—and selfishly. He should have no slavish political affiliation but should vote for "men and measures," solidly, if needs be, for local, state and national self-interest. . . .
>
> America and the world are power-conscious. Few people act on an impulse of brotherhood and unselfish service to others despite our ancient pratings on the beauty of the unselfish, devoted life of self-sacrifice in the interest of others. Legislative bodies act when public opinion demands action. One gets the respect of his fellows not when the man speaks but when his money talks. This is not as it should be, but *it is* as *it is*.[27]

The League had some ideas about bringing Afro-American power to bear on the federal establishment. It was T. Arnold Hill who put them into effect.

25/Grass-Roots Action

"There had developed simultaneously with the depression," observed
T. Arnold Hill in 1935, "the psychology that only by organized pressure
could minorities and unpopular causes secure recognition."

> Thus, two factors—a large urban population and the pressure device—
> made it both possible and logical to rally Negroes in defense of their eco-
> nomic rights. The National Urban League decided to follow the American
> pattern, advised Negroes to "go thou and do likewise," undertook the task
> of organization. . . . It did not abandon its activities with organized
> labor, nor did it give up its appeals to employers. But it did conclude
> that both employers and employees might be more willing to listen to the
> demands of 5,500,000 [black] workers than they would to the suggestions
> of a social service organization.[1]

The first move of NUL in this drive was to "galvanize sentiment" in a
letter and telegram campaign aimed at government leaders.

The second phase was more ambitious. It was the organization and
launching of the Emergency Advisory Council for Negroes. The NUL
news release in August of 1933 told the basic story:

URBAN LEAGUE FIGHTS EVASION OF NRA
SPAULDING TO HEAD NATION-WIDE ORGANIZATION
FOR NEGRO WORKERS

> Deluged with bitter complaints from all sections of the country to the ef-
> fect that Negro workers are being systematically excluded from the benefits
> of the NRA and in many cases discharged to make room for white workers,
> T. Arnold Hill . . . announced upon his return from the Washington of-
> fice of the League, that Emergency Advisory Councils for Negro Workers,
> to be designated by the initials EAC, were in the process of formation by
> the Urban League throughout the country. . . .
>
> The EAC will organize public opinion and inform Negroes as to the
> benefits to which they are entitled under the various acts.
>
> Jesse O. Thomas, Southern Field Director of the Urban League is now
> making personal investigation of complaints that by subterfuge and evasion
> the Negro in the south is denied participation in the plans for recovery.[2]

Though the EAC's were actually operating as early as October 1933 in some areas, the formal kick-off was a week-long drive in December. The focus of the EAC effort was the NRA, but the administration's relief activities were included. EAC objectives were:

I. To conduct a nation-wide educational program for acquainting Negroes with the laws respecting industrial codes, emergency relief, reemployment, mortgage loans, housing projects, public works, subsistence homesteads, etc., and the methods to be followed in securing these benefits.

II. To enlist the interest and support of Negroes in complying with the provisions and regulations of the NRA.

III. To receive complaints on violations of codes and other Federal activities.

IV. To sensitize the Negro population on economic and industrial problems, to the end that their significance will be understood and discussions leading to their improvement be given constant consideration.[3]

To do these things, a national advisory council was established. It consisted of the chairmen of state EAC councils and fifteen members appointed by NUL. C. C. Spaulding, president of the North Carolina Mutual Life Insurance Company of Durham, North Carolina, was chairman of the national EAC. He also was chairman of the National Negro Business League and an NUL board member. Spaulding was responsible for appointing the state EAC chairmen, with NUL approval. The state chairmen in turn appointed the heads of the EAC's in the cities of their state. The executive secretary of each local League automatically was the advisor for the EAC in his area. The EAC's were to be strictly voluntary and nonpolitical and the national council had the final say on all selections of EAC officers. Fund-raising campaigns were specifically outlawed, except for money for stamps, stationery, etc.

The *EAC Handbook* recommended setting up subcommittees on (1) survey or data collection; (2) code research, to study all laws and regulations relating to blacks to interpret them; put them in simple language and distribute them to the masses, and to point out how and where to bring pressure to bear concerning these codes; (3) public information —to keep developments and EAC action before the black population; (4) complaints—to investigate and rectify them if possible, or to submit them to the state or national EAC; (5) public works—to call on major and minor officials to get black jobs on all projects; (6) home loans—to help blacks take advantage of the Home Owners Loan Act; (7) agricultural service—to help blacks share in the benefits of the Agricultural Adjustment Act and services of the Department of Agriculture.

With this action framework outlined, the *EAC Handbook* went on to

"What's what in the emergency legislation and how to go about getting it." In the pages that followed, Ira Reid and Hill spelled out the essential facts about the National Recovery Administration, Public Works Administration, Federal Emergency Relief Administration, Civilian Conservation Corps, Agricultural Adjustment Administration, Tennessee Valley Authority, Federal Home Owner's Loan Corporation, United States Employment Service and the Emergency Railroad Transportation Administration. In each case the *Handbook* told the legal purpose of the agency, the provisions of the act that brought it into being, the name and address of the federal administrator and local branches if any. In some cases the *Handbook* specified the titles of additional literature and the names of bureaucrats assigned to give out information about projects and policies.

The proliferation of agencies was so rapid and varied that the period was truly a time of federal alphabet soup. It was the foresight and common sense of T. Arnold Hill, who spent alternate weeks in Washington during the critical early days of the New Deal, that gave NUL its intimate knowledge of the new agencies. The practical approach to these agencies was clearly drawn in the *EAC Handbook*. For example, in the FERA spell-out, the Transient Service Bureau, services for sick unemployed, education, the Federal Surplus Relief, and the Civil Works Administration were described briefly. The Transient Service Bureau, said EAC, "was devised not to aid in the sending of transients on to the next town but to stabilize the transient jobless. . . . States securing Federal allotments for this purpose have been instructed to deal with each individual on the basis of need and to help as many as possible of the migratory jobless to stabilize themselves."

Concerning the Civil Works Administration, the *Handbook* suggested "that local Councils of the EAC work out with the Civil Works Administrators suitable projects that will offer employment to Negro men and women. All such projects can be determined by local CWA representatives and do not have to be passed upon by Washington authorities."

Since the United States Employment Service was to be the channel for 2,000,000 jobs, the EAC advised "it is therefore important that the EAC acquaint Negroes with the location of offices of the United States Employment Service in their respective localities; also that connection be made with the staff of the Service on behalf of equal opportunity for Negro workers. Negro employees should be a part of the personnel of these offices, and the EAC should make an effort to have them appointed." [4]

By December 1933 the League had organized 196 EAC's in thirty-two states and the District of Columbia. This network, added to the Urban

League family of more than forty local Leagues, provided a structure for coordinating and communicating with black Americans. The fact that the National Industrial Recovery Act had been financed with an astronomical appropriation of $3,300,000,000 had captured the attention of the nation and raised the hopes of dispirited millions across the land, as the programs were implemented and jobs and relief were distributed locally.

As early as October 1935 the EAC sent out to city chairmen a three-page memo (the first of scores of such bulletins) calling for action on four points. In it, T. Arnold Hill as the EAC national adviser exhorted local EAC's to write General Hugh S. Johnson, NRA administrator, and Frances Perkins, urging them to name a qualified black to the Labor Advisory Board of the NRA. Hill pointed out the importance of this board and the fact that the AFL, which had "large representation" on the board, "cannot be expected to represent Negroes enthusiastically and earnestly." [5]

A similar situation existed in each local community, Hill pointed out, with the compliance boards set up by the NRA. These committees were to adjust code violations and Hill spurred the EAC's to act immediately to secure appointment of blacks on each such board. He mentioned that the EAC in St. Louis had succeeded in getting a black on the compliance board in that city.

Hill wanted the EAC's to use their strength to influence the AFL. Since blacks were barred from union membership, said Hill, they would be disadvantaged in securing work "now that organized labor has been elevated to such high favor in the Recovery Administration." AFL President Green had been asked by NUL time and again to adjust differences between black workers and organized labor "with little or no result." So NUL was turning to the Department of Labor and calling on it to use its influence to break down organized labor's barriers against blacks. To help with this, Hill asked the EAC's to write Madame Perkins calling her attention to the injustice of the AFL attitude, "requesting that she use her influence to bring about a 'new deal' for Negroes on the part of organized labor." [6]

The fourth matter in the 1935 memo was the Civilian Conservation Corps. The former experiences of blacks with this relief service were not satisfactory, Hill said, without going into the dismal details that had been spread widely on the pages of the black weekly newspapers. The NUL protests to Washington had resulted in beneficial changes, but Hill wanted the EAC's to bring their pressure to bear also. So in addition to writing the director of the USES asking for opportunities for blacks, Hill advised contacting the local relief organizations that were to enroll men

for the camps and equally important, carrying out an educational campaign among young blacks to let them know what the camps were all
about and how to apply for them. This was typical of the memos sent to
the EAC's.

"The EAC is an organization of Negroes for Negroes," said the suggested talk sent out by NUL's Industrial Department during the kick-off
Education for Recovery Week, December 3–10, 1933.[7] This coordinated
promotion under the direction of the EAC's across the country gave as
the councils' purpose

> to inform and make known to every colored man, woman, and child, what
> the NRA is, and what their rights are under it, and to use every honest
> and intelligent means to secure those rights. They include:
> 1. The right to work under the code adopted in an industry as to hours
>   and wages.
> 2. The right to work on all Public Works—Federal, State or Municipal—
>   which receive funds from Federal, State or Municipal governments.
> 3. The right to share in the loans which the Government is making to
>   home owners and farm owners.
> 4. The right to secure adequate relief, food, clothing and shelter from all
>   agencies receiving Federal or State or Municipal funds.
> 5. The right of representation on the Labor Advisory Board of the NRA at
>   Washington, the local Compliance Boards, relief committees, and those
>   bodies which are in charge of reemployment in local communities.[8]

To the individual black citizen who wondered how the New Deal affected him, the EAC held out a helping hand. Citizens who wanted a
civil works or public works job were invited to go to the EAC; workers
who had not been treated according to the NRA Code were advised to
report to the EAC. So also were those who had been refused employment
because they were not union members, or were fired without satisfactory
reason; or were turned down for relief aid; or were denied a government
loan to help save home or farm; or had found prices were higher on
goods in one neighborhood than another. Then, through the 196 EAC's
in the nation the complaints and questions would funnel into local
Leagues and, if necessary, from them to NUL in New York where T. Arnold Hill, Ira Reid and their assistants (two) would attempt to bring
about changes or know the reason why. Therein lay the fatal weakness of
the structure: without sufficient staff, it was impossible to service the system set up and without sufficient money, it was impossible to expand the
staff. Since May 6, 1932, the NUL staff had been "donating" a day's pay
per month. This was boosted to 5 percent of their salary from December
16; the executive staff also had voted 1 percent of their paycheck for a

sixtieth birthday gift for L. Hollingsworth Wood.[9] Considering such handicaps, the EAC effort was all the more valiant and the achievements, limited though they were, the more remarkable.

Economy forced cancellation of the League's annual conference in 1933 in favor of regional conferences at Columbus, Chicago and Newark and a special National Emergency Advisory Council Conference at Tuskegee, December 5 and 6, to launch the nationwide EAC Week. It brought together representatives of many regional organizations and government agencies.

What the EAC's meant to the black population is illustrated in the report for 1934 of Jesse O. Thomas. In January of that year the southern field director covered the cities of Tampa, St. Petersburg, Sarasota, Lakeland, Bradenton and Miami, conferring with the local councils, speaking at mass meetings in the churches, auditoriums and courthouses to white and black citizens. He helped organize an EAC in Miami and, under the auspices of five of these EAC's, put together a two-day district EAC conference at Lakeland.

This conference brought together more than a hundred social workers and professional people and concentrated on nuts and bolts information given by specialists. The three major subject categories were the Federal Emergency Relief Administration and integration into a permanent welfare program; the NRA and reemployment; and the New Deal and the forgotten man.[10]

The FERA panel explained the ERA and family welfare, casework and case aid work (by the social service director of the Polk County ERA); nursery and adult illiteracy, health, hygiene and sanitation (by the director general of the Hillsborough County ERA); recreation and personnel training (by the state director of public recreation); transients and migratory labor (by the state director for transients).

The NRA and better participation by Negroes was discussed by the assistant secretary of the Tampa NRA Compliance Board; collective bargaining and benefits to Florida Negroes were the subjects for the president of the Tampa Labor Assembly, who also was a vice president of the state federation of labor; re-employment aid for all citizens was explained by the assistant state director of re-employment.

The manager of the Home Owners' Loan Corporation talked about this agency and advised on "how to make it more effective for Negroes." The mayor of Lakeland spoke about homestead planning in decentralizing urban Negro groups in Florida. And Farm Credit Bureau aid to small farmers was outlined by a county agent.

There were discussions of each of these subjects led by trained leaders. The program included speeches by the mayor of Lakeland, the associate director of the Florida ERA, the general chairman of the Tampa NRA, and Jesse O. Thomas.

What came of it all? In addition to sharper understanding of the emergency relief activities and ways in which they could be used to benefit blacks, there were direct, positive results. Example: the assembly passed resolutions calling on the state administrator to add blacks to the administrative staffs of each county and city relief organization and city administrators to add black caseworkers to local staffs. The case supervisor for Lakeland proved that the message had gotten across by hiring two black social workers for her staff before the conference ended. There were similar moves by other administrators in the state.

In February 1934 the southern field director traveled to Oklahoma City where, at the invitation of Roscoe Dunjee, EAC state chairman, the two men covered twenty-four cities of the state intensively in an educational campaign that extended more than a thousand miles. Dunjee was editor of *The Black Dispatch,* an outspoken black weekly newspaper, and also was a prominent NAACP member, serving as chairman of its national resolutions committee.

Thomas and Dunjee had four goals in their campaign: (1) to explain to blacks the different relief and recovery programs and counsel them on the method of approach to the agencies involved; (2) to influence cities and counties to hire trained black social workers through conferences with case supervisors; (3) to help local EAC officials organize projects that could be financed by FERA funds; (4) to spread the word through mass meetings; interpreting the New Deal and explaining who had responsibility for what.

Thomas and Dunjee reached 11,472 people in their campaign, giving them first-hand information about the national recovery program. The EAC's were, as Thomas reported, "the only medium through which colored people have been able to intelligently approach Relief Administrators and directors of the CWA and PWA projects." [11]

They conferred with CWA, PWA and FERA officials about hiring black staff persons. In four cities, casework supervisors agreed to add black professionals to their staffs.

Other specific EAC achievements included the appointment of an adviser on Negro affairs for the CWA and FERA for the State of Virginia after the EAC had called on state officials of the federal bureaus. [12]

The EAC's in Illinois brought pressure to bear to move a Federal Production Credit Association from the town of Anna, Illinois, where hostility to blacks was palpable, to Harrisburg. Applications from black farmers for production loans were received favorably, as a consequence.

In St. Louis, the United States Employment Service bureau was registering blacks only for common labor and domestic jobs even though the USES had responsibility for all placements on projects financed in part or entirely by federal funds. The local EAC moved in and this discriminatory pattern was overturned.

In Atlantic City the EAC helped get wage boosts for blacks before the NRA codes were adopted and wages frozen.

The Philadelphia EAC sponsored a slum clearance housing project for blacks and registered to secure federal financing. A farm subsistence project in Huntersville, Missouri, was developed through the sponsorship of the state EAC. Four blacks were placed in the Bureau of Transient and Homeless in Atlanta as a result of EAC action. In New Bedford, Massachusetts, four black women were appointed as census takers and a teacher was hired for the "Opportunity Classes" given by the school system, thanks to the EAC. And "instances are too numerous to mention where trained Negroes at the requests of various EAC Councils were employed on the staffs of county and city social service organizations to administer various phases of emergency programs," reported John T. Clark.[13]

In spite of considerable achievements, Hill was disillusioned about the prospects for major change through the EAC's.

The needs of black Americans, he charged, demanded "the support of that large group of [black] business and professional men who have corralled neither their money nor their intelligence on behalf of these basic factors involved in the adjustment of race relations. It is with difficulty that the National Urban League, with its prestige, its long years of service and practical program, can secure a thousand dollars from Negroes on any issue. The amount of money and time consumed in raising such an amount equals in money the amount of cash received. Our experience in getting the Emergency Advisory Council for Negroes organized . . . and in keeping them busy when once organized, is a sad commentary on the willingness of Negroes to support a program which they themselves admit is necessary." [14] (In 1935 NUL solicited the scores of Fellows it had helped put through professional training over the span of twenty-five years, asking them for quarter-century contributions. The total contributed was $130.87.) [15]

As noted, some of the EAC's were active and accomplished much good. Some withered away without a trace. The NUL interest in them waned after 1936 as the agency's support dried up and it shifted its emphasis to labor and vocational guidance.

26/Organizing the Unorganized

What could be expected of an administration, in terms of rooting out discriminatory practices, establishing differential wage scales, and so on, if it had no stomach for enforcing the Fourteenth and Fifteenth Amendments? asked Jesse O. Thomas in 1934. He roasted the "alphabet agencies" in the pages of *Opportunity* in January 1934. As far as benefits to southern blacks from the New Deal agencies were concerned, Thomas said that the administration of relief or job-giving could have been handled just as well by the KKK. He then pointed out specific examples illustrating why the NRA did not work for black citizens. The differential wage system was basic. Thomas cited Macon, Georgia, where a black teacher had to teach *forty years* to reach the salary level of a *beginning* white teacher. Members of boards of education in such circumstances would not, said Thomas, "be enthusiastic about seeing that blacks received equal pay with whites in industry." [1]

Among the most painful abuses of the New Deal were those that flaunted race as a factor. Thomas cited the 300 blacks in Jacksonville who were given work cards for a CWA (Civil Works Administration) project. The cards stipulated that they would receive 40 cents per hour; when they were paid, it was at the rate of 30 cents. In the New Orleans Federal Land Commissioner's office Thomas saw more than 700 clerical employees—all of them white except for a maid and a porter. Skilled and semiskilled work on black school buildings in Jackson, Mississippi, was done by whites, not blacks, under a CWA program. [2]

What recourse was there? There were the germs of a viable approach in St. Louis. In the depths of the Depression all city work in the building trades was assigned to white unions that adamantly refused to allow any black mechanics to work with them. There were seventeen black schools in the city, and not one black man was allowed to earn a dime on repair or construction work on them. Conferences and appeals to the union brought only evasion.

Then a $2,000,000 black hospital, built with city and federal funds, was begun in the middle of the city's black belt without a single black skilled worker on the job. The black community boiled over at this affront. The St. Louis League, capitalizing on the situation, drew together black workers and helped them organize a building trades union. Called the International Laborers and Builders Corporation, it numbered some 300 skilled workers. It was an instant success. Contractors who formerly turned their backs on black workers immediately accepted these organized black mechanics.[3]

With this kind of organized power in mind T. Arnold Hill wrote after one year of the New Deal: "The future of Negro workers will be unprotected under any plan without adequate representation of their case. This they have not now in the A F of L nor in the machinery of the NRA. But they do have it among the 5,000,000 Negro workers whose organized resistance could not possibly be ignored. It is to be hoped that leadership for such an effort will soon be found, and that Negro workers already organized will form the nucleus." [4] These are the words of a man for whom temporizing is over. What did Hill have in mind? Was he giving up on organized labor?

The man's own words indicate that he saw that there had been a New Deal indeed, and that at the table were big business, government and big labor. Of these three, only one, labor, was likely to give voice to black citizens' needs—but not so long as the major factor in the field, the AFL, continued to turn its back to blacks. What to do about it? Breaking open the AFL had been a fruitless effort for the NUL for twenty years. It could not be abandoned or written off. But neither could the AFL be relied upon as a possible channel for black representation. The imminent congressional consideration of the Wagner Labor Act would increase labor's power, giving it representation on NRA code authorities, for instance, in addition to broad new legal advantages in organizing and bargaining. In the light of labor's historical bigotry, this, said Hill, was a matter that gave blacks concern over the new labor bill and the advantages it would grant labor.

"If the labor representatives on the board set up in the Wagner Bill should come from the AF of L they might come from one of the Federation's nationals which permit no Negroes to join its ranks," Hill underlined. "The Wagner Bill elevates labor to the dominant position of an active, operating co-partner with the employer and the public, each having equal rights and authority. If . . . [the NRA] . . . has permitted labor unions to continue their restrictions against Negroes, what might not be expected when organized labor is given greater prestige and control?" [5]

As Hill indicated, the AFL had proved, through the years, in every kind of economic situation ranging from the high-riding days of World War I to the depths of Depression during the Hoover administration, that it was the agency of white workers. The NUL's efforts since 1913 had netted minimal results, only copious sanctimonious statements from Gompers, Green and their associates. Little or no help could be expected from the AFL for the benefit of black workers.

Thus on March 8, 1934, the acting executive secretary of the NUL proposed that the agency organize all existing black labor union groups into a federation. Further, the organization of "additional units of Negro workers" would be encouraged and this federation hopefully "would broaden into many as time goes on." [6]

As observer Charles Lawrence analyzes it, "It seems almost incredible that at a time when . . . the Negro population was losing ground economically, the National Urban League should go on the offensive with a program of worker education and a bolder approach to trade union integration. Yet, this was a period when there was so little left to defend in terms of the Negro population's participation in the general economy that the League hardly had an alternative. At the same time, the recrudescence of trade unionism, with the official blessing of the government made it mandatory that Negro workers become identified with organized labor if they were to survive." [7]

Hill's federation of workers was to be only the means to an end. It "would be the instrument through which we hope to obtain appropriate action on behalf of Negro workers, rather than the end itself. Our principal objective would be, first, the awakening of consciousness among Negro workers as to their own strength; and, second, the use of this strength to secure for them recognition in all the ways that labor is being recognized today." [8]

In addition to bringing black workers together, Hill perceived the NUL role to be one of continuously keeping in touch with the movement, feeding to it matters of vital interest to workers with practical plans for their participation. Also into this effort would go the Vocational Opportunity Campaigns, concentrating on the secondary schools and colleges.

Hill had worked out a scheme for launching this program at minimum cost—he estimated that $2,250 would cover. A committee of 100 was to be formed, with R. R. Moton as chairman, to raise funds and sponsor the new NUL program. It was to be an all-black committee and it was to carry on a fund-raising effort among blacks. John T. Clark would be borrowed from the St. Louis League to organize the project and Jesse O. Thomas would be moved to the New York office "to work out the relationship of the EAC and assist with other administrative details." Albon

L. Holsey of Tuskegee and the National Negro Business League would be hired to direct the financial campaign. Field contacts would be the existing black unions, EAC's, local Leagues and the National Negro Business League branches.

The NUL Steering Committee approved, and Hill moved forward with the project. John T. Clark and Jesse O. Thomas came to the national office and set to work. Hill had to rejigger his program slightly; he secured Robert S. Abbott, publisher of the Chicago *Defender,* as chairman of the new Committee of One Hundred for Negro Workers, and he assigned to the business manager of *Opportunity,* Lester B. Granger, a young, militant newspaper columnist and former Los Angeles League secretary, the responsibility for the new program.

Jesse O. Thomas went after money, composing and mailing 1,100 appeal letters over Chairman Abbott's name, inviting persons to join the Sponsoring Committee and asking them to contribute at least $5 each. Thomas followed up with another mailing and claimed that of the 149 people who accepted membership on the Sponsoring Committee, 118 were brought on by his efforts. He then traveled to seven border and southern cities to secure more sponsors.

John T. Clark's experienced hand quickly shaped the outlines of the new program. By mid-April it was ready to launch and on the nineteenth an "open letter" addressed to "The Five Million Negro Workers in the United States, Employed and Unemployed," was released. Workers' Councils would be formed around the nation, it was announced, to "crystallize their activity and develop their bargaining power in the labor market." [9]

"You must organize to compel the breakdown of discriminatory barriers that keep you out of unions," said the letter, "and, consequently, out of employment. You must organize to prevent the passing of legislation that will be a further aid to discrimination-practicing unions and employers. You must organize to demand, with other workers, a new deal for labor."

Hill's horizons were broad: the workers were to come from every stratum of employment, including domestics, porters, chauffeurs, mechanics, building tradesmen, clerks and musicians. And once organized the councils were to be managed and controlled by the workers themselves.

In the statement issued by NUL, the councils would consider and plan corrective programs for:

1. Handling of grievances within the ranks of Negro workers.
2. Including Negro workers in unions that now excluded them.
3. Planning ways to overcome discrimination and exclusion.
4. Participating in labor programs in the community.

5. Interesting Negro workers in social legislation for old age pensions, unemployment insurance, minimum wage, sickness insurance, and hours
and conditions of work.
6. Educating the Negro community, the white community and white workers in the history of Negro labor and Negro workers.[10]

Moving into the field of labor was not like a stroll in the Easter parade. It had its difficulties, even dangers. The history of organizing black
workers had been amply studded with violence and repression: the New
Orleans dock strikes; the sentencing of Angelo Herndon to twenty years
on the chain gang for trying to organize workers to fight for unemployment relief in Georgia; the death penalty for "inciting to insurrection
against the state of Georgia" facing six members of the National Textile
Workers Union for organizing black and white workers and demonstrating against unemployment.

But the young man who was to head the effort to organize the Negro
Workers' Councils had courage, energy and the gift of brilliant expression to contend with the drawbacks and dangers. "Yesterday's standards
have proven unfit for application today," said Lester B. Granger.

> Let us then forget both yesterday and today, and plan for a fast ap-
> proaching Tomorrow. . . . The Negro Workers' Councils have an unusual
> opportunity for mass education through their workers' institutes. An educa-
> tional program at the start will disappoint those who yearn for the soap
> box banner parade but after all, Negro youth is planning for tomorrow.
> . . . Simply stated, this means that Negroes will try to educate themselves
> about labor's problems, will organize for race betterment, and will try to
> break into or break up white unions which exclude them. This is a very
> different policy from that followed by our diplomatic old gentlemen and
> lady leaders of yesterday, but it is vitally necessary. Industrial America is
> organizing steadily through governmental action and labor maneuvers, but
> Negroes are being left out of the picture. They see a wall of protection
> being erected for white workers while unorganized black labor is left out-
> side, exposed to the dangers of bitter class conflict. This is no time for soft
> words and seeking after interracial amity at the expense of the race's fu-
> ture.[11]

Such outspoken statements may have been a jolt to staid Urban Leaguers, but they were no more revolutionary than the actions of some of
the most venerable Leagues and most reliable League leaders at this
time. The initial Workers' Council was a case in point. This was in St.
Louis, where John T. Clark had followed the organizational formula he
had drafted for the councils. The local effort had been kicked off with an
institute, in which national and local labor problems facing American
workers in general and black workers specifically were reviewed and dis-

cussed by economists, government officials, labor leaders and blacks. Following the institute, the St. Louis Workers' Council was established, with particular strength from building trades workers and maintenance employees. By the fall of 1934 the St. Louis council had staged monster picketing demonstrations on city jobs where black workers had been refused work. A protest parade with John T. Clark leading the march was successfully executed as part of the activity.

All of this was a giant step from the traditional Urban League tactics of only a few years before. Though the Committee of One Hundred, the sponsors of the Workers' Councils, consisted of the old Urban League regulars (the national board members, local board members and prominent blacks from various additional cities), there was an added dimension in the National Advisory Committee, which included black labor leaders such as Clarence R. Johnson, general chairman of the Dining Car Employees Local 582; Rienzi B. Lemus, Brotherhood of Dining Car Employees; Benjamin Fletcher, former organizer for the IWW; R. L. Mays, secretary of the National Association of Railway Employees; and Harry E. B. Davis, treasurer, Eastern and Gulf Marine Cooks' and Stewards' Union.

The central secretariat for the Workers' Councils was the Workers' Bureau, a grandiose designation for Lester Granger and his secretarial assistant. As Granger saw it, his job was "to inundate the Negro working public with arguments in favor of trade unions . . . not warnings against what unions will do to you, which was the routine treatment, but warnings of what will happen to you if you are not a member of the labor movement . . . our message was you've got to organize, preferably with white workers in unions of your own choosing—or, if you can't do that, you've got to organize outside of them and use your organization to pressure your way in. For the day is gone when unorganized workers can protect themselves." [12]

Granger found that it was an uphill fight. The avenues traditionally open to the League, the black weekly newspapers, were themselves hostile to unionization of Afro-Americans. So, though the newspapers printed the Workers' Council releases, they usually did so with minimal treatment. Granger wrote a series of pamphlets aimed at black workers, in which he took out after black misconceptions and discriminatory practices of unions and government in the labor field. Granger packed a great deal of verbal dynamite into these little leaflets and they were mailed out by the hundreds to people who had been suggested as key persons.[13]

But campaigning by mail and by newspaper was not enough. Except for the International Ladies' Garment Workers Union (ILGWU) and the Amalgamated Clothing Workers of America, Granger found, white union officials did not want the League to carry through this project. White businessmen were against it—"they didn't want blacks corrupted with trade union infection." Blacks—middle-class businessmen, white collar workers, civil servants—opposed this activity because they saw the unions as the natural enemy of black workers. "And the Negro workers themselves were so discouraged, and so embittered they thought we were going up a blind alley. . . . And so," summed up Granger, "we had no public. We had to make a public." [14]

This was done by taking the message on the road from city to city. However, it was difficult to find persons to call together a group. In Detroit, only the prestige of John Dancy made a meeting possible after the YMCA canceled use of its facilities when it learned the subject matter of the gathering. It was, after all, at the height of the organizing activity when the unions were fighting Ford, GM and Chrysler tooth and nail. The YWCA opened its doors to the meeting, and about one hundred attended. Granger, an Auto Workers official and a minister spoke in favor of joining the unions and organizing a Workers' Council. John Dancy, considered the "arch reactionary" of the Urban League movement and a "protegé" of the Ford interests, was chairman of the meeting.[15] After the speeches, Dancy announced that he personally endorsed and approved the Workers' Council as being necessary to the industrial welfare and employment prospects of blacks in Detroit. "The meeting sat there appalled," reports Granger, "and Dancy made his endorsement even stronger."

Granger covered the major cities of the north and found that in Chicago and New York there was opposition from existing groups of black unionists; in Pittsburgh the reception was too warm—the council formed there had to be closed down after a short life under Communist domination, and re-activated when the Reds were thrown out. In the winter of 1936 Granger drove into the south to contact some of those who had responded to the mailings and help them set up councils. He had no idea how vulnerable he was nor how dangerous his mission until he was in the backwoods of Arkansas, Georgia, Mississippi and Tennessee. One night in the Arkansas "outback" he attended a meeting of a tenant farmers union local:

> We had parked the car and walked a considerable distance . . . through the woods to a sharecropper's residence, a cabin, and we met by candlelight, covered by blankets, and during the meeting a man came in with the regular knock and he was admitted and in great excitement he told us that the sheriff's deputy posse had raided a meeting west of there . . . and they had shot through the walls first; they hadn't killed anybody but maybe they

injured someone, and they were "headed thisaway." . . . I will never forget the cool way in which the chairman disposed of the meeting.[16]

In Jackson, Mississippi, a Workers' Council had been organized and was ready for recognition. Granger gave his usual speech about the goals of unionization and of the councils. The next morning the chairman of the committee rushed over to Granger on the street. "Glad to find you, Brother Granger. I've been looking for you. When you leaving town, Brother Granger?"

"I think tomorrow," Granger replied.

"Oh, oh. You leaving tomorrow?"

"Yes, tomorrow." But Granger noticed that the Mississippian was terribly uneasy. "You think I should leave town earlier?"

"Yes, I reckon you better," he encouraged. "You know, some of those folks at that meeting might not have just understood the things you've said, and maybe they've talked to some of the white folks and they got the wrong idea of what the meeting's about, and if this was so, maybe you'd find yourself in jail not even knowing what happened. You'd better leave town before it's too late . . ."

"Brother ——, when do you think I ought to leave?"

"Well, I reckon right about now you ought to leave." And, with the man's nervous assistance as lookout, Granger picked up his belongings and sped out of town.

This, reports Granger, was typical of conditions he met in the south. He went on to Atlanta and Birmingham where he conducted meetings. But he decided it was unfair for him to contact blacks in the small towns, endangering their livelihoods if not their lives. He had no more Workers' Councils organizing meetings in the south. However, there were some strong councils formed in places such as Little Rock, Memphis and St. Louis, and some "hole-in-the-wall secret organizations in various cities" which, by request of their leaders, were never named in the Workers' Council roster.[17]

Granger found himself busy on many fronts in his Workers' Bureau activity, sometimes to the discomfort of his boss. On two occasions he actually participated in strikes—once in 1935 when he joined a longshoremen's picket line (and met maritime leader Joe Curran) and another time when he joined such notables as Heywood Broun to picket the New York *Amsterdam News* on behalf of the Newspaper Guild strike. E. K. Jones was "distressed." His judgment was that Granger should not get involved. "The League should be in a position to give service to people without taking part, direct part, in strike situations. We should be in a position to join and talk with management and talk with labor." [18]

When Granger spoke in Cleveland his remarks were printed in the black newspaper. He called on Afro-Americans to drop their rigid hostilities toward organized labor and oppose those elements that were anti-Negro but seek chances to join even if a union generally opposed black membership, because you couldn't vote to change a union except from within. This statement infuriated the head of a Cleveland corporation that had regularly given $100 a year to the NUL. This man wrote E. K. Jones asking if the speech represented the policy of the NUL. Jones called Granger in, asked him if he thought it represented the agency's policy. "I certainly do," the Workers' Bureau secretary answered.

"On what basis?" Jones asked.

Granger showed how it tied in with established policies and official statements of the NUL and offered to bring in the notes from which he had spoken. Jones reached across the desk and slapped him on the shoulder.

"I wanted to see if you really believed it. If you believe it, and can back it up—that's Urban League policy." He wrote the Clevelander, endorsing Granger's speech, and that was the end of that $100 contribution —at a time when the NUL was on the ropes financially, with a debt of $14,000, and $100 represented a sizable portion of a payroll.[19]

The energetic surge of Communist grass-roots action in the major cities was a definite threat. Granger explains:

> We could not broadcast organizational needs and organizational methods. If we did, the first to answer would be communists, because they knew what potential importance resided in this idea of organizing Negroes on the basis of their employment interests. And they didn't have the direct access that the Urban League had, but they'd ride our boat. And so after the first few unfortunate experiences, we carefully chose leaders who would in turn carefully screen out communists. Now, this made for a non-communist-controlled operation, but it also made for a severely impaired program of recruitment.[20]

The League effort at the 1935 AFL convention followed up the favorable omens of 1934 AFL action. Picketed by NAACP activities, the AFL 1934 convention had approved appointment of a Committee of Five "to investigate the conditions of colored workers of the country and report to the next convention." [21]

During the summer of 1935 the Committee of Five held hearings in Washington to which NUL sent a delegation to testify. Reginald A. Johnson presented the League's position paper, covering succinctly the AFL history of exclusion and bigotry in its locals while its leaders and conventions passed platitudes of brotherly love. Johnson charged that the greatest handicap to organizing blacks was organized labor itself—its policies, practices and prejudices. He noted that there was evidence of rank-and-file acceptance of blacks that was thwarted by reactionary leaders and he gave examples. The alienation of blacks from the AFL was distinctly possible, he said, for Afro-American labor was "in a state of flux . . . unparalleled in former history." There were strong movements toward dual unionism, company unionism, anti-AFL unionism, Johnson stated, and definite and positive action by the AFL was needed immediately.

NUL called for strong action to expel or discipline AFL unions that refused to comply with pronouncements of the AFL executive council on interracial brotherhood. It endorsed also Philip Randolph's resolution calling for appointment of black organizers and a program of worker education among blacks. NUL and its Workers' Councils, reported Johnson, were at the service of the AFL, and were even then working to discourage dual unionism, fighting antilabor sentiment and instilling in black workers appreciation of the benefits of unionism and working to get them into existing labor organizations.[22]

Coordinating with this presentation, Workers' Councils around the nation put the heat on the AFL by letter, telegram and personal calls. They appealed to AFL officials and to local labor unions and central trade bodies. Such undignified action upset AFL officials and President William Green accused the councils of promoting dual-unionism and anti-AFL attitudes and of domination by radicals. Lester Granger rejected these charges point by point and stressed the fact that "a majority of our National Advisory Committee (which is our policy-making group) are members in good standing of unions affiliated with the American Federation of Labor."[23]

Hill and Granger organized an Urban League lobby at the 1935 AFL convention in Atlantic City to urge action against AFL bigotry. Edward S. Lewis; James H. Hubert, secretary of the New York League; Donald Wyatt, industrial secretary of Philadelphia's Armstrong Association; and Lester Granger, representing the NUL and the Workers' Councils, attended the 1935 convention of the AFL. In addition, twelve of the Negro Workers' Councils sent telegrams and letters, held meetings and worked in their own localities to let the AFL know action was demanded. These councils were in Avon Park and Palmetto, Florida; Camilla, Georgia; Seattle; Columbus, Ohio; Lutcher, Louisiana; St. Louis, Kansas City, Philadelphia, Pittsburgh, Newark, and New York.

Granger reported that the communications and lobbying by the on-scene black delegation, the distribution of literature (circulars entitled "Fools and Cowards Cut Their own Throats—Are American Workers Fools or Cowards?" and "Expel the Traitor! Kick Out Jim Crow!")

to each delegate made some of the AFL officers angry, some of them sympathetic, but all "were impressed with the determination of Negro workers to break down the bars which have prevented their free entry into organized labor." The AFL Committee of Five brought in a report recommending a three-level program. The elements proposed were (1) that the biased unions shape up, review their practices and "harmonize" their rules and practices to conform with AFL statements upholding equality of treatment; (2) that charters to biased unions would not be issued; and (3) that an educational campaign be established by the AFL "to get the white worker to see more completely the weakness of division and the necessity of unity between white and black workers to the end that all workers may be organized." [24]

The true attitude of Green and the AFL was revealed by the treatment of this report. The AFL president turned it over to the tender mercies of George M. Harrison, president of the lily-white Railway Clerks Union, one of the most retrograde and recalcitrant bodies in the federation. Harrison watered it down to the point that only the education recommendation remained. In this anemic form the remains of the Committee of Five's report were withheld by Harrison until 10 p.m. on the final night of the convention, then tossed into the inevitable log-jam of last-minute items brusquely considered and quickly rejected by exhausted delegates.[25]

However, out of this convention grew the Committee for Industrial Organization (CIO), which was based on the concept of bringing everyone in a factory or industry into one big labor organization. This inclusive approach rejected exceptions on the basis of race or nationality. Self-interest dictated that *everybody* in the plant be unionized—the interdependence of all workers in the place was evident, and a new, democratic evangelism entered labor organization efforts at this point. When the CIO broke away and became independent under the name Congress of Industrial Organizations the competition for members quickly made the AFL more friendly to blacks. The advantages to black workers from this competiton and the new opportunities presented by the CIO were outlined in Workers' Council *Bulletin* No. 7 in December 1935, under the heading "Hope for Negroes in Industrial Unions." [26]

Urban League secretaries and Workers' Council leaders looked at the CIO development as offering real opportunities. At NUL Workers' Institutes, industrial relations secretaries of the League strongly endorsed the CIO and black participation in it. Some saw it as the wave of the future, in which white workers would see where their "real interests" lay. They believed the CIO would bring equality of industrial opportunity for blacks and would be the vanguard of an inevitable socialist economy in the nation. Others recognized no change in the attitudes of white workers but urged CIO membership for blacks to help change antiblack attitudes, and to insure that when and if backlash set in black workers would be safely entrenched in the new labor organization.

In December of 1935 Granger wired the Negro Workers' Councils commending the moves of John L. Lewis (whose United Mine Workers had some 65,000 black members) against racial discrimination in unions. Granger offered Lewis the aid of the fifty-three Workers' Councils in twenty-six states.[27]

Four months later Granger wrote Lewis, Sidney Hillman, Louis Zaritsky, John Brophy and other founding fathers of the CIO. The CIO, he suggested, could "at this time perform a fine service to Negro labor, and greatly increase its own potential strength by doing what the AFL has thus far refused to do: appoint some Negroes to its staff for educational and organizing work." Holding out the bait that several international unions, not at that point supporters of the CIO, had large black memberships, Granger suggested that such membership might be sufficient to "easily decide the Internationals' policies" in the case of the hod carriers and longshoremen. Black personnel on the CIO staff would, Granger advised, increase tremendously the chance of the CIO to win support of additional internationals at the upcoming AFL convention. Such staff members would have "the active cooperation of the Negro Workers' Councils and their approximately 30,000 members," said Granger, and sent along the names of two qualified persons for consideration.[28]

By the end of 1936 there were seventy-three Workers' Councils on the roster, and in Illinois and Florida state networks were particularly effective. Granger was able to pull together a committee of black tobacco workers in the North Carolina towns. A Tobacco Workers' Council was formed, cooperating with a group of white workers who were dissatisfied not only with their own wages and work conditions, but with the corruption and indifference in the leadership of the Tobacco Workers' International Union. Here was evidence that blue-collar whites and blacks could act together for mutual benefits, even in the south.

The uphill struggle to organize effective Workers' Councils, the "new ball game" opened up by the rise of the CIO and its conflict with the AFL, the financial prostration of the NUL (in 1934 it spent $62,000 and was in debt $14,000; in 1935 it held expenditures to the same figure but debts increased to $16,000; staff numbered fourteen) took the steam out of the Workers' Councils drive. Though the project continued under the administration of Reginald A. Johnson after Lester Granger went on leave in September 1937, NUL went back to more conventional paths, concentrating its efforts on vocational guidance and opening civil service jobs to blacks.

Concrete results from the Workers' Council efforts? There were many, perhaps the greatest of which was the teaching of protest and organizing techniques.[29] As Dr. Charles Lawrence observes, the Workers' Council program of the National Urban League served an important function during its few years of existence. It was probably the first time that a social service organization had made a frontal attack on the integration of Negroes into trade unions. The league itself, along with the NAACP and other organizations, had made repeated overtures to AFL leaders and to the leaders of international unions; but here was a program which was aimed at the "grass roots." It is estimated that 8,000 Negro workers secured admission into unions from which they had previously been barred —at least in their localities. Scores of former participants in Workers' Councils are holding positions of leadership in local and international unions of the AFL and CIO.

"The Workers Council programs seem to have been in tune with the times. The adult education movement was beginning to take a more direct hand in workers education . . . for participation in the labor movement. . . . Most important in whatever success the program had, however, was the widespread need felt among Negro workers." [30]

27/ Transition

The greatest single NUL accomplishment of 1935, said T. Arnold Hill in reviewing that year, was the added popularity of the organization, free from attack by conservatives, radicals, the press and other critics. This was all the more remarkable he said, inasmuch as the League had "pursued aggressively, highly controversial endeavors." The agency had been spared criticism, Hill declared, because the public agreed with the agency's policies, both local and national. These were "not new policies, nor new program, nor even a new statement of the program—but a more active participation in seeing them through." [1]

Anyone who accepted Hill's estimate of the agency at face value was likely to be misled. For the entire tenor of the NUL had changed. No longer was it the diplomatic go-between, operating behind the scenes and speaking in public only in polite terms, if at all, while it met in offices and council rooms with the power structure to open new opportunities to black workers. Far from it. Under Arnold Hill, the agency was kicking up a fuss about discrimination and demanding a rightful share for blacks. The language was not always polite, but the facts were indisputable. Furthermore, it was not Hill alone who was speaking out; he had organized the Emergency Advisory Councils, which were raising their voices in 201 communities. Not only that, but Workers' Councils were sounding off in some seventy-three places around the country. (It was a fact that both these programs were all-black, contrary to the time-honored Urban League policy of interracial action.) And not only was the agency attacking government bias at all levels, it had abandoned the kidglove approach to organized labor. An indication of this new aggressiveness was the following extraordinary resolution:

> That the Executive Board of the National Urban League puts itself on record as approving the appointment of a Legal Committee, and that we ask the local organizations and Workers' Councils to submit to the League's Legal Committee, the facts in any cases in which discrimination has arisen that affects the industrial worker.[2]

Thus the agency signified its intention of moving into another area, legal action, a vineyard previously conceded to the NAACP. (Apparently the resolution was never implemented.)

Also, a new realization of the vast expansion of government and the churning that was going on in the New Deal prompted Hill to set up a temporary Washington office in the summer of 1935.

The shift from social work to citizens' rights had been made without tearing the agency apart. The needs of the day and the avenues for achieving them dictated the response, and the response was protest, pressure and civil rights action. Social service, after all, was becoming largely a government responsibility. As such, it had a commitment (unfulfilled) to provide aid to all needy citizens. The League was anxious to see that responsibility carried out.

T. Arnold Hill's moves revitalized the agency. It was Rosenwald Fund official Dr. M. O. Bousfield, NUL board member from Chicago, who had made the point in an executive meeting that if NUL had a more positive program it could secure additional funds. He said he did not know which way it should go.[3] T. Arnold Hill agreed, saying that he thought the approach to more money for the NUL was through program, and if the program could be made more aggressive, there were both whites and blacks who would give to the agency. Then he went on to outline a $500,000 fund-raising campaign, designed to give the NUL a basic annual $50,000 budget. For good measure, he recommended establishment of a $25,000 Ruth Standish Baldwin Fellowship Fund in memory of the late president of the agency. (She had died in 1934.) Such proposals must have been staggering to directors of an agency that was at that time unable even to eke out $65,000 to keep itself afloat.

It was at this meeting that a national advisory board was approved. Each local League was asked to nominate one of its board members.[4]

Hollingsworth Wood, surveying the terrain highlighted by Hill, remarked that he did not see sufficient board and staff personnel to handle the responsibilities now resting on the League (much less in the future). E. K. Jones pointed out the need for staff and the crippling handicap of no funds. New sources of revenue were needed, he said, and suggested gently that board members help in approaching foundations and other donors. Past performance, however, indicated that the prospect for adequate financial support from this group was dim.

At this time the so-called Twenty-fifth Anniversary of the agency was up for discussion, and it was recommended that a mammoth fund-raising campaign be conducted in all League cities through the cooperation of the newly established NUL advisory board.

The possibilities of attracting fresh sources of funding through program activities with wider appeal seemed sensible. If Hill was right, the new, aggressive path down which he was taking the NUL should have resulted in added support as well as the accolades he claimed. The proof would, therefore, be not in headlines alone, but in dollars in the NUL treasury.

Hill had learned one bitter lesson from his unsuccessful run for office in Chicago. He had found that the endorsement of the women's clubs was of minor value in a popularity contest when your opponent was slugging away, building an image as an aggressive fighter for black rights and striking at "gut issues" such as food, clothing, shelter and jobs.[5]

In his two and a half years in the NUL driver's seat, Hill had changed the agency. In late 1935, it was clear that, as Dr. Bousfield suggested, a more distinct impression had to be made on the black community and those whites who were willing to take an interest. Choices must be made; directions must be followed. The question was, which was the agency to be—more radical or more conservative?

> The problems of today fall directly in our field. They have been brought to our doorstep by the depression. The solution of them takes us into the field of action. There is no escape from it if we are to meet the challenge. The Negro throughout the country must be led to utilize the personnel and physical resources at his command if he is to share equally with others the public benefits made possible by public funds. We must help him employ articulate, aggressive devices which today assure more effective protec-

tion than do the warranties of the constitution itself. The information and leadership to promote an awareness and such action seem logically to be ours now after a service of twenty-five years in the field of race relations.[6]

Obviously T. Arnold Hill was aiming for an increasingly militant, action-oriented course for the NUL. But in spite of Hill's confidence that the agency had increased its popularity in 1935, the hoped-for concomitant—increased financial support—failed to materialize. Quite the reverse: the agency finished 1935 with expenditures of $62,000 and a comparatively huge $16,000 debt. This threatening financial situation staggered Kinckle Jones. By the end of April 1936 he had cut back to one day a week his Commerce Department work and resumed direction of the national office. On July 1, T. Arnold Hill took off for Europe on a four-month leave of absence at full salary with traveling expenses underwritten by the Rosenwald Fund. There he studied adult education, vocational training and cooperatives. After his return Hill continued as NUL industrial secretary but accepted appointment as a member of the New York State Board of Social Welfare for a three-year term.

E. K. Jones quickly slammed on the brakes and NUL reverted to a more sedate approach to black problems in the nation. The executive secretary concentrated his attention on fund raising. At the end of 1936, Jones reported with a touch of pride that the deficit had been reduced by more than $6,000. It had been accomplished by scrimping along on $59,000, of which more than 10 percent was the salary of the executive secretary.

It was in his address to the NUL annual meeting in 1938 that Kinckle Jones enunciated his conception of the League's role after ten years of depression (for blacks it had started in 1928):

> The most important responsibility of our movement is that of discovering social trends, gauging the Negro's capacity for accommodating himself to forward movements and finding out the best methods to be followed in aiding him to condition himself for the change and preparing himself helpfully and creditably to participate in bringing about desirable social mutations. No less important, probably, is the work of conditioning the public mind to realize that no helpful social change is permanent without programs that offer all mankind equal and full integration.[7]

This "accommodating" approach, with its quaint throwback to social Darwinism in the reference to "social mutations" could scarcely have been calculated to contrast in a more extreme fashion to the action-oriented drive of Hill's pronouncements.

Kinckle Jones applied a checkrein to League activities—the most effective kind of checkrein—a tight money policy. NUL's major efforts in industrial relations during the years 1937–1940 were focused on a new elaboration of and emphasis on the Vocational Opportunity Campaign, which brought the extraordinary organizing talents of Ann Tanneyhill to the fore; on developing programs for qualifying black workers for civil service posts; on continuation, on a diminishing scale, of the Workers' Councils effort; and on individual vocational counseling which became a placement service for professional social workers and a civil service career launcher.

The Industrial Relations Department, according to Jones, "kept constant contact with employers, employees, white and Negro, and various Governmental agencies." There had been a worldwide current to improve the economic and social conditions of workers through trade unionism, Jones observed. This opportunity the League had "freely grasped with the hope that the pleasant relationships between [white and black workers] would result in better occupational opportunities for Negro workers." [8] (He referred to the new initatives of the CIO.)

At the beginning of 1937 E. K. Jones listed three goals for the agency: (1) getting jobs for blacks; (2) impressing federal authorities with the importance of guarding the interests of black workers; (3) improving NUL staff efficiency and techniques. Income that year totaled $63,000 and the deficit was shaved to $8,000.[9]

The following year, Jones shifted the emphasis to "(1) a five-year program . . . to organize new cities and coordinate the local activities of the movement; and (2) expansion of the Vocational Guidance and Counseling Service." Income dropped to $57,000, and the deficit rose to $14,000.[10]

When the Axis nations clanked onward in their conquests and takeovers in 1938, the United States Congress voted a billion-dollar naval building program to shore up long-neglected defenses. This, plus other military expenditures and the purchases in the United States by other nations gave the economy the impetus that began to bring it out of the long, deep freeze of the Depression.

In January 1939 another $552 million was requested by President Franklin D. Roosevelt for improving fortifications and defense establishments. Meanwhile France became a major purchaser of military goods, and the United States set out to build 600 military planes for French armed forces. The pace of American industry quickened. Output picked up; more men moved into production lines; money began to circulate. The workers hired and nearly all the families benefited were white.

In the world's largest black city, New York, there were 327,000 Afro-Americans residents in 1930. That year they bought goods at the rate of $150,000,000 and owned $65,000,000 worth of real estate in Harlem alone. But when the industrial machine ground to a halt, it crushed the blacks: their median family income went from $1,808 in 1929, to $1,019 in 1932, to $837 in 1935 (median white income in 1935 in New York City was $1,814).[11]

Unemployment reached epidemic proportions in New York, blighting the lives of an estimated 5,000 to 10,000 black workers in the 1920–1929 period, 17,848, in 1930, 20,000 in 1932, and 50,000 in 1939.

The impact of the Depression revolutionized Afro-American life in New York even more than elsewhere. The Negro Renaissance shriveled as Harlem ran dry of money and more than half of New York's black families depended on home relief or work relief for subsistence. In 1927, 2,000 black New York families were on relief; in 1930, there were 20,000, and in 1939, 40,000.

The disproportionate impact of Depression and discrimination was evident in the fact that New York City's annual direct relief payments totaled $100,000,000 in 1939 and of that amount one fifth went to black citizens, though they numbered only one twentieth of the city's population! But if New York was tragic, the conditions in the rest of the country were disastrous:

Nationwide, the median take-home pay of American men in 1939 was $1,112 if they were white. You could hire two and a half blacks for this amount—the median wage for black men was $460. White women earned $676 annually; black women received $246 in median wages.[12]

Two out of every five black families in the nation's cities were on relief. They were the fortunate ones; many in the cities and most in the rural areas received no regular aid.

Things had to improve; they could scarcely have deteriorated further for Afro-American citizens. So it seemed, anyhow, but 1939 was, on the domestic front, a year of fits and starts, unexpected reverses and unpredicted advances.

It was the year that gave Marian Anderson the opportunity to upstage the Daughters of the American Revolution by singing at the Lincoln Memorial (thanks to Secretary of the Interior Ickes) instead of Constitution Hall, in the same month that Mississippi Senator Bilbo introduced a back-to-Africa bill for blacks. Far more serious, it was in 1939 that WPA was suddenly and drastically chopped back in an administration effort to find funds for defense preparations. Defense industries were taking up the slack for whites who were lopped off WPA. But the WPA shutdown spelled calamity for hundreds of thousands of blacks. The cutback had, editorialized *Opportunity*, "accelerated misery, family disorganization and moral disintegration on a scale which is alarming to those who are interested in the welfare of Negro citizens." [13]

Summing up the WPA, *Opportunity* admitted it had been staggeringly expensive and had had defects, but thought it was worth the cost in terms of its preservation of "human values of dignity and self respect which employment—regular employment—gives to the man and woman who can not find a job in private industry." This, it said, was the fate of the great mass of black workers, even though business was supposed to be on the upswing. If American industry was beginning to hum, said Elmer Carter, editor of *Opportunity,* blacks did not hear it because the doors of industry were closed to them.[14]

WPA had given black white-collar workers their first real chances to use the skills they had learned in school and college. Also, WPA had made it possible to expand social work in black communities where it had been inadequate and extend it to others where it had never existed. So the cutback not only ended vital jobs but abruptly ended civic and social work to the black community. "The evidence of poverty and want and suffering is not hard to find," said Elmer Carter, "but those who are inclined to probe beneath the surface will be shocked by the growing despair which seems to be prevalent among all groups and all classes. Relief is not enough . . . bare subsistence and weary days of enforced idleness —is apt to discourage any normal person. From discouragement sometimes comes desperation. And after that, who knows." [15]

At the beginning of 1939, Kinckle Jones emphasized the need for expansion: "No more important service can be rendered by our national office than that of establishing more local organizations. The League's ideals can best be spread and established through local contact with the problem, and with those people of intelligence and influence through whom the Negro masses can best be helped. . . ." [16] Priorities for 1939 were predicated on money, but were, in order: (1) extension of the League to twenty-five to fifty more cities; (2) a special vocational and educational guidance program at $10,000 a year; (3) a special household workers' improvement program at $10,000 a year.

But all of Jones's predictions went out of the window the night of March 3, 1939. Returning from an exhilarating WPA theater performance of *The Hot Mikado,* Jones was stricken with a grave case of tuberculosis, signaled by hemorrhaging. It was his first serious illness in forty-two years. Hospitalized with one lung collapsed, the executive secretary was in mortal danger—and so was the National Urban League. A replacement was urgently needed and the logical candidate—experienced, seasoned, vigorous and with great prestige among other League executives, government, industry and the social work profession—was T. Arnold Hill.

Instead, Hollingsworth Wood wired Jesse O. Thomas, then in the midst of a campaign to raise the third year's budget for the New Orleans

League, to come to New York and take over as acting executive secretary of NUL. This, Thomas commented later, "was an unenviable position, because I was very much in the position of a strike breaker." [17] He amplified this in his autobiography:

> It developed that between Mr. Jones and T. Arnold Hill . . . there had developed a schism akin to mistrust and suspicion. Information accumulated while Mr. Jones was serving as adviser to Mr. Roper, Secretary of Commerce, made it appear that Mr. T. Arnold Hill, who was second in authority at national headquarters, was seeking to undermine Mr. Jones and replace him as Executive Secretary. This impression became sufficiently convincing for Mr. Jones to resign the position in Washington and return to New York and assume his position as executive head of the organization. . . . If Mr. Hill was trying to take his job while he was well and giving part-time supervision to the organization, he would be more successful if he were put in charge while Mr. Jones was seriously and dangerously ill. It was in that kind of situation that I became acting Executive Director of the National Urban League. I never held a job where I exercised less of my imagination and where I was less aggressive in the discharge of my functional responsibilities. This was true for two reasons: (1) I knew there were persons in the office who would keep Mr. Jones informed of what was happening, and I did not want to militate against his recovery by giving any basis for his informant to becoming suspicious of any ambition that I might entertain of becoming Executive Secretary; (2) I knew of the possibilities of a reconciliation between these two erst-while boyhood friends, in which event I would find myself "a lost ball in high weeds." On this account, I adopted a middle-of-the road policy and did the best job possible under the circumstances. [18]

Under the uneasy guidance of Jesse O. Thomas the NUL continued on its way. New locals were opened or under development in Washington, D.C., Providence, Greenville, South Carolina, Chester, Pennsylvania, Oklahoma City, Durham, North Carolina, Portland and Miami. The seventh VOC was bigger and better than ever. Three League Fellowships were awarded, bringing the total number of full-time NUL Fellows up to ninety. *Opportunity* completed its seventeenth year, with outstanding articles by authors such as Pearl Buck, Alain Locke, Melville Herskovits, William Grant Still, Claude McKay and Rayford Logan. The annual conference was held at the Green Pastures camp belonging to the Detroit League, to discuss "The Urban League Movement Faces New Frontiers."

It was at this annual conference that a group of the local League executives got together and formed an executive secretaries council. Their major concern was expressed in a letter signed by twenty-one of them and addressed to Hollingsworth Wood:

Without further ado, may we state, in what we think is logical sequence, some of the factors that are of pressing concern to all of the secretaries that assembled at Green Pastures:

1. There now seems to be a lack of the close relationship that once existed between the local branches and the National office.

2. This lack of contact and specific knowledge about certain matters is fostering fear, suspicion and a lack of faith in the National office.

3. The apparent lack of inclination to make the logical placements in the Administrative Staff of the National has contributed to a widespread misunderstanding, such as the recent shift in Executive direction of the National office even though it be on a temporary basis.

4. The round-about method through which Executives are informed of either impending or completed changes has made it most embarrassing in the field, such as the constant shift of National officers to other organizations without any knowledge of the same coming to the local branches save through the press or public rumor.

5. The lack of ability to explain such matters to our friends in the local fields authoritatively creates community uncertainty about our future.

6. Unfortunately, this lack of coordination has seemed to inspire, in some cases, a decided lack of loyalty within the Urban League family.[19]

The secretaries requested the board's reaction to this bill of particulars and offered to cooperate with the board and staff "in any future matters of policy, program planning and financing."

Almost immediately after this Hollingsworth Wood mailed one of his typically lofty, proprietorial letters to the executive of the Carnegie Corporation, Dr. Frederick P. Keppel. "My Dear Fred," he wrote,

I hope, with your additional degrees, that you still have sufficient of the common touch to remember my Negro responsibility, shall I say, as well as affections.

Last January, my redoubtable Executive Secretary, Eugene Kinckle Jones, wrote you about the work of the Urban League and in April . . . I confided to you the distressing news that Mr. Jones had been stricken with tuberculosis and was out of the picture for the time being at least.

We have been struggling along since that time in the National Urban League keeping the manifold helpful activities going and the staff has been incredibly loyal in spite of the failure of salary checks.

I have just returned from the Conference of Secretaries, etc. . . . I had to appear before them with their knowledge that the national treasury was empty, with consequent criticism, though unspoken, of my management.

Eugene Kinckle Jones' doctor tells me that he has made miraculous progress and will in a few months be back, so that I have been deferring making changes which might startle him and retard his progress, and this accounts for all the criticism on the part of ambitious young men who would like to take his place.[20]

Wood appealed for $10,000 from the Carnegie Corporation for the National Urban League and "its contribution to cooperative solidarity of our American people." [21]

T. Arnold Hill was still on the staff and, in fact, had celebrated his twenty-fifth anniversary with NUL during the summer. *Opportunity* had saluted him with a laudatory editorial. He was spending a significant amount of time in his several state and federal government consulting posts, especially as consultant to the Wage and Hour Division of the Department of Labor. But no longer was Hill actively expressing the League's position on economic developments in articles in *Opportunity*. The EAC's and Workers' Councils were things of the past as the national defense program began to take up the slack. Hill was understandably unhappy that he had not been named acting executive secretary during Jones's illness. He confided his "considerable resentment" to those he considered his similarly minded friends. The white board member whose views and approaches most closely matched Hill's, Roger Baldwin, archliberal head of the American Civil Liberties Union, was one to whom Hill unburdened himself. Baldwin's reaction, however, was unsympathetic "concern" over Hill's "attitude." To Hollingsworth Wood, Baldwin wrote:

> I know, of course, why he was not appointed acting secretary and I go even further and raise the question whether he is really suited for our staff. He strikes me as a careerist without any fundamental loyalty, and ambitious at the expense of his associates. Jesse Thomas rather confirmed that view.
> Couldn't he be eased out? I would raise even the whole question as to whether his conduct of his department makes it desirable for him to come back. Anyhow I just leave my concern in your hands. [22]

At this defection by one of Hill's more consistent NUL board supporters, Wood registered surprise that had to be shared. "Look what Roger has written!" he noted on the letter, as he passed it on to William H. Baldwin, NUL board secretary.

In January 1940 E. K. Jones reported to the office at 1133 Broadway for "limited service." He had been recuperating for ten months and, as he put it, "while the League's work went on apace, its expansion was limited, fund-raising had been retarded by the adoption of a policy of borrowing [1939 expenditures, $57,000; debt, $9,000] . . . and the work indicated need of drastic reorganization." In mid-February he reported to the NUL annual meeting on 1939's accomplishments and underscored two areas for emphasis in 1940—(1) expansion of vocational and educational guidance services so that the national office would be a "first-class experimental station" to serve as a model for secondary schools and colleges; and (2) improvement in NUL's supervisory services to local communities.[23]

A month later, according to Kinckle Jones, T. Arnold Hill dropped by his home one Tuesday night. Hill was in a good mood, said he was buoyant and contented because he had decided to tender his resignation to the League. He was in a blind alley, said Hill, and wanted to get into something where promotional schemes that he had in mind could be carried out before he got too old. His resignation was to be submitted the following day and he wanted to make it clear that it was not presented with the idea of encouraging any concession.[24]

Hill's resignation letter was sent on March 13 to E. K. Jones, with copies to each member of the NUL Steering Committee. He was divorcing himself from the NUL movement, he said, after more than a quarter-century of uninterrupted service with great reluctance and deep regret. Yet, he noted, the reasons that impelled the decision were of such great concern to contentment of mind that he felt he must make whatever sacrifice was entailed and suffer whatever losses might ensue. Acknowledging the support of board members for giving him the opportunities to grow and develop, and with appreciation to E. K. Jones, Hill wished all of them long years in service.

A quickly called special meeting of the Steering Committee was held on March 15 to consider the resignation. Few members were present. E. K. Jones presented the background cited above, and Hill's resignation was accepted unanimously with appreciation of his "long, devoted, and extremely able service to the NUL and the UL Movement throughout the many years of your association with us." Hill's resignation would be effective June 1, as he had suggested, and his salary would be paid to that date. "We referred to Mr. Jones the adjustment of the matters which you have in charge, and I shall rely upon you for your best service in advice and information out of your wide experience. . . . I know I need not express to you my appreciation of the long-standing friendship which I, at least, have so much enjoyed and from which I have received so much valuable information. With best wishes for your future wherever it may lead you, I am, very truly yours, L. Hollingsworth Wood, chairman, NUL." [25]

Five days later E. K. Jones sent a uniform letter to all local executives notifying them of the resignation and its acceptance. "Suffice it to say," wrote Jones, "that the League is deeply appreciative of the years of efficient and constant service performed by Mr. Hill, and we trust that his future will be in every way successful and as he would have it. Mr. Hill's successor has not yet been named. I wanted to make sure that you received this information from the National office rather than to have it come to you through other channels." [26]

Thus the news officially became public. There was an immediate tempest. An outcry was heard from a dozen of the more vocal League secretaries, led by John T. Clark and William Conners and joined by George Goodman and Edward S. Lewis, each questioning the wisdom of allowing Hill to resign at such a critical juncture. Some based the need to retain him on Hill's obvious qualifications to lead, others on Jones's apparent physical infirmity; all of them stressed the need of the organization for Hill's capabilities.

The League's executive board members also questioned the move, especially the haste with which it was rammed through the Steering Committee without referral of so vital a matter to the board. Long-time League stalwart Caroline B. Chapin, who had been a member of Hill's Industrial Committee in the early thirties (along with Charles Poletti, John W. Davis, Abraham Lefkowitz, W. R. Valentine and Corliss Lamont) promptly resigned from the Steering Committee, writing Hollingsworth Wood:

> Though I am resigning from the committee, I do suggest that every possible care should be given to arrange a time long enough in advance of the meeting so that a full attendance may be secured—an agenda to accompany the call, which shall be a notice in writing, not just a telephone call —that any action taken be immediately reported to the absent members— and that the Steering Committee have only power to recommend action to the board in any important matters such as this resignation of Mr. Hill's or the involvement of the board in any new financial undertakings.[27]

She also reluctantly agreed that Hill's resignation would have to be accepted, inasmuch as matters had gone so far, but that he should receive a letter of appreciation for his long years of valuable service and that he be paid "two or three months' salary as an expression of Board appreciation."

C. C. Spaulding was vigorous in his opposition to the resignation and wrote Hill that the Industrial Relations Department of the League was the most effective unit and Hill was responsible for it. Furthermore, Hill had managed the office in Jones's absence in Washington while carrying on his industrial responsibilities. "A number of your friends have never understood why you were not placed in charge of the office during Mr. Jones' absence due to illness. I am among that group. I think this whole matter needs to be ironed out by the executive committee before any action is taken on your resignation." [28]

Board member P. B. Young, publisher of the Norfolk *Journal and*

Guide, wrote that he hoped the board would withold acceptance of Hill's resignation; Mrs. Mary McLeod Bethune was disturbed at the possibility of losing Hill, because of his years of experience and the critical time for the NUL. Hubert Delaney questioned whether it was in the League's best interests to accept Hill's resignation.

Letters came from outside the League family from mutual friends of Hill, Jones, Wood and the organization, urging a reconciliation. The president of the New York State Conference on Negro Welfare, A. G. Fallings, was one who wrote in this vein, as did Samuel A. Allen, former industrial secretary of the New York Urban League and at that time supervisor of racial problems in the New York State Department of Social Welfare.

There was at least one letter backing Jones in this matter. It came from Robert L. Vann, publisher of the Pittsburgh *Courier* and godfather of Jones's son, after the NUL board meeting approved the action of the Steering Committee. Vann applauded the quick acceptance of the resignation, saying that if Hill had grievances he should have brought them before the committee and asked for a hearing. If the committee refused to grant him relief, then he should have resigned. Since he had not followed this procedure, but simply handed in his resignation, the whole matter "was closed." As Vann said, "Gene, it looks as though somebody has been trying to muddy the water, and they have seized upon this matter of Hill's resignation as an opportunity to display disloyalty. I am glad to note that the matter has been closed and the people who are in such sympathy with Mr. Hill now have an opportunity to find him employment, assist him financially, or follow his leadership into whatever fields his fortunes may allow." [29]

Jones's reply summed up his attitude:

> Dear Bob: As ever, you are uncanny. You have diagnosed the situation correctly in regard to the incidents of the last Urban League Board Meeting. Your advice is timely, and my procedure is as suggested: I must forget the whole thing for the welfare of the work as well as of my self. I shall certainly be looking forward with pleasure to seeing you as early as you can arrange to come this way. I'm getting better and will be ready before long for more active duties.[30]

Jones's letter acknowledged serious problems of confidence within the board, and the groundswell of concern from local League executives was another sector requiring assiduous attention. Yet, as Jones recognized, he was not physically well enough to shoulder the burden of internal problems which would complicate the demanding requirements of the NUL's ongoing program in a period of national peril.

The local League executives were extremely concerned. It was therefore an aroused NUL annual conference in 1940 that shifted from scholarly social work discussion to active policy-making. The League executives assembled in convention and went on record about the organization's most urgent problems.[31]

They passed sixteen resolutions calling for NUL action and submitted them to the agency's executive board. Among the resolutions, a few called only for endorsement, such as the one commending federal public housing for giving work opportunities as well as living quarters to blacks. Another resolution of this sort was the notification of the National Conference of Social Work that the League opposed any change in NCSW's policy of meeting only where blacks could be accommodated freely.

Other resolutions were more far-reaching. One called for more frequent expressions by the NUL on national matters related to blacks. One urged a petition to the President and War Department against Jim Crow. Another called for the League to go after youth by hiring a youth guidance secretary and appointing a committee on a national youth program (as had been recommended the previous year). Still another resolution called for implementing block unit and neighborhood improvement programs at the local level with the help of national staff members. A gathering of major agencies concerned with Afro-Americans was recommended, to discuss "possible joint action in regard to the economic, political and social welfare" of blacks in the United States.

Expressing serious concern about the future of the League's industrial program (leaderless since the departure of T. Arnold Hill on June 1) the delegates endorsed stronger support and direction from the national office by adding persons with experience and influence in industrial relations to an industrial relations committee and to the executive board. They also recommended that the Industrial Department be enlarged to provide staff assistance to local branches; and that a Washington listening post *cum* representation office be maintained.

All of the above resolutions were approved or endorsed or put in abeyance by the executive board. But the problem of executive direction of the agency remained. T. Arnold Hill was gone and was irretrievable. Yet he had left his stamp on the agency and it was indelible. What was to be the fate of the NUL? Was there room at the top for anyone but Jones? If so, whom?

In a master stroke, Jones prevailed on Hollingsworth Wood and the board to bring back Lester B. Granger, Hill's protegé and former head of the Workers' Bureau to be assistant executive secretary in charge of industrial relations. Thus those who wanted Hill's spark and drive, his articulateness and vigor would be (and were) pleased.

Granger was born in Newport News, Virginia, in 1895 and grew up in Newark, New Jersey. His parents were both professionals—his mother was a teacher and his father a doctor. Lester, the youngest of six brothers, was considered the black sheep of the family in that he alone did not become either a doctor or dentist. He was graduated from Dartmouth College in 1918 and almost immediately went into the United States Army.

Though no one matched Hill's experience, Granger's association with the League stretched back to 1919, when as a newly discharged AEF artillery lieutenant, he took the post of industrial secretary of the New Jersey Urban League in Newark. His job was finding work for returning veterans. It was a thankless, discouraging task, for the jobs were just not to be had. He quit and went south, then came back and took a job as director of extension work for the Bordentown, New Jersey, state vocational school. While there he began to take courses at the New York School of Social Research. When the post of executive secretary of the Los Angeles League opened up, E. K. Jones, a fellow tennis player, offered it to Granger. He went to the coast on a year's leave of absence, got his fill of California and returned to Bordentown. Then in 1931 he was hired as business manager for *Opportunity* magazine and moved from that to head the Workers' Bureau the next year.

Granger had traveled to all the League cities in his *Opportunity* job, promoting sales of the magazine, calling on local Leagues to buy 100 or 200 copies, visiting college campuses to find sales agents. Then, as Workers' Bureau chief he had traveled even more extensively, helping form councils, speaking before groups of laborers, social workers, League board members and staff persons. For years he had attended the NUL annual conferences. He was, therefore, well known among the local secretaries, and widely respected for the tough job he had tackled so effectively in the Workers' Councils activity.

With Hill, Granger had received a thorough grounding in techniques of reaching government leaders and applying pressure at sensitive points. And in his two years as secretary of the Standing Committee on Negro Welfare of the Welfare Council of New York City, Granger got to know not only the agencies and their programs but almost everybody of importance in social welfare and politics in the city and state, and many of national importance as well. In his view, "there couldn't have been a better apprenticeship for the job of executive director of the League." [32]

For those who looked askance at Lester Granger as a wild-eyed pink for his liberal and class-struggle-oriented statements about labor and capital in the thirties, his performance at the 1940 National Conference of Social Work was reassuring. The Hitler-Stalin pact in 1939 had soured any sympathies Granger might have held for the Communists and quickly exposed fellow-travelers. Though he, like millions of others, admired the achievements of the Communists in defending the Scottsboro boys, he was appalled at the Reds' ideological rigidity. At the NCSW 1940 meeting the isolationist and pro-Communist social workers held a rally under the banner "The Yanks Are *Not* Coming." Granger and others led a counter-rally promoting "Aid to Britain" and for their efforts were brought up for disciplinary measures before the board of the local chapter of the American Association of Social Workers.[33]

Granger took the NUL job in 1940 with no illusions. Buzzing in the back of his head were the words of the black New Deal social scientist who had said, "Well, in a few years there won't be any Urban League. . . . The New Deal will be taking over." [34] And, having experienced the lean paydayless months in the NUL, he was aware of how bad things could be. He stepped into an agency that was starving financially and demoralized and shaky from the Jones illness, the Jesse O. Thomas regency and the T. Arnold Hill exit. NUL appeared to be spiraling downward to oblivion.

In mid-1940 the NUL was $15,000 in debt and needed $24,000 more to keep afloat through the last half of the year. Hollingsworth Wood, usually the epitome of jaunty confidence, confessed that the world situation made him feel that it was difficult to seek support at the time. He admitted he was at a loss as to how to proceed and asked for suggestions and advice from members of the NUL Steering Committee.[35]

A call on Arthur Packard of the Davison Fund brought a flat refusal when it was suggested that Nelson and John D. Rockefeller III be approached for support of the league. Packard would consider it only if the NUL could submit definite plans to put its financial house in order.[36]

A month later, Hollingsworth Wood reported to the Finance Committee that he had written the forty-two NUL board members asking each to be responsible for raising $100 in his own community for the NUL treasury. The results were absolutely zero.

Even the NUL Thirtieth Anniversary Dinner, with the nation's First Lady, Eleanor Roosevelt, as the headlined speaker, managed to backfire financially—it drew only 300 attendees, cost $776 and took in $640 for a net deficit of $136.

It was into this seemingly hopeless situation that Lester B. Granger stepped officially October 1, 1940, and set about reversing the League's decline.

LINDSLEY F. KIMBALL
President, NUL (1964–1968).

Blackstone-Shelburne N.Y.

JAMES A. LINEN
President, NUL (1968–   )

GEORGE EDMUND HAYNES
Founder, chief executive,
CUCAN (1910), and its successor NLUCAN (1911). Resigned
in 1918 to enter federal government service

EUGENE KINCKLE JONES
Field Secretary, CUCAN (1911);
associate chief executive,
NLUCAN (1912); Executive
Secretary, NUL (1917–1941);
General Secretary (1941–1950)

T. Arnold Hill
Acting Executive Secretary
(1934–1936) during E. K.
Jones's leave of absence for
government service

Lester Blackwell Granger
Assistant Executive Secretary
(1939–1941); Executive Director (1941–1961)

WHITNEY MOORE YOUNG, JR.
Executive Director, (1961–1971)

28/Another Pilot

If ever there was a man in the middle, it was Lester Granger when he came back to the NUL in 1940. Generally speaking, he was considered a good man with an organization that was a loser. The National Urban League's credit standing with both black and white communities at large was nearly exhausted.

Blacks viewed it as practically impotent: after all, what victories did it have to tout while the NAACP won battle after battle in the Supreme Court? What visible outpouring of benefits for blacks had the NUL been able to release?

White leaders measured the League against their usual criteria and found it far short: they saw little evidence of solid black support and no evidence of support by the black masses. The League had few members; its black constituents gave it little in contributions. Its vital statistics were definitely not reassuring—its budget was infinitesimal, its reserves were nonexistent, its size was inconsequential, its black leaders were practically unknown and few of them wore the "old school tie," whites on its board were mostly do-gooders and even its address—1133 Broadway— was *déclassé*.

The attitudes and misconceptions of both blacks and whites bear further examination because they were fundamental to the prospects for Granger's success or failure in his efforts for NUL survival.

As executive of the nation's oldest interracial agency, Granger had to walk the tightrope between the white and black communities as they became increasingly polarized. As spokesman for the interracial NUL, Granger was a prime target for the vituperation of both groups.

Whites generally distrusted interracial or black organizations: they were always stirring up trouble; after all, what was the difference between the NAACP and NUL anyway? The gnarled stereotype that "blacks cannot be trusted with money" applied to the NUL, as it had to the Garvey movement, to the fly-by-night store-front businesses, and to the radio comedians Amos and Andy in their various (supposedly) humorous business misadventures. Perhaps one white in 100,000 knew of any successful, large-scale black business such as the major insurance companies.

Those who had some exposure to the League generally misunderstood its specialized functions. What did it do that the local employment agency (YMCA, community center or council of social agencies) was not already doing, better? Board members as well as persons outside the organization suffered from such doubts. Some whites projected from their own local Leagues the nature of the NUL and in cases where the local League was weak, the vision of the national suffered accordingly.

Whites, until the late 1960's, were generally unaware of and unwilling to accept the charge that they were inherently guilty of racism against blacks. They were, therefore, unaware of the varieties and depths of bigotry that shackled blacks. Also, whites psychologically blind or unwilling to see their current and past guilt for racism placed an impenetrable wall of defense between themselves and the criticism of blacks, whether it was the wild charges of a demagogue or the measured, supportable, constructive criticism of a Lester Granger.

The critical nature of the period in which Granger came on the scene made his calls for change subject to white discount as "divisory" and "untimely" (wait until after the war; wait until after the emergency; wait until after the Korean "Police Action," and so on). Patriotism and priorities were handy and convenient counterarguments, never far from reach when Granger called for action in these years.

But in the black community priorities and patriotism were almost the mirror image of those of the white majority. As Ralph Bunche said, the necessity for Afro-Americans to fight for democracy was an empty question, "for that which does not exist cannot be saved." The fight was "to maintain those conditions under which people may continue to strive for realization of the democratic ideals." [1] And where was the NUL in that fight? To most blacks, it was "nowhere," or so it seemed.

The League had a number of good-sized mountains between it and its black constituents' understanding of its functions. These constituents were in three main groups—the black public, the press and the intellectuals. Some in each simply failed to comprehend the League; some misunderstood it, and some savored (prematurely) its downfall for reasons best known to themselves.

NUL was handicapped to begin with in putting across its story. It was not a mass movement or a membership organization (like the NAACP), therefore, it had a relatively small number of board members. Furthermore, League successes seldom seized the headlines. Its activities usually were complex, intricate and time-consuming, concerned with fine print rather than headlines. The League activities usually affected specific subgroups of blacks, not the entire black population in the way that the NAACP's white primary victory or antilynching campaigns affected all Afro-Americans.

There were other handicaps, inherent in the NUL organization and its program. The further it advanced toward the goal of community organization, the further it receded from direct services, thereby becoming more remote from black constituents. Additionally, since government had become a major factor in black urban survival after the onset of the Depression, achievements of the League in moving government agencies to action were claimed by politicians; shortcomings and failures to deliver were blamed on "ineffectual" black leaders and their agencies, such as the League.

Many of the most influential black intellectuals saw the League as beneath consideration. Their contemporary writings reflect this: few of them mention the League, and their rare mentions are frequently negative. Black intellectuals and academicians conveniently ignored the League's consistent efforts to work with organized labor and preferred instead to think of the agency as a handmaiden of industry or a "captive of capitalism" because of its efforts in job-seeking and placement. Many intellectuals closed their eyes to the decided shift in League focus from jobs, to better jobs and upgrading, to vocational guidance and training. The impact of Marxism and the surge of Communist thought in the thirties caused convenient categorizing of the League as a "bourgeois, reactionary, capitalist tool."

To these highly articulate black opinion leaders, the League's white leadership was hopelessly bourgeois and ineffective, hamstringing any serious advances and achievements on behalf of blacks. The League's black leadership was considered little better, composed mainly of persons who had a Booker T. Washington mental set and were dependent on whites and white initiatives.

To black intellectuals the establishment, by its "enslavement" of blacks, was corrupt; not to condemn it, therefore, made one suspect. But to work *with* that establishment bordered on treason to black interests at worst and foolhardiness at best.

Those who turned away from revolution saw clearly that blacks had to be placed in decision-making positions in the establishment. Yet black intellectuals glossed over the League role in placing blacks in government and, in fact, the unique importance of the League as a training ground and cadre from which government recruited trained and experienced Afro-Americans.

Between the black leaders and their public was that powerful vehicle of opinion-making, the black press. These newspapers administered weekly shots of adrenalin to the black urban masses, compensating in words and pictures for the lack of political and economic power of their readers. The black press during the Depression years had reached a high point of development as an institution through which the fury and frustrations of Afro-Americans were vented. The subject matter was essentially the news not found in the white press; it included news of crime, divorce, scandal and especially news of white crimes against blacks, flagrant cases of discrimination, bigotry, and bias, unequal justice and denial of civil rights, especially by the government; social or society news, uplift and achievement; and news of Asians and Africans in the United States and human rights, national and international.

Year in, year out the concentration was on white racism in its infinite variations—not theory but the reporting of flesh-and-blood case after case after case. In this context, the League reports and/or critical statements were mild indeed. The slashing attacks of the NAACP against restrictive covenants, white primaries and educational bias were right in the emotional and combative framework of the black press and rated front-page headlines. The subject matter and tone of the League reports were frequently out of synchronization in both topicality and timeliness with the major black interests and League news wound up buried on ·an inside page or rated merely a mention on the editorial page. Thus the League had a serious handicap in reaching black constituents.

(It should be noted that radio directed to black audiences was almost nonexistent until the fifties, and magazines aimed at black readers did not blossom until after World War II.)

Clearly, with factors such as these to contend with, Lester Granger would have had his hands full even if the NUL had been a model of strength, organization and solvency.

When he came back to the National Urban League at the end of 1940 his position was anomalous: he had accepted the job only with the understanding that he would be the chief executive officer of the agency, yet his title was "assistant executive secretary in charge of industrial relations." E. K. Jones still retained the title of executive secretary, and it was he who reported on the year's work at the next annual meeting, February 19, 1941. Mrs. Philitus W. Joyce, E. K. Jones's administrative assistant for twenty-two years, who had kept Jesse O. Thomas in a state of continuous discomfort for fear he might overstep the bounds of his charge "to aid in administration, advice and counsel and other activities subject to direction of the steering committee," was still very much on deck, and watchful.[2]

Granger, the liberal, the organizer of black labor, the protegé of T. Arnold Hill, the advocate of action, not rhetoric, the sharp-witted polemicist and newspaper columnist, was expected by his associates in labor and social work to move the NUL off dead center. But only Granger and those at the helm of the agency knew how rickety was the NUL vessel and how close to capsizing.

What the old ship needed most of all was a thorough overhaul, new crew, new engines, new courses and a firm hand on the tiller. Basic to such fundamental changes was money. And in 1940 a black man heading an agency dependent on contributions from white donors, philanthropists and businessmen could not steer a leaky tub into heavy seas and expect to survive.

29/March Time

During 1941 fate took a hand in reshaping the NUL. E. K. Jones had returned to his desk for limited service in January 1940, ten months after his severe illness. For seventeen months he continued on the job but on June 13, 1941, he had a relapse that forced him to take to his bed for a period that stretched into 1943. In October, Jesse O. Thomas was granted a leave of absence to take a position with the United States Treasury Department Defense Bond Sales to the black community.

At the November 1941 board meeting, Lester Granger was named executive secretary of NUL "with full authority and responsibility for conducting the League's program" during E. K. Jones's sick leave. He took over an agency that was seriously in debt, with a total income in 1941 of $54,000 ($45,000 in contributions). Its professional staff consisted of research director Warren M. Banner, *Opportunity* editor Elmer A. Carter and his two assistants, vocational guidance secretary Ann Tanneyhill and an industrial relations specialist on loan from the Phelps-Stokes Fund, Franklin O. Nichols.

Plans for restructuring the NUL board were presented. A "National Committee" was formed consisting of NUL "elder statesmen," regional representatives, and inactive board members. An executive board of fifteen was selected, persons who would be active and available for monthly board meetings. The Steering Committee was to be dropped. The officers of the agency were trimmed to four, with William H. Baldwin succeeding Hollingsworth Wood as League president (1941–1945). Wood continued as a member of the executive board and became chairman of the new National Committee of thirty-eight, which would be "restricted in scope and importance only by his abundant persuasiveness." [1]

Granger told this new board that the point of diminishing returns had been reached in current activities. The League's approach to problems of blacks should be altered in keeping with changing trends, he said, and he proposed new fund-raising action and a revision of program activities. He called for the hiring of an industrial relations field secretary and a community organization field secretary to work with national welfare agencies and with local Leagues, their boards and staffs and councils of social agencies to develop better understanding of the criteria for local League programs. Granger recommended establishing a formal public relations program with a director responsible for publicity, publications, the interpretation of NUL program and financial appeals. [2]

He also suggested establishing within the Industrial Relations Department a bureau of guidance and placement for year-round activity. To cover communities outside the League network, he proposed volunteer committees modeled on the Emergency Advisory Councils of a decade before. These would be served by a field secretary to help them in their communities. NUL's southern program needed a new approach, he suggested. An advisory board of southerners responsible to the NUL executive board and carrying out active field work and fund-raising was mentioned.

Granger challenged the League Fellowship program on its current basis, maintaining that the method of selection should be restudied. It might be best, he suggested, to award the fellowships to persons specializing in fields not adequately served, rather than simply in social work in general.

Of all these proposals, the board approved only one outright—the establishment of a bureau of guidance and placement with Ann Tanneyhill as its secretary—inasmuch as this involved no additional expense.[3]

As Lester Granger looked at the situation in 1941 he decided top priority had to go to a program to counteract the near-total exclusion of black workers from the nation's defense efforts. To dramatize this exclusion and to move the federal authorities to action, Granger at the NUL annual conference organized a task force of local League executives. With national staff members, local executives from twelve Leagues, plus representatives of the United Transport Service Workers' Union and the Committee on Participation of Negroes in the National Defense Program, Granger went to Washington in November 1941.[4] For two days they made the rounds, demanding full integration of black workers into defense employment, training and housing. The delegation met with administrators of ten federal agencies and to each presented a formal memorandum (drawn up by Warren M. Banner, the NUL research director) on which to base discussions with department members. One League executive was delegated to be spokesman on each of the ten topics tackled.

Sidney Hillman told the Urban Leaguers that the AFL and CIO had agreed to "lift bans against employment of Negroes in defense industries." He further promised that as discrimination against blacks appeared in defense plants, his office "would correct these cases as rapidly as facilities permitted."

The commissioner of public buildings of the Federal Works Agency assured the group that black labor would receive "equitable consideration" in construction of defense housing, using the policy guidelines of the United States Housing Authority in its low-rent housing projects. (At its best, this policy provided jobs for blacks in proportion to percentage of population.)

The delegation brought the defense housing coordinator up short with information that less than 3 percent of housing so far built under his program was occupied by blacks. He promised to insure occupancy in proportion to black numbers in the working population.

Local offices of the Bureau of Employment Security would be instructed to emphasize placement of skilled black workers in defense industries, promised that bureau's director. Furthermore, in-service training of local office personnel was scheduled to correct inequities such as faulty referral of black job applicants.

There was good news from the NYA deputy administrator. He said enlarged appropriations meant that NYA could expand work experience programs for black youths in preparation for defense jobs.

The influence of the United States commissioner of education was promised to help secure appointment of blacks to advisory committees working with local boards of education on vocational training programs in the public schools. He also promised to talk with employers in key industries to urge the hiring of blacks who had received defense industry vocational training.

The assistant secretary of labor was nailed to the wall with charges that the department had delayed giving the United Transport Service Workers (Redcaps) proper representation on the Railway Labor Adjustment Board. The official promised speedy action.

Inadequate facilities and equipment provided by the Civil Aeronautics Administration to train black pilots were lambasted by the delegation. Representatives of the CAA assured them that aspects of the program under CAA control would be corrected, but passed the buck to the army. The delegation charged that the army was secretly opposed to the training program and was dragging its heels.

WPA discrimination against blacks at the local level, especially in professional and service projects, was described to the Federal Works Agency bureaucrat. A bill of particulars including specific and general complaints was reviewed and promises of investigation and action were made by the government representatives.[5]

There were concrete results from this expedition. Some of the officials and agencies did follow through as they promised. By the end of the year, the League could see evidence of results, such as the hiring of black assistants in several defense agencies, and a revised approach by the Bureau of Employment Security in its placement of blacks, following the suggestions made in the League memo. The defense housing coordinator acted on suggestions for housing of black workers. And local Leagues developed and/or reinforced contacts with federal agencies.[6]

The "Washington expedition" was a solid beginning in the process of renovating NUL.

But perhaps the major achievement of Lester Granger in 1941 was to set the agency's course by his public statements and activities. His key effort was his address to the National Conference of Social Work that year on "The Negro and Economic Opportunity," in which he rebuked social workers and other social scientists:

> We find social agencies falling into repetitious error when confronted with problems, or fancied problems, involving race. We find recreational

workers unable to plan for professionally sound group work programs because they insist on seeing differences between white and Negro children
instead of likenesses between human beings. We find "research scholars,"
comparing the health records of a poverty-stricken Negro neighborhood
with those of a middle-class white community, and drawing conclusions
therefrom regarding "physiological differences" between races. We find
housing authorities trembling in panic before the momentous question of
whether Negroes and whites can live together in the same low-cost housing
project, when they have lived together in tumble-down neighborhoods for
generations.[7]

If that had not awakened them, he commandeered their attention with
this statement: "I am obliged to declare that the gravest single subversive
movement in this country today is to be found in the anti-Negro policies
tolerated by the Federal Government and practiced directly through the
military and naval arms of defense." He went on to demand that army
and navy barriers against employing blacks be destroyed, and called for
similar action by the civil service. Then he proceeded to delineate how
bigotry in government hiring was "a standing encouragement to private
employers throughout the country to practice similar discrimination.
Under these conditions small wonder indeed that the OPM [Office of
Production Management] finds itself handicapped in its almost tearful
pleas to employers not to discriminate against Negroes in the present
emergency. As long as discrimination is rife in the very building where
the OPM is housed . . . the efforts of this war-emergency agency must be
handicapped." [8]

With defense the paramount concern of the nation and government
the prime mover in defense, Granger leveled his guns at government and
fired broadside after broadside into the culpable federal edifice. The
United States Employment Service was scored for failing to give equal
employment opportunity to all applicants, for not "educating" employers
who were backward or biased. OPM was blasted for not putting a clause
in defense contracts whereby employers who discriminated would be pe-
nalized. OPM insisted that this was not practical, but Granger cited the
success of the Public Works Administration and United States Housing
Authority in doing so on low-cost housing projects all over the nation.

Granger slammed organized labor for blocking entrance of blacks into
defense industry, pointing out that the twenty-four international unions
that barred blacks from membership in 1930 had only one "actual honest
change of policy" among them. The NUL executive called for amendment of the National Labor Relations Act to outlaw from its protection
any union that discriminated by race, religion or nationality.

Then he summarized the thinking that fueled him and the League in the defense emergency:

> America is giving birth to new ideas overnight. Old habits of thinking are being destroyed. Old principles and ideals are being refurbished and a new understanding of them is being developed. While America's thinking is being renovated, we have an opportunity to shake to pieces this mental stereotype which has frozen public opinion into a highly patternized and undemocratic kind of racial thinking. The Negro will never have a better argument for increased economic opportunity than the need for total national defense. Not again for a long time will he find training facilities so plentiful as today. He may never again find enlightened industrial leadership or Federal and state governments so deeply concerned with the most effective use of all labor. The extent to which the Negro can be integrated into the defense program can be considered as a measure of his chances for economic opportunity in the country of which he is part by birth, by tradition and by personal devotion.[9]

Race leaders, still driving centripetally toward integration, knew the journey was yet a long and arduous one and were determined to cover as many miles as possible during this revolutionary moment. Wise white citizens, said Lester Granger early in 1942, "have supported Negroes in these efforts, aware that the racial discrimination that destroys national unity might easily be the Achilles' heel of our nation's defense." Said he:

> We have accepted the fact that the leadership of our national Government in this period of war will be the most important single influence in the country. Reflecting public opinion, the Government's leadership will also develop and shape that opinion in turn. Thus, one of the League's principal objectives has been to insure that our national leadership shall remain aware of the special problems faced by Negro citizens in connection with the war effort and shall frame effective policies for solving those problems. Our frequent conferences with governmental officials and communications addressed to department heads have already influenced important decisions affecting the welfare of the Negro population and the soundness of public policy.[10]

In support of this assertion Granger cited consultations with the United States Office of Education resulting in instructions to state units to give blacks equal access to defense training courses, the federal housing agencies for defense housing for blacks, the federal works administrator, who issued an administrative order protecting rights of blacks to work on defense housing contracts, and the United States Employment Service, to place blacks as well as whites in all jobs for which they were qualified.

He also mentioned the success in placing blacks on draft boards in southern cities.

It was during this period that a "board of strategy" of race leaders was formed. Consisting of Granger, Walter White for the NAACP, Channing A. Tobias for the YMCA (who was also a member of the National Selective Service Board), A. Philip Randolph and Mrs. Mary McLeod Bethune, then director for Negro Affairs in the NYA, the group spent several days in Washington during the winter of 1940–1941.

They met with directors of bureaus and departments, even President Roosevelt, asking action by government to wipe out discrimination in defense work and the armed forces. Philip Randolph described these conferences as "genial, gracious and reassuring" as officials voiced their opposition to bias. But the net result, noted Randolph, was that blacks got no jobs.[11]

In a 1941 meeting in Chicago to explore the possibilities of broadening the effort into a national council of Negro organizations, Granger and the other leaders presented the facts to a large group of black spokesmen. The minimal progress in getting government action was reported and discussed. Then one irate black woman got to her feet and addressed the gathering:

> "Mr. Chairman, we ought to throw 50,000 Negroes around that White House, bring them from all over the country, in jalopies, in trains and any way they can get there, and throw them around the White House and keep them there until we get some action from the White House." This was the first time such a radical thought had been suggested. It was picked up by Phil Randolph, who thereupon said, "I agree with the sister. I will be very happy to throw [in] my organization's resources and offer myself as a leader of such a movement." The meeting then voted to carry through this demonstration, and so the March on Washington (I) was born.[12]

A few weeks later in New York ten black leaders, including Lester Granger, met with Randolph to make further plans. Each of the organizations represented put $25 into a kitty to cover expenses and a call was issued for a mass meeting to generate some steam behind the idea. They formally organized as the March-on-Washington Committee, New York Division, with headquarters at Harlem's Hotel Theresa. It was at this session that somebody questioned how many should be called for and the first figure mentioned was 5,000. "Five thousand is ridiculous," hooted a listener. "You can get 5,000 Negroes right in Washington." So the figure was raised to 10,000. Then Randolph said "Fifty thousand—if we get less than 50,000 it will be a failure." Benjamin McLaurin, Randolph's associate in the Brotherhood of Sleeping Car Porters, said dryly, "By the time

10,000 get there it will look as big as 50,000 to the press, so it will be safe to announce 50,000." There was general laughter. Granger went along with the 50,000 figure in the belief that to get 25,000 you had to ask for 50,000. Finally, the call for 100,000 blacks to march on Washington was issued in early June. It went out over the names of Layle Lane, vice president, American Federation of Teachers, Walter White for the NAACP, Lester Granger for the NUL, Frank Crosswaith, general organizer, ILGWU, Adam C. Powell, Channing H. Tobias, Henry Pope and A. Philip Randolph for the Brotherhood of Sleeping Car Porters, as chairman. The National Negro Congress and Communist-tinged organizations were conspicuously absent throughout.[13]

The core of the call to march was in this paragraph:

Negroes, by the mobilization and coordination of their mass power can CAUSE PRESIDENT ROOSEVELT TO ISSUE AN EXECUTIVE ORDER ABOLISHING DISCRIMINATIONS IN ALL GOVERNMENT DEPARTMENTS, ARMY, NAVY, AIR CORPS AND NATIONAL DEFENSE JOBS. [Emphasis in original.] [14]

The spell-out of actual inequities, shortcomings, evasions and oversights by the administration, the solid guts of the call to march, the background for demands, were supplied by the NUL, which prepared the roll-call and documentation of these items. Local Leagues all over the country backed the march and the NUL board endorsed it.

"Nothing took off," said Granger, "and caught the imagination of Negroes like getting on a train or a bus or in your car and going to Washington and marching around the White House and challenging the American democracy for inequities practiced in the name of democracy, and refusing to defend the security of the country because of mean racial prejudice." [15]

The threat of a black Coxey's Army descending on the Executive Mansion was more than the administration could endure. The confrontation of the March-on-Washington Committee with President Roosevelt, the secretaries of the War and Navy departments, Mayor Fiorello A. LaGuardia, Sidney Hillman, William S. Knudsen of the Office of Production Management, Anna M. Rosenberg of Social Security and Aubrey Williams of the NYA is well known. The high drama of the confrontation in the White House has been thoroughly reported elsewhere. The Negro community saw presidential action on this matter as signifying whether America really believed in the Constitutional rights of its black citizens. Therefore, Roosevelt's signature on Executive Order 8802 June 25, 1941, was historic, though hardly the "second Emancipation Proclamation" as it was labeled by some enthusiasts.

The Executive Order established in the Office of Production Manage-

ment a Committee on Fair Employment Practice to "receive and investigate complaints of discrimination in violation of the provisions . . . and
to take appropriate steps to redress grievances which it finds to be valid."
That was the fundamental provision, though it also directed that "all departments and agencies . . . concerned with vocational and training programs for defense production shall take special measures appropriate to
assure that such programs are administered without discrimination." Further, it said, "All contracting agencies of the government . . . shall include in all defense contracts hereafter negotiated . . . a provision obli-
gating the contractor not to discriminate against any workers." The
President also stated, "It is the duty of employers and labor organizations
to provide for the full and equitable participation of all workers in the
defense industries without discrimination." [16]

Though Granger hailed the Executive Order as "truly momentous" at
the time, he was candid in stating that it did not end discrimination in
national defense per se, that watchdog action was still necessary, that discrimination in private industry could not permanently be checked by the
government, even in defense production, "as long as the Government sets
an unwholesome example by practicing racial discrimination in its own
Civil Service." [17]

After its first year Edward S. Lewis, executive of the Baltimore League,
evaluated the committee on Fair Employment Practice in *Opportunity*
and found its accomplishments valuable but few and its shortcomings
many. The committee (FEPC) had held only three public hearings and
had certified no cases of discrimination in government to the President;
the President had canceled no defense contracts, in spite of concrete evidence of discrimination exposed by the FEPC. "On the plus side," stated
Lewis, "FEPC has done an excellent job of focussing public attention on
the problems of racial discrimination in employment. . . . For the first
time in our history some of the vicious employment policies of large corporations . . . have been exposed in front page articles by the press." [18]

The weaknesses of FEPC were many. It was severely hampered by low-
prestige chairmen, by a minimum budget and staff, by inability to cover
more than a relative handful of cases and, most of all, by no powers of
enforcement. Thus, when it slapped an employer on the wrist for bigoted
practices he would promise to mend his ways, hire several "token" blacks
and forget it. "Employers and labor union leaders," said Lewis, "are *'real
politikers.'* They are not going to move until contracts are suspended or
until charters of unions are actually withdrawn." [19]

The pressures against such drastic action were stupendous. After all,
how could a committee take action that would halt production on vital
war material? Both labor and management knew that it would not and

acted accordingly. The only coercive weapon available to the FEPC was exposure through hearings and reports of its findings and these it used with considerable effectiveness. Still, something more than FEPC was needed to protect the rights of black workers during a period of international crisis. On that score, the League had considerable experience.

30/The War Emergency

In 1942 Lester Granger hired a full-time field secretary but lost editor Elmer A. Carter and Edward Lawson, *Opportunity*'s managing editor. NUL income totaled $48,000 in contributions; by year's end the agency owed $7,200 in loans payable, $6,800 in bills unpaid and was fully $5,200 behind in paying its employees their salaries. (In February 1943, Jesse O. Thomas wrote NUL for back pay and petty cash owed him since October 1941. The board resolved to liquidate the debt by regular payments.)

Faced with these hard facts the executive board, considering plans for 1943, turned down the recommendation that the budget be increased by $13,000. Experience indicated, the directors agreed, that the League's fund-raising capability seemed to have a $60,000 ceiling and therefore expenditures should be held to this figure until more money was in sight to permit expansion. For guidance, the board established priorities: (1) an industrial relations secretary (to be hired); (2) a research department; (3) *Opportunity* and public relations; (4) the southern field, where no more than minimum expenses were to be incurred until expansion money was in sight.[1]

Lester Granger was not at this board meeting. He was in a hospital, undergoing a minor operation. Hearing of this situation, E. K. Jones, recuperating from his illness, urgently requested permission to return to active duty. William H. Baldwin advised that such a return in winter would be unwise and the board voted to carry Jones on half-salary for the first half of 1943 or until his return to duty, if earlier.[2]

Both the agency and its executive leaders were in shaky condition as the year 1942 ended. Furthermore, the restructuring into an executive board and national committee had, from a financial viewpoint, been disappointing if not a failure. There were on these two panels fifty-two persons and among them they were unable to raise $60,000 to meet the NUL's modest expenses. This was frightening when it was considered that some of the nation's leading liberals and wealthy families were represented: Chester Bowles, Lloyd K. Garrison, Mrs. Albert D. Lasker, Mrs. William S. Paley, Mrs. Joseph M. Proskauer, Winthrop Rockefeller, Mrs. George W. Seligman. If men and women such as these could not manage to raise the League's budget, what hope was there? In fairness, the men were quickly caught up in the events of the war by government or the military. The women helped—Mrs. Proskauer sent out a covering letter with a solicitation from Granger. The results were poor. They and others lent cash to the League to tide it over paydays.

Granger saw his (and the NUL) dilemma as a balancing act:

> It would be easy for the League Movement to make capital of this situation for selfish or short-sighted ends. As "rabble-rousers," we could inflame the already angry mood of those with whom we work thereby becoming popular spokesmen of the moment with certain rewards appertaining thereto. As opportunists of another sort, we could ignore the Negro man-in-the-street, offer the counsel of postponement and appeasement, and thereby win grateful approbation from the camp of the timid souls.[3]

At this time there came a request from the Workers' Defense League that NUL join in an *amicus curiae* brief in support of the case of sharecropper Odell Waller before the United States Supreme Court. In self-defense, Waller had killed the white man on whose farm he worked. He had been found guilty by the all-white Virginia jury. The Workers' Defense League, led by Norman Thomas, A. Philip Randolph and Frank P. Graham, was joined by the NAACP in an appeal to the Supreme Court. Liberals made it a *cause célèbre* as an example of the interlocked injustices of the south: sharecropping and the poll tax, which effectively excluded blacks from jury duty as well as from voting. Granger had checked with Baldwin and several other board members who approved and so NUL had been listed as one of the agencies endorsing the brief.[4]

The situation brought before NUL's board the question of how far the League was prepared to go in galvanic cases such as this. It was agreed that in future board members should be polled by letter or telephone before such endorsement. Granger, perhaps foreseeing the increasing necessity to commit the NUL one way or another on controversial public issues, asked the board to establish an advisory committee on legislation, composed of lawyers or persons experienced in government work. Such a committee would act as a panel to pass judgment on "policies aimed at remedying conditions with which the League is actively concerned."

Though the board approved it, Granger was cautioned that such activities should be carefully restricted to avoid endangering NUL's tax-exempt status and knock out the charitable contributions on which the agency was dependent. Granger was authorized to ask New York State Assemblyman William T. Andrews to chair the committee, but the whole idea hung fire until a decade later.[5]

Early in 1942 Baldwin asked a fund-raising expert to study NUL. The analysis, in brief, was that the agency had a core of loyal supporters who renewed their giving year after year. However, "certain of our supporters are giving relatively much less than their known interest in the interracial problem would indicate," and efforts to broaden the base of support had been ineffectual. In 1941 some 365 new contributors had been added for a total of $12,000 in "new money," but this was more than offset by the loss of other substantial contributions. By mid-December of 1942, a new momentum was evident. The League counted some 600 new contributors, but the total of contributions had flattened out at a disappointing $44,000.[6]

The National Urban League Guild, an auxiliary of socially prominent women (and a few men) was formed in 1942 for the express purpose of drumming up financial support for NUL via fund-raising events. Its Beaux Arts Ball in New York was an instant success and became an annual feature of the social scene. It grew to be the largest volunteer group associated with the League and raised and turned over to the League hundreds of thousands of dollars over the years.

The key element in solving the NUL's money crisis was the series of social disasters—riots—against which the League had worked and warned. "To many of us who know the stresses," Hollingsworth Wood had written the Carnegie Corporation in January of 1942, "the sensation of dread lest some spark should set off the dreadful series of race riots, is a daily experience when we open our newspapers." [7] President William H. Baldwin, in his foreword to the 1941 NUL annual report, was filled with foreboding: "North and South, East and West, country and city, interracial relations are approaching a tension where only wise guidance can (if anything can) forestall serious incidents."

Lester Granger at the end of 1942 had scored reactionary spokesmen and administration leaders whose efforts, if any, were to placate black dissatisfaction rather than remove its causes. Granger lambasted liberals also, for counseling that black advancement be put on ice until the "greater struggle" against the Nazis was won. The League's job, he said, is

> to work with the man in the street, and his family at home, offering the
> kind of guidance that will direct his resentment into constructive channels

of thinking and action. It *is* our responsibility to remind the Negro community that blind hatred is a dangerous social weapon, one that strikes back upon its user as often as it injures an opponent. It is also our job constantly to prod a blind or neglectful public opinion that would shelve the cause of interracial democracy at home out of a short-sighted concern for world democracy among nations.[8]

The League carried out these jobs, as Granger put it, warning, advising and assisting community leaders to eliminate or ameliorate the most pressing problems arising from worker migration. These covered the waterfront—from recreation to public deportment—and included the basics—housing, health and employment conditions. Many of the NUL formal studies done by Warren Banner served as guides for community improvement. But in many communities the improvement was undertaken late or halfheartedly if at all.

Granger attacked specific conditions. He put before his professional social work colleagues their responsibility to speak out against the concerted campaign of group vilification carried on by the New York daily press in early 1943. Granger and a group of black concerned citizens also called on New York editors. The Sunday editor of the city's largest daily excused his paper's policy saying that crime by blacks was played up because it was the kind of news the public liked to read. His response was typical. The cumulative effect was to present a picture of Harlem as "a seething center of mounting violence and crime." [9]

This racial misrepresentation and distortion affected younger blacks intensely, pointed out Granger. It reinforced feelings of rejection, tended to develop something of a mass psychosis in which aggressive attitudes might result, or caused retreat into group seclusion.

Granger also moved to counsel national leaders. One aspect of this move was "A Minimum Federal Program to Assure the Maximum Contribution of the Negro to Winning the War," a four-page memo delivered to presidential assistant Jonathan Daniels in April 1943. It called for the President of the United States to develop in a formal address to the nation: (1) the implications of race and color and the role of Afro-Americans in winning the war and the peace; (2) a program of educating the public as to the cost of racial discrimination in a nation at war "at once," through war information agencies and all media; (3) a slate of objectives announced as national policy, covering the armed forces, manpower, civilian defense and morale and postwar planning.

Essentially, these objectives included breaking open all branches of the armed forces to blacks and opening all assignments to them; using black manpower to the fullest and providing for training, housing, evaluating and placing workers; bringing Afro-Americans into Civil Defense operations at all levels and using blacks to plan for the postwar period.

In February 1943 Granger added Julius A. Thomas to the national staff as industrial relations secretary. Before the end of the year he had hired five other professionals (including field secretaries Reginald A. Johnson and Dr. Alphonse Heningburg); reactivated the southern field office under Franklin O. Nichols; assigned volunteer Ann Mather as secretary to tend the newly created service councils; put two assistants in the research department and welcomed E. K. Jones back to active duty. In mid-year funds were so scarce that a request by Ann Tanneyhill for $90 to cover the cost of a six-week radio workshop course was turned down by the board despite her extraordinary success in producing VOC network radio programs. Board members felt the money was just not available. Yet, expenditures before the year's end increased until they almost reached the level of 1929, totaling $74,000.[10]

Coming generations, wrote Lester B. Granger in mid-1943, would "regard as incomprehensibly childish the attitudes of 130,000,000 Americans who took time out from fighting the Axis powers and fought among themselves over segregated housing, war transportation, job assignments in defense industries and the use of parks and toilets." [11]

Granger was reacting to the explosion of riots that began in May 1943 and ripped the social fabric of Mobile, Alabama; Beaumont, Texas; Los Angeles, Detroit and New York's Harlem. They were not unexpected, he charged, but were the "violent snapping of tensions" that had grown without hindrance for the previous three years. They were "the inevitable outcome of a *laissez-faire* policy followed by governmental leadership, irresponsible or indifferent attitudes by many leaders in private life and a concentrated bitter resentment shared by a large proportion of the white population, and an actual majority of Negroes." [12]

The riots each had their own characteristics. In Mobile, though there was a pool of thousands of unemployed black workers, thousands of whites were imported to work in shipyards where the shortage of skilled laborers was acute. Housing, health, recreation and transportation facilities were strained to the point of collapse by this influx.

Then, under pressure from the FEPC, the CIO Union of Marine Shipbuilders and the unmet need for skilled workers, the Alabama Drydock and Shipbuilding Company promoted blacks to welding jobs. They worked the night shift of May 24 without incident, but when shifts changed on the twenty-fifth, mobs of white workers attacked all blacks and drove them out of the shipyards. It took troops to restore order, and by that time an estimated fifty blacks and at least one white had been severely injured, 25,000 workers had downed tools and untold vital man hours of ship production had been lost.[13]

The NUL was able to respond quickly. When the riot broke out at Alabama Drydock and Shipbuilding Company, the NUL's southern field director was on the scene the same afternoon. He gathered facts from the police department, the War Manpower Commission, the company, and the local news media. To each he pointed out their responsibilities for stopping violence and protecting black workers. To white and black leaders he outlined a program to relieve local tensions by action on local problems that aggravated conditions.

To those who recalled the past, the event smacked all too strongly of East St. Louis in World War I. To those who looked to the future, the impact on world opinion of this incident cast a long and dreadful shadow ahead. The immediate situation was resolved after the War Manpower Commission, the Maritime Commission, FEPC, management and the CIO union pasted together an agreement by which a segregated workyard was set up. In this Jim Crow arrangement blacks could advance as far as their skills would take them, with whites working only until blacks could be trained to replace them. Other shipways were subsequently added to this one, and there was some interchange with the "white" shipways, when blacks with needed skills were transferred to them.[14]

The major incident in that summer of biliousness in the American domestic body politic was the Detroit riot. Detriot had the proper mixture of ingredients for an explosion: tens of thousands of blacks and southern whites had flocked to the Motor City to compete for the defense jobs that were available. Housing, always a headache in Detroit, had gone from acute to impossible. Blacks were hedged in by savagely defended white areas with their "improvement associations" (often tightly organized groups of householders and young toughs who used intimidation, violence and even bombs against black "encroachment") and antagonistic real estate operators. The history of race friction in housing stretched back to World War I. Whites in Detroit had been stirred by the siren songs of several ganders whose honking had aroused native *fascisti*, bigots, reactionaries and haters. The long words and short vision of Fritz Kuhn, William J. Cameron, Father Charles Coughlin, Frank J. Norris and Gerald L. K. Smith were poisonous food for thought and violent action.

Two days of murderous rioting broke out, in which mobs of white men and boys took over the main streets of downtown Detroit, halting cars, overturning them and beating blacks. Blacks roamed the main street of the black community's business area, "Paradise Valley," looting white businesses, beating whites and rolling their cars over. Both whites and blacks used stones, knives, bottles, guns, torches and all other available weapons until federal troops arrived on June 21 and ended the small war. The toll: twenty-five black and nine white dead; 500 injured; 1,300 blacks and 500 whites under arrest; forty-three autos gutted by fire; property damage estimated at $1 million. The loss in manhours of work in the arsenal of the nation was in the hundreds of thousands. The loss to American prestige was incalculable. The nation that was battling Axis racism abroad was conspicuously guilty of it at home—that was the message of the riot.[15]

There was a new element in the Detroit riot: it was the symbolic attack on the white man through destruction of his property. It had been seen in the 1935 Harlem riot, and was to spread.

In the Detroit holocaust everybody pinned the blame for the riot on someone else. The police commissioner and Wayne County prosecutor blamed the black newspapers and organizations; Negro nationalist agitators were accused by others; the city administration blamed the black community; the executive secretary of the National Negro Congress blamed it on the Fascists and the Ku Klux Klan; enemy agents working among whites were cited by others, blacks demanded a grand jury investigation but the city administration rejected the idea.

William H. Baldwin, NUL president, Julius A. Thomas and Dr. Warren M. Banner arrived while the ashes still smoldered. They called on leaders of the city administration, the white and black community, giving the NUL viewpoint on the steps taken following the riot.[16]

John Dancy, executive of the Detroit League, had written the NUL on its behalf requesting Banner's services in helping to set up and put in operation a recreation program in districts where blacks were concentrated. The limitations of the request had set off a spirited discussion in the NUL executive board meeting. Banner had studied Detroit in 1941 and had recommended at that time that the city extend education and recreation facilities, among other things. These recommendations had not been acted upon. There was little reason to have Banner repeat his 1941 performance, but the NUL board approved sending him to give whatever assistance might be required through the Detroit League.[17]

Afterward, the NUL staff developed a special bulletin to local affiliates outlining specific steps to take in their communities as riot precautionary measures.

The next body blow to American moral superiority came Sunday, August 1, when a white policeman and a black military policeman wounded one another in an altercation in a fifth-rate Harlem hotel as the white cop was trying to arrest a black woman for disorderly conduct. A crowd gathered in the hotel lobby and followed when the wounded were taken to the hospital for treatment. There the crowd grew and the rumor mill ground out its grisly worst: "A white cop shot a black soldier" degenerated into "a white cop has killed a black soldier." [18]

Some 3,000 blacks were milling about outside the hospital when a bottle, thrown from a roof top, smashed into the street, followed by another, then several more. This scattered the crowd, which broke up into groups of men and boys who spilled into the main streets of Harlem, breaking store windows as they rushed down the avenues. Before long looting began. Vandalism and destruction became more focused, and white-owned businesses were deliberately attacked while those identified as black-owned were spared. The prime targets were "whitey's" businesses and merchandise, not whites as such.

Mayor LaGuardia moved to a Harlem precinct headquarters to direct the police effort to quell the riot, and the New York police with great restraint brought the riot to a close. They were helped by black leaders who went on the radio with LaGuardia to appeal for peace, and the mayor, joined by prominent black leaders, toured Harlem in a car, talking to residents and crowds with a public address system.

The toll in Harlem was five dead—all blacks; nearly 600 injured (hospitals treated 561), most of them black; 500 arrested, nearly all of them black; property damage totaling close to $5,000,000, all of it in the black neighborhood. Because there were no pitched battles with whites, Mayor LaGuardia and others denied that this had been a race riot. The selective attack on white property, however, proved otherwise. One analyst called it a riot of poor young blacks against racism, property and authority represented by the white-owned stores (80 percent of Harlem's businesses) and New York's police (only 132 of the 18,200 policemen were blacks). By any name, the Harlem debacle was another staggering blow to American prestige and an ominous indication of festering conditions that were not unique to Harlem; resentments and pressures that, as in Detroit, could explode in dozens of American cities.

Harlem exploded in 1943 because, as E. Franklin Frazier had stated in his report on the 1935 Harlem riot:

> economic and social forces created a state of emotional tension which sought release upon the slightest provocation. As long as the economic and social forces which were responsible for that condition continue to operate, a state of tension will exist in Harlem and recurrent outbreaks may occur.[19]

The "forces" Frazier listed included: (1) discrimination against blacks in employment; (2) overcrowded housing and exorbitant rents; (3) dearth of

school, playground and health facilities; (4) discrimination against black
professionals in city institutions; (5) inferior city services, such as garbage
collection and police protection; (6) police brutality and abuse of civil
rights.

In 1943 these same factors were still major causes of black community
unrest. Lester Granger observed that white Americans must learn that
they could not fight Hitlerism in Europe without attacking "domestic
manifestations of the Hitler spirit—an American type of racialism every
whit as dangerous and of even longer historical standing." [20] There was
grave danger, he said, in allowing the struggle of blacks for citizenship
advancement to become a racial one. "To permit this isolates the Negro
community and leaves it to be exploited by the street-corner rabble-
rousers—the peddlers of racialism who match in vicious distortion the
white Negro-phobes who preach their native brand of Nazi Aryanism." [21]
It took race riots in five great cities to awaken white America to the dangers of race conflict, he charged. And the Harlem riot had shown, said
Granger, that a Negro mob could be every bit as bad as a white mob.

The President of the United States finally commented. He condemned
race conflict, saying, "We cannot stand before the world as a champion of
oppressed peoples unless we practice as well as preach the principle of democracy for all men. Racial conflict diminishes war production, cuts
down the flow of guns and planes and increases the toll of American
lives. Racial strife destroys national unity at home and renders us suspect
abroad." [22]

Under the circumstances, League action was urgently needed. After the
Detroit conflagration, the NUL executive wired the secretaries of the forty-seven affiliates.

URGE LOCAL URBAN LEAGUES TO CALL SPECIAL MEETINGS OF BOARDS TO-
GETHER WITH REPRESENTATIVE LABOR, POLITICAL AND CIVIC LEADERS TO
PREPARE COUNTER OFFENSIVE OF PUBLIC OPINION AGAINST OUTBREAKS IN
LEAGUE CENTERS. MEETINGS SHOULD HAVE WIDEST POSSIBLE PUBLICITY.
URGE THAT YOU REPORT FULLY TO NATIONAL OFFICE ON LOCAL DEVELOP-
MENTS. [23]

The local Leagues responded. Thirty-six of them worked with their
city administrations to form city-wide committees representing a cross-sec-
tion of the community. Their purposes were to study tension situations
—pressure points—and come up with planned procedures to deal with
them. A unity for victory committee sponsored by the Baltimore League
brought together eighty-six religious, labor and civic agencies, and
held a demonstration and meeting at a local park in August to which
some 15,000 white and black citizens came. In Washington, the local

League organized a committee consisting of some 100 community groups in the city.[24]

One of the most ambitious moves by the NUL was the deliberate expansion of the 1943 annual conference into a major national event. With the theme Victory Through Unity, the conference was the most widely publicized and biggest interracial meeting in the nation's history, with attendance above 3,800. The conference opened with a greeting from President Roosevelt, who found it timely to affirm the importance of interracial harmony. Ten governors and a number of mayors proclaimed the conference period "Victory Through Unity Week." Delegates from twenty-six states attended and a highlight was a management-labor luncheon at which 288 industry, labor and League representatives discussed black industrial employment. The conference achieved a breakthrough not only in numbers but in coverage by the press. Some two hundred newspapers printed day-by-day reports and correspondents from the New York *Times*, Associated Press, Associated Negro Press and Chicago newspapers were on hand throughout. An added dimension was given by a nationwide broadcast on the NBC network. It featured a talk by Edward G. Robinson on the conference theme.

The historic relations between the League and the black newspapers made the press a valuable resource at this critical time. Through the black press League activities, news releases and statements by League officials were carried into the black community with new prominence. In this way the Afro-American public was constantly aware of the enormously important fact that black leadership was joined by an important body of white opinion and leadership in efforts to correct injustices suffered by blacks throughout the nation. This fact, in terms of morale building and as a deterrent to extreme reactions, had a highly significant, though unmeasurable, effect.

Meanwhile, NUL addressed letters and telegrams to mayors in a hundred cities and governors of thirty states urging that committees such as Detroit's be established. These broadly representative committees were a further extension of the old Booker T. Washington doctrine of bringing together the best whites and blacks for mutual understanding and, hopefully, progress on matters affecting race relations in the communities. The NUL formally proposed to mayors and governors that these committees have on their agendas the analysis of tension conditions and action to clear up factors that threatened to blow up.

The response went far beyond NUL's expectations. In the first place, more communities accepted the idea than NUL anticipated. Over three hundred finally established what later came to be known as "human relations commissions." Furthermore, they were set up on a continuing, rather than emergency basis, and often were legal entities or quasi-legal bodies assigned to the specific area of race relations. They evolved into something that Lester Granger, for one, had not foreseen and would not have encouraged. "It's one thing," he said later, "to have prominent citizens financed and staffed for a job controlled by the citizens [i.e., a private, voluntary agency]; it's another thing to have the civil service operation set up under the city government to take the leadership in such a delicate situation as racial friction. There's too much danger of being politicalized." He was commenting on the "professionalization" of these human relations committees and their placement within city or state governments with permanent staffs, a movement that came after the war, as a result of what Granger called "the self-interest of some and the considered judgment of others." (He favored permanent, voluntary citizen committees rather than "civil service staff operations" because of the greater prestige and effectiveness of the former.) [25]

The NUL also announced a community counseling service under its research director, to make its experience available to community leaders in cities with or without Leagues. The service was to include field visits and consultations with local authorities and other national agencies, especially those in the fields of social work.

Moreover, the agency entered into a federation with five other national organizations to coordinate efforts to serve war communities. The other agencies were the Child Welfare League, Family Welfare Association, National Institute for Immigrant Welfare, National Organization for Public Health Nursing and the national board of the YWCA. The group called itself the American War-Community Services.

It worked out a cooperative program of pooling information and resources to help communities in greatest need of social services. In its first year AWCS served ninety-one communities and had 200 on its waiting list. AWCS actually went into a city, diagnosed needs and helped construct organizations and locate leadership to cope with health, welfare, and recreational conditions. (In one case, a town that had grown in population from 30,000 to 75,000 had but one hospital in which it was attempting to make do by assigning two patients per bed! AWCS helped organize and institute a visiting nurse service that took the immediate pressure off.)

This association with five other national agencies gave NUL and the local Leagues instantaneous access to reports, information, studies and follow-up action in communities throughout the nation where the vast shuffling of the American population had put pressure on existing community resources. The League also benefited from its association with the blue-ribbon sponsors of the AWCS in terms of prestige and broader dis-

semination of knowledge of the League program. Several League directors and executive Granger served on the AWCS board and Committee
of Sponsors. NUL President Baldwin became AWCS treasurer.

The AWCS was approved by the President's War Relief Control Board
and the Community Chests and Councils endorsed it as a "forward-looking experiment in joint planning, coordination, budgeting, fund-raising
and interpretation on a national level," deserving of support by those interested in more effective social welfare action by national agencies.[26]

NUL was active in still a third way, developing a program of local action under the label "Service Councils of the National Urban League." A
national twenty-five-member blue-ribbon sponsoring committee headed
by Dr. Charles A. Wesley of Howard University was organized to provide
strong leadership to this effort. These councils were to coordinate local
organization efforts and to receive NUL bulletins, guidance and field service. It was all on a volunteer basis, with the local organizers under the
general national supervision of Dr. Banner and his associates Harold A.
Lett and Ruby Bryant Yearwood.

Over a period of two years about a hundred cities called on the NUL
for guidance and help. In five of them Leagues were organized; in an additional dozen or so, service councils were set up. In others, local Leagues
developed in later years. All in all, there was considerable evidence that
Granger had succeeded in reinvigorating his patient, the NUL, after
three years as its chief executive.[27]

In totting up the positive contribution of the League to improving
race relations, Granger estimated that during 1943 League staff and
board members reached 500,000 Americans in face-to-face meetings, conferences, counseling, and so on, exclusive of radio and printed messages.
Though many of these meetings dealt with specifics of housing, jobs,
health and play facilities, many others looked at the current and future
black-white picture and focused attention on it. This meeting-and-confer-
ence activity Granger put under the heading of "quiet and undramatic,
but nonetheless effective programs of public education." [28]

Early in 1945 Lester Granger received word from Secretary of the Navy
James Forrestal inviting him to Washington. When he met Forrestal,
Granger and the navy secretary discovered it was a case of mistaken
identity. Forrestal, a Dartmouth graduate, had thought he was contacting
an old classmate, Lester Granger's elder brother. (Three Grangers had
preceded Lester at Dartmouth.) However, it *was* the Urban League Granger whom Forrestal wished to see. He was concerned about his efforts to
integrate the navy and wanted Granger's help. It was his plan to send the
race relations expert on a tour of inspection of all major navy installations for an honest appraisal and report on the progress of integration of

the service. Granger was given leave of absence by the League from July 1 until the end of October 1945 to carry out the assignment.[29]

He traveled the length and breadth of the navy examining facilities, housing, recreation, battle conditions, shore and ship, topside and below decks. He went to all twelve major naval installations in the United States, to Pearl Harbor and the Pacific bases, then on to the Philippines, and to other bases. Granger's technique in arriving at a base was to get together with the black sailors, take note of their own comments and criticisms, then meet with the top brass on the base, relating the important points in such a way as to protect the enlisted men who had told him specific things. This session generally brought forth a variety of responses, admissions, rejections, denials, agreement, interested acceptance, and so on. Following this meeting, Granger would again get together with the black sailors to go over what he had been told by the white officers. Thus, as he put it, "the black sailors got two chances, the white officers one, to tell their story." Following this he wrote out his notes, from which he later made up his report.

Ultimately Granger reported directly to Forrestal on the entire matter. He was convinced of Forrestal's absolute integrity in carrying through integration in the navy. Granger met with top navy brass and briefed them on his findings, and the endorsement of Admirals King and Nimitz was secured. Forrestal followed up with two directives that wiped out race as a factor in the navy as far as possible. Forrestal did one more thing that indicated his good faith—he granted executive clemency to the Mare Island mutineers and the Guam rioters (all but one), ordering them returned to active duty.

For his help, Lester Granger received the navy's highest civilian award, the Distinguished Service Cross.

Another war service award went to NUL industrial relations head Julius A. Thomas. It covered far more than personal service. It signalized the importance of NUL's efforts to plan ahead for 1,000,000 black veterans by coaching the armed forces concerning their needs and producing materials and programs for training separation center specialists in counseling blacks. The award given Thomas was the Selective Service Medal authorized by Congress,

> for the significant contribution which you have made to the operation of the Selective Service System by making yourself available for continuous consultations regarding occupational and employment matters concerning Negro veterans, and for the Urban League studies of Negro employment which have helped the Selective Service System to understand the occupational and employment problems of Negro veterans.[30]

31/New Forms of Social Action

In 1940 there were 657,000 blacks working in manufacturing in the United States, according to the federal census of occupations. Most of these, it must be remembered, were in unskilled and menial jobs. The attitude of major employers toward black workers was, by and large, negative. J. H. Kindelberger, president of General Motors' subsidiary North American Aviation, typified the prevailing level of industrial statesmanship with his statement in mid-1941: "Regardless of their training as aircraft workers, we will not employ Negroes in the North American plant. . . . It is against the company policy." North American was not alone, of course. Other headlines of that year read: [1]

Row Over Negroes Stops Truck Plant
3,000 War Workers Sent Home As 350 Protest at Chrysler Unit in Detroit

No Jobs For Negroes Says Plane Builder
Boeing Representative in Chicago Rejects Race Workers

War Department Employs Negro Radio Expert:
Fires Him On Learning His Race [2]

The roll-call of American industry in 1941 would have yielded equally depressing responses from nearly all major corporations. But, as World War I had proved, prejudice is a sometime thing. When contract deadlines demand production workers and there are none available—except blacks—prejudice plays second fiddle to profits.

By mid-1942, with the nation at war and the psychology as well as the impetus to produce drastically altered, many of the companies that had publicly denounced hiring blacks or taken adamant stands against Afro-Americans on their payrolls had done an abrupt about-face. "Our Negro workmen have turned out swell. The spirit of these men is just as good as you'll find. They work hard and they know we are at war," announced North American Aviation's president Kindelberger in May 1942 without a trace of sheepishness.[3] But it had taken a concentrated campaign by the Kansas City Urban League, leading the Kansas City Citizens' Defense Committee in a protest rally and marshaling the cooperation of the NAACP, public and private, national and local agencies, that finally caused North American to reverse its policy.

Bell Aircraft Corporation, whose headquarters were at Buffalo, New York, was building a bomber production plant near Atlanta. NUL secured a commitment from Bell to hire 2,000 black workers. However, they had to be skilled workers and Atlanta authorities refused to train blacks.

The Atlanta League registered 5,000 Afro-American citizens as proof that defense job training was needed and desired. NUL and local League representatives huddled with War Production Board, Office of Education and FEPC officials to cut through the tangle of red tape thrown up by Atlanta industry. It took four months of sustained Urban League effort, but finally the city fathers established training courses for blacks. This opened the way in the south for blacks to move into aircraft manufacturing.

In Brooklyn, manufactuers had signed for $300,000,000 in war contracts by the end of 1941, but blacks were practically excluded from these factories. The Brooklyn League pulled together a citizens' committee that organized all the agencies interested in combatting discrimination in defense. Inside of one year, the committee's pressure had cracked plants, factories and shops that historically had closed out blacks and caused them to hire 791 Afro-Americans.

Sometimes the unions were the stumbling blocks. Defense construction was lagging in Kansas City because the projects hired only union labor and the unions refused to admit blacks. There were qualified black carpenters, cement finishers, bricklayers and painters—all with skills needed on local projects. The Kansas City League patiently asked union officials in the area to open their memberships to blacks. The unions hauled out their hoary hypocrisy and said "impossible." The League then went after congressmen, international union officials, the War Department, the army's quartermaster general, federal, state and local government agencies. It finally took the threat of court action under a local ordinance prohibiting discrimination in defense employment to shake the unions loose. They capitulated, blacks received union cards and immediately went to work on the defense projects. Thus the headlines in 1942 showed a distinct change for the better: [4]

> RCA Establishes Plan To Hire Without Bias
> Hudson Fires Four in 'Hate' Strike
> Bethlehem-Fairfield Co. Drops Bars, Hires 10 men

Ordnance Plant Plans Negro Training School
Visitor At Winchester Plant Finds 1200 Negroes Working
General Motors Hires Negroes

And yet, as late as June 1942, the Bureau of Employment Security reported that "over 500,000 Negroes who should be utilized for war production are now idle because of the discriminatory hiring practices of war industries." [5] The whole subject was considered important enough to warrant an "off-the-record" panel discussion during an American Management Association conference on industrial production in November 1942. (In this conference and the report published afterward, AMA relied heavily on NUL and praised its "realistic and practical" approach.) As AMA saw it, "Today's urgent need for manpower effectively removes Negro employment in industry from the realm of *social reform*. Employers need only to approach the matter practically and objectively, using the proved rules of good management practice as a guide." [6]

It was in this context that Charles S. Johnson called on Lester Granger in 1943. Johnson was then head of the Sociology Department at Fisk University and had been counselor to many federal government departments and foundations over many years. The sociologist praised Roosevelt's FEPC policy but recommended a project to "permanentize" the gains blacks would make during the war.[7]

He harked back to his own experience in the Chicago League and NUL offices at the end of World War I and spoke of the great loss blacks suffered after that war. If black workers were cast aside once again then they had wasted time so far as their long-term situation was concerned. But if the NUL could be used as a device to build into the industrial structure of the nation on a continuing basis a large body of black industrial workers it would have made a most significant contribution to the race—and the country. Such was Johnson's thesis and the genesis of the NUL's Industrial Relations Laboratory.[8]

Julius A. Thomas had been brought to the NUL staff in February 1943 to serve as industrial relations secretary. Thomas, loquacious and unflappable, always a magnificent example of sartorial elegance, had been the executive secretary of the Louisville League for years, and before that the head of the Jacksonville affiliate. Thomas, Granger and Dr. Charles S. Johnson worked out the basic framework of the industrial relations laboratory. It was to be a device for integrating industrial work forces "for following placements and assisting employers and workers toward mutually satisfactory work-production experience." [9]

They decided that inclusion in the project must be voluntary, that the employers represented should include big, medium and small industries operating in cities as well as small towns and that all sections of the country should be covered. Another basic guideline was that fair employment was not the question, but the enlightened self-interest of the employer—i.e., was he getting his money's worth from black workers?

The plan was presented to the Julius Rosenwald Fund, which agreed that the need was evident, the plans sound and allocated a grant of $7,500. Consequently, through the local Leagues and additions to the NUL staff, some 2,000 war plants were reached. From this roster, NUL selected 300 plants for the laboratory project. They were located in twenty-five states and 120 towns and cities around the nation and employed a total of 150,000 blacks. They constituted a good cross-section and were purposely chosen for that reason.

The cooperating managements had nothing to lose and much to gain by their participation. NUL representatives called at the plants, interviewed and counseled management and labor representatives, used questionnaires with the stated goals of improving (1) job status; (2) work performance; and (3) postwar prospects of black workers. It was, in many aspects, a continuing counseling service, helping solve personnel problems, breaking down union restrictive policies, improving on-the-job relations between blacks and whites and advising blacks on their working and living problems. This last was necessary, as it had been in World War I, for again many of the black workers were unfamiliar with the big cities, big factories, big unions, big work forces and the crowding, makeshift living conditions that came with wartime shortages and all-out production.

By early 1944 a summary report was complete, covering the performance of Negro workers in 300 war plants.[10]

The key question was, what did management think of black workers? Officials in 215 of the 300 plants stated that they were satisfied with their work. Fifty plant spokesmen said they were "fairly satisfactory," and in nine plants the report was that they were not as good as white workers. Follow-up by League specialists revealed that without exception plants with progressive personnel policies for all workers had the most satisfactory experience with black workers.

What about postwar employment of the black workers? Managements of 253 industries declared that, based on current experience, they would continue to employ them after the war. Twelve plants reported no decision, and the rest declined to go on record.

Management was candid in reporting problems. However, only 142 plants listed difficulties. Most often cited was high absenteeism (sixty-seven plants).

A second survey was made in 1944 to check on upgrading of black workers and the employment of black women in these plants. Information on this follow-up study came from 252 of the original 300 industries, employing some 100,000 blacks.[11]

Six months after the first study the sixty-seven plants that reported excessive absenteeism among black workers were visited by League staff members. In thirty-seven absenteeism was no longer a serious problem. Management said the improvement was due to better adjustment of the workers after they became familiar with their jobs. In the remaining plants factors that affected blacks and whites equally caused absenteeism among both groups to run high.

The close relationship developed by the League with the companies in and out of the Industrial Relations Laboratory gave invaluable counsel and assistance to management, black workers and labor. The League was pleased with the results of its Industrial Relations Laboratory project, and it won the plaudits of knowledgeable observers. Professor Charles R. Lawrence, for one, called it "one of the instances of the Urban League strategy at its best. The instrument of action-research, combined with the availability of trouble-shooting services was utilized to get into the record commitments of future employment . . . the League hoped to obviate the kind of stereotypical and unfavorable judgments which might be made after the fact. Over and over during the war the staff of the National Urban League demonstrated a great capacity for imaginative and creative thinking in the area of Negro employment." [12]

In another part of the forest significant growth was observed. The NUL had stressed civil service as an area for careers for black citizens since the twenties. Untold hours of counseling, coaching and training of aspiring civil service applicants were invested by League workers over the years. (The League even lent them typewriters to use in the exams.) These efforts were augmented by literature, press releases, and systematic broadcasting via the Leagues and the black press, about the upcoming examinations for civil service positions at all levels, but particularly federal.

In addition to assistance to individuals in their efforts to qualify, the League was largely responsible for changing the mental set of Afro-Americans toward government jobs. For so many decades the civil service had been such a white preserve that blacks scarcely gave it a passing glance as a career possibility. Civil service jobs were simply considered off limits for blacks. Then the League, the temper of the thirties, the exclusion of blacks from private industry and the inadequacy of emergency work programs pushed thousands of Afro-Americans to make the effort required to attempt the civil service exams. The League was active on the other side also, pressing to place black examiners and members of hearing committees, and was slowly but increasingly successful. The results of this prosaic work shone through in the government civil service figures for 1938 and 1944.

In 1938, 9.8 percent of all federal workers and 8.4 percent of those in the District of Columbia were black. In that year, 90 percent of all the black civil servants in the District were in custodial jobs. The remainder consisted of the highly conspicuous top-level professional and subprofessionals (.5 percent) and a scattering of clerical-administrative, fiscal or clerical-mechanical positions (9.5 percent).[13]

By 1944 vast changes had taken place. There were some 300,000 blacks on federal payrolls, comprising about 12 percent of all government workers. But the distribution of these blacks, according to skills, was practically revolutionary. More than 60 percent had escaped the mop and broom brigades: 1.1 percent were professionals or subprofessionals, 9.9 percent were clerical-mechanical and nearly half—49 percent—were clerical-administrative and fiscal.[14]

As Julius Thomas pointed out, an increase in black government workers in wartime had happened before. The extraordinary factor in this World War II increase, however, was that it "exceeded in quality anything that has happened in the past." It was obvious, said Thomas, that much of the wartime progress in the employment of Negroes in government service resulted from the Executive Orders establishing FEPC.[15]

It was the war that revolutionized the position of blacks within the labor movement. Ira deA. Reid had found only 110,000 black union members in 1930. By 1935 it was estimated that the number had increased to 180,000. By 1945 there were 1,250,000 blacks carrying union cards. The CIO claimed 500,000 of these and the AFL said it had 650,000 black members.[16]

Julius Thomas emphasized that numbers alone were not the measure of black unionism. The CIO, he observed, had been much more aggressive in protecting the rights of black members in promotions, upgrading, holding office and other privileges of union members. Furthermore, the CIO had taken note of the NUL bill of particulars urged on the AFL for so many long years without results.

The CIO had formed a national antidiscrimination committee composed of top CIO officials and directed by a black executive. An active educational campaign had been carried out by the committee in CIO unions to fight bias and promote democratic practices. A manual dealing with race relations in industry was prepared by the NUL's industrial relations department entitled *Working and Fighting Together;* it was printed and adopted by the national CIO Committee to Abolish Racial Discrimination for wide distribution. This handbook gave guidelines for labor officials in settling or avoiding racial problems within unions.

At the same time the League presented a formal proposal (again) to the AFL executive council with the endorsement of President William Green that formal machinery be established within the AFL to adjust and eliminate discrimination within AFL unions.[17]

It was during World War II that the Vocational Opportunity Campaigns of the League really hit their stride. Under the seasoned, imaginative leadership of Ann Tanneyhill, the program of organizing the week-long campaigns to reach black youths expanded and enlisted outstanding Americans from the President down. In the VOC of March 1941, in addition to coordinating the usual activities—the public meetings and special counseling at schools and colleges, literature distribution, local radio and dramatic shows, displays and exhibits—she put together a nationwide hour-long radio "spectacular" on the CBS network promoting both vocational guidance and education. The program featured headliners including Marian Anderson, Joe Louis, John Kirby, Louis Armstrong, Canada Lee, Ethel Waters, Bill "Bojangles" Robinson, "Rochester," Eddie Green, Duke Ellington, Eddie South and Edward Matthews.[18]

The following spring, the nation was at war, and the VOC took on deeper significance. Its theme was "Speed Defense Production," a slogan deliberately chosen to drive home the point that blacks who had needed skills were available for defense work.

Lester Granger contrasted the needs of war industries in 1942 with those of 1917. In the earlier war strong bodies and willing hearts were qualifications enough and millions of blacks had them, he said. But a quarter-century later industry demanded higher skills. Fortunately, he pointed out, more than a million black workers were skilled and available to serve in the war effort. More than 112,000 had been trained in 1941 alone, 5,000 of them with college degrees. The major problem at that date (March 1942) was still bigotry in industry but "one by one, under the persistent hammering of Negro workers and their spokesmen, the pressure of public opinion and the influence of governmental representatives, management heads are induced to come in line and include Negro workers on their rolls. . . . Vocational opportunity," Lester Granger stated, "was more than an exhortation to black youth, it was a challenge to the American nation; testing its innermost determination to wage all-out war." [19]

This approach—tying the VOC's in with tactical goals for black advancement—carried through from this time forward. In 1943 the theme was "Womanpower is Vital to Victory." The immediate purpose was to focus attention on hiring women in defense efforts, for the League had found that black women were not being employed to the extent necessary and possible. So the VOC riveted public attention on the contributions of black women in the nation's earlier wars and the need to use them in this one.

In addition to the traditional techniques, Ann Tanneyhill worked with the editors of *Opportunity* to bring together a special "Negro Womanpower Issue." [20] It began with a special letter of endorsement from President Roosevelt and carried sixty-four pages of special articles, including two by Anna M. Rosenberg, now New York regional director of the War Manpower Commission, and Mary Anderson, director of the Women's Bureau of the United States Department of Labor.

Radio again carried the League message nation-wide, via the Mutual Network, various local stations and especially through "spectaculars" over the CBS and NBC networks. The CBS show was called "Heroines in Bronze" and featured Anne Brown (of *Porgy and Bess*), Fredi Washington, Canada Lee, Mary McLeod Bethune, Addie W. Hunton and Willa Brown, portraying black heroines such as Phyllis Wheatley, Harriet Tubman and Sojourner Truth. The NBC offering was a moving performance of a special epic poem, "Freedom's Plow," written by Langston Hughes for the occasion and read by Paul Muni with the accompaniment of the Golden Gate Quartet. Through radio the VOC message had become a major vehicle to put across the NUL program goals to millions of Americans.

In 1944 and 1945 the VOC theme was "The Future Is Yours—Plan and Prepare" and the observance expanded into more communities, schools, colleges and homes. This theme became the basis for the VOC's in the postwar years as well, and undergirded the NUL's activities in the field. Cooperation in the annual VOC's came from the respected professional societies in the field—the National Education Association, American Teachers' Association and American Council on Education.

In 1946 a $26,500 grant from the Volker Charities Fund of Kansas City, Missouri, made it possible to put vocational guidance on a year-round basis and to hire a vocational guidance worker to assist the southern field director, working out of the Atlanta regional office.

In 1944 NUL went to the General Education Board with a three-year project proposal and received an initial grant of $35,000 to launch it in September. Called the "Community Relations Project for Interracial Social Planning," it brought together fourteen other national social service agencies for a task-force approach to combining social work procedures with positive action to improve race relations. They were the American Public Welfare Association; American-War Community Services; Boy

Scouts of America; Child Welfare League of America; Community Chests and Councils; Family Welfare Association of America; Girl Scouts of America; National Committee on Housing; National Federation of Settlements; National Health Council; National Organization for Public Health Nursing; National Probation Association; National Tuberculosis Association; National Committee for Mental Health.[21]

NUL was the organizer and administrative agent of the project and Dr. Banner headed it. J. Harvey Kerns and Dr. William H. Dean were brought in as assistants and five other specialists were added to the payroll.

The procedure was for a city to invite NUL's Race Tension Project Committee to come in and survey local conditions affecting race relations and welfare of blacks.

Sponsorship of the local Council of Social Agencies was important. It took the project out of the realm of politics, insured city-wide participation and interest, and made it a professionally responsible and respected operation. In each community covered, a local sponsoring committee was organized, representing black community agencies, general civic leadership and the Council of Social Agencies itself. At the national level, there was an advisory board composed of representatives of the fifteen cooperating agencies.

This unique association with fourteen other national agencies gave NUL and local Leagues instantaneous access to reports, information, studies and follow-up action in communities throughout the nation where the vast shuffling of the American population had put pressure on existing community resources.

In its three-year existence and with a total expenditure of $110,000, the Community Relations Project put thirteen American cities under the social action microscope. Each was a city with severe problems and acknowledged serious tensions between blacks and whites. In its first year, the CRP covered New London, Connecticut, Gary, Indiana, Dayton, Houston, Oklahoma City, Tulsa and St. Petersburg. This was possible because Dr. Banner developed a technique for analyzing a city in one month, with J. Harvey Kerns's assistance. When the report was returned to the committee in the city, Banner or Kerns would accompany it and explain the findings. After everyone arrived at a common understanding of the problems, the NUL specialists in housing, public health, recreation, social work and employment would then come in and work with the local agencies responsible for correcting the problems uncovered in the Banner survey.[22]

After the task force returned to New York each specialist made out his report and gave it to Banner, who bound them along with the original survey and sent the package back to the sponsoring committee as the final report on racial conditions in the city, with recommendations for future progress. In many cities this final report came to be known as "the Banner Bible," and in many ways had unprecedented prestige.

In Chattanooga, a year after the report had been received, the Chattanooga *Times* reprinted the findings and recommendations together with an editorial and item-by-item report on what the city had done to live up to the challenge of the study.

Some CRP cities admittedly had tinderbox situations and were chosen to receive NUL attention before others where conditions were not so pressing. The remarkable success of the CRP was evident in that *none* of the cities studied had any race riots or community flareups, although Gary came close. J. Harvey Kerns's CRP study and the local League that grew out of it headed off disaster there.

An example of Gary's level of leadership at the time of the CRP study was the fact (revealed by the study) that the city's public health officer was a veterinarian. The CRP task-force medical specialist, Paul Cornely, M.D., of the Howard University School of Medicine, pointed out to the mayor and others that what suited Gary's horses wasn't necessarily safe for its humans.

The CRP study exposed the fact that blacks in the city were far less healthy than whites and pinpointed the specific shortcomings and remedies. It also revealed that Gary's whole public health program was inadequate. On the basis of the CRP findings the city health department's budget for the following year was nearly doubled.

Gary was a bad town for black workers. The dominant steel industry was thoroughly unionized and Afro-Americans had been barred from many jobs and apprenticeships for better trades and crafts. After the CRP study the boards of eleven locals of the United Steel Workers in the city adopted a resolution calling for black apprentices, opening jobs to them and endorsing them in positions as high as plant supervisor. By this action, the immediate and postwar job picture for blacks in the city's steel industry was transformed.[23]

The Gary study uncovered serious race antagonism in a large junior high school attended by both blacks and whites, and predicted a racial explosion unless changes were made. Before the suggested remedies could be put into effect white students called a strike. They demanded transfer of black pupils from the school and refused to attend until this was done. It was evident that the youngsters were reflecting their parents' attitudes. The student strike hit front pages all over the nation—and overseas as well. The CRP study had prepared the city for such an outbreak. City authorities, backed by community leaders, refused to give in to the strikers.

A local League was in process of formation in Gary at the time. Its president was H. B. Snyder, editor of the conservative daily Gary *Post-Tribune,* who had been chairman of the CRP study group in the city. Unfortunately, development of the League was not far enough along to prevent the student strike, but when the executive secretary reported for duty, he brought both factions together for discussion of the situation. Catholicism was the dominant religion among whites in Gary. The League executive was Catholic and had on his board of directors a highly respected Catholic priest. The priest joined the black League executive in sitting down by turns with the white students and their parents, then the black students and their families in conferences at League offices. The youths were convinced, finally, that on their shoulders was the major responsibility for building citizenship standards in the city by demonstrating that young blacks and whites could study and play together. The leaders signed and released a pledge reconciling their differences. Its language seems quaint by the standards of a quarter-century later, but it was an effective force in knitting a fast-unraveling community. It stated, in part:

> We believe a satisfactory solution of all problems at Froebel School can be effected through an organization composed of representative parents, teachers, students and area citizens. We pledge our support of such a group. . . . Further, we express our confidence in its ability to cope with current questions.
>
> We strongly urge the Board of Education . . . to issue a statement of policy providing for the enrollment of all students, regardless of race, creed or color, to attend whatever school is located in the zone of their residence.
>
> Further, we urge that complete facilities, activities, clubs, and programs of all schools be made available to all students.
>
> Finally, to all Gary, we say, begin now to live the American way of life —by deed rather than by word.
>
> Signed,
> STUDENTS' COMMITTEE

At the offices of the Urban League of Gary, March 2, 1946.[24]

The CRP closed at the end of three years when the General Education Board funding stopped. In its refinement of techniques and task-force survey approach to communities CRP brought to a peak the sophistication of the social work diagnostic instruments that were basic in the League's earliest efforts, back in 1905 and 1906.

With considerable justification Lester Granger viewed the format, methods and results of the Community Relations Project as a "shining example of the maneuverability of a social agency devoted to breaking precedents and reforming practices hampering the emergence of the good community.' " [25]

A somewhat more objective endorsement of the League was published the same year that the CRP was launched. It was in the Carnegie Corporation sponsored study of American black-white relations called *An American Dilemma*, written by Dr. Gunnar Myrdal. NUL had helped Myrdal and his associates collect information for the study. T. Arnold Hill had canvassed some two dozen local Leagues, securing data that Myrdal requested.

Myrdal's thoroughgoing study instantly made other reports about black Americans obsolete and/or fragmentary by comparison and was universally hailed for its scholarship and insight. Myrdal had some kudos for the League:

> What the Urban League means to the Negro community can best be understood by observing the dire need of its activity in cities where there is no local branch. The League fills such an unquestionable and eminently useful community need that—were it not for the peculiar American danger of corruption and undue influence when something becomes "political"—it is obvious that the activity should be financed, and financed much more generously, from the public purse: by the city, the state and the federal government. . . .
>
> There are few informed persons in America, among either whites or Negroes, who do not appreciate the social service work done by the League. . . .[26]

The influence of such an authoritative statement was immeasurable. It did bring the action recommended—more generous financing—as it reassured prospective contributors, serving as an unimpeachable endorsement. Myrdal also quoted criticisms of the League by Dr. Ralph J. Bunche, charging that it had not defined its program, never came to grips with the fundamentals in American racial conflict, and followed a policy of "racial expediency . . . [and] extreme opportunism." [27] Also cited was criticism by E. Franklin Frazier that the League's efforts to reach workers had been inadequate and misdirected.

Dr. Myrdal's riposte was:

> The Negro leaders who see the need for a Negro movement with a broader and more radical economic program should not—from their own point of view—spend their time in criticizing this useful social service agency which has been able to solicit so much help from the whites and to soothe so much suffering among the Negro people. They should, instead, appreciate what is obvious to any impartial observer: namely, that this organization,

even though its tasks have been lowly, has been able to maintain a fighting spirit. It has been, and is now more than ever, pressing and fighting, intervening and proposing, educating and propagating for ideas and measures which—even from the point of view of its critics—are headed in the right direction even though they are not drastic enough in their opinion." [28]

As for the criticism that the NUL was opportunistic, Lester Granger recalled that E. K. Jones "wholeheartedly endorsed opportunistic methods" by the League. "[Jones] said, 'The woodchopper doesn't have to be opportunistic; there's a hunk of wood there, he's got an axe that can handle it—he chops into it. That's being authoritative. But if you haven't got an axe, you've got to figure how you can split this damn thing. That's an opportunistic approach.' " [29]

32/Housing Pioneers

The guest speaker at NUL's annual meeting in February 1946 was housing specialist Charles S. Abrams, consultant to the Federal Public Housing Authority and noted author of *Man's Struggle for Shelter in an Urbanizing World*.[1] His subject was racial aspects of reconversion after World War II, but his focus was housing.

The intervention of the federal government in housing, he said, had set far-reaching patterns of segregation by means of the acceptance of segregation and restrictive covenants and the refusal of the Supreme Court to review "gentlemen's agreements" through which segregation was "written" into housing contracts. He warned that blacks must watch housing more than anything else, since mass movements of people could and did lead to permanent patterns of discrimination.

Working in the field of housing was not new to the League. The earliest activities in 1905 of its predecessor, the NLPCW, were, after all, concerned with safe and sanitary lodgings for the young black girls who came to New York and Philadelphia.

The CIICNY had been active in the field also, helping finance the San Juan Hill area tenements at West 63rd Street built by the City and Suburban Homes in 1908.[2] And in April 1911 the NLUCAN had held a conference to discuss social needs of Harlem blacks, with the principal discussion centered on "improper sanitary and moral conditions of the Negroes' homes growing out of the neglect by the City Departments and the indiscriminate mixing in of respectable and questionable tenants in apartment houses." [3] In other words, there was no enforcement of existing housing and sanitation laws by city officials, and police indifference to gamblers and prostitutes moving into family-type apartment houses was scandalous.

The result had been formation of the League's Housing Bureau, with John T. Clark as its staff secretary. As Clark saw it, his first task was to "arouse among the Harlem residents a moral consciousness which will speedily remedy the evils of the neighborhood." He found, however, that he needed reliable facts on which to base a more definite and practical program, and so the first survey of Harlem was carried out, with results noted earlier.

From that time on, League-conducted or inspired surveys laid bare the ugly facts of housing blight and race in America's cities. League executives were leaders in efforts to secure decent housing for blacks. John Dancy in Detroit opened up to Afro-American occupancy entire sections in and near that city during and after World War I. [4] James Hubert in New York brought housing needs to the attention of John D. Rockefeller, Jr., and suggested building homes for blacks. The ultimate result of this was the construction by Rockefeller of the pioneer Dunbar Apartments in Harlem. [5]

As Harold A. Lett, official of the New Jersey Department of Public Instruction, Division Against Discrimination, wrote in 1945, "Urban League secretaries and board members have written articles and influenced local programs as have no other private agency representatives; and Urban League files, from the National office to the newest branch, contain authentic histories of local and national housing conditions that are the severest indictments of America's short-sightedness in its mishandling of the so-called Race Problem." [6]

Through local studies, such as that in Harlem, the 1919 study of Newark's Third Ward, studies in Chicago, Kansas City, Buffalo and other major cities, League research exposed free enterprise in housing as freedom to exploit the unfortunate, uninitiated and unorganized. It was a freedom that held back the civic development of entire communities and the social growth of entire groups of people while endangering the health of great cities, as Lett pointed out. League research in housing was constantly cited in interpretation of trends by local secretaries, national staff and the media. These, plus special publications, testimony and counsel of League staff all had a cumulative effect. They brought to public notice the inescapable responsibility of government for action in this area to protect the well-being of its citizens. In its first issue in 1923, *Opportunity* held up to observation the probable effects of the (then) new zoning ordinances on current and future housing for blacks.

Few blacks could escape the ghettoes or change them fundamentally, so the local Leagues pursued programs to improve and protect the housing blacks were forced to occupy. This rationale was behind the widely promoted League campaigns of clean-up and home beautification, brought to their highest points of development in Baltimore, Pittsburgh and St. Louis especially.

It was the League that had the facts about black living conditions in the nation and put them before housing experts in 1931 when President Hoover called a conference on home building and home ownership. Thirty-one of the studies and articles used as references in the report of the Committee on Negro Housing to the conference came from the League research and/or *Opportunity* magazine.

At this 1931 conference Hoover told more than 1,000 delegates that the nation had, in his opinion, "fairly creditably solved every other segment of our credit structure more effectively than we have solved that of housing." [7] His proposals for solving this problem shriveled in the economic desiccation of the Depression. The vast majority of blacks were renters, not owners (people were sentimental about homes but "never sing songs about a pile of rent receipts," noted Hoover).[8] Hoover's unclear attitude toward their problems is apparent in his statement on slum clearance:

> There is scarcely a city where, if the health and building laws were adequately enforced, a large part of the slums would not be empty of tenants. There is no provision in morals or freedom or the Constitution that building owners be allowed to collect income from the pollution of public health and morals in the name of private property.[9]

What he expected to do about the conditions of life or the supply of housing for the unfortunate slum dwellers was unspecified. It was the League in the thirties that consistently brought to the attention of public officials and social agencies the impact of the Depression on black citizens. As the mortgage foreclosures and tenant evictions dumped thousands of Afro-Americans on the streets, it was the League that insisted attention had to be paid. It was the League that spread on front pages the side-stepping policies of the Home Owners' Loan Corporation and the Federal Housing Authority, pointing out that these agencies, in their "safe and sane" ultraconservative policies were avoiding black residential areas as poor risks.

The NUL's own E. K. Jones, in his post with the Department of Commerce during the early New Deal years, made certain that black enumerators and technicians were included in the Real Property Inventory of 1934 under the Emergency Relief Administration. This survey covered every major city in the nation. It was by interpreting the plight of black citizens that national and local project directors made sure that the study was objective and complete in its presentation of the nation's housing needs.

League staff members were on deck in 1936 and 1937 when the federal government through the Public Works Administration moved into public housing for the first time in the nation's peacetime history. The League counseled and advised, argued, chivvied and cajoled the PWA and United States Housing Authority officials on the national and state levels to include black citizens to the utmost in the projects. The efforts were aimed at two fundamental aspects: securing jobs for blacks in construction of these public-funded housing units; and opening the finished dwellings for black occupancy.

The League and its allies in this campaign succeeded in bringing the federal housing officials to set local employment and occupancy ratios for Afro-Americans in these projects. League influence had mixed results. In some cities, such as Buffalo, Jim Crow won; in others, such as Springfield, Illinois, the League and open occupancy won; in others, there were various arrangements, including separate buildings for blacks in the same project. The significant, basic fact is that by keeping on top of developments in this field the League influenced the ultimate result: 7,500 PWA units and 41,000 USHA project apartments for blacks, which measured a full one-third of all dwellings built through mid-1942.

In that year the League's annual conference received a report from its Commission on Housing analyzing the present and future roles of NUL in that field. Twenty-three branches were engaged in aggressive campaigns to stimulate interest in public housing in their cities. Ten League executives had a quasi-official "tie-up" with the local housing authority; nine locals had staff or board members serving as members of the local housing authority; League staff members were on advisory committees in eight cities; in fourteen cities they were on citizens' housing councils and in six cities were on local rent-control committees.[10]

Twenty-six local Leagues reported that they had "applied pressures which had served to guide the formulation of local housing policies." And many of the locals had helped the housing authority advisory committees, citizens' councils and rent-control committees select black staff members. The commission made the point that one-sixth of all black citizens lived in the thirty-one League cities covered by its report. And it took the position that NUL, "as the recognized spokesman for the Negro group," had to take an active interest in housing. It saw the postwar future of public housing "up for grabs" with evidence that antihousing influences were seeking to control it. The future of "this significant social program," it said, would depend on mobilizing housing proponents into a strong, alert, articulate body of public opinion, of which the NUL executives must be in the vanguard. "Possessing the broad, social perspective and first-hand knowledge of the evils of poor housing and equipped with the tools for social research, the League can and should be the focal center of local housing interest," the commission stated. Consequently, the Leagues, it solemnly charged, had a grave responsibility to prepare essential social and housing data, study and graph community growth and development, set up spot maps showing morbidity, mortality and delinquency, chart the correlation of minority group islands with blighted housing areas to educate the community and lead in securing needed housing.[11]

The League took this charge seriously and the action of its locals and the national office confirm this. NUL published *Racial Problems in Housing* in 1944 as a review of conditions in the field and this booklet went through three printings before mid-1945. Looking back on that year, however, Lester Granger ticked off the basic situation: 80 percent of blacks living in substandard dwellings; trends toward increasing segregation in housing; increased government activity in building low-income housing. In the face of these developments the League had not been able to provide adequate leadership, he acknowledged.[12]

The agency's goals would be to check the "suicidal trend toward racial ghettoes observed in the spread of restrictive property owners' covenants" and the spawning of segregation in new areas by erecting separate public housing projects. Health and sanitation codes with teeth in them must be enacted, he demanded, to correct the deterioration and decline of existing black neighborhoods. Neighborhood leadership, of course, had its part to play in this. Black home-owners were to be advised and assisted to purchase property and protect neighborhood standards.[13]

The League had a further interest in the housing field: jobs for black workers. In the postwar reconversion period the housing industry, curtailed during the war, was a likely candidate to take up the slack in employment. Emphasis on housing, therefore, made good sense. And it was with this in mind that the NUL industrial relations department canvassed the locals on the employment status of black workers in their cities in early 1946.

The survey showed a mixed pattern, but standard conditions included scanty apprenticeship opportunities, and few veterans enrolled in training programs. Wilson Wyatt, the National Housing Agency administrator, had recommended recruitment and training of one and one-half million more construction workers by mid-1947. The NUL, therefore, sent its survey, *Negro Workers in the Building Trades in Selected Cities,* to the Housing Agency's director of labor and to others (including the press) interested in what was going on in construction in twenty-one of the nation's major cities.[14]

Housing was a major focus of the NUL annual conference in 1946. It was held in St. Louis and John T. Clark's Block Units were among the sponsors. A full day's program of the conference was devoted to housing. The morning session was "Mobilizing the Community to Meet its Housing Needs" and had as discussion leader Frank S. Horne, assistant to the administrator of the National Housing Agency. His panel consisted of experts—League secretaries who had wrestled with the hydra-headed housing monster for years—William Evans of Buffalo, William Ashby of Springfield, Illinois, Joseph Douglass of Washington, D.C., and Clyde Malone of Lincoln, Nebraska. The luncheon speaker was Wilson W. Wyatt, the NHA chief, talking about meeting housing needs. He was the headliner for the conference that year—the highest-ranking government official on the program.

Though jobs and training preoccupied NUL's limited staff in the years that followed, by 1950 Lester Granger sensed a new emphasis on housing in the nation. Housing had become a key factor in the nation's racial problem. During the decade from 1940 to 1950, 1,600,000 blacks had flocked to the cities, more than in the first thirty years of the century. The impact of the newcomers plus the high birth rate of those already settled in the cities had turned the black enclaves into huge black cities-within-cities, thanks to segregation in housing. In 1950, said Granger, the sociologists and city planners, even the city fathers, were beginning to realize that the future of the city depended on enlightened housing policies to cope with the steadily growing Afro-American population. He thought there was evidence that progress was being made.

San Francisco, Chicago, and Newark led the way in outlawing segregation in public housing. Others barred discrimination in urban redevelopment plans. In New York and Chicago, the New York Life Insurance Company, the Metropolitan Life Insurance Company and Levittown finally gave in to insistent demands to allow blacks into their mammoth housing projects as residents as well as domestics. New York's Bowery Savings Bank, led by long-time League director Henry Bruere, took the initiative and built a modern community complex of stores, offices and apartments in Harlem.

It was about this time that the bulldozer impact of urban renewal on black population centers was raising storms of resentment. Atlanta cut a new superhighway through its center and wiped out the homes of 2,000 blacks in the process. New housing accommodated only half of these. There were some positive factors: the black citizens moved into new areas, a new housing market—Afro-Americans—was "created," and black administrators or staff officials were appointed to municipal housing authorities in several cities.

Local Leagues were victorious in many lengthy, enervating battles to secure housing and to write bigotry out of public housing plans. In Omaha, the League finally prevailed on the local housing authority to end segregation in city public housing units. In Tampa the League turned the city around: the previous policy of ignoring blacks in new housing plans was reversed and a $5.5 million low-rent housing project was set for the heart of Tampa's "shanty town."

Perhaps the most spectacular success was that of the Buffalo League: William Evans's fifteen-year struggle to get decent housing for blacks won city council approval of a $26 million public housing project, 80 percent of which was to be allocated to a district that was primarily Afro-American. Evans had pushed persistently for the city to drop its segregation policies in public housing, and won. He had faced and beaten racist realtors and demagogues who had whipped up antiblack sentiment, using the classical scare techniques. And he had managed to educate and indoctrinate public housing officials, city councilors and the public to the needs of black citizens. As a second and essential element in his strategy, Evans had stimulated construction of private low-cost housing for blacks. These two elements—public and private housing—went far to relieve the immediate overcrowding of the rapidly increasing black population. Evans's success was so striking and the techniques he used were so widely applicable that NUL printed a forty-four page report on the Buffalo housing story. This was widely distributed and guided local League executives in their housing campaigns.[15]

At the end of 1951 the NUL board decided to formalize activities in housing. A board committee was established and Reginald A. Johnson was named director of housing activities for NUL. His mission was to expand and encourage housing for blacks, with emphasis on privately built and financed construction. A tougher area of activity could not have been chosen, for it was in the private market that there was least leverage and most latitude for every kind of prejudice, ignorance and manipulation to be exercised by financing institutions, real estate operators, dealers, sellers, builders and unions.

The League did not forgo the public housing area, however. On the contrary, it coordinated efforts to move public housing agencies as well as private interests to increase construction of open-occupancy housing. NUL sponsored regional "Housing and Home Finance Institutes" in Omaha and in Grand Rapids–Muskegon, Michigan, and brought to builders, public officials and black community leaders the straight, unvarnished facts about housing for Afro-Americans—the needs, opportunities, fears and bottlenecks.

The neglect of this black market was overwhelmingly evident. There had been nine million units of housing built in the period 1935–1950. But out of this total only 100,000 units—less than 1 percent—were available to nonwhites. The League's goal was, therefore, to open such housing to blacks, not only on the basis of ability to pay and in areas of individual choice, but also according to standards that limited crowding and irresponsible tenant activities, that provided decent maintenance standards and services.

The first two NUL Housing Institutes uncovered a promising amount of interest from developers who had projects ranging from $250,000 to $12,000,000 they wished to finance. All of these plans, Lester Granger noted caustically, could have been financed locally if they had not provided for black residents or were not breaks in the restricted—that is, "white"—area pattern. The League succeeded in bringing these development plans to "a more favorable mortgage market for financing." Actually, Reginald Johnson managed to land mortgage assistance for some nine projects around the nation, three of them through the Federal National Mortgage Association.

The League's Housing Committee, consisting of Mrs. Samuel Rosenman, Robert W. Dowling, president of City Investing Company of New York, Walter "Chief" Aiken, Atlanta builder, and Housing Director Reginald A. Johnson, met with the new federal housing commissioner in Washington in 1952. The committee submitted a five-point plan calling on the Federal Housing Administration to respect the United States Supreme Court's 1948 decisions against restrictive covenants in its financing and building operations and to add black personnel to its staff. Commissioner Walter L. Greene pledged full cooperation, promised a "realistic extension" of FHA services and expanded black staff. He later repeated these assurances before the NUL annual conference, promising to extend equal housing opportunity.[16]

During these years the NUL housing director buttonholed builders, developers, mortgage brokers, city, state and federal officials. He met with executives of the National Association of Real Estate Brokers, the Mortgage Bankers Association and the National Association of Home Builders to move them to positive action in minority housing instead of remaining the massive roadblocks they had been. Johnson also worked up recommendations for the President's Advisory Committee on Housing Policies and Programs and took part in planning discussions of the Federal Housing and Home Finance Agency in projecting future housing needs. Pressing forward on the local fronts, NUL developed program aids to guide local Leagues in mounting neighborhood housing clinics and housing and home finance institutes. Johnson participated in housing conferences at Prairie View, Texas, Baton Rouge, Louisiana, and Washington, D.C.[17]

League action in housing ranged from victories in Warren, Ohio, to an opening wedge in New York. In Warren, Co-Op Homes, a project sponsored by the local League, secured $432,000 in mortgage money. Furthermore, the League moved the city fathers to pass a zoning ordinance prohibiting industrial inroads in a black residential neighborhood. In New York, a "mortgage clinic" to discuss financing of housing for blacks attracted builders and lenders and exposed them for the first time to the facts about black needs and financial abilities. Other League cities began to score; Muskegon pushed through a 200-unit home development, Phoenix opened three developments to blacks; Forth Worth pulled together the elements that made possible three housing projects open to blacks.[18] And so the emphasis on housing increased in League cities as the concentration of attention and circulation of information and know-how through the League pipeline accelerated.

But it was the Supreme Court's decision desegregating the schools that added an element of urgency. Lester Granger told the NUL board three days after the court's announcement that most southern states would probably attempt delaying tactics. An obvious segregationist strategy would be to attempt to continue segregated schools by concentrating black neighborhoods more closely than ever. This dictated that the League apply itself even more to housing activities. To offset the strategy, Granger called for League action to stimulate private home financing, cooperative building, regulation of urban development programs, the changing of policies of public housing authorities to make them more favorable, and so on. Moreover, he recommended efforts to get the White House to assume a leadership role, suggesting a White House conference on unmet housing needs for nonwhites.[19]

The NUL resolved to go to the top on housing. It addressed a "Blue Paper" to President Eisenhower in 1954. Pinpointing government responsibility, the NUL outlined *The National Housing Situation as it Affects the Non-White Population* [20] and called for a White House conference to increase the supply of housing for blacks. "Housing," it said, "is the only commodity in America that Negroes cannot buy in the open market in the same way that food and clothing, and cars and radios are purchased by those who have the money and the desire to buy." [21] The reasons this was so, NUL noted, were because of such practices as:

—refusal of mortgage financing to nonwhite buyers or use of exorbitant rates;

—subterfuges whereby a trustee held title to blocks of individually owned properties to control sales, transfers, and occupancy;

—requirement of a cash bond from property owners, whereby the bond would be forfeited if the property were sold to nonwhites;

—censuring and intimidating of brokers who sold without restrictions;

—"gentlemen's agreements" to keep nonwhites out of "restricted" areas;

—threats, intimidation, vandalism, arson and violence.

Federal commitment to break down these factors was important on many counts, but particularly because increasingly larger proportions of new housing construction used one or more forms of federal assistance (such as FHA and VA financing or refinancing). Furthermore, government, said NUL, should lead in awakening public consciousness and the enlightened self-interest of American business in open housing.

The result of this NUL approach to Eisenhower was a shortfall, but a productive one. The administrator of the Housing and Home Finance Agency did call a conference in December. Forty representatives of twenty-eight national organizations, including the builders, bankers, real estate operators and unions as well as religious and minority agencies, met with government officials for two days of off-the-record discussion.

NUL accused the federal government of guilt in depriving black citizens. Congress had created the Federal Housing Administration in 1934 "to encourage improvement in housing standards and conditions, to provide a system of mutual mortgage insurance, and to exert a stabilizing influence on the mortgage market." But, NUL pointed out FHA not only tolerated, it established definite anti-Negro policies that resulted in almost completely turning the building industry away from the black housing market. Realtors were threatened with loss of their licenses if they sold homes outside the racial ghettoes to black families. Builders found it difficult if not impossible to get mortgage financing if their structures included minority occupancy. Properties occupied by blacks, even those located near black-occupied houses, were appraised from 10 percent to 20 percent lower in value by FHA appraisers and subsequently by private appraisers.[22]

Reginald Johnson judged that the Washington conference was "of great significance" because it marked the first time that housing industry organizations had met with civic and service agencies and federal officials to examine ways of eliminating hurdles to open housing. Johnson believed the conference "established the federal government's commitment to its own responsibility in this important phase of the nation's housing needs. It also produced the first comprehensive review of the . . . racial problems in housing." [23]

Johnson made a breakthrough earlier in the year when he "integrated" the forty-first annual meeting of the Mortgage Bankers Association. He addressed the group in an agenda presentation on "Minority Housing and Redevelopment," the first time it had formally faced such a subject. The association also established a committee on minority housing.

Johnson produced a white paper (*Mortgage Financing for Properties Available to Negro Occupancy*) that was widely circulated and quoted in the industry. And he succeeded in drawing from the National Association of Home Builders acknowledgment of responsibility for increasing housing for blacks to the extent of 150,000 homes in 1954. Quotas were to be recommended to NAHB's regional committees, reported Lester Granger, "with pressure on their local members." [24]

As a government-industry team toured the country studying and promoting urban renewal in 1955, NUL stimulated local Leagues to demand "equal time." And when a Congressional committee on urban renewal barred public interest groups, the League pressured until League staff members were allowed to testify in Philadelphia and New York. During this period the League had the expert guidance of both nationally known real estate specialist Robert W. Dowling, who served as NUL president from 1952 to 1956, and James Felt, head of James Felt, Inc., a dynamo in the New York office space management field and NUL and New York League board member. Felt initiated a host of demonstration projects in New York City in property management and in concentrated slum rehabilitation and real estate workshops in the black community.

NUL continued down this road conducting regional institutes in various parts of the country on the subject of urban renewal. It projected a series of ten such institutes in 1956 then had to cancel seven because of lack of money. To these institutes the local Leagues sent board and staff representatives and urged local housing and real estate officials to attend. NUL was represented by Reginald Johnson, who brought in representatives (usually regional directors and their top staff people) of the Urban Renewal Administration, FHA, Housing and Home Finance Agency, the Veterans Administration, and Public Housing Administration. The value of these conferences was emphasized by one League executive's comment: "One of the most informative sessions that I have ever attended in housing. I learned more about the available government housing aids in two days than in the last five years." [25]

The broad goals of NUL efforts in the fifties were to expand the housing supply for blacks, to conserve their current shelters and to prevent eviction, dislocation and hardship for black citizens faced with urban renewal and slum clearance action. Workshops and institutes were initiated by local Leagues throughout the country. League after League conducted housing studies to get the facts and presented the results to officials and public for action. City after city directed new attention to minority housing needs, some of them establishing city offices to deal with needs and problems. In Tulsa, for instance, the League forced the public to look at outdoor privies and sanitation unworthy of Hogarthian London, conditions endangering city drinking water. In Gary the League brought construction defects in newly built black houses to FHA attention, a move which resulted in corrective action. Even in the south, Leagues managed to push ahead. Blacks in Miami benefited from ninety new Veterans Administration housing units after the League gave facts to authorities. Louisville's Municipal Housing Commission built an integrated project for large families, using League data as a basis.[26]

In some cities the League action was preventive. In both Detroit and New York relocation projects were affected by League community action. Detroit brought affected businesses and families together and submitted recommendations to city commissions. In New York, the League forestalled redevelopment of an area until acceptable provision for relocation of residents could be made.

The League capitalized on favorable developments such as the release in 1959 of the extraordinary study of the independent, prestigious Commission on Race and Housing. The results of this exhaustive research showed conclusively and impartially that black ownership did *not* decrease property values. So important was the study that NUL brought together 400 specialists in a housing conference in New York to analyze the report. Among those present were top federal, state and city officials, leading housing experts and race leaders. Local Leagues sponsored similar meetings in Denver, San Diego, Tulsa and Cleveland, among others.[27]

Constant NUL discussions, presentations, correspondence, interviews, memoranda, conferences and petitions to the FHA brought some response in 1959. The agency revised its regulations on federally insured low-cost housing, dropped racial classifications on 221 relocation housing projects and opened opportunities for better living quarters for black families.

Every indication pointed to housing as a crucial factor in the structure of discrimination in America. Though breakthroughs were few and gains were modest, the League continued to devote a significant proportion of its energies to its housing activities.

33/Enlisting Industry

In early 1947 NUL's executive board recommended joint action with the NAACP to plan for the inevitable impact of farm workers who would be migrating to the cities in the following five years "because of the mechanization of the south's farming and subsequent job cancellations." [1] (The NAACP's Washington bureau suggested a delay pending more complete information from the National Planning Association and the CIO.)

There were three factors the NUL could not foresee: (1) the unprecedented effectiveness of chemical agents in agriculture—equal to if not more important in their impact than the most far-reaching mechanical advances, and equally as devastating in their revolutionizing of postwar agriculture; (2) the continuation of industrial prosperity with only a breathing-space recession in 1949 thanks to depression-suppressed, war-denied consumer demand; and (3) the Korean conflict with its acceleration of industrial demand, war economy, and so on.

In other words, because of these factors the old push-pull mechanism was at work on blacks (as it had been in World War I) from 1942 straight on through the Korean conflict: the push of southern discrimination and poverty and the pull of economic promise in the cities of the north and west. Hundreds of thousands responded.

The domestic impact of the Korean conflict was felt in communities throughout the land. The shifting of people scrambling for jobs, industry's hurried assembling of factories and giant complexes of processing and production facilities, roads and highways, water and electric plants and railroads, supply and service facilities—all of these were complicating life in the Republic by the end of 1950.

Remembering the problems of wartime living conditions, the National Social Welfare Assembly and Community Chests and Councils jointly decided that a special approach was needed. So in January 1951 United Community Defense Services was formed to help towns and cities meet defense-created needs. UCDS was a federation of fifteen national agencies particularly suited to help in health, welfare and recreational services.

NUL was one of the founding agencies and played an extremely active role in UCDS's functions.

The UCDS operated as a task force, sending a team of experts where requested to help communities organize and finance social welfare programs. It also established emergency programs, recruited nurses and social workers, carried out research and cooperated in "developing the resources and potentials of all minority groups." [2]

During 1951 NUL experts worked in consultation with 135 cities in every region of the nation. Consultation required 372 staff visits and 199,000 miles of travel, and half of the cities served did not have local Leagues; many of them had no organized social services.

A major example of both the impact of change and the remedial effort by the League and UCDS was the Savannah River Project of the United States Atomic Energy Commission. Around Ellenton, S.C., a small farm village of six hundred, 200,000 acres of land were bought by the AEC for a billion-dollar production facility. The tiny town was wiped out by the project, and so were the few job opportunities and housing for blacks. Nelson C. Jackson, who moved from NUL southern field director to NUL director of community services and its UCDS coordinator, went to the site. He met with industrialists, state employment service officials and labor union leaders to find out what the basic policies of each of these elements was in the situation. His objective was to open up jobs for blacks.

Beginning on August 1, 1950, and repeatedly during the months after that, staff members called on the AEC or its contractors, General Electric, DuPont or Union Carbide and Carbon Company to pin down just what the racial policies were to be in the AEC operations. These calls involved visits to the Paducah, Kentucky, project, the Savannah River Project, Oak Ridge, Tennessee, Pasco-Kennewick-Richland, Washington, Seattle, Wilmington and other sites, interviewing company officials, AEC bureaucrats, labor union representatives and community leaders.

The NUL found that blacks were being closed out, that the AEC was taking a passive attitude, leaving policy-setting up to the corporations that signed the contracts and were going to run the operations. As the AEC representative at Savannah River said, "When we hired the DuPont Company, we hired their employment policies." And DuPont stated officially that all employment policies would be determined by local project management with due consideration of prevailing racial customs and practices. [3]

An exhaustive, documented NUL memorandum was prepared and sent to President Harry S. Truman in July 1951. As Lester Granger made clear in his covering letter, "We have exhausted the last possibility of improvement to be expected from negotiations with responsible officials.

. . . We strongly urge that your office take appropriate steps to eliminate all forms of racial discrimination presently in practice at these projects." [4]

Following this memorandum the AEC changed its hands-off approach and the League, working with management and union officials, brought about changes in AEC personnel policies and hiring practices of the corporate contractors.

Conference after conference, months of checking and studying and close cooperation with labor unions and contractors finally succeeded in reducing the resistance to hiring blacks in skilled, semi-skilled and unskilled jobs. By January 1953 out of some 29,000 workers, 6,500 were Afro-Americans, thanks to the League. The picture in housing, health and recreational facilities was similar; in each case openings for blacks went from zero to a sizable proportion of those available.

An indication of the improvement was the hiring of blacks at the Savannah River project and the action of top AEC and Company personnel officials in serving as consultants at some of the NUL-sponsored career conferences. These visits to campuses of black colleges resulted in recruiting of engineers and other technical and professional college graduates.

Other UCDS aid went to communities such as the west coast seaport city of Vamport, which mushroomed from 25,000 in 1940 to 125,000 ten years later. The city had only 300 blacks in 1940. They worked as janitors and domestics, living in a peaceful four-block area. But during World War II, workers from the south were brought in by the thousands and growth of the black population went up by an astonishing 7,555 percent. The blacks were employed in defense installations so unemployment was no immediate problem. The major difficulties were shamefully inadequate housing and social services.

A study by the NUL coordinator pointed this out and carefully underscored the sensitive, highly explosive situation that these conditions caused. The community organized a citizen's committee to take action and, as a stopgap, made arrangements with a nearby city to hire specialists to work on the problems until the city could develop its own services for blacks.

In another significant development, the General Electric Company gave full approval for and cooperated with the NUL research director to study its practices at twenty-five company installations around the United States. As Lester Granger reported about one phase of the study (in Hanford, Washington),

> [It] was carried on with the full cooperation of the General Electric Company, representatives of the Atomic Energy Commission and leading citizens in the tri-community area. . . . The local Citizens Advisory Committee formed to sponsor and participate in the study is continuing at work to

effectuate the recommendations made by the League's Study Director. Thus in a previously isolated valley community, now heavily affected by a mammoth industrial enterprise, a laboratory experiment in human relations has been instituted by the National Urban League which can produce results of deep significance to other American citizens in no matter what state.[5]

If you were a black, university-trained chemist and could not find a job, what could you do? In the year 1944, you went to your local Urban League. The League's industrial secretary checked you out, then contacted a nearby plant, part of a huge national corporation. A place was found for you on the payroll—as a laborer. Would you take the job? You would, for you, the League and the corporation all knew that it was an "entrance job," that the League's industrial secretary would be working with management and with you to see that you were upgraded just as fast as possible and ultimately assigned to your target—the laboratory.

That was the way it was done, and at that time that was the way it had to be done to crack the color line in top-level jobs in most American corporations. The approach required to make these placements was agonizing and humiliating on several levels, not the least of which was the amount of League time and effort invested for each such "success." Yet, follow-through by the League was both logical and necessary. After all, the agency had since 1930 stressed the importance of staying in school, studying and preparing for better occupations. If it did not help open up the opportunities that it had urged black youngsters to seek, it could only be condemned for heartlessly misleading its constituents. So it was that the NUL institutionalized its approach to upper-echelon job-finding in 1947. It called this the Pilot Placement Project and it was underwritten by the Rosenwald Fund.

The theory behind it, according to Lester Granger, was that blacks were being hired largely on the basis of an employer's previous experience with them.[6] Still, since many employers could not be persuaded to change their policies and hire blacks simply on the basis of the success of some other employers or the results reported in accurate studies, no matter how careful, another technique had to be found. Once again, Professor Charles S. Johnson brought his wisdom to bear. He suggested a device whereby blacks should, with League assistance, get a toehold (perhaps "fingernail-hold" would be more accurate) in a company. The technique would be to induce an employer to accept one or more blacks in key spots as "pilots" for the possible entrance of other Afro-Americans in other jobs, based on their success.

The League's goal would be to place at least fifty blacks per year in fields where Afro-Americans seldom, if ever, had been hired. Each of these "pilots" would be specially trained or qualified. The NUL industrial relations department would carry on the program, listing and analyzing the job potentialities of this blue-ribbon group of blacks.

Each of the placements was to be followed and noted, case-study fashion, to record the effects on (a) white workers associated for the first time with a black colleague; (b) the employer and his hiring practices; (c) the black "pilot's" progress up the job ladder; and (d) the black worker himself—the entering wedge for additional black placements. "The acid test of the usefulness of this project," wrote Granger, ". . . lies in the continuing effect which such initial placements have upon the employment attitudes of management and upon the determination of aspirant Negroes to secure the ultimate in training." [7]

The project was successful from the beginning because, said Granger, there always had been a large number of very promising and capable young people who came to the League to look for jobs. It was Julius A. Thomas's assistant director of industrial relations, LeRoy W. Jeffries, who managed the Pilot Placements. The qualifications of each job applicant were recorded at NUL and this became the roster of eligibles for the project. As Thomas made his rounds of American industrial moguls, often one would mention that his company could use an engineer or physicist or research person. At this the NUL executive would thumb through his list of eligibles and frequently, by happy coincidence, discover that he had just such a person available. (More often than not the person was in a job that was beneath his skills and welcomed the possibility of working at his profession.)

It hardly ever was as simple as this, of course. In the first year of the project, twenty-four colleges and universities were contacted to recruit "pilots." And 165 industrial companies were visited to discuss possible placements. How did it work out?

> Local Leagues cooperated with the NUL industrial relations department and a Chicago engineer was placed in Denver; a Denver chemist found a place through the Cleveland League. A Chicago bank hired a teller and an accountant. An executive trainee was placed in a large New York department store; college-trained office secretaries were hired by a mammoth foundry corporation in New Jersey. A draftsman went to work for a New York engineering firm. St. Paul's department stores hired black saleswomen and 8 engineers were placed on the payroll by the nation's largest electrical research laboratories.[8]

Such was the box score on Pilot Placement's first year. The following year, 1949, the Project was pushing forward with a full head of steam: 261 black men and women, "unusually significant placements," had been located in American industry in what Lester Granger accurately described as "new opportunities and responsibilities for members of their race . . . serving as pilots for the subsequent entrance into business and industry of uncountable thousands." Those Pilot Placements, he said, had given new emphasis and importance to the NUL's entire industrial relations approach. The clincher was his estimate of the total income of this one-year crop of Pilot Placements: $3,600,000, or better than $13,000 per pilot.[9]

This emphasis on the "Talented Tenth" (as DuBois had called them) had led the NUL into new pathways and shifted the emphasis in its entire industrial relations operation, according to Lester Granger. Seeking openings for the highly qualified caused the NUL to undertake an approach far more systematic than had been required in earlier times. Julius Thomas became an avid reader of the reports of the National Industrial Conference Board and thus learned, among other things, that the General Electric Company was at that time the largest single recruiter of college personnel in the nation. GE's 1949 goal was 1,000 college-educated youngsters.

Thomas called on Maynard Boring, GE's chief of technical personnel, and showed him NUL's file on Pilot Placement candidates. This led to discussion of GE's recruiting techniques and Boring confessed that to his knowledge GE had never set foot on a black college campus in its search for talent.

"No other American business has for that matter," commented Thomas. "Why don't you include Howard University on your recruiting schedule?"

The GE executive pulled out his college directory and noted that Howard had an accredited engineering school. "Well, I'll tell you," he said, "I'll go to Howard myself and I'd appreciate it if you would set the dates for me." Thomas agreed with alacrity, and that was the seed from which sprang another League pioneering effort—Career Conferences.

Julius Thomas extended the concept of GE recruiters visiting Howard to encompass other major corporations with an interest in graduate engineers. And he gave the concept a creative new twist beyond simple recruitment by proposing that an occasion be structured in which American industry could learn about Howard, its engineering faculty and students and *vice versa*. Each had plenty to learn from the other.

Using his Commerce and Industry Council contacts, Thomas persuaded General Cable and Radio Corporation of America to join GE in the project. Then he went to Washington and talked to the officials at Howard. He suggested a convocation of the Engineering School. It was to be a first: nobody from American industry had ever addressed the school. The topic was to be "The Future of Technical Personnel in the

Life of an Expanding Economy." The heads of the school agreed enthusiastically.

Thomas then went to Dr. Mordecai Johnson, president of Howard, and told him of the arrangements thus far, pointing out that it might be of interest and benefit to the heads of other departments or disciplines as well, and suggesting that it might be useful to invite them to luncheon with the industry officials. Dr. Johnson was wary. What, he wanted to know, was the National Urban League going to get out of this? The League, responded Thomas, was going to get at least one black university faculty alerted to what was currently going on in American industry and what skills were being sought.

Dr. Johnson approved, set up a luncheon and presided himself. After the convocation and luncheon, corporation officials interviewed Howard engineering seniors and made job offers to a number of them. It was a breakthrough: these were the first white recruiters on the campus of Howard or any other black college. This was followed later in 1949 with a platform appearance by major American business and industry representatives before the presidents of Negro land-grant colleges, arranged by the League. As Thomas recalled,

> I wrote a field report on [the Howard recruitment visit], mimeographed it and I think we sent it to about 200 corporation vice-presidents, describing the day's activity at Howard University and the fact that these kids had received job offers. Well, then, it was just like taking the lid off. . . . Pretty soon there were a dozen or so companies that had decided they'd go down to Howard to see what this was all about. And this was the beginning of the recruitment of Negroes on Negro college campuses. Today [1969] there are now some 3,000 companies and government agencies beating the bushes. They are now out-bidding each other.[10]

That was the beginning also of a program of career conferences on campuses of various black colleges. To each, the League brought top corporation executives who injected a welcome note of reality into the orientation of too-long insulated and isolated students and faculty.

"Thus," Lester Granger declared, "a whole new vista was opened for aspirant Negro youth: a new field of trained technical manpower was revealed to American business and industry. . . . None of this was accomplished by arm-chair theorizing or empty public fulminations. It required teamwork *plus* legwork—in many cases, patient plodding by scores of board, staff and committee members on rounds of visits to offices of corporations and labor unions. There were recorded 5,022 such visits to management offices and 1,066 to union headquarters."[11]

In the south alone, NUL representatives had visited more than 200 high schools and colleges to advise on guidance programs geared to current national conditions and career possibilities. The Vocational Opportunity Campaign was reaching nearly 300,000 black youths—students in colleges and high schools, out-of-school youngsters, veterans and adults—in meetings conducted by local Leagues or cooperating organizations. More than 600 guidance activities were carried on at sixty-five schools and colleges that reported their VOC programs in detail.

To open doors and counsel the NUL on its dealings with unions and others (such as schools and guidance counselors, for instance) regarding organized labor and its policies and practices, the League formed a Trade Union Advisory Council in mid-1949.

To cultivate the labor field, said professional fund-raising counselors and friendly union officials, someone from the labor movement itself should represent the League. Consequently, the agency hired first Robert Kinney and later Carleton Yeldell as secretary of its TUAC. The results were disappointing in each case because, as Granger saw it, they were given an impossible task: to establish the kind of relationships with organized labor that would change attitudes toward the League, with the end result of making organized labor partners in the NUL operation. One index of partnership was financial support. On both counts the NUL effort failed miserably. Attitudes toward the League remained fixed and contributions were not forthcoming.

As an example, the United Auto Workers in its Communist-dominated period under R. J. Thomas gave up to $10,000 annually to the Negro Labor Victory Committee. When Walter Reuther took over and swept out the Reds he dropped the Labor Victory Committee, of course, but no black organizations supplanted it as major beneficiaries. The UAW made small contributions to the NAACP and little or none at all to the League, on a national basis, in effect ignoring the sizable black membership in the Union.[12]

From the vast majority of unions, local as well as national, the NUL received little other than words of encouragement. Notable exceptions were the laundryworkers' adjunct of Amalgamated Clothing Workers, the International Ladies' Garment Workers and the United Mine Workers. These three gave more than all the rest of the labor movement combined. All three had large black memberships.

The situation with business was altogether different. The prime mover in developing greater business participation in NUL activities was Winthrop Rockefeller, son of John D. Rockefeller, Jr. "The [Rockefeller] family," John D. Rockefeller III, wrote NUL vice president Charles Poletti in 1938, "have always had a special interest in the problems of the Negro race. Because of this interest I have myself kept in touch through the Davison Fund with the activities of the League." [13]

He could have related a lengthy chronicle of Rockefeller concern, beginning with the Underground Railway and coming up to date in the Dunbar Apartments and Dunbar National Bank established as modern examples of enlightened philanthropy in New York, not to mention the General Education Board and other funds that had dispensed aid and support to black institutions over the years. Thus it was not considered extraordinary when Winthrop Rockefeller was elected to the board at the NUL's annual meeting in 1940.

Rockefeller aide Arthur Jones noted in a memorandum:

> The most fundamental contribution Mr. Winthrop could make at the present time [1940] would be to reserve any decision with regard to a contribution and instead to make himself thoroughly acquainted with the problems of the League with a view to determining whether it would be desirable to take such action as might lead the League to a reorganization of personnel, an orientation of program and development of a new financial plan.[14]

Before "Mr. Winthrop" could thoroughly acquaint himself with the League he was caught up in World War II. He returned after the war and resumed his place on the NUL board in 1946. Through his inspiration and active assistance the NUL formed its Commerce and Industry Advisory Council in the fall of 1949, composed of high-ranking officers of major corporations. The League wanted companies with big employment rosters and men with major influence on corporations that had such payrolls.

Winthrop Rockefeller thought the League could work more effectively if it had the organized assistance and cooperation of outstanding industries and businesses, through inclusion of their officers on the Advisory Council. He insured its launching by securing a grant from the Rockefeller Brothers Fund for its initial operation. And he invited friends to membership on the council. Among these were Bernard Gimbel and Henry Luce.

The Commerce and Industry Council became the nucleus of business support for the League. Through Commerce and Industry Council members the program of the League was put before business leaders at luncheon meetings and their cooperation solicited. Winthrop Rockefeller was an active participant in these and in fund-raising ventures. When he met with local managers of the ILGWU and asked for support of NUL, International President David Dubinsky presented him with a check and sighed, "When I became interested in union work and the welfare of the laboring man, I never dreamed that it would entail giving money to a Rockefeller." [15]

The usefulness of the Commerce and Industry Council was reflected in the NUL's 1950 record of activity with business. The panel of companies engaged in the Pilot Placement Project included such giants as GE, GM, Ford, DuPont, Standard Oil (New Jersey), RCA, Union Carbide, Gimbels, Macy's, Allied Stores, Adam Hat, Royal Typewriter, Doehler-Jarvis, United States Steel, International Harvester, Woolworth, Safeway Stores, A & P, Socony-Vacuum, Wright Aeronautical, NBC, CBS, Metropolitan Life, and Time, Inc.

In addition, some 200 national corporations were in constant touch with NUL's industrial relations department. The relationship was such, said Lester Granger, that, as an example, it was possible for the League to get action via the headquarters staff of GE, Western Electric, RCA, Curtiss-Wright, GM, General Cable and others on "discriminatory or otherwise unsatisfactory employment conditions in any and all of the company's plants throughout the country." [16]

This was a revolutionary change from seven or eight years before when blacks could not even get past the front gates of major American corporations.

34/Civil Rights

At the 1948 Democratic party convention southern delegates rebelled against a party platform that called for extending civil rights to black citizens. Leader of the Dixiecrat revolt was South Carolina's nineteenth-century museum-piece Senator J. Strom Thurmond, who fancied himself a reincarnated Wade Hampton. Wrapped in dudgeon, Thurmond was stopped and questioned by a reporter as he pranced from the convention floor: the Democratic party had perennially included a civil rights plank in its platform from 1932 onward. Why was Thurmond walking out, since "President Truman is only following the platform that Roosevelt advocated?"

"But Truman really means it," snarled the senator.[1]

There was considerable evidence that he really did. His record as a senator, supporting the CCC and NYA in the face of vindictive attempts to end these programs because of their "race-mixing" was one indication of his views. But still more clear-cut were his actions in issuing Executive Orders concerning civil rights. The first was his Order 9808, December 5, 1946, appointing a fifteen-man committee to investigate and recommend better protection of the civil rights of Americans. He took this action because of the repeated antiminority incidents immediately after the war in which homes were invaded, property was destroyed and a number of innocent lives were taken. "I wanted," said Truman, ". . . to see that the law was strengthened, if necessary, so as to offer adequate protection and fair treatment to all of our citizens." [2]

Truman's committee included Mrs. Sadie T. M. Alexander, NUL Board secretary and famed black lawyer from Philadelphia. Both the committee and Truman acted as if they meant business. The committee's report, *To Secure These Rights*, was presented to the President in October 1947 and recommended ten important actions, including creation of a permanent commission on civil rights, a civil rights division in the Justice Department and a joint Congressional committee on civil rights; setting up a permanent FEPC; protection of the right to vote and federal protection against lynching; home rule for the District of Columbia and voting rights for its residents. The committee spotlighted and condemned the shortcomings and bias in the operation of the United States Employment Service, police brutality, and on-the-job discrimination by both labor and management.

"The national government should assume leadership in our American civil rights program because there is much in the field of civil rights that it is squarely responsible for in its own direct dealings with millions of persons," said the report, citing the fact that the government was the largest single employer in the nation and that its employees dealt with millions of citizens daily. Thus it set a model for other employers. "The choice . . . between legislation and education as to the means of improving civil rights is an unnecessary one. In our opinion, both approaches to the goal are valid, and are, moreover, essential to each other."

Harry Truman placed these recommendations before Congress in his message on February 2, 1948. He also threw the weight of his office behind desegregation of government and public transportation facilities in the nation. The Republican-dominated Congress—which he called the "do-nothing, Eightieth Congress"—pigeonholed his civil rights package. So Truman took it to the Democratic convention and it was the basis for the civil rights plank in the party platform, the "loyalty-oath" move by Senator Hubert Humphrey and liberal Democrats, and the bolt of the Dixiecrats.

Truman was, in this "Fair Deal" effort, the first President to try to define the status of black Americans and their relationship to the federal government since Reconstruction. His was an attempt to bring the weight of the federal establishment to bear on behalf of Afro-Americans in a comprehensive fashion. That the attempt failed should not detract from the effort nor from Truman. In these principles a new national plateau of expectations was established. The implementation took considerably longer. Truman used his executive authority to issue other Executive Orders—one on discrimination in government, another concerning integration of the armed forces and a third on compliance by government contractors with regulations prohibiting discrimination.

In mid-1948 A. Philip Randolph had organized the League for Non-Violent Civil Disobedience Against Military Segregation to dramatize the bitterness of black Americans against the American Jim Crow armed forces. Within weeks President Truman issued an Executive Order abolishing discrimination in the nation's armed forces and naming a committee to study and recommend ways of implementing this order. Lester Granger was one of those appointed to the President's Committee on Equality of Treatment and Opportunity in the Armed Forces. Granger viewed it as a campaign device,[3] but the initial meeting with the President gave great promise. "I know you have a tough assignment, I'm behind you all the way," rasped Truman. "If I have to knock some heads together to get the action that you need, I'll knock heads together."[4]

The goal, so far as Granger and his fellow committee members were concerned, was complete integration in the nation's armed forces. Granger's burning dedication to this goal stemmed from personal experience as a young lieutenant in World War I where he observed and felt the sting of army racism. He had seen its dangerous effects in World War II and had warned of them in his first major address as executive of NUL:

. . . As long as our major arms of defense, maintained and controlled directly by the Federal Government, are allowed to operate [with biased] policies, what right have we to be surprised when their example is followed by employers and unions in private industry? . . .

One reason for the almost complete exclusion of their race from [civil] aviation transportation and industry is the fact that in the last World War, the United States army rigidly banned Negroes from any kind of aviation service, whether flying or ground. Thus commercial aviation naturally inherited the army's color bar. This is another example of how careless thinking develops into a mental stereotype and makes the readjustment of ideas on a more intelligent level almost impossible.

Moreover, Negroes suffered for a full decade after the World War from the kinds of attitudes and opinions developed among impressionable young white soldiers through their exposure to despicable racial policies. Young whites saw Negroes herded off in army camps and given the least desirable

living quarters; saw them provided with inferior equipment, or given none
at all; saw Negro college men reduced from fighting units and assigned to
labor battalions with ignorant, Negro-hating white corporals in charge, in
keeping with the best traditions of the plantation south. Negroes experienced all these things and saw their result; for it would have been impossible for 2,000,000 young whites to witness and share in so undemocratic a
procedure without readjusting their ideas of what was right and proper in
a democratic society.

. . . Army and navy service today is the greatest single conditioning program in the country; because our military oligarchy has the power to say,
within tremendous limits, what our boys of today are going to be like tomorrow; because that power is being used today with potentially vicious results to democratic thought in America. . . . Thus one step in expanding
economic opportunity for Negroes in America is to proceed immediately to
break down the employment barriers erected by the biggest employers of
them all, the United States army and navy.[5]

Granger later described the Truman committee's activities. The navy
came in to report, and thanks to Secretary Forrestal's 1945 determination,
its policies were in pretty good shape and it was moving to erase remaining pockets of bias. The air force came in and reported that it had been
separated from army control and as an independent branch it would accept the navy example and improve on it. The army came in and smugly
reported that it was satisfied with what it had and was not going to
change.[6]

The committee met regularly, did its work, sent in its reports and recommendations for integrating the military forces. According to Granger,
Harry Truman paid no attention to the committee, its reports, nor its
recommendations.

Nevertheless, in January 1950 Gordon Gray, secretary of the army,
called the committee together in Washington. Distinguished in appearance, Gray, the retired chancellor of the University of North Carolina,
told the group that he had two announcements. First, when he had met
with the committee the previous year he had committed himself to a position that the committee opposed—continued segregation in the army.
"I did so on the advice of my military adviser," said Gray. "I've since
then become convinced that I had bad advice. I've changed my mind."
The second announcement was that the army would integrate its training
schools first. "I realize I'm spelling an end to segregation in the army and
I for one am glad of it."

That was the key, Granger stated. The committee's recommendation
had been that in assigning men to and from army schools race be ignored. It was the pilot placement principle applied to the army. The

committee figured that if black graduates of army schools were assigned into army outfits the way would open up for the rest.

The committee chairman wrote to President Truman reporting on the group's successes and failures and pointing out that army integration would take years. With this in mind, he recommended that the committee be continued or another named to replace it in order to "watchdog" the operation. In response, the committee members received a "mimeographed" note from Truman accepting the report, saying he was aware of the good work of the group but felt it was now proper to let the army police itself. To Granger, this abrupt shutoff meant that the army would be allowed to coast at its own speed for decades. He was heartbroken that the black press ignored this Presidential inaction and continued to champion Truman.

The astuteness of Harry Truman as a practical politician, however, was never more evident than in his various moves to put civil rights on the national agenda.[7] Only strong support from the black community pulled him through in his narrow victory in the 1948 election. The increasing importance of the urban black voters was a factor now apparent to all, and from this strength grew consequences in terms of political representation and consideration for blacks.

Lester Granger's reaction to the civil rights package Harry Truman presented to Congress was negative. True, Granger was then ardently Republican, but moderate enthusiasm might have been expected for the first such legislative proposals in seventy years. Granger's reaction was based on an upbeat assessment of race relations possibilities in the south.

Truman's civil rights message, the League executive observed, had brought the political pot to a boil. "Many latent animosities and suspicions have been brought to the surface, and have already hampered constructive efforts in fields of social interest that should be far removed from politics." [8]

Ironically enough, this disturbance takes place at the very time when a number of southern developments have proven that leadership elements are ready and available for effective action to lessen the economic and cultural gaps between whites and Negroes of the South. Aggressive and imaginative steps must be taken at this time to capitalize upon this "state of flux" or the Urban League and similar movements will be so crippled as to require years of patient rebuilding before the losses suffered can be repaired. One problem only prevents our moving forward along these dual lines of action, bringing fresh ideas and methods into the vocational guidance field and stimulating the imagination of southern leadership with the vision of what *can* and *should* be done, rather than what it is feared *cannot* be done. That problem is financial.[9]

Granger asked the General Education Board for $24,000 for a demonstration project in vocational guidance in the south. The answer was no.

Granger was reflecting the reports of southern field director Nelson Jackson, who wrote "the climate here is torrid and agin [*sic*] Civil Rights programs. I have every reason to believe that it has temporarily slowed us down." [10] As an example, Jackson cited a letter from James G. Hanes of Hanes Hosiery Mills, "deploring what the politicians have done" and hoping that "the air can be cleared soon, so that we might be able to do something constructive again." Hanes was one of the employers in the south who had cooperated with the League in bringing black workers into production jobs. Jackson continued:

> My candid opinion is that the sooner this Civil Rights mess dies, the better we will all be. . . . I re-emphasize the approach of the Urban League is one which is continuous and at the "grass roots" level. The job of chronicling achievements will, in the long run, gain more converts, I believe, than an approach which ties our activities up to a controversial situation such as the Civil Rights issue. This week, the representatives of the Southern Democratic organizations are meeting in Atlanta to draw up a platform protesting the Civil Rights pronouncement. I still believe it is all a tempest in the tea pot and that it will soon boil dry. [11]

The pronouncement drawn up in Atlanta was a "Southern Manifesto" signed by more than 110 Dixie congressmen opposing Truman's civil rights legislation. As the "tea pot" of civil rights boiled up, the Urban League in the south was scalded by a segrationist surge. When the NAACP brilliantly scored success after success in winning federal court decisions to strike down white primaries, inferior public accommodations and education, the frustration and backlash of southern whites increased.

The changes in the status of blacks in the south in a short time were visible. Their political power had increased tremendously: Even in the deepest of the Deep South—Louisiana and Georgia—there were by 1952 dozens of black candidates for offices ranging all the way up to governor. And there had been great increases in numbers of registered Afro-American voters. The purchasing power of blacks had grown from just over $1 billion in 1939 to at least $3.5 billion by 1949. The forced-draft construction of schools for blacks had improved educational facilities and expanded educational and vocational training opportunities, with obvious implications for better career and employment possibilities. Large amounts were pouring into housing for blacks in the south—at long last. Health and welfare of blacks had become a matter of community concern, rather than just the crusade of black social workers, as industry came to the area.

Nelson Jackson brought all these points to the attention of the NUL board in late 1951, explaining that the southern field division was the only agency either qualified or equipped to serve in the field of health and welfare. In the south, he reminded the board, 63 percent of the nation's black population still lived; one fifth of the League's branches were there but only one tenth of the League's budget went to that area. The opportunities, he said, were great, if the League would but invest the money and manpower to move into the region with concentrated effort.[12]

Money and manpower, however, were the two things the agency had least of.

35/Money Problems

Not introspection but serious concern caused the NUL board of trustees in 1948 to secure a $15,000 grant from the Carnegie Corporation for a diagnostic look at the League. A company specializing in analysis of corporate organizations and functions was hired for the project. After several months of study in which all national staff members, many board members, and a number of local League executives were interviewed and operations were studied, the experts reported in 1949 on *The Structure and Operation of the National Urban League.*[1]

The major weaknesses of the agency, said the experts, were the lack of "integration and cohesion" between national and local Leagues and the shortage of staff and money to carry out programs. The money shortage appalled the investigators:

> At our visit to the Southern Field Office on December 8, pay checks for December 1 had not arrived, nor had there been any notice or explanation of the matter. In previous months there had been similar occurrences. One staff member was in Florida, had completed his assignment, but did not have the money to return home; he had to make two long distance telephone calls at his own expense before he received money to permit his return. Another worker was having to advance from her own money expenses for a League trip at a time when her salary check was a week overdue. Other members were at this same time endeavoring to borrow from the director, who was in no position to lend. While the staff continued with remarkable loyalty, nevertheless such situations cannot fail to tell on morale and efficiency.

There is a continuous problem respecting traveling allowances. They have no assurance that the "revolving" funds for this purpose will "revolve" —i.e., be reimbursed—and often plans are made which cannot be carried through. Last year they spent a great deal of time arranging an extended tour of a national and regional staff member—making speaking engagements, arranging for school assembly periods, arranging schedules for conferences with agencies and groups—only to have to call the whole matter off because of lack of money. The waste and confusion in such situations are obvious.[2]

What the experts failed to grasp was that the financial drought that caused such incidents was chronic and that most of their recommendations for greater effectiveness were academic as long as the agency was close to financial disaster.

So the solution offered by the specialists to what they saw as the number one problem—the relationship between national and local Leagues—was as ludicrous as Marie Antoinette's "let them eat cake" remedy for the bread riots in Paris. The management analysts recommended that the League set up five regional offices around the nation, each one of them with professional and clerical staff to function as scaled-down replicas of the NUL home office in New York. These regional staff members were to be competent in industrial relations, community services, public relations, organizing, fund-raising, and other traditional League functions. This recommendation—calling for a staff increase of at least ten—came at a time when the entire NUL staff numbered twenty-nine (including the office boy) who were suffering "voluntary" pay cuts and deferred paydays, to say nothing of program curtailment. The "Rich Report" (after its executors, Raymond Rich Associates) seemed aptly named to the staff and brought raucous hoots of derision from some.

There had been serious attempts to secure more money for the League. The most significant step in this direction had been in 1945 when NUL moved to professionalize its fund-raising. Elmo Roper, the well-known public opinion analyst, had interested himself in the League and agreed to head a "united Urban League Service Fund" which would raise money for the NUL and Urban League of Greater New York in New York City, and for NUL outside the city. A budget of $35,000 for the effort was approved by the boards of both the New York and the national Leagues, and professional fund-raisers were hired to carry out the campaign. A panel of important sponsors was signed up (including such nationally prominent persons as Governor Thomas E. Dewey, Henry Ford II, James Forrestal, William Green, the Reverend John LaFarge, S.J., Fiorello LaGuardia, Philip Murray, Donald M. Nelson, Eleanor Roosevelt, William Jay Schieffelin, Robert E. Sherwood, Dr. Channing H. Tobias), and labor, corporation, foundation, women's, New York and out-of-town committees were organized.

Scores of fund-raising events were held, tens of thousands of letters were sent and thousands of telephone calls were made. But for all the vigorous activity, the cash register rang with disappointing infrequency. "It was," said Roper, "very discouraging that this was regarded as an outcast, radical organization . . . it was not respectable." [3]

> The largest single number, if you divided up attitudes, was "Gee I think that's a wonderful thing you're doing, Elmo; you know in the business I'm in I just can't do that, but I think it's wonderful that you're doing it."
>
> I think the next largest number was, "It's wonderful you're doing it and if I can do anything to help, let me know."
>
> And the third largest group . . . was that we were disreputable troublemakers and if we had any good sense we wouldn't be besmirching our names by this close affiliation with Negroes. [4]

Though the financial results were poor, the organizational activity served an invaluable purpose in developing a coordinated fund-raising drive and extending the NUL's name and information about its program into new fields, especially in top echelons of business and industry. The NUL's income had reached an unprecedented $147,000 during 1945, though the greatest increase had come as earmarked grants ($12,000 from the American War-Community Service cooperative activity and $43,000 from specific foundation grants).

In 1946, its first full year of operation, the fund was headed again by Elmo Roper and was better organized and more efficiently run. But it yielded NUL a painfully small net $14,000 total. Though its income from all sources rose to over $186,000 NUL nevertheless racked up a substantial deficit. The staff director for the fund was replaced at the end of the year.

From the time it put its fund-raising in professional hands in 1945 the agency had recognized a special relationship with the Urban League of Greater New York. Both NUL and ULGNY existed in the same geographical area; the major multiplant national corporations headquartered in the city rightfully should have supported both the New York and National Urban Leagues, for obvious reasons. To eliminate duplication and overlap, a joint NUL–ULGNY fund-raising unit was established. A formula was drawn up under which NUL and ULGNY split all receipts by the ratio of 17 to 13. In addition to the dismal failure of the fund drives in the first years, later years were marked by incessant arguments over the formula and its inequities to one or the other organization and excursions by one or the other into unilateral fund-raising events prohibited under the agreement.

Henry R. Luce, editor-in-chief of Time, Inc., accepted chairmanship of the Urban League Service Fund in 1947 and with Lester Granger and Lloyd Garrison made flying visits to League cities to raise funds. Garrison, who had made a similar trip twenty years before with Hollingsworth Wood and E. K. Jones, found it sad that so little progress had been made in two decades. A conversation with Harvey Firestone stamped this impression in his mind as Firestone described how his rubber factories were about to put two black Pilot Placements from the local League on the production line (previously all blacks in the plants had been sweepers). Firestone considered this "an act of great boldness . . . and the outcome was awaited with trepidation." Everything went well and over the years blacks were hired in all kinds of jobs by Firestone.[5]

(Another measure of Firestone's courage and Akron, Ohio's, backwardness was shown in the report to the Akron League executive earlier that same year. A member of the League's Committee on Equal Job Opportunities, who was president of a local lumber company, stated flatly that the committee as organized was impotent in Akron. He pointed out that local businessmen felt that the effort to get Negroes into better jobs was subversive and inspired by Reds. The best way to kill this suspicion, he believed, was to get the rubber industry people and other industrial leaders involved in the League program.) [6]

Again the results of the fund-raising effort fell short. The basic reason, Granger believed, was that Henry Luce "simply has not been willing to throw himself into this campaign as he has in some others." [7] Nevertheless, Elmo Roper was convinced that the association of Luce (whom he had persuaded to succeed him as chairman) was valuable: "As far as gilt-edge names were concerned, this was quite a forward step from Elmo Roper to Harry Luce. And he had his circle of friends then and even if they were a little skeptical they would say 'Well, if Harry's for it, it can't be all bad and I'll go along.' " [8]

At the end of 1947 the financial pinch was considerable. The NUL had spent $21,000 more than its income of $168,000. Granger wrote southern field director Nelson C. Jackson:

> Your tight situation is only a reflection of an equally tight condition here. You ask, "why don't we get a chairman?" It is the same old story— getting a man big enough to be useful who is willing to take a public position in our field. . . . Garrison, Roper and Rockefeller are working now [March 3, 1948] trying to line up someone so that we can get going no later than next week. It is heartbreaking to have this same delay occur year after year simply because we can't find the lay leadership with sufficient conviction and enterprise to make things move.[9]

It was, Lloyd K. Garrison (NUL president, 1947–1952) remembered, a hand-to-mouth existence. There were financial crises, one after another, with too many payless paydays. From month to month the question was how the organization was going to survive. It was growing, nevertheless, and moving ahead, but the job of the executive, Garrison observed, had expanded to an almost impossible task. "Lester Granger ate his heart out doing all the things that had to be done at the executive level . . . helping set up new local Urban Leagues, dealing with personnel, and fund-raising problems of various other local Urban Leagues and arranging for annual conferences and responding to constant calls from industry and government for information and advice. And on top of all this he had to give some time to fund raising because he was by far the most impressive and eloquent spokesman for the League." [10] In an effort to relieve Granger, R. Maurice Moss, the effervescent executive of the Pittsburgh League, was brought in as associate executive director.

The next year, 1950, saw some changes. The staff director of the Urban League Service Fund was ousted and Frank C. Montero, the public relations director of the Urban League of Greater New York, who had been liaison person between that agency and the fund, moved into the vacated post. This cleared the air in at least one respect, for until this point the fund director had been receiving two and a half times the salary of the NUL executive and even the number two and three persons on the fund staff had been paid more than Granger. That heavy drain in salaries ended forthwith. Montero's pay was in line with League salaries.

This change gave a lift to staff morale. "For some crazy reason or other," said Granger "I have a feeling that [1950] is going to be a good year now that we've scraped off the 'goo' and 'gunk' of the UL Fund and gotten rid of the hustlers who have been fattening off us for the last several years." [11] Granger's hopes were not realized. Income in 1950 fell to $165,000 and expenses were held to $176,000, leaving obligations of $47,000 for the new decade.

Frank W. Abrams, board chairman of Standard Oil Co. (N.J.), had followed Henry R. Luce as chairman of the League's fund drive. "This was stepping up, as far as the corporate world is concerned, at a rather rapid rate from Roper to Luce and from Luce to Abrams . . . the association of those names, of those people, that were willing to take what risks there were, either of business or social opprobrium, helped," judged Elmo Roper. And Abrams was followed by Robert W. Dowling, head of the City Investing Company in New York. (Dowling was elected president [1952–1956] of the NUL when Lloyd K. Garrison stepped down in 1952.)

During this period Winthrop Rockefeller involved himself with the

League increasingly. He participated in fund-raising, helping bring corporate leaders out for luncheons and breakfasts at which Lester Granger and Julius Thomas could indoctrinate them.

Rockefeller's strong interest in the League was proved by his Christmastime 1953 gift to NUL of $124,000 worth of stock toward purchase of a permanent national headquarters building for the agency. The $350,-000 structure at 14 East 48th Street in New York was dedicated in June 1956, in memory of Rockefeller's mother, Abby Aldrich Rockefeller. (In reviewing accomplishments of the League from 1910 to 1960 NUL labeled this "perhaps the most important single accomplishment of this decade.") [12]

In spite of the participation of business and industrial leaders of the top echelon, the NUL's finances were less predictable than the weather. By 1954 the financial drought was so severe that staff cuts were unavoidable and all departments were grounded—no travel was to be undertaken unless it was paid for by the community visited.[13]

Weekly breakfasts at NUL board member (later New York League President) Sophia Jacobs's Manhattan apartment brought together the presidents and executive directors of the New York and national Leagues and the director of the Urban League Fund. The figures on income or rather, lack of it, were often so catastrophic that, like a body blow, a stomach spasm would force Granger to rush to the bathroom and throw up. Thanks to the persuasiveness and ingenuity of James Felt or Lloyd Garrison or Robert W. Dowling an emergency contribution or loan of a few thousand dollars would be extracted from a hastily impressed friend of the League expressly for one of the frequently overdue payrolls.[14] At the beginning of 1958 the executive director was functioning with the unhappy knowledge that in his national office his professional colleagues were owed $12,500 in back salaries, $1,852 in unreimbursed petty cash, and the clerical staff members had $2,445 in wages due.[15]

At the 1956 annual conference the executive secretaries had presented a resolution asking the national office of the League to upgrade its pay scale. The local Leagues were suffering from depressed salary schedules and were complaining that such low pay made it impossible to attract and keep good professional staff members. All of this related back to the national's pay scale, because local community chests took that as the acceptable standard.

Fund-raising was the crucial factor. Salaries remained low and payrolls were unpredictable. (By September of 1960 there were at least ten professional staff vacancies at various local Leagues, not to mention many junior and clerical posts.) [16]

It proved almost impossible to secure from others the consistent understanding and faithful support supplied by such standbys as Carnegie Corporation and the Rockefeller philanthropies. The philosophy of John D. Rockefeller, Jr., and the Rockefeller Brothers Fund was solid:

> In recognition of this [NUL and ULGNY] progress, support was raised to $12,500 for 1946 with the thought that every effort should be made to encourage expansion of their programs . . . to bring consistent and conservative effort to bear upon all fields of Negro advancement.[17]

It was with this in mind that the General Education Board had given $110,000 for the Community Relations Project and the Rockefeller Brothers Fund continued its support after that. The Rockefeller interests were backing integration which they defined as:

> Reduction of racial discrimination to the point where those Negroes who are competent to do so may participate freely in the life of the white community and its institutions, while the Negroes who choose to center their lives around Negro communities such as Harlem may do so without compulsion, economic or social, and receive the same standard of service in their local medical, educational, recreational, religious and social welfare institutions as the rest of the city.[18]

This was a forward position for 1946, and one that would have been sincerely embraced by many black spokesmen of that day. The League was one of the institutions that was clearly and consistently working toward such ends. Furthermore, leadership such as Lester Granger's in the forties was rare: he was a man of integrity who had standing in the black community.

The enlightened white man who wrote that race relations memo to John D. Rockefeller, Jr., in 1946 described the dilemma that faced Lester Granger:

> The whole Negro community suffers from a lack of leadership, white and colored. On the whole, Negro psychology at present discourages the development of conservative or practical leadership. Once a person becomes identified as a race leader, he becomes subjected to pressures which to a large degree nullify his usefulness as a constructive worker.[19]

The key question was, without sufficient support, how long could Granger and the League stave off the howling pressures that swept about them?

Perennially during Granger's incumbency there was the soap opera of NUL finances: Will the poor deserving agency cover its expenses this year? Will the plucky employees find a paycheck in their envelopes next month? Will Lester Granger move the big foundation (or company) to give that contribution? Will the fund find a dynamic chairman who can put the clamp on big givers? And also: Will NUL and the New York League be able to divide up the fund receipts without a fight?

The answers were definitely "who knows?" The results were wildly erratic: in 1948 NUL spent $209,000 and had an income of only $182,000, and an accumulated deficit of $14,000. In 1949 a 10 percent salary cut was imposed and outgo was pared back to $160,000; income jumped to $196,000, which, when accumulated debts were paid off, left a surplus of $9,000. One fact stood out: Despite huge fluctuations, Lester Granger's first decade of leadership had brought NUL from a $60,000 level of operations to a plateau three times that. The pity was that the needs were so much greater still.

36/Social Engineering

The winds of change in the fifties moved the NUL into vital new areas of need. They had brought the agency attention and assistance from new quarters and new attention from old quarters. These changes were evident in League efforts directed at sponsoring foster homes and adoptions; cracking the brewery industry; "cultivating" southern industry; emphasizing black role models; pointing youth toward science; mobilizing religious leaders behind equal opportunity; and establishing new public relations and fund-raising ventures.

The genesis and development of the Foster Home and Adoptive Services project illustrated the new sophistication of the League movement in organizing to meet a need on a national basis. This particular project came up at the 1953 NUL annual conference in the sessions of one of the councils of League professionals.[1]

The sessions concentrated on appraising trends and programs, comparing notes and techniques and, as in this example, in recommending a coordinated effort on a particular problem. In 1953 the Community Organization Council of NUL voted to concentrate on finding homes for black infants and children. In doing so, the council's humanitarian concerns overcame its philosophical position against establishing or encouraging Jim Crow operations. The policy position of the agency was that social agencies should serve all "clients" without regard for race. But in the case of black "parentless" children (the word "orphan" no longer adequately described the many black infants abandoned or relinquished to institutions), there was a specific and urgent need and it was being sidestepped by the agencies in the field. The League concluded, therefore, that, as in its earliest days, it should act to move the appropriate organizations to shoulder their share of the responsibilities.

The situation was this: in the black ghettoes of the major cities the birth rate among Afro-Americans had climbed and was higher than that of whites. A sizable percentage of the births was illegitimate. Because of depressed economic conditions—lack of jobs, inadequate housing, undependable income, and meretricious welfare regulations, among others—many of these children were not in wholesome, stable family situations. The adoption and child care agencies were geared to place and serve white infants and parents and shunned the black babies. The problem of caring for these tiny black citizens was acute and nearing the disaster stage.

The reluctance of the adoption agencies to move into this huge and growing area of need could be understood but not condoned. Most of them had lily-white boards, staff and clients and limited budgets and facilities. With white babies, they were in a "sellers' market," for there were not enough to fill the demand from adoptive parents—in fact, a "white market" in babies developed to meet the demand. With black babies the situation was just the opposite. There were far too many babies for the available adoptive homes. Therefore, reasoned the agencies, to go into this field and accept black infants would mean turning adoptive agencies into child care agencies, since, they thought, only a fraction of the infants would be adopted.

With Nelson Jackson as coordinator (he was then director of community services of NUL), the League moved to open and expand foster home and adoption services for black children. Twenty-three Leagues were in at the outset and their major goal was to demonstrate how the communities could care for these neglected black babies.

Nelson Jackson worked at the national level to backstop the local Leagues with information and reports to help them develop local programs, and he worked with the national headquarters of child care agencies, bringing to their attention the need and the approaches being explored by the local Leagues. The locals went at the basic problem in a variety of ways.

Kansas City landed a foundation grant to underwrite a two-year study of adoption needs and methods best suited to that community.

Seattle organized a citizens' committee on foster homes and adoption and through it sensitized the city to the needs. The League succeeded in placing a black social worker—its first—on the staff of the key children's home in the area. Thus a qualified professional was assigned to this work.

Some Leagues, such as those in Essex County, New Jersey, and Pittsburgh, held institutes and seminars, bringing together all of the interested civic, religious, fraternal and social agencies in their regions to educate them to the facts and discuss ways and means of tackling the situation.

In New York, the local League rounded up all the major adoption agencies in the metropolitan area in a project called "Adopt-A-Child." Backed with a $49,000 foundation grant, an organization with full-time director and secretary was established and a distinguished board of directors enlisted, representing all faiths, boroughs and major adoption agencies. The project went after the media and got extraordinary cooperation from the black and Spanish press, radio and TV, major daily newspapers and *Ebony, Jet, Our World,* and *Life* magazines. This activity resulted, in short term, in bringing together more than fifty organizations (some 250 persons) for community conferences on the problems and methods. The publicity stimulated 240 local families to apply, and more than 200 from outside New York inquired and were referred to agencies in their own states.

The impact of the entire project was not to be judged locally or for the short term. Over the years that followed, this impetus by the League literally revolutionized thinking and action in the adoption-foster homes field. Some of the nation's oldest and most conservative agencies, notoriously all white, overturned their outmoded policies and replaced exclusivity with humanity. They brought blacks onto staffs and boards and made the major needs—those of Afro-American children—the needs that they undertook to meet. They also moved strongly into foster home care as a promising alternative to the slow and limited potential of adoption to get the infants out of institutions into homes. This meant commitment to the principle that homes, though temporary, were preferable to long years in an institution before adoption—if, indeed, adoption resulted— and this was a revolutionary concept in the child welfare field.[2]

The League introduced a "revolutionary concept" into another field in 1951. The concept was that Afro-Americans should be at work in the brewery industry. It was revolutionary, apparently, to management and the unions in that industry, for during the eighteen years since the repeal of Prohibition this $5,000,000 industry of upwards of 80,000 workers had a total of 500 blacks in it. And only a handful of those (less than twenty-five) were in sales or promotion for the black market. The facts were indisputable, for NUL's assistant research director J. Harvey Kerns had documented them in a painstaking study that had taken him to ninety-nine breweries and twenty-four cities in six major producing states and had included interviews with brewery officials, the United States Breweries Foundation and the International Union of the United Brewery Workers, CIO.[3]

In 1933 the NUL had approached the brewery industry as it opened up after repeal. But the lily-white traditions, the contention by the brewers that skilled workers were mandatory and the hard-pressed, understaffed League's preoccupation with vast, rapid changes in the federal government and relief, caused NUL to concentrate on more urgent matters until this detailed inspection nearly two decades later.

Kerns's report painted "a grim picture generally," said Lester Granger. But the brewery industry acted quickly and before the report was off the press brewers in Milwaukee and New York had taken steps to hire black production workers. The Breweries Foundation, sensitive to the public relations aspects of the study, counseled member companies to act positively. And the executive board of the Brewery Workers Union reviewed the NUL survey and stated that it was "opposed to discrimination in employment based on race. . . . We recognize that the time has come to give careful consideration to the situation in light of developments during the past several years. The International Union will give guidance and assistance to our local unions in finding solutions." [4]

Compared with conditions and attitudes a few months earlier, therefore, Kerns and NUL had wrought a small revolution. The black clerical workers, economists and consultants as well as production workers who were added to brewery payrolls were proof of it.

Research during these Granger years was particularly effective in laying the foundation for new Leagues. There had been thirty-seven locals in 1940. After the Service Councils, the American War-Community Services, the Community Relations Project and the community surveys following that concentrated effort, Dr. Banner could point to a roster of fifty-six cities studied during the two decades. New Leagues had developed in eight of them.[5] In the remainder, councils of social agencies or similar groups were following the "Banner bibles" to improve their communities. Expansion had dried up in the Depression years, but the extraordinary number of Leagues formed after 1940 owed much to solid grounding based on NUL research.

Pinpoint research to open up "closed" industries or job situations was a powerful NUL tool, limited only by money and manpower. As in the brewery industry, NUL surveys of the music industry and the airlines resulted in incontrovertible proof of discrimination. Faced with the evidence, employers opened their doors and changed their hiring policies to include some blacks.

Another case, and a wearying one, was the assault on Jim Crow in the federal General Services Administration public building service. From 1933 to 1960, GSA had built literally hundreds of millions of dollars worth of federal buildings in Washington, D.C., without letting one pair of black hands touch any of the electrical wiring installed in them. What made it even more outrageous was the fact that during that time Washington was a city whose black population doubled from 27.1 percent to 53.9 percent of the total.

Using New Deal Secretary of the Interior Harold Ickes's rule of thumb that the absence of black workers in such circumstances was *ipso facto* evidence of discrimination should have been sufficient. But with union complications and petttifogging bureaucratic buck-passing it required literally years of conferences, interviews, checking of records, screening of personnel and examination of contracts, and finally, an appeal to the President's Committee on Government Contract Compliance. There was a skein of collusion between the local union, which excluded blacks, the contractors and the General Services Administration. GSA's compliance division was all too compliant with contractors and unions. White-run and white-oriented, GSA was insensitive at best to the situation of black electrical workers. It compared contractors' statements with applicants' qualifications and ruled "no discrimination" when black electricians were invariably turned down.[6]

The League stepped in, nailed down the "acceptable" specifications, then went out and screened, tested and interviewed dozens of men until it found the pilot for this placement. He had everything but angel's wings: he was a thirty-four-year-old Korean war veteran, father of four, skilled, experienced and a union member. He was hired, and so cracked the race barrier in what the League called a "small but immensely significant miracle—for hundreds upon hundreds of skilled Negro workers still materialize behind this man's lead." [7]

In 1957 when the Soviets lofted Sputnik I and jolted America out of its complacency it also moved the League to call again for full use of American manpower. The statement had a ring reminiscent of 1941, when blacks were excluded from defense industries, but the problem now had another dimension. In 1941 the big push was to get blacks on payrolls— any payrolls. In 1957 the horizon had lifted, and the goal was to educate, guide and place highly trained Afro-Americans in top positions in business, industry and government.

With this in mind, and the clear evidence that black youths had shied away from science and engineering because they saw few if any career opportunities there, NUL deliberately set out to reverse that situation. Lester Granger dreamed up the idea for "Tomorrow's Scientists and Technicians," candidly described as an "attack on the twin problems of frustration and unrealistic training" inflicted on black youths.

Labeled TST for short, the program was launched with the school year in September 1958. It sought out talented youngsters and by guiding, inspiring and demonstrating the potentialities to them, encouraged more black youths to complete their training and education at the highest levels achievable, aiming at the best careers they could anticipate—especially in technical and scientific fields. The goal was to reach 500,000 boys and girls in the junior and senior high schools and 50,000 black college students. A national advisory committee of noted scientists and technicians, both whites and blacks, was enlisted to help guide the program. In more than twenty-six cities the TST program stimulated schools to organize career clubs with the help of 400 blacks who had made good in science and technology. Some forty career clubs, enrolling more than 2,000 youngsters from the seventh grade up, were in operation by 1960.

TST operated in a logical, straightforward way. Teachers, ministers and others who worked with youth referred exceptionally talented youngsters to special committees assembled by local Leagues. These students were brought together in the career clubs. They went on field trips to plants, factories, offices, colleges and cultural centers, to observe the advantages of education. The youngsters were in constant contact with well-educated people who took a sincere interest in them, giving incentive for study. The local TST committees also searched out scholarship and other financial help for worthy youngsters. Typical career club programs included parent and pupil conferences, where fathers and mothers learned about career potentials in order to enlist their enthusiasm in propelling their offspring into better careers.

The NUL vocational guidance team did its part in developing filmstrips, printed materials and a widely heralded half-hour youth incentives film called "A Morning for Jimmy." This was shown on network television to an audience of more than four million. It was a searching documentary about a black boy who faced educational and growing-up problems and met them courageously. The film was in the tradition of the two pioneer youth incentive publications sponsored by the League back in 1950 and 1951. These were comic books entitled *Negro Heroes* and in them the lives of famous black men and women were given the irresistible cartoon-strip treatment. Nearly 500,000 copies of each of these were produced and distributed in cooperation with *Parents Magazine*. The second one was underwritten by Delta Sigma Theta sorority.

New bonds were fashioned between the League and major black fraternal organizations during the fifties. The Prince Hall Masons were particularly active. Through their Supreme Council they underwrote and
helped sponsor demonstration vocational guidance institutes in Birmingham, Baltimore, St. Louis and Pittsburgh. The state Grand Lodge
in Oklahoma, together with the black Greenwood Chamber of Commerce, actually helped organize and finance the brand-new Tulsa Urban
League.

Churchmen had played an important role in early League history,
from the Reverends William H. Brooks, Samuel H. Bishop, John Haynes
Holmes, and A. Clayton Powell, Sr., onward, but it was not until 1956
that NUL institutionalized the church-League relationship. It did this at
the initiative of Dr. John Paul Jones, long-time board member and early
head of the League's industrial relations committee. Jones made headlines in the spring of 1956 when he exchanged congregations in Manhattan and Brooklyn. Buses carried parishioners from white to black
churches and vice versa, and the novelty and impact of the project received wide media coverage in New York.

Later that same year Jones, who had rotated off the NUL board, was
put on part-time retainer, and Mrs. Edward W. Macy, former president
of the National Board of the YWCA, was engaged to head a new NUL
"Church and Race Relations" project. Its purpose was to consult with
church groups, especially committees of Urban Leaguers and local
church leaders. These committees would then work out programs with
three general elements: (1) exchange of congregations; (2) a forum for presentation of League ideas, with the goal of making Urban League work a
recipient of church support; and (3) wider use of League personnel in
church programs.[8]

The project, Religious Resources, formally organized a committee and
received an infusion of additional vigor in 1959 when a women's committee was developed to extend it. These volunteers used correspondence,
workshops and institutes in their communities to help improve the race
relations climate, with League leadership giving direction.

Through its southern field division, NUL attempted to do something
about the lag in industrial personnel practices in the south, which were
about twenty years behind the rest of the nation. It initiated in 1953 a
Southern Industry Project, with grants from the Philip Murray Memorial
Foundation, the Marshall Field Foundation and the Fund for the Republic. Nelson C. Jackson, Harry Alston and Mahlon T. Puryear garnered the cooperation of twenty-five of the nation's largest companies
with plants in the south. And they also brought into the project the international and local unions concerned.

The project's purpose was to help management and labor leadership increase the use of black manpower in the expanding industries of the region. The survey that marked its initial phase showed that in 265 typical (for the south) plants, there were 261,000 workers. Of these, 10 percent were Afro-Americans, though blacks constituted fully 25 percent of the work force of the region. (These plants were more advanced than most, for across the south only 5 percent of industrial workers were black.) As could have been predicted, 85 percent of the black workers in the surveyed plants were at the bottom of the heap, in unskilled and low-paying, semiskilled jobs.[9]

The NUL attacked this sorry situation circuitously as well as frontally. Julius Thomas and his Commerce and Industry Council under the chairmanship of Ralph L. Mason, employee relations manager of Standard Oil Company, New Jersey, called together the fifteen largest employers of manpower in industry. These giant, multiplant corporations each had sizable operations in the south and plans for further expansion there. The first meeting was in 1953 and the featured presentations were the true success stories of International Harvester, Radio Corporation of America, General Cable Corporation and others that had integrated their southern work forces without difficulty. The message to America's leading corporations was that the work situation has its own sociology—it does *not* have to reflect the social structure and mores of the community.

The Commerce and Industry Council meetings grew bigger and involved more important corporations each year. By 1958 NUL had established strong working relationships with fifty multiplant corporations who employed more than 4,000,000 workers. The local Leagues extended this network to scores more of the nation's top corporations. With this growth there was corresponding spread of the equal opportunity gospel. But it had a lot of distance to cover. As an instance, in Atlanta, the most enlightened part of the south, one of the nation's more enlightened companies, Southern Bell Telephone and Telegraph, was adamantly opposed as late as April 1961 to opening job categories to blacks and initiating other equal opportunity policies.

Mahlon T. Puryear, then NUL's southern field director, called on Southern Bell's president, B. S. Gilmer, and personnel director, W. A. Thompson, about "merit employment." The personnel director abruptly stopped the interview until Puryear and his associates identified themselves, giving their birthplaces, background and education to make sure they were "southern" blacks. Following Puryear's presentation, Messrs. Gilmer and Thompson blandly stated why Southern Bell would not initiate any program to eliminate discrimination in employment practices. The reasons were classics: the company already employed lots of blacks who had been on the payroll long years; community custom could not be breached; worker relationships posed a serious problem and the company had no responsibility to change social customs; it did have a responsibility, however, to the wishes and rights of the employees already working for it. The company was not intransigent, however. As proof that it was willing "to change with the time," it reported, "we have desegregated our luncheon facilities in Louisville, Ky." [10]

But the south was on the move, if cautiously. Five months later Clarence Coleman, assistant director of NUL's southern field division, was in Mr. Thompson's office again, at Thompson's request. Southern Bell had decided to upgrade some of its black employees and wanted to report this to Coleman and his associates (a Citizens' Committee on Employment and Economic Opportunity). Most of its black employees were "house service workers" (i.e., janitors) or unskilled laborers. Two blacks, each with ten years' service, had been promoted—hence this conference: one was moved from janitor to "Equipment Maintenance Service Man," (corporate gobbledygook for house mechanic); the other was upped from laborer to auto mechanic.

Coleman and the employment committee congratulated Southern Bell on this bold step. It was then suggested, among other things, that there were "forces and agencies at work in the community who are concerned with equal employment opportunities which would likely be communicating with the company regarding the employment situation, but would utilize other methods for accomplishing this objective." The committee offered cooperation of the national and local Leagues for recruitment and screening of job candidates.[11]

During the Granger years the way in which the agency communicated with the "outside world" was institutionalized. In 1941, the pages of *Opportunity*, occasional statements and public appearances by the executive and industrial secretaries and the annual report were the major channels to project the League program and accomplishments. By the end of the two decades of Granger's leadership a department of public relations, established in 1946 with Guichard Parris as director, had developed into an effective communications instrument. League publications, press releases, speech reprints, annual conference arrangements and publicity and major public relations events cleared through it. In cooperation with the fund-raising staff, the public relations department helped develop several attention-getting projects during this period.

The Fund in 1948 and 1949 conducted the first fund-raising art exhibitions and sales in the country. Featured were oils donated by amateurs ranging from Joe Louis and Pancho Gonzalez to (then) General Dwight D. Eisenhower. The events were highly successful and were followed later (1959) by a prestigious exhibition of the private collections of the Rockefeller brothers, David, John D., III, Nelson and Winthrop, also for the benefit of the League.

But the most effective public relations events of this period were the "Two Friends" and the "Equal Opportunity Day" awards.

The Two Friends award was established in 1945 to signalize outstanding achievement by an interracial team for the benefit of the American community. It began as a commemoration of the friendship and teamwork of E. K. Jones and L. Hollingsworth Wood, who had worked together for more than three decades as leaders of NUL. A medal was presented to them at a League banquet.

The medal with the profiles of the first recipients—Jones and Wood—was afterward given to a white and a black whose joint achievement was voted by the NUL board as worthy of signal honor. The second recipients were H. B. Snyder, editor of the Gary *Post-Tribune,* and H. Theo Tatum, principal of Gary's Roosevelt School, for their joint action in creating harmony out of chaos in their city during the critical days of 1944–1945. The next honorees were the Reverend James H. Robinson of the Presbyterian Church of the Master, and Harry G. Oppenheimer, New York textile executive, for their leadership in reorganizing Sydenham Hospital as the first interracial voluntary hospital in the nation.

In 1948 the Two Friends award went to Jackie Robinson and Branch Rickey of the Brooklyn Dodgers, for integrating major league baseball. Dwight R. G. Palmer, president of General Cable Corporation, and John H. Sengstacke, publisher of the Chicago *Defender,* both NUL trustees, received the award in 1950 for their teamwork on the President's Committee on Equality of Treatment and Opportunity in the Armed Forces. The awards were presented in other years to New York's Mayor Robert F. Wagner and Welfare Commissioner James Dumpson; Chicago UL president Dr. Nathaniel O. Calloway and NUL trustee H. B. Law; and basketball stars Jack Twyman and Maurice Stokes of the Cincinnati Royals.

In 1956 the first Equal Opportunity Day was celebrated on the anniversary of Lincoln's Gettysburg Address, November 19. A dinner was held in New York. The President, governors and mayors of major cities were asked to issue proclamations observing the significance of the day. Twenty-two governors and 100 mayors did so. Labor Secretary James P. Mitchell attended and read a message from President Eisenhower.

Equal Opportunity Day caught on. In 1957, the dinner honored Labor Secretary Mitchell and Amalgamated Clothing Workers president Jacob S. Potofsky. Dinner chairman was New York Governor Nelson A. Rockefeller, and President Eisenhower issued a formal statement on the eve of the observance, calling on Americans to "join in the effort to abolish all artificial discriminations. . . ." Meanwhile, local Leagues around the country held similar observances and fund-raising dinners in their cities. The event became a central rallying point and the major fund-raising event for the year.

In 1958 the honorees were Benjamin F. Fairless, chairman of the American Steel Institute and former president of the United States Steel Corporation, and David J. McDonald, United Steelworkers president. George Meany, AFL–CIO president, and Lee H. Bristol, chairman of Bristol-Myers Company, received awards in 1959 for "their contributions toward the Urban League's goal of equal opportunity." Coverage of the event by the three major TV networks signaled that the EOD dinner had hit the "big time."

The capstone public relations achievement of the Granger years was the preparation and distribution of special newspaper supplements about the agency and race relations. Thanks to a special grant from the Taconic Foundation for the specific purpose, the League was enabled to prepare a tabloid-sized illustrated supplement entitled "America, His Hope, His Future . . ." for the New York Sunday *Times* in January 1960. It featured articles by Attorney General William Rogers, anthropologist Margaret Mead, Congressman Chester Bowles, historian John Hope Franklin, reporter Carl T. Rowan and others.

The second supplement, headlined "A Family with a Future," examined the strengths and needs of black families and the functions of the Urban League network in supporting and helping. This feature supplement was distributed across the country by some forty black newspapers in April to commemorate the League's Founders Day. In this, said NUL, it was speaking to the black community as a friend and a brother, as it so often had through the pages of the black press. Both supplements, the agency found, "broadened the contact still further among thoughtful men and women of all races as to what America is . . . what Americans are." [12]

37/Under Attack

Black Americans recall with clarity where they were and what they were doing on May 17, 1954, when they first heard the news of the Supreme Court's decision striking down the "separate but equal" doctrine of 1896.

Scowling segregationists called it "Black Monday," and Afro-Americans, all but dancing in the street, jubilantly agreed. It was a landmark victory of a black plaintiff represented by a black lawyer appealing for justice in a court of nine white men according to laws written by whites. The unanimous decision left no doubt for segregationists as to the future of "separate but equal" and/or challenges to the decision. That the decision was unequivocal was the greatest boost to Afro-American morale in generations and a signal visible throughout the land that justice was possible in these United States. Faith in the basic concepts of democracy and the workings of the democratic process took on new life that day.

In the narrowest sense, the Supreme Court ruled only that "separate educational facilities are inherently unequal." But so doing, it knocked the legs from under the feverish school building program southern states had indulged in during the early fifties in their effort to prevent or forestall a drastic decision such as this.

NUL staff and board members saw the decision as epochal. At the League annual conference in September 1954, a lengthy statement was prepared by a special committee purposely appointed to "reaffirm" League purpose "in the light of present day developments." [1]

The Supreme Court's decision went far in removing the last vestige of legal sanction for segregation. Therefore, NUL "refuses to recognize segregation as a lawful practice anywhere, and pledges its determination to remove the blight and stain of segregation from our national life."

> The truth of the . . . decision is not a new truth. Segregation has not suddenly become wrong. It has always been wrong. The wrong has been suffered by minorities and inflicted by the majority. Both minority and majority have been conditioned to a pattern that should never have been, and which must be eradicated. [2]

The League called for immediate public school integration, said it recognized the magnitude of problems, but could not tolerate evasion of this fundamental issue. It showed concern for teachers, calling for use of instructors without regard to race. Furthermore,

> We ask that the nation bear in mind that work and homes are key factors in the integration of minorities. If the ghetto pattern of segregation in housing can be enforced, school integration may be defeated. If discrimination in employment continues, minorities can be prevented from entering into the cultural life on the basis of education, character and refinement. . . . Integration in education cannot proceed unrelated to integration in housing and employment and the national life as a whole. [3]

The court gave the south a year to present plans for compliance with the decision. Southern leaders vied with rednecks in shouting "Never!" and "Massive resistance!" The pillars of southern society, those who had always abided by the law and clucked nervously about lynching, left the public arena to the demagogues and the rabble rousers.

The one man in the nation whose immense prestige could have helped bring Americans together at this time of contention was intellectually and emotionally unreachable on this subject. Dwight David Eisenhower, thirty-fourth President of the United States, was a product of a segregated society and the training and experience instilled by a segregated United States army. He had appointed Governor Earl Warren chief justice of the United States Supreme Court as a political payoff and the 1954 action of the Court was one of its liberal decisions that made Eisenhower wonder if Warren's appointment had been one of his greatest mistakes. Temperamentally and philosophically opposed to a strong presidency, filled with the conviction that laws could not change human nature, that segregation was a local issue to be decided "in the hearts of men," Eisenhower resolutely refused to take any official stand on the court decision or on segregation. His personal friendship with one of the white men who portrayed the black buffoons "Amos 'n Andy" was well known, however. And wading through the labyrinth of Eisenhower press conference syntax, the south rejoiced to learn that the President could foresee no circumstances that would prompt him to send federal troops into that region.

Local level, "hands-off policy," not laws but human hearts, no federal troops—the Eisenhower doctrine added up to an encouragement of intransigence. In this, as in his tolerance of attacks on such men as General George C. Marshall by Senator Joseph McCarthy, Eisenhower encouraged the forces of repression, vigilantism and character assassination.

In the rest of the country the quiet, God-fearing, well-meaning, law-abiding white people, the mainstays of status quo and racial superiority, shook their heads about the south and did nothing about de facto segregation in their local schools. In the south, whites shook their fists and did nothing about de jure segregated schools. The Supreme Court had ruled that segregation was outlawed and blacks had rejoiced. But as the days stretched into years, rejection and resistance by whites revealed the racist basis of white American society in a raw, unconcealed way no longer excusable as backed by the law of the land. And as the Supreme Court had stripped white adherence to segregation of the last vestiges of legality, bone-deep disillusion set in among millions of black Americans. Deep-seated distrust of whites spread as blacks were forced to pry their rights to equal education out of recalcitrant school boards almost on a school-by-school basis. The NAACP and liberal whites who had counseled blacks to rely on gradualism and the power of law suffered a staggering blow to their credibility from which many never fully recovered.

Throughout the nation the liberals were on the defensive and the chill of the McCarthy witch hunts blighted promising social developments and shriveled existing ones. The combination of backlash resistance to the Supreme Court's desegregation decision and the McCarthy-reactionary offensive against humanitarian elements of American life struck the Urban Leagues, particularly in the south.

A concerted drive to knock out the National Urban League was launched at this time. Along with the White Citizens Councils, the Ku Klux Klan and other race-hate agencies such as the Columbians leaped into action.[4]

In the past, the KKK had mobilized the rednecks and welded them into a despicable force of brutality, sadism and every degree of intimidation from murder to economic reprisal. The "best people" in the south had in more recent years turned away from this uncouth, besmirched and bloody organization.

The White Citizens Councils, however, were a serious threat because they organized from the top instead of from the bottom. They brought into their ranks the respectable elements of the community, and mobilized the business, industrial, religious and government leaders with the good wishes, if not the active leadership, of the highest officials of the various southern states, up to and including the governors. In Mississippi, the councils were supported with annual appropriations of tens of thousands of dollars of state funds for several years.

By organizing the leadership of the community the Citizens Councils effectively paralyzed resistance and silenced opposition from moderate and substantial white elements, giving the field to the reactionaries and haters. And since the members of the councils were the financial and social leaders of southern communities, their opposition could break an agency dependent on white public support for its on-going budget. The local Urban Leagues in the south were such agencies. They depended on their Community Chests for their income and were prohibited from independent fund-raising. Thus, Urban Leagues could be strangled by the cutting off of their Community Chest support. That pressure point was the target of the racists' attacks.

In a leaflet entitled *The South Under Siege* (which should have been called "The Urban League Under Siege") NUL cited the Little Rock case as typical.[5] After Governor Orville Faubus defied the United States Supreme Court and was forced by President Eisenhower's action to open Little Rock's high school to blacks, Faubus's alliance with hate groups gave them tremendous strength and prestige, completely changing race relations in the city.

Moderates who at first stood fast for law and order are now [1958] silenced; some are in public retreat from the mob. Business men who only
yesterday were working wholeheartedly to advance the Urban League's employment program are now being told to fire their Negro workers or face
economic boycott.

Before violence erupted at Little Rock Central High School, the Arkansas
AFL–CIO Council publicly pledged support to the elected school board's
program of gradual integration. But in the hour of crisis, when community
church, and civic leaders called for a day of prayer, labor was silent. Union
members began joining the white citizen's council and candidates for labor
offices vied with each other in bigotry. . . .

Two months later, just before the November elections, came the Community Chest drive for local health and social welfare needs. Renewing its attacks on the League, the [White Citizen's] council so intimidated the
Chest's volunteer workers that the success of the drive was imperiled and
the pressure on the member organizations became intolerable. . . . To ease
the situation the Little Rock Urban League decided to withdraw [from the
Chest] voluntarily. To have acted otherwise, the local Board believed,
would have endangered not only the Chest's drive for local health and social welfare needs, but also the League's future sources of independent support. . . . The segregationists continued their pressure on the League, and
for the first time its supporters began sending their contributions anony-
mously.[6]

Spearheading the attack on the Leagues was an organization styling itself the National Citizens Protective Association, with headquarters in St.
Louis. It carried on, through its publication *White Sentinel,* a continuous
campign of hate against the League and individual board and staff members.[7]

By 1955 the Citizens Protective Association had linked with other
hatemongers in a number of other southern cities. Richmond, Jacksonville, Little Rock, New Orleans and Washington were cities where the attacks were vigorous. Chain telephone call campaigns demanded boycott
of the Community Chest unless the League was kicked out. Lester Granger reported on the situation to the officers and directors of the National
Newspaper Publishers Association,[8] indicating that the reaction chosen
by Leagues and Community Chests was dignified public silence. Meanwhile, the New Orleans Chest estimated that it lost several thousand dollars in contributions in the 1955 campaign as a result of this smear attack.

In the hate literature of 1956 the charges against the League had
grown to twenty-one items. They included Communistic activity, being a
tool of the bosses and an unprincipled agitator for black rights, union-
busting, illegal use of funds in political activity and serving as a channel

for money to support the NAACP. This broad-brush smear technique also tarred unions, industrial companies that cooperated with the League in hiring blacks and social agencies that hired or served blacks.

The campaign spread as far north as Baltimore and even Boston. By July of 1956, the racists could gloat over a major success: The New Orleans United Fund (which raised money for the Community Chest) announced that after that year, "Contributors to the United Fund are assured that none of the money raised will go to the Urban League." This success was featured news in a widely distributed leaflet that also headlined: "COMMUNITY CHESTS SUPPORT RACE-MIXING: Gives [sic] Urban League over $2,000,000 a year," which repeated the smears and focused on the dependence of local Leagues on the Community Chest in their cities. Typical was the statement:

> The Urban League is a political, race-mixing pressure group. Not one cent from the charity funds collected by the Community Chests and United Funds should be used to promote race-mixing and mongrelization. Notify your local Chest or the plant at which you work that you will not give any more money as long as it supports the Urban League.[9]

In a memo to local executives at the end of 1956, Granger predicted that the attacks would be renewed before the Community Chest campaigns in 1957 and that they would spread. Some executives, he noted, had not even discussed the *White Sentinel* literature with their own boards. In some cities executives and board members had not gone over the situation with Community Chest leaders. He urged that they do so immediately.[10]

Another somber development was cited by Granger in this memo. It was labeled the "Big Four Project" and referred to an effort directed from a small California town. It was aimed at revoking the tax-exempt status of the League, the American Jewish Committee, the Anti-Defamation League and the NAACP. Granger alerted local executives to the sobering fact that the Kansas City League had suddenly received notice that its tax-exempt status was under review. It had been called upon to produce records, statements and documents concerning the amount of "legislative" activity it had undertaken over the years.[11]

The *White Sentinel* worked to institute boycotts against companies that supported the NUL. Years before, an official of Philip Morris, the cigarette company, had presented a contribution check to Lester Granger. "Johnny," Philip Morris's advertising symbol, had been photographed with Granger and the cigarette company official at the presentation. The *White Sentinel* found this photo in one of the black newspapers, republished it and demanded a boycott of Philip Morris cigarettes. The power of the racist rag was apparent when the public relations director of the company reported to Granger that Philip Morris had lost 35 percent of its sales in Alabama and 45 percent in Mississippi. The company continued to support the League, nevertheless, and the public relations director was vehement: "We are not going to let a bunch of nitpickers tell us who to give our money to." [12]

This kind of calumny and corroding assault at both national and local levels had, inevitably, a diminishing, contracting and cautionary effect on the League, its officers, board members and programs. Persons who in other times would not have hesitated to associate themselves with the agency now thought twice about board membership. Activities that normally would have been feasible now required doubly close examination before launching—first to determine whether their cost could be covered; second to gauge whether they would "make it" in the highly charged, racially tense atmosphere.

Inevitably, the local Leagues "pulled in their horns," dropping the marginal activities and cutting back on costly or high-visibility sensitive projects. The essential programs were continued and to reach necessary goals community organization procedures were used. This meant that the local executives worked increasingly behind the scenes, involving other social and civic agencies. They mobilized them to achieve purposes that the League, because of its interracial nature, could not hope to accomplish without dividing the community and perhaps detonating an explosion that would prevent attainment of the goal and possibly destroy the League itself. It meant also that local Leagues relied increasingly on NUL staff to circumvent their obstacles. The Leagues purposely put a premium on discretion. Thus in this period of upheaval in black-white relationships during the late fifties the local Leagues were out of the spotlight for both tactical and strategic reasons. The result was a popular impression in both black and white communities that the League was either AWOL ("absent without leave") or asleep at the switch. Yet the measure of effectiveness to the League was not the amount of newspaper space it rated for its achievements. This attitude continued, though there was much head-wagging about the increasing tendency of the news media to make sensations out of overnight wonders who splashed into the news one day and disappeared the next.

The headlines for breakthroughs in smashing bias and forcing the hiring of blacks often were sacrificed by the League in deference to the wishes of the "reformed sinner"—a company that hired blacks after long years of resistance. Months of intricate, costly and painstaking effort were invested by NUL in achievements that garnered little if any glory in the media. When the airlines finally were cracked by NUL they wished to minimize publicity that would expose the degree of their former bigotry in excluding blacks. The League cooperated, in the belief that the positive achievement of unbiased hiring was the true goal, not publicity for the agency. Consequently, the news stories at the time played up the positive aspect: "Miss Xyz has been hired by Flyway Airlines, their first black stewardess, etc."

Typical of the unobtrusive approach to problems in a community was the Baltimore League's technique. As a member and major factor in the Greater Baltimore Committee, the strongest citizen power group in the city, the League tackled the long-standing, critical problem of housing. A nonprofit corporation was established to "promote access to the whole housing market" for all qualified citizens. The actual words "open occupancy" were avoided, but the purpose was, in truth, to open the housing market to blacks. Through this new corporation Baltimore banks and real estate interests were approached for cooperation in a far more effective way than if the League—or any one of the agencies backing the corporation—had "gone it alone."

Another Baltimore League initiative was development of a Coordinating Council of Civic Unity in the fall of 1954 after neighborhood disturbances occurred around four newly integrated public schools. Consisting largely of white organizations, the council served as an information clearing house and "fire brigade," on the alert for other racial friction.

Elsewhere, the hate mongers scored some successes. The Jacksonville League was dropped from the Community Chest when it refused to disaffiliate from NUL. The Richmond League was "persuaded" to resign from the Community Chest in that city a few days later. There were some victories for courage, however. In Fort Worth the city's largest industrial plant first boycotted the Community Chest campaign under pressure from its employees, then reversed itself and exceeded its own quota by 6 percent. The Oklahoma City Chest took a firm stand against the White Citizens Council and the Community Chest drive went over the top.

One NUL response to the hate campaigns was announcement of "an emergency fund of $100,000" to meet what Lester Granger called "this fresh threat against our national safety and decency" in southern cities. It was, he said, a "struggle to-the-death between organized bigotry and aspiring democracy" that depended upon establishing and maintaining interracial communication and cooperation of the sort provided by the Leagues. A fund-raising letter was sent over Granger's signature to stimulate contributions to this new war chest.[13] The results were disappointingly meager in spite of the disconcerting slogan used in the solicitation: "Give to the Urban League now—tomorrow may be too late." [14]

38/A Reexamination

Out of the ferment and friction and cross-hauling that was visible, as well as that which was covert, came the progress report in mid-1954 of NUL's Board Committee on Urban League Policy. Chaired by Lloyd K. Garrison, the committee had taken long strides toward setting down a League philosophy statement as recommended in the Rich Report five years earlier. The committee made the point that over the years policy pronouncements had issued from the NUL executive director, board and annual conferences. It summarized major social issues on which public statements had been made for the previous five years (as if in rebuttal of those who accused the League of being tongue-tied on such matters).

Those cited were statements: (1) for ending discrimination in the armed forces; (2) for establishing "open occupancy" in housing; (3) for extending Social Security to workers not covered by the act; (4) for establishing fair employment laws at state and/or federal levels; (5) for passage or stronger enforcement of civil rights laws throughout the nation; (6) against segregation in all forms, specifically including public facilities, in the nation's capital and in the public schools; and (7) against segregation and discrimination in housing financed in any way by public funds.[1]

On the hot question of whether the agency could or would promote action or take action itself on politically sensitive subjects, the committee reported that "policy decisions have sometimes been to support . . . legislation directly. When the latter has been the case, NUL's course has been guided by the Board's position concerning 'lobbying.' "

It had been the deliberate choice of the executive, stated the report, "to err, if at all, on the side of caution in interpreting this ruling—caution being dictated by the experiences of other national agencies and certain local Urban Leagues." (The National Housing Conference, of which NUL had long been a member, had lost its tax exemption for lobbying; the Kansas City League was under investigation by the Internal Revenue Department at this time.) The League "sought to act in the role of expert consultants," stressing the importance of certain legislation as part of NUL's "educational and interpretive" program. "What we have sought to avoid," it underlined, "has been any activity which could be interpreted as 'button-holing or nailing' legislators in an attempt to line up votes." [2]

In light of this preamble, the committee recommended that NUL staff develop procedures to keep abreast of current legislative questions and public issues and report to the board on them and on NUL collaboration with other organizations on such matters. Recognizing recent changes and expecting more, the committee recommended a mid-winter conference to review NUL's "place and function in the national racial scene and of ways in which that place and function can be strengthened."

On one point, however, the committee had its own recommendation: more research. "We believe that never before in our history has it been possible to obtain such instant public recognition of accurate factual studies of racial conditions conducted by organizations well-known for their scholarly and reliable work. We believe that public understanding of the aims and purposes of the League would be greatly furthered, and that avenues for increased activity and responsibility on the part of Board members, both nationally and locally, would be opened up." To finance research projects the committee recommended going after foundations.[3]

Out of this committee report grew a major self-examination of the agency the following spring. It was an attempt to shake the agency loose from the pathways of the past and, with navigational aid from outside experts, to chart the directions of NUL's future. Called the Board Convention, the meeting was held in Kansas City in mid-April 1955 and was underwritten by the Rockefeller Brothers Fund.

When the convention opened, all sixty Leagues were represented through 157 delegates. Each League had been briefed in advance and had received background material from NUL setting out the current situation of the agency and its programs, finances, personnel and problems.

The delegates received advance texts of papers by five resource specialists: Harry S. Ashmore, editor of the Little Rock *Gazette,* discussing "The Racial Climate in the Wake of Segregation"; Columbia University Professor Eli Ginzberg analyzing "Better Preparation for Better Jobs"; Professor William Haber of the University of Michigan covering "The Economic Position of the Negro Wage Earner"; Fisk University President Charles S. Johnson dissecting "Race Relations and the Dynamics of Cultural Change in the United States"; and Elizabeth Wickenden, consultant to the American Association of Social Workers, looking at "Race Relations as a Welfare Function." NUL Board member Ira DeA. Reid served as discussion leader, chairman of the panel presentation and presided over the closing session.

The papers of Professor Ginzberg and Dr. Johnson provided especially valuable insights.

Dr. Johnson warned against mistaking improvement in the status of blacks for improvement in race relations. The status of all Americans had improved, he said, but relatively blacks might have gone downhill. The accurate measure was whether harmony in race relationships involved the well-being of both groups or whether one had to accept a disadvantage to gain the harmony. "Changes . . . in the Negro's status . . . have come in the matrix of changes in American society and culture, and especially in its thought forms and institutional patterns," he stated.

> At this point of history, the power structure is increasingly weighting the side of non-segregation and fuller incorporation of Negro workers into the total economy. The recent Supreme Court decision . . . is the first unequivocal affirmation of civil rights expressly involving Negro citizens that has come out of our government in ninety years. It is now politically expedient, nationally and internationally, to support by actual example the principle of full democratic status for all people.[4]

But only system-shaking events could be expected to influence the culture, Dr. Johnson insisted. "These system-shaking experiences appear to be the essential prerequisites for the initiation of purposive action directed specifically toward improvement of the Negro status, or of race relations." Cited as a "system-shaker" example was the use of black workers in World Wars I and II—"customs and folkways that ordinarily govern recruitment and training had to go into the discard—a sacrifice to the common good." Other examples were migrations from agriculture to industry and the impact of the Depression in the south.

In Dr. Johnson's view the two important power structures in the nation were government and industry. Fundamental changes in society and culture, he said, owe less to personal persuasion and conversion than to the institutions. Changes were dictated by the power structures in the interests of preserving that power. Such preservation, however, now (1955) depended on national and international as well as local and domestic conditions. This was so because of the government's new role as leader of the democratic forces of the world and the necessity of demonstrating at home its ability to put into practice the principles it would hold up to all peoples as a way of life. From this, Johnson insisted, "phenomenal changes in racial policy and even economic policy" had already come.

> The most strategic leverage for changes in Negro economic opportunity is through work with the personalities and instrumentations of these power structures. This is a task of social and political statesmanship, and not merely of public exhortations, and those individuals whose techniques are

limited to protest meeting and personal litigation are merely examples of the obsolescence of this personal strategy, within our current cultural context.[5]

Thus Dr. Johnson endorsed the League's basic approach and gave the back of his hand to agencies more prominent in the headlines than in solid achievement.

Professor Ginzberg, a nationally-acknowledged expert on manpower uses, challenged the League to increase opportunities for blacks to become skilled workers and technicians. In 1955, he stated, 9 percent of all male workers in the United States were blacks, but they represented only 4 percent of the skilled workers and technicians.

He counseled that acquiring the needed skills was a process, not a single exposure or experience, and that it began in early childhood and stretched through young adulthood at least. The process included influences of home, school, military service, apprenticeship and opportunities on the job. The League should, therefore, move to aid blacks at key places in this process. The major handicap, he emphasized, was poor educational background—many more whites than blacks graduated from high school. The League, he suggested, should shift its emphasis from the job market to a "more deliberate concern" with family structure, community influences and basic schooling. "Unless the Negro's native potential can be developed during the course of his childhood and adolescence, many opportunities that are being opened up will never come within his grasp," he said.[6]

(Dr. Ginzberg's recommendations were rapidly translated into NUL program emphases, as noted in other chapters. Furthermore, he became so interested in this subject that he wrote a significant book on it, expanding his paper and drawing upon the aid and assistance of Ann Tanneyhill, among others, to produce *The Negro Potential.*)[7]

The delegates resolved that "the goal in all areas of community activity should be the complete integration of the Negro in community life, whether in terms of where he lives, the services he receives, the job he performs or his role as a citizen." They voted that the League should continue to use its full resources to eliminate racial discrimination in employment, housing, education, health and welfare services.

To this end they passed resolutions on public education and information; research and social action; training and guidance; employment and industrial relations; health and social welfare; housing; and national/local League relationships. In two words, they called for "more" and "better" in each category, but program priorities and staff actions were specified.[8]

In the highly sensitive social action area, the delegates said the dynamic American culture and economy placed a heavy responsibility on research for information, analysis and interpretation as the very foundation of intelligent social planning, action and community education. A national research advisory council was recommended to counsel and to secure foundation funds.

A committee on social issues was recommended. It would provide reports to local Leagues and to the annual conference. Locals were advised to establish such committees also. NUL was urged to redefine its policy, methods and techniques dealing with social action. These include (1) giving expert testimony before governmental bodies; (2) attending and participating in national meetings on issues within NUL's field of concern; (3) making public statements in support of issues within the area of League operations; and (4) providing information from UL research and experience to agencies, both private and governmental, dealing with matters in the League's area.

The health and social welfare resolutions set forth a priority list: (1) housing; (2) availability of health services, including mental health; (3) adoption and foster care; (4) problems of the aging; (5) leisure time activities; (6) public welfare programs.

The League's job in these "community services" areas was to identify unmet needs of black citizens and to persuade the people and agencies with the power to take action to meet these needs. Delegates reaffirmed that the League's primary effort should be toward community planning and social action. Priority of effort was to be evaluated by weighing key situations: (1) those in which a very limited investment of effort might bring especially large returns; (2) those which could bring about a maximum compounding of progress by paving the way for other changes; (3) those which are at a crucial point of development (education, as a result of the Supreme Court decision, for example); (4) those in which there is special current national or local interest; (5) those on which the agency has specialized competence or knowledge.[9]

The convention was, in Lloyd Garrison's opinion, "a landmark in the history of the Urban League." What impressed Garrison particularly was the contrast between the League's formative years when its problems were "stark and crude: how to get jobs—any job; how to get housing—any housing" and so on. The contemporary problems facing the League were more complex and more subtle.

Accepting the recommendations of the experts and League delegates that the agency move into more urgent areas, Garrison was reminded of the Spanish explorer "who sailed across one ocean only to see before him from the peak in Darien another and vaster one." The message of the convention, as he saw it, was "not to abandon our vessel, for we have built well and soundly, nor to alter our course toward the promised land, but to trim ship, take on fresh provisions, enlarge the crew, and in all ways ready ourselves for a voyage at once more difficult and more hopeful than the one we have so far completed." [10]

39/After the Landmark

It was a hostile environment.

That, in a word, described black existence in the United States of 1960. It was not news to blacks, nor to whites with any sensitivity. But it was the decade of the sixties that put across to the majority of Americans some understanding of the Afro-American experience. It got across, it bridged the gap between black life and white obliviousness until by 1963 there were few, if any, who did not have some awareness of what it meant to be black in red-white-and-blue land.

It had taken a century, but the unsettled question of the status of black men in the United States had returned to center stage. And this time the credits revealed it to be an Afro-American production—staged, directed, produced and performed by blacks, most of them young. They had moved from the Jim Crow peanut gallery to take over the theater, and their production was a super-epic, played in hundreds of scenes on thousands of sets with a cast of literally millions. It was not a production to be ignored, though the reviews were mixed.

There were those who thought the times were out of joint. There were others who thought the venerable agencies in race relations—particularly the NAACP and the NUL—were out of synchronization with the needs of the day. At the League's 1959 annual conference one of the young dissidents, the hard-driving, brilliant executive secretary of the Chicago League, Edwin C. "Bill" Berry, laid it on the line: he called on the NUL to take a daring new approach. Black Americans, he said, had emerged from two and a half world wars with a new dimension of personal significance.

They are at war with the status quo and will no longer accept the leadership of any agency or organization that does not know this and will not act on it forthrightly.

A good Urban League program should drop the old casework approach, should base itself on scientific research, should accept the risk of irritating some people who cling stubbornly to the status quo. . . . This old canard about the Urban League working "quietly and without fanfare" is rubbish.[1]

The Washington *Afro-American* editorialized on Edwin C. "Bill" Berry's criticism and the traditional Urban League approach:

Militancy is a necessary element in the war for first-class citizenship, but militancy can be both a virtue and a fault. The successful prosecution of any war calls for both frontal attacks and strategic holding actions. It takes storm troopers to wage a breakthrough and non-combatants to mop up and consolidate the gains. This seems good strategy. . . . There is no doubt that the popularity of the League with the masses could be enhanced by a more dramatic approach but the job of the League at this point is not so much histrionics as it is to sell the public both on the necessity for and an appreciation for the type of service the League is rendering.[2]

Lester Granger denounced those who disparaged the League for lack of aggressiveness. "Militancy," he said, "has an inner meaning which is far deeper [than picket lines and placards and the hurling of epithets and denouncing of public figures]. In such a sense it is determined by faith in a cause, by willingness to endure assaults instigated by opposition to the cause, by determination to stick to a job until completed, and not to be distracted by glory parades and soft sitout corners. In this sense I challenge any national organization in the country to match its record for militancy with that of our Urban League." [3]

His application of this emphasis was to recommend in 1960 a series of projects in League cities, planned to demonstrate the community organization process at work. The projects would be in fields such as housing, vocational guidance, leader training, adjustment and acculturation of black newcomers. Yet, NUL's major impact that year was made through none of those channels. It became startlingly relevant partly by chance, when the "Feed the Babies" campaign developed, centered on the New Orleans Aid to Dependent Children emergency.

One of the bills passed by the Louisiana state legislature in June 1960 summarily cut off relief benefits to any woman who had a child born out of wedlock while she was receiving relief or whose home was declared "unsuitable" for child rearing for any reason. The law struck not only the illegitimate children, but all children in such a family. And it summarily cut off aid practically without warning, ending such relief aid three days after passage of the bill. This caused an upheaval among the 23,000 women and children affected by this law (about 97 percent of them were black).

Throughout the state, but particularly in New Orleans, the thousands of cast-out mothers, herding their tattered children, frantically beat on the doors of the welfare agencies literally begging for food. These agencies were not equipped to dole out food, and in the days that followed the refuse piles in Louisiana took on a new look as little children and their mothers fought rats and maggots for food scraps and foraged in garbage cans.

The New Orleans League was appalled. No welfare agency or spokesmen protested the inhumanity of the new state law for fear of bringing down the wrath of the governor and/or state legislature. The League immediately wrote the governor pointing up the inhuman hardships the new law created and urging relief be granted to alleviate the suffering. The League's letter was not given the courtesy even of an acknowledgment.

Simultaneously, the League called together forty ministers to tell them the facts of the situation and organize their efforts to help in the emergency. A committee of the ministers was appointed to join League executive J. Harvey Kerns in a conference with New Orleans's mayor to request emergency action. The mayor was moved by the facts and authorized the city's welfare department to use $4,000 of its annual "emergency purposes" appropriation to help the 5,000 citizens in the city who were affected by the cutoff.

The following Sunday the ministers appealed to their flocks in more than 100 churches, raising some $6,000 and by the end of that week an additional fifty churches had joined in.

Meanwhile, the New Orleans League was forced to put aside its "normal" activities and devote its attention to the ADC emergency. It brought together the League board of directors in emergency session along with representatives of social, civic, business, fraternal and religious organizations. An action program was developed. The crisis was to be publicized, not hidden, by going to the local news media with the facts. The national press was to be contacted, hopefully to bring the spotlight of public opinion throughout the nation to bear and to encourage outside assistance. The federal Department of Health, Education and Welfare was to be informed and requested to intervene immediately. Finally, the NUL was to be enlisted.

For two weeks the New Orleans League had been the chief dispensary for relief. Now one relief headquarters was set up by the Baptists, another by the Methodists and the League organized three others in the suburbs. As the local papers dug into the story citizens began to respond to the need. The International Longshoremen's Association contributed twen-ty-five tons of potatoes. Taxi drivers put on a campaign. They asked every fare they picked up to contribute to the emergency. They brought in more than a ton of canned food plus clothing.

Harvey Kerns wrote to the Secretary of the Department of Health, Ed-ucation and Welfare urging federal intervention in the situation inas-much as $21 million of the $28 million spent by Louisiana for public as-sistance in New Orleans came from the national treasury. He also pointed out that the purpose of the ADC program was violated by the new state law. HEW Secretary Arthur Flemming replied, scoring the ac-tion of Louisiana's governor and legislature and promising "investigation and quick action."

The emergency was sixty days old when the NUL annual conference convened after Labor Day. Harvey Kerns and several staff and board members of the New Orleans League attended and press conferences were set up to tell the nation the grim facts. Though it had not been sched-uled, the Louisiana situation was described in a general session of the NUL conference and on the spot a "Feed the Babies Project" was launched. To national and international press media—newspapers, radio and TV—Kerns and the Louisiana League colleagues described the needs and appealed for funds, food and clothing.[4]

With that, contributions began to pour in. The first received was from English women who chartered a TWA plane and shipped food, medicine and money "to shame the governor of Louisiana for the dastardly thing he did to the Negro children." Local Leagues and UL guilds put on cam-paigns and shipped busloads of food and clothing. So did unions, welfare employees in cities such as Chicago, and conscience-stricken people from twenty-two states and four foreign countries.

The promised "quick action" by federal authorities did not materialize —perhaps because the 1960 Presidential election was approaching and the Republican administration hoped to avoid alienating potential Nixon supporters. The net result was that hundreds of families were evicted from their meager homes for nonpayment of rent money; hundreds were ill because of hunger, exposure, and lack of medical care. The League lost patience and a delegation, consisting of NUL president Henry Steeger, southern field director Nelson Jackson and J. Harvey Kerns met in Washington and called on HEW Secretary Flemming.

"I explained to him what happened," recalls Kerns, "and we appealed for help."[5]

"Well," he said, "Mr. Kerns, this is one of the most unconscionable things that I have ever heard of. I will have an investigation made. I'll have them send me a report on this thing immediately."

"Well," said Kerns, "Mr. Secretary, I have absolutely no confidence that the true facts will be stated in any report that will be sent to you . . . I'd like to suggest that you send your own investigators in there to validate what I'm saying to you."

He looked at Kerns and said, "Well, you may be right."

Within two weeks, reports Kerns, there were twenty-four investigators all over the state of Louisiana looking into the situation. "We had representatives from at least 24 papers throughout the country together with members of the press from other countries. After the investigation was made we had a hearing in Washington. At that hearing I also appeared. The NUL joined in: Lester Granger and Lisle C. Carter Jr. [NUL Legal Counsel], were there. We were able to pull in other organizations also— The Family Welfare Association, Child Welfare League of America, New Orleans Social Welfare Planning Council, Family Service Society and Tulane University." The controversy heated up, with hundreds of letters from all over the nation pouring into the Louisiana governor's office and that official making statements to the press that "there are no starving children in Louisiana as a result of the Law." Reporters from wire services, networks and international news services covered the situation intensively and the New Orleans League was a focal point for their orientation and fact-gathering. J. Harvey Kerns was quoted by the press as saying the governor's statements were irresponsible and indicated a gross lack of information. He directed reporters to cases that easily disproved the governor's callous claims.

It was not until January 1961 that the New Orleans welfare officials restored about 90 percent of the ADC cases to the welfare rolls. It took much longer in the rest of the state. And it was not until July 1961, that the Kennedy administration's commissioner of social security issued changed regulations covering ADC, barring state plans from putting in eligibility requirements that would cut off assistance to needy children because home conditions were deemed "unsuitable" where the child continued to live in that home. The Louisiana law conflicted with this, of course, and the state was given until September 1962 to shape up or be cut off from federal subsidies.[6]

This extraordinary crisis had far-reaching implications for the New Orleans League. It mobilized the community programs to strengthen black family life. Many of the churches opened their doors for programs, recreational classes and lectures and special activities dealing with family life. Teachers, housewives and civic leaders joined in community self-surveys to pinpoint major problems affecting black families adversely. And the city-wide black PTA moved its chapters to devote major efforts to programs to plan and carry out activities that would strengthen family life.

The local League, through its three area councils, sponsored family life programs in church, social and civic groups, supplying help in planning and securing specialists. The result was, as Bill Berry had predicted, a local League with wider and stronger support in its community.[7]

Clearly, as the sixties began, life in the nation was in the process of jet-propelled metamorphosis. A major propellent was the drive of blacks for not-to-be-denied civil rights. The aim was still centripetal, toward inclusion in the society. Conditions in the world and the nation had changed sufficiently to give blacks a fighting chance to change the system.

There were, by 1960, tens of thousands of college-educated Afro-Americans to provide the leadership for civil rights efforts. There were blacks in law and politics where they could interpret and guide efforts. There were pressures on the white establishment to show cause why Afro-Americans were not included. Such pressures came from the skepticism of other nations who judged us hypocritical for our professions of democracy and denial of it to black citizens. Similar pressure came from whites who were conscience-stricken at the sight of black children braving murderous white mobs to enter public schools in what had been considered law-abiding communities.

There were other changes in the nation that gave blacks considerably more weight in the thinking of the Establishment than in the past. Some of the changed factors were demographic, some were economic, some were psychological.

On the demographic side, the black migration had continued during the fifties. Another one and one-half million pushed off from the south and went north, east and west. They went to the cities, until, as the census showed, blacks were no longer primarily agricultural workers living in rural areas—they were overwhelmingly city dwellers. Even in the south, nearly 60 percent lived in cities. In the north, 96 percent of blacks were city dwellers; in the west the figure was 93 percent.

The fact that all these Afro-Americans were piled into the cities had consequences recognized by the white men with their hands on the levers of power—the bankers, politicians, presidents of the major industrial and utility and retail companies. They looked at the statistics and saw the great metropolises of the nation with huge black cities within the cities; and they projected current trends to the future (see table opposite).

An old maxim states that the infantry is the queen of battles because control of terrain wins the war. Even without a war there were enough black citizens living in the major cities to control vast sections of them. This powerful fact dictated many relevant conclusions. Among them:

1. You don't mistreat with impunity 1,000,000 black citizens as you might have 60,000 half a century before. They *will* have their represen-

Black Population of Ten Major U.S. Cities [8]
(In Thousands)

City	1960 Population	Percent of Total City Population	1970 Population	Percent of Total City Population
New York	1,085	14	1,667	21
Chicago	813	23	1,103	33
Los Angeles	335	14	504	18
Philadelphia	529	26	654	34
Detroit	482	29	659	44
Houston	218	23	317	26
Baltimore	328	35	420	46
Cleveland	251	29	288	38
Washington, D.C.	412	55	538	71
St. Louis	214	28	254	41

tatives and they *will* be a political force that can profoundly affect the cities and states, even the nation.

2. As an economic force, they can make or break—as they demonstrated in the Montgomery bus boycott and the "selective buying" boycotts against Sun Oil, Gulf Oil, Tastee Baking, Pepsi Cola and others.

Therefore, politically, economically, tactically, and realistically—not to mention morally—astute leaders of the Establishment realized that they must desegregate the institutions and even their own sanctuaries of power, whether banks, businesses, utilities or quasi-public agencies such as hospitals, universities, social service units, and so on.

In the space of less than six years after the Supreme Court's landmark decision there had been a veritable revolution of thinking, of action, of drive, and of techniques—not to mention development of shock troops —in the battle by Afro-Americans for first-class citizenship.

Where fifty years before on the bleak and forbidding topography of black life in America there had been a few towering black promontories such as DuBois, Washington, Bulkley and Trotter, there now had developed a landscape liberally dotted with black citizens of strength and courage, with constituents alert, sensitive, aware of and demanding their citizenship rights. And between the promontories in 1954 there was a resilient network, an infrastructure of agencies, institutions, personal relationships, tactical and strategic coalitions, formal and informal, that created a higher plateau on which black ambitions could travel faster and move more broadly than ever before. The overall impetus was still overwhelmingly centripetal toward the goal of integration into the American mainstream. The major questions seemed to be "How fast?" and "Using what avenues?"

The initiative on the second question was with young blacks, who, in 1960, triggered the sit-ins in the south. There had been sit-ins in the north and in border cities before, but when four black North Carolina A & T students sat at the lunch counter in the Greensboro Woolworth store, the shock wave of student sit-ins hit the beach.

Within ten days sit-ins were under way in fifteen cities in five southern states. In the next year and a half some 70,000 black and white students had taken part in sit-ins in twenty states and over 100 cities. It was at this time that the Student Non-Violent Coordinating Committee was formed with the guidance of the Reverend Martin Luther King, Jr.

Why the sit-ins? And why did black citizens back them? One answer lies in Julius A. Thomas's experience in trying to break through the walls of bigotry in Charleston, West Virginia, years before.

Thomas had gone to Woolworth's Charleston store in 1949. This had recently been reopened, following reconstruction after a fire that had burned out the building and killed seven firemen (two of them black). Several black organizations and the widows of the black firemen petitioned for more and better jobs for blacks and a change in the store's Jim Crow food-serving policy at the lunch counters.

The NUL industrial relations specialist had talked with Woolworth's public relations people in New York about this situation. They had authorized him to tell the local manager that Woolworth's would change its policy if other stores in the city would do likewise. So Thomas talked to leaders of the black community, then the variety store people and the local Retail Merchants Association. He made absolutely no progress. He called on the Woolworth store manager and found him visibly afraid to make even a small commitment concerning any policy change. He was certain that any hiring of blacks for positions other than maid, dishwasher and menial tasks would result in terrific loss of business.

Thomas briefed him on employment changes in other parts of the country and the situation in other Woolworth stores. He suggested that instead of the bitter criticism the manager anticipated, the reaction would probably be warm applause by the people of the area. Thomas reported:

> I suppose I lost a great deal of my pleasant demeanor because a few weeks ago [the manager] had employed a very attractive young woman, a graduate of the West Virginia State College, and had assigned her to the pot-washing department. She complained that the work was too heavy so they promoted her to the dish-washing machine. She worked two weeks and they discovered that there weren't too many dishes to wash. She was dropped from the staff. . . . I pointed out to Mr. Swazee that I thought he should be ashamed to ask any college-trained young woman to take a job of

this kind. I told him that I doubted that there was a college-trained white woman in the entire work force of 125 people. He admitted that there was not, as far as he knew. He had no excuse, however, for offering the young woman the job. He said that he couldn't afford to employ her in any other capacity.[9]

Julius Thomas's experience, like that of William Ashby in Newark during World War I, was all too typical. Now young blacks, by their actions moved to end such bigotry. The sit-ins and other nonviolent demonstrations brought on retaliation and in Chattanooga, Jacksonville, Biloxi, and Orangeburg, South Carolina, there were race riots and mass arrests. Television brought not only the *word* of these happenings to millions of Americans, it actually brought into living rooms the clubbings, fighting, firehoses, cattle-prods and killer dogs. The difference in impact between the printed word of the newspaper and the lurid violence witnessed on television was a quantum leap. Americans received a crash course about the uncivil wrongs that passed for civil rights for blacks. Public opinion polls found a new awareness among whites of black goals, and a rapidly growing belief that Afro-Americans should not be denied their civil rights. In this educative role television was tremendously effective.

It was unexpectedly effective also in placing before black citizens the tantalizing picture, seemingly accurate, of how white Americans really lived. The dramas and soap operas, variety programs, talks and quiz shows, commercials and news programs showed a white world in which blacks intruded only as entertainers, clowns, athletes or "disruptive" demonstrators. The effects of television programs on viewers have been bitterly debated. On certain fundamentals it may be possible to agree: generally TV until quite recent years portrayed middle-class white Americans living in pleasant, clean homes surrounded by creature comforts and afflicted with peculiar fixations on personal cleanliness, patent medicines, food, drink, cars and cigarettes. When observed from the vantage point of a ghetto basement apartment with its sweating walls, cold water and faulty sewage, skittering roaches, rats in the night and dependence on frequently stolen or undelivered welfare checks such programs have an educative effect that may not motivate all slum viewers to positive behavior at all times. As the National Commission on the Causes and Prevention of Violence staff report pointed out,

> Learning to be Negro in a white-dominated society meant one thing to the socially isolated sharecropper's child; it means something else to the child in the urban ghetto with access to a television set, and its new meaning can easily include violent rejection of anything regarded as a token of continued white dominance. The ghetto dweller's child has abundant op-

portunities to see whites in roles other than landlord and overseer, and he has abundant opportunities to see how other Negroes are going about the business of breaking down racial barriers. If television gives him more glimpses of violent ways than of the non-violent ways, he must be expected to learn accordingly.[10]

Additionally, though TV itself was lily-white, it found that black protest leaders were good box office. Thus in the early sixties the TV talks and news programs turned increasingly to articulate protesters. It quickly became apparent that instant fame was available to the leader who put together a protest and was its spokesman. Electronic demagogues flourished along with genuine representatives of black citizens' needs. The TV industry, with neither lines nor roots into the black community, found that it could not tell one black leader from another, in terms of his significance, validity or following.

Lester Granger, for one, thought the media were "criminally reprehensible" for giving wide circulation to the "fringe" spokesman—black powerites, Black Muslims, black nationalists. When Granger went abroad in 1961 he knew Malcolm X as a streetcorner speaker "of great ability, but he had the ordinary streetcorner crowds. He broke no records." When the League executive returned from his trip, he found "all Negro Americans talking about Malcolm X; I couldn't imagine what had happened. One television show by Susskind did it." [11]

In 1960 few well-informed citizens questioned TV's considerable power to influence men's minds. There were decisive demonstrations of its power that year, particularly in the political arena. John F. Kennedy's bid for election was one outstanding proof of this, from the primary battles with Hubert Humphrey, where Kennedy superiority in money and use of the medium paid off, to the TV debates with Richard M. Nixon, widely conceded to have tipped the scales to Kennedy.

But there was also the essential media role that enabled Kennedy to overcome his poor voting record on civil rights (which had earned him the lowest rating by blacks, of all leading Democratic candidates for the nomination).[12] He wooed black voters—calling on Eisenhower on August 8, 1960, to issue an executive order on equal opportunity in housing; denouncing the Nixon Committee's record on government contract compliance; carrying his campaign into black neighborhoods and including blacks conspicuously in his entourage.

Nixon, apparently having written off the black vote, was silent or equivocal on civil rights matters when it counted, and refused even to appear in Harlem. For many black citizens the contest was decided when Martin Luther King, Jr., was arrested in Atlanta in the final days of the campaign. King was jailed for participating in a sit-in and Kennedy immediately telephoned Mrs. King to tell her how concerned he was. He dispatched his brother Robert to Atlanta to confer with the judge who had jailed the head of the Southern Christian Leadership Conference. The following day King was released, the media featured this event and Kennedy benefited substantially at the polls a few days afterward.

The evidence was strong that Kennedy's appeals to black voters gave him the edge in his narrow win in 1960:

Item: In Illinois, about 250,000 blacks voted for Kennedy; he won the state by a bare 9,000 votes.

Item: Some 250,000 blacks voted for Kennedy in Michigan; he took the state by only 67,000 votes.

Item: Even in South Carolina the black vote was the deciding factor. With Strom Thurmond splitting the traditional Democratic vote in his States Rights party bid, Kennedy squeaked through with a 10,000-vote plurality—and 40,000 of his total was from black citizens.

Item: Seven out of every ten black voters cast their ballots for Kennedy.

Politicians and plain folk alike saw a new aggregation of Afro-American power in such results. The box score was yet another index that a new climate, encompassing new factors favorable to civil rights, was abroad in the land. The National Urban League determined to capitalize on this new climate. Its first move was a month after the presidential election. NUL placed in the hands of the President-elect a memo entitled "The Time Is Now." In it the League challenged John F. Kennedy to move boldly against segregation and discrimination: [13]

> The Urban League believes that beyond all other consideration it is the power, the will, the talent of the President that will cause the nation to face up to these problems most quickly, most efficiently.
>
> A faltering start in "the right direction" or "deliberate speed" is no longer good enough. There must be full speed ahead. And the leadership must come from the top.
>
> Tomorrow may be too late—THE TIME IS NOW.

The admonishment applied with equal urgency to NUL itself.

40/Afflictions of Leadership

During his twenty years as executive secretary of the National Urban League, Lester Granger reminisced, he had been called "everything . . . from a bandana-wearing Uncle Tom to a bushy-tailed Communist to a Machiavellian conniver." [1] Those were only a few of the names. They give some of the flavor if not the substance of the pressures directed at both the executive and the NUL. Granger, as leader and public spokesman, was both the symbol and actual target. And he was on the receiving end increasingly in the late forties and throughout the fifties, from many directions and factions, for many reasons. Fortunately, during these years he could depend upon the loyalty of his staff and especially his able, tactful administrative assistant and confidential secretary, Mrs. Enid C. Baird, who served him and the organization from 1940 onward.

The Lester Granger who had thundered at government iniquity in excluding black workers from defense jobs in 1940 and 1941 seemed muted by the end of the forties. It was not entirely so. There had been a diffusion of black interest and concern. In 1940 and 1941 jobs were the number one concern of all blacks. And in this area the League was in the vanguard speaking out and leading boldly. By the end of the decade civil rights, especially segregation and discrimination in education and public accommodations were absorbing Afro-American attention.

Though the NAACP scored success after success in gaining court decisions against segregation and discrimination, it became clear that affirmative action by government agencies was highly important if not mandatory to insure blacks their citizenship rights. The League was concentrating on "Pilot Placements" and guidance and housing and said little about civil rights matters, while the NAACP and other black leaders spoke out incessantly. The situation concerning fair employment practices illustrates the positions taken, and the ferment Granger faced.

The original Fair Employment Practice Committee (FEPC) expired in 1946, but even before its demise black citizens were organizing to make it permanent under a federal law. FEPC was an emotion-charged rallying cry in the black community, symbolizing a square deal for blacks and a commitment of the power and prestige of the federal establishment on the side of, rather than opposed or blind to, Afro-American rights. To be against FEPC was anathema in the black community, akin to opposing motherhood and advocating sin at the same time. By 1952, FEPC had become the touchstone by which blacks judged political parties and candidates as well as lesser mortals. And by this test, Lester Granger and NUL were judged equivocal at best.

The NUL executive was pressed by staff, board and annual conference delegates to take strong public positions in favor of a national FEPC. Granger declined, explaining why in memos to the local League executives and presidents.[2]

Actually, Granger's opposition to deeper NUL involvement on FEPC originally was based on convictions (1) that FEPC had been relatively weak and ineffective; (2) that a federal FEP law was not going to be passed by Congress in the foreseeable future; and (3) since these conditions obtained, a meaningful NUL effort would not only be too demanding but a diversion of precious resources that the agency could ill afford in its precarious financial condition.[3]

All-out public statements and concerted campaigns in favor of federal FEP bills were out, Granger stated publicly, for one very good reason— "the bite of the sharply-whetted official axe" of the Internal Revenue Service could decapitate NUL's tax exemption and kill the agency. This would happen if NUL was adjudged guilty of using undue effort in trying to influence legislation. Hence NUL's cautious approach to such matters.[4]

This condition vexed a number of vitally concerned people—including some local League executive secretaries. Among these men a group of "young Turks" developed. This group wished to see NUL play a more aggressive and creative role on the national stage as it had in earlier years. The group included Edwin "Bill" Berry of Portland, Oregon, Leo Bohanon of St. Louis, Omaha's Whitney Young, Alexander J. "Joe" Allen of Pittsburgh and Sidney Williams of Chicago. Calling themselves the "Disturbed Committee," they pressed Lester Granger for change. Essentially their goals were few but important: they wanted to relate more to civil rights developments and to the civil rights agencies. Many of the executives served on boards of the NAACP in their communities and were distressed that NUL relations with the national NAACP were not as warm and cooperative as between their locals.[5]

A number of local League executive secretaries had been industrial secretaries previously and were dissatisfied with the progress in integrating work forces. They wished to speed up placement of black workers and called for new and different approaches. Sidney Williams, for instance, recommended that the League certify as "equal opportunity employers" those companies whose personnel policies and hiring of blacks were up to NUL standards. This was suggested as an alternative to the permanent FEPC, which all of them favored, in case the FEPC did not become law.

The "Disturbed Committee" also called for a tightening of standards within NUL so that the affiliates would be carrying out a coordinated program or parallel projects with greater cumulative impact.

Bill Berry presented these views for the "Disturbed Committee" in 1949, all but demanding that the League take strong positions on the major issues of the day. To fail to do so would weaken the organization by separating it from its black constituents, he argued. And, he stressed, it was imperative that the League throw its efforts into the balance in favor of the FEPC act, using all pressure short of actual political action. The Young Turks saw the importance of such action from the standpoint of its effects on Afro-Americans' perception of the League. "This and later attempts to move Lester Granger," observed one of the "Disturbed Committee," "simply exasperated him." [6]

As Granger saw it, the "Disturbed Committee" got more attention from him than from the other executive secretaries. "Their 'recommendations' were more 'gripes' than realistically oriented proposals, in that almost all called for considerable budget additions or elimination of standard and successful program features, if competent staff were to be secured," believed Granger. "In a session with the Executives' Council I went into all this and won the understanding of the great majority." [7]

There were others who were calling on NUL to change directions. In mid-1954 representatives from the Anti-Defamation League (ADL) met with NUL staff members and urged them to assume new responsibilities. Since the United States Supreme Court's school decision, it was imperative that a "Negro" organization should be in the forefront of education activities, they argued. League spokesmen outlined the difficulties involved, including "lack of adequate resources" though they conceded the desirability of such an undertaking. [8]

The ADL representatives continued their advocacy, however, saying that the League had the reputation, contacts and staff to assume such new responsibilities. Furthermore, they volunteered, ADL would assist in any educational activities the League might undertake, if requested. [9]

What the League spokesmen did not say was that any such major change in program might literally have been suicidal. NUL had ten professionals on its national staff. The agency was torn by internal dissension in its board, was under vicious attack from the reactionary right at both the local and national level and was gasping on the ropes financially.

Within weeks, Granger requested a "voluntary" staff pay cut of 10 percent.[10]

Pressure on Granger came also from highly vocal board members who refused to accept the "cautious" approach. Most of these were outspoken blacks who had come on the board in the late forties. They included NUL vice president Judge Irvin C. Mollison of the United States Customs Court; Dr. George Cannon, physician; psychologist Dr. Kenneth C. Clark; A. Philip Randolph's associate Theodore Brown from the Brotherhood of Sleeping Car Porters and Dr. John E. Moseley, physician. Sidney Hollander, a white Baltimore industrialist and philanthropist who was a leading figure in social work, also sided with them.

Before NUL's 1953 annual conference Judge Mollison asked about the absence of the FEPC question from the conference agenda. Granger was opposed to including it and said it was then too late to get anyone to appear to discuss the subject. Mollison disagreed, insisting that it was possible, even on five minutes' notice. Granger challenged this, asking who could be found at the last minute. The judge replied "Bill Berry, for one." [11] Naming a leader of the "Disturbed Committee" did not strengthen Mollison's argument from Granger's point of view, and his discussion with the judge escalated into a shouting match that steamed the windows and singed the woodwork in the League's offices.

Granger was unyielding; the judge was incensed and other "militants" on the board were deeply upset. They challenged Granger on FEP support repeatedly and found him consistently and firmly opposed to committing the agency to work for it, always on the tax jeopardy excuse, even when board members pointed to activities by other tax-exempt organizations of which they were directors.[12]

Since the executive director avoided strong public statements on major issues, the annual conference took on added importance as a channel to place on record the concern of the Urban League movement. The resolutions adopted by the conference were, in a sense, attempts to register with the outside world Urban League views that its chief spokesman neglected to utter or to emphasize. Thus, at the fall meeting in 1953 the NUL board took up annual conference resolutions on civil rights; condemning segregation in the District of Columbia; blasting appointment of South Carolina segregationist James Byrnes to the UN Commission on Human Rights; and urging enactment of a federal FEPC bill "with clearly defined powers to enforce the outlawing of discrimination and segregation in employment." [13] The board approved all the resolutions except the one on FEPC, which it tabled until it could hear Lester Granger, who was absent, on the subject.

The December board meeting had unusually large attendance. There were twenty-one members present. Lester Granger "reiterated his feeling that the NUL should be extremely cautious in protecting its tax-exempt status." [14]

The minutes of the meeting continue:

There was general acceptance of Mr. Granger's statement, except on the matter of "extreme caution," as some of the members present felt that the League's executive director had been overcautious in protecting the League's interests. Dr. [Kenneth] Clark stated that there was great danger in concentrating on methods to such an extent as to defeat and frustrate the object to be obtained. A number of board members said the basic question was not a specific bill but for the principle of federal FEPC legislation containing sanctions and penalties. Mr. Granger agreed to this concept.

Fullest opportunity was given to all of those who wished to speak.

Afterward, the board authorized the establishment of a committee on NUL policy and appointed a Committee on Social Action Machinery, to keep abreast of these situations and report to the board when necessary.[15]

At its next meeting the board heard a report from Nelson C. Jackson, NUL's community services director, about the concern expressed in the National Social Welfare Assembly (of which NUL was a member agency) over the impact of the federal government on social welfare. The assembly had appointed a committee to inform national agencies of legislation and to confer with them and keep them alert to upcoming developments. The committee would be charged with supporting the legislation considered valuable and working against the bills inimical to social welfare.

Sidney Hollander noted that there were sixty agencies in the assembly, twenty-eight of them similar to NUL. These agencies, he said, felt strongly that they had a responsibility to play an effective part in influencing legislation in social welfare, discrimination and housing. He proposed that NUL establish a committee on public affairs to participate formally in these activities and report back to the NUL board for action. This was done.[16]

It was this committee, with William H. Baldwin as its chairman, that appeared in May 1955 before the Senate Subcommittee on Labor and Public Welfare, testifying in favor of an increase in the minimum wage. The committee continued for several years, with Lisle C. Carter, Washington, D.C. League executive, its paid staff consultant.[17]

Meanwhile, beginning in 1952 with Granger's leadership, the League had taken up the cudgels against United States Steel in a confrontation originally concerned with housing. U.S. Steel was constructing a huge new plant in Bucks County, Pennsylvania, which would have some 3,600 workers. In addition, a subsidiary of U.S. Steel was building some 6,000 homes. Levitt, the builders who had thrown up thousands of dwellings on Long Island's potato patches after World War II, planned to duplicate that feat in Bucks County.

These two factors together—U.S. Steel and Levitt—were going to set housing and employment patterns not only locally, but, black leaders were convinced, for years to come and with national repercussions. Levitt had already announced a lily-white policy for his 6,000 houses and was adamant when the NUL tried to get him to change it. Both U.S. Steel and Levitt were self-financed projects, so no question of misuse of government financing could be invoked. Therefore, Steel, with its many black workers, was the logical company with which to try to establish an open occupancy policy.

The result of nearly a year and a half of effort was near-total frustration of both the League's original and secondary goals—integration of the U.S. Steel housing development and placement of high-level black employees in the Bucks County works. (U.S. Steel, as the nation's largest employer of blacks at all levels, was comparatively impregnable to attack on the charge of discrimination; and since the qualification for housing was upper-level employment at the Bucks County plant, the entire case rested on Steel's decision not to assign blacks in such positions to the new plant—a matter of company policy that NUL failed to budge.)

"Militant" board members were infuriated. They wanted to cite U.S. Steel before the President's Committee on Government Contracts, popularly called the Nixon Committee, and hold a press conference blasting the huge corporation. Granger and Julius Thomas opposed these countermoves and the board voted against such action. Judge Mollison, Theodore Brown and the other "progressives" were irate.[18]

This soured Mollison and several other board members on Granger's leadership. But it was an address by the NUL executive to 5,000 black members of the North Carolina Teachers Association in April 1954 that really caused an uproar. In that talk Granger said: "It looks as if the Negro is almost at the place where he will begin to be fully integrated in the American life of which he has been a part for 300 years. . . . The question is, are we ready for it?"[19]

As Granger saw it, "Integration was a final step; desegregation was the first [step] . . . desegregation could be imposed; integration couldn't. It had to be people coming together and thrust into work together. . . . 'Obviously, the Negro is not ready for integration, and obviously the whites are not ready either.' And the only way to get ready is to desegregate, make desegregation work, then we can begin to work with each other. . . ."[20] A black reporter in the audience flashed Granger's words to the weekly press and overnight the NUL executive was roasted in the black newspapers for denying that blacks were ready for integration.[21]

The "progressives" on the board were enraged. Granger's words confirmed their worst suspicions of him. Innuendos and accusations against Granger and the League blossomed in the black press. Columnists spoke of "collusion" between Granger and League president Robert W. Dowling, who was identified as "one of the nation's biggest real estate manipulators," and accused Dowling of having close connections with both U.S. Steel and Levittown.[22] (Dowling was NUL president from 1952 to 1956. He was a director of numerous corporations, including two banks and the Home Insurance Company, had been a consultant to the Metropolitan Life Insurance Company in its vast apartment house developments in New York and a power in the real estate field as chairman of the New York City Citizens Zoning Committee, president of the Citizens Budget Commission and chairman of the Borough of Manhattan Planning Board.) The source of the calumnies, NUL staff discovered, was Theodore Brown, who had been a member of the NUL Bucks County committee dealing with U.S. Steel. Granger, however, believed that Judge Mollison was the "evil genius" behind the attacks.[23] (Fifteen years later Granger was certain that Mollison was a "low conniver" who had financed and carried out a "vendetta" of "scurrilous, anonymous attacks" with his associate Theodore Brown.) [24]

The agency's annual meeting, June 10, was a scorcher. The nominating committee, of which Brown was a member, had met previously and dropped Brown for re-election by a vote of 5–2. The stage was set for a fight on that matter plus others.

Brown had charged in a newspaper interview the week before the meeting that the League had no program for blacks, that it had taken them for granted "in its haste to get money from big business firms," that it did not keep pace with local Leagues and was lagging behind labor and black workers in their fight for jobs.[25] Granger, after giving his annual report on NUL's year, blasted the charges and Brown for this "knife-in-the-back" attack on the NUL. He deplored the "scandal-mongering and libelous, underhand, anonymous" attacks and said three members of the board itself were responsible, naming Brown specifically as an instigator.

Election of officers brought open controversy. The nominating committee filed its list of new and to be re-elected board members without Ted Brown's name. An attempt from the floor to question this was turned aside on grounds that the discussion in committee was confidential. A move to add the name of Judge J. Waties Waring to the slate of nominees was beaten back as out of order. The slate was then elected. Immediately after this, Judge Waring was nominated from the floor and elected.[26]

Mollison then asked what Granger had said to that audience of 5,000 black teachers in Raleigh, North Carolina. This brought on a heated denial by Granger that he had ever said in so many words that blacks were not ready for integration and a complaint that his statement had been lifted out of context.

The upshot was that Brown was dropped from the board, the executive was unconvincing in his defense of his North Carolina talk and though the annual meeting was adjourned, the controversy was transferred by the "progressives" to a broader platform. The following week, Judge Mollison and Dr. Cannon both resigned, sending letters to the NUL board and to newspapers questioning the integrity of the officers, the makeup of the board (calling it nonrepresentative of blacks and overweighted with whites, thereby explaining its "non-progressive stance").[27]

The departure of Cannon, Brown and Mollison was the beginning of more than a year of coordinated, well-financed harassment that included a running series of letters to the editors of the *Amsterdam News* and *Afro-American,* telegrams and letters to important and influential people (such as leaders of the New York State Federation of Labor who at its annual convention denounced the League as being anti-labor). There were inspired stories in black weeklies and mailings to local League executives and presidents of critical articles, editorials and letters to the editors clipped from the black press. These were mailed in unmarked post office envelopes almost weekly to all Leagues for several months.

The black weeklies "played the thing up to the full" because, as one of Granger's friends in the press told him, "This is the first time there's been a scandal in the Urban League. . . . This is news." [28] For a while the League's "problems" were popular gossip in the black community. Months later Granger's friends Dr. Kenneth C. Clark and Dr. John Mosely resigned, purposely disassociating themselves from the Mollison group, but nonetheless convinced that they could not serve as board members in a meaningful way so long as the executive director was inflexibly opposed to involving the League in some of the great issues of the time.[29]

Granger summarized the events at the next board meeting. He also read letters from board members, local executives, supporters and friends who expressed their confidence in the organization. During the discussion that followed the focus was why the board members had resigned. There was a consensus that some of the criticism was justifiable, particularly about "admitted weaknesses in League operations." Failure to develop board participation in League affairs through committee activities was mentioned as the outstanding example of this.[30]

Granger saw the challenges of dissident board members and "disturbed" executive secretaries as a threat to the very survival of the agency.

Mollison's group, he said, wanted the League to do a radical about-face as an organization, to transform the whole structure. This, he contended, would have spelled an end to the kind of staff the League had, the largest ever assembled in the world in this field of interest.[31]

Granger and the League countered the press fusillade by stressing NUL achievements in news releases and in an appearance by Granger before the National Newspaper Publishers Association plus a two-hour off-the-record session with the black press executives afterward. Confidential memoranda were sent to influential friends of the League and major supporters. In such a memo to the Rockefeller Brothers Fund Granger outlined the brouhaha and concluded that attacks on the League would, understandably, receive some support. "One reason is that the social work function of the League is still understood by a too-small proportion of the public. Not understanding this function, that public which is agitated as never before over the possibilities of 'militant action' is apt to be impatient with any interracial program not so labeled." League leadership, he continued, believed that the agency's basic purpose and function were unchanged but that changing times called for adaptation and alteration of approaches to conform to trends and developments.[32]

To the NUL board it seemed clear that the agency needed assistance in changing course or in making its current course more meaningful. There were few indices that were reassuring. Neither the black or white press gave headlines or featured treatment to League programs or statements—they were predictable and all too familiar. Financial support, never reliable, was even more uncertain. Expenditures and contributions fluctuated in the $209,000 to $315,000 range.

Thus at a time when local Leagues were being battered by hate drives and squeezed out of local Community Chests the national office was in no position to help. It was in these circumstances that Granger bravely announced a $100,000 rescue fund campaign to aid Leagues whose support had been turned off. But it was a case of "physician, heal thyself." And the doctor, in this case NUL, seemed to many to be almost beyond recovery.

41/A New Pilot

The future of the National Urban League rested with four individuals during the summer of 1960. They were the members of the board's selection committee named to screen applicants for the post of NUL executive director. On the committee were two blacks and two whites: Mrs. Henry Lee (Mollie) Moon, stylish, perennial president of the National Urban League Guild; Mrs. Regina M. Andrews, head librarian of the Washington Heights branch of the New York Public Library and long-time board member; Burns W. Roper, president of Elmo Roper & Associates, public opinion analysts, who had been associated with the League for a decade as board and public relations committee member; and NUL president Henry Steeger, Sr. (1960–1964), publisher of *Argosy, Lawn Tennis,* and other magazines. White-maned, ever-smiling and gracious, Steeger had succeeded labor mediator Theodore W. Kheel (1956–1960) as president at the 1960 annual meeting. Steeger was chairman of the selection committee.

The task was to find a man to take the helm from Lester Granger when his mandatory retirement took place in October 1961. After the word went out that applications were being received, the NUL suddenly discovered that it was more popular than it had realized. All but one of the professionals on the NUL headquarters staff applied for the job; a number of local League executives put in their bids; several educators and other prominent blacks also let it be known that they might be interested. The committee narrowed the field to twelve principal candidates who were seen as a group and interviewed individually. (One candidate bowled the committee over with his opening: "You don't want me. You want Ralph Bunche, at $65,000 a year, or you want Bob [Robert C.] Weaver at $55,000. But if you can't get them, I'm your next best bet!") [1]

The field was brought down to four, then to two and finally the committee by unanimous vote chose Whitney M. Young, Jr., thirty-nine-year-old dean of the Atlanta University School of Social Work.

It was a long trail from the time when, as a boy, Whitney had glimpsed Julius A. Thomas, then executive secretary of the Louisville

Urban League, resplendent in one of his expensive suits, surrounded by attentive listeners at a League meeting. "I don't know who he is or what he does," a dazzled Whitney Young had told his father, the president of nearby Lincoln Institute, "but that's what I want to be."

Whitney Moore Young, Jr., was born and reared in Lincoln Ridge, Kentucky, where his father was president of the Institute and his mother taught school. It was a small town, a peaceful enclave, and Whitney was spared the trauma of white racism as a youngster. Tutored at home, he entered second grade at age five, was graduated from high school at fourteen and from Kentucky State College at nineteen. He played basketball, studied pre-med courses, met his future wife and was elected class president in college.

Caught up in World War II, Young was sent to Massachusetts Institute of Technology in an army specialized training program in engineering. When this was terminated he was assigned to a segregated construction outfit in Europe. Quickly made sergeant, Young soon found himself exercising his latent gifts as negotiator between sullen, resentful black enlisted men and the jumpy, inexperienced southern white officers in charge. The experience caused him to decide on race relations as a career.

After the war he enrolled at the University of Minnesota and earned his master's degree in social work, married his childhood sweetheart, Margaret Buckner, who was teaching in Minneapolis, and participated in student demonstrations to desegregate eating places near the university campus. In 1947 Young became industrial relations secretary of the St. Paul Urban League and scored some substantial successes, integrating the city's transit system, its taxicabs and department store work forces. From this post he went to Omaha in 1950 as executive of the League and a charter member of the "Disturbed Committee" of League executives. He took up his duties as dean of Atlanta University's School of Social Work in 1954.

During his years in Atlanta, Young was vice president of the state NAACP and, with Dr. Samuel Williams of Morehouse, was among the closest advisers of Martin Luther King, Jr., and of the black students who tested their mettle in sit-ins in Atlanta. Thus he was extraordinarily well equipped by background and experience to direct a forward-looking, advancing League movement attuned to current dynamics.

Young's record at Atlanta was phenomenal. He arranged for the school's students to do their field work at the leading social service institutions in the area and he succeeded in fund-raising to such a degree that he doubled the school's budget and boosted faculty pay some 60 percent. His achievements were considered impressive enough to win for him the top social work prize in the nation, the National Conference of Social Welfare's outstanding achievement award in 1959. That same year he appeared on an NUL annual conference program in Washington, D.C., and impressed the Urban Leaguers with the vigor and fundamental soundness of his presentation.

One of those who observed him then was a new man on the NUL board, Lindsley F. Kimball, doyen of foundation executives, who had served as a long-time philanthropic counselor to John D. Rockefeller, Jr., and his sons through posts at the Rockefeller Foundation and later at the Rockefeller Brothers Fund. Through Kimball and the Brothers Fund a year's sabbatical was arranged for Young at Harvard. It was from this intensive, self-structured program that he came to the League, accepting the post of executive director on January 26, 1961, reporting for orientation on August 1 and assuming his duties on October 1, 1961.

In the eyes of many black social workers, this meant that Whitney M. Young, Jr., had scaled Mt. Everest. As Dean James Dumpson of Fordham's School of Social Work said:

> When I was a beginning professional, I looked and saw that Lester [Granger, as president of the National Conference of Social Work] was *the* top Negro professional in my field. . . . He was a couple of rounds ahead of our expectations as professionals; the League itself had that kind of cloak of statuesque acceptance and status in the professional field and I suppose one of the greatest things that a Negro social worker . . . could aspire to was to have been first a League secretary, then a field secretary and to think that some day you would aspire to be the executive director of the Urban League was like a poor white boy aspiring to be President of the United States.[2]

That was the way some assessed the position Whitney Young assumed when he succeeded Lester Granger as NUL executive director.

Though the selection committee had nominated and the board had confirmed Young without outside pressures, it was true that Lester Granger had suggested Whitney, along with a few others. And as far back as 1958 he had told C. F. McNeill of the National Association of Social Workers, "Mac, I'll tell you what I think of Whitney Young. I hope he's going to be my successor."[3]

The conditions that faced NUL and its new executive were epochal. A fundamental change had taken place during the final years of the Eisenhower administration, a shift as profound as that of the New Deal era. There was a parallel. During the Hoover years the existing voluntary welfare agencies were overwhelmed by the basic social needs of millions of citizens. The only institution with the resources, organization, prestige, discipline and ability to deal with the situation was the federal government. Consequently, government moved into the social welfare field even under Hoover, and more quickly, broadly and deeply under Roosevelt.

After the Supreme Court decision in 1954, the currents in race relations quickened from a trickle to a thundering torrent and again private agencies were inadequate to deal with the civil needs of millions. Government at all levels began to react—sometimes astutely, sometimes appallingly—and the judicial, executive and legislative departments of the federal government grew in importance in this field. Government activities and influence in race relations expanded as Federal influence and action in welfare and labor relations had during the New Deal years.

In these times of vast and rapid change, a private organization seeking to register valid views had to strive mightily to achieve significant impact.

The solid but quiet gains scored by individual Leagues in many cities appeared isolated and were not perceived as part and parcel of a vital, moving, all-encompassing program coordinated by a powerful, highly respected, prestigious national agency in the forefront of the struggle for Afro-American rights. NUL was not perceived that way by black constituents or white citizens for one good reason. It simply was not those things.

As a national organization, operating high visibility, effective, coordinated campaigns in many communities simultaneously across the nation, NUL existed only during the celebration of Equal Opportunity Day and in activities such as the vocational services campaigns and the annual conference.

In the slower, milder days before the acceleration of the fifties, the NAACP had been considered the militant, even the radical organization. The United Negro College Fund was considered the staid, arch-conservative agency. And the Urban League was seen as middle-of-the-road and hopelessly middle-class. The sudden outcropping of brash, outspoken leaders and groups as uncompromising as DuBois and Trotter had been in their times had shunted the NAACP aside. Now the NAACP itself was considered old-hat, stick-in-the-mud, hopelessly middle-class. If yesterday's tiger shrinks to today's tabby, what becomes of yesterday's house cat? That was the NUL's quandary.

"To a good many people," Whitney Young observed in 1961, "the Urban League appears to be 63 or 64 local affiliates with so much local autonomy it is sometimes difficult to identify local activities as part of a nationwide program or movement. These people frequently see the NUL office as an independent 'super' local Urban League. In my opinion, this should not be—and we have taken the first steps toward correcting it." [4]

The first step was a revision of the terms of affiliation, prepared by a special committee and approved by the NUL delegate assembly at the 1961 annual conference. The new national/local League contract, said Young, set the stage "for much closer collaboration and planning between the National office and our affiliates . . . the National office will have more responsibility for the standards of performance in local Leagues and local Leagues are pledged to assume more responsibility for development of the total League program." [5]

The annual conference would have new importance as Young outlined it. There the Urban Leaguers would identify problems of current importance on the American scene and decide which should have top priority in the following year for specific programs centered on those problems. "Then we are able to go to press with an Urban League position that is truly an Urban League position, and with a clear statement of the Urban League's participation and degree to which the League will be involved." [6]

Both planning and implementation would be cooperative, Young said. National projects would be planned with locals and would involve them. Special projects that were discussed would receive final planning and implementation decisions would be made at a national conference, thus committing the various affiliates to work toward the success of the project for which they were going to be held responsibile. He then described how task forces drawn from Local League board and staff members would have assignments (such as urban renewal) and would propose the official League position, program and participation in that area. The national conference would then come to decisions on the proposals.

This would increase the importance of field visits by NUL staffers to local Leagues in the coming year, for they would concentrate on execution of programs adopted at the conference.

There had been considerable discontent among the local Leagues in the past, contending that they receive little from the national office but printed matter and promises. Field visits were rare, except in emergencies; strong direction and assistance on projects and programs were available generally when they coincided with those of several other locals but were infrequent otherwise. Except for the annual conference, the vocational guidance campaigns, the regional institutes or special conferences, the locals saw distinct limits to national office usefulness. They conceded that NUL was handicapped by lack of money and staff, but also, many of them believed, by its leadership. They welcomed Whitney Young's exposition of the terms of affiliation: [7]

> I feel the passage of these new terms [is] crucial to the kind of movement we want to develop. I would hope [local Leagues] would see in them

not threats in terms of demands for service and demands from them for
more materials and harder work [but] in terms of the commitments we are
making for greater service to them. I would hope that they would look at
them objectively, in terms of the movements we are trying to push ahead.
But . . . we intend to follow [them] to the letter.[8]

The executive-designate counseled the local executives on two points
—performance and psychology.

The day had passed, he said, when League professionals could "play it
by ear." Now they would have to study to be knowledgeable; as intelligent people, working according to the book, they were not theorists, but
executives who had to have a planned, thoughtful approach to a job.
Local League public relations would be observed more closely by NUL
—the local's reports, letters, publications, and so on, would be evaluated
and "if these are shoddy, we'll say so."

"We have been suffering too long from 'self-hatred'—we have for too
long talked or permitted people to talk too long about the fact that we're
'no good.' We've talked out of the family about other Leagues. Nothing
succeeds like success. Certain things we must say about unevenness of
quality in staff, but we've got to project a public impression of believing
in ourselves . . . we must start being more positive about each other. I
still think that with all of our failings we have a history that we can be
proud of and a future that has unlimited possibilities—but it is going to
be projected by ourselves, by our saying we are doing something." [9]

Two days later Whitney Young made his first public statement as executive-designate when he addressed the annual conference. At stake, he
said, were the future and reputation of NUL, the commitment and dedication of thousands of volunteers and staff members who, "reflecting on
the urgency of the times, and witnessing dramatic new approaches, are
understandably experiencing moments of doubt, uncertainty and indeci-
sion about our program and the future." [10]

"I am no different from 99 percent of those with whom I talk or from
whom I hear in believing that the League needs greater visibility—
greater public understanding and more dramatic interpretation of its
program." Then he ticked off guideposts for the League: first, the "honest and real needs" of the black masses; second, the interracial structure
and unique resources of the League's national network; third, the
League's relationship to other race relations organizations—the League
program, "different in method and meeting an unduplicated need,"
would at no time compete with or reject the responsible activities of others. Fourth, equality of opportunity was not enough—remedial steps
must be taken to insure true equality of competition. Society, which had
given the special consideration of *ex*clusion of blacks for over 300 years,

now must give special treatment to insure their *in*clusion as citizens able to compete equally with all others.[11]

The League must be effective, understood and supported in coming to grips with these matters. It would be so by:

1. Action-oriented research on the extent of social disorganization and on attitudes.

2. Communicating dramatically "to the total community and its power-structure" a frank presentation of the true causes of problems and the alternative solutions.

3. Fact-finding on remedies and resources in the communities, state and federal programs and services.

4. Informing black constituents of and helping them use the total resources available to them.

5. Developing unique and tangible League programs to involve both blacks and whites. "Some will be aimed at the problems of youth, but will be so designed as to show awareness of the relationship to the total environment."

6. Initiating a program recognizing that the black family as a unit must be strengthened. "In the final analysis, the primary rocket which thrusts the human being into social orbit is the family, and until we effectively direct our attention to this total unit, our society will be guilty of fragmentizing its efforts and . . . alienating and dividing, rather than solidifying, what is still our most basic social institution." Young wound up his presentation on a note of aggressive determination:

> I think that we need to recognize that as a movement we will be at war —at war against prejudice and discrimination, against apathy and indifference, against rationalization, greed, selfishness and ignorance—and we will not hesitate to identify our enemies in this war, whether they be Negro or white, confident that by rendering this service to our communities our financial support will be increased, not diminished.[12]

Those who heard Whitney Young's address were not certain whether it was most like a physician prescribing a healthier regimen or a cavalry officer sounding the charge but few doubted that under the new leader fundamental changes were imminent for NUL.

42/"Operation Rescue"

If the first step to a strong, national organization was passage by NUL's delegate assembly of the new terms of affiliation, the second step had to be to locate a money tree quickly and shake it hard. With 1961 income at the 1952 level, down fully $161,000 from the previous year, the agency's condition was grave. Whitney Young told Rockefeller Brothers Fund executive and NUL board member Lindsley Kimball, "I knew the League was in bad shape (financially) but I had no idea it was *this* bad." He secured a promise that Kimball would round up financial support for NUL for 1962 in order to give the new regime a fair chance to get underway.

Kimball called his special effort to tap the coffers of foundations "Operation Rescue." He was acerbic with the NUL board when he told them about it, describing his own concern over the League's financial experience, the incomprehensible financial statements and the displeasure of Winthrop Rockefeller over mortgaging of the NUL building. He foresaw possibly $350,000 in foundation support for the next year. He spoke of imperative new emphasis on corporate support through a series of luncheons for top business leaders. The first was to be hosted by David Rockefeller of Chase Manhattan Bank and A. L. Nickerson of Socony Mobil Oil Company. The goal was to expand corporation giving under a "fairshare" formula with projected receipts from corporations to be $250,000 for the year ahead. Board members were urged to contribute and to make personal appeals on behalf of the League. Mollie Moon immediately responded with a pledge of $20,000 on behalf of the NUL Guild.[1]

Young then pulled together the Commerce and Industry Council, representing twenty of the nation's largest and most affluent corporations and, against the advice of some, put the NUL's case to them candidly. The agency, he said, was going to improve its image and performance from the national office to its most distant local League; it planned to strengthen and expand industrial relations and vocational services. It was going to increase its activity in health, housing and welfare services. He told them he had been "amazed" at the variety and volume of services industry had received from NUL even with its limited staff. Such services were to be expanded and extended down to the local plant level.

He then put to their enlightened self-interest the alternatives to a viable National Urban League, as he was to do often to representatives of the power structure. Reminding them that blacks were suffering disproportionately from the rapid onset of automation and that black family income relative to white family income remained in 1960 where it had been in 1950, at 54 percent—he said:

> You recognize, I am sure, that federal, state and local government agencies are vitally concerned about the situation. Negroes themselves are concerned. The sporadic attempts to change discriminatory hiring practices in many communities through pressures of various kinds are a matter of public record. But at this point in history, we should come up with better plans for bringing about these changes—and I am confident we can.[2]

The implications seemed clear enough to his auditors—other strong programs by the "moderate" NUL or more government or more protest demonstrations. On that psychological pinnacle Young turned the meeting over to newly appointed associate executive director for administration, Alexander J. Allen. Lanky, Lincolnesque "Joe" Allen briefed the businessmen on the League's finances. He pointed out that in 1960 there had been only 136 commerce and industry gifts of $100 or more, totaling $85,000 or about one fourth of the agency's budget. He introduced a formula for giving scaled from $500 to $5,000 or more, based on gross sales of the corporation. And he asked business to double its support in 1962.

This head-on, outright request for money to finance the agency contrasted with the indirect and unsatisfactory approaches of the past in which erstwhile contributors were treated with such deference and "delicatesse" that results were downright distressing.

The astonishing thing about Whitney Young's frontal approach to prospective donors was that it worked and worked well. Here was a straightforward, businesslike presentation of the agency's needs, its program in the field of interest to the listeners and its expectations from them. The approach to industry was refined by Bill Simms, Whitney Young and that veteran of fund-raising pitches, Lindsley Kimball. They worked on this with NUL senior vice president Malcolm Andresen, tax counsel of Socony Mobil, and Ramon S. Scruggs, manager of personnel relations, American Telephone & Telegraph, a longtime League board member in Detroit before transfer to New York where he became an NUL board member.

The pattern was to form a Special Gifts Committee of a dozen chief executive officers of top-level corporations. They were to serve for one year

only. Each agreed to host one luncheon for corporate tycoons at which
no appeal would be made or pressure brought to bear, but Whitney
Young would present the League story with a specially developed chart
talk. The "bite" came in a later follow-up by Bill Simms and the chairmen
of the committee. It succeeded beyond expectations. By 1963 the contributions "formula" that had been worked out in 1961 to encourage industry
to increase its giving was abandoned. Gifts outran the formula. NUL
income hit $661,000 in 1962 and rocketed to $1,126,000 in 1963.

In other ways, Whitney Young was restructuring NUL. He established
weekly "cabinet" meetings of his department heads, with minutes kept
and decisions, discussions and recommendations recorded, along with the
crucial matter of responsibility, item by item. This strengthened communication within the top ranks and it was mirrored by regular meetings of
program staff members, carried on in a similarly businesslike fashion.
Minutes of the cabinet meeting were shared with program staff to give
them running background on developments and policies.

A development of fundamental significance was the mounting attack
on segregation in the public schools. The scene of battle was beginning
to shift by 1961, from the (formerly) segregated-by-law south to the segre-
gated-by-bigotry north.

In this situation, NUL policy was clarified by action centered about a
small but influential book, *Slums and Suburbs,* written by former Harvard president James B. Conant. In his perceptive study of education in
the cities, Conant had observed that millions were dropping out of school
and that this problem was far more serious for black youths. He found
that in one large slum 70 percent of the youths were out of school and
out of jobs; in another slum the figure for boys was 59 percent. High
school graduates (male) were 48 percent unemployed; the rate for drop-
outs was 63 percent.[3]

Dr. Conant's suggested solution to inferior education for blacks included this statement:

> . . . Antithetical to our free society as I believe de jure segregation to be,
> I think it would be far better for those who are agitating for the deliberate
> mixing of children to accept de facto segregated schools as a consequence
> of a present housing situation and to work for the improvement of slum
> schools whether Negro or white.[4]

Elated segregationists, north and south, picked up Conant's argument
and used his authority and prestige to combat efforts to integrate schools.
Black educators and leaders were alarmed, the weekly press had whipped
up a furor over the "racist" conclusions: it was a hot issue. NUL, therefore, invited Dr. Conant to meet with a group of specialists to review this

situation.[5] They disagreed with Conant's contention that integration was a political issue, that bussing was no answer to unequal education and that "open enrollment" was not essential to quality education.

The consensus of the group was that open enrollment was one important step that was essential, that segregated schools are inherently inferior and cannot provide adequate education. The school, they said, as an important institution in a free society, has the responsibility of helping develop wholesome democratic programs and shaping democratic attitudes in all its students. This is impossible in all-white or all-black schools.

Furthermore, black families should have the opportunity to select schools of their choice away from the ghetto, the NUL spokesmen stated. Because the black neighborhood is artificially created and deliberately circumscribed, free movement of black citizens is prevented and the "neighborhood school" concept is not applicable in such ghettoes. Black parents should have the opportunity to send their children to a school more representative of the total American community. Transcending this, there are important psychological and moral issues involved in the right to free choice that is fundamental to open enrollment programs.

And finally, the group rejected Conant's statement that inferiority of present all-black schools can be completely corrected by better staff and facilities. This would be a return to "separate but equal" and a refutation of the Supreme Court's desegregation verdict. A statement reviewing the discussion was circulated to local Leagues and released to the press, giving a consistent League point of view around the nation on this controversial subject—a vivid contrast with NUL action in the recent past.

In the fall of 1961 unemployment (running about 7 percent) afflicted millions of Americans. The automobile capital, Detroit, was in the doldrums and black workers, especially, were feeling the pinch as employees were laid off. The reports from many Leagues told the same story and NUL, therefore, did a quick survey of fifty cities. The data showed that the unemployment rate among black workers was roughly double that of whites. In St. Louis, 20 percent of the Afro-American wage earners were out of work; in Detroit the rate was a frightening 39 percent.

Vice President Lyndon B. Johnson in his capacity as head of the President's Committee on Equal Employment Opportunity had requested NUL representatives to meet with him. This NUL saw as an important opportunity in the circumstances. The fear was that in a recession, "pecking-order" bumping would take place, that is, blacks, usually the last hired, would be laid off first and whites would take jobs formerly held by Afro-American workers. Labor Secretary Arthur Goldberg made arrangements for the meeting with Lyndon Johnson and a delegation from the League went to Washington. Whitney Young and NUL president Henry

Steeger were accompanied by Mrs. Cernoria Johnson, Guichard Parris and Mahlon T. Puryear, who had just succeeded newly retired Julius A. Thomas as industrial relations director.

Vice President Johnson, in his responsibility for opening new jobs in industry through the "Plans for Progress" operation of the President's Committee on Equal Employment Opportunity, could and should play a highly visible and effective role in opening up more jobs for blacks, thereby narrowing the disparity in Afro-American unemployment, reasoned the NUL. One of the major headaches was the roadblock in the building trades against black journeymen. The League delegation had this on its list to discuss, along with other points that boiled down to too few jobs for blacks.

Ushered into Johnson's Capitol Hill offices, the delegation was seated around a table with the Vice President and several of his aides. After the amenities, Young and Steeger went over their list of particulars, complaining that progress had been too slow and that not enough blacks were being placed, urging that Johnson's committee move to correct the situation. Johnson called for his files and began to read from them to the group. Steeger remembers that the meeting became increasingly uncomfortable:

> [Johnson] then proceeded to pinpoint all of the jobs which had been placed and all of the industries which the government had opened up to Negroes under his administration of the President's Committee. It was most impressive. In fact, as he reviewed the figures, he seemed to become incensed with what appeared to be our unreasonable demands. So instead of our delegation holding him to account for a job not sufficiently well done, the situation was reversed and we found ourselves on the end of the scolding we had intended for him.[6]

The NUL delegation was duly impressed with Johnson's executive ability, with the work his committee was doing, and with the energy he was devoting to the task. But it was able to put across to the Vice President its concern with the fact that not enough had been done and that too many blacks were unemployed, were not hired for jobs at upper levels—or starting jobs either, for that matter—and were not promoted equitably. The NUL group and the Vice President parted amicably, with renewed respect for one another and determination on Young's part never to allow the League to be caught without full information again.

This relationship with the Vice President grew over the years, and put his Plans for Progress staff into intimate contact with the League movement. (Johnson was the featured speaker at the League's 1962 Equal Opportunity Day dinner at which Thomas J. Watson, Jr., of International Business Machines and A. Philip Randolph were honored.) Again, the establishment of direct ties at the top was all-important for future League activity.

By mid-January 1962 Urban Leaguers had appeared four times to testify before the House Subcommittee on Labor and, thanks to former NUL board member Louis E. Martin, the vice chairman of the Democratic National Committee, a meeting with President Kennedy was set. Whitney Young and Henry Steeger went to the White House and pledged the League's resources and cooperation to the administration. They carried with them a statement about progress for the nation's blacks.

The timing of the visit was opportune. Less than ten days before the United States Civil Rights Commission had issued a report charging the government itself with heavy responsibility for discrimination because of its complicity as a silent partner in so many federally sponsored, financed or operated activities. This added importance to Young's and Steeger's call on the President.

Theirs was the last appointment on Kennedy's calendar, suggesting opportunity for full and unhurried discussion, and that was exactly the case. The President met them on the stairs and accompanied them into his second-floor office. They presented recommendations calling for greater federal involvement in aiding blacks in health, welfare, education, vocational training, guidance, apprenticeships, employment and housing. "I'll go for that," said President Kennedy, agreeing that the federal government could do more.

Who, asked Young, would be responsible for implementing such programs? Kennedy replied at once, "Vice President Johnson."

They talked about legislation in these various fields and the President ran through the probable support and opposition for each measure, indicating which senators would be for or against. He asked the Urban Leaguers if they would be willing to speak with some of the legislators about the pending bills. Though they met with House Speaker McCormack, they declined to lobby for legislation.

In the statement delivered to Kennedy, the League pressed him to issue his promised Executive Order outlawing unfair housing practices. During the campaign Kennedy had repeatedly criticized President Eisenhower, saying the President could end discrimination in housing with "a stroke of the pen," ostentatiously promising that a new Democratic administration would do so.

NUL had picked him up on this point in its special memorandum, *The Time Is Now,* sent to Kennedy within a month of his narrow election. More than 25 percent of the memo concentrated on housing and urban renewal.[7] Zeroing in on urban renewal, the League charged it with disregarding people and having a "crushing impact on minority citizens."

At the time of this meeting with President Kennedy in the winter of 1962 the housing industry—builders, contractors, the producers of building materials and especially real estate brokers—were panic-stricken at the prospect of Presidential action against discrimination in housing. These forces of status quo and reaction mounted an intensive nationwide public relations and publicity campaign against any such Executive Order.

The American economy at that time was in a trough and the building industry was wallowing in its own archaic practices and rigid, reactionary policies. In mid-year the National Association of Home Builders issued a scare bulletin in which it directly opposed any presidential order against discrimination in housing, stating that such action would cut the rate of home construction by more than 50 percent.

NUL housing specialist Reginald Johnson prepared a white paper on *The Home Building Industry,* refuting this wildly irresponsible statement.[8] He pointed out that basic conditions alone disproved the contention. In cities and states that had ordinances barring discrimination, housing construction had not dried up—it had increased.

The white paper scored the housing industry for failing to adjust to the change from seller's to buyer's market; with continuing a pernicious dual market system that excluded blacks from bidding on available housing; for being victims of their own stereotype of race; and for reluctance, if not refusal, to recognize the successful experiences with integrated housing documented by the Commission on Race and Housing and the United States Civil Rights Commission. The industry's spurning of moral responsibility in favor of selfish exploitation was cited and the paper wound up with one irrefutable conclusion: "As long as it can make money and there is a demand for housing, the housing industry will continue to build," whether or not an Executive Order was issued.[9]

It was November before Kennedy issued the Executive Order against racial or religious discrimination in federal public housing. This affected only a minor portion of the housing market, for public housing building programs were declining and the overwhelming majority of homes was built by private builders and sold under FHA mortgages. It was this huge sector of home building that was left untouched by the President's unsatisfactory housing order.

In other areas the White House call of Young and Steeger on President Kennedy was more beneficial. The NUL representatives recommended involving the League in more federal activities and suggested that it would be useful to bring all local League executives and NUL professional staff to Washington for a briefing on government programs and response-interaction sessions to determine how the League could play a constructive role in advancing those efforts that were aimed at black progress. Kennedy was enthusiastic. He instructed one of his aides to arrange appointments with the Secretaries of Labor and of Health, Education and Welfare and appropriate agency heads. And he said he would see if the government had funds to help underwrite such a program.

From this grew an unprecedented NUL Washington conference four months later, cosponsored by the Departments of Labor and Health, Education and Welfare plus the Housing and Home Finance Agency. Labor Secretary Arthur Goldberg, HEW Secretary Abraham Ribicoff and HHFA Administrator Robert Weaver and their top aides sat down for three days with eighty-nine NUL and local League executives and other staff. The conference, having been initiated at the White House, elevated NUL's prestige, established direct lines of communication between the highest levels of these key government departments and League professionals, and gave the bureaucrats a short course in the current conditions and needs among blacks in major cities of the nation. It was invaluable in putting the newly established NUL Washington Bureau operation on a "first name" basis with key Labor and HEW agencies.[10] It gave to leading administrators the benefits of League experience and expertise and brought these qualities to bear on developing government programs and policies. The League was moving on Kennedy's "New Frontier."

The whole operation was top-level and fundamental; it was typical of the Whitney Young approach. It fit into his oft-repeated philosophy at this time: "You can holler, protest, march, picket, demonstrate, but somebody must be able to sit in on the strategy conferences and plot a course. There must be the strategists, the researchers and the professionals able to carry out a program. That's our role. That's what we're prepared to do." [11]

43/ Turning Point

In the first week in May 1962 NUL reached a symbolic and psychological turning point. The occasion was formation of a statewide committee on human rights in New York, under the state's Civil Rights Bureau.

The plan was to hold regional conferences to discuss local leadership responsibility for civil rights. It was bona fide and promised to be as bland and safe as such talk-fests usually are, but the point at issue for the NUL was whether to adhere to its traditional self-designation as a social service or social welfare agency or to put itself on record in this official state document as a civil rights agency.

There was no lengthy discussion: To Whitney Young and the five members of the NUL cabinet present there was no question; it was as if the matter had been settled when Young had been chosen as executive director.[1] It was a historic moment, but it went unheralded. More than a year was needed to accomplish emphatically and conclusively what was here decided so easily. The formal, dramatic emergence of NUL as a civil rights agency occurred in the second March on Washington, on August 28, 1963. There were major passes to navigate before that continental divide, however.

The year 1963 was special. It marked the passage of 100 years since Abraham Lincoln penned the Emancipation Proclamation. For several years before the centennial the NAACP had been using the slogans "Free in '63" and this slogan had become firmly implanted in the minds of blacks throughout the nation. Of all the expectations in this era of rapidly cresting black expectations, this—freedom—was central and deepseated, the emotional accelerator of righteous courage in Afro-Americans.

Black citizens had proved their mettle in the encounters of this climactic year of what some called Civil War II. Birmingham, Cambridge, Maryland, Savannah and Americus, Georgia, Danville, Virginia, and Selma, Alabama, were major battle sites in the crusade for civil rights. There were battles in the north, too—in Chicago, Boston and New York, where de facto segregation was targeted. It was the year in which nonviolent action reached a peak—10,000 demonstrations were carried out, causing an estimated 5,000 Americans to be arrested.[2]

In response to the nonviolent, peaceful methods of the civil rights protestors, a full gamut of savagery was employed by racist adversaries—fire hoses, police dogs, electric cattle prods, clubs, axe-handles, ball bats, whips, guns, and bombs. As the photos of unrestrained mayhem against blacks by racist civilians and police leaped from front pages of newspapers in the nation and abroad, the parallel with Nazi Germany of a generation earlier stung the consciences of many whites. There was a pronounced shift of white public opinion in support of black demands for their rights. White educators, students, religious and civic leaders, housewives and postal workers joined the protests. Meanwhile, the Ku Klux Klan surfaced once again. The John Birch Societies indoctrinated thousands with hatred and loathing of national leaders, including the Supreme Court and presidents past and current, who were smeared as dupes or tools of Communism.

The Supreme Court in 1963 threw out the conviction of sit-in demonstrators and the Justice Department initiated court action to halt discrimination by southern voting registrars. The Kennedy administration had succeeded in stimulating the economy and putting more Americans to work. But the great majority of those who had benefited during the decade past were white. Blacks had lost ground. The figures showed it clearly: In 1963, black males earned only 57 percent of median white male wages—a drop from 62 percent in 1951. The NAACP threatened to launch demonstrations for jobs in federal building projects, and the administration responded with a presidential order that federal construction programs be reviewed to end discriminatory hiring and admit young blacks to federal apprenticeship programs.

Early in June 1963, the NUL executive sent a special memorandum to the local executives because of the "dynamic and explosive" racial situation. The broad coverage by the mass media of black citizens in community after community demanding justice and equality disturbed him, Young said, not because of black action, but because Afro-Americans were winning real victories without local Leagues ever being mentioned as participants at any level in what he called "this most significant dialogue and social revolution." [3]

This did not mean, he added, that he expected local Leagues to initiate or participate actively in picketing or boycotting. But he expected League staffers "to be sufficiently involved . . . so that at all times there is rapport and communication between the responsible actionist groups and the Urban League, to the extent that we maintain the respect of the Negro community and a leadership role in the resolution of some of these crisis situations."

> Unlike three, five or ten years ago, when the power structure might have taken a dim view of our active identification with these groups, that same power structure today would not only desire that we have some communication with and relationship to these groups, but would feel that unless we do we are of little value to them on those matters that concern them most. [4]

Young cast a wary glance at newly organized human relations commissions, particularly in League cities, saying it was inconceivable to him—but apparently true—that these groups were playing roles that should be the League's. This reflected on "our smugness, lack of skills, naivete . . . or else that we are, in fact—as some would suggest—overly compromising."

Young sketched his picture of the League's ideal role in the current critical period. It was to be skillful and adequately fortified with know-how, to continue as fact-finder, arbitrator and effective liaison between action groups and the power structure. Act immediately, he suggested to the League executives, "to secure the appropriate visibility" for the local League. He asked to be kept informed of what was happening in the local community and what the executive was doing in relation to it.

He proposed three broad areas of action that local Leagues could pursue and still keep within their program focus:

> First and foremost—secure all the facts about present inequities in the community and make them available publicly with a warning of potential dangers unless corrective measures are taken.
>
> Second, the Leagues should be informed of tension areas and community attitudes and should point these out to city officials, publicly.
>
> Third, Leagues should offer their services in the immediate correction of these inequities, indicating willingness to participate in a negotiating role.

"I was never more convinced," he asserted, "that the opportunity for the Urban League to play a significant role was never greater then it is right now; and if we show some real imagination, creativity and honest-to-goodness sweat this could well result in the doubling and even tripling of our budgets and staffs." [5]

This statement signaled a revolutionary change in League policy. And yet it had a reminiscent ring. In fact, it had antecedents stretching back more than three decades. In the depths of the Depression, Chicago League official O. O. Cox wrote to NUL "the time has come for a more aggressive attitude on the part of Negroes. We, of the Chicago Urban League, realize that fact, and our future programs will be far more aggressive than they have been in the past." [6]

"Throughout the Depression," note Drake and Cayton in *Black Metropolis*, "the Urban League gave its moral support to the younger radicals who were channelizing the discontent of [Chicago] into non-violent patterns of aggressive action." The Chicago League, they note, had always been considered the "citadel of safe leadership." But when the Bronzeville masses began to picket for jobs, the League "not only gave its sanction to the movement, but placed the facilities of its offices at the disposal of the leaders." [7]

True, 1963 was not 1930, but for thousands of unemployed black citizens in the slums it was almost as bad.

Another factor of significance was President Kennedy's special message at the end of February 1963 on civil rights. In it he listed the administration's priorities: (1) voting rights, with referees; (2) aid to desegregate school districts; (3) elimination of "separate but equal" from the Morrill land-grant colleges act; (4) extension of the Civil Rights Commission for four more years. Useful as these measures might be, race leaders looked at them as puny and peripheral in terms of the gigantic requirements of the moment. And even limited as they were, there was serious doubt that Congress would enact them.

Stemming from Whitney Young's statements in his speech to the NUL annual conference in September 1961, there had been staff discussions about his concept of "compensatory activity." By April 1, 1963, "Joe" Allen had completed a second draft of a statement on this subject and it was circulated to NUL cabinet members for comments and suggestions so that it could be revised for review by the agency's executive committee that week. At the cabinet meeting it was agreed that "one concept which should be added is that of emphasis on the responsibility of individual minority group members themselves to make special effort." [8]

This was the draft of the program that came to be known as the NUL's domestic "Marshall Plan." Its debut in the NUL executive committee meeting was inauspicious. It was greeted with suspicion, if not outright hostility, from several board members who saw it as a reversal of the interracial foundation of the League, and a spurning of the time-honored concept laid down by Ruth Standish Baldwin: "Let us work not as colored people nor as white people for the narrow benefit of any group alone." The heart of the Marshall Plan concept was that *special effort* was needed for and by black citizens if they were ever to catch up. Its ten points called for:

1. Special effort to overcome the serious historic handicaps of black citizens.

2. Moves to develop the potential of Afro-Americans.

3. Assignment of the best educational talent and facilities to teach and motivate black youngsters.

4. Conscious effort to put blacks in entrance jobs in all types of employment, including upper and lower management positions.

5. Open housing for all and elimination of racial ghettoes.

6. Concentration of the best health and welfare skills where needed most—to help needy blacks in the ghetto.

7. Placement of black citizens on boards, commissions and panels that make policy in health, education, welfare, housing and employment.

8. Action by blacks themselves to seize every opportunity for education, advancement and strengthening of the black community.

9. Government, foundation, labor and business support and backing for preventive programs carried on by established, responsible black leadership organizations.

10. Responsible participation by Afro-Americans in every phase of community life.[9]

Introduction of these sweeping proposals was a shock to the NUL board. Many board members huddled in small groups to discuss them; several called NUL President Henry Steeger about this "inflammatory" business. Several opposed the program because it would "tarnish the image" of the League as an interracial agency and charged Steeger with responsibility to get Whitney Young to drop the whole wild scheme. Steeger had several conferences with the NUL executive and with various board members concerning suggestions to "bridge the gap" but discovered that Young was adamant. He believed that such a program was absolutely imperative to help overcome black handicaps and poverty. He was a persuasive advocate and convinced Steeger.[10]

The "compensatory activity" program went through several revisions and became known as the "special consideration" plan. To several board members it was still a mackerel regardless of its label and they refused to swallow it. Meanwhile, the siege of Birmingham, Alabama, led by Martin Luther King, Jr., was under way, and headlines from around the nation reported blacks demonstrating and protesting against second-class citizenship. In mid-May the President sent troops to Birmingham after a shattering riot.

This was the situation, then, when Whitney Young appeared at a testimonial luncheon on June 9, 1963, honoring the extraordinary lady who had negotiated the integration of black nurses into the American Nurses Association, Inc. and their professional acceptance in the medical field. She was Mabel K. Staupers, R.N., retired president of the National Association of Colored Graduate Nurses, and the turnout in her honor consisted mainly of her nursing colleagues. Health and welfare and human interest reporters were present from the daily papers and the black press. A press conference had been held before the luncheon. After saluting Mrs. Staupers, Whitney Young took his future in hand, went on to his second subject and read a prepared statement announcing an NUL call for a domestic Marshall Plan.

This was the program that had stirred the NUL board and left it divided. Young had now announced it without board approval, so his neck was in the noose. The proposal was page one news in the major daily papers and was featured on radio and TV. The New York *Times* covered it thoughtfully and favorably, as did many others. But many tore the proposal to shreds, attacking it as a request for "reparations" and "indemnification" and denouncing Young for these "outrageous demands."

Apparently NUL board members saw the favorable news accounts for there were no criticisms of the plan at the next meeting nor were any sent directly to Steeger.[11] The public response was immediate and intense, with much controversy, a great deal of thoughtful consideration and extensive applause from black constituents.

At the NUL cabinet meeting the following day program staff members were asked to develop applications and expositions of the Marshall Plan concepts for their specific areas of interest. An all-day conference in July was planned in order to work out ways and means of bringing the Marshall Plan idea into all discussions at the annual conference. And Joe Allen was designated to talk with NUL's legal counsel and The Reverend Dr. M. Moran Weston of St. Phillips Episcopal Church of Harlem to explore the possibility that precedents or bases of some consequence might be found in English common law for the plan.[12]

The release of the NUL Marshall Plan position paper appeared to be a master stroke. At a time when the cities of the nation were shuddering with confrontations in the streets the League offered constructive alternatives, clearly differentiating itself from the action-protest groups. The plan was responsible and could not conceivably be attacked as a "sellout" by any but the most impossibly alienated blacks. It at once put the nation on notice that there was a strong voice, respectable and determined, that must be considered. It was a bid not only for League recognition but a bid to the nation to turn a corner in confrontation politics.

For the first time from a national forum and with such emphasis, the NUL advanced from its traditional position of asking "not alms, but opportunity," or simply for equal opportunity. It recognized and admitted the impossibility of blacks to compete equally because of historic handicaps and called for similar recognition by society. It took the case an additional, essential step—demanding that remedial attention be administered to these handicapped citizens. This was special pleading without apology. Whitney Young had moved the League a long, long way down the road to "militancy," putting the League in the headlines in the role of "respectable radical." And such was his strength with his board of trustees that there was no move either to censure or displace him.

The media, particularly the television and newspaper reporters, were busy with their antic game of gossip doubled and redoubled as they hounded civil rights leaders that summer. The favored ploy was to ask the leader of the NAACP about CORE's latest move, then rush that comment back to the leader of CORE, SCLC and the NUL for countercomment, and so on, ad infinitum, with an occasional break in the rhythm for Congressman Adam Clayton Powell or Malcolm X to denounce all other black leaders. Thus it was with more than nominal dismay that the reporters discovered a meeting on July 22 of Whitney Young, Roy Wilkins,

Martin Luther King, Jr., James Farmer and Jack Greenberg of the NAACP Legal Defense and Educational Fund, under the aegis of the Taconic Foundation. Out of it came a new grouping, called the United Council of Civil Rights Leadership, or simply UNITY, with Whitney Young as the chairman.

The basic thought was that strategic planning was needed in the civil rights field and that bringing the various leading organizations together would make possible some division of labor and long-range viewing. Stephen Currier, head of the Taconic Foundation, believed there was a need to develop position papers mapping out the road ahead, describing the needs. These papers would place the anticipated problems before government agencies and/or foundations which would underwrite programs to deal with them.

The UNITY meetings were to figure how additional financing could be obtained to develop the strategies, provide guidance and prevent overlap. The goal was $1,500,000, of which $800,000 had been pledged, with a major portion of it assigned to NUL. Some of the money was to be available to the League to underwrite new Leagues in the south and to pay salaries for additional staff persons in Chicago, Washington and New York.

From the UNITY meetings, with pictures and headlines about the civil rights leaders, came additional prestige for NUL and clear evidence that it was very much alive and ranked with the biggest, as well as the most active of the civil rights organizations.

Not in boast but to move his NUL associates to use this prestige Whitney Young told them in July that "we can get anybody we want now to sit down and meet with us. . . . We should do [this] in all our program areas. . . . We wouldn't have any trouble getting top people and alerting them to what they might expect. This is the way I would like to see you capitalize on the new image we have with the [Negro] revolution." [13] (This was a considerable change from slightly over a year before when Young had complained that Urban Leaguers had trouble getting appointments with the assistant to the third assistant in some companies.)

Meanwhile, the nation's shock at the brutality in Birmingham had brought the President of the United States before a nationwide television audience on June 11, in the first direct presidential appeal in history to American citizens to end discrimination.

The nation faced a moral crisis, Kennedy declared, that "cannot be met by repressive police action. It cannot be left to increased demonstrations in the streets. It cannot be quieted by token moves or talk. It is time to act in the Congress, in your state and local legislative body, and, above all, in all of our daily lives."

This was a landmark in the lives of black citizens. It was an unequivocal statement by the Chief Executive endorsing the cause of Afro-Americans. The justifiable elation of black citizens at this new plateau of federal concern was marred by the rejection of Kennedy's appeal by some—underscored by the infamous murder of Mississippi state NAACP secretary Medgar Evers only seven hours after the President's plea.

Eight days later John Kennedy, who had taken office believing that executive orders and executive action would be the only really effective tools to accomplish anything in civil rights, sent to Congress a proposed civil rights law. The temper of the times had shifted sufficiently to override Kennedy's reluctance to put a civil rights bill before a conservative Congress. He had believed such a measure had no chance and would simply jam the machinery, preventing action on other vital legislation. The civil rights bill was promptly pigeonholed by the House Rules Committee, and the March on Washington that followed was a major effort to dislodge it.

The first mention of such a second March had been made in February 1963 by A. Philip Randolph. The Negro American Labor Council, which Randolph formed in 1960, backed the project and other organizations were invited to participate. Whitney Young brought the matter to the NUL cabinet meeting on April 1, 1963, passing Randolph's letter around. The tentative date set for the March was June 13 and the League was asked to cooperate. The six NUL staff members present agreed that if the League was to be involved it should be on the basis of cosponsorship rather than cooperation in someone else's project. Furthermore, they decided, it should be interracial and its objectives should be sharply defined.[14]

When Joe Allen and Mahlon Puryear, for the NUL, met with Philip Randolph and representatives of both the Negro American Labor Council and CORE nine days later, the project's name had been changed to "Emancipation March on Washington for Jobs" and it had been rescheduled for October. At the next NUL cabinet meeting in mid-April Joe Allen reported these facts plus the reaction of the NUL executive council (critical of League participation on the basis proposed) and news that NAACP did not plan to participate in the march.[15]

Meanwhile, around the nation local Leagues had been pressed to join in picketing and demonstrations carried on by black citizens. There was a lengthy debate of the subject at the NUL program staff meeting on June 26, 1963.

Reginald Johnson said that recently in Detroit he had advised the local League not to join a march without board approval, but agreed that Urban Leaguers as individuals were free to demonstrate. Nelson

Jackson spoke of the decision of the New York League that joining picket lines was against policy. It was not the League's role, he said, to carry picket signs, but rather to collect facts to be used by those who did in order to achieve "our mutual goal." It was national's job, he stressed, to instill in locals their responsibility to maintain such information and the know-how to use it.

The staff decided to differentiate between peaceful demonstrations or parades where black and white Americans marched in the name of human dignity and picket lines designed to bring economic pressure to bear. "It was felt that the former was a part of the job of the Urban League." [16]

This neat delineation was put to the test only a few days later when Baltimore League executive Furman Templeton landed in jail and in the headlines for picketing. He had done so as a member of a Presbyterian church group in which he was prominent, not as an Urban Leaguer. The action was in character for him, however, and at the next NUL program staff meeting the limits of individual action were probed: Templeton was involved in an improper action, according to the League's definition, Whitney Young said. His involvement was understandable, however; he had to be engaged because of his position. "But this does not change our basic policy against picketing and boycotting. . . . You are no good to us in jail. You must decide which is more important to you. Some people are better suited to work for organizations such as CORE and the NAACP rather than the Urban League. This the person must decide for himself." [17]

This discussion, it should be noted, took place just a month before the March on Washington. It was in this meeting that Whitney Young explained the evolution of the march project. The concept had been mentioned after the White House meeting of civil rights leaders. The Leadership Conference on Civil Rights had met afterward and decided to set up an office and devise programs to support Kennedy's civil rights legislation. A March on Washington was discussed as a possibility, depending on the way the legislation moved.

Later, Philip Randolph's American Negro Labor Council decided on a March for Jobs, stressing the plight of black workers, and set the date for October. After meeting with Martin Luther King, Jr., and several local groups, Randolph's organization shifted to August 28. Legislation was added as a goal. CORE, NAACP and NUL were not invited at this stage. Furthermore, the basic League position was to stay out of things in which it did not have a planning role.

However, when leaders of the Big Six civil rights organizations got together,[18] they agreed that they should join in order to give the demonstration a constructive purpose and prevent it from hurting the chances of legislation by getting out of hand. Young volunteered that the League would cooperate and participate up to the point of lobbying activity. He agreed to speak at the rally and march down the street on three conditions: (1) that the group would be broad based, representing the policy-making bodies of churches, labor unions, and so on; (2) that it must be interracial; (3) that there be no activity around the Capitol that could be called civil disobedience.[19]

Congressmen were to be invited to meet the leaders. The group planned to assemble on Pennsylvania Avenue and march to the Lincoln Memorial. All participants would be asked to come that morning and leave the same night. There could be "no guarantee that no one will be out of line," said Young, "but we are trying to plan an all-night vigil of the White House for the SNCC group."

This threw the meeting open to a serious discussion of the basic significance of such participation to NUL's future. Young stated that he believed this decision was consistent with the NUL policy: picketing and boycotting were out, for they were directed primarily at affecting the economic life of specific institutions. Demonstrations in which a broad spectrum of responsible people addressed themselves to an overall social evil and concerned themselves with general inequity, were activities in which NUL should be represented and identified.

What about local Leagues, asked one staff member, with their dependence on their Community Chests? The Chests had not gotten around to discussing these problems and the local Leagues were trying to protect their pocketbooks.

"It is a matter of proper interpretation," Young said.

> We have to make a decision. We must keep the respect of the Negro people and provide some leadership. The revolution is here. Should we divorce ourselves and let it go as it [is], or intervene and try to bring our experience to bear in these matters? Unless we are in communication with the people we are not in a position to advise those who give us money on matters of the Negro. . . . We recognize that on the national level we are dealing with bigger men who understand the larger aspects of the problem. We also recognize that it is a calculated risk either way we go, and we must have proper communication with other groups and impress upon them the value of the Urban League's program.

"If we are officially part of the march and SNCC gets out of hand at the White House, what will this mean for the League?" asked another staff member.

What is more important, responded the executive director, is the damage to the cause if they get out of line. "I must think in terms of the larger thing. The best way to keep them in line is to be involved in it and try to guide its direction toward something constructive."

Cernoria Johnson observed that the level of the March had been raised by the decisions made in the leadership conferences and by the church groups and national organizations that had announced they would participate. "The League's image has come through clearly as being responsible for bringing the idea of the March into focus, and it has been expressed adequately in the press." We must take a stand, she continued, and let the locals know NUL is wholeheartedly for the August 28 March. She recommended an announcement that Whitney Young would speak and League members were free to march if they chose. The League must take the risk of someone getting out of hand, she argued. "We must play our part in this fight or lose our ground and our status among Negroes."

"We will not only lose status among Negroes, but with white liberals and the country as a whole," Young added.

Planning meetings multiplied before the March on Washington and as the date approached tension rose. Newspapers and broadcast media were more and more apprehensive. Interviews with political, business and other spokesmen were full of dire predictions. Southern congressmen denounced the march, vowing that Congress would not be "swayed by threats."

Under the direction of Bayard Rustin intense efforts were put into organization of the march. Joe Allen represented NUL. The civil rights leaders met and Whitney Young's influence was exercised to keep the program focused on positive statements.

The event itself was historic. From all parts of the nation blacks and whites poured into Washington, D.C., and, in a spirit of concern and determination marched proudly to the Lincoln Memorial. There the civil rights leaders spoke, in turn. Whitney Young marked the formal emergence of the National Urban League as a transformed organization, in the forefront of the civil rights struggle, with these words:

> The National Urban League is honored to be a participant in this historic occasion. Our presence here not only reflects the civil rights community's increased respect for, and awareness of, the Urban League's role, but most important, it says, and I hope loud and clear, that while intelligence, maturity, and strategy dictate that as civil rights agencies we use different methods, we are all united as never before on the goal of securing first-class citizenship for all Americans—NOW. . . . This is the real significance of our March on Washington today. . . . Our march is a march for America. It is a march just begun.[20]

The march was an awesome demonstration of black determination and discipline. It was clearly within the democratic tradition of peaceful assembly and petition. It was also an undeniable demonstration that the civil rights drive had acquired solid white support, in the persons of the 50,000 white citizens who joined 200,000 Afro-Americans in witnessing that day. Not to be overlooked was the prominent participation of the National Council of Churches, the American Jewish Congress and the National Catholic Conference for Interracial Justice plus the United Auto Workers' Walter Reuther (though the AFL-CIO executive council refused to endorse the march) representing the AFL-CIO Industrial Union Department. The euphoria of the stunning dignity and successful, unmarred execution of the march was contagious. Pollsters found that whites were impressed. Blacks had gained new allies. And this new coalition for civil rights extended the range of responsible advocacy, adding weight to the efforts to move Congress to action.

Retaliation against the local Leagues for NUL participation in the march was insignificant. In reply to a specific inquiry sent to local Leagues no cutoff of support by United Funds or Community Chests was reported though there were some negative statements in southern cities.

NUL had been a conspicuous leader in the most controversial national demonstration of the year, yet it had not only weathered it. It had emerged without the scurrilous and devastating attacks of the fifties. It had come through strengthened and with enormously enhanced prestige. Whitney Young had led the League across still another Rubicon.

44/Federal Commitment

Though the March on Washington was a singular achievement in American civic action, the incidents and violence of the remainder of the year proved that blacks were still only in the foothills of freedom.

The demonstrations had shifted northward in the fall of 1963 when a massive boycott of Chicago schools was organized. Some 220,000 black children—half of Chicago's total enrollment—protested de facto segregation. In Boston in June of 1963, 3,000 students had boycotted the public schools for the same reason. A school boycott in New York pulled nearly half a million students out of classrooms in February 1964 and 267,000 in March. Once again Chicago and Boston schools were struck and Cleveland, Gary, Kansas City, Chester, Pennsylvania, Milwaukee and Cincinnati were also sites of major school protests.

White reaction was swift, as groups of parents organized to protect the status quo, using "neighborhood schools" as a rallying cry. It was a rationale that made segregated schooling supportable for northern whites who had clucked smugly when the bigots of Little Rock and New Orleans and other southern communities had defied orders to integrate their public schools.

Another significant development in the fall of 1963 was the first successful rent strike in New York. Tenants of slum properties were organized into the Community Council on Housing and refused to pay rent to slum-lords until heat was furnished, leaky roofs were mended, plumbing was fixed and the buildings were legally inhabitable under the city's housing and sanitation codes. The strikers won a stirring victory when the courts upheld their action, refusing to support landlords until they repaired their buildings. This small but significant breach in the walls of Property caused a sharp intake of breath in the banking and finance sector where slum-lords and real estate operators were preferred credit risks. The rent strike spread to Chicago and then on to other major cities. On the other side of the ledger, California voters in a trickily worded referendum voted to repeal the state's fair housing law by a margin of two to one.

Another event that sent the tempers of thousands of white middle-class Americans rocketing and caused apoplectic bursts of outrage was the wildcat sit-in staged by the East River (New York) chapter of CORE on the Triborough Bridge at the height of rush-hour traffic. The net results of this new dimension of civil disobedience were nil, but the power structure suffered another palpitation as it realized the vulnerability of the nation's vital cities and realized also that unpredictable elements in the black community had discovered this truth.

The sickening event that symbolized white rejection of integration and demonstrated the depths of racist depravity occurred in Birmingham that fall. A bomb in a Birmingham church Sunday school destroyed four tiny black girls. (It was the twenty-first bombing of blacks in Birmingham since 1955; the fiftieth since World War II—all "unsolved.") President Kennedy sent federal mediators to Birmingham to reconcile continuing differences between black protests against Jim Crow and white intransigence.

Six weeks later many pro-segregationist southerners won office in the November elections. Scarcely two weeks after that John F. Kennedy was assassinated in Dallas. The immediate reaction of blacks was a great sense of loss. Kennedy, after all, had stated that regardless of how long it took, passage of a strong civil rights bill was imperative. Now he was gone, succeeded by a Texan, Lyndon B. Johnson. Johnson's drawl was enough to make Afro-Americans apprehensive, and the new President knew it.

President Johnson threw himself into action to bridge the confidence gap. Within forty-eight hours of taking the oath of office he had called all the major civil rights leaders by telephone. He phoned Whitney Young twice that first weekend, and summoned him and other civil rights leaders to the White House. For days the media carried photos of the President meeting with first one, then another black leader. Doubts about Johnson's commitment to civil rights were reduced when the new President pledged that he would do his utmost to pass pending civil rights legislation.

Some blacks who knew Johnson's record as a young New Dealer and Texas congressman remembered his consistent support of NYA and measures benefiting "the little man," whether black or white, as consonant with his egalitarian, populist background. They recalled also that he, as majority leader during the Eisenhower years, was largely responsible for moving the two civil rights bills of that administration through a reluctant Congress. Now, with "Let Us Continue" as the poignant slogan for his presidency, Johnson capitalized on the upsurge of grief and guilt to push through Congress the stalled civil rights bill.

NUL senior vice president Malcolm Andresen arranged for Whitney Young to meet with Senator Everett Dirksen, the Republican leader in the Senate. The visit ranged over many topics and it was the NUL executive's conclusion that while no one thing changes a person, this interview influenced Dirksen's attitude on several points. It was at a crucial time, for the civil rights bill came up for a vote at the end of June and was passed in July, with Dirksen casting an "aye" and influencing other Republican senators to do likewise.

This law, called by historian John Hope Franklin "the most far-reaching and comprehensive law in support of racial equality ever enacted by Congress," [1] was mistaken by naïve millions of Americans as the solution to the nation's deep racial travail. Even such hard-bitten campaigners as the NUL were caught up by unqualified enthusiasm for the act, declaring that it "levels all barriers to first-class citizenship and equal opportunity for Negroes save those erected in human hearts." [2]

It was a good law, a quantum leap forward in federal acknowledgment of responsibility for the rights of black citizens. The Freedmen's Bureau and the Fourteenth and Fifteenth Amendments to the Constitution had dealt with basic rights of the black population. This Civil Rights Act of 1964 was the first decisive proof that after a century the black citizen had moved to center stage in the concerns of the federal establishment and that the prestige and weight of the government were to be brought to bear on behalf of Afro-Americans. Its provisions allowed the Attorney General to protect citizens from discrimination in education, public accommodations and voting; set up a Community Relations Service to troubleshoot civil rights wrangles; gave the Office of Education power to help with school desegregation; ruled out Jim Crow in programs financed with federal money; set up an Equal Employment Opportunity Commission; and gave the Civil Rights Commission an extension of nearly four years.

Yet good as it was, this law could not and did not solve all of America's race problems. It did not quiet smoldering black discontent or eradicate white racism. Racism, in fact, acquired new currency with the all-but-overt appeals of Senator Barry ("In Your Heart You Know He's Right") Goldwater to reactionary and segregationist elements during his 1964 campaign for the presidency. Outdone only by the redneck racism of George Wallace, who openly courted the bigots in the primary campaign, Goldwater talked about "law and order" which seemed to translate into "keep the blacks in their place."

Landmark though it was, the Civil Rights Act of 1964 was clearly identified as Kennedy legislation. The new President was searching for programs that would establish his own identity and leave his imprint on history. He discovered elements that he sought in incomplete plans and formulations prepared for Kennedy's consideration.

In its first two years the Kennedy administration had reduced unemployment from about 7 percent in early 1961 to 5.3 percent. The economy was picking up perceptibly. Yet studies in the spring of 1963 (by Robert Lampman of Wisconsin University) showed that the rate at which individuals were throwing off the yoke of poverty was slowing.[3] President Kennedy devoted a cabinet meeting in June 1963 to examining unemployment among blacks and in September a Task Force on Manpower Conservation was appointed to tackle the problems of poverty in the nation. Labor Secretary Willard Wirtz was chairman of the committee, with Secretary of Defense Robert McNamara, HEW Secretary Anthony Celebrezze and Selective Service Chief General Lewis Hershey as members.

Kennedy told Walter Heller, the chairman of the Council of Economic Advisers, in November that his key legislative objective in 1964 would be an attack on poverty.[4] Two elements of this went into the legislative hopper and were passed by Congress before the end of 1963: the Manpower Development and Training Act and the Vocational Education Act. The rest was still in the form of staff reports and position papers when Lyndon Johnson succeeded Kennedy.

The attack on poverty had the broad potential for which Johnson was hunting and he seized it eagerly, announcing on January 7, 1964, in his State of the Union Message to the Congress: "I shall shortly present to the Congress a program designed to attack the roots of poverty in our cities and rural areas. . . . This war on poverty . . . will not be won overnight." Before the end of January, Sargent Shriver, the Peace Corps chief, had been appointed special assistant to the President for the War on Poverty and within six weeks the proposed legislation was sent to Capitol Hill for congressional action. For the most part, the programs were developed by the "JD"—Juvenile Delinquency—team in Robert Kennedy's Justice Department and by experts outside government.

If ever there was an open invitation to the Urban League professionals, this legislation appeared to be it. The areas of action specified were those in which the League had decades of experience and the target group— the poor—included, by income definition, half of all black citizens. NUL made sure that it kept up with the fast-breaking developments in the antipoverty war in two significant ways: Whitney Young met with Sargent Shriver and his aides, advised on the bill and the timetable for its implementation and testified on April 14 as an expert witness in Congressional hearings on the legislation.

Before the end of May 1964 five of the NUL program staff specialists went to Washington to meet with the top administrators of the still-to-be confirmed Office of Economic Opportunity. Their mission was to make certain that the League had, in detail, the exact procedures to be followed in securing grants, and to check out program possibilities thoroughly before making the input of effort for participation in the OEO projects. It was expected that NUL might be a prime contractor for some programs that would then be subcontracted to local Leagues for execution.[5]

The Economic Opportunity Act of 1964 was passed August 8, 1964, to a drumroll of riots ripping Harlem, Brooklyn, Patterson, Jersey City and Elizabeth, N.J., Jacksonville, Rochester, Chicago and Philadelphia. Largely confined to the black ghettoes, these were outpourings of protest against police brutality, of distress and impatience by blacks who agreed with the fiery words of Malcolm X, damning white racism, even if they rejected some of his remedies. Direct action was fragmented, with demonstrations in many cities across the nation but no single focal point of black unrest or sustained pressure for civil rights. In fact, so hot had the "long hot summer" become in the steaming ghettoes of the north that Whitney Young and other worried black civil rights leaders issued a joint statement denouncing riots and calling for a "moratorium" on demonstrations that might get out of control and flare into riots. (With an eye on the approaching election contest between Johnson and Goldwater and with "law and order" the Goldwater refrain, White House aides contended that every additional bottle broken in a street encounter meant another vote for Goldwater.)

Some black leaders spoke disparagingly of demonstrations as group therapy, blowing off steam. They pointed to the fact that the victories won by demonstrations were few and far between, in terms of real improvements in black living conditions, in jobs, housing and integrated education. Whitney Young called for "tangible victories" and adroitly exploited white anxieties about the possibilities of black violence getting out of hand, with pointed reminders in his speeches to business and labor leaders. Responsible black leaders needed support and evidence that the power structure was moving to include Afro-Americans, he would say, with significant emphasis in his delivery. Then he would follow up with the comment that if his suggestions for special effort to secure more jobs, training, housing, and so on, seemed like irrational demands of an unrealistic black spokesman, his audience had no idea of the demands that would be presented by extremist black leadership which was just "waiting in the wings to step in and take over."

The Economic Opportunity Act had two main parts. Title I contained three youth programs, Title II covered something new: a community action program (CAP). This new program was to mobilize and utilize resources, "public or private . . . in an attack on poverty." It was to provide "service, assistance and other activities of sufficient scope and size to give promise of progress toward elimination of poverty or a cause or causes of poverty through developing employment opportunities, improving human performance, motivation, and productivity, or bettering the conditions under which people live, learn and work." These were to be "developed, conducted, and administered with the maximum feasible participation of residents of the areas and members of the groups served; . . . conducted, administered, or coordinated by a public or private nonprofit agency (other than a political party), or a combination thereof." [6]

Based on its intimate involvement with the new antipoverty program NUL decided it was imperative to bring together black leadership for better understanding of the measures. The heads of black sororities, fraternities, trade organizations, service groups, and agencies from national to precinct level were invited to a conference in Washington. The purpose was to share quickly and with maximum accuracy the specifics, the implications, ramifications and limitations of both the new Civil Rights Law and the antipoverty program. Also part of the conference's purpose was to reestablish in the minds of black citizens that the League was "the knowledgeable and appropriate agency with the greatest concern in this area." [7]

The NUL's Community Action Assembly was held December 9–11, 1964, in Washington. It brought together more than 350 black leaders representing national organizations and civil rights agencies. The conclave had the full attention of the Johnson administration, from the address by the President himself to the attendance at special sessions of Secretaries Weaver, Wirtz and Celebrezze, Sargent Shriver and key aides. Guidelines were developed for grass-roots black leadership to make use of the federal programs in the areas of employment, civil rights and antipoverty legislation.

A direct outgrowth of the assembly was a series of antipoverty workshops sponsored by NUL's southern regional office. Through twelve such workshops conducted in cooperation with other prominent black organizations in the region, some 3,000 conferees came together to learn how to participate in the programs provided for in the Economic Opportunity Act. The League brought to these workshops government representatives from federal and state agencies who gave authoritative counsel to people who would be the "field officers" in the so-called "War on Poverty."

Evaluating the assembly, Whitney Young described to NUL board members the two-way impact it had made. Black leaders were impressed by the caliber of people brought together. Cabinet officers and other government officials were given a unique opportunity to meet and talk with leaders of national black organizations. It succeeded in its basic function, that of quickly bringing the necessary information and counsel to hundreds of communities via their representatives who returned to their homes and set to work developing antipoverty programs to be funded by OEO.

The community action portion of the Economic Opportunity program, which was unquestionably one of the most creative developments in social welfare ever to be launched in the nation, soon ran into problems. The language of the act called for "maximum feasible participation of residents of the areas and members of the groups served," and the next section ruled out political parties as coordinators, administrators and contractors for the projects.

It did not sound revolutionary. But when the "disadvantaged" were brought onto the governing boards in the CAP projects (one third of a board was reserved for poor people) as the OEO directives insisted, politicians in cities from Chicago south suddenly felt an unfiltered blast of indignation from those long by-passed by the system. Not that the politicians were unaccustomed to criticism, but over this program, as originally operated, they had no control. The money went directly from Washington to the local CAP agency. The fundamental orientation of the administrators of the CAP was anti-Establishment. The operative concept was that city hall and public services, especially the schools, welfare and employment agencies, were parts of the Establishment and instead of truly serving the needs of the poor gave them the run-around, treating their cuts and abrasions but never treating their deep-seated mortal illness of poverty.

So the community action programs put the squeeze on the established agencies for action. If prompt and effective action was not forthcoming, the new CAP organization might—and often did—raise a howl that resulted in headlines on page one with painful fallout on local political leaders. This led, inevitably, to changes in the administration and structure of OEO and its programs.

The League had some criticism of the War on Poverty. In brief, the primary *caveats* were that the federal antipoverty program was diffuse and uncoordinated, operating as it did through the Departments of Labor, Commerce, HEW and HUD as well as the OEO. Inevitably there were duplications, competition and wide gaps. Sargent Shriver, said Young, "working with extremely limited resources . . . and laboring under the necessity to mobilize a major effort in an exceedingly short period of time, has done a most commendable job." [8]

But, with 22,000,000 Americans living in slums (versus 21,000,000 on farms) the total federal effort was akin to using a Band-Aid as a cancer cure, said Young. He deplored the fact that limited funds forced the antipoverty war administrators to react to crisis (as when they poured resources into Watts in Los Angeles after the huge riot) rather than act positively and preventively. The suspicion was alive that a riot was a necessary prelude to remedial action on poverty.

Closer to home was his criticism that there had been a consistent government practice of funneling funds for programs into new local agencies —green, untried, assembled for the express purpose of receiving funds. Too many of these, charged Young, had been hastily conceived and hastily manned and had generated uproarious quarrels over who was to run them. He said that too often jobs had been given out as political rewards rather than to those with experience and competence.

Civil rights agencies, some of them with fifty years of experience and with thoroughly representative boards and the confidence of their communities had received little or nothing from the federal program. If they had, Young reported, they would have been strengthened and could have implemented some of the tangible results sought in the ghettoes. The influence of these agencies would have been increased, making it possible for them to channel understandable anger and impatience in constructive rather than destructive directions.

Young could not resist pointing out that even though some of these agencies had been left out of the picture, they were still the first ones to which the authorities turned when civil disorder threatened to replace realistic and orderly procedures, "and the first ones upon which extremists turn because they cannot deliver on the meat, bread and potatoes programs fast enough." [9]

Many and perhaps most of the existing health and welfare agencies needed challenging, admitted Young. They should be forced to re-examine their programs, assess whether they were really reaching the needy, and make their policy boards more representative. But it was the NUL executive's view that it would have been better to establish coordinating bodies to work through the existing agencies, capitalizing on their years of experience and know-how—*if* they met the criteria on program, clients, personnel and representation at policy levels.

An example of this approach was NUL's part in OEO-financed Project ENABLE in cooperation with the Child Study Association of America and Family Service Association. ENABLE was the acronym for Education and Neighborhood Action for Better Living Environment, a multiphase approach to hard-core poverty neighborhoods in sixty-one cities. Major areas of action were child-rearing, employment and education. Perhaps the most striking innovation of ENABLE was recruitment and training of 150 "social work aides." These people, from the ghetto areas they were to work in, were, in effect, junior social workers serving some 120 families each. Their primary duty was to guide slum families to existing agencies—public or private—equipped to aid the "client." The aide was trained to research the community services in his area and to deal with the agencies supplying them. If the agency proved unresponsive, the ENABLE professional staff was on call to apply the necessary persuasion or pressure to get results. ENABLE reached and helped more than 30,000 parents in its three years.[10]

Dr. Orville G. Brim, president of the Russell Sage Foundation, gave ENABLE a warm endorsement: "The richest material now available on working with lower class parent motivation, interests, themes discussed, and the like, now should be based on the information collected in that project, which is surely the largest parent education effort with lower income groups in history." [11]

The event of maximum importance in 1964 was the Presidential election. Between 60 and 70 percent of northern blacks and only 38 percent of southern Afro-Americans of voting age were registered. In the south the registration ran from a miniscule 6.7 percent in Mississippi to a high of 67.2 percent in Tennessee.

In 1962 NUL had hired Heman Sweatt, hero of the Supreme Court case that desegregated the University of Texas law school in 1950, to assist southern field director Clarence Coleman. Sweatt's primary assignment was coordination of the League's participation in a "Non-partisan Voter Education Program" in Winston-Salem, Richmond, Little Rock, Fort Worth, Birmingham and New Orleans. The project was limited in time and scope, but results were considered good.

That experience was of fundamental importance when, in 1964, the League organized a far more ambitious Voter Education Project financed with $100,000 from the Taconic Foundation. Sterling Tucker, the nervous dynamo who was at that time executive of the Washington, D.C., League, was put on temporary assignment to head the project in August. Using the ready-made infrastructure of the local Leagues across the nation and concentrating particular attention on fifteen target cities, Tucker and the League team were extremely effective in educating and motivating blacks to register and vote. Tucker reported that in the fifteen target cities 253,597 blacks were added to the voting rolls in neighborhoods covered by the Leagues. This was an increase of 48 per cent. In thirty-nine nontarget cities that reported, 98,644 additional black voters were registered.

The program had additional benefits for the local Leagues, said Tucker, in that "the leadership structure, the power structure, centers of influence and the Negro masses were brought together." [12]

It was a significant project that was to influence Tucker and the future direction of the League. NUL board members commended Tucker and the staff for avoiding the pitfalls some had anticipated in the project. "The value of continuing with a project that would make use of the volunteers and machinery brought about in this project, and some type of consumer education program [were] suggested." [13]

In the 1964 Presidential election, 95 percent of Afro-American votes went to the Johnson-Humphrey ticket. Senator Goldwater had alienated blacks with his widely publicized vote against the Civil Rights Act of 1964 and his promises to curb "crime in the streets," a transparent reference to the demonstrations for civil rights.

Not only did Afro-American voting strength reach a new peak—6 million votes—but black citizens were elected to office in unprecedented numbers from precinct level to Congress. Black political power was too important to ignore. President Johnson took his overwhelming vote to be a mandate and addressed himself to further action to aid Afro-Americans.

45/The Mood Shifts

"There can be no question of the American Government's full and complete commitment to the cause of racial justice in all of its aspects—legal, political, economic and social" declared the NUL delegate assembly and board of trustees on August 2, 1965.[1] This extraordinary statement with its hint of incredulous euphoria went on to note that "during the last few years, the national Government has, by precept and example, accepted the principle of equality for all American citizens," and cited the passage of the Civil Rights Acts of 1964 and 1965 and Lyndon Johnson's two uncompromisingly strong statements of March 14, 1965 (calling for passage of the "Voting Rights Act" and concluding with the watchwords of the Negro revolution, "We Shall Overcome"), and June 4, 1965 (his Howard University commencement address) in support of this conclusion.

The NUL was not alone in this belief that a millennium of sorts had arrived: SCLC official Reverend James Bevel told that organization's August 1965 convention, "There is no more civil-rights movement. President Johnson signed it out of existence when he signed the voting-rights bill [signed August 2, 1965]." [2]

Lyndon Johnson's speech at Howard University kindled great enthusiasm among blacks and liberals not only because of its rare eloquence but because it promised to lead beyond civil rights to a new goal.

To redress the balance, said the President, jobs and decent homes in decent surroundings, a chance to learn, welfare and social programs and care of the sick were necessary. An "understanding heart by all Americans" also would be a large part of the answer.

Other answers were still to be found, Johnson stated, and not all the problems were understood. Therefore, he announced, "a White House conference of scholars, and experts, and understanding Negro leaders—men of both races—and officials of government at every level" would be held in the fall on the theme "To Fulfill These Rights."

> Its object will be to help the American Negro fulfill the rights which, after the long time of injustice, he is finally about to secure.

To move beyond opportunity to achievement.

To shatter forever not only the barriers of law and public practices but the walls which bound the condition of man by the color of his skin.

To dissolve, as best we can, the antique enmities of the heart which diminish the holder, divide the great democracy, and do wrong—great wrong —to the children of God.

I pledge you tonight this will be a chief goal of my administration, and of my program next year, and in years to come. And I hope, and I pray, and I believe, it will be a part of the program of all America.

In this remarkable speech President Johnson asserted his leadership of a movement that presumably would supersede the civil rights movement. He was, as some put it, "leapfrogging the [civil rights] movement," seizing the initiative from its leaders. This was a unique situation in a nation where every advance by blacks, almost without exception, had been yielded by the Establishment only in response to pushing, pressing and protest by Afro-Americans on their own behalf.

President Johnson's Howard University "manifesto" was based in large measure upon the concepts outlined in NUL's domestic Marshall Plan.

In our plea for such a domestic Marshall Plan, we are asking for special *effort*, not for special privileges. Our program is designed to reverse economic and social deterioration of urban families and communities and to help develop the tools and understanding that will prevent such deterioration in the future.[3]

This was the rationale Whitney Young had used in announcing the ten points of the domestic Marshall Plan in June 1963. He had said the Marshall Plan was necessary because

the "discrimination gap" caused by more than three centuries of abuse, humiliation, segregation and bias has burdened the Negro with a handicap that will not automatically slip from his shoulders as discriminatory laws and practices are abandoned. . . . Our Negro citizens, after only grudgingly receiving the barest minimum in health, education, welfare, housing, economic and cultural opportunities cannot conceivably compete equally for, or share in, the full rewards and responsibilities of our society simply by an announcement, with impressive flourishes, that now a state of equal opportunity exists.[4]

Another major source for Johnson's speech came from Daniel Patrick Moynihan, then assistant secretary of labor in charge of the Office of Policy Planning and Research. Moynihan espoused the concept of "preferential treatment" focused especially on two areas of black need—families and jobs. He developed a report for key Johnson administration officials on the same topic, *The Negro Family: The Case for National Action.* In this paper, dated March 1965, Moynihan stated that a new era in civil rights was beginning.

> In this new period the expectations of the Negro Americans will go beyond civil rights. Being Americans, they will now expect that in the near future equal opportunities for them as a group will produce roughly equal results, as compared with other groups. This is not going to happen. Nor will it happen for generations to come unless a new and special effort is made. . . .
>
> The thesis of this paper is that these events in combination, confront the nation with a new kind of problem. Measures that have worked in the past, or would work for most groups in the present, will not work here. A national effort is required that will give a unity of purpose to the many activities of the Federal government in this area, directed to a new kind of national goal: the establishment of a stable Negro family structure.[5]

Moynihan's report struck home. It was intended to stimulate federal consideration of action, hopefully the adoption of a policy

> to bring the Negro American to full and equal sharing in the responsibilities and rewards of citizenship. To this end, the programs of the Federal government bearing on this objective shall be designed to have the effect, directly or indirectly, of enhancing the stability and resources of the Negro American family.[6]

The report was distributed within the top echelons of the Johnson administration at a most opportune time. The President was eagerly seeking domestic programs that would help him rank in history with his hero, Franklin D. Roosevelt. Moynihan had purposely avoided recommending remedies to avoid detracting from his basic thesis. The thesis impressed the President and his closest advisers as valid and as having the necessary potential. Moynihan and Richard N. Goodwin were assigned the task of incorporating it in the speech delivered by the President at Howard University.

Meanwhile, back at NUL, a fundamental review of the agency's goals, functions and structure was under way. One of Whitney Young's innovations had been an annual gathering of the national staff in a two-day "retreat" at which it could examine itself in terms of its past, current and future activities and effectiveness. The third of these retreats, held in November 1964, brought the staff face to face with the questions of where the agency was and where it could and should go. President Lindsley Kimball and NUL consultant Dr. John B. Turner, later dean of the School of Social Work at Western Reserve University, were on hand as resource persons.

It was in this "think-tank" that the Urban Leaguers concluded that their long-held basic goal of equality of opportunity for every American was not enough. The new goal of the League, they decided, should be to "eliminate inequality in the life chances of Negroes and other Minority Groups," or, more succinctly, to eradicate the gap between the life chances of black and white citizens. This, they agreed, meant helping create community policy (governmental and voluntary) at local, state and national levels, designed to provide (a) services and/or programs which would help the Negro to develop needed social, political and economic skills; (b) protection of basic liberties; and (c) equal access to opportunity.

The discussion went into this matter in great detail and it was agreed that for the League to tackle the goal of equalizing life chances it must shift its approach, emphasis and organization. The organizational changes had been started with decentralization into five regional offices and appointment of Mahlon T. Puryear as deputy executive director.

The shift in approach and emphasis proposed by Dr. John Turner was to problem-oriented rather than program-oriented action. Thereby, staff would have to be flexible and sharpen their awareness and knowledge of conditions and "be much more sensitive in development of agency resources as well as the resources of all levels of community." [7] This would require thorough planning by board and staff members to (a) determine priorities for concerted action; (b) assess how the team would work to resolve the problems; and (c) develop new yardsticks to measure effectiveness of action to close the gap.[8] The change of approach was adopted by the NUL staff.

In this setting, President Johnson's Howard University speech on June 4, 1965, seemed to be a beacon into the future. Not until months later could it be seen as the apogee of Johnson's commitment and concern for civil rights. Only two days afterward, on June 6, 1965, the administration announced that American forces in Vietnam would no longer be restricted to advisory roles, but would perform "combat-support" missions. By the end of the month United States troops had been in offensive action for the first time. Thus began the momentous shearing action that was to cut President Johnson loose from primary consideration of civil rights and subordinate all other concerns to Vietnam.

The attention and interest of the President in the problems of black citizens descended and his obsession with and commitment in the Vietnam debacle rose. There was an inverse emphasis in presidential rhetoric, as Johnson continued throughout 1965 to give all-out verbal backing to the antipoverty war, to civil and living rights and to the promise of the upcoming White House Conference on rights. Meanwhile, Johnson was not only terse but misleading in telling the American public about involvement in Vietnam. As Vietnam escalated in men, materiel, money and in presidential attention, civil rights passed it on a descending escalator.

By the time Johnson signed the Voting Rights Act of 1965 on August 2, 150,000 United States troops had been ordered to Vietnam, and within days the President asked Congress for an additional $1,700,000,000 to pay for Vietnam action.

On August 11, Afro-Americans in Watts cut loose and turned that section of Los Angeles inside out. More than 4,000 were arrested, 1,032 injured and thirty-four killed in the rioting, looting and burning before 13,000 National Guardsmen brought the outbreak to an end. Property damage reached some $40,000,000 as 200 businesses were totally destroyed and 700 damaged heavily. Reaching for quick answers rather than decisive action, the administration released the Moynihan report to the public and noted that the White House Conference was intended to come up with solutions that would help prevent such eruptions as Watts. Since little antipoverty money had been assigned to Watts, the War on Poverty could not be discredited as having failed in this instance.

The Watts blowup was one more of those highly visible manifestations of deep-rooted problems and festering discontent that had shaken the nation with increasing frequency. It was an indication that there existed what came to be labeled a "credibility gap" between Johnson promises and Johnson delivery.

Among civil rights leaders there was not only uneasiness, there was a mounting concern about developments. The administration pointed to the Moynihan report not only as an explanation of the causes for eruptions such as Watts but the focus of the up-coming White House Conference. Thus this limited-purpose paper came under intensive examination, dissection, misinterpretation and attack.

Moynihan's focus was the black family and, to oversimplify the case, he contended that the major problems of Afro-Americans could never be solved until black families were strengthened so as to enable them "to raise and support [their] members as do other families." [9] In making his case, Moynihan cited statistics on delinquency and educational attainment, occupational data, a profile of black families including data about maternal dominance, illegitimacy, broken homes, and so on.

Some black leaders were openly hostile to aspersions they found in the data about broken homes and illegitimacy rates, and quickly condemned the report. Deeper distrust was voiced by several leaders who saw the proposed White House Conference as a device to concentrate on black families and abandon other necessary efforts. A mid-September "sweetness and harmony" outing with Vice President Humphrey on the presidential yacht in the Potomac turned into a heated wrangle between civil rights leaders and Humphrey's staff. Clarence Mitchell, head of NAACP's Washington Bureau (and a former Urban League Fellow) and Floyd McKissick of CORE attacked the administration for not following up the Voting Rights Act in the south. In some areas, McKissick charged, "When we got masses to go, there were no [federal] registrars. That made us waste a whole damn summer of work. And then they go turn to the Moynihan Report." [10]

Scarcely more than a week later, on September 24, the President's Council on Equal Opportunity and the President's Committee on Equal Employment Opportunity were abolished and their functions redistributed in a reshuffle that dealt various civil rights responsibilities to the Departments of Labor and Justice and the United States Civil Rights Commission. That added uncertainty to confusion. Meanwhile, the Moynihan report continued to draw lightning from civil rights leaders, commentators and columnists. The White House Conference was deferred until the following year and a planning meeting for the conference was scheduled in November, to be chaired by A. Philip Randolph.

When it convened the planning conference was upstaged both by its chairman and the President. Philip Randolph unveiled an elaborate and thoroughgoing "Freedom Budget for All Americans." It was the distillation of several months of effort by a panel of experts led by Leon Keyserling, former economic adviser to Harry Truman, and sponsored by the A. Philip Randolph Institute. Its purpose was to budget American resources in the decade 1966–1976 "to achieve freedom from want" in the nation.

With evident inspiration from the domestic Marshall Plan and other social planning documents, it set specific goals and timetables for attacking poverty, slums, health, education, training, housing, rural life and welfare problems. It also made specific recommendations for use of government budgetary and policy powers. Though it called for outright expenditures at the rate of only $1 billion in 1970 and $2 billion in 1975, its major thrust was a restructuring of the federal budget in socially productive ways, with anticipated enlargement of it from $104 billion in 1967 to $155 billion in 1975. This was about $355 billion more than anticipated normally over the decade. The increase was to come out of the powerful growth of the American economy during the period and would actually represent a *decrease* in the proportion of the federal budget relative to the size of the total economy during that period.

The Freedom Budget made sense to many leaders, especially liberals, and more than two hundred prominent men endorsed it. [11] The program was praised for its thorough approach and consigned to that special limbo set aside for things so outrageously exorbitant that "prudent men" refuse to consider them.

The planning conference was further obscured in national news by President Johnson's action overruling United States Education Commissioner Francis Keppel, who had cut off federal funds to Chicago's school system because of its de facto segregation. Mayor Richard Daley had taken the decision to the White House and Johnson responded according to political realities rather than moral or legal principles. He ordered a study of de facto segregation in the schools. Civil rights leaders and black citizens in general viewed this as a weakening of administration resolve, bringing into question its pronouncements favoring tough enforcement of the laws against discrimination.

The planning conference had originally been intended to bring together a few dozen black and white specialists to map out the larger White House Conference the following year, focusing primarily on ways of strengthening black families. But the planning conference expanded to 150 attendees and became a forum for discussion. There were even attempts to pass resolutions. Instead of concentrating on the black family and bringing blacks into the mainstream, the delegates attacked or rejected the first and castigated the Johnson administration for not accomplishing the second.

Having crossed off the family as a convenient entree to organizing new and greater federal initiatives, the delegates came up with many and varied suggestions but no outstanding, fundamental ideas that could conceivably supply the overarching conceptual umbrella necessary. Nearly all concerned, therefore, considered the planning conference a fiasco. The administration received chastisement rather than consensus, blacks distrusted the basic premises of the meeting, and white delegates apparently were puzzled that there was far more emotional criticism of the Moynihan report than agreement on far-ranging concrete principles to "get on with the job."

There was something else beneath the surface, however. The holocaust of Watts had staggered a nation which believed that the succession of civil rights, legal and legislative victories had given blacks what they wanted. Watts also caused many black leaders to admit privately what the black extremists had been saying all along: the major black and interracial organizations did not have strong roots in the ghetto communities. The academicians and the administration's specialists saw this and were agitated that the planning conference did not come to grips with this significant fact in a way that would lead to new initiatives at the

White House Conference. Black leaders pointed out that the civil rights laws and the War on Poverty had made little change (Watts was Exhibit A) and would not unless the administration redoubled its efforts.

In short, each was dissatisfied with the other and all were dissatisfied with the administration.

46/Crisis and Commitment

The "civil rights mood" at the beginning of 1966 was described by Whitney Young as one of "watchful waiting." [1] Direct demonstrations had been temporarily suspended in hopes that the civil rights laws of the past two years would be so effective that more tangible gains would result. Consequently, civil rights groups were most concerned with pressing for full implementation of the laws and this, said Young, gave the appearance of a "lull."

There was a further complication, however. Some of the civil rights organizations were in serious financial trouble. In some cases this was because there was at the moment no "crisis element," the foundation on which many organizations based their programs.

There was a need to shift to a new emphasis. This was a blow to those who had been skilled at a day-to-day job of protest but now were forced to think in terms of less dramatic, long-range activity. "Nothing could be worse for the Urban League," Whitney Young stated, "than for every rights organization to disappear from the scene or become so weak as to be unable to function." Much of the success of the League in recent years could be traced to the existence of the other organizations and the threats which many associated with them, he confided to the NUL board. For this reason, as well as others, Young felt an obligation to help keep the civil rights organizations both responsible and focused on civil rights and where possible even to help them get resources. (This had been attempted in the case of James Farmer's ill-starred Community Action Education Centers program.)

The League, too, was "in trouble" he said, because its size and position imposed overwhelming responsibilities not only on the executive and staff but also on the board. There was the basic problem of greater recognition by and involvement of the masses, interpreting to them the League's importance in changing their lives and destinies. The local Urban Leagues needed strengthening. The League should expand to additional cities, particularly in Mississippi, Texas and Alabama.[2]

The League movement was suffering from personnel depletion. As far back as mid-1962 the new climate for professionally trained blacks had changed drastically. From the administration in Washington to local city and county governments, from national business and industry to private, voluntary health and welfare organizations in many parts of the land, the impact of black expectations and demands had been felt. There was a scramble for trained Afro-Americans and the result was an acute shortage, for there were not enough to go around.

NUL felt the pinch in two ways: first, it and its locals were handicapped in competing with the salaries and benefits being offered by business and education and some of the more affluent welfare agencies and government units. League recruiting was, therefore, hampered. Second, a major preserve where experienced professionals were to be found was— the League. Thus as NUL and the locals assumed greater responsibility and needed more manpower to serve the imperatives of the Negro Revolution, the movement was losing many of its most experienced hands.

Whitney Young told NUL board members of his surprise to find that in a meeting with eight government officials about the Skills Bank six of them were former Urban Leaguers![3] The League was a happy hunting ground for government and business recruiters and this extended clear to the top. Young, commenting on rumors that he was going to depart for a government job, confirmed that the Johnson administration had approached him to take a post in the War on Poverty program. He decided against it and the board unanimously backed him in that decision, suggesting he reply that he could serve best from the "outside."

A few months later the siren call from Sargent Shriver's domain was turned on southern field director Clarence Coleman, to the alarm of Young and others in the national office who saw it as part of an all-too pervasive (and enticing) pattern. Coleman plugged his ears with the wax of "higher and more effective duty" through continued service as an NUL staff executive, but many others were lured to the federal service. In fact, by early 1966 NUL's situation had grown so desperate that the regional directors drew up a memo calling for immediate action to counter the mass departure of League staff personnel. It amounted, said the directors, to raids on UL staffs by government and other organizations who held out the irrefutably tangible advantages of higher salaries and benefits. Since this had reached serious proportions, the regional directors asked for a thorough review of local and national office salaries.

League president Kimball also urged wiring presidents of local Community Chests suggesting they boost salaries of League professionals in their next budget reviews. Whitney Young wryly observed that in many cities the Chest people had the idea that a local League executive's salary should be comparable to that of the local Boy Scout or settlement house executive. This was absurd, he contended, for there was no comparison in terms of responsibilities and training.[4]

Meanwhile, this very function of serving as a skilled labor pool, a training ground and cadre for industry, education and government was cited by Ford Foundation representatives as unique and as one of the League's greatest contributions in the entire race relations area. This was of passing consolation when the agency was feeling the hot breath of the "raiders" even though it had expanded to the point where NUL was "big business." Young directed his board members' attention to the need to (1) strengthen local Leagues, with better supervision and personnel assistance from NUL's regional offices and help in getting more money for locals; (2) accelerate staff training and recruitment to compensate for loss of staff to higher paid positions in government and private industry.

The spring and summer of 1966 brought several significant events that caused a shift in the "civil rights mood."

Whitney Young apprised NUL board members of the changeover that was taking place in the agency's approaches. The first thirty years or so of the League's history had, of necessity, been devoted to direct services because the health and welfare agencies excluded blacks, he said. This had changed in the past twenty years, but even with new laws and new resources there was still serious neglect and masses of disillusioned black citizens. The League was, therefore, coming "full circle" in its operations, moving again to the direct services-personal contact level as an antidote to the bone-deep disbelief and cynicism that were afflicting more and more blacks.[5]

The NUL executive director deplored the nation's "expediency" fixation that was more concerned with "cooling" blacks during hot summers than in reducing year-round human misery, suffering and exploitation that produced ghetto riots. The League had studied the needs and its capabilities and the demands upon it and decided that it must make problem-solving rather than program its basic orientation.

In recent years, the League had operated on the basis that a "minimum program" was necessary in each UL city for a local League to be considered truly part of the NUL movement. This meant that at least some effort was being put forth in each of the basic UL program areas— employment, vocational services and education, health, welfare and housing. However, this principle was unworkable, if not impossible. In the

first place, some local Leagues were very small, with only one or two professionals on their staffs. It was unreasonable to expect that such limited
operations could manage creditable programs in all five program areas.
Moreover, if the urgency of local conditions demanded concentrating attention on one area of UL expertise—such as a local housing crisis—it
was senseless to require that the local League carry out a balanced program in the other four fields to the detriment of the overriding local
need for housing action, simply to meet NUL specifications.

Whitney Young had stated at the 1965 NUL annual conference "our
major goal is to eliminate inequality in the life chances of Negroes and
other minority groups." Though the overall NUL movement now numbered seventy-six local Leagues, a staff of 600 and more than 6,000 volunteers, operating on a budget of about $6 million (of which one fourth was
for the national office), these resources were still woefully inadequate to
rehabilitate the nearly 10 million neediest black brothers. With new
problems, new tools and new resources, said Whitney Young, it could
well be a waste of energy and time for UL to try to program in all areas.
It would be much better to develop a systematic way of identifying major
problems in the local community in relation to services available to attack such problems.[6]

On June 1, 1966, the much-heralded White House Conference, "To
Fulfill These Rights," convened in Washington. Some 2,400 delegates assembled, split up into twelve unwieldy groups to discuss a 104-page position paper prepared by a Conference Council in advance and to throw
their suggestions and criticisms into the hopper. After discussion of housing, economic security, welfare, education and justice, the delegates
turned the position paper recommendations and their suggestions over to
the Conference Council again. This group of eight businessmen, seven
civil rights leaders, and fifteen lawyers, judges, labor leaders, government
officials and scholars, presented the summary findings to President Johnson.

The conference had been picketed by "militants," boycotted by SNCC,
attacked as a "hoax" by delegate Floyd McKissick of CORE, and condemned as a waste of time by scores of blacks who attended. Instead of a
vast, new "grand design" for "closing the gap" as President Johnson had
suggested in his Howard University speech one year earlier, the White
House Conference rendered a report that one observer called "a hodge-
podge of every idea that had been advanced so far, with no analytic structure underlying it." [7] To many it seemed that the administration was attempting to "spin off" responsibility to others.

Running through the conclusions was the unmistakable theme that the
federal government, as Berl I. Bernhard, the Conference's general

counsel, stated, "cannot be saddled with the whole task of solving all the nation's civil rights problems." [8] As the report put it in one of its conclusions, the central issue was that the national government's response had not been matched by state and local governments, business and labor, housing, industry, educational institutions and the "wide spectrum" of voluntary agencies "who, through united effort, have the power to improve our society." [9]

One man who publicly disagreed with these emphases was a recent top-level Johnson administration "dropout," McGeorge Bundy. In his first major public statement as president of the Ford Foundation, Bundy told the NUL annual conference in August 1966 that the most urgent domestic concern of the nation was full equality for Afro-Americans and that "the greater share of the burden of effort falls now and must fall in the future, upon Government at all levels, and upon the business concerns whose role it is to provide new opportunities for all Americans."

As the most influential man in philanthropy in the world because of the Ford Foundation's astronomical assets and millions of dollars in annual grants, Bundy's words carried special significance when he committed his foundation to supporting stronger and deeper white and Negro leadership for peaceful progress. It was a commitment that beckoned other foundations to reassess their programs and turn their attentions from peripheral matters to the core of American life. (In a related aside, NUL president Kimball pointed out to conference delegates that Community Chests across the country had increased the budgets of Campfire Girls by a greater increment than the support for local Leagues. "Perhaps," he said, "communities as they assess damage may conclude that it is cheaper to provide a fence at the top of a cliff than to maintain an ambulance at the bottom.")

The Ford Foundation had granted NUL $1,500,000 in the spring of 1966 for an eight-city project in housing called Operation Equality. Through this, segregated housing patterns were to be attacked, and programs with existing local fair housing committees were to be strengthened and expanded. In the first year, the local Leagues, cooperating with the New York Operation Equality project, registered 2,800 open occupancy listings, responded to 2,900 requests for housing services and helped 481 families to buy or rent homes in integrated neighborhoods.

The NUL conference in 1966 was notable for statements by Whitney Young and David Rusk (son of Secretary of State Dean Rusk) and a crucial shirt-sleeve session led by Dr. John B. Turner.

Whitney Young in his keynote speech proposed a reordering of private and governmental criteria and action in an "Operation Urban Survival." New commercial, industrial and government buildings should deliberately be placed in slum areas as part of an integrated social rehabilitation and development program. Using as an example the relocation of the World Trade Center from lower Manhattan to Harlem, Young described how it would bring construction and office jobs to the community, would bring whites back into Harlem, would improve police, sanitation and other inadequate city services so grudgingly supplied, would include low and middle-income housing and the opportunity to turn ghettoes into "urban showcases of strength and vitality." [10] It was a radical proposal, Young agreed, but radical problems demanded radical solutions and the efficacy of such investment in rehabilitation was evident in the miraculous transformation of the slums where Lincoln Center and the United Nations headquarters are located. (Later, New York Governor Nelson Rockefeller announced that a state office building would be built in Harlem. This was responsive only to a portion of Young's proposal and the project promptly became a center of controversy in the community.)

In a work session with board, staff and volunteers from NUL and the local Leagues around the nation, League consultant John Turner went through the step-by-step process of assessing urgent problems of Afro-Americans and mobilizing a community to take relevant action to solve them.

And in another conference event young David Rusk, associate director of the Washington, D.C., League, startled Urban Leaguers with proposals far more radical than Whitney Young's. In a witty address that had his audience alternating between waves of laughter and shock, Rusk (who sardonically styled himself the UL's "WASP-in-residence") asked the basic question, "What is the UL to be?" The message from the ghetto was that blacks were demanding meat and potatoes; whites were willing only to provide pablum. The League, he said, must not continue its "traditional role as an interracial communications link, a mediator, an interpreter" and, as such, a producer of social pablum.[11] He described the kind of League action he would advocate, using the goal of halving the unemployment and dropout rates in a League city as an example:

> The conservative mayor and city council are holding down city taxes and the school budget. You campaign to throw them out . . . get a bond issue passed . . . a commuter tax to support the schools. You beat the state capital and Washington unmercifully for every aid-to-education penny you can get.
>
> Your school superintendent and board of education are running a discriminatory school system. You organize your black masses . . . picket . . . boycott . . . force resignations . . . bring court actions . . . bring in the feds . . . force curriculum changes, pupil redistricting, reallocation of more funds and teachers to Negro slum schools.

Your companies don't offer jobs to the kids; you go to work on their job descriptions and personnel practices . . . build new entry requirements . . . on-the-job training . . . give the full FEP treatment to that company who isn't hiring Negro kids; if your chamber of commerce is lousy, you go out and bring new industries into town.

Your vocational education program is antiquated and useless . . . you sack the administrator . . . get the industries and unions to design and run vocational education programs . . . give the full FEP treatment to that union who isn't admitting Negro kids; if your labor standards are lousy, you go out and bring new labor organizers into town.

And so on. You keep your eyes fixed on your goals. You [are] ruthless about cutting back on the other UL "fringe" activities. And you fight to win.[12]

Young Rusk admitted that the UL might "take an awful beating in the process" and held up to view the whole range of traditional League bogies: (a) loss of tax-exempt status (to be offset by "pulling a whole community along in your support"); (b) ouster from the local United Fund (which "would cost the United Fund more than the UL"); (c) building enemies ("if you have no enemies you probably aren't doing anything worthwhile"). But the crisis of the cities demanded that the League become "a relentless, dedicated, driving force at the heart of social change," David Rusk insisted.[13]

In these radical recommendations Rusk sounded like nothing less than one of the members of the "Disturbed Committee" of eight years before, or Lester Granger as head of the NUL Workers' Bureau and T. Arnold Hill as acting NUL executive secretary a generation earlier.

The difference was that the tide had changed and now was running in the direction of Rusk's signals. As background counterpoint to this "call to the barricades," ghetto riots exploded anew in Chicago, Waukegan, Lansing, Benton Harbor, Brooklyn, Omaha, Cleveland and Dayton. Rusk's polemic grew out of his experience with the aggressive and successful program of the Washington League and simply articulated thoughts that had occurred to many Urban Leaguers and been discarded as impossible. Yet, within two years the entire organization moved drastically in the direction Rusk had suggested.

As the riots of 1966 escalated white jitters to the level of near-hysteria, candidates for office in the fall elections played cheap and loose with their constituents' futures by appealing to white backlash sentiment. The public opinion polls and editorial comments around the nation showed an unmistakable drop in white sympathy for black civil rights and an illogical linking of black protest, however peaceful, with riots and "crime in the streets." In an attempt to set the record straight Whitney Young and six other civil rights leaders issued a statement in mid-October head-lined "Crisis and Commitment." [14]

To underlying white racial prejudices the events of the year had added confusion and uncertainty, the statement began. The result had been in-tensified resistance to change at the very time when such change was most needed. It was because of these conditions that a restatement of the prin-ciples of the civil rights movement was necessary.

> 1. We are committed to the attainment of racial justice by the democratic process. . . . We propose to win genuine partnership for all our people . . . within the framework of this nation's constitution.
> 2. We repudiate any strategies of violence, reprisal or vigilantism, and we condemn both rioting and the demagoguery that feeds it. . . . Defense of one's family, home and self against attack is not an issue; it is a basic American principle and must not be perverted into a cover for aggressive violence.
> 3. We are committed to integration, by which we mean an end to every barrier which segregation and other forms of discrimination have raised against the enjoyment by Negro Americans of their human and constitu-tional rights.
> 4. As we are committed to the goal of integration into every aspect of the national life, we are equally committed to the common responsibility of all Americans, both white and black, for bringing integration to pass. We not only welcome, we urge, the full cooperation of white Americans in what must be a joint endeavor if it is to prosper.[15]

It was not condoning riots to cry out against ghetto conditions, the statement insisted. Nor was it condoning riots to report the steady wors-ening of the average Afro-American's lot while others enjoyed unprece-dented prosperity. "It is not an abdication of responsibility . . . to say that society cannot perpetuate discrimination against Negroes and then blame the victims or their leaders for the outbursts of those who have been made desperate." [16]

All of American society was obligated to take the massive actions that were required to reverse black economic trends. The mass media would have to moderate "their obsession with sensation and conflict and to help create a climate of genuine knowledge and understanding in which perspective is restored." Perspective was understanding that for every black who tossed a Molotov cocktail in a ghetto riot there were a thou-sand fighting and dying on the battlefields of Vietnam, said the civil rights leaders.

The signs that America was retreating from national commitment to racial justice were everywhere evident. Bigotry had been elevated to a major political instrument by exploiting the so-called "white backlash."

"Sometime friends" had pulled back in full retreat and yielded to "battle-field scavengers" ground which could have been held if fought for, the statement continued. Determined that the tragedy of the post-Reconstruction era should not be repeated, the leaders called on all countrymen "to move with us." [17]

There was no stampede by men of goodwill to this call for action. On the contrary, the 1966 elections three weeks later produced a Congress in which the "conservative coalition" of southern Democrats and conservative Republicans was strengthened. The *Congressional Quarterly* predicted that in the House, labor, open housing, poverty program and Great Society bills all could be beaten handily by the new opposition lineup. It appeared to be a poor season for commitment.

47/Beyond Civil Rights

At the beginning of 1967, NUL board members asked Whitney Young the question that nagged many Americans: was the civil rights movement dying? The patient's condition was critical, admitted Young, but this was due largely to the fact that organizations historically are born for a specific purpose, and use specific tools and methods to attain their specific goals. When those goals are achieved, the organizations pass off the scene and new organizations emerge to meet new problems. It was Young's belief that the immediate objectives of demonstrations and marches had, for the most part, been achieved and the organizations which had been engaged primarily in using those methods must now attempt to shift their constituents to something else.

At heart, the civil rights struggle was a battle for domestic programs. The real danger, he ventured, was that many liberals who historically had fought for those programs had been diverted and obsessed by Vietnam. He was impatient with those who now took the position that until Vietnam was solved they could not involve themselves in domestic programs.[1]

This position was based on the conviction that the civil rights movement's resources were too slim to be diluted or diminished by investing them in anti-Vietnam activity. (Young visited Vietnam in 1966; returned with praise for United States army troop integration, condemnation of the disproportionate burden of battle borne by blacks—20 percent of United States troops in Vietnam were Afro-Americans—and determination to aid discharged black veterans.) NUL set up a Veterans Affairs Office in 1967 with cooperation of business, labor and the federal government, to care for the needs of black vets. That same year President Johnson insisted that Young serve as a member of the team of Americans which observed the South Vietnam presidential election of General Thieu and Marshal Ky. (Neither Young nor the League issued endorsements of American involvement in Vietnam during these years but it was not until 1968 that NUL's Delegate Assembly called for prompt withdrawal of United States forces.)

Young's outlook grew even more somber. He felt compelled, he told the NUL Board in May 1967, to indicate the League staff's grave concern about the critical nature of race relations at that time. There was a deep sense of pessimism, if not depression, he said. The pessimism was not confined to the Urban League (except that the problems were so overwhelming and League resources were so limited) but applied to the whole area of race relations.[2]

A "defensive posture" had become necessary for civil rights, he declared, because of such headlines as those about the peccadillos of Adam Clayton Powell, the widely publicized and highly unpopular positions taken by Muhammad Ali, *né* Cassius Clay, and Martin Luther King's diversionary move in opposing American involvement in Vietnam. He confessed to a sense of frustration from the fact that so many were using Vietnam as an excuse to cut back their support of domestic programs. Additionally, many friends were failing to speak out on critical issues. Nevertheless, he emphasized the importance of the League's holding to its basic commitment.

The inevitable question about the summer ahead drew a balanced response: Young considered predictions of riots and violence risky, but would be "less than candid" if he didn't say that it would be a miracle to go through the summer without them if there was no organized preventive effort. The experiences of many communities in 1966, however, showed that "cool summers" could be achieved.[3]

Unfortunately, not enough communities were moving fast enough to immunize themselves against racial outbursts. The summer of 1967 was the most violent in American race relations history. There were riots in Nashville, Tampa, Atlanta, Cambridge, Maryland, Winston-Salem, San Francisco, Cincinnati, Toledo, Roxbury, Massachusetts, Newark, Plainfield, New Jersey, Cairo, Illinois, Minneapolis, Buffalo, Syracuse, Detroit,

Grand Rapids, South Bend, Chicago, East St. Louis, Milwaukee and New Haven.

Some of these were cities where violence was least expected because progress had been substantial—New Haven and Detroit, especially. The week after the Detroit riot, Vice President Hubert H. Humphrey called for a domestic Marshall Plan to aid the slums of the cities. Senator Jacob Javits and Dr. Martin Luther King, Jr., echoed Vice President Humphrey. (This was four years after Whitney Young's original announcement of the concept.)

The big city riots of 1967 were truly awesome. Their impact on the minds of Americans was immediate and strong. When the smoke died in Detroit there were forty-three dead, 2,000 injured, 7,200 arrested and damage had not been confined to the black ghetto; it hit the heart of the business district. So, too, in Newark, where twenty-three died, 1,200 were injured and 1,300 arrested. In Detroit, the rebellion was not quelled until 14,000 paratroopers using machine guns and tanks joined National Guardsmen and local police. The damage was estimated at $43 million. In Newark it came to more than $10 million.

The shock wave of the riots struck heads of the nation's major business and industrial corporations as nothing had previously. The most prominent of them hurriedly met in August to organize to "reorder national priorities, provide emergency work programs and provide jobs in the cities." More than 800 mayors, business, labor, church and civil rights leaders, including Whitney Young for the NUL, gathered in Washington for this purpose and formed the Urban Coalition, headed by former HEW Secretary, John W. Gardner. The first definite widely publicized result of joint action of NUL and the coalition was the pledge by the nation's insurance industry of $1 billion for aid to black ghettoes.

Other factors complicating conditions were the inflammatory appeals of SNCC leaders Stokely Carmichael and H. Rap Brown. Carmichael had urged Fisk University students to "take over" the school and the following day a police incident triggered rioting in the city. Carmichael went to Atlanta, refused a police order to move on, was arrested and a riot erupted.

Rap Brown had advised blacks to "burn this town down" when he appeared in Cambridge, Maryland, if city leaders refused black demands. Brown was wounded by a shotgun blast and Cambridge blacks went on a rampage. In Washington, D.C., Brown urged Afro-Americans to get guns because the white man was the enemy and "you got to destroy your enemy." And in East St. Louis he helped heat the black community to the kindling point with an incendiary speech. He was a national sensation when he said "violence is as American as cherry pie."

In white minds, Rap Brown and Stokely Carmichael with their shouts of "black power" were the scariest manifestations of black *anomie* yet. Incomprehensibly implacable, they seemed to be offspring of Malcolm X's most fevered exhortations to reject and suspect everything white. Their open calls to kill and burn "whitey" sent shivers of fear and fury through whites around the nation. They also raised the question of whether the urban riots were spontaneous or were ignited by *agents provacateurs*. A shock wave of fear and doubt swept the land and when it hit 1600 Pennsylvania Avenue, Washington, D.C., Lyndon Johnson appointed a National Advisory Commission on Civil Disorders to investigate.

SNCC was not the only far-out group of irreconcilables. The Black Muslims and Black Nationalists had been out there for years but the first was noted for its strong discipline and the latter had alienated more blacks than it had recruited. There were other more recent groups, however, and among them were the Deacons, a group of southern blacks who armed themselves for self-defense, and the Lowndes County, Alabama, protective association, whose emblem was the black panther. Many others were springing up.

A black terrorist group was exposed in New York in June 1967, just a month after Whitney Young's briefing concerning "defensive posture." It was of more than ordinary concern, for it was not the usual group of nuts and crackpots who bomb railroad station lockers or blast a rival organization's headquarters. This group, called RAM (Revolutionary Action Movement), consisted of twelve men and four women, several of them middle-class intellectuals, one of them a public school official. Their scheme was to hasten polarization of blacks and whites by eliminating the moderates: assassinate Roy Wilkins and Whitney Young. The plot was thwarted by the arrest of the group on June 21. NUL hastily hired a bodyguard for Whitney Young and initiated security measures at NUL headquarters.

Responding to general comments and specific queries of NUL board members, Whitney Young in the fall of 1967 answered criticism that the riots were evidence that the League was not reaching Afro-Americans at the grass roots. More than anything else, he said the question reflected the fact that there was "inadequate communication." It was a fact that with eighty-five local Leagues in the nation, each seeing an average of twenty-five persons a day—and some Leagues seeing many times that number—on the basis of a five-day week, fifty-two weeks a year, more than 500,000 people were aided annually by NUL. These were people in search of jobs, housing, assistance with welfare, education and a myriad of other problems—persons seen on a one-to-one basis.

In addition, there were scores of League grass-roots programs that reached out into the ghettoes: the Harlem Street Academies; ENABLE (Education and Neighborhood Action for Better Living Environment); Leadership Development Program; On-the-Job Training; the Washington, D.C. Clean-Up Effort, Pride, Inc., and Alert (which placed seven youth leaders as field coordinators in sensitive police precincts to put neighborhood people in touch with the League and other helping agencies). Young cited the San Diego League's action with the Neighborhood Youth Corps. And he could have cited five dozen more broad-ranging, specific programs deeply involved in black community betterment.

There was at this time, Young estimated, more segregation, more concentration of blacks physically than ever before in the nation's history. Realistically there were no other organizations equipped to do the job that demanded action. The League remained committed to the principle of integration, he insisted, but on the basis of options: that the individual ought to have the right to decide for himself where he wanted to live, where he wished his children to learn, and so on, instead of having these choices foreclosed by discrimination and bigotry.[4]

On the positive side, Whitney Young counted the election results in Boston, Cleveland and Gary. In Boston, the racist who made a nationally publicized bid for mayor on a "neighborhood schools" platform had been defeated. In Cleveland and Gary black mayors had been elected, and Young stated that he found it difficult to convey in words the profound importance of these victories in terms of continuing leadership and impact on disaffected citizens. Their election proved, he said, that it was possible for blacks to secure positions of power and the support of many whites and also demonstrated the emergence of mature, politically organized blacks.

To Mayor Carl B. Stokes, Young gave credit for organizing the black community of Cleveland, with conspicuous success in avoiding a riot that seemed almost inevitable. The building-in of internal discipline and control were, he said, important features of Mayor Stokes's victory and were basic features of the domestic Marshall Plan, illustrating that it worked.[5]

Stokes benefited from an extraordinarily effective League activity carried out in Cleveland and thirty other cities. The tightly knit political group that worked so successfully for Stokes's election learned its skills through the League's Leadership Development Program. This program was based on the conviction that the black community was a reservoir of leadership talent that could be developed and tapped. A three-year demonstration project was underwritten with $450,000 from the Rockefeller Brothers Fund.

Cleveland was one of ten cities in the original Leadership Development Program. In each city a series of four intensive, ongoing seminars was organized with up to 150 people enrolled. Recruiting and selecting the participants for these seminars was done with great care. The trainees ranged from housewives and sales clerks to ministers, industrial engineers and teachers; some were on welfare, others had dropped out of school in the primary grades; some had lived all their lives in the ghetto. All were highly motivated and had indicated achievement potential.

In the study phase, the groups met and learned the facts about how their city was organized, how it ran and what the real power positions were. In the second phase the trainees went into action. They put together organizations that monitored the local socio-economic-political horizon for lapses and opportunities. Not only did they alert the black community to vital matters that affected its future (such as pending school bond issues with analyses of what share of the results would benefit blacks, as in Springfield, Illinois), they brought informed, incisive criticism to bear (as in hearings on charter revision in Cleveland).

In their communities the trainees formed action teams to coordinate the efforts of local civic groups. They worked out methods of monitoring complaints of police brutality, school bias, violations of housing and zoning codes and discrimination in hiring, employment and housing. Here the Cleveland LDP was a standout. The program's graduates worked up an "information bank" on community issues and public figures for instant reference by members of the black community.

The result, in the final phase of the LDP, was intense, eager and knowledgeable grass-roots participation (the kind envisioned by the theoreticians who designed the community action programs for "maximum feasible participation" of the citizens concerned). Because the LDP "graduates" had solid training, they knew how to "take on city hall" and win. Many of the LDP participants ran for local commissions and boards and won election. Others were named to civic and social agencies. One was elected mayor of his small town. Others, as in Cleveland, provided the nucleus for moving into office political candidates who were responsive to ghetto needs. In Carl Stokes's case the link was unusually close: his campaign manager, Dr. Kenneth W. Clement, was an adviser to the Cleveland LDP group and a local Urban Leaguer (Clement was elected to the NUL board of trustees in 1968).

The "successes" achieved as a result of the LDP project were numerous. The Reverend Channing Phillips played a prominent role at the 1968 Democratic National Convention and Ernest Morial made history as the first black elected to Louisiana's legislature since Reconstruction. Both of these men had been chairmen of Leadership Development Advisory committees in their respective communities.

In Miami, through the LDP, the expertise gained by the local League in organizing community leadership resulted in special grants from local government agencies, the U.S. Department of Housing and Urban Development, and even from private industry (Westinghouse Urban Systems Design). The local League had become a nerve center for organizing coalitions to achieve results.

The LDP in Springfield, Ohio, organized an Information Council that documented community situations and drafted position papers on them. It also pulled together a United Black Coalition that challenged the local public housing authority on location of a development, stopping construction. Alternatives were recommended. Wittenberg College was brought into a program to develop opportunities for black businessmen, conducting management seminars to train them. Springfield's United Fund actually underwrote the salary of the LDP project director.

In Washington, D.C., the LDP brought to an end the system of appointing members of the District of Columbia school board (they now are elected). It also organized a Council for Negro Progress in Government with the local League. LDP activities included supplying facts about cooperative enterprises; organizing residents to testify before the Public Services Commission about discrimination against low-income consumers and helping organize a tenant council among residents of a public housing development.

One extremely successful NUL project during these years was a 1960's version of its earliest efforts—job placement. The difference was not only one of scale and scope but of levels and approaches. Called the "National Skills Bank," the project was originally launched in 1963 under the leadership of Mahlon T. Puryear as a demonstration project with outposts in twenty-six cities. Optimistic estimates reckoned that the job profiles of perhaps 2,000 to 3,000 highly qualified blacks from all over the nation would be "deposited" in the "Bank." Within weeks of its launching the Skills Bank superseded those figures and the flood of registrants, demands from industry and government upset all forecasts.

In its first year of operation the Skills Bank spread to fifty-six local Leagues and screened more than 50,000 blacks, of which 33,600 had "saleable or usable skills in a wide variety of occupations." [6] Furthermore, more than 5,300 registrants were placed in new or better jobs and League staffers went out to industry and government and developed "orders" for 10,000 black employees.

The Skills Bank was unquestionably one of the all-time great League success stories. Year after year it served as the key national clearinghouse for highly skilled positions for blacks. By 1968 the emphasis had shifted largely to upgrading black workers, finding openings commensurate with the skills and experience of Afro-Americans. In 1967 alone, the Skills Bank operation was responsible for moving more than 18,000 blacks into better jobs. Skills Bank and Economic Development director Adolph Holmes, was key man in the operation's success. The other key person was a career woman—placement officer Mrs. Ruth Allen King. (Ruth King began as a NUL clerical worker in 1929 and for years assisted Julius A. Thomas and his successors.)

Another extraordinary League success story was performance under its contract to the United States Department of Labor. In 1964 the League was awarded an $8 million Manpower and Training Act contract to train jobless blacks for industrial work. Nearly nine out of ten of those trained were hard-core unemployed. Thirty-eight local Leagues participated in this on-the-job training program and in four years 26,000 workers were trained at an average cost of $550 to $1,100 each, as contrasted with similar programs elsewhere that cost the United States government up to $8,000 per worker trained. (The League found it necessary to keep super-accurate, doubly-documented records on the project. This was because the original contract was awarded to NUL without the concurrence of the chairman of the House Labor and Education Committee. This gentleman was so incensed that he ordered special monitoring of the League's contract performance and implied dire consequences if it failed to deliver.)

Many Leagues turned out to be rate-breakers in this project: Gary contracted to train and place 400 workers and placed 976. Seattle contracted for 145 and placed 184. In New York, NUL contracted for 500 and placed an astonishing 1,102. Atlanta contracted for 300 and placed 382.

At the end of February 1968, the ugly dynamics of American black-white relations were thrust before the eyes of all citizens when the President's National Advisory Commission on Civil Disorders (also called the Riot Panel or Kerner Commission) issued its stark, epochal report. Black alienation, the centrifugal move away from integration, away from inclusion, had indeed become a grave matter, said the Commission. The nation, it found, was "moving towards two societies, one black, one white, separate and unequal." The reason, shorn of verbiage and qualifications, reduced to its unvarnished minimum, was white racism.

This indictment of American society, coming from a blue-ribbon panel of moderate, middle-class citizens, was the end of an era of clouded vision and self-delusion and the beginning of a new, clear-eyed view of the fundamental factors in race relations in the United States.

The massive study covered more than just the riots; it looked into what had happened, went into why—from a historical and practical point of view—and examined the factors of community, police, justice, media, government and other institutions. It made recommendations for action. The panel's remedial suggestions came down to this summary:

> . . . The only genuine, long-range solution for what has happened lies in an attack—mounted at every level—upon the conditions that breed despair and violence. All of us know what those conditions are: ignorance, discrimination, slums, poverty, disease, not enough jobs. We should attack these conditions—not because we are frightened by conflict, but because we are fired by conscience. We should attack them because there is simply no other way to achieve a decent and orderly society in America . . .[7]

Those words, however, were not the commission's but President Johnson's on the day he appointed the commission. The major value, then, of the seven months of intensive effort by the Commission and its army of staff workers, its expenditure of $47,000 (not including the hundreds of thousands spent by congressional committees) and uncounted man-hours, was not alone that it confirmed the conclusions of the President but that it laid on the table under unimpeachable auspices what blacks had been saying since Frederick Douglass: White racism was the root cause.

The grave danger of the slide into separate societies could be halted and reversed, as the commission and the President suggested. The only difference in their remedies was one of degree: the commission called for specific, massive action, expensive in time and money, difficult in likelihood of legislative approval and therefore, from the standpoint of a President who had made perhaps more civil rights progress than all of his predecessors combined, not only unlikely, but impossible at the federal level. The impetus for civil rights legislation had run its course, in the view of politicians. Furthermore, the competition of the bloody Vietnam quagmire for national attention and national resources doomed any major efforts for civil rights progress.

48/New Thrust

In 1968 the world's mightiest nation was fighting two wars and losing them both. The devastating Tet offensive by the Vietcong and North

Vietnamese in South Vietnam had impressed millions of Americans with the gap between the rosy claims of America's military leaders and the realities of that war. A similarly harsh revelation was in store concerning the domestic War on Poverty.

By mid-February 1968, the program specialists of NUL, with the expert counsel of John Turner, had developed a proposal for a $300,000 program that (they expected) would make "significant progress in grappling with the problems of urban planning." [1]

The new approach was to be three experimental Urban Leagues that would give "intensive care" to specially chosen communities to link the white and black "haves" with the black "have-nots" of the ghetto. In meticulous detail the plan outlined the three-phase approach in which task forces and program committees would bring into play the resources of the whole NUL movement in "serious attempts . . . to organize and strengthen each city's black ghetto and change the basic structural systems which impede racial progress."

As outlined, each of the experimental Leagues would have a special staff of five (plus consultants), would work for three years developing the program, each aspect of which would be carefully supervised and evaluated. At the end of the three-year period the entire program and findings of the experiment would be weighed and compared with racial progress in other similar cities to discover and isolate programs, procedures and policies that had proved most efficient. It sounded like an excellent project and a cinch for foundation support.

But, on April 4, 1968, the world changed. Martin Luther King, Jr., head of SCLC, Nobel Peace Prize winner and leading symbol of the civil rights movement, was assassinated by a white man in Memphis.

In the week that followed, riots and attacks on property exploded in 125 American cities. The nation awoke to the fact that the so-called War on Poverty had failed. The cost of the rioting was staggering: forty-six killed (only five whites); more than 3,500 injured; $45 million worth of property lost, stolen or destroyed; more than 20,000 arrests; and deployment of 68,887 troops to cope with the emergencies in the cities. The streets of the nation's capital had to be retaken from rioters and the steps of the Capitol itself were desecrated with machine-gun emplacements. Not a few were sure that the end of the American nation was imminent. In the view of NUL, the country had been brought to the brink of racial disaster. [2]

(It was in this climate that the Civil Rights Act of 1968 was hurried through Congress and signed by the President on April 11. At last federal law banned discrimination in some 80 percent of apartment and house rentals and sales.)

The mood in the nation seemed to favor an end to involvement in both wars as speedily as possible, Americans were inclined to end the shooting war in Vietnam by negotiation and, ironically, to stop the poverty war by force. NUL was convinced that any such simplistic approach to domestic problems would be a grave error.

It was in these seething circumstances that Sterling Tucker urged on Whitney Young an immediate, crash program by NUL. The contemplated experimental Leagues project, with its methodical pace and laboratory aura was too limited and too slow to meet the demands of the moment. Three years of experiment during which hundreds of black communities might rip apart was too much of a luxury. What was needed, argued Tucker, was swift, forceful, curbstone-level action of the kinds that had proved so effective in the Leadership Development Program and in the best of the OEO community action projects. The extraordinary achievements of such programs plus the grave state of affairs convinced Whitney Young and the NUL program staff. The result was a momentous shifting of Urban League gears.

NUL called an emergency national meeting of presidents and executives of local Leagues in New York for a two-day session (April 27–28, 1968) to consider dynamic new approaches to the problems of the ghetto. It was in his keynote address to a grimly sober and expectant gathering of League leaders that Whitney Young assessed the race relations state of the nation.[3] The League's prime responsibility in this critical hour, he said, was nothing less than to help halt the nation's self-destructive course. (The presidential primary campaign of Senator Eugene McCarthy, which rallied thousands—particularly young people—had a similar avowed purpose.) Recent events not only demanded but created the opportunities to so move. That necessity was evident from several basic conditions:

1. First and foremost was the reality of current life in America for black citizens; the gap—in all areas—was widening, not narrowing.

2. The attitude among blacks toward that condition was a mixture of bitterness, anger and loss of faith in the American system and in people —both blacks and whites.

3. Among blacks a lack of discipline, patience and restraint was evident. Acting out of frustration and demonstrations were increasing.

4. The assassination of Martin Luther King and the attitudes toward it in black and white communities were significant: blacks were not particularly interested in apprehension of the killer—except to confirm that the killer was a white American. Blacks believed that King's murder was the death knell of the possibility for a black man to exist in this society even when he exemplified love and nonviolence.

5. The polarization of the community continued; there was increasing segregation, increasing willingness of white bigots to articulate their prejudices. The bigots felt they could operate with impunity in spewing their vitriol; the hostile and contemptuous attitude of both black and white young toward American society was based on their belief that the system would not respond to normal channels of expression and dissent.

6. More suppression, more force was being marshaled than ever before. The statements of congressmen and others (such as Mayor Richard Daley of Chicago, who ordered police to shoot to kill looters) were typical of widespread attitudes.

And yet, there was evidence that more humane and sensible views did exist. The Riot Commission's report was outstanding in this respect. It was, in effect, a social audit. It squarely faced up to the fact that equal opportunity for citizens as severely handicapped as black Americans was not enough. The commission stressed the imperative that there must be honest sharing of the rewards and responsibilities of this society, that blacks must be given a stake in the system, sharing in its action, its decision-making and results. The report made clear the futility of attempting to achieve equal results for black Americans by separation (and inspection of the seven existing all-black communities in the country would confirm this). And finally, Afro-Americans had a spiritual stake in all of the things of the nation.

The power structure controlled wealth, communications, military and political power. Since this was so, blacks trapped in the ghetto were not likely to escape their current fate unless they were helped—they needed a massive booster to get them out of their ghetto orbit, away from its gravitational pull. Therefore, the League must work with the black community—those within it must mobilize their own power. And for this the League had the staff to help with the job. Urban Leagues would now plunge into this effort in what Young called a "New Thrust." [4]

Wiry, professorial Sterling Tucker, who had directed the successful NUL voter education project in 1964, had been leader of the task force to develop the New Thrust. It was Tucker who presented the program to the audience of Urban Leaguers.

As preamble, Tucker said that though the NUL commitment to interracial teamwork and an open society remained, the agency now was to direct itself to the black ghetto. Lasting solutions to minority problems could be achieved only through integrated effort.

The new fundamental objective of the Urban League would be equalization of life results between black and white America.

Tucker described two philosophies that were currently splitting the civil rights movement. The first called for attacking racial or socio-economic barriers in the general society, using judicial, legislative and political tools and heavy reliance on the active participation of the federal government. Integration was the goal in this approach and primary strength came from the leverage and support of the liberal-labor-religious-black coalition that had made the advances of the past decade.

The alternative strategy developed out of the War on Poverty community action programs (CAP) and the black power movement. This emphasized building the internal economic, social and political strength of the black ghetto. Integration was either rejected or relegated to a low priority. Biracial cooperation and cooperative relations with the power structure were "deemphasized" or even eliminated. Basic support would come from mobilization of the black masses. (The black intellectuals and militant antipoverty professionals were the theoreticians for this approach.)

The League's traditional strategy of removing barriers and the NAACP's drive to provide the legal basis for integration would, said Tucker, "continue to benefit mainly middle class individuals able to take advantage of opportunities and will leave the masses of black poor locked into the ghetto."

Tucker acknowledged that "the debate on whether the UL should be devoting its major attention to activities designed to change basic institutions and practices or to service-rendering programs has raged for years." The time had come, he declared, to decide in favor of social change. The reasons?

1. "No massive expansion of social services alone within the existing social framework can eliminate all the ghetto's problems. . . . Ultimate solutions for the urban crisis cannot occur without basic changes in many of the ways in which our society operates."

2. The human needs were so immense that UL-provided services could not make any substantial dent in the problem. Concentration on service would be inefficient use of the UL's unique but limited resources.

3. "If the forces repressing and perpetuating the ghetto are inherent in the system, the principal leverage . . . for changing them lies with the community's principal opinion and decision makers." The League with its contacts could bring together ghetto dwellers and such leaders in combined efforts to effect basic institutional reforms.

The primary emphasis would thenceforth be on "systems-changing confrontations." Tucker's definition of confrontation was "moving beyond remedies for individual distress, moving to a full-scale attack on the entire system that causes such distress time and time again." [5]

He used housing as an example: the common problems were high rents, easy eviction, physical disrepair, overcrowding, courts serving as rent collection or eviction agencies rather than dispensaries of justice. Usually tenant complaints led to eviction, while landlord repairs automatically meant higher rents. Though relief to individual tenants in distress was important, even more important was breaking the whole system of landlord exploitation—through carefully planned landlord/tenant confrontations with the protagonists prepared to follow through by going to court to change the rules.

The test of success would be in the results—in evidence that the problem tackled was solved or substantially reduced, not in the effort invested or the number of individuals served.

Tucker bombarded the Urban Leaguers with definitions, concepts and new compass readings that would demand radical revision and revamping of ongoing programs. The delegates then passed a resolution the force and tone of which had never previously been recorded in National Urban League formal assemblies.[6]

WHEREAS the black ghettos, created by white society, have been spreading in size and in the degree of frustration, and

WHEREAS there is a compelling need to organize the black masses in the ghettos and other poverty areas to give a voice to the voiceless, power to the powerless, to strengthen pride and dignity in the dispossessed of these communities, and,

WHEREAS the black masses must participate in the decisions made concerning their lives and must speak for themselves in matters concerning their community, and,

WHEREAS the Urban League movement through its Board and staff structure has proposed a plan for working more directly with the black masses and other minority groups trapped in the ghetto and to develop black economic, social and political strength, and,

WHEREAS white America must abandon racism in all of its evil forms and actively support our efforts to create a better interracial climate and a truly open society, and,

WHEREAS this concept was endorsed by the National Urban League's Board of Trustees meeting in Indianapolis . . .

BE IT RESOLVED that the Delegate Assembly of the NUL most emphatically supports the 'New Thrust' defined at the Strategy Meeting and endorsed by the NUL Board of Trustees.

BE IT FURTHER RESOLVED that financial, structural and other internal "tooling up" required to implement this program carry the highest priority as of the adoption of this Resolution.

Whitney Young announced that the NUL expected to have $1,500,000 in foundation funds to apply to the New Thrust effort. He also announced that forty-four-year-old Sterling Tucker was to be majordomo of the program, assisted by a staff of at least five specialists. Tucker's title would be NUL associate executive director for field services.

The remainder of the two-day meeting concentrated on moving and coaching local Leagues to "build Ghetto Power."

Where and how should they start the New Thrust effort in their cities? The manual developed by Tucker and his collaborators had a step-by-step outline.[7] First step was to set up review panels consisting of local League board representatives and experts from the areas of action under consideration and possible areas of involvement. (In the early days of the organization, similar reviews and program direction were conducted by volunteer committees.)

Next, the local League was advised to make a "Racial Gap Survey," bringing together existing information from available sources. (Here was a principle fundamental to both the Associations for the Protection of Colored Women and the Committee for Improving the Industrial Conditions of Negroes in New York in 1905 and in 1906.)

Relevant experiences would be pulled together, sifted and reported to the local Leagues by the national and regional UL offices. A thorough analysis of existing programs and policies of voluntary agencies and local government should be made through studies or "problem-centered" conferences preferably by the local Health and Welfare Council. (This was a throw-back to the basic precept of the Committee on Urban Conditions Among Negroes in 1910.)

Local colleges would be brought into direct contact with the urban crisis by working out arrangements for course-credit seminars via research topics suggested by the UL. (This echoed George Haynes's original prospectus for establishing field work at Fisk in 1910, with his stress on bringing the strengths of the campus to bear on the slums.)

An element labeled "community input" was listed as "a most important aspect of planning." Where the local League had members living in the ghetto community, these members would "be elevated to primary influence in program planning"—that is, "community input." (In 1913, the National League on Urban Conditions Among Negroes' "clients" made plenty of "community input." When the "tenderloin" pushed into black neighborhoods, NLUCAN's housing bureau organized black immigrants to channel their rage and defend themselves.)

Conferences with neighborhood groups, local community action assemblies, and so on, were also recommended to get the community pulse and participation. (The first public activity of the newly formed National League on Urban Conditions Among Negroes, December 4, 1911, was the first gathering of social workers who served the black community for just such purposes.)

A technique that was listed with its pluses and minuses was the demonstration project to illustrate a new approach to providing a service or solving a problem. (Many aspects of NLUCAN's early programming—travelers' aid work, then shelter, employment, vocational guidance, health and welfare, recreation and interceding with the law—started as demonstration projects.)

Urban Leaguers were warned that demonstration projects often devoured staff time and effort, were frequently more service-oriented than change-oriented. "In the final analysis," said the staff paper on the subject, "most social institutions have been reformed, not by example, but by outright challenge." (That sounded like Frances Kellor's philosophy. It was a fundamental precept employed in 1906 when the first League met head-on and destroyed the interstate system that was recruiting, shipping and selling black girls into the brothels of the big cities.)

It was consistent with the New Thrust philosophy that when the Poor People's Campaign, led by the Reverend Ralph D. Abernathy, headed for Washington, D.C., and what appeared to be an imminent debacle (because of lack of pre-planning and organization) the NUL came to its aid. Sterling Tucker was detached for emergency assignment to help the campaign find facilities, secure government permission and assistance, and organize the June 19, 1968, Solidarity Day rally at the Lincoln Memorial climaxing the event. Whitney Young represented the League at the rally, pledged increased League exertion on behalf of the poor.

Back of the New Thrust and "black power" shift of the Urban League course was, said Whitney Young, the fundamental League approach of coming to grips with reality. Historically, the agency's goals had been integration and it had programmed and planned on the assumption that this was coming about, was actually taking place. The reality—looking at conditions overall—was that by and large this was not happening and nowhere was this fact more evident than in the zooming growth of the suburbs and the black center city populations. The blacks were filling the cities and the whites were fleeing to the "white noose" of suburbs that ringed them. The races were more, not less, segregated.

Furthermore, the institutions that should have been serving the city's citizens were not doing the job. It was true in the cities in general, but even more of a lapse was evident with regard to the black community. Whatever the indices, there was a shortfall in the ghettoes: school dropout rates higher; achievement levels lower; chronically maximal disease and mortality rates; peak unemployment; transportation inadequate; housing abominable; and on and on.

The League was not alone, of course, in this view. Indeed, from the national headquarters of the United Community Funds and Councils of

America went an extraordinary statement and checklist of activities in May concerning what it called the "unparalleled domestic crisis." [8] This time, instead of condoning ejection of local Urban Leagues from Fund membership as it had a decade before, the Fund headquarters endorsed "substantial increase in subsidy to the local UL" and "formation of and providing for operational needs of an UL in communities where it does not exist."

Another extraordinary action in mid-year was the appearance of Whitney Young as a featured speaker at CORE's convention. Under Floyd McKissick's leadership CORE had become xenophobic and thus Young's attendance was almost as startling as his address. The coming 1968 presidential election, said the NUL executive, made necessary the highest degree of unity among those "seeking opportunity and equal results for all Americans." He had, Young stated, come to the CORE convention convinced that the mutual goals of CORE and the League were greater than their differences. He praised CORE's frontal attacks on problems for making a "negotiable or a legislative solution by the UL or the NAACP possible." What is important, he stressed, is that "each do his thing well, understanding fully his dependence on the other. . . . To negotiate across the table, or to engage in political activity, is sometimes more militant and effective than continuing to picket . . . no war is ever won unless there is an intelligent division of labor with each respecting the other."

Black power, Young said, is not lung power or fire power, but brain power, political power and economic power. These come from a "new sense of pride, of dignity, of destiny, as well as roots [and] . . . a new sense of unity of community." [9]

> We support as legitimate and historically consistent a minority's mobilization of its economic and political power to reward its friends and punish its enemies. . . . We do not believe in cultural absorption but rather cultural exchange. We believe black people have in the past given much to America which we insist all our educational systems must record and teach for both blacks and whites. We believe blacks are giving much to the present society and will contribute even more to the future if there is to be a future for America or mankind. [10]

He warned against being trapped in the "trick bag" of generalizing on the basis of race.

> Most black people have been beautiful, but some black men killed Malcolm X; your associate director Roy Innis' son; and daily exploit their people either as employers, landlords or merchants. Most white people, as the Kerner Commission report pointed out, are racist but some are not. Particularly among young people do we witness an attempt to rid themselves of the disease of prejudice and a willingness to challenge the institutions and

the systems which have perpetuated racism. Significantly, an increasing number of top corporate leaders and public officials have demonstrated a flexibility and a desire for change. . . . We must continue to fight and reject those white racists, and . . . revolutionists who would send us back to Africa or establish a more formal American apartheid.[11]

The League, Young said, "does not apologize for its past contributions to our black brothers. We were for many years the only resource to which black citizens could turn for jobs, welfare, housing, education and recreation." Considering the limitations of law, public attitude and the League's resources, it had achieved miracles. But yesterday's programs and methods were not good enough for today. That was why the League had announced a New Thrust, shifting from "our role as honest power broker to that of providing technical assistance to the ghetto to help it organize, document its needs, select its own leadership and arrange for creative confrontations with appropriate officials." Young also mentioned League plans and programs aimed at middle-class blacks and at white racism, and formed to reach and expand the number of black leaders, businessmen, campus leaders, and ghetto youth groups.

This carefully defined embracement of black power brought the CORE convention to its feet at the end of Young's talk. Delegates shouted "The brother has come home; the brother has come *home!*" This address, in which Young seemed to loft the black power banner, jolted moderates—white and black—and "shook up" establishmentarian friends of the League.

To alienated blacks, this was further reassurance that the League was a viable agency sympathetic to their goals and methods. It was the logical extension of the League action they witnessed in their neighborhoods. As a Dayton Black Power leader had told a mass meeting that summer, "I can't give the League hell any more because it got fifteen jobs for my boys. I'm not calling them names any more. I'm calling them espionage agents for the black people!" [12]

49/Building Ghetto Power

It was NUL's 1968 annual conference in New Orleans in July that brought together the small army of professionals most concerned with propelling the New Thrust into meaningful action. At New Orleans more than 2,100 industry, government, labor, education, health and welfare experts came together and focused their brain power on the problems of building ghetto power. Lindsley F. Kimball, who had done so much to put the League on a sound financial footing, to open doors in high places and find it a new, modern national headquarters building, stepped down after four years as NUL president. He was succeeded by James A. Linen, president of Time, Inc., and former leader of NUL's corporate support campaign.

Linen electrified his NUL conference audience by endorsing black power. He carefully qualified it, however, excluding black terrorist power, black power for vengeance or the kind that withdraws into sterile isolationism or nationalism. "Only black political power, black economic power, black social power and black educational power can insure progress toward a truer democracy," he declared.

> Not only am I for it because it is right, but also because in a pluralistic society, as opposed to a monolithic power system, that black power—or ghetto power—or soul power—will succeed. . . . It will succeed if black Americans push into the world rather than withdraw from it.[1]

Linen endorsed the goals of the New Thrust program, which Whitney Young defined further for conference delegates. "It is racial and community pride and experience in competent management that will free the black community from its traditional and quasi-total dependency on the institutions of the white society," he pointed out.[2]

> So the UL pledges its all-out support to the creation and the support of black groups which can speak for a united community, and who will be able to bring about a "dialog of equals" with the representatives of the power structure outside the black community. We pledge our help in giving a voice and a structure to the just demands of the ghetto. . . .
>
> We will build the economic institutions of the ghetto through the development of black-owned businesses, cooperatives, consumer unions and black-owned franchises.
>
> As we intend to devise the means by which white involvement replaces guilt and fear, we intend to devise the means whereby black involvement replaces bitterness and despair. The emerging black middle-class will be called upon to aid their brothers in the slums, for here is a vast untapped strength within the black community. The resources, expertise and know-how of these brothers who have made it have to be applied to solving the problems of the ghetto.[3]

To provide a sense of urgency and fundamental reality, sessions of the conference dispersed to New Orleans's Carrollton, Central City, Desire and Lower Ninth Ward slum areas. There workshops on housing, education, employment family and welfare were carried on with ghetto residents participating shoulder-to-shoulder with nationally known experts.

Another blast of urgency and reality was provided by youths at the conference. Young people, including gang leaders and university students, had been invited to attend. They came in force and nearly "broke up the place." Sporting Afro and "natural" hair styles, wearing dashikis and/or casual clothes, the youths knew their own minds and went aggressively about their activities. They scandalized a few highly conservative Urban Leaguers when they announced a boycott and picketed the restaurant, bar, lobby concessions and drug store at the conference headquarters hotel "because of racism." But that was only a starter.

The youths presented two pages of "Proposals for the New Thrust" that looked suspiciously like an ultimatum. Among the proposals were these:

> The UL should support existing black community groups morally and financially.
>
> NUL should finance a conference of black youth organizations to define problems and plan programs for ghetto youth action.
>
> UL should recruit members from the black community; it should become a membership organization with democratic control in the hands of members. All policy-making bodies of the UL Movement should be 80% black; 20% should be radical whites. The Youth Community (persons under 25 years) is to have 30% representation; another 20% of the boards should be between 25 and 35 years.
>
> NUL should provide $1,000,000 for scholarships to be distributed by affiliates.
>
> UL programs in Housing and Employment duplicate existing city services. These should be abandoned and UL should make tax-supported agencies benefit black people.[4]

Needless to say, such outspokenness was a stunning change from the NUL Youth Community statements of a couple of years earlier and caused heated reactions and some decidedly constructive action.

At the 1963 NUL conference Marcia Young and Nancy Steeger, daughters of the NUL executive and president, had sparkplugged formation of an Urban League Youth Community "to develop . . . understanding of race relations and to train [youths] for community responsibilities." Main activities of the youths were projects ranging from voter education drives and parent-student seminars to human relations workshops and tutorial work with slum children. By 1965 some thirty-five cities had ongoing programs under the Youth Community banner.

Members of the UL Youth Community attended the annual confer-

ences and had their own sessions, presented resolutions and attended
open sessions of the conference. An NUL program specialist was assigned
to advise, coordinate and arrange regional meetings and oversee publication of a newsletter for the Youth Community. By the time of the 1966
conference some 4,000 young people had gone through UL orientation
seminars, thirty-seven cities had organized Youth Community chapters
and twelve more were in formation.

Up through 1966 Youth Community members were predominantly
well-scrubbed, neatly groomed, well-spoken, well-intentioned and impec-
cably dressed middle-class youngsters. They were invariably polite and observed the amenities as they discussed their projects in colloquiums and
panels.

The shift in tone, articulateness and relevance of youth participation in
League activities was indicative of the forces surging within and without
the NUL. To keep abreast, NUL elected three black twenty-year-old students to its board of trustees. Each of them was a leader of new militants
on his college campus. And NUL initiated a program whereby thirty-
three black students from twenty-five colleges came to national headquarters for a period of intensive orientation, then fanned out to special projects in the slums of ten League cities. They lived and worked in the
slums, organizing residents for social and economic activity. It was part of
the New Thrust and it benefited both the slum dwellers and the college
youths.

The youngsters discovered, as one of them put it, "that expressing
black anger and frustration in college is different from transforming that
energy into constructive programs in the slum neighborhoods." [5]

In Atlanta, they organized domestic workers into a union; in San
Diego, a food-buying club, aiming toward a consumer cooperative. In
some cities they taught classes in black history and tutored. In one city
they succeeded in forcing the local government to pave streets and light
them. The project was a further link between the UL and young black
leaders and was expanded later.

The brash demands presented by the Youth Community militants at
the annual conference stung some of NUL's most outspoken advocates.
Senior vice president Ramon S. Scruggs spoke not only for himself when
he said, "It is time that the UL ceases to try to placate people who cannot be placated, and make clear that this is not going to be a black organization." Whitney Young agreed that the League "will not be a black
organization, philosophically, practically, or any other way," nor would it
"run away from the white racism issue as the basic cause of society's
evils." [6]

Staff members had been assigned to work with the youths and would continue to do so, said Young. It was of primary significance that the agency was not only carrying on a dialogue with outspoken youth, but enlisting their efforts constructively in League programs and bringing them into the inner chambers of League policy-setting—the NUL board of trustees and the Delegate Assembly. "A voice must be given at the highest levels of the civil rights movement to young people," Young said. "We want and need their counsel in setting our policy." [7]

There was, in the view of NUL professionals and others, profound merit in the Community Action Program concepts of involving the poor and changing the systems. The League had, for much of its existence, been forced by lack of resources compounded by the obtuse intransigence of white Americans and the incomplete awareness of blacks themselves, to concentrate on ameliorative efforts—basically trying to keep Afro-Americans alive. By 1968 these factors had changed drastically and, from the standpoint of possible remedial action, favorably.

In the early days, the League had a handful of professionally trained workers at most, and their skills and experience were circumscribed. Sixty years later the agency had a small army of professionals, the best-trained and most experienced in the nation.

For most of its existence the League, like Sisyphus, struggled repeatedly against overwhelming odds. The forces of the government at local, state and federal levels had been hostile, indifferent or minimally cooperative for the most part. Business and industry, labor, foundations and the private sector had, by and large, been disinterested, uncooperative or hostile, with notable exceptions. This situation had been almost reversed; now those who would not cooperate were the exceptions.

The League's constituents had changed considerably in six decades also. No longer illiterate, impassive peasants shunted aside into small enclaves, they were now volatile, knowledgeable citizens aware of how society had short-changed them. They were no longer cowed by white power or economic superiority—and they occupied key sections of the nation's most important population centers.

All of these were elements that collectively caused a shift of gears in the Urban League movement, a shift to a new level of relevancy, the most urgent and far-reaching move in NUL history.

But could the New Thrust hope to change society? In the months following, the answers to that became apparent, as the five regional offices and ninety-five Leagues reported their results in eight categories of New Thrust action: (1) environment—housing and community development; (2) black business development; (3) education; (4) political action; (5) employment; (6) police-community relations; (7) community organization; and (8) welfare.

During the year forty-two new projects were launched, many of them multicity projects. The major difference in the New Thrust programs, compared with previous NUL efforts, was the uncompromising targeting of major objectives and unswerving determination to achieve them. Many, if not all, of the projects were direct challenges to the Establishment. They had to be, explained Whitney Young, because black powerlessness had to be ended.

An example was a study of decision-makers in Chicago by the UL. It revealed that blacks held fewer than 300 of the 11,000 policy-making positions in Cook County, though one third of the population was black. This was merely one instance of incredible underrepresentation that left the levers of power in the hands of people who lived outside the ghetto and made their decisions in snug, isolated board rooms. Such decisions were often if not always unresponsive to the needs of blacks for education, welfare, sanitation, health and other primary life requirements.

The problems and approaches of a militantly aggressive local League were illustrated in Miami. There the UL was organizing the black community around the issue of housing abuses and continued crumbling of the ghetto. With members of block clubs in a thirty-block central city renewal area, the UL was attacking lax enforcement of the city housing code, neglect of buildings by landlords, lack of garbage pickups and increasing infestation of rats and vermin.

Such problems, said Whitney Young, do not exist in white middle-class communities. When they do, only a phone call or angry letter is required to correct them. But the powerlessness of the black community is apparent, he noted, when such "proper" means of protest produce no results. Petitions and complaints had been tried in Miami, with no success. Therefore, other methods would be used: refusal to pay garbage collection fees; tenant clean-up crews with "salaries" supplied by deducting amounts due from rent payments; and withholding of rents.[8]

The short-term goal of such confrontation techniques would be the improvement of living conditions in the area. Long-term goals included building cooperation leading to formation of an area council of block clubs (such as John T. Clark had pioneered in St. Louis) to move on other neighborhood problems. This, said Young, was unity-building. Where the ghetto developed self-awareness and confidence to exercise power responsibly it could move into many projects, such as economic development, education and recreation. The constants in the equation, as the League analyzed it, were the necessity of organizing the black community and of developing authentic leadership and institutional strength.[9]

The resentment of blacks about the inadequacy of education became the motive power for confrontation action in fourteen UL cities. Results? Community control in Seattle; halt of construction of a de facto segregated school in Fort Wayne, and curriculum changes in Elkhart, Indiana; organization for specific changes in Riverside and San Diego, California, St. Louis, Miami and others.

One of the most celebrated League projects (and justly so) was the Street Academies. With profound significance not only to the students and the black community but to American education, the Street Academies proved beyond doubt that the educational system deserved failing marks, not (in many, many cases) the students.

Operated by the New York League, the first Street Academies in Harlem were designed as a college entrance program for hard-core teenage dropouts. Students were recruited by League workers in ghetto pool halls, bars, and "shooting galleries." In 1967 alone, 107 Street Academy graduates entered Ivy League and other prestigious colleges around the nation. The academies were justifiably proud of the fact that 100 percent of their graduates won acceptance to these colleges. They were expanded into a system that included a Harlem prep school and more than a dozen storefront Street Academies sponsored by major United States corporations. Similar Street Academies were initiated in Hartford, South Bend, Detroit, Pittsburgh and Los Angeles.

This education program proved that students abandoned by the public school system were not only educable but, when taught relevant material in a relevant curriculum, could and did qualify for colleges. The system-changing implications of this "demonstration" were profound. In New York, the Board of Education installed League-supervised Street Academy programs in five high schools of the city. Furthermore, seven of the city's teachers were assigned to UL Street Academies for training and orientation—important steps toward changing an ossified system of education that had sloughed off slum youth.

In forty cities the League instituted crash voter education projects to bring blacks to the polls. In Rochester, black voter turnout increased from 64 percent in 1964 to 87 percent in 1968—and the UL executive led other candidates by 5,000 votes in election to the Board of Education.

The New Thrust added a dimension beyond the ghetto to NUL's major programming in 1968. In its first adequately supplied effort to move against a long-neglected source of urban problems the League went into the countryside. Taking a cue from William H. Baldwin, Jr., nearly seventy years before, the NUL began a project to make a backward, rural southern county a model of black rural development. If successful, it might slow migration to the cities and make the rural area viable.

In Hancock County, Georgia, three-fourths of the population of 10,000 were black, steeped in poverty (median income, below $2,500, as compared with national median income of $8,318), and dependent on agriculture. Thanks to the Voting Rights Act of 1965, blacks won two of three seats on the county's Board of Commissioners in 1968. With this interracial sharing of power, the commissioners asked the League for help. A field office was established in Sparta, the League spearheaded a town meeting (otherwise known as a mass rally), brought in representatives of federal and state agencies plus a major bank and explored avenues of assistance. Calling for a federal task force to make a concentrated effort on behalf of the poor in Hancock County, Whitney Young spotlighted the community. There were promising beginnings when the Economic Development Administration put up money for an economic development study: a catfish farming business was proposed for local black management. A concrete block plant was built and other developments were in the offing. Hancock County was on the move, thanks to NUL intervention.

In employment, the New Thrust in Washington, D.C., pressed the United States Government Printing Office, a major employer of blacks. After a series of carefully escalated confrontations with the administrators, a rally of 500 black employees was held. Upshot: appointment by the Civil Service Commission of an outside arbitration panel to monitor GPO action on personnel complaints—a breakthrough.

In Jacksonville, fourteen major banks were faced with documentation of their lily-white hiring (above janitorial level) and a quiet, community-wide boycott of noncomplying banks to force hiring of blacks. Results: blacks hired for counter positions by ten banks plus a Chamber of Commerce training program for others.

Newark established a Welfare Rights Center for building an informed, aggressive welfare clientele to challenge the system. In Little Rock, a coalition placed a welfare recipient on the county welfare board—a first. Fort Wayne's UL organized mothers and children on welfare into a power group that took legal action in federal court against unlawful local welfare practices and started action to change the archaic town trustees system of local government.

By the end of 1968 more than thirty Leagues were deeply involved in organizing their black neighborhood communities into block clubs and councils and forming ghetto coalitions. Example: Blacks in Racine, Wisconsin, were incensed when the city council substituted a zoo for a previously approved recreation center for the ghetto. The UL played a major role in transforming reaction from this incipient riot into constructive action. The black community channeled its anger into a boycott of the existing recreational facilities and organized bussing of 200 black children to the nearest white center. Confrontation with the police resulted in three injured police, twenty-five arrests and minor damage. A curfew was imposed and the National Guard put on alert in Racine's outskirts. The black community was convinced the results were worth the dangers: the city council reinstated plans for the ghetto center, hired an architect and purchased the land. Moreover, the black community, reported the local UL executive, was "reborn" with a new sense of unity and purpose. New awareness had been instilled in white leadership and communication was flowing through new channels.

Evidence of this awareness was the statement by one top corporation executive to Whitney Young: " [Building ghetto power] is the best thing the UL has done. By becoming more involved in organizing, you're helping to tackle these problems more effectively. That's what we need. My company can't do business in a city in which so many people are too poor to buy our goods or who lack the education to work for us." [10]

The New Thrust in 1968 moved the League into the mainstream of relevancy in serving black constituents. By the year's end scores of local Leagues had established storefront outposts in the ghettoes, operating around the clock to help Afro-Americans. They were there, corners of strength, with hot-lines to the resources of the local, regional and National Urban League offices.

By returning to the slums and organizing ghetto power to change the hostile environment, the League had gone back to its beginnings.

It had truly come home.

50/A Final Word

Around the turn of the century America's cities suffered a vicious and mysterious plague each summer. It was an unpredictable and devastating "summer death" that struck down babies in the teeming industrial communities. Race, ethnic background and religion were of no consequence to this invisible murderer that seized the tiny citizens as the summer's heat intensified each year. Heat itself was thought to be the culprit and for years high temperatures were blamed for the deaths of thousands of city infants.

The blame was, however, misplaced. Public health specialists found that not heat but impure milk caused the deaths. With that vital finding, social scientists, social workers, and public health authorities teamed to devise methods for purification of milk, its reliable, sanitary delivery and distribution (through establishment of milk stations) to the poor especially, plus intensive campaigns to teach mothers the crucial importance of pure milk. In this way the mysterious "summer death" was overcome.

The founders of the Urban League were among those social workers, progressives and reformers who scored this victory, and so many others of fundamental, historic importance in the fields of housing, health and education. These men and women had the divine effrontery to believe that they could solve the problems of blacks in America's cities in the same manner that they so vigorously and successfully used to clean up other social problems. If they knew, they refused to be intimidated by the fact that they were tackling the most complex and sensitive matter in American life. Their knowledge and their tools, their manpower and their resources proved inadequate. The problems in this area expanded far beyond their capacities and they failed. It was a noble, not ignominious, failure and it was not surprising. Even the immense power and prestige of the government of the United States of America failed in this.

However, the courage and determination of the League founders did not falter. The agency, its staff and volunteers carried the torch and passed it on. Today, as in the beginning, the League's goal is not amelioration (though it recognizes that necessity) but changing root causes. Now, as then, this is neither a popular nor safe path. While some critics have denounced the League as too ineffectual to achieve such changes, others have disagreed and attacked it violently for being too "militant": recently the home of the Warren, Ohio, executive was bombed; the Seattle executive was assassinated on his doorstep; the national executive was the target for assassins.

The founders and leaders of the League were animated by great visions of the future that might be. Toward these goals they strove and toward them they made measurable progress. The tyranny of racism vitiated many of these visions and sent them to unmarked graves. American racisim often has prevented American citizens from joining together as they did to overcome the "summer death." America has paid an agonizing toll for that incomprehensible irrationality—and continues to do so. This obtuseness appalled Urban Leaguers but they pressed forward undaunted.

Social movements rarely leave conventional monuments to mark their trajectory. The League, like most social movements, has been geared to performance. Its monuments have been its accomplishments and these have been changed lives—the lives of black constituents directly improved and enhanced by Urban League action, and the lives of unaware hundreds of thousands in the cities who, but for League action, would have suffered even more from the inevitable consequences of unmitigated black migration.

We ended our summary of the League's history with the year 1968. It was an arbitrary ending point but an appropriate one. For 1968 was the year in which the martyrdom of Martin Luther King, Jr., seared American society, the federal commitment to black progress wound down, black separatism reached a new plateau of viability—and the League shifted to its New Thrust program. The League's traditional role of power broker was transmuted into that of coach and strategist, "convener" of confrontations; member of coalitions to achieve change and, paradoxically and most significantly, working partner with business, labor government, social and civic organizations and, above all, with the black community.

In its new roles, the League has moved with increased resources, velocity and effectiveness since 1968. The League has not been and cannot be content simply with reflecting or repeating the past. The men and women who shape the agency's present and future have developed modern methods to meet contemporary needs. But that, it seems to the authors, is another vital and exciting chapter that warrants a separate chronicle. That record will reveal achievements relevant to the urgent needs of the times, achievements foreshadowed and made possible by the dedicated struggle of thousands of League staff, board and volunteers who prepared the way.

A Note on the Sources

Chapter References

Officers and Board Members of the
National League on Urban
Conditions Among Negroes
and of the
National Urban League

Index

A Note on the Sources

A number of basic sources were used in this work. The most valuable is the extensive National Urban League collection at the Manuscript Division of the Library of Congress. It contains vital board and committee minutes, financial records, correspondence and other documents for the years 1910–1960.

The reports of activities issued each year by the National League on Urban Conditions among Negroes, known later as the National Urban League, carried a variety of cover titles. In the earliest years the reports covered a fiscal year and were issued as *Bulletins;* in later years they covered a calendar year, and in still others a combination of two or three years. Some were issued as "Year-end Reports." In order to minimize the confusion to the reader, the authors have called each of these published reports of activities the "Annual Report," indicating the period covered.

The income and expenditure budget figures cited in this study were taken from official documents containing the League's audited financial statements on file at the League's national headquarters office in New York. These figures differ sometimes from those in the agency's annual reports and other publications.

The L. Hollingsworth Wood Papers, in possession of his widow at Mount Kisco, New York, have invaluable correspondence and documents for the years 1915–1941—the years of Mr. Wood's presidency of the organization.

The George Edmund Haynes Papers in the Fisk University Library Negro Collection; and the Robert R. Moton Papers at Tuskegee Institute contain a wide range of correspondence and materials that are not found elsewhere. Other papers and documents of Dr. Moton are found at the Collis P. Huntington Library at Hampton Institute. Additional correspondence and papers of Dr. Haynes are in the possession of his widow in Mount Vernon, New York. The unpublished "Memoirs" and "Abridged Autobiography" of Eugene Kinckle Jones, in the possession of

his widow at Flushing, Long Island, were an extremely important resource. Typescripts of speech notes for about 150 addresses by Mr. Jones,
delivered from February 19, 1919, to January 11, 1938, are in the possession of Guichard Parris. The National Archives in Washington, D.C., has
correspondence and reports of the United States Department of Labor,
Division of Negro Economics in 1918–1919 by Dr. Haynes, Forrester B.
Washington and others.

The Peabody Collection at the Hampton Institute Library contains
newspaper and magazine clippings bound in book form, that provide
hundreds of items from scores of publications bearing directly on the
growth and development of the National Urban League.

Columbia University's Oral History Research Office in the Library's
Special Collections contains the "Reminiscences" of Roger N. Baldwin,
Lester B. Granger, Will W. Alexander, Benjamin F. McLaurin and
George McAneny.

The William Edward Burghardt DuBois papers are in the custody of
Herbert Aptheker, Director of the American Institute for Marxist Studies.

The Rockefeller Family Archives (in New York), the Carnegie Corpo-
ration of New York Archives (in New York) and the Julius Rosenwald
Papers at the University of Chicago Library provided valuable National
Urban League documents, reports and correspondence. The archives of
the New York School of Philanthropy, now the Columbia University
School of Social Work, contain pertinent material relating to the estab-
lishment and development of the National Urban League's Fellowship
Program from 1910 to date.

It is not possible to list all of the periodicals and reports used but the
following were especially helpful:

Armstrong Association of New York, *Annual Reports,* 1896–1910; New
York Association for Improving the Condition of the Poor, *Annual
Reports*—especially 1903–1919; Charity Organization Society, *Annual
Reports,* particularly for the years 1903–1919; Hampton Negro Conference, *Reports,* 1896–1920; *Opportunity* magazine, the Urban League's of-
ficial organ from 1923 to 1949, which contains articles and news items by
and about Urban League Board and staff members not found elsewhere;
The early issues of the National Association for the Advancement of Col-
ored People's *The Crisis* magazine (1910–1930) are important sources for
reports of National Urban League activities; The National Conference of
Social Welfare, *Proceedings* (title varies), especially 1911–1925; New York
City Mission and Tract Society, *Monthly Bulletin,* especially 1902–1910;
The *Southern Workman,* 1897–1920; The *Survey* magazine, a Journal of
Constructive Philanthropy (title varies); especially 1904–1930, and At-

lanta University Publications; especially Numbers 2, 1897; 14, 1910; and 17, 1912.

The important contemporary periodicals in the Schomburg Collection of the New York Public Library containing pertinent items on the National Urban League are the Chicago *Defender,* Pittsburgh *Courier,* Baltimore *Afro-American,* New York *Age,* the *Messenger* and the New York *Amsterdam News.* Microfilms of these were made available to us through the courtesy of 3M Company International Microfilm Press.

The Schomburg Collection is also the repository for the unpublished reports, notes and memoranda used in Gunnar Myrdal's *An American Dilemma.* The reports by Dr. Ralph J. Bunche and Dr. Guion G. Johnson throw light on the National Urban League movement. Also, valuable reports and summaries gathered by T. Arnold Hill, at the request of Dr. Myrdal, from local Urban Leagues throughout the nation are available in the collection.

The following persons generously granted interviews and answered inquiries about their association with the National Urban League and its activities:

Sadie T. M. Alexander, Alexander J. Allen, Joseph V. Baker, Roger N. Baldwin, Philip Benjamin, Edwin C. Berry, Ralph J. Bunche, Chester Burger, Elmer A. Carter, Kenneth C. Clark, James R. Dumpson, Robert J. Elzy, Raymond B. Fosdick, Lemuel L. Foster, John Hope Franklin, Andrew F. Freeman, Lloyd K. Garrison, Eli Ginzberg, Lester B. Granger, William Haber, Charles Hamilton, Louis Harlan, Olyve Jeter Haynes (Mrs. George Edmund), James H. Hubert, Nelson C. Jackson, Sophia Yarnall Jacobs, Reginald A. Johnson, Charles Flint Kellogg, J. Harvey Kerns, Lindsley F. Kimball, Mary Emlen Metz, C. F. McNeil, Dwight R. G. Palmer, Jacob S. Potofsky, Burns W. Roper, Elmo Roper, Ramon S. Scruggs, William R. Simms, Donald Slaiman, Raymond Smock, Sandford Solender, Arthur B. Spingarn, Mabel K. Staupers, Henry Steeger, Arvarh E. Strickland, Ann Tanneyhill, Julius A. Thomas, Sterling Tucker, Betti Whaley, Mittienell A. Wheeler, Roy Wilkins, Jack Wood, Ruby Yearwood, and Whitney M. Young, Jr.

Chapter References

Chapter 1: Ladies First

1. Mary E. Richmond, "The Inter-relation of Social Movements," National Conference on Charities and Correction, *Proceedings* (1910), pp. 212 f.
2. Ibid.
3. Lillian Brandt, *Growth and Development of AICP and COS* (New York: Charity Organization Society, 1942), p. 280; see also the Charity Organization Society, *23rd Annual Report* (July 1, 1904–September 30, 1905), p. 91.
4. Mary K. Simkhovitch, quoted in R. H. Bremmer, *From the Depths* (New York: The University Press, 1956), p. 64.
5. Frances A. Kellor, "To Help Negro Women," Boston *Traveler* (May 31, 1905).
6. Kellor, "Evils of the Intelligence Office System," *Southern Workman* (July 1904), p. 378.
7. Kellor, "Southern Colored Girls in the North," *Charities* (March 18, 1905), p. 585.
8. Kellor, "Agencies for Prevention of Crime," *Southern Workman* (April 1903), p. 207.
9. See also her illustrated feature article in the New York *Times* (March 19, 1905). The *Bulletin* of the Inter-Municipal Committee on Household Research, New York (May 1905), devoted this special issue to black girls in the city.
10. *Out of Work: A Study of Employment Agencies, Their Treatment of the Unemployed and Their Influence on Homes and Business*, (New York: G. P. Putnam, 1904).
11. Ibid.
12. *Bulletin* of the Inter-Municipal Committee (March 1906), pp. 3 f.
13. Ibid.
14. Victoria Earle Matthews, ed. (New York: Fortune and Scott, 1898), with an introduction by T. Thomas Fortune.
15. "Mrs. V. C. Matthews and the White Rose Mission," New York *Age*, (June 6, 1905); and "Dangers Encountered by Southern Girls in Northern Cities," Hampton Negro Conference, *Proceedings* (July 1898), pp. 62 f.
16. *Bulletin* of the Inter-Municipal Committee (May 1905); Frances A. Kellor, "Associations for the Protection of Negro Women," (June 10, 1905), p. 825.
17. *Charities* (June 10, 1905), p. 825; "Assisted Emigration from the South," *Charities* (October 7, 1905); see also, "Associations for the Protection of Colored Women," New York *Age* (January 27, 1910).
18. Frances A. Kellor, "Associations for Protection of Colored Women," *The Colored American* (December 1905), pp. 695 f. The October 7, 1905, issue of *Charities* devoted its entire ninety-six pages to the subject.
19. Ibid.
20. New York *Age*, March 7, 1907. (In November 1905 the organization changed its name to Inter-Municipal Research Committee.)

21. National League for the Protection of Colored Women, *Annual Report*, New York (November 1910), Wood Papers.

Chapter 2: The Industrial Concern

1. Frances G. Peabody, *Education for Life: The Story of Hampton Institute* (New York: Doubleday, Page & Co., 1918). This book provided the information about the associations.
2. Letter, New York City Department of Education to William L. Bulkley, November 4, 1906. See also "Some High School Teachers of New York City," *The Crisis* (July 1926), pp. 137–140.
3. William L. Bulkley, "The School as a Social Center," *Charities* (October 7, 1905), pp. 76–78.
4. William L. Bulkley, "The Industrial Condition of the Negro in New York City," *Annals of the American Academy of Political and Social Science* (May 1906), pp. 590–596.
5. "Industrial Campaign," New York *Age* (April 26, 1906).
6. Letter, William J. Schieffelin to J. C. Phelp Stokes, May 24, 1906, Stokes Mss. (Box 18), Columbia University Special Collections. The estimates of the blacks in New York during the period 1906–1909 ranged from 60,000 to 90,000
7. New York *Age* (May 17, 1906).
8. *Charities and the Commons* (June 23, 1906), p. 378.
9. Ibid.
10. The May 17, 1906, issue of the New York *Age* reported the May 11th event extensively in a front-page story.
11. Ibid.
12. CIICNNY leaflet, Introductory, Booker T. Washington Papers, Library of Congress.
13. Letter, Mary White Ovington to W. E. B. DuBois (May 20, 1906), American Institute for Marxist Studies.
14. Letter, W. E. B. DuBois to Mary White Ovington (undated), American Institute for Marxist Studies.
15. CIICNNY leaflet.
16. Ibid.
17. *Charities and the Commons* (October 13, 1906), p. 109.
18. New York *Age* (September 27, 1906).
19. *Charities and the Commons* (October 13, 1906), p. 109.
20. New York *Age* (September 27, 1906).
21. Ibid.
22. New York *Age* (March 7, 1907).
23. Ibid.
24. New York *Age* (May 14, 1908).
25. Ibid.
26. Ibid.
27. *Survey* (October 2, 1909), p. 5.
28. Ibid.
29. Letter, J. T. Emlen to A. J. Kennedy, June 18, 1945, in possession of his daughter, Mrs. Mary Emlen Metz, Philadelphia. See also Armstrong Association of Philadelphia, leaflet (Philadelphia, 1908), Russell Sage Collection, College of the City of New York Library.
30. Richard R. Wright, *87 Years Behind the Black Curtain* (Philadelphia: Rare Book Co., 1965), pp. 157 f; see also, Armstrong Association of Philadelphia, *Annual Report* (1909).

Chapter 3: The Social Concern

1. The monthly series from May 1907 to August 1907 carried the title "Color Line in the South"; and from February 1908 to September 1908, "Color Line in the North."
2. Letter, Ruth S. Baldwin to Ray Stannard Baker (January 4, 1910), Ray Stannard Baker Papers, Manuscript Division, Library of Congress.
3. New York *Age* (January 27, 1910); and Brooklyn *Eagle* (January 21, 1910).
4. Ibid.
5. Ibid.
6. Ruth S. Baldwin, chairman; Elizabeth Walton and the Reverend Henry Phillips, vice chairmen; Dr. Schieffelin, treasurer.
7. Mary L. Stone, president; the Reverend William Brooks, vice president; Mrs. John Wesley Johnson, member.
8. Quoted in Adam Smith, *The Money Game* (New York: Dell Publishing Co., 1968), p. 250.
9. George E. Haynes, "Memoirs" (c. 1950), unpublished autobiography in the possession of his widow. This is the source of much of the information.
10. Roi Ottley and William J. Weatherly, *The Negro in New York* (New York: Oceana Publications, Inc., 1967).
11. Mary White Ovington, *Half a Man: The Status of the Negro in New York* (New York: Longmans, Green and Co., 1911).
12. Richard R. Wright, *87 Years Behind the Black Curtain*, (Philadelphia: Rare Book Co., 1965), pp. 148 f.
13. Haynes's doctoral dissertation was "The Negro at Work in New York City," Columbia University (1912).
14. G. E. Haynes, *The Birth and Childhood of the National Urban League* (NUL, April 20, 1960; mimeograph posthumous publication).
15. Haynes, "Memoirs."
16. Committee on Urban Conditions Among Negroes (CUCAN), Minutes (September 29, 1910), NUL papers, Manuscript Division, Library of Congress. See also Fisk University, *Catalog 1910–1911*.
17. CUCAN, Minutes (September 29, 1910).
18. Haynes, *The Birth and Childhood of the National Urban League.*
19. Ibid.
20. "Sketch of George Edmund Haynes," undated manuscript, Haynes Papers.
21. CUCAN, Prospectus (c. May 1911), Wood Papers.
22. National League on Urban Conditions Among Negroes, "Annual Report for 1910–1911."
23. CUCAN, Memorandum, no title (c. October 1, 1910), Wood Papers.
24. CUCAN, Minutes (September 29, 1910). Officers were: Edwin R. A. Seligman, chairman; William L. Bulkley, first vice chairman; Mrs. Ruth S. Baldwin, second vice chairman; L. Hollingsworth Wood, treasurer; Paul D. Cravath and Frances A. Kellor, executive committee members.
25. CUCAN, Memorandum (October 1, 1910).
26. "The Common Welfare," *Charities and the Commons* (August 13, 1910), p. 703.
27. CUCAN, Memorandum (October 1, 1910).
28. Haynes, *The Birth and Childhood of the National Urban League.* Lee was one of the three trained black social workers in the nation. Haynes and Eva D. Bowles were the other two.
29. "Suggested Outline of Research for Mr. Houstoun" (c. 1910), Haynes Papers.
30. "Eugene Kinckle Jones: A Biography," Wood Papers. The first page of this unpublished manuscript bears a penciled notation "for Benchley." Robert Benchley was an NUL board member.

31. E. K. Jones, "Memorandum for Mrs. Baldwin" (1920), Wood Papers.
32. Letter, the Reverend A. Clayton Powell to G. E. Haynes (May 12, 1911), Haynes Papers.
33. CUCAN, Memorandum (July 1911), Wood Papers.

Chapter 4: A New Era

1. Charity Organization Society, *31st Annual Report* (1913).
2. Memorandum, "Plan for Uniting the Social Betterment Organizations among Negroes," Wood Papers.
3. Ibid.
4. Letter, the Reverend Samuel H. Bishop to George E. Haynes (September 13, 1911), Haynes Papers.
5. Ibid.
6. National League on Urban Conditions Among Negroes, "Annual Report for 1910–1911."
7. Booker T. Washington suggested the formation of NLUCAN to Mrs. Baldwin, according to E. K. Jones, (E. K. Jones, National Urban League Twenty-fifth Anniversary speech, 1935.)
8. Letter, Charles W. Anderson to Booker T. Washington (June 25, 1906), Booker T. Washington Papers, Library of Congress, Manuscript Division.
9. Letter, Booker T. Washington to Charles W. Anderson (October 1, 1907), Booker T. Washington Papers.
10. The executive committee of the new agency (NLUCAN) included Dr. Felix Adler, the Reverend Samuel H. Bishop, the Reverend William H. Brooks, Paul D. Cravath, Frances A. Kellor, Mrs. F. B. Leaf, Abraham Lefkowitz, Dr. E. P. Roberts and Mrs. Haley Fiske. The finance committee consisted of Edwin R. A. Seligman, Edward E. Pratt, A. S. Frissell, L. Hollingsworth Wood, William J. Schieffelin and Fred R. Moore.
11. Letter, Ruth S. Baldwin to E. R. A. Seligman, October 23, 1910, Seligman Papers, Columbia University Special Collections.
12. NLUCAN, "Annual Report for 1910–1911; Announcement 1911–1912." The quotations and information in the next few pages are taken from this report.
13. *The Survey* (October 28, 1911), p. 1080. *The Survey* was formerly *Charities*, and later *Charities and the Commons*.
14. NLUCAN, "Annual Report for 1910–1911."
15. Ibid.
16. Ibid.
17. Ibid.
18. NLUCAN, Audited Statement, fiscal year ending September 30, 1912, NUL Headquarters, 55 East 52nd St., N.Y.
19. Ibid.

Chapter 5: Black City Pioneering

1. NLUCAN, *Bulletin* (November 1915).
2. April 23, 1915.
3. NLUCAN, *Bulletin* (October 1916).
4. NLUCAN, *Bulletin* (November 1913).
5. Gilbert Osofsky, *Harlem: The Making of a Ghetto, New York, 1890–1930* (New York: Harper & Row, 1966) p. 7.
6. NLUCAN, *Bulletin* (November 1913).
7. John C. Dancy, *Sand Against the Wind* (Detroit: Wayne State University Press, 1966), pp. 124 f.

8. NLUCAN, *Bulletin* (November 1913).
9. Ibid.
10. Letter, E. K. Jones to L. H. Wood (June 23, 1915), Wood Papers.
11. Letter, Jones to Wood (January 19, 1917), Wood Papers.
12. NLUCAN, Minutes (December 16, 1914), NUL Papers, Library of Congress.
13. Ibid.
14. E. K. Jones, "Memoirs," unpublished manuscript (c. 1948), in the possession of his widow, Mrs. Blanche Jones, Flushing, Long Island.
15. NLUCAN, *Registration Bureau of Tenements* (leaflet, n.d.).
16. NLUCAN, Minutes (December 16, 1914).
17. "Housing Conditions Among Negroes in New York City," NLUCAN, *Bulletin* (January 1915).
18. "Planning to Solve Negro Housing Problems," New York *Times* (December 19, 1915).
19. NLUCAN, Minutes (December 16, 1914).
20. New York City Conference of Charities and Correction, *Proceedings* (May 25–27, 1915), pp. 169 f.
21. Ibid.
22. City and Suburban Homes Company, Memorandum (December 28, 1915), Wood Papers.
23. Ibid.
24. "Housing Conditions Among Negroes in New York City," NLUCAN, *Bulletin* (January 1915).
25. New York *Home News* (December 13, 1915).
26. New York *Times* (December 19, 1915).
27. Ibid.
28. Osofsky, *Harlem: The Making of a Ghetto*, p. 42.
29. NLUCAN, Report of the Director for June, July, August to September 22, 1913, NUL Papers, Library of Congress. This report provides the information in the pages which follow.
30. Ibid.
31. Ibid.
32. Ibid.

Chapter 6: Beginnings

1. NLUCAN, "Annual Report for 1910–1911."
2. Letter, Ruth S. Baldwin to E. R. A. Seligman (October 23, 1912), Seligman correspondence, Columbia University Special Collections.
3. In its first year the Philadelphia Armstrong Association placed 124 in jobs valued at a total of $24,000. (Armstrong Association of Philadelphia, *Annual Report,* 1909.)
4. NLUCAN Certificate of Incorporation (February 20, 1913), with a handwritten note "draft not used," Wood Papers.
5. NLUCAN, *Bulletin* (May 1913).
6. NLUCAN, Constitution (May 1913), NUL Papers, Library of Congress.
7. Interview with James H. Hubert, July 19, 1968.
8. Letter, Elizabeth Walton to L. H. Wood (October 18, 1915), Wood Papers.
9. NLUCAN, Minutes (December 16, 1914).
10. Draft letter, L. H. Wood (December 24, 1914), Wood Papers.
11. Letter, Ruth S. Baldwin to G. E. Haynes (undated), Haynes Papers.
12. Memorandum (undated), Wood Papers.
13. Ibid.

Chapter 7: Inside Story

1. Lilian Brandt, *Growth and Development of AICP and COS* (New York: Charity Organization Society, 1942), p. 233.
2. NLUCAN, *Bulletin* (November 1915).
3. Letter, Ruth S. Baldwin to G. E. Haynes (February 9, 1914), Haynes Papers.
4. Letter, Ruth S. Baldwin to G. E. Haynes (February 5, 1915), Haynes Papers.
5. Letter, Baldwin to Haynes (May 3, 1914), Haynes Papers.
6. Letter, Baldwin to Haynes (June 6, 1914), Haynes Papers; see also NLUCAN, Minutes (October 1913), NUL Papers, Library of Congress.
7. Letter, Baldwin to Haynes (July 8, 1914), Haynes Papers.
8. Letter, Ruth S. Baldwin to L. H. Wood (June 1, 1915), Wood Papers.
9. Ibid.
10. Ibid.
11. Ibid.
12. NLUCAN, *Bulletin* (November 1915).
13. Letter (draft), NLUCAN executive committee to Ruth S. Baldwin (undated), Wood Papers.
14. NLUCAN, Minutes (June 8, 1915).
15. Letter, L. H. Wood to A. J. Lacy (June 28, 1933), Michigan Historical Collection, Ann Arbor.
16. Letter, E. K. Jones to Dr. Carter G. Woodson, printed in *Journal of Negro History* (April 1924), pp. 232 f.

Chapter 8: Migration and Expansion

1. NUL memorandum, "Beginning of the Exodus of 1916–1917" (undated), NUL Papers, Library of Congress.
2. Ibid.
3. Ibid.
4. Letter, E. K. Jones to L. Hollingsworth Wood (June 2, 1916–1917), Wood Papers.
5. Quoted from NUL memorandum, "Beginning of the Exodus of 1916–1917."
6. Ibid.
7. NLUCAN, *Bulletin* (November 1915).
8. E. K. Jones, "Summary Report of Associate Director on Western Trip, November 2, 1915, to November 25, 1915" (n.d.), Wood Papers.
9. "Abridged Autobiography" of Eugene Kinckle Jones (c. 1940); and "Memoirs" (c. 1948). Much of the information concerning his trips comes from these two unpublished documents, both in the possession of his widow, Mrs. Blanche Jones, Flushing, Long Island.
10. Ibid.
11. Ibid.
12. "What the League Is?" unsigned Memorandum (October 7, 1916), Wood Papers.
13. "Reasons for Making Nashville Model Training Center in Southern Field," Memorandum (July 1914), Wood Papers.
14. Ibid.
15. Ibid.
16. Ibid.

Chapter 9: Anatomy of a Conflict

1. Letter, Eugene K. Jones to L. Hollingsworth Wood (February 23, 1916), Wood Papers.

2. Letter, G. E. Haynes to L. H. Wood (March 15, 1916), Wood Papers.
3. Letter, Haynes to Wood (July 21, 1916), Wood Papers.
4. NLUCAN, Minutes (April 11, 1917), NUL Papers, Library of Congress.
5. G. E. Haynes, "Suggestions for Further Executive Organization of League Work," Memorandum (1916), Moton Papers.
6. Ibid. This memorandum is the source for much of the information and the quotations which follow.
7. Ibid.
8. Ibid.
9. Ibid.
10. Ibid.
11. Letter, Ruth S. Baldwin to L. H. Wood (July 9, 1917), Wood Papers.
12. Letter, Roger N. Baldwin to L. H. Wood (July 1, 1917), Wood Papers; see also Letter, Thomas Jesse Jones to L. H. Wood (July 16, 1917), Wood Papers.
13. Letter, E. K. Jones to L. H. Wood (July 7, 1917), Wood Papers.
14. Ibid.
15. Letter, G. E. Haynes to Roger N. Baldwin (July 20, 1917), Wood Papers.
16. Ibid.
17. Ibid.
18. Ibid.
19. Letter, E. K. Jones to L. H. Wood (August 3, 1917), Wood Papers. (The outline has been lost, though it was accepted by E. K. Jones, who discussed it with Baldwin and told Hollingsworth Wood that the recommendations were satisfactory to him.)
20. Letter, James H. Dillard to L. H. Wood (August 6, 1917), Wood Papers.
21. Draft Memorandum, no title (1917), Wood Papers.
22. "Conference Held at the Educational Building," Memorandum, Washington, D.C. (August 29, 1917), NUL Papers, Library of Congress.
23. Letter, G. E. Haynes to L. H. Wood (November 3, 1917), Wood Papers.
24. Letter, L. H. Wood to G. E. Haynes (November 12, 1917), Wood Papers.

Chapter 10: Farm to Factory

1. New York *Age*, February 1, 1917.
2. *Southern Workman*, Vol. 46, p. 133.
3. Ibid.
4. John T. Emlen, "Report for the National Conference on Migration" (January 1917), NUL Papers, Library of Congress.
5. Ibid.
6. New York *Evening Post*, July 13, 1917, which carries much of the information on Washington's report.
7. Ibid.
8. NLUCAN, "Annual Report for 1917."
9. Ibid.
10. New York *Evening Post*, July 13, 1917.
11. *Report of the National Advisory Commission on Civil Disorders* (New York: Bantam, 1968), pp. 217 f.
12. New York *Evening Post*, July 14, 1917.
13. E. K. Jones, quoted in New York *Evening Mail* (February 6, 1918).
14. Ibid.
15. Ibid.
16. Ibid.
17. NUL Papers, Library of Congress. (Paul G. Prayer was the social worker.)
18. Letter, G. E. Haynes to L. H. Wood (November 21, 1917), Wood Papers.

19. Quoted in *Opportunity* (November 1935), p. 348; originally from the Detroit *Leader* (May 4, 1918).
20. Information obtained in an interview with William Ashby, June 20, 1968.

Chapter 11: The Federal Government Enters

1. Giles B. Jackson, Petition to the Secretary of Labor, January 14, 1918, National Archives (RG. 174, chief clerk's files, 8/90-8/102c-17).
2. Ibid.
3. Letter, Secretary of Labor, National Archives (RG. 174, chief clerk's files, 8/90-8/102c-17).
4. New York *Age* (February 9, 1918).
5. NLUCAN, Minutes (February 1, 1918).
6. George L. Boyle, "The Department of Labor and the Negro Problem," *Lumber World Review* (April 10, 1919), p. 23.
7. National Archives (RG. 174, chief clerk's files, 8/90-8/102c-17).
8. Memorandum, Honorable Louis F. Post to Secretary William B. Wilson, National Archives (RG. 174, chief clerk's files, 8/90-8/102c-17).
9. George E. Haynes, "Memoirs" (c. 1950), unpublished manuscript in the possession of his widow, Mt. Vernon, N.Y.
10. National Archives (RG. 174, chief clerk's files, 8/90-8/102c-17).
11. G. E. Haynes, *The Negro at Work During the War and During Reconstruction*, U.S. Department of Labor (Washington: Government Printing Office, 1921), p. 13.
12. Haynes, "Memoirs."
13. Ibid.
14. John H. Kirby, "Labor Problems in the South," *Lumber World Review* (April 10, 1919), p. 25.
15. G. E. Haynes, *The Negro at Work During the War*, p. 14.
16. Ibid.
17. Boyle, "Department of Labor and the Negro Problem," p. 25.
18. Kirby, "Labor Problems in the South."
19. Letter, Secretary William B. Wilson to G. E. Haynes (July 1, 1919), National Archives (RG. 174, chief clerk's files, 8/90-8/102c-17).
20. Draft letter, G. E. Haynes to L. H. Wood (July 2, 1919), copy sent to R. R. Moton, Moton Papers.
21. Letter, L. H. Wood to G. E. Haynes (July 1, 1919), Moton Papers.
22. Ibid.
23. Letter, E. K. Jones to R. R. Moton (July 5, 1919), Moton Papers.
24. Letter, G. E. Haynes to E. K. Jones (July 10, 1919), Moton Papers.
25. Ibid.
26. Haynes, "*The Negro at Work*," pp. 135 f.
27. Letter, L. H. Wood to G. E. Haynes (July 14, 1919), Moton Papers.
28. Letter, L. H. Wood to R. R. Moton, August 6, 1919, Moton Papers.
29. Ibid.
30. Letter, L. H. Wood to G. E. Haynes (August 7, 1919), Moton Papers.
31. Draft letter, unsigned and undated, marked "Haynes," Moton Papers.
32. Letter, E. K. Jones to G. E. Haynes (undated), National Archives (RG. 174, chief clerk's files, 8/90-8/102c-17).

Chapter 12: World War I Readjustment

1. NLUCAN, Minutes (December 4, 1918).
2. NLUCAN, "Annual Report for 1917–1918."

3. Ibid.
4. These tributes are from the New York *Times,* Chicago *Defender* and Philadephia *North American,* quoted from the NLUCAN "Annual Report for 1917–1918."
5. New York *Times* (October 20, 1918).
6. Letter in NUL Papers, Library of Congress. See also Letter, E. K. Jones to L. H. Wood (April 23, 1917), Wood Papers.
7. Draft letter, E. K. Jones to the Carnegie Corporation of New York (undated), Wood Papers.
8. Ibid.
9. Ibid.
10. NLUCAN, Minutes (December 5, 1917), see also Financial Statement, National and New York Urban Leagues, January 1 to December 31, 1920, NUL Papers, Library of Congress.
11. Letter, R. R. Moton to L. H. Wood (October 13, 1919), Moton Papers.
12. NLUCAN, Minutes (December 4, 1918).
13. Ibid.
14. Ibid.
15. "Recommendations for a Reconstruction Program to the Second Annual Conference of the National Urban League," Memorandum (n.d.; no author), Wood Papers.
16. NLUCAN, Minutes (December 12, 1918).
17. Ibid.
18. Ibid.

Chapter 13: Moving West

1. Eugene Kinckle Jones, "Memoirs," unpublished manuscript, in the possession of his widow, Mrs. Blanche Jones. The material in this chapter, except where indicated, is based on this document.
2. Ibid.
3. Ibid.
4. Ibid.
5. Ibid.
6. Ibid.
7. Ibid.
8. Ibid.
9. Ibid.
10. Chicago *Defender,* editorial (January 15, 1916).
11. Arvarh E. Strickland, *History of the Chicago Urban League* (Urbana: University of Illinois Press, 1966), pp. 40 f.
12. Ibid.
13. Memorandum, William C. Graves to Julius Rosenwald (November 23, 1917), Rosenwald Papers, University of Chicago Library.
14. E. K. Jones, Report to the Executive Board (October 24, 1919), Moton Papers.

Chapter 14: A Reorganization

1. NLUCAN, Report of the Special Committee (January 1918), Moton Papers. Other committee members were Ella Sachs, John T. Emlen, John Hope, the Reverend William H. Brooks and Abraham Lefkowitz. This report provided the materials for the quotations and information on the next pages.
2. NUL, Minutes (December 12, 1918), NUL Papers, Library of Congress.
3. Report of the Special Committee.

4. Report, "Committee on Standardizing Work" (January 31, 1918), Moton Papers. The quotations following on the next pages are from this report.
5. E. K. Jones, "The NUL and Its New Outlook," notes for speech delivered in Chicago, October 19, 1921.
6. Report, "Committee on Standardizing Work."
7. Letter, J. O. Thomas to P. J. Bryant (June 12, 1920), NUL Papers, Library of Congress.
8. NUL, *Bulletin* (February–June 1920), NUL Papers.
9. Ibid.
10. Letter, L. H. Wood to Morse (November 21, 1922), Rosenwald Papers, University of Chicago Library.
11. Ibid.
12. Letter, L. H. Wood to William C. Graves (November 28, 1922), Rosenwald Papers.
13. Ibid.
14. Ibid.

Chapter 15: Wooing Organized Labor

1. NULCAN Conference: "The Work of the National Organization," and "Negro Labor in America" (January 29–31, 1918). The New York *Age* (February 9, 1918) reported extensively on the meeting and is the source for the pages that follow.
2. Ibid.
3. Ibid.
4. Letter, Samuel Gompers to Robert R. Moton, *et al.* (March 25, 1918), NUL Papers, Library of Congress.
5. Letter, E. K. Jones to Secretaries of Affiliated Organizations (April 8, 1918), NUL Papers, Library of Congress.
6. John T. Clark to Robert R. Moton, Memorandum (February 9, 1918), Moton Papers.
7. Ibid.
8. Ibid.
9. Letter, George E. Haynes to R. R. Moton (April 10, 1918), Moton Papers.
10. Letter, E. K. Jones to R. R. Moton (April 8, 1918), Moton Papers.
11. Draft Letter, E. K. Jones to Samuel Gompers (May 28, 1918), Moton Papers.
12. NLUCAN, Minutes (May 24, 1918).
13. Quoted in Ira deA. Reid, *Negro Membership in American Labor Unions* (New York: National Urban League, 1930), pp. 27 f.
14. Ibid.
15. Letter, E. K. Jones to R. R. Moton (November 15, 1918), Moton Papers.
16. Letter, John C. Dancy to Alexander L. Jackson (May 15, 1919), NUL Papers, Library of Congress.
17. Quoted from "The Negro and the Labor Union: An NAACP Report," *The Crisis* (September 1919), pp. 240 f.
18. Ibid.
19. Fred R. Moore, "Letting Him into the Labor Union," *World Outlook* (October 1919), p. 28.
20. Ibid.
21. Ibid.
22. *The Crisis* (August 1919), p. 182.
23. Quoted in NUL, Twenty-fifth Anniversary Souvenir Booklet (November 1935).
24. NUL news release, "Negro Workers Urged to Organize" (November 15, 1919), Moton Papers.
25. NUL, Minutes (June 14, 1920), NUL Papers, Library of Congress.
26. Reid, *Negro Membership*, p. 30.
27. NUL, Minutes, June 14, 1920.

Chapter 16: The "New Negro"

1. NUL, "Statement on Race Conditions at the Present Time" (August 5, 1919), Wood Papers.
2. Ibid.
3. Edward J. Brundage, speech to the Chicago Association of Commerce, LaSalle Hotel, Chicago (n.d.), Wood Papers.
4. Chicago Commission on Race Relations, *The Negro in Chicago: A Study of Race Relations and a Race Riot* (Chicago: University of Chicago Press, 1922), pp. 45 f.
5. Letter, E. K. Jones to R. R. Moton (August 12, 1919), Moton Papers.
6. Chicago Commission of Race Relations, *The Negro in Chicago.*
7. October 5, 1919.
8. Arvarh E. Strickland, *History of the Chicago Urban League* (Urbana: University of Illinois Press, 1966), p. 63.
9. NUL, "Annual Report for 1919."
10. Ibid.
11. Unsigned article, "New Leadership for the Negro," *The Messenger* (May–June 1919).
12. *The Messenger* (July 1919).
13. *The Messenger* (August 1919).
14. Though Owen was the first of its Fellows to turn on the League, he was not the last. Two others who distinguished themselves later and followed a similar path were Abram L. Harris and E. Franklin Frazier.
15. New York, National Association for the Advancement of Colored People, 1919.
16. NUL, "Annual Report for 1919."

Chapter 17: A Change in Pilots

1. From the "Abridged Autobiography of Eugene Kinckle Jones" (c. 1940), typescript in the possession of his widow, Flushing, Long Island.
2. Ibid.
3. E. K. Jones, "The Day," notes for speech delivered in Baltimore, April 6, 1919.
4. NUL, "Annual Report for 1919." By the end of the year there were thirty-two local Leagues with an aggregate budget of $149,000.
5. E. K. Jones, "Problems of City Life" notes for speech given at Greensboro, N.C., Summer, 1919.
6. E. K. Jones, "The Day" and "Problems of City Life" notes for speech given at Indianapolis, Ind., November 20, 1919.
7. E. K. Jones, "Extension of the Urban League Work," Memorandum (March 27, 1919), NUL Papers, Library of Congress.
8. Ibid.
9. Letter, E. K. Jones to the executive board (June 12, 1919), Moton Papers.
10. Jesse O. Thomas, *My Story in Black and White: The Autobiography of Jesse O. Thomas* (New York: Exposition Press, 1967), p. 29.
11. Letter, E. K. Jones to J. O. Thomas (July 11, 1921), NUL Papers, Library of Congress.
12. Letter, J. O. Thomas to E. K. Jones (March 4, 1922), NUL Papers, Library of Congress.
13. E. K. Jones, "Memoirs," unpublished manuscript in the possession of his widow, Flushing, Long Island.
14. Thomas, *My Story in Black and White,* p. 103.
15. Ibid.

Chapter 18: The Spread of Information

1. E. K. Jones, "Memoirs," unpublished manuscript in the possession of his widow, Flushing, Long Island.
2. Ibid.
3. Letter, E. K. Jones to J. R. Angell (December 27, 1920), Carnegie Corporation of New York Archives.
4. Ibid.
5. Charles S. Johnson, "Public Opinion and the Negro," address delivered at the National Conference of Social Work, Washington, D.C., May 23, 1923. Printed in *Opportunity* (July 1923), pp. 201 f.
6. Letter, J. O. Thomas to E. K. Jones (November 1, 1929), NUL Papers, Library of Congress.
7. Ibid.
8. Ira deA. Reid, *Negro Membership in American Labor Unions* (New York: National Urban League, 1930), p. 5.
9. Ibid.
10. Ibid.
11. NUL, *The Urban League Bulletin* (December 1921); see also unsigned article, "Twenty-six Years of *Opportunity*," *Opportunity*, special issue (Winter 1949), pp. 4–7. (Publication of the magazine was suspended with this issue.)
12. *Opportunity*, Editorials (February 1923), p. 3.
13. Ibid.
14. Quoted in *Opportunity* (June 1925), p. 187.
15. Interview with Elmer A. Carter, September 20, 1968.
16. Arna Bontemps, "The Schomburg Collection of Negro Literature," *The Library Quarterly* (July 1944), p. 190.
17. *Opportunity*, Editorials (January 1925), p. 2.
18. *Opportunity*, Editorials (October 1928), p. 293.
19. Jones, "Memoirs."
20. Charles S. Johnson, "The Urban League's Responsibility to the Future," keynote address delivered at NUL's 1949 annual conference in Denver (New York: National Urban League, 1950).

Chapter 19: Focus on Industry

1. NUL, *The Urban League Bulletin* (December 1921).
2. E. K. Jones, "The Negro in Industry," notes for speech delivered at Atlantic City, June 2, 1919.
3. E. K. Jones, "The Negro's Future in Northern Industry," notes for speech delivered at Pittsburgh, February 19, 1920.
4. Ibid.
5. E. K. Jones, "Extension of the Urban League Work," Memorandum (March 27, 1919), NUL Papers, Library of Congress.
6. Letter, E. K. Jones to John D. Rockefeller, Jr. (January 31, 1923), Rockefeller Family Archives, New York.
7. Memorandum, Kenneth Chorley to John D. Rockefeller, Jr. (November 2, 1923), Rockefeller Family Archives, New York.
8. Letter, L. H. Wood to William C. Graves (March 17, 1924), Rosenwald Papers, University of Chicago Library.
9. Arvarh E. Strickland, *History of the Chicago Urban League* (Urbana: University of Illinois Press, 1966), p. 80.

10. T. A. Hill, "Duties of the National Industrial Secretary," Memorandum (n.d.), Wood Papers.
11. Ibid.
12. NUL news release (n.d.), NUL Papers.
13. Ibid.
14. New York *Age*, Editorial, "A New Industrial Program" (undated clipping), NUL Papers.
15. T. A. Hill, "Prospective Immediate Program," Memorandum (June 24, 1925), NUL Papers.
16. T. A. Hill, "Report to the Executive Board" (October 28, 1925), NUL Papers.
17. Ibid.
18. Peter M. and Mort N. Bergman, *The Chronological History of the Negro in America* (New York: Mentor, New American Library, 1969), p. 414.
19. Hill, "Prospective Immediate Program."
20. Ibid.
21. A. Philip Randolph, "The Negro and Economic Radicalism," *Opportunity* (February 1926), p. 63.
22. Ibid.
23. Quoted in T. A. Hill, "The Dilemma of Negro Workers," *Opportunity* (February 1926), p. 39.
24. E. K. Jones, "The Pullman Porters," notes for speeches delivered in New York, January 20, 1926, and November 30, 1926.
25. Ira deA. Reid, *Negro Membership in American Labor Unions* (New York: National Urban League, 1930), p. 131.
26. *Opportunity* (February 1926), p. 75.
27. T. A. Hill, "Work of the Department of Industrial Relations from March 15, 1925 to December 31, 1927," Memorandum, NUL Papers.
28. William Green, "Why Belong to the Union," *Opportunity*, special issue (February 1926), pp. 61 f.; T. A. Hill, *American Federationist* (Washington, D.C., 1925), pp. 915–920.
29. Hill, "Work of the Department of Industrial Relations."
30. "Survey," *Opportunity* (January 1928), p. 26; see also Reid, *Negro Membership in American Labor Unions*, p. 131.
31. "National Negro in Industry Week," Memorandum (1927), NUL Papers.
32. Ibid.
33. Ibid.

Chapter 20: Black Social Workers

1. NLUCAN, Minutes (December 14, 1913), NUL Papers, Library of Congress.
2. Letter, Ruth S. Baldwin to Dr. Richard Cabot (March 11, 1915), Wood Papers.
3. George E. Haynes, Report to the Executive Board of NLUCAN (February 12, 1916 to June 15, 1916), Moton Papers.
4. Atlanta *Independent* (June 23, 1917).
5. NLUCAN, "Annual Report for 1917–1918."
6. NLUCAN, Minutes (December 4, 1918).
7. E. K. Jones, speech notes, October 15, 1919.
8. Indianapolis *Recorder* (December 6, 1919).
9. Letter, J. O. Thomas to E. K. Jones (November 1, 1929), NUL Papers.
10. Letter, J. O. Thomas to E. K. Jones (December 21, 1929), NUL Papers.
11. New York *Times* (February 6, 1926).
12. J. O. Thomas, "In the Path of the Flood," *Opportunity* (August 1927), p. 237.
13. Ibid.
14. "The Urban League Conference in Philadelphia," *Opportunity* (May 1928), p. 142.

Chapter 21: Other Forces at Work

1. Will W. Alexander, "Reminiscences," Oral History Research Office, Columbia University Special Collections, 1956.
2. Ibid.
3. George E. Haynes, *Toward Interracial Cooperation* (New York: Federal Council of Churches, 1926).
4. Charles S. Johnson, *The Negro in American Civilization* (New York: Holt, 1930), p. v.
5. *Opportunity*, Editorials (February 1929), p. 36.
6. Ibid.
7. NUL, "Annual Report for 1928."
8. Arvarh E. Strickland, *History of the Chicago Urban League* (Urbana: University of Illinois Press, 1966), p. 98.
9. Ibid.
10. Interview with Lloyd K. Garrison, April 9, 1969.
11. Telegram, quoted in the Philadelphia *Tribune* (December 16, 1933).
12. James Weldon Johnson, *Negro Americans, What Now?* (New York: Viking Press, 1934), pp. 35–40.
13. Memorandum, Alfred K. Stern to Julius Rosenwald (October 15, 1929), Rosenwald Papers, University of Chicago Library.
14. Ibid.
15. Strickland, *History of the Chicago Urban League.*
16. Letter, Will W. Alexander to Thomas B. Appleget (July 15, 1929), Rockefeller Family Archives, New York.
17. Letter, Charles S. Johnson to Thomas B. Appleget (July 11, 1929), Rockefeller Family Archives.
18. Memorandum (March 26, 1931), Carnegie Corporation of New York Archives, New York.
19. "Conversation with Mary Van Kleeck," Memorandum (October 7, 1932), Rockefeller Family Archives.
20. Ibid.

Chapter 22: Anchor and Hope

1. T. A. Hill, "The Present Status of Negro Labor," *Opportunity* (May 1929), p. 143.
2. Ibid.
3. Hill, "The Present Status of Negro Labor," p. 144.
4. Hill, "Labor," *Opportunity* (October 1928), p. 311.
5. Hill, "The Present Status of Negro Labor," p. 143.
6. Ibid.
7. E. K. Jones, "Industrial Unpreparedness," speech delivered in Cincinnati, November 21, 1919.
8. Ibid.
9. Ibid.
10. Hill, "Proposals for Enlarging the Industrial Relations Department of the National Urban League" (January 5, 1929), NUL Papers, Library of Congress.
11. Ibid.
12. Quoted in "Survey of the Month," *Opportunity* (May 1930), p. 155.
13. Hill "Proposals for Enlarging . . ."
14. Conference Memorandum (September 28, 1929), NUL Papers.
15. Ibid.
16. Letter, W. Robert Smalls to T. A. Hill (September 28, 1929), NUL Papers.

17. "Vocational Opportunity Campaign," Memorandum for Executive Board (n.d.), NUL Papers.
18. NUL, *Vocational Opportunity Campaign*, leaflet (April 20–27, 1930).
19. Hill, "Labor," *Opportunity* (March 1930), p. 92.
20. Ibid.
21. Dean S. Yarborough, "Facing the Future After Twenty," *Opportunity* (July 1930), p. 208.
22. *Opportunity*, Editorials (May 1930), p. 135.
23. Hill, "Labor—Vocational Opportunity Campaign," *Opportunity* (April 1931), p. 117.
24. *Ever Widening Horizons* (New York: National Urban League, 1951).
25. E. K. Jones, speech at New York Urban League, New York, April 18, 1932.
26. *They Crashed the Color Line* (New York: National Urban League, 1935). The Vocational Opportunity Campaign used several significant publications issued by NUL. In 1933 three pamphlets in "The Color Line Series" were published. They were prepared by Ira deA. Reid, T. Arnold Hill and Elmer A. Carter. Titles were: *The Forgotten Tenth; 5,000,000 Jobs—The Negro at Work in the United States;* and *He Crashed the Color Line!* In 1935 two additional titles were published: *Occupational Opportunities for Negroes* and *They Crashed the Color Line!*

Chapter 23: The Great Leveler

1. NUL, *Unemployment Among Negroes . . . Data on 25 Industrial Cities* (New York: National Urban League, 1930).
2. Ibid.
3. The replies from some governors were classics. To wit, from Albert Ritchie, governor of Maryland (January 19, 1931): "Dear Sir, I received your favor of January 1st with regard to the employment of Negroes on road work and other public improvements. I have never heard it suggested that the Negroes do not get their fair share of public work in this State."
4. Quoted in *Opportunity* (January 1931), p. 25.
5. Letter, J. O. Thomas to mayor of Atlanta (January 9, 1931), NUL Papers, Library of Congress.
6. Letter, executive secretary of mayor of Atlanta to J. O. Thomas (January 14, 1931), NUL Papers.
7. NUL, "Annual Report for 1930."
8. Ibid.
9. Memorandum, T. A. Hill to E. K. Jones (December 29, 1930), NUL Papers.
10. NUL, "Annual Report for 1931."
11. Ibid.
12. NUL, "Annual Report for 1932."
13. Ibid.
14. Ibid.
15. Letter, J. O. Thomas to E. K. Jones (March 14, 1932), NUL Papers.
16. Letter, J. O. Thomas to E. K. Jones (October 28, 1932), NUL Papers.
17. NLUCAN, *Bulletin* (November 1914).
18. Ibid.
19. John T. Clark, "When the Negro Resident Organizes," *Opportunity* (June 1934), pp. 168–170.
20. Ibid.
21. Ibid.
22. NUL, "Annual Report for 1932."
23. Ibid.
24. Telegram (January 13, 1932), NUL Papers.
25. T. A. Hill, "Labor: Yesterday and Today," *Opportunity* (August 1932), p. 250.
26. Letter, J. O. Thomas to E. K. Jones (February 19, 1932), NUL Papers.

27. Letter, J. O. Thomas to E. K. Jones (1932), NUL Papers.
28. Ira deA. Reid, "*Opportunity* Presidential Candidates Poll, Analysis," *Opportunity* (April 1932), p. 115.
29. "The Candidates Speak" (in answer to a question as to their position in employment of blacks in public works), *Opportunity* (November 1932), pp. 238–240.
30. Ibid.

Chapter 24: Focus on Washington

1. T. A. Hill, "Labor—The Situation in Washington," *Opportunity* (November 1933), p. 347.
2. NUL, Twenty-fifth Anniversary Souvenir Booklet.
3. Quoted in "Memorandum of Experiences of Negroes in Connection with the Program of the NRA" (1933), NUL Papers, Library of Congress.
4. "Memorandum of Experiences" (May 19, 1933).
5. Ibid.
6. Letter, Secretary Frances Perkins to E. K. Jones, Washington, D.C. (April 27, 1933); published in *Opportunity* (June 1933), p. 169.
7. Ibid.
8. T. A. Hill, "Labor—Economic Status of the Negro," *Opportunity* (June 1933), p. 185.
9. E. K. Jones, notes for speech delivered in Washington, D.C., May 11, 1933.
10. Letter, E. K. Jones to local executive secretaries (April 1933), NUL Papers.
11. T. A. Hill, "Activities of the NUL Industrial Relations Department for 1933," Report (December 18, 1933).
12. Ibid.
13. "The Social Adjustment of Negroes in the United States: A Special Memorandum Submitted to the President, Franklin Delano Roosevelt" by the National Urban League for Social Services Among Negroes, 1133 Broadway, New York (April 15, 1933); 43 pages and covering letter mimeographed.
14. Ibid.
15. Ibid.
16. Ibid.
17. *Opportunity*, Editorials (November 1933), p. 327.
18. Letter, E. K. Jones to Frederick D. Keppel (September 10, 1934), Carnegie Corporation of New York Archives.
19. E. K. Jones, notes for speech to the graduate students in social work, Bryn Mawr College, June 1, 1936.
20. NUL, "Annual Report for 1934."
21. NUL, "Annual Report for 1935."
22. NUL, "Annual Report for 1936."
23. E. K. Jones, newsletter to executive board (July 19, 1937), NUL Papers.
24. T. A. Hill, Quarterly Report (March 31, 1938), NUL Papers.
25. "Special Memorandum to the President of the United States—The Negro Working Population and National Recovery" (January 4, 1937); see also letter, President Franklin D. Roosevelt to C. C. Spaulding, White House, Washington, D.C. (July 5, 1935), NUL Papers.
26. Ibid.
27. E. K. Jones, "The Negro and the Economic World," excerpts from an address delivered on October 19, 1935, NUL Papers.

Chapter 25: Grass-Roots Action

1. T. A. Hill, quoted in NUL Twenty-fifth Anniversary Souvenir Booklet (November 1935).

2. NUL news release (August 12, 1933), NUL Papers, Library of Congress.

3. EAC Handbook (December 1933), NUL Papers.

4. Ibid.

5. EAC Memorandum (November 14, 1933), NUL Papers.

6. Ibid.

7. "The NRA and the EAC," draft of typical speech for use in campaigns (November 28, 1933), NUL Papers.

8. Ibid.

9. Letters, E. K. Jones to J. O. Thomas (June 23, 1932 and August 3, 1933), NUL Papers; E. K. Jones to Frederick D. Keppel (December 18, 1933), Carnegie Corporation of New York Archives. See also NUL "Annual Report for 1933."

10. EAC District Conference Program (January 24–25, 1934).

11. J. O. Thomas, "Activities of the Southern Field Director," for the year 1934, NUL Papers.

12. EAC, *Newsletter* (March 10, 1934), NUL Papers.

13. EAC, *Newsletter* (April 25, 1934).

14. T. A. Hill, "The National Urban League," *Southern Workman* (May 1936), p. 138.

15. NUL, Audited Statement for 1935 and 1936, NUL Headquarters Office, New York.

Chapter 26: *Organizing the Unorganized*

1. J. O. Thomas, "The Negro Looks at the Alphabet," *Opportunity* (January 1934), pp. 12–14.

2. Ibid.

3. Lester B. Granger, "Negro Workers and Recovery," *Opportunity* (May 1934), pp. 153 f.

4. T. Arnold Hill, "Briefs from the South," *Opportunity* (March 1934), p. 89.

5. Ibid.

6. Ibid.

7. Charles R. Lawrence, "Negro Organizations in Crisis," unpublished Ph.D thesis, Columbia University (1952), p. 292.

8. NUL, Minutes, "Memorandum on Proposed Labor Plan" (March 8, 1934), NUL Papers, Library of Congress.

9. *Opportunity* (June 1934), p. 183.

10. Ibid.

11. "Step-Children of the Depression," *Opportunity* (July 1934), pp. 218 f; see also NUL Workers Council pamphlet, Series No. 1 (June 1934), NUL Papers.

12. Lester B. Granger, "Reminiscences" Oral History Research Office, Columbia University Special Collections, 1963, p. 119.

13. Ibid.

14. Ibid.

15. Interview with Granger, June 28, 1969.

16. Interview with Granger, June 29, 1969.

17. Ibid.

18. Granger, "Reminiscences," p. 133.

19. Interview with Granger, June 29, 1969.

20. Interview with Granger, June 29, 1969; see also NUL, Minutes, October 26, 1934, NUL Papers.

21. American Federation of Labor, *Proceedings*, 1935, quoted in Herbert Northrup, *Organized Labor and the Negro* (New York: Harper and Brothers, 1944), p. 11.

22. "The Urban League and the A.F. of L.," *Opportunity*, August 1935, p. 247. This statement was read by Reginald A. Johnson at the Hearing of the A.F. of L. Committee of Five to deal with Negro problems, Washington, D.C., July 9, 1935.

23. Letter, Granger to William Green (August 13, 1935), quoted in Lawrence, "Negro Organizations in Crisis," p. 278.

24. American Federation of Labor, *Proceedings* (1935), p. 809, quoted in Northrup, *Organized Labor and the Negro*, p. 11.
25. Northrup, *Organized Labor and the Negro*, p. 12.
26. Quoted in Lawrence, "Negro Organizations in Crisis," pp. 281 f.
27. Telegram, Granger to John L. Lewis (December 3, 1935), NUL Papers.
28. Letter, Granger to John A. Brophy (April 17, 1936), NUL Papers.
29. Lester B. Granger, "What Objectives Shall the League Set for the Next Five-Year Period in the Field of Organization in Industry," speech at NUL annual conference, November 27, 1935, NUL Collection.
30. Lawrence, "Negro Organizations in Crisis," pp. 272 f.

Chapter 27: Transition

1. NUL, "Annual Report for 1935."
2. T. A. Hill, newsletter to League executives (June 5, 1935), NUL Papers, Library of Congress.
3. NUL, Minutes (May 15, 1935), NUL Papers.
4. Ibid.
5. See Arvarh Strickland, *History of the Chicago Urban League* (Urbana: University of Illinois Press, 1966).
6. T. A. Hill, "The National Urban League, Which Way After 1935?" *Southern Workman* (May 1936), pp. 135 f.
7. NUL, "Annual Report for 1937," NUL Papers.
8. Ibid.
9. NUL, Audited Statement for 1937 NUL Headquarters, New York.
10. NUL, Audited Statement for 1938 NUL Headquarters, New York.
11. Statistics from the Welfare Council of New York City, "The Negro Worker in New York City," Committee on Negro Welfare (New York, 1941).
12. Peter M. and Mort N. Bergman, *The Chronological History of the Negro in America* (New York: Mentor, New American Library, 1969), p. 483.
13. *Opportunity*, editorials (November 1939), p. 322.
14. Ibid.
15. Ibid.
16. NUL, "Annual Report for 1938."
17. J. O. Thomas, *My Story in Black and White—The Autobiography of Jesse O. Thomas* (New York: Exposition Press, 1967), p. 109.
18. Ibid.
19. NUL, Minutes (September 28, 1939), NUL Papers.
20. Letter, L. H. Wood to Frederick P. Keppel (September 21, 1939), Carnegie Corporation of New York Archives.
21. Ibid.
22. Letter, Roger N. Baldwin to L. H. Wood (June 29, 1939), Wood Papers.
23. NUL, "Annual Report for 1939."
24. NUL, Minutes (March 15, 1940), NUL Papers.
25. Letter, L. H. Wood to T. A. Hill (March 15, 1940), NUL Papers.
26. Letter, E. K. Jones to League executives (March 20, 1940), NUL Papers.
27. Letter, Caroline B. Chapin to L. H. Wood (March 27, 1940), NUL Papers.
28. Letter, C. C. Spaulding to T. A. Hill (March 30, 1940), NUL Papers.
29. Letter, R. L. Vann to E. K. Jones (June 24, 1940), NUL Papers.
30. Letter, E. K. Jones to R. L. Vann (June 27, 1940), NUL Papers.
31. NUL 1940 Annual Conference, *Proceedings*.
32. Lester B. Granger, "Reminiscences," Oral History Research Office, Columbia University Special Collections, 1963, p. 140.
33. Granger, "Reminiscences," p. 85.
34. Ibid.

35. NUL, Minutes (May 21, 1940), NUL Papers.
36. NUL, Minutes (June 18, 1940), NUL Papers.

Chapter 28: Another Pilot

1. Ralph J. Bunche, "The Political Status of the Negro," *Journal of Negro Education* (July 1941), p. 582.
2. NUL, Minutes (March 5, 1939), NUL Papers, Library of Congress.

Chapter 29: March Time

1. NUL, "Annual Report for 1941." The committee consisted of Sadie T. M. Alexander (secretary), Regina M. Andrews, Roger N. Baldwin, Wm. H. Baldwin, M. O. Bousfield, Helen E. Cromer, Hubert T. Delany (vice president), Mrs. David M. Levy, Myles A. Paige, Mrs. Joseph M. Proskauer, Roger William Riis, Mrs. Alfred H. Schoellkopf (treasurer), Dorothy Straus, W. R. Valentine and L. Hollingsworth Wood.
2. NUL, Minutes (November 25, 1941), NUL Papers, Library of Congress.
3. Ibid.
4. NUL, "A Summary of the Activities of the National Urban League, January 1 to December 31, 1941" (1942), New York, NUL Papers.
5. "Survey of the Month," *Opportunity* (November 1940), p. 344.
6. NUL, "Summary of the Activities of the National Urban League," January–December 31, 1941, NUL Papers.
7. "The Negro and Economic Opportunity," National Conference on Social Work, *Proceedings* (1941), p. 75.
8. "The Negro and Economic Opportunity," p. 76.
9. "The Negro and Economic Opportunity," p. 87.
10. NUL, "Annual Report for 1941."
11. News Release by A. Philip Randolph, quoted in Charles R. Lawrence, "Negro Organizations in Crisis," unpublished Ph.D thesis, Columbia University (1952), p. 337.
12. Lester B. Granger, "Reminiscences," Oral History Research Office, Columbia University Special Collections, 1963, p. 304 *et passim*.
13. Charles R. Lawrence, "Negro Organizations in Crisis," p. 338.
14. Ibid., p. 339.
15. Interview with Granger, July 1, 1969.
16. L. B. Granger, "The President, the Negro and Defense," *Opportunity* (July 1941), p. 204 *et passim*.
17. Ibid.
18. *Opportunity* (May 1942), pp. 135–136.
19. Ibid.

Chapter 30: The War Emergency

1. NUL, Minutes (November 17, 1942), NUL Papers, Library of Congress.
2. Ibid.
3. NUL, "Annual Report for 1942."
4. P. Murray and Murray Kempton, *All for Mr. Davis* (New York: Workers Defense League, 1942).
5. NUL, Minutes (June 9, 1942), NUL Papers.
6. Letter, William H. Baldwin to Walter A. Jessup (March 23, 1942), Carnegie Corporation of New York Archives.

7. Letter, L. A. Wood to Robert M. Lester (January 15, 1942), Carnegie Corporation of New York Archives.
8. NUL, "Annual Report for 1942."
9. Lester B. Granger, "Crime in Harlem," *Better Times* (New York, April 16, 1943).
10. NUL, Minutes (June 3, 1943), NUL Papers.
11. "Victory Through Unity," *Opportunity* (October 1943), p. 147.
12. Ibid.
13. Charles R. Lawrence, Jr., "Race Riots in the United States, 1942–1946," *Negro Year Book: A Review of Events Affecting Negro Life, 1941–1946* (Tuskegee Institute, Alabama, 1947), pp. 233 f.
14. Lawrence, "Race Riots in the U.S.," p. 235.
15. Lawrence, "Race Riots in the U.S.," p. 241.
16. NUL, Minutes (June 3, 1943), NUL Papers.
17. Ibid.
18. Harold Orlansky, "The Harlem Riot: A Study in Mass Frustration," *Social Analysis, Report No. 1* (New York, 1943), pp. 5 f.
19. *Report of Commission on Conditions in Harlem, N.Y.* (1936). This report was never released by the mayor's office but leaked out to the New York *Amsterdam News* and other papers.
20. "Victory Through Unity," *Opportunity* (October 1943), p. 150.
21. Ibid.
22. Letter, Franklin D. Roosevelt to L. B. Granger (September 7, 1943), NUL Papers.
23. NUL, *Racial Conflict—A Homefront Danger* (New York: National Urban League, 1943).
24. NUL, "Annual Report for 1943."
25. Interview with Granger, July 1, 1969.
26. American War-Community Services, *United for Country and Community* (New York, American War-Community Services, Inc., 1944).
27. NUL, *Adventures in Community Cooperation* (New York: National Urban League, 1943).
28. NUL, "Annual Report for 1943."
29. Quoted in *Negro Year Book, 1947,* p. 353.
30. Interview with Granger, July 1, 1968; subsequently in a letter to the authors Granger calls this project a "significant partnership" between the navy and the National Urban League.

Chapter 31: New Forms of Social Action

1. NUL, *Bulletin,* "Employment Problems of the Negro" (April 1944), NUL Papers, Library of Congress.
2. NUL leaflet, *Putting Victory First!* (1944).
3. Ibid.
4. Ibid.
5. Bureau of Employment Security, Federal Security Agency, *The Labor Market* (Washington, D.C., June 1942), p. 9.
6. American Management Association, *The Negro Worker* (New York, 1942), p. 2.
7. Interview with Lester B. Granger, June 28, 1969.
8. Ibid.
9. NUL, "Annual Report for 1948."
10. NUL, Report, *Performance of Negro Workers in 300 War Plants* (February 1, 1944).
11. Julius A. Thomas, "The Negro in the National Economy, 1941–1945," *Negro Year Book: A Review of Events Affecting Negro Life, 1941–1946* (Tuskegee Institute, Alabama, 1947), p. 138.

12. Lawrence, "Negro Organizations in Crisis," Ph.D. thesis, Columbia University (1952), p. 358.
13. Thomas, "The Negro in the National Economy," p. 141.
14. Fair Employment Practice Committee, *The Wartime Employment of Negroes in the Federal Government* (January 1945).
15. Ibid.
16. Labor Research Associates, *Labor Fact Book No. 7*, p. 146.
17. NUL, "Annual Report for 1943."
18. *Opportunity*, Editorial (March 1941), p. 66.
19. Lester B. Granger, "Vocational Opportunity and the Victory Goal," *Opportunity* (March 1942), pp. 74–77.
20. March 1943.
21. American War-Community Services, *United for Country and Community* (leaflet, 1944).
22. NUL, *Six Times a Year* (New York: National Urban League, September, 1947).
23. NUL, *Spotlight on Gary* (New York: National Urban League, 1946).
24. NUL, "Annual Report for 1945."
25. Letter, L. B. Granger to authors (August 30, 1970).
26. Gunnar Myrdal, *An American Dilemma: The Negro Problem and Modern Democracy*, Vol. 11 (New York: Harper & Brothers, 1944), p. 839. See also "Digest and Analysis of Questionnaires Submitted by Urban League Secretaries for 'The Negro in America'" unpublished manuscript, by T. Arnold Hill, Schomburg Collection, New York Public Library (New York, 1940).
27. Myrdal, *American Dilemma*, p. 835 and footnotes.
28. Myrdal, *American Dilemma*, p. 841.
29. Interview with Granger, June 30, 1969.

Chapter 32: Housing Pioneers

1. Cambridge: M.I.T. Press, 1964.
2. NLUCAN, *Bulletin* (January 1915).
3. Ibid.
4. John C. Dancy, *Sand Against the Wind* (Detroit: Wayne State University Press, 1966), pp. 57 f.
5. Letters, James H. Hubert to John D. Rockefeller, Jr. (March 1924 and October 2, 1925), New York: Rockefeller Family Archives. See also interview with Mr. Hubert, July 19, 1968.
6. *Opportunity* (Fall 1945), p. 215.
7. Herbert Hoover, *Memoirs* (New York, Macmillan Co., 1951), p. 257.
8. Ibid.
9. Ibid.
10. NUL conference, Report of the Commission on Housing (September 1942), quoted in *Opportunity* (Fall 1945) p. 217.
11. Ibid.
12. NUL, "Annual Report for 1945."
13. Ibid.
14. Prepared by the Department of Industrial Relations (1945).
15. William L. Evans, *Race Fear and Housing in a Typical American Community* (New York: National Urban League, 1946).
16. NUL, minutes (September 18, 1952), NUL Papers, Library of Congress.
17. NUL, "Annual Report for 1953." NUL Papers.
18. NUL, "Annual Report for 1953."
19. NUL, Minutes (May 20, 1954), NUL Papers.
20. NUL pamphlet (June 18, 1954).
21. Ibid.

22. L. B. Granger and R. Maurice Moss, "Statement to the NUL Staff" (April 1, 1955).
23. Reginald A. Johnson, *A Documented Report on Housing* (New York: National Urban League, 1955).
24. NUL, Minutes (May 20, 1954), NUL Papers.
25. Reginald A. Johnson, Memorandum to NUL executive secretaries (July 6, 1956).
26. NUL, "Annual Report for 1958" (covering the three years 1956–1958).
27. Ibid.

Chapter 33: Enlisting Industry

1. NUL, Memorandum to executive board (May 9, 1947), NUL Papers, Library of Congress.
2. NUL, *New Frontiers in the Atomic Age* (New York: National Urban League, 1951).
3. "A Protest Against Current Racial Employment Practices in Atomic Energy Projects," Memorandum, NUL (July 5, 1951).
4. Ibid.
5. NUL, "Annual Report for 1951."
6. Interview with Granger, June 29, 1969.
7. Quoted in NUL, "Annual Report for 1947."
8. NUL, "Annual Report for 1948."
9. NUL, "Annual Report for 1949."
10. Interview with Julius A. Thomas, March 21, 1969.
11. NUL, "Annual Report for 1949."
12. Interview with Granger, July 1, 1969.
13. Letter, John D. Rockefeller 3rd to Charles Poletti (January 3, 1938), Rockefeller Family Archives, New York.
14. Memorandum, Arthur Jones to John D. Rockefeller 3rd (August 12, 1940), Rockefeller Family Archives, New York.
15. Quoted in *Six Times a Year* (New York: National Urban League, September 1947).
16. NUL, "Annual Report for 1950"

Chapter 34: Civil Rights

1. Harry S. Truman, *Memoirs* (New York: Doubleday & Co., 1956), Vol. 11, p. 183.
2. Ibid.
3. Interview with Granger, June 29, 1969.
4. Ibid.
5. L. B. Granger, Address at the National Conference of Social Work, 1941.
6. Interview with Granger, June 29, 1969.
7. See Professor H. Sitkoff, Address before the Organization of American Historians, New York City, May 20, 1970, in which Truman's "Northern Strategy" is detailed.
8. Letter, Granger to R. D. Calkins, General Education Board (March 17, 1948), NUL Papers.
9. Ibid.
10. Letter, Nelson C. Jackson to Granger (April 13, 1948), NUL Papers, Library of Congress.
11. Ibid.
12. NUL, Minutes (September 20, 1951), NUL Papers.

Chapter 35: Money Problems

1. Raymond Rich Associates, *The Structure and Operation of the National Urban League* (New York, February 1949).

2. *Structure and Operation of NUL.*, pp. 73–74.
3. Interview with Elmo Roper, September 12, 1968.
4. Ibid.
5. Interview with Lloyd K. Garrison, December 21, 1968.
6. Memorandum, J. A. Thomas to L. B. Granger (1947), NUL Papers, Library of Congress.
7. Letter, L. B. Granger to Nelson C. Jackson (March 3, 1948), NUL Papers.
8. Interview with Roper, September 12, 1968.
9. Letter, Granger to Jackson (March 3, 1948), NUL Papers.
10. Interview with Garrison, December 21, 1968.
11. Letter, Granger to Jackson (March 9, 1950), NUL Papers.
12. *The Urban League Story: 1910–1960,* Golden Fiftieth Anniversary Year Book (New York: National Urban League, 1961).
13. Memorandum, L. B. Granger to national staff (September 1954), NUL Papers.
14. Interview with Sophia Yarnall Jacobs, April 18, 1969.
15. NUL, Minutes (January 16, 1958), NUL Papers.
16. Memorandum, Administrative Department (September 20, 1960), NUL Papers.
17. Memorandum, Dana S. Creel to John D. Rockefeller, Jr. (July 3, 1946), Rockefeller Family Archives, New York. Rockefeller's contribution was raised frcm $5,000 to $12,500 and the Rockefeller Brothers Fund gave an additional $5,000.
18. Ibid.
19. Ibid.

Chapter 36: Social Engineering

1. Over the years the staff people from the local and national League offices gathered to discuss common problems. This was institutionalized in five councils formed by the executive secretaries, the industrial secretaries, vocational guidance specialists, community organization workers, and administrative and clerical personnel.
2. Nelson C. Jackson, "Foster Home and Adoptive Services for Minority Children," unpublished report, 1956; NUL Papers, Library of Congress.
3. NUL, "A Study of the Employment Opportunities for Negroes in the Brewery Industry in the United States," NUL Papers (New York: National Urban League, 1951).
4. NUL Release, September 12, 1951, NUL Papers.
5. NUL, Department of Research, *A Partial List of Community Studies: 1940–1967* (New York: National Urban League, n.d.).
6. NUL, Minutes (May 19, 1960), NUL Papers.
7. NUL, "Annual Report for 1960."
8. NUL, Minutes (October 1956), NUL Papers.
9. NUL, "Annual Report for 1956."
10. Memorandum, Clarence Coleman to M. T. Puryear (April 19, 1961), NUL Papers.
11. Memorandum, Coleman to Puryear (September 27, 1961), NUL Papers.
12. *The Urban League Story: 1910–1960,* Golden Fiftieth Anniversary Year Book (New York: National Urban League, 1961), p. 26.

Chapter 37: Under Attack

1. Statement Submitted to the Annual Conference (September 9, 1954), NUL Papers, Library of Congress.
2. Ibid.
3. Ibid.
4. NUL, *The South Under Seige* (New York: National Urban League, 1958).
5. Ibid.

6. Ibid.
7. National Citizens Protective Association, St. Louis, Mo. (leaflet, n.d.), NUL Papers.
8. Memorandum, L. B. Granger to the National Newspaper Publishers Association (October 13, 1955).
9. *White Sentinel,* National Citizens Protective Association.
10. Memorandum, L. B. Granger to local executive secretaries (November 28, 1956), NUL Papers.
11. Ibid.
12. Ibid.
13. Letter, L. B. Granger (October 29, 1957), NUL Papers.
14. *The South Under Seige.*

Chapter 38: A Reexamination

1. NUL, Progress Report of the Committee on Urban League Policy (July 22, 1954), NUL Papers, Library of Congress.
2. Ibid.
3. Ibid.
4. NUL, *The National Urban League Re-examined* (New York: National Urban League, 1955).
5. Ibid.
6. Ibid.
7. Eli Ginzberg, *The Negro Potential* (New York: Columbia University Press, 1956).
8. *The National Urban League Re-examined.*
9. Ibid.
10. Ibid.

Chapter 39: After the Landmark

1. Washington, D.C., *Afro-American* (September 12, 1959).
2. Ibid.
3. L. B. Granger, "The Story Thus Far," address at a testimonial luncheon in his honor, New York, October 3, 1961.
4. NUL Memorandum, *The Current Attack on ADC* [Aid to Dependent Children] *in Louisiana* (September 19, 1960), NUL Papers, Library of Congress. This document was circulated extensively throughout the nation and to the representatives of the 593 national organizations gathered in Washington at the Golden Anniversary White House Conference on Children and Youth. These leaders were urged to communicate with the President, Secretary Flemming and the Louisiana Board of Public Welfare "your concern and strong protest."
5. Interview with J. Harvey Kerns, March 13, 1969.
6. Ibid.
7. Ibid.
8. Prepared by the Research Department of the National Urban League from 1970 Census data in *U.S. Department of Commerce News,* Bureau of the Census, CB 71-22 (February 10, 1971).
9. Memorandum, J. A. Thomas to L. B. Granger (May 1950), NUL Papers, Library of Congress.
10. William R. Catton, Jr., "Mass Media as Activators of Latent Tendencies," *Mass Media and Violence,* Vol. XI, A Report to the National Commission on the Causes and Prevention of Violence (Washington, D.C.: Government Printing Office, 1969), pp. 306 f.
11. Interview with Granger, July 1, 1969.

12. Theodore H. White, *The Making of the President, 1960* (New York, Pocket Books, Inc., Cardinal edition, 1962), p. 424.
13. "The Time Is Now," a special memorandum presented to the President of the United States, John F. Kennedy, by the National Urban League, December 6, 1960.

Chapter 40: *Afflictions of Leadership*

1. L. B. Granger, "The Story Thus Far," address at a testimonial luncheon in his honor, New York, October 3, 1961.
2. L. B. Granger, Memorandum to presidents and executive secretaries of NUL (June 12, 1952), NUL Papers, Library of Congress.
3. Interview with Granger, June 29, 1969.
4. L. B. Granger, Memorandum to executive secretaries (October 10, 1954), NUL Papers.
5. Interview with Alexander J. Allen, May 21, 1970.
6. Ibid.
7. Granger, Letter to the authors (August 30, 1970).
8. NUL, Minutes (July 22, 1954), NUL Papers.
9. Ibid.
10. Letter, Granger to Harry L. Alston (October 7, 1954), NUL Papers.
11. Interview with Granger, June 30, 1969.
12. Interview with Kenneth C. Clark, April 18, 1969.
13. NUL, Minutes (November 19, 1953), NUL Papers.
14. NUL, Minutes (December 15, 1953), NUL Papers.
15. Ibid.
16. NUL, Minutes (January 21, 1954), NUL Papers.
17. Letter, Granger to Lisle C. Carter (April 2, 1956), NUL Papers.
18. NUL, Minutes (March 17, 1954), NUL Papers.
19. Baltimore *Afro-American* (June 19, 1954).
20. Interview with Granger, July 1, 1969.
21. Baltimore *Afro-American* (June 19, 1954); Chicago *Defender* (April 24, 1954); New York *Amsterdam News* (July 3, 1954).
22. New York *Amsterdam News* (July 3, 1954), and Baltimore *Afro-American* (June 19, 1954).
23. Interview with Granger, July 1, 1969.
24. Letter, Granger to the authors (August 30, 1970).
25. Baltimore *Afro-American*, June 19, 1954.
26. NUL, Minutes (June 10, 1954), NUL Papers.
27. Interview with Granger, July 1, 1969.
28. Ibid.
29. Interview with Kenneth C. Clark, April 18, 1969.
30. NUL, Minutes (July 22, 1954), NUL Papers.
31. Interview with Granger, July 1, 1969.
32. Memorandum, Granger to Dana S. Creel (August 4, 1954), Rockefeller Family Archives, New York.

Chapter 41: *A New Pilot*

1. Interview with Henry Steeger, December 2, 1968.
2. Interview with James Dumpson, April 3, 1969.
3. Interview with C. F. McNeill, October 7, 1968.
4. Whitney M. Young, Jr., Statement to the NUL Commerce and Industry Council (October 30, 1961).
5. Ibid.

6. Ibid.
7. NUL, "Terms of Affiliation for Local Urban Leagues," adopted September 5, 1961.
8. Executive Secretaries' Council, Minutes (September 2, 1961), NUL Papers, Library of Congress.
9. Ibid.
10. Whitney M. Young, Jr., "Threshold of Tomorrow," address at the NUL annual conference, Dayton, Ohio, September 4, 1961.
11. Ibid.
12. Ibid.

Chapter 42: "Operation Rescue"

1. NUL, Minutes (November 11, 1961), NUL Papers, Library of Congress.
2. Whitney M. Young, Commerce and Industry Statement (October 30, 1961).
3. James B. Conant, *Slums and Suburbs* (New York: McGraw-Hill, 1961), p. 34.
4. Conant, *Slums and Suburbs*, p. 31.
5. The group included Elmer A. Carter, former chairman, New York State Commission Against Discrimination; Dr. Kenneth B. Clark, noted psychologist; Dr. Eli Ginzberg, director of Columbia University Conservation of Human Resources Project; Edward S. Lewis, executive director, Urban League of Greater New York; Hylan Lewis, director, Child Rearing Study of the Health and Welfare Council of Washington, D.C.; Dr. John B. Morsell, assistant to the executive secretary, NAACP; Frederick H. Williams, director, Bureau of Human Relations, New York City Board of Education; and NUL staff members Otis Finley, Guichard Parris and Whitney Young.
6. Henry Steeger, *You Can Remake America* (New York: Doubleday, 1969), p. 50.
7. New York: National Urban League, December 6, 1961.
8. New York: National Urban League, July 21, 1962.
9. NUL, "The Home Building Industry" (July 21, 1962).
10. Early in 1962 NUL opened a Washington Bureau to facilitate liaison with federal government agencies and District of Columbia offices of national organizations in health, welfare, labor, industry and religion. Mrs. Cernoria Johnson, veteran of seventeen years as executive of the Fort Worth, Texas, and the Oklahoma City League affiliates, was selected to head the bureau.
11. Whitney M. Young, *Jet* (May 16, 1963), p. 17.

Chapter 43: Turning Point

1. NUL Cabinet Notes, May 7, 1962, NUL Headquarters, New York.
2. Peter M. and Mort N. Bergman, *The Chronological History of the Negro in America* (New York: Mentor, New American Library, 1969), p. 579.
3. Whitney M. Young, Jr., Memorandum to Executive Directors (June 7, 1963).
4. Ibid.
5. NUL, Cabinet Notes (September 3, 1963), NUL Headquarters. (NUL's income hit $1,226,000 before the year was over.)
6. Quoted in St. Clair Drake and Horace R. Clayton, *Black Metropolis: A Study of Negro Life in a Northern City* (New York: Harcourt, Brace, 1945), p. 734. The date of the letter was October 9, 1930.
7. Ibid.
8. NUL, Cabinet Notes (April 1, 1963), NUL Headquarters.
9. NUL, "A Statement by the Board of Trustees" (June 6, 1963).
10. Henry Steeger, *You Can Remake America* (New York: Doubleday, 1969), p. 43.
11. Steeger, *You Can Remake America*, p. 46.
12. NUL, Cabinet Notes (June 10, 1963), NUL Headquarters.

13. NUL Program Staff, Minutes (July 18, 1963), NUL Headquarters.
14. NUL, Cabinet Notes (April 1, 1963), NUL Headquarters.
15. NUL, Cabinet Notes (April 16, 1963), NUL Headquarters.
16. NUL Program Staff, Minutes (June 26, 1963), NUL Headquarters.
17. NUL Program Staff, Minutes (July 23, 1963), NUL Headquarters.
18. Big Six members were: National Association for the Advancement of Colored People (NAACP), Congress of Racial Equality (CORE), Southern Christian Leadership Conference (SCLC), Student Non-Violent Coordinating Committee (SNCC), National Urban League, and A. Philip Randolph in his several organizational roles.
19. NUL Program Staff, Minutes (July 23, 1963) provide most of the information and direct quotation for the following pages, except where indicated.
20. Whitney M. Young, Jr., Address at the March on Washington rally at the Lincoln Memorial, Washington, D.C., August 28, 1963.

Chapter 44: Federal Commitment

1. John H. Franklin, *From Slavery to Freedom* (New York: Alfred A. Knopf, 3rd ed., 1967), p. 635.
2. NUL, "Annual Report for 1964–1965."
3. John C. Donovan, *The Politics of Poverty* (New York: Pegasus, 1967), pp. 23 f.; his book is the source of much of what follows on this subject.
4. Ibid.
5. NUL, Minutes (May 24, 1964), NUL Headquarters, New York.
6. Section 202 (a) (1–4) of the Economic Opportunity Act.
7. NUL, Minutes (August 6, 1964), NUL Headquarters.
8. Whitney M. Young, Jr., "Testimony before the Subcommittee on Executive Reorganization of the Senate Committee on Government Operations," December 14, 1966 (Washington, D.C.: Government Printing Office).
9. Ibid.
10. NUL, "Annual Report for 1966," NUL Headquarters.
11. NUL, "Annual Report for 1967," NUL Headquarters.
12. NUL, Minutes (November 17, 1964), NUL Headquarters.
13. Ibid.

Chapter 45: The Mood Shifts

1. NUL, Policy Statement 1965-1, August 2, 1965.
2. Quoted in Charles E. Silberman, "Beware the Day They Change Their Mind," *Fortune* (November 1965).
3. Whitney M. Young, Jr., *To Be Equal* (New York: McGraw-Hill, 1964), p. 28.
4. Young, *To Be Equal*, pp. 22 f.
5. United States Department of Labor, Office of Policy, Planning and Research, *The Negro Family: The Case for National Action* (1965), Preface.
6. Ibid.
7. John B. Turner, "Suggested Revision of the Ad Hoc Committee Report on Goals, Functions and Structure of the National Urban League," Memorandum (July 27, 1965).
8. Ibid.
9. *The Negro Family*, pp. 47 f.
10. Quoted in Lee Rainwater and William L. Yancey, *The Moynihan Report and the Politics of Controversy* (Cambridge: M.I.T. Press, 1967), p. 196.
11. Including Whitney Young, Daniel Bell, Ralph Bunche, Stokeley Carmichael, Kenneth Clark, Eugene Callender, John K. Galbraith, Robert Heilbroner, Martin Luther King, Jr., John Lewis and Burke Marshall.

Chapter 46: Crisis and Commitment

1. NUL, Minutes (February 8, 1966), NUL Headquarters, New York.
2. Ibid.
3. NUL, Minutes (November 19, 1963), NUL Headquarters.
4. NUL, Minutes (May 17, 1966), NUL Headquarters.
5. Ibid.
6. Ibid.
7. Quoted in Lee Rainwater and William L. Yancey, *The Moynihan Report and the Politics of Controversy* (Cambridge: M.I.T. Press, 1967), p. 290.
8. Ibid.
9. Ibid.
10. Whitney M. Young, Jr., Address to the NUL annual conference, Philadelphia, July 31, 1966.
11. David Rusk, Address to the NUL annual conference, Philadelphia, July 31, 1966. (Note: WASP is an acronym for white, Anglo-Saxon Protestant.)
12. Ibid.
13. Ibid.
14. "Crisis and Commitment" appeared as a full-page advertisement in the New York *Times* (October 14, 1966).
15. Ibid.
16. Ibid.
17. Ibid.

Chapter 47: Beyond Civil Rights

1. NUL, Minutes (February 7, 1967), NUL Headquarters, New York.
2. NUL, Minutes (May 16, 1967), NUL Headquarters.
3. Ibid.
4. NUL, Minutes (November 17, 1967), NUL Headquarters.
5. Ibid.
6. Henry Steeger, *You Can Remake America* (New York: Doubleday, 1969), p. 127.
7. Lyndon Baines Johnson, Address to the Nation, July 27, 1967.

Chapter 48: New Thrust

1. Draft Memorandum, "Experimental Urban Leagues" (February 16, 1968), NUL Headquarters, New York.
2. NUL, Memorandum to local Urban Leagues (April 28, 1968), NUL Headquarters.
3. Whitney M. Young, "The New Thrust," keynote address before the assembled League top leadership, New York, April 27, 1968.
4. Ibid.
5. "A New Thrust for the Urban League Movement," Working Paper, NUL Headquarters, New York. This paper was delivered on April 27, 1968.
6. The resolution was approved subsequently by the NUL board of trustees at a meeting on May 17, 1968, and by the Delegate Assembly, July 31, 1968.
7. NUL, Minutes, Delegate Assembly (July 31, 1968), NUL Headquarters.
8. United Community Funds and Councils of America, *United Fund Campaigns and the Current Domestic Crisis,* statement and attachment (New York, May 17, 1968), 23 pages.
9. Whitney M. Young, Jr., address before the Congress of Racial Equality (CORE) Convention, July 6, 1968.

10. Ibid.
11. Ibid.
12. Quoted from "UL Action in Summer Crisis," NUL, *Newsletter* (September 1967), p. 2.

Chapter 49: Building Ghetto Power

1. NUL, *Newsletter* (October 1968).
2. Ibid.
3. Ibid.
4. Ibid.
5. New York *Times* (August 30, 1968).
6. NUL, *Newsletter* (October 1968).
7. Ibid.
8. Whitney M. Young, Jr.," Ghetto Power," *Business Today* (Summer 1969).
9. Ibid.
10. Ibid.

Officers and Board Members

Index